NBER
Macroeconomics
Annual 2003

NBER
Macroeconomics
Annual 2003

Editors
Mark Gertler and
Kenneth Rogoff

THE MIT PRESS
Cambridge, Massachusetts
London, England

NBER/Macroeconomics Annual, Number 18, 2003
ISSN: 0889-3365
ISBN: Hardcover 0-262-07253-X
ISBN: Paperback 0-262-57221-4

Published annually by The MIT Press, Cambridge, Massachusetts 02142-1407

Standing orders/subscriptions are available. Inquiries, and changes to subscriptions and addresses should be addressed to MIT Press Standing Order Department/BB, Five Cambridge Center, Cambridge, MA 02142-1407, phone 617-258-1581, fax 617-253-1709, email standing-orders@mitpress.mit.edu

In the United Kingdom, continental Europe, and the Middle East and Africa, send single copy and back volume orders to: The MIT Press Ltd., Fitzroy House, 11 Chenies Street, London WCIE 7ET England, phone 44-020-7306-0603, fax 44-020-7306-0604, email info@hup-MITpress.co.uk, website http://mitpress.mit.edu

In the United States and for all other countries, send single copy and back volume orders to: The MIT Press c/o Triliteral, 100 Maple Ridge Drive, Cumberland, RI 02864, phone 1-800-405-1619 (U.S. and Canada) or 401-658-4226, fax 1-800-406-9145 (U.S. and Canada) or 401-531-2801, email mitpress-orders@mit.edu, website http://mitpress.mit.edu

This book was set in Palatino by Achorn Graphic Services, Inc., Worcester, Massachusetts and was printed and bound in the United States of America.

10 9 8 7 6 5 4 3 2 1

Relation of the Directors to the Work and Publications of the NBER

1. The object of the NBER is to ascertain and present to the economics profession, and to the public more generally, important economic facts and their interpretation in a scientific manner without policy recommendations. The Board of Directors is charged with the responsibility of ensuring that the work of the NBER is carried on in strict conformity with this object.

2. The President shall establish an internal review process to ensure that book manuscripts proposed for publication DO NOT contain policy recommendations. This shall apply both to the proceedings of conferences and to manuscripts by a single author or by one or more co-authors but shall not apply to authors of comments at NBER conferences who are not NBER affiliates.

3. No book manuscript reporting research shall be published by the NBER until the President has sent to each member of the Board a notice that a manuscript is recommended for publication and that in the President's opinion it is suitable for publication in accordance with the above principles of the NBER. Such notification will include a table of contents and an abstract or summary of the manuscript's content, a list of contributors if applicable, and a response form for use by Directors who desire a copy of the manuscript for review. Each manuscript shall contain a summary drawing attention to the nature and treatment of the problem studied and the main conclusions reached.

4. No volume shall be published until forty-five days have elapsed from the above notification of intention to publish it. During this period a copy shall be sent to any Director requesting it, and if any Director objects to publication on the grounds that the manuscript contains policy recommendations, the objection will be presented to the author(s) or editor(s). In case of dispute, all members of the Board shall be notified, and the President shall appoint an ad hoc committee of the Board to decide the matter; thirty days additional shall be granted for this purpose.

5. The President shall present annually to the Board a report describing the internal manuscript review process, any objections made by Directors before publication or by anyone after publication, any disputes about such matters, and how they were handled.

6. Publications of the NBER issued for informational purposes concerning the work of the Bureau, or issued to inform the public of the activities at the Bureau, including but not limited to the NBER Digest and Reporter, shall be consistent with the object stated in paragraph 1. They shall contain a specific disclaimer noting that they have not passed through the review procedures required in this resolution. The Executive Committee of the Board is charged with the review of all such publications from time to time.

7. NBER working papers and manuscripts distributed on the Bureau's web site are not deemed to be publications for the purpose of this resolution, but they shall be consistent with the object stated in paragraph 1. Working papers shall contain a specific disclaimer noting that they have not passed through the review procedures required in this resolution. The NBER's web site shall contain a similar disclaimer. The President shall establish an internal review process to ensure that the working papers and the web site do not contain policy recommendations, and shall report annually to the Board on this process and any concerns raised in connection with it.

8. Unless otherwise determined by the Board or exempted by the terms of paragraphs 6 and 7, a copy of this resolution shall be printed in each NBER publication as described in paragraph 2 above.

Contents

Editorial, NBER Macroeconomics Annual 2003

This year's *Macroeconomics Annual* provides a mix of cutting-edge research and policy analysis on various topics.

Arminio Fraga, Ilan Goldfajn, and André Minella give an overview of how to think about "Inflation Targeting in Emerging Market Economies." Until recently, all three authors have been affiliated with the Central Bank of Brazil. Arminio Fraga took over as governor of the bank in the wake of the country's 1999 financial crisis. He is widely credited with having overseen a period of monetary stability unprecedented in the modern history of a country that has experienced one full-fledged hyperinflation and one borderline hyperinflation over the past two decades. The idea that inflation targeting could work in any form in a country with such supposedly weak institutions, and where fiscal dominance had been the norm, surprised many observers, as did the country's success in making a transition to a managed floating exchange rate regime. In their paper, the authors look not only at Brazil's experience but also at those of inflation targeters around the world. They try to draw lessons going forward. This paper is important precisely because in 1999 Brazil did not seem to many observers to have the prerequisites for a successful transition to inflation targeting. There are some (the editors of this volume included) who are skeptical of the claims of some of the more zealous inflation-targeting proponents, especially considering that almost every country in the world has experienced a significant drop in inflation over the past 15 years, including those that would seem to flout the basic principles of inflation targeting. This broad-ranging paper, combined with the balanced discussion that accompanies it, provides a major contribution to the debate. Fraga, Goldfajn, and Minella make a credible case that Brazil has adopted a thoughtful and meaningful version of inflation targeting rather than "inflation targeting lite," as some have maintained.

Pierpaolo Benigno and Michael Woodford take a complementary theoretical approach to analyzing macroeconomic policy. Their paper offers an analytical method for studying optimal monetary and fiscal policy in a modern new Keynesian monetary model. In economics, as in many other disciplines, the growing power of computers has led to a wholesale shift away from analytical methods toward computation-based approaches. This adaptation to technological progress is a welcome and natural one, but as one can see from the Benigno and Woodford paper, much is still to be gained from analytical approaches in terms of intuition and insight. Using their general framework, they tackle several classic policy issues—including optimal tax-smoothing, time consistency with government debt, and coordination of fiscal and monetary policy rules—with startling simplicity and clarity. As one can see from the subsequent discussion, methodological debates in economics can be quite intense, but the *Macroeconomics Annual* has long prided itself on providing a forum for such debates, and the present one is illuminating.

Perhaps one of the most exciting areas of intellectual growth in economics over the past ten years has been in the area of behavioral economics, as recognized by the recent Nobel prize awarded in this area. The field of finance has been perhaps the most eager consumer of this new approach. Yet there is considerable skepticism within the economics profession as a whole about what can be gained by abandoning long-established basic principles. Many argue that, whereas experimental evidence of irrationality may be convincing in the small, it is not at all convincing when it comes to explaining the behavior of important markets that aggregate across many individuals. Perhaps for this reason, many broad areas of research have not yet been significantly affected by behavioral economics. Annette Vissing-Jorgensen's paper takes a critical yet balanced look at some of the field's strongest claims of success. She argues that direct observations of investor expectations and actions are essential to sort out competing claims. Using a novel dataset, courtesy of Union Bank of Switzerland (UBS)/Paine Webber/Gallup, she finds that irrational behavior seems to diminish significantly as wealth rises, strongly suggesting that transaction costs might be a much simpler explanation for many supposed anomalies (such as limited investor diversification). Once wealth is taken into account, it would appear that surprisingly modest transaction costs can explain limited investor participation in stock markets.

N. Gregory Mankiw, Ricardo Reis, and Justin Wolfers use survey data to highlight the heterogeneity in investor expectations about inflation, a property that few modern macroeconomic models include. They argue that their empirical evidence provides additional strong support for the Mankiw and Reis model of sticky expectations as an explanation for observed business-cycle dynamics and for aggregate responses to monetary policy. (Mankiw, of course, is presently on leave from his professorship at Harvard University to serve as Chair of the President's Council on Economic Advisers. His decision to write a paper for the *Macroeconomics Annual* should be seen as a reflection of his infectious enthusiasm for this exciting recent line of work.) Although the paper certainly stirred widespread discussion, there was broad agreement that it raises two fundamental questions: (1) Why is there such a dispersion of expectations about a basic macro variable, and (2) should macroeconomists be working harder to explain it?

Conventional wisdom is that the United States has enjoyed much higher productivity growth than Europe has, in no small part because of more flexible labor and product markets. But as Susanto Basu, John G. Fernald, Nicholas Oulton, and Sylaja Srinivasan note in their paper, "The Case of the Missing Productivity Growth, or Does Information Technology Explain Why Productivity Accelerated in the United States but Not in the United Kingdom?" this popular explanation does not explain why productivity growth in the United Kingdom—with its relatively flexible markets—has also lagged. The paper gives a clear and cogent overview of the various competing theories of U.S. and U.K. productivity growth, employing new evidence and new data for the latter country. The conclusion of the paper is that, because investment in technology yields high returns only with substantial lag, the fact that the United Kingdom began investing heavily in information technology (IT) well after the United States may explain disparities in productivity to date. The cautious prediction of the paper is that the United Kingdom is likely to see a sharp rise in productivity growth, echoing the boom in the United States, sometime over the next several years.

Finally, Dirk Krueger and Fabrizio Perri ask how the much-vaunted increase in cross-sectional earnings variability in the United States has affected individual welfare. In their paper entitled "On the Welfare Consequences of the Increase in Inequality in the United States," they begin with the premise that welfare ought to be based on consumption variability as opposed to income variability. Then they present some startling evidence to suggest that the rise in cross-sectional consumption variability has been much less dramatic than the rise in income variability. Using this information to help delineate the key parameters, they proceed to use a simple quantitative variant of the standard lifetime-utility framework to calculate the welfare losses associated with the modest rise in consumption variability. They find that these losses, overall, have not been large, and they cite increased access to credit markets as a potential reason that consumption variability has remained relatively immune to the rise in income variability. As the conference discussion indicates, the authors' results are striking and clearly warrant additional investigation into the measure and nature of idiosyncratic consumption volatility.

The authors would like to take this opportunity to thank Martin Feldstein and the National Bureau of Economic Research for their continued support of the *NBER Macroeconomics Annual* and its associated conference; the NBER's conference staff, especially Rob Shannon, for excellent logistical support; and the National Science Foundation for financial assistance. Doireann Fitzgerald did an excellent job again as conference rapporteur and editorial assistant for this volume. This volume marks her last *Macroeconomics Annual* in this capacity, although we expect to see her name appear as an author sometime in the future.

Mark Gertler and Kenneth Rogoff

Abstracts

The Case of the Missing Productivity Growth, Or Does Information Technology Explain Why Productivity Accelerated in the United States but Not in the United Kingdom?

SUSANTO BASU, JOHN G. FERNALD, NICHOLAS OULTON, AND SYLAJA SRINIVASAN

Solow's paradox has disappeared in the United States but remains alive and well in the United Kingdom. In particular, the United Kingdom experienced an information and communications technology (ICT) investment boom in the 1990s, in parallel with the United States, but measured total factor productivity (TFP) has decelerated rather than accelerated in recent years. We ask whether ICT can explain the divergent TFP performance in the two countries. Stories of ICT as a general purpose technology (GPT) suggest that measured TFP should rise in ICT-using sectors (reflecting either unobserved accumulation of intangible organizational capital, spillovers, or both) but perhaps with long lags. Contemporaneously, investments in ICT may in fact be associated with lower TFP because resources are diverted to reorganization and learning.

In both the United States and the United Kingdom, we find a strong correlation between ICT use and industry TFP growth. The U.S. results are consistent with GPT stories: the acceleration after the mid-1990s was broadbased—located primarily in ICT-using industries rather than ICT-producing industries. Furthermore, industry TFP growth is positively correlated with industry ICT capital growth in the 1980s and early 1990s. Indeed, as GPT stories would suggest, if we control for past ICT growth, industry TFP growth appears negatively correlated with increases in ICT use in the late 1990s.

A somewhat different picture emerges for the United Kingdom. TFP growth does not appear correlated with lagged ICT investment. But TFP growth in the 1990s is strongly and positively associated with the growth of ICT capital services, while being strongly and negatively associated with the growth of ICT investment. If unmeasured investment in complementary capital is correlated with ICT investment, as we argue, then this finding too is consistent with the GPT story. Comparing the first and second halves of the 1990s, however, the net effect of ICT is positive, suggesting that ICT cannot explain the observed

TFP slowdown. On the other hand, our results do suggest, albeit tentatively, that the United Kingdom could see an acceleration in TFP growth over the next decade.

On the Welfare Consequences of the Increase in Inequality in the United States

DIRK KRUEGER AND FABRIZIO PERRI

We investigate the welfare consequences of the stark increase in wage and earnings inequality in the United States over the last 30 years. Our data stems from the Consumer Expenditure Survey, which is the only U.S. dataset that contains information on wages, hours worked, earnings, and consumption for the same cross section of U.S. households. First, we document that, while the cross-sectional variation in wages and disposable earnings has significantly increased, the overall dispersion in consumption has not changed significantly. We also show that households at the bottom of the consumption distribution have increased their working hours to a larger extent than the rest of the population. To assess the magnitude and the incidence of the welfare consequences of these trends, we estimate stochastic processes for earnings, consumption, and leisure that are consistent with observed cross-sectional variability (both within and between education groups) and with household mobility patterns. In a standard lifetime utility framework, using consumption and leisure processes (as opposed to earnings processes) results in fairly robust estimates of these consequences. We find that about 60 percent of U.S. households face welfare losses and that the size of these losses ranges from 1 to 6% of lifetime consumption for different groups.

Perspectives on Behavioral Finance: Does "Irrationality" Disappear with Wealth? Evidence from Expectations and Actions

ANNETTE VISSING-JORGENSEN

This paper discusses the current state of the behavioral finance literature. I argue that more direct evidence about investors' actions and expectations would make existing theories more convincing to outsiders and would help sort behavioral theories for a given asset pricing phenomenon. Evidence on the dependence of a given bias on investor wealth/sophistication would be useful for determining if the bias could be due to (fixed) information or transaction costs or is likely to require a behavioral explanation and for determining which biases are likely to be most important for asset prices.

I analyze a novel dataset on investor expectations and actions obtained from UBS/PaineWebber/Gallup. The data suggest that, even for high-wealth investors, expected returns were high at the peak of the market, many investors thought the market was overvalued but would not correct quickly, and investors' beliefs depended strongly on their own investment experience. Then I review evidence on the dependence of a series of "irrational" investor behaviors on investor wealth and conclude that many such behaviors diminish substantially with wealth. As an example of the cost needed to explain a particular type of "irrational" behavior, I consider the cost needed to rationalize why many households do not invest in the stock market.

Disagreement about Inflation Expectations

N. GREGORY MANKIW, RICARDO REIS, AND JUSTIN WOLFERS

Analyzing 50 years of inflation expectations data from several sources, we document substantial disagreement among both consumers and professional economists about expected future inflation. This disagreement shows substantial variation over time, moving with inflation, the absolute value of the change in inflation, and relative price variability. We argue that a satisfactory model of economic dynamics must address these important business-cycle moments. Noting that most macroeconomic models do not endogenously generate disagreement, we show that a simple sticky-information model broadly matches many of these facts. Moreover, the sticky-information model is consistent with other observed departures of inflation expectations from full rationality, including autocorrelated forecast errors and insufficient sensitivity to recent macroeconomic news.

Optimal Monetary and Fiscal Policy: A Linear-Quadratic Approach

PIERPAOLO BENIGNO AND MICHAEL WOODFORD

We propose an integrated treatment of the problems of optimal monetary and fiscal policy for an economy in which prices are sticky (so that the supply-side effects of tax changes are more complex than in standard fiscal analyses) and the only available sources of government revenue are distorting taxes (so that the fiscal consequences of monetary policy must be considered alongside the usual stabilization objectives). Our linear-quadratic approach allows us to nest both conventional analyses of optimal monetary stabilization policy and analyses of optimal tax-smoothing as special cases of our more general framework. We show how a linear-quadratic policy problem can be derived which yields a correct linear approximation to the optimal policy rules from the point of view of the maximization of expected discounted utility in a dynamic stochastic general-equilibrium model. Finally, in addition to characterizing the optimal dynamic responses to shocks under an optimal policy, we derive policy rules through which the monetary and fiscal authorities may implement the optimal equilibrium. These rules take the form of optimal targeting rules, specifying an appropriate target criterion for each authority.

Inflation Targeting in Emerging Market Economies
ARMINIO FRAGA, ILAN GOLDFAJN, AND ANDRÉ MINELLA

This paper assesses inflation targeting in emerging market economies (EMEs) and develops applied prescriptions for the conduct of monetary policy and inflation-targeting design in EMEs. We verify that EMEs have faced more acute trade-offs—higher output and inflation volatility—and worse performance than developed economies. These results stem from more pronounced external shocks, lower credibility, and a lower level of development of institutions in these countries. To improve their performance, we recommend high levels of transparency and communication with the public and the development of more stable institutions. At an operational level, we propose a procedure that a central bank under inflation targeting can apply and communicate when facing strong supply shocks, and we suggest a monitoring structure for an inflation-targeting regime under an International Monetary Fund (IMF) program.

Susanto Basu, John G. Fernald, Nicholas Oulton,
and Sylaja Srinivasan

UNIVERSITY OF MICHIGAN AND NBER / FEDERAL RESERVE
BANK OF CHICAGO; CEP, LONDON SCHOOL
OF ECONOMICS;* AND BANK OF ENGLAND

The Case of the Missing Productivity Growth, or Does Information Technology Explain Why Productivity Accelerated in the United States but Not in the United Kingdom?

1. Introduction

After the mid-1990s, labor and total factor productivity (TFP) accelerated in the United States but not in most other major economies. A growing body of research has explored the robustness of the U.S. acceleration, generally concluding that the acceleration reflects an underlying technology acceleration. This research, along with considerable anecdotal and microeconomic evidence, suggests a substantial role for information and communications technology (ICT).[1]

In this paper, we seek fresh insights into the nature of the U.S. experience in an international comparative perspective. First, we focus narrowly but more deeply on the relative productivity performance of the United States and the United Kingdom. Second, to understand

---

*This work was undertaken while the author was at the Bank of England.
1. See Jorgenson (2001) or Jorgenson, Ho, and Stiroh (2002) for reviews of the empirical literature on the productivity acceleration and the role of information technology. We discuss this literature in greater detail later.

comparative productivity performance better, we do detailed growth accounting at an industry level for both countries. Third, we focus on the role of ICT, which many see as being at the heart of the productivity acceleration.

Why do we take this approach? First, the U.K. experience provides an intriguing counterpoint to both the U.S. and continental European experiences. In particular, overall macroeconomic performance looks similar to that of the United States, but productivity performance looks similar to that of the rest of Europe.

In terms of late 1990s macro performance, output growth in both the United States and the United Kingdom rose, investment surged, inflation moderated, and unemployment rates fell to levels that seemed implausible just a few years earlier. In the U.S. case, many commentators attributed this strong macroeconomic performance to the strong productivity growth. But in the U.K. case, both labor and total factor productivity growth *de*celerated rather than *ac*celerated. Hence, understanding the U.K. experience may provide insights into the U.S. experience.

In terms of cross-country productivity evidence, van Ark et al. (2002) and Gust and Marquez (2002), among others, document that TFP and labor productivity growth decelerated in the European Union overall and in Japan.[2] To the extent that one expects ideas—especially when embedded in easily traded physical capital—to diffuse easily across borders, the lack of a strong response abroad surprised many observers. Hence, understanding the lack of a productivity acceleration in the United Kingdom may provide insight into the anemic productivity performance elsewhere.

Second, we build up from industry data in order to understand the aggregate picture. Because of data limitations, most cross-country comparisons have used aggregate data. But many hypotheses about relative productivity growth—e.g., about the role of ICT—are observationally equivalent in aggregate data. To implement this bottom-up approach, we construct a new industry-level dataset for the United Kingdom that includes industry use of information technology. This approach allows us to isolate the sources of U.S. and U.K. productivity growth at an industry level.

Third, we seek to understand better the myriad roles of ICT in both countries. Much discussion has focused on the distinction between the use and production of ICT. In standard neoclassical growth accounting,

2. Gust and Marquez look at 13 industrialized countries. Compared with the 1980–1995 period, their data show a positive TFP acceleration in 1995–2000 for the United States, Finland, Sweden, Australia, and Canada.

the use of ICT leads to capital deepening, which boosts labor productivity. TFP growth in producing ICT goods shows up directly in the economy's measured TFP.

This standard growth accounting framework leads to the first question we ask of the data, for both the United States and the United Kingdom: were the 1990s a time of rising total factor productivity growth outside the production of ICT? Although existing work often seems to consider this an open question, our industry data strongly support the view that most of the TFP acceleration reflects an acceleration *outside* the production of ICT goods and software.[3] Even when we focus on arguably well-measured sectors (Griliches, 1994; Nordhaus, 2002), we find a substantial TFP acceleration outside ICT production.

The productivity acceleration in sectors that use ICT raises a deeper question: does ICT itself explain some or all of the measured acceleration in TFP in sectors using it? This question is at the heart of the debate over whether computers are a new general-purpose technology. Helpman and Trajtenberg (1998), for example, argue yes; Gordon (2003), rejects this notion. The main feature of a general-purpose technology (GPT) is that it leads to fundamental changes in the production process of those using the new invention. Chandler (1977) discusses several examples, such as how railroads allowed nationwide catalog sales, which in turn transformed retailing. David and Wright (1999) also discuss historical examples.

Indeed, the availability of cheap ICT capital is likely to effect truly major changes only if firms can, as a result, deploy their other inputs in radically different and productivity-enhancing ways. That is, if cheap computers and telecommunications equipment stimulates an ever-growing series of complementary inventions in industries using ICT, thereby continually shifting out the demand curve for ICT capital, then innovations in the production of ICT can have substantial long-run effects before diminishing returns set in.

Why do we focus so intently on relatively subtle arguments about the role of ICT? An important reason is that other explanations for the U.K. experience fall short. In particular, in this case of the missing productivity growth, we round up and interrogate the plausible suspects. Some are routine and can be dismissed quickly; others require deeper investigation, as the paper discusses. The suspects include the following:

---

3. In our view, more studies than not find a widespread acceleration in technology. See, for example, Basu, Fernald, and Shapiro (2001); Baily and Lawrence (2001); Bosworth and Triplett (2002); Council of Economic Advisers (2003); Jorgenson, Ho, and Stiroh (2002); Nordhaus (2002); Oliner and Sichel (2000); and Stiroh (2002a, 2002b). Gordon (2003) remains a skeptic.

1. Cyclical mismeasurement of inputs. Productivity is generally procyclical, rising sharply in the early phase of a business cycle upswing. Basu, Fernald, and Shapiro (2001) and the Council of Economic Advisers (2003), using different methods, conclude that the level of unobserved labor effort and capital utilization probably fell in the United States after the mid-1990s. For example, both capacity utilization and hours per worker fell over the second half of the 1990s. In the U.K. case, macro performance was stronger in the second half of the 1990s than in the first, making it unlikely that business-cycle considerations held down measured productivity.

2. Differences in national accounts methodology. The United States employs hedonic methods for some crucial ICT price indices (e.g., for computers), while the United Kingdom and many other countries do not. Also, the United Kingdom has only recently included software as a form of investment in gross domestic product (GDP). Is it possible that part of the difference between U.S. and U.K. performance is a statistical illusion? The dataset we use for the United Kingdom addresses this issue by using U.S. methodologies.[4]

3. Differences in regulation of product and labor markets. Many people suggest that inflexible labor and product markets prevent European countries from benefiting from new technologies and innovations. Gust and Marquez (2002), for example, find that countries with a more burdensome regulatory environment—particularly regulations affecting labor market practices—tended to adopt information technologies more slowly and also had slower total factor productivity growth. Gust and Marquez suggest that economies with more flexible labor and product markets should benefit first, and to a larger extent, than less flexible economies.

But many of the institutional features—such as the extent of the labor and product market rigidities emphasized by Gust and Marquez—are similar in the United Kingdom and the United States. Thus, this suspect seems completely absent from the scene.

4. U.K. unemployment fell sharply. When unemployment falls, low-skilled workers are often the ones drawn disproportionately into the labor force, reducing measured labor and total factor productivity. We control for labor quality, but the productivity puzzle remains.

5. Differences in the size of the high-TFP-growth ICT-producing sectors. A larger ICT sector in the United States could explain at least some of the aggregate gap in productivity growth. But relative to GDP, the ICT-producing sectors are about the same size in the two countries (Oulton, 2001b). And even when outside ICT production, the U.S. data still

---

4. A detailed description of the sources and methods used to construct the U.K. dataset is available at www.nber.org/data (see the *Bank of England Industry Dataset*).

show a sharp productivity acceleration, whereas the U.K. data show an even sharper deceleration.

6. Intensity of competition. Although measures of regulation look similar across sectors, some commentators think that many sectors of the U.K. economy have less competitive pressure, and that this feature retards pressure for innovation. See Nickell, 1996, Lovegrove et al., 1998.[5]

7. Disruption costs associated with investment. Investment accelerated in both the U.S. and the U.K. data in the second half of the 1990s. Much of the literature suggests that because of various adjustment costs, measured output and productivity are lower in the period in which the investment takes place. Basu, Fernald, and Shapiro (2001) argue that in the second half of the 1990s, considerations of adjustment costs raise the magnitude of the U.S. acceleration in "true" technology relative to measured productivity; a similar calibration reduces the magnitude of the slowdown in U.K. productivity growth. But such calibrations don't resolve the puzzle, in part because they increase the acceleration in U.S. productivity at the same time.

8. The GPT nature of ICT capital. Benefiting from ICT requires substantial complementary investments in learning, reorganization, and the like, so that the payoff in terms of measured output may be long delayed. This is our main hypothesis. As it turns out, the evidence is much stronger for the United States than for the United Kingdom, where the evidence remains mixed. Much of the evidence for this hypothesis is circumstantial—the suspect's fingerprints are all over the crime scene.

What is the evidence for the GPT hypothesis? To begin, once we have confirmed that measured U.S. TFP accelerated strongly in non-ICT-producing industries during the late 1990s, we assess whether the acceleration in measured TFP is related to the use of ICT. We find that the U.S. results are quite supportive of the joint hypothesis that ICT is a GPT—i.e., that complementary investment is important for realizing the productivity benefits of ICT investment—and that, because these complementary investments are unmeasured, they can help explain the cross-industry and aggregate TFP growth experience of the United States in the 1990s. Specifically, we find that industries that had high ICT capital growth rates in the 1980s or early 1990s (weighted by ICT revenue shares, as suggested by theory) also had high TFP growth rates in the late 1990s. If we control for lagged capital growth, however, ICT capital growth in the late 1990s

---

5. A long literature has, of course, explored how competition affects innovation. Aghion et al. (2002) provide recent theoretical and empirical work and suggest that over some range, greater competition raises innovation.

was *negatively* correlated with contemporaneous TFP growth. These results are consistent with—indeed, predicted by—a simple model of unmeasured complementary capital investment.

Bolstered by these encouraging results for the United States, we ask whether complementary capital accumulation can explain the missing TFP growth in the United Kingdom in the second half of the 1990s. The aggregate data are encouraging: the United Kingdom had a huge ICT investment boom in the late 1990s—by some measures, a larger boom than the one labeled historic in the United States over the same period. The United Kingdom had had much lower ICT investment in the early 1990s due to a severe recession. And the U.S. results say that current TFP growth is positively correlated with lagged investment but negatively correlated with current investment—and on both counts measured U.K. TFP growth should have been low in the late 1990s.

However, results using industry-level U.K. data are more mixed. TFP growth does not appear correlated with lagged ICT capital growth, which could mean that lagged ICT capital growth is a poor proxy for unobserved U.K. complementary capital accumulation. Contemporaneously, rising ICT capital growth is positively, not negatively, correlated with the industry's TFP acceleration, although ICT *investment* growth (as the proxy for unobserved complementary investment) is negatively correlated. If the lags between ICT investment and unobserved complementary investment are shorter in the United Kingdom, then this finding, too, is consistent with the GPT story. However, the magnitude of the negative investment effect is too small to explain the pervasive TFP slowdown in U.K. industries. On the other hand, our results do suggest, albeit tentatively, that the United Kingdom could see an acceleration in TFP growth over the next decade.

In sum, we search for suspects in this case of the missing U.K. productivity growth. The crime is of particular interest because the most obvious suspect—differences in labor and product market regulations—appears to be absent from the scene. In our search for clues, we ask which sectors account for the productivity acceleration in the U.S. data, and explore whether those same sectors show an acceleration in the United Kingdom. We explore the role of ICT in the United States and the United Kingdom.

Although our tentative and incomplete answer to the puzzle emphasizes explanation 8—the GPT nature of ICT capital, and the different timing of U.S. and U.K. investment in ICT—more than one of the suspects may have conspired in the crime. For example, our explanation takes as given U.K. complementary investment and leaves open the question of why the timing differs. Other suspects may bear greater responsibility for that situation.

The organization of the paper is as follows. Section 2 compares recent U.S. and U.K. macroeconomic experience and makes some broader observations on the U.S. versus European experiences. Section 3 presents data and basic TFP results and also discusses some augmented growth accounting. Section 4 focuses more specifically on the potential role of information technology as a GPT. Section 5 provides empirical evidence on the importance of ICT in the United States and the United Kingdom, and provides some preliminary empirical results suggesting that the GPT story fits at least some of the facts. Section 6 concludes.

2. Comparative U.S., U.K., and Continental European Macroeconomic Performance

2.1 THE UNITED STATES AND THE UNITED KINGDOM

The U.S. economy performed admirably in many dimensions in the late 1990s. As Table 1 shows, output growth rose, investment surged, inflation moderated, and unemployment rates fell to levels that seemed implausible just a few years earlier. Many commentators attributed this macroeconomic strength to rapid productivity growth—linked particularly to information technology—which rose at a rate nearly double that of the preceding years. For example, the Council of Economic Advisers (2001, page. 245) stated that:

The economy this expansion has created is not just greater in sheer size but "new" in its structure and performance. It is dramatically more information intensive and more technology driven, more productive and more innovative. Today's economy utilizes new, more efficient business practices and has redefined many traditional relationships between suppliers, manufacturers, investors, and customers to achieve ever-greater efficiency. The cumulative result of these trends and their interactions is a New Economy, one that is currently providing Americans of all walks of life the benefits of high growth, low inflation, high productivity, rising incomes, and low unemployment.

As Table 1 shows, however, the United Kingdom shared many of these desirable macroeconomic features. Output rose more quickly than in the preceding period, investment boomed, unemployment rates fell sharply, inflation moderated. But in the United Kingdom, productivity growth does not appear to be the explanation for this strong macroeconomic

Table 1 MACRO PERFORMANCE: UNITED STATES VERSUS UNITED KINGDOM (ANNUAL PERCENTAGE CHANGE)[1]

United States

		Whole economy					Private nonfarm business	
	GDP	Bus. Fixed Inv.	Equip. and Soft. Inv.	Hours	Unemployment	PCE[2] Inflation	Output/hour	TFP
1980–1995	2.9	5.7	3.3	1.7	7.1	3.8	1.5	0.5
1980–1985	3.1	6.8	4.5	1.4	8.3	5.0	1.8	0.5
1985–1990	3.2	4.1	1.1	2.1	5.7	3.7	1.4	0.5
1990–1995	2.3	6.2	4.3	1.7	6.7	2.7	1.5	0.6
1995–2000	4.0	10.5	8.4	2.5	5.4	1.9	2.5	1.1

United Kingdom

		Whole economy					Private nonfarm business	
	GDP	Bus. Fixed Inv.	Equip. and Soft. Inv.	Hours	Unemployment	RPIX Inflation	Output/hour	TFP
1980–1995	2.5	3.1	3.7	0.0	9.9	5.4	3.4	1.2
1980–1985	2.1	3.2	3.9	−0.3	11.1	7.1	3.5	1.4
1985–1990	3.1	7.0	6.5	2.0	9.0	5.2	2.6	0.6
1990–1995	1.8	−0.8	1.1	−1.5	9.5	3.9	3.9	1.7
1995–2000	2.8	6.4	10.0	0.8	6.7	2.5	2.9	0.8

Sources: For the United States, GDP, business fixed investment, equipment and software investment, and PCE inflation are from the Bureau of Economic Analysis and (except for business fixed investment) refer to whole-economy averages. Unemployment rates are from the Bureau of Labor Statistics and are averages over the respective periods. Hours, output per hour, and TFP are from the Bureau of Labor Statistics multifactor productivity dataset, and cover the private nonfarm business sector. TFP incorporates an adjustment for labor quality.

1. For the United Kingdom, output, business fixed investment, hours, unemployment, and inflation are from the Office of National Statistics and (except for business fixed investment) refer to whole-economy averages. Equipment and software investment is from the Office of National Statistics and Oulton and Srinivasan (2003a). Output per hour and TFP are derived from the U.K. dataset constructed for this paper and cover the private nonfarm business sector. While the hours data match the aggregate, the output data differ from the national accounts because of adjustments to ICT investment in each industry and the output of the financial services industry. TFP incorporates an adjustment for labor quality.

2. PCE = personal consumption expenditure and RPIX = retail prices index excluding mortgage interest payments.

performance. Both labor and total factor productivity grew more slowly in the second half of the 1990s than in the first half.

2.2 BROADER REFLECTIONS ON EUROPEAN CONVERGENCE AND DIVERGENCE

Van Ark et al. (2002) provide a fairly comprehensive comparison of the European Union (E.U.) and the United States, using aggregate national accounts data. Their results cover 12 of the 15 E.U. countries, comprising 95 percent of E.U. gross domestic product (GDP) in 2000 (Belgium, Luxembourg, and Greece are excluded), for 1980–2000. They find that labor and total factor productivity grew much faster in the European Union than in the United States in the 1980s and the first half of the 1990s. Labor productivity rose by nearly 2½% per year, about 1¼ percentage points faster than in the United States. But in the second half of the 1990s, productivity decelerated in Europe, while the opposite occurred in the United States. As a result, in 1995–2000, labor productivity grew about ¾ percentage point per year faster in the United States than in the European Union.

With more detailed growth accounting, van Ark et al. find that some of this U.S. advantage reflected the higher contribution to labor productivity from ICT use, and some reflected a larger contribution of ICT production to TFP growth. But another important factor was that TFP growth in the non-ICT part of the economy fell sharply in Europe but rose in the United States. As we shall see, our consideration of the United Kingdom and the United States shows the same picture.

The recent divergence reflects a reversal in convergence forces. Until the 1990s, labor productivity generally grew more rapidly in Europe than in the United States. The reason seemed clear: the European productivity *level* was lower, so the Europeans were catching up. Table 2 shows that, in 1999, the level of labor productivity in the market sector of the United Kingdom lagged France and Germany as well as the United States. In particular, the United States led the United Kingdom by 39 percent, France by 22 percent, and Germany by 19 percent.

Intuitively, it is easier to grow when all you have to do is copy a successful example. And the neoclassical growth model predicts that countries with a lower level of capital will grow faster along the transition path. From this perspective, it was a surprise when the productivity gap between the United States and Europe started to widen again starting in about 1995.

Many popular accounts stress the U.S. strength in basic science and technological innovation. In addition, a vibrant venture capital industry is always eager to commercialize the results of the latest research. Hence,

Table 2   LABOR PRODUCTIVITY IN THE MARKET SECTOR, 1999 (UNITED KINGDOM = 100)[1]

Country	
United States	139
France	122
Germany	119
United Kingdom	100

1. Market sector is GDP, excluding public administration and defense, health, housing, and education, per hour worked, measured at purchasing power parities.
Source: O'Mahony and de Boer (2002, Table 7).

one popular interpretation of the productivity acceleration is that the United States benefited from rapid leading-edge creation of knowledge in producing high-tech goods; other industries then benefited from the presumed relatively cost-free adoption of these new technologies, i.e., by capital deepening.

Such an account is not altogether compelling. First, some of the basic technological innovations were, in fact, European in origin. For example, if any one person can be said to have invented the World Wide Web, that person was an Englishman, Tim Berners-Lee (not Al Gore). In the 1980s, Berners-Lee created the essential elements of the Web—URLs, HTML, HTTP, and Web browser and Web server programs—while employed at CERN, the European center for research in particle physics.[6]

Second, if the difference were just science and basic innovation, with technology adoption by other sectors, one could reasonably expect the revival to diffuse relatively quickly—e.g., personal computers (PCs) and other new technologies developed in the United States could be quickly installed in Europe as well. In other words, if the issue were simply that the ideas were initially developed and implemented in the United States, then the European failure to experience a comparable revival would be particularly puzzling.

Third, as we discuss in Section 3, much of the measured productivity acceleration reflects an acceleration in TFP in sectors *other* than those producing ICT. So the U.S. story goes beyond simple capital deepening, which in principle could be easily replicated elsewhere.

6. See Berners-Lee (1999). Of course, the Web relies on the Internet, which provides the physical infrastructure and low-level software protocols like TCP/IP. In the 1970s, the U.S. Defense Department funded the Internet, and initially its commercial use was banned. But the government did not claim ownership of the intellectual property, and it permitted key personnel to quit and set up companies to exploit the new technology (Abbade, 1999).

If the U.S. advantage is not simply its capability in basic science and technological innovation, then what is it? As we discuss later, many stories of the benefits of ICT emphasize that adopting new technologies requires substantial complementary investments (such as reorganizations) and co-inventions. Gust and Marquez (2002), following Greenspan (2000) and Feldstein (2001), promote essentially this story in arguing that labor and product market regulations prevent many countries in Europe from benefiting fully from new technologies because the regulations inhibit necessary reorganizations.

2.3 STRUCTURAL REFORM IN THE UNITED KINGDOM

If the United Kingdom has not yet benefited from ICT to the same extent the United States has, it is not because of inflexible labor markets, burdensome regulation, or the dead hand of government control of industry—all those factors summed up under the label "Eurosclerosis." The United Kingdom now ranks highly on measures of competitiveness, labor market flexibility, ease of starting a business, and freedom from burdensome regulations; in all these areas, Card and Freeman (2001) argue that the United Kingdom's rank is similar, and sometimes superior, to that of the United States.

Why does the United Kingdom appear to have a more flexible economy than does continental Europe? The rise of Margaret Thatcher to power in 1979 set in motion an extensive program of structural reform. This program continued under her Conservative successor, John Major, prime minister from 1990 to 1997. The elements of reform most relevant in the present context were fivefold. First, the government abandoned the attempt to control inflation through wage and price controls; these methods had been employed in increasingly restrictive form since the 1950s but had become particularly important in the aftermath of the first oil shock in 1973. Second, it reduced the legal privileges of the trade unions (e.g., secondary picketing was banned), while also increasing the rights of individual members vis-à-vis their own union (e.g., requiring ballots before strikes could be called). Third, it began privatizing the "commanding heights" of the British economy—steel and telecommunications, and later the utilities (gas, electricity, and the water supply), coal mining, and the railways. Where elements of natural monopoly existed, as in telecommunications and the utilities, independent regulators were set up. Fourth, it announced that it would cease to "bale out lame ducks": no company was now "too important to fail." This new policy was largely adhered to and was cemented by selling off commercial companies that had for various reasons fallen into government ownership (e.g., Rolls Royce, British Aerospace, British Airways, and the United Kingdom's national champion in the car industry, then known as British Leyland). Fifth, financial markets were deregulated and almost all exchange controls were abolished.

The Labour government that came to power in 1997 announced in advance that it did not intend to reverse the reforms of the Thatcher-Major period. It has continued the process of privatization. For example, air traffic control services are now supplied by a private company, not a government agency as in the United States. Immediately after it came to power, the new government gave the Bank of England operational independence in monetary policy. A Monetary Policy Committee was established at the Bank with the remit of meeting a target for inflation set by the chancellor of the exchequer: this target was (and has continued to be) 2.5% per annum as measured by the Retail Prices Index excluding mortgage interest payments (RPIX). The new government also announced a framework of rules for fiscal policy.

Apart from law and order, defense, health, and education, the government owns or directly controls little of the economy. In 1999, less than 30% of the labor force were members of a trade union, down from 50% in 1980; collective-bargaining agreements now cover fewer than 36% of the labor force, down from 68%, over the same period (Nickell and Quintini, 2001). The bulk of union members work in the public sector; as in the United States, private sector union membership is now quite low. The kind of regulation found in some European countries, which makes it costly to close plants, does not exist in the United Kingdom.

In sum, as Card and Freeman (2001) argue, the United Kingdom's reform program has reversed the process of relative economic decline that became apparent in the 1960s and 1970s.[7] Nor does weak U.K. productivity performance reflect a failure of macroeconomic policy. Inflation peaked at an annual rate of about 9½% in late 1990 but then declined steadily toward what became the target rate of 2.5% in mid-1997; since then, inflation has fluctuated in a narrow range. The unemployment rate (the internationally comparable International Labour Organization definition) peaked in early 1993 at 10.7% and has been reduced by half since.

Lest this should seem too rosy a picture, one long-standing weakness continues to hamper the U.K. economy: a low level of skills (see Table 3). In 1999, the share of the U.K. labor force with a college degree or higher was little more than half the U.S. share. Although the U.K. share was sim-

7. The underlying weaknesses of the U.K. economy and the extent to which these have been alleviated by policy are discussed in Bean and Crafts (1996), Oulton (1995), and Crafts and O'Mahony (2001). O'Mahony and de Boer (2002) compare productivity levels and growth rates across countries.

ilar to France and Germany, the U.K. proportion with vocational qualifications was also much lower.

Other aspects of policy may also be relevant. For example, some have argued that U.K. town and country planning laws limit the expansion of new forms of retailing (Lovegrove et al., 1998). More generally, Nickell (1996) argues that competition promotes productivity growth. But historically, U.K. law has been much more lenient toward uncompetitive behavior than has been the case in the United States. (This situation may now be changing with the coming into force in 2000 of the 1998 Competition Act.)

3. Data and Preliminary Empirical Results

We begin with results from standard growth accounting to establish some stylized facts. Doing so will help us dismiss a few potential explanations for the productivity divergence and hence help motivate our later focus on the general-purpose nature of ICT.

We focus on disaggregated, industry-level results for total factor productivity. Even if one is interested in aggregate outcomes, such a disaggregated approach is helpful. Any number of stories can be told to explain a single time series like GDP or GDP per worker. It is often difficult to reject a particular hypothesis using just aggregate data. Here sectoral and industry data can help. In addition, if one wishes to explore the differences between the ICT-producing and ICT-using sectors, then it is natural to disaggregate.

In this section, first we describe briefly our datasets; then we discuss results. Finally, we consider and reject several sources of measurement error as explanations for our results.

3.1 U.S. DATA

We use a 51-industry dataset that updates one used in Bosworth and Triplett (2002) and Basu, Fernald, and Shapiro (2001). For industry gross

Table 3   LABOR FORCE SKILLS, 1999

Percentages at different levels	Higher: college degree level or higher	Intermediate: post–high school vocational qualifications	Low: high school only or below
United States	27.7	18.6	53.7
France	16.4	51.2	32.4
Germany	15.0	65.0	20.0
United Kingdom	15.4	27.7	56.9

Source: O'Mahony and de Boer (2002, Table 5).

output and intermediate-input use, we use industry-level national accounts data from the Bureau of Economic Analysis (BEA). For capital input—including detailed ICT data—we use Bureau of Labor Statistics (BLS) capital input data by disaggregated industry. For labor input, we use unpublished BLS data on hours worked by two-digit industry. Gross output is not available before 1977, and for some industries is not available before 1987.[8,9]

Several issues should be kept in mind. First, we do not have industry measures of labor quality, only raw hours. We do incorporate an aggregate adjustment for labor quality in our top-line numbers, using an index calculated by Aaronson and Sullivan (2001). (Their index is relatively close to that produced by the BLS.) Second, the BEA industry data come from the income-side of the national accounts, which accelerated faster than the expenditure side in the late 1990s, as is well known. It is not clear which side of the national accounts is more reliable; the Council of Economic Advisers, for example, takes an agnostic view and uses a geometric average for growth accounting. This approach is not possible with industry-level data.

The detailed industry definitions differ a bit from those in the United Kingdom. To simplify comparisons in summary tables, we aggregate to approximately a one-digit level, where definitions are reasonably close.

3.2 U.K. DATA

We use a new industry dataset, developed at the Bank of England, containing data for 34 industries spanning the whole U.K. economy and running from 1979 to 2000.[10] For each industry, we have gross output

8. We thank Jack Triplett for sending us the industry dataset that merged the BEA and BLS data. We updated the BEA data to incorporate November 2002 national income and product account (NIPA) industry revisions and also removed owner-occupied housing. The BEA labor compensation data do not include proprietors or the self-employed, so we follow Bosworth and Triplett in using BLS data that correct for these omissions. We thank Larry Rosenblum at the BLS for sending us unpublished industry hours data, which makes adjustments for estimated hours worked by nonproduction and supervisory employees as well as the self-employed. We updated the BLS capital data from http://www.bls.gov/web/prod3.supp.toc.htm (accessed December 2002). We follow Bosworth and Triplett and exclude several service sectors where consistent input or output data are unavailable: holding and other investment offices, social services, membership organizations, and other services. We *do* include those industries in the ICT capital-by-industry data reported later in the paper.

9. Jorgenson, Ho, and Stiroh (2002) use different industry data sources; unfortunately, their dataset was not publicly available as of November 2003. The Brookings Institution (2002) discusses key differences across datasets.

10. Outton and Srinivasan (2003b) describes the industry input, output, and ICT capital data and is available on request.

and inputs of capital services, labor services, and intermediates, in both nominal and real terms. Capital services cover three types of ICT and four types of non-ICT capital. The non-ICT assets are structures, plant and machinery (equipment), vehicles, and intangibles. The three ICT assets are computers, software, and communications equipment. The real capital input index is a rental-price weighted average of the growth rates of these asset stocks. The real intermediate index is a weighted average of purchases from all the other industries and from imports.

Labor services are measured as hours worked and are built up in several steps. First, we estimate total usual hours for each industry. Second, we apply two aggregate adjustments. The first is to constrain the growth of total hours to conform with the official index of aggregate hours worked. This method allows for cyclical variability in hours, though at the same rate in all industries. The second aggregate adjustment is to apply a correction for changes in labor quality, mainly due to rising levels of educational attainment (quality change is discussed below).

Prior to several adjustments described below, the dataset is reasonably consistent with the official U.K. national accounts in both real and nominal terms, which is important because otherwise any story based on industry data will not be convincing as an explanation of what is happening at the macro level.

For making comparisons with the United States, we need to use the same methodology to derive ICT capital services in both countries. Therefore we assume that computers and software depreciate geometrically at rates similar to those used in studies of the United States (e.g., Jorgenson and Stiroh, 2000), which are in turn based on those used by the Bureau of Economic Analysis. We also employ U.S. price indices, converted to sterling terms, to deflate investment in current prices. U.S. ICT price indices generally fall faster than those in the United Kingdom, which means that our ICT capital and investment measures will grow more rapidly. The United Kingdom is also an ICT producer, so we have made corresponding adjustments to the growth rates of output of the ICT industries.

In addition, we have made a large adjustment to the official nominal level of software investment, multiplying it by a factor of 3, for reasons discussed by Oulton (2001b) and (2002). Compared with the United States, official software investment is very low relative to computer investment, and a much lower proportion of the sales of the computer services industry is classified as investment. The "times 3" adjustment can be justified as putting the two countries on the same footing methodologically.

3.3 EXONERATING TWO OF THE SUSPECTS

We briefly expand on two broad data issues related to the challenge of cross-country data comparability. First, the official U.K. statistics do not control for hedonics in the same way or to the same degree that the U.S. national accounts do. Second, the United Kingdom had an even larger decline in unemployment than the United States did, which could reduce overall productivity if those pulled into the labor force have lower-than-average skills and productivity. Neither story explains the divergent performance of U.K. and U.S. productivity because, as noted above, our U.K. industry data incorporate adjustments for these two issues.

First, what difference do the computer hedonics make? National accounts in Europe (including the United Kingdom), have, so far, lagged in introducing satisfactory methods for measuring ICT, leading to implausibly large variation across countries in computer price indices (Schreyer, 2002). Indeed, the main weakness of U.S. methods of measuring ICT is that they don't go far enough. For example, there is no true price index for investment in custom and own account software (two-thirds of the total), only for prepackaged software (Parker and Grimm, 2000). And within telecommunications, hedonic methods are only just starting to be introduced (Grimm, Moulton, and Wasshausen, 2002).

A related issue is that, although measured GDP in both Europe and the United States now includes software investment, different method-ologies lead to substantial differences in estimated levels (Lequiller, 2001). Hence, cross-country comparisons again need to use a compara-ble methodology.

Most researchers have dealt with these issues by applying as far as pos-sible U.S. methods to other countries. However, this approach does not necessarily transform European productivity performance because inputs as well as output grow faster (see again Schreyer, 2002). Oulton (2001b) finds that U.S. methodology raises the growth rate of U.K. GDP by about one-third of a percentage point per annum in the last half of the 1990s. Despite this, aggregate labor productivity still slowed down over this period.[11]

Second, why isn't declining labor quality quantitatively important in explaining the divergence? We apply an index of U.K. labor quality (con-

---

11. Gust and Marquez (2000) and van Ark et al. (2002) also find that differences in national accounts methodology cannot explain the productivity growth gap between the United States and Europe.

structed by Burriel-Llombart and Jones, 2004). As is standard, we define labor quality as the growth of quality-adjusted labor input minus the growth of unweighted total hours.[12] The unemployed do tend to have below-average skills or qualifications and falling unemployment indeed contributed to a lower growth rate of labor quality from the first to the second half of the 1990s. But other factors affected U.K. labor quality, such as increasing female participation; declining participation by older, unskilled men; and (of particular importance) the retirement or death of older, less qualified people and their replacement by younger, better qualified workers. In both countries, we find that labor quality growth was positive throughout the 1990s, though in both the rate of growth also decelerated.[13]

3.4 RESULT FROM TRADITIONAL GROWTH ACCOUNTING

Tables 4 and 5 provide standard estimates of TFP for various aggregates, including the one-digit industry level. The first three columns show TFP in gross-output terms. Since aggregate TFP is a value-added concept, we present industry TFP in value-added terms as well; by controlling for differences in intermediate input intensity, these figures are scaled to be comparable to the aggregate figures. The final column shows the sector's nominal value-added share.[14]

We start by discussing the U.S. results in Table 4, focusing on the value-added measures. The top line shows the sizable acceleration in TFP growth, from about 0.6% per year to about 1.9%.[15] These calculations incorporate labor quality adjustments from Aaronson and Sullivan (2001), shown in the second line. Labor quality growth grew more slowly in the second half of the 1990s, when the booming economy drew lower skilled workers into employment. Hence, adjusting for

12. Quality-adjusted hours is a Törnqvist index of hours worked by 40 groups, where each group's hours are weighted by its share of the aggregate wage bill. The groups consist of four qualifications groups (degree, A level, O level, and "other") and five age groups (covering ages 16–65), for each gender.
13. See the second line in both Tables 4 and 5. It is labeled "(adjusted for labor quality)."
14. With Törnqvist aggregation, aggregate TFP growth is a weighted average of industry gross-output TFP growth, where the so-called Domar weights equal nominal industry gross output divided by aggregate value added; the weights thus total more than 1. In continuous time, this is equivalent to first converting gross-output residuals to value-added terms by dividing by (1 minus the intermediate share), and then using shares in nominal value added. (In discrete time, using average shares from adjacent periods, they are approximately equivalent.) Basu and Fernald (2001) discuss this aggregation and its extension to the case of imperfect competition; see also Oulton (2001a).
15. As noted earlier, the acceleration exceeds that in the product-side BLS data shown in Table 1.

Table 4 UNITED STATES: TOTAL FACTOR PRODUCTIVITY (TFP) GROWTH BY INDUSTRY IN PRIVATE NONFARM BUSINESS, 1990–2000 (Percentage change, annual rate)

	Productivity (gross output terms)[2]			Productivity (value-added terms)[3]			Share of nominal value added (2000)
	Pre-1995	Post-1995	Acceleration	Pre-1995	Post-1995	Acceleration	
Private nonfarm economy (adjusted for labor quality)[1]	0.30	0.98	0.68	0.59	1.92	1.32	100.0
Contribution of labor quality	*0.16*	*0.09*	*−0.08*	*0.32*	*0.16*		
Private nonfarm economy (*not* adjusted for labor quality)	0.47	1.06	0.60	0.91	2.08	1.17	
Mining	1.61	−1.16	−2.77	3.08	−2.15	−5.23	1.6
Manufacturing	0.86	0.97	0.11	2.40	2.76	0.36	20.6
Nondurables	0.34	−0.39	−0.73	1.02	−1.20	−2.22	8.7
Durables	1.34	2.08	0.74	3.47	5.61	2.14	12.0
Construction	0.22	−0.58	−0.80	0.39	−0.98	−1.38	6.1
Transportation	0.83	0.77	−0.06	1.69	1.53	−0.16	4.2
Communication	1.47	0.01	−1.46	2.31	0.15	−2.16	3.7
Electric/gas/sanitary	0.27	0.11	−0.16	0.42	0.17	−0.25	2.9
Wholesale trade	1.08	3.39	2.32	1.66	5.37	3.71	9.2
Retail trade	0.49	3.23	2.74	0.83	5.33	4.50	11.8

Finance and insurance	0.24	1.95	1.72	0.44	3.39	2.96	10.7
Finance	0.86	2.96	2.10	1.31	4.90	3.59	7.5
Insurance	-0.81	0.05	0.86	-1.49	-0.06	1.44	3.2
Business services and real estate	0.68	0.24	-0.45	1.12	0.40	-0.72	13.9
Business services	0.41	-0.89	-1.30	0.60	-1.40	-2.00	7.1
Real estate	0.87	1.27	0.40	1.55	2.34	0.79	6.8
Other services	-1.19	0.05	1.24	-1.89	0.08	1.97	15.2
ICT-producing[4]	2.41	4.43	2.02	5.52	11.02	5.50	5.3
Non-ICT-producing	0.32	0.80	0.48	0.61	1.54	0.93	94.7
Well-measured ind.[5]	0.82	1.44	0.62	1.80	3.17	1.37	54.2
Well-measured (excluding ICT-producing)	0.62	1.04	0.42	1.35	2.24	0.88	48.9

1. For productivity purposes, our definition of private nonfarm business excludes holding and other investment offices, along with miscellaneous services, because consistent input and output data are unavailable for these industries.

2. A sector's gross output TFP growth is calculated as a weighted average of the industry-level gross output TFP growth rates; the weight for each industry is the ratio of its Domar weight to the sum of the Domar weights for that sector.

3. Value-added TFP growth is defined as (gross output TFP growth)/(1 − share of intermediate inputs). Implicitly, this uses the Törnqvist index of value added for a sector.

4. For the United States: ICT-producing includes industrial machinery and electronic and other electrical equipment sectors.

5. For the United States and the United Kingdom: Well-measured industries include mining, manufacturing, transportation, communication, electric/gas/sanitary, and wholesale and retail trade.

Table 5 UNITED KINGDOM: TOTAL FACTOR PRODUCTIVITY (TFP) GROWTH BY INDUSTRY IN PRIVATE NONFARM BUSINESS, 1990–2000 (Percentage change, annual rate)

	Productivity (gross output terms)[1]			Productivity (value-added terms)[2]			Share of nominal value added (2000)
	1990–1995	1995–2000	Acceleration	1990–1995	1995–2000	Acceleration	
Private nonfarm economy with quality adjusted labor input	0.79	0.35	−0.44	1.72	0.78	−0.94	100.0
Labor quality adjustment	*0.39*	*0.21*	*−0.18*	*0.84*	*0.48*	*−0.37*	
Private nonfarm economy with nonquality adjusted labor input	1.18	0.56	−0.62	2.56	1.25	−1.31	100.0
Mining	5.69	0.89	−4.79	9.20	1.34	−7.86	3.8
Manufacturing	1.11	0.51	−0.59	3.03	1.42	−1.61	23.2
Nondurables	1.04	−0.03	−1.07	2.81	−0.07	−2.89	15.7
Durables	1.26	1.57	0.31	3.52	4.57	1.05	7.5
Construction	0.67	−0.31	−0.98	1.77	−0.84	−2.61	6.6
Transportation	1.62	0.50	−1.12	3.46	1.18	−2.28	6.5
Communication	3.26	2.61	−0.65	4.83	4.77	−0.06	3.9
Electric/gas/sanitary	1.22	0.99	−0.24	3.11	2.61	−0.50	3.1
Wholesale trade	2.22	2.13	−0.09	3.44	3.71	0.28	6.8
Retail trade	0.38	−0.58	−0.96	0.73	−1.17	−1.90	13.0

Finance and insurance	0.90	1.56	0.66	1.89	3.87	1.98	6.2
Finance							
Insurance							
Business services and real estate	0.64	0.53	-0.11	1.13	0.99	-0.14	21.0
Business services							
Real estate							
Other services	1.06	0.10	-0.96	2.05	0.19	-1.86	5.7
ICT-producing[3]	1.45	3.75	2.30	3.82	10.46	6.64	3.3
Non-ICT-producing	1.16	0.41	-0.75	2.52	0.93	-1.59	96.7
Well-measured ind.[4]	1.38	0.59	-0.79	3.10	1.37	-1.73	60.5
Well-measured (excluding ICT-producing)	1.37	0.37	-1.00	3.90	0.45	-3.45	57.2

1. A sector's gross output TFP growth is calculated as a weighted average of the industry-level gross output TFP growth rates; the weight for each industry is the ratio of its gross output weight to the sum of the Domar weights for that sector.
2. Value-added productivity growth equals (gross output productivity growth)/(1 – share of intermediate inputs).
3. For the United Kingdom: ICT-producing comprises electrical engineering and electronics (SIC92 30–33).
4. For the United Kingdom: well-measured industries comprise mining, manufacturing, transportation, communication, electricity, water and gas supply, wholesale, retail trade, and waste treatment.

labor quality growth heightens the magnitude of the TFP acceleration calculated with raw hours (shown in the third line, calculated as the appropriate weighted average of the industry TFP growth rates shown in the table).

The remainder of the table shows various subaggregates (none of which incorporate a labor quality adjustment), including the one-digit SIC level. Our dataset shows clearly that acceleration was not limited to the ICT-producing sectors. First, if we focus on the non-ICT producing sectors (third line from the bottom), they show an acceleration of nearly one percentage point. In an accounting sense, these sectors contribute about 0.9 percentage points of the 1.2 percentage point total (non-quality-adjusted) acceleration. Major non-ICT sectors contributing to the acceleration include wholesale trade, retail trade, finance, and insurance.

Second, Griliches (1994) and Nordhaus (2002) argue that real output in many service industries is poorly measured—e.g., it is often difficult even conceptually to decide on the real output of a bank or a lawyer; as another example, in health care, the hedonic issues are notoriously difficult. Nordhaus argues for focusing on what one hopes are the well-measured (or at least, better measured) sectors of the economy. The acceleration in TFP in well-measured industries is even larger than the overall acceleration; the acceleration is sizable even when we exclude ICT-producing sectors.

Table 5 shows the comparable table for the U.K. economy. Between the first and second halves of the 1990s, productivity growth fell in the U.K. private nonfarm economy by about one percentage point, even after adjusting for the much slower growth in labor quality in the second half of the 1990s. Looking at major industries, TFP growth (unadjusted for labor quality) rose substantially in finance/insurance and manufacturing durables, but it was flat or it declined in most other major sectors.

By contrast, aggregate productivity growth rose in the United States by 1.3 percentage points per annum (Table 4), so the difference in acceleration was about 2.3 percentage points. Given this broad difference, there are some similarities in the sectoral pattern across the two countries. For example, the productivity acceleration was much faster in durables than in nondurables; finance and insurance surged.

A closer look at the sectoral data shows a major difference between the United States and the United Kingdom in the trade sectors, especially retail. U.S. retail value-added TFP growth *rose* by 4.5 percentage points per year; U.K. TFP growth *fell* by about 1.7 percentage points.

Nevertheless, they are not the entire story. Even excluding them, the U.S. data still show an acceleration, whereas the U.K. data still show a deceleration.[16]

The fact that the U.S. productivity acceleration was broadbased is consistent with a growing body of recent work. For example, the Council of Economic Advisers (2003) reports that between 1973–1995 to 1995–2002, non-ICT TFP accelerated sharply, with its contribution to U.S. growth rising from 0.18 percentage points per year to 1.25 percentage points, roughly in line with the figures here.[17] Bosworth and Triplett (2002) focus on the performance of service industries and find a widespread acceleration. Jorgenson, Ho, and Stiroh (2002) also find that TFP accelerated outside ICT production, although by a smaller amount.

3.5 AUGMENTED GROWTH-ACCOUNTING CONSIDERATIONS

Some researchers have investigated whether the results cited here are robust to deviations from the standard assumptions of growth accounting, generally concluding that they are. Using different methodologies, Basu, Fernald, and Shapiro (2001); the Council of Economic Advisers (various years); and Baily and Lawrence (2001) find that cyclical mismeasurement of inputs plays little if any role in the U.S. acceleration of the late 1990s. Basu, Fernald, and Shapiro (2001) also find little role in the productivity acceleration for deviations from constant returns and perfect competition.

Basu, Fernald, and Shapiro (2001) do find a noticeable role for traditional adjustment costs associated with investment. Because investment rose sharply in the late 1990s, firms were presumably diverting an increasing amount of worker time to installing the new capital rather than producing marketable output. In other words, if adjusting the capital stock incurs costs and faster growth leads to higher costs, then true technological progress was faster than measured. These considerations strengthen the conclusion that the technology acceleration was broadbased because

16. Wholesale and retail trade account for about three-quarters of the U.S. acceleration (Domar weighted industry TFP growth) and one-third of the U.K. deceleration. The McKinsey Global Institute (2001) provides anecdotal as well as quantitative evidence on the transformation of wholesale and retail trade; Foster, Haltiwanger, and Krizan (2002) link the retail industry data to firm-level developments. Note that Jorgenson, Ho, and Stiroh (2002), who use output data from the BLS Office of Employment Projections, do not find as important a contribution from the trade sectors.

17. The CEA methodology is very similar to that of Oliner and Sichel (2002), who report *no* TFP acceleration outside ICT production. But Oliner and Sichel discount their finding on this score because their method takes non-ICT TFP as a residual. Because the Oliner and Sichel endpoint is a recession year, 2001, they point out that any cyclical effects on productivity are forced to show up in non-ICT TFP. In addition, the CEA measure of labor productivity is a geometric average of income- and product-side measures of output per hour.

service and trade industries invested heavily in the late 1990s and hence paid a lot of investment adjustment costs.

The United Kingdom had even more sharply rising investment than did the United States, so conceivably adjustment costs might be masking an underlying improvement in U.K. productivity growth. From 1990–1995, aggregate investment in the U.K. private nonfarm economy fell at 0.45% per year; over 1995–2000, it rose at 8.60% per year.[18] So how much of the decline in U.K. productivity growth might be attributable to adjustment costs? Following Basu, Fernald and Shapiro (2001), we calibrate these costs as a parameter ϕ times the growth rate of investment; following Shapiro (1986), they take ϕ to be 0.035.[19] This calibration implies that investment adjustment costs held down measured TFP growth by about 0.30 percentage points per year over 1995–2000, but boosted it by 0.02 percentage points over 1990–1995. Hence, the slowdown in true productivity growth was about 0.63, not 0.95, percentage points per annum, and adjustment costs might account for about one-third of the observed productivity deceleration.

Of course, the same correction would raise the U.S. technology acceleration by a bit under 0.2 percentage point.[20] Hence, although this correction makes a larger difference to the U.K. data, it doesn't reverse the U.K. decline or even noticeably narrow the gap with the United States.

4. Industry-Level Productivity Implications of ICT as a New GPT

The U.S. productivity acceleration coincided with accelerated price declines for computers and semiconductors but, as we just saw, most of the TFP acceleration appears to have taken place outside ICT production. Can ICT somehow *explain* the measured TFP acceleration in industries using ICT? We first discuss broad theoretical considerations of treating ICT as a new general-purpose technology (GPT) and then present a simple model to clarify the issues and empirical implications.

18. This estimate uses the same data employed to estimate capital services in the United Kingdom at the industry level.

19. Shapiro does not estimate different values of ϕ for IT and non-IT capital; one could imagine that the values differ. We hope to estimate these values in future work.

20. These numbers are qualitatively the same but smaller than those reported in Basu, Fernald, and Shapiro (2001) for three reasons. First, we have added an extra year of data (2000) in which investment growth was weak. Second, data revisions have reduced the growth rate of investment in the second half of the 1990s. Third, Jason Cummins and John Roberts pointed out a mistake in our conversion from Shapiro (1986)'s framework to ours. This led us to reduce our estimate of ϕ from 0.048 in Basu, Fernald, and Shapiro (2001) to 0.035 in this work.

4.1 GENERAL-PURPOSE TECHNOLOGIES: "SPOOKY ACTION AT A DISTANCE"

Standard neoclassical growth accountants identify several effects of ICT on aggregate labor and total factor productivity growth. Faster TFP growth in *producing* ICT contributes directly to aggregate TFP. In addition, the *use* of ICT contributes directly to labor productivity through capital deepening: by reducing the user cost of capital, falling ICT prices induce firms to increase their desired capital stock.[21]

Standard growth accounting does not presume that the use of ICT has any particular effect on TFP. By contrast, many microeconomic, firm-level, and anecdotal studies suggest that there are important—but often indirect and hard to foresee—potential roles for ICT to affect measured production and productivity in sectors using ICT. Conceptually, one can separate these potential links into two categories: purposeful co-invention, which we interpret as the accumulation of complementary capital, which in turn leads to mismeasurement of true technology; and externalities of one sort or another.

These indirect effects arising from general-purpose technologies such as ICT are akin to what Einstein, in the context of particle physics, called "spooky action at a distance": quantum physics predicts that, in some circumstances, actions performed on a particle in one location instantaneously influence another particle that is arbitrarily far away. In terms of the effects of ICT, an innovation in one sector, ICT, often causes unexpected ripples of co-invention and co-investment in sectors that seem almost arbitrarily far away. Many of the GPT stories (e.g., Bresnahan and Trajtenberg, 1995; Helpman and Trajtenberg, 1998) fall in the "spooky action" camp. (Of course, Einstein's spooky action was instantaneous; the effects of GPTs are not.)

First, firm-level studies suggest that benefiting from ICT investments requires substantial and costly co-investments in complementary capital.[22] For example, firms that use computers more intensively may reorganize production, thereby creating intangible capital in the form of organizational knowledge. These investments may include resources diverted to learning; they may involve purposeful innovation arising from research and development (R&D). As Bresnahan (undated) argues,

21. Tevlin and Whelan (2000) and Bakhshi et al. (2003) provide econometric evidence for the United States and the United Kingdom, respectively, that falling relative prices of ICT equipment fueled the ICT investment boom.
22. See, for example, Brynjolfsson and Hitt (2000) and Bresnahan (undated) for a discussion of the kinds of complementary investments and co-invention that firms undertake to benefit from ICT, given its general-purpose attributes. David and Wright (1999) provide a historical reflection on general-purpose technologies.

"[A]dvances in ICT shift the innovation possibility frontier of the economy rather than directly shifting the production frontier;" that is, ICT *induces* co-innovation and co-investment by firms using the technology, with long and variable lags.

The resulting organizational capital is analogous to physical capital because companies accumulate it in a purposeful way. Conceptually, we can think of this complementary capital as an additional input into a standard neoclassical production function; it differs from ordinary capital and labor because it is not directly observed but must somehow be inferred.[23]

Second, the GPT literature suggests the likelihood of sizable externalities to ICT. For example, successful new managerial ideas—including those that take advantage of ICT, such as the use of a new business information system—seem likely to diffuse to other firms. Imitation is often easier and less costly than the initial co-invention of, say, a new organization change because you learn by watching and analyzing the experimentation, the successes, and the mistakes made by others.[24] Indeed, firms that *don't* use computers more intensively may also benefit from spillovers of intangible capital. For example, if there are sizable spillovers to R&D, and if R&D is more productive with better computers, then even firms that don't use computers intensively may benefit from the knowledge created by computers.

These GPT considerations are completely consistent with the traditional growth accounting *framework* but suggest difficulties in implementation and interpretation. In particular, these considerations suggest that the production function is mismeasured because we don't observe all inputs (the service flow from complementary, intangible capital) or all outputs (the investment in complementary capital). Hence, TFP is mismeasured.

Note that the spooky action nature of the co-inventions and externalities suggests that we should not expect the benefits of ICT to diffuse quickly across borders. First, if large complementary investments and innovations are necessary, diffusion will inevitably take time. Second, Bresnahan and Trajtenberg (1995) note that co-invention often requires

---

23. Much of Brynjolfsson's work tries to quantify the role of unobserved complementary capital. Macroeconomic studies of the effects of organizational capital include Greenwood and Yorokoglu (1997), Hornstein and Krusell (1996), Hall (2001), and Laitner and Stolyarov (2001).

24. Bresnahan (undated) discusses the channels for externalities to operate. Bresnahan and Trajtenberg (1995) highlight both vertical externalities (between general-purpose technology producers and each application sector) and horizontal externalities (across application sectors).

"coordination between agents located far from each other along the time and technology dimension" (p. 3), so that institutional arrangements and market structure—which affect the ability to contract successfully in an environment with asymmetric information and uncertain property rights—are likely to matter; these factors are likely to differ across countries. Third, adoption costs may differ across countries, just as they seem to differ across firms, so that low adjustment/adoption cost countries may adopt new technologies first. These differences in cost may reflect the presence or absence of complementary factors—business school–trained managers, for example—or the vintage structure of the existing capital stock.[25] Finally, spillover effects may be stronger at closer distances (e.g., within Silicon Valley).

In looking at the United States versus the United Kingdom, this discussion makes clear the difficulty of the task at hand: we need to find a way to infer unobserved complementary investments. That is, the United States could be benefiting from past intangible investments in knowledge and reorganization, leading to high measured TFP growth; the United Kingdom might have begun heavy intangible complementary investment only more recently, diverting resources from production of market output and appearing to have low TFP growth. We now turn to a formal model that suggests variables that might act as proxies for these unobservables.

4.2 INDUSTRY-LEVEL IMPLICATIONS OF ICT AS A NEW GPT: A SIMPLE MODEL

The last ten years, and especially the last five, have seen an explosion in papers modeling the effects of general-purpose technologies (GPTs) and interpreting the ICT revolution as the advent of such technology.[26] But it is quite difficult to derive industry-level empirical implications from this literature. For example, it is often unclear how to measure in practice some of the key variables, such as unobserved investment and capital;

25. Chandler (1977), for example, highlights the rise of professional managerial skills. In addition, new technologies may be somewhat specific to a country's particular cultural and institutional arrangements—society's general organization, infrastructure, social capital, and the like. In other words, appropriate technology may matter even in comparisons of U.S. versus U.K. companies. This is related to the literature on factors that affect the costs of adopting a new GPT. Helpman and Trajtenberg (1998), for example, have some interesting examples of which industries adopted semiconductors first—e.g., hearing aids and computers, where the existing technology was inadequate—and which adapted late, notably telecom and automotives, with a large body of vintage capital.

26. An incomplete list is Caselli (1999), Greenwood and Yorukoglu (1997), the collection of papers edited by Helpman (1998), Hobijn and Jovanovic (2001), Jovanovic and Rousseau (2003), and Laitner and Stolyarov (2001).

and even for observed variables, measurement conventions often depart from those used in national accounting.[27]

On the other hand, conventional industry-level growth-accounting studies of the sort reviewed and extended in Section 3 are typically hard to interpret in terms of GPT considerations because they generally lack a conceptual, general equilibrium framework to interpret movements in TFP. Although some studies try to look for a "new economy" in which ICT has indirect effects on measured TFP in ICT-using industries, in the absence of clear theoretical guidance, it is not clear that many would not know if they had, in fact, found it.

Finally, as discussed above, a large empirical literature, often using firm-level data or case studies, stresses the importance and costly nature of organizational change accompanying ICT investment. This literature, while important and insightful, rarely makes contact with economywide productivity research.[28] In many ways, our empirical work below is a tentative attempt to make just that connection. The model below provides the bare bones of a theoretical framework to capture some of the key issues, focusing on cross-industry empirical implications. Our model takes as given the arrival of a particular GPT, which here is taken to be the production of ICT capital at a continuously falling relative price. The distinguishing feature of a GPT is that its effects are general—going well beyond the industry of production—but require complementary investments by firms for its use to be truly beneficial. For empirical implementation, we focus on industries that use the GPT.

Value added in industries that use, but do not produce, IT is given by[29]:

$$Q_{it} \equiv Y_{it} + A_{it} = F(Z_t G(K_{it}^{IT}, C_{it}), K_{it}^{IT}, L_{it}) \tag{1}$$

where, $i = 1 \ldots N$, and F and G are homogeneous of degree 1 in their arguments. Z is a technology term that each industry takes as exogenous. We discuss the distinction between A and Y shortly. For simplicity, we ignore materials input (although we add it back in our empirical work), imperfect competition, increasing returns, and capital adjustment costs. All could be added, at the cost of considerable notation.

---

27. For example, capital is typically measured as foregone consumption, which is sensible for an aggregative model but difficult to relate to industry-level capital accounts that deal with capital heterogeneity and quality change by measuring (attempting to measure) capital input in efficiency units. Howitt (1998) attempts to bridge the two conventions.

28. An exception is Brynjolfsson and Yang (2001).

29. With constant returns and competition, one can speak of firms and industries interchangeably. "An industry does x" is our shorthand for "all firms in an industry do x."

Each industry rents ICT capital K^{IT} and non-ICT capital K^{NT} in competitive, economywide markets. The aggregate stocks of the two types of capital evolve as:

$$K_t^{JT} = I_t^{JT} + (1 - \delta^{JT}) K_{t-1}^{JT} \qquad (2)$$

where

$$J = I, N$$

Industries must, however, individually accumulate their stocks of complementary capital, C. We think of this capital as business and organizational models or training in the use of IT, and the investment flow A as the time and resource cost of training and creating new business structures.[30] Industries forego producing market output Y to accumulate this capital:

$$C_{it} = A_{it} + (1 - \delta_C) C_{it-1} \qquad (3)$$

We assume that investment in all three kinds of capital is irreversible. Because both A and NT investment goods cost the same to produce, the economic difference between the two types of capital is that they interact in different ways with the ICT capital stock. The difference from the point of view of measurement is that Y is measured in the national income accounts, but A is not.[31]

The main economic implication of the separability assumption built into equation (1) is that the marginal productivities of K^{IT} and C are closely tied to one another. We assume that the elasticity of substitution between the two inputs in the production of G is relatively small. We also assume Inadalike conditions such that the marginal productivity of each input is very low if the level of the other is close to zero. Thus, when the GPT arrives and ICT capital starts getting cheap, the incentive to accumulate C is also very strong.

Note that conceptually and as traditionally construed, innovation can take two forms. First, we lump purposeful innovations into C (indeed, we have assumed that *all* purposeful innovation is closely linked to ICT). Second, we interpret Z as all exogenous increases in technology, including, for example, the component of organizational change that spills over from the sector of origin—for example, the idea of using individual

---

30. Chandler (1977) discusses innovations in inventory management made possible by railroads. Wal-Mart's inventory management system provides an example of innovations made possible by ITC.

31. Some fraction of A is probably measured, for example, consultant services and many forms of software. It is not clear how much of what is measured is properly capitalized, as required by equation (3).

electric motors at each workstation in a factory rather than relying on the single drive train of a steam engine.

4.3 TFP MEASUREMENT WITH UNOBSERVED INPUTS AND OUTPUT

What are the implications of complementary capital accumulation for the measured TFP of ICT-using industries? Differentiating, we can write the production function in growth rates as:

$$\Delta q = \frac{F_{K^{IT}} K^{IT}}{Q} \Delta k^{IT} + \frac{F_C C}{Q} \Delta c + \frac{F_{K^{NT}} K^{NT}}{Q} \Delta k^{NT} + \frac{F_L L}{Q} \Delta l + s_G \Delta z \tag{4}$$

Because we have made Solow's assumptions of constant returns to scale and perfect competition, we have

$$\frac{F_{K^{IT}} K^{IT}}{Q} + \frac{F_C C}{Q} + \frac{F_{K^{NT}} K^{NT}}{Q} + \frac{F_L L}{Q} = 1 \tag{5}$$

If we observed total output Q, and knew the required rates of return to capital, we could back out the elasticity of output with respect to complementary capital, C:

$$\frac{F_C C}{Q} = 1 - \frac{WL}{PQ} - \frac{P_K^{IT} K^{IT}}{PQ} - \frac{P_K^{NT} K^{NT}}{PQ} \tag{6}$$

Without independent information on the flow of A or the stock of C (perhaps from stock market valuations), one cannot implement this procedure using measured output, Y^{NT}. Rewrite equation (6) as:

$$\frac{F_C C}{Y^{NT}} = \frac{Q}{Y^{NT}} - \frac{WL}{PY^{NT}} - \frac{P_K^{IT} K^{IT}}{PY^{NT}} - \frac{P_K^{NT} K^{NT}}{PY^{NT}}$$

Because Q/Y^{NT} is not observed, within broad limits we are free to believe that complementary capital is arbitrarily important in production by assuming that an arbitrarily large share of the true output that firms produce is not counted in the national accounts.

Some algebraic manipulations of equation (4) yield an expression for the conventional Solow residual:

$$\Delta y^{NT} - \frac{P_{K^{IT}} K^{IT}}{PY^{NT}} \Delta k^{IT} - \frac{P_{K^{NT}} K^{NT}}{PY^{NT}} \Delta k^{NT} - \frac{F_L L}{Q} \Delta l \equiv \Delta TFP =$$

$$\frac{F_C C}{Y^{NT}} \Delta c - \frac{A}{Y^{NT}} \Delta a + s_G \Delta z \tag{7}$$

We see that omitting complementary inputs can cause us either to overestimate or to underestimate TFP growth. When unmeasured *output* is growing ($\Delta a > 0$), TFP growth is underestimated (the 1974 story) as resources are diverted to investment. When unmeasured *input* is growing ($\Delta c > 0$), TFP growth is overestimated. In a steady state, of course, the accumulation equation implies that $\Delta c = \Delta a$, which in turn implies that the steady-state mismeasurement is

$$\frac{C}{Y^{NT}} \left[F_C - \frac{A}{C} \right] g = \frac{C}{Y^{NT}} \left[(r^* + \delta_C) - \frac{g + \delta_C}{1 + g} \right] g$$

where r^* is the steady-state real interest rate. In a dynamically efficient economy, the mismeasurement is necessarily positive: true steady-state TFP growth is *lower* than measured, not higher.

This point is a simple one, but it is a quantitatively important correction to statements in the existing literature (e.g., Bessen, 2003).[32] Of course, if one corrects only output mismeasurement (Δa), then ICT will appear fantastically productive, far beyond what is ordinarily measured. But firms choose to divert resources to unobserved investment Δa to create an intangible capital stock that contributes to future production. The resulting unmeasured flow of capital services implies a bias in the other direction. The net bias may be either positive or negative at a point in time, but it is positive in the steady state.

We now seek an observable proxy for unobserved investment in, and growth in the stock of, complementary capital. In light of the firm-level evidence, observed growth in ICT capital provides a reasonable proxy. Suppose G takes a CES form:

$$G = \left[\alpha K^{IT\,(\sigma-1)/\sigma} + (1 - \alpha)\, C^{(\sigma-1)/\sigma} \right]^{\sigma/\sigma-1}$$

We consider the optimization subproblem of producing G at minimum cost, which firms solve every period. The solution of the subproblem is:

$$\Delta c_t = \Delta k_t^{IT} + \sigma \Delta p_t^{IT} \tag{8}$$

where Δp_t^{IT} is the change in the relative rental rate of ICT capital to C capital. This equation implies a direct link between growth in complementary capital and growth of observed ICT capital.

---

32. Laitner and Stolyarov (2001) also stress the importance of including complementary capital in a growth accounting exercise.

We can use the accumulation equation to express unobserved investment Δa in terms of current and lagged growth in unobserved capital Δc:

$$\Delta a_t = \frac{C}{A} \left[\Delta c_t - \frac{(1 - \delta_C)}{(1 + g)} \Delta c_{t-1} \right]$$

Substituting the last equation and equation (8) into equation (7), we have in principle an equation for TFP growth that indicates the importance of complementary capital accumulation:

$$\Delta TFP = \left[\frac{F_C C}{Y^{NT}} - \frac{C}{Y^{NT}} \right] \left[\Delta k_t^{IT} + \sigma \Delta p_t^{IT} \right]$$

$$+ \left[\frac{C}{Y^{NT}} \frac{(1 - \delta_C)}{(1 + g)} \right] \left[\Delta k_{t-1}^{IT} + \sigma \Delta p_{t-1}^{IT} \right] + s_G \Delta z \qquad (9)$$

The first term is proportional to $(r^* + \delta - 1)$, so under reasonable circumstances it is negative. The second term, on the other hand, is clearly positive. Hence, our GPT-type framework implies that firms or industries that invest substantially in GPTs have lower current measured output but higher future measured output; that is, other things being equal, industries that are making large IT investments today will have low measured TFP growth, but those that made such investments in the *past* will have high measured TFP growth. (This discussion is independent of any externalities, which may also be important.)

As an estimating equation, equation (9) has the difficulty that industries are likely to differ in their long-run C/Y^{NT} ratios. Using the CES assumption for G, the cost-minimizing first order condition implies that:

$$\frac{K^{IT}}{C} = \left[\left(\frac{1 - \alpha}{\alpha} \right)^{\sigma} \right] \left(\frac{P_K}{P} \right)^{-\sigma}$$

or

$$\frac{C}{Y^{NT}} = \frac{PC}{P_K K^{IT}} \frac{P_K K^{IT}}{PY^{NT}} = \left[\left(\frac{1 - \alpha}{\alpha} \right)^{\sigma} \right] \left(\frac{P_K}{P} \right)^{1-\sigma} s_{K^{IT}}$$

In the convenient Cobb-Douglas case, the C/Y^{NT} ratio is proportional to the observed ICT share; other things being equal, the mismeasurement of complementary capital is more important in those industries where ICT capital is used to a greater extent—a reasonable conclusion.

$$\Delta TFP = \left[F_C - 1 \right] \beta \tilde{k}_t + \left[\frac{(1 - \delta_C)}{(1 + g)} \right] \beta \tilde{k}_{t-1} + s_G \Delta z \qquad (10)$$

where $\tilde{k}_t = \left(\frac{P_K}{P} \right)^{1-\sigma} s_{K^{ICT}} \left[\Delta k_t^{ICT} + \sigma \Delta p_t^{ICT} \right]$

$$\beta = \left(\frac{1 - \alpha}{\alpha} \right)^{\sigma}$$

As an alternative way of implementing equation (7), can we take ICT investment as a direct proxy for unobserved complementary capital investment? Combining the accumulation equations for complementary capital and ICT capital implies:

$$\frac{A_{it}}{C_{it}} = \frac{I_{it}}{K_{it-1}} + \left(\delta_C - \delta_{ICT}\right) + \sigma\Delta p^{ICT}$$

If $\delta_C = \delta_{ICT}$ and $\sigma = 0$, then $\Delta a = \Delta i^{ICT}$, which implies:

$$\Delta TFP_{it} = F_C \tilde{k}_{it} - \left(\frac{PA}{P_I I}\right)\left(\frac{P_I I}{PY}\right) \Delta i_{it}^{ICT} + s_G \Delta z_{it}$$

$$= F_C \tilde{k}_{it} - b\tilde{i}_{it} + s_G dz_{it} \tag{11}$$

where $\tilde{i}_{it} = s_{it}^I \Delta i_{it}^{ICT}$

Note that the capital and investment terms incorporate the income share of complementary capital and the share of complementary investment in output, which are likely to differ greatly across industries. So we are assuming that the complementary shares are correlated across industries with the ICT shares.

When is equation (10) preferable to equation (11)? The key issue is the lag between ICT investment and complementary investment. For example, suppose a company invested heavily in an expensive enterprise resource management system in the mid-1980s and then spent the next decade learning how best to reorganize and thus benefit from the improved information availability. Then equation (10)—with long lags—should work well. By contrast, if the reorganization were contemporaneous with the ICT investment, then equation (11) should work well (assuming the other conditions involved in deriving it are not too unreasonable) and there might not be long lags.

Our method of using cost-minimization conditions to act as proxies for unobserved variables from observables is common in the literature on cyclical productivity with unobserved factor input (utilization).[33] As in that literature, the method can imply a fairly elaborate proxy, which may not be easy to estimate. Given that fact, should we try to follow Hall (2001) and several other authors, who measure the importance of organizational capital from the gap between firms' stock market valuations and the replacement values of their physical capital?[34]

We do not do so, for two reasons. First, given the importance of the issue, it is interesting to investigate a different approach to estimation and see if we get roughly the same answer. Second, given the recent large swings in equity markets, we are wary of any attempt to impute the real

33. See, for example, Basu and Kimball (1997).
34. See Brynjolfsson and Yang (2001) for an example of this alternative approach.

service flow of the stock of organizational capital from stock-market valuations. Setting aside the usual concerns about stock-market bubbles, suppose the recent fall in equity prices is due to the realization that much of the current ecapital will become obsolete sooner than previously expected. This information will appropriately lead to a lower market value of the capital, but it does not imply that its current real service flow into production must be lower.[35]

4.4 EXTENSIONS TO THE BASIC FRAMEWORK

Clearly, the implications of a new GPT for measured productivity growth are subtle and may be hard to distinguish from alternatives. But the theory does suggest that one needs lags of ICT capital growth in the TFP equation, in addition to the current growth rate.[36]

One complication is that the externality captured in Δz can be a function of industry C_i as well as aggregate C. In that plausible case, one can no longer tell whether the capital growth terms in equation (9) represent accumulation of a private stock, or externalities that are internalized within the industry. Similarly, if we find that lagged Δk^{IT} is important for explaining current productivity growth, we do not know whether that finding supports the theory we have outlined or whether it indicates that the externality is a function of lagged capital.

In addition, a free parameter is the length of a period, a point on which the theory gives us no guidance. The lagged Δk^{IT} may be last year's ITC capital accumulation or the last decade's. Furthermore, equation (3) for the accumulation of complementary capital has no adjustment costs or time-to-build or time-to-plan lags in the accumulation of C. But such frictions and lags are likely to be important in practice, making it even harder to uncover the link between ICT and measured TFP.

One additional concern is whether other variables should enter the production function for A, which we do not account for here. Our framework implicitly assumes the same production function for A and Y. But it is possible, as many have recognized, that the production of complementary

---

35. Formally, capital aggregation theory shows that the service flow of capital is proportional to the value of the stock only if depreciation occurs at a constant, exponential rate. A large, one-time capital loss is an excellent example of a nonconstant depreciation rate. Jovanovic and Rousseau (2003) make exactly the same argument about changes in stock-market valuation when a GPT is introduced. But given the false starts and dead ends that often accompany a recently introduced GPT, their logic should apply equally to episodes after the GPT is introduced but before it has become a mature technology. (Think, for example, of DC power generation in the United States.)

36. Hence one needs to generalize the approach followed by, e.g., Stiroh (2002b), who argues against a spillovers/GPT story by regressing TFP growth on only the current-year growth rate of IT capital. Brynjolfsson and Hitt (2002) also find significant lags in firm-level data, which dovetails our more aggregative evidence.

capital is particularly intensive in skilled (i.e., college-educated) labor.[37] This hypothesis is particularly interesting given the noticeable difference between the United States and the United Kingdom in the fraction of skilled workers that we documented in Table 3. If true, the hypothesis implies that the relative price of accumulating complementary capital may differ significantly between the two countries (and perhaps among industries within a country) in ways that we may not be able to capture.

5. Evidence for the GPT Hypothesis

5.1 EMPIRICAL EVIDENCE ON THE ROLE OF ICT

We concluded earlier that much of the U.S. acceleration in measured TFP reflects an acceleration outside the production of ICT products. TFP can move around for many reasons unrelated to ICT. For example, it could be that the United States experienced broadbased managerial innovations that raised TFP growth throughout the economy. Nevertheless, the previous section suggests that the acceleration—and managerial innovations—could be associated with the use of ICT.

Several studies explore whether TFP growth across industries is correlated with ICT intensity. In contrast to firm-level studies, these industry studies rarely find much correlation between ICT capital and TFP growth (e.g., Stiroh, 2002b; Wolff, 2002). But given the GPT nature of ICT, the contemporaneous correlation need not be positive—even if ICT is, in fact, an important contributor to measured TFP.

Wolff does find that U.S. industries investing heavily in ICT have greater changes in their occupational mix and the composition of intermediate inputs, consistent with substantial reorganization. Gust and Marquez (2002) find that, in a sample of industrial countries, those with a more burdensome regulatory environment—particularly regulations affecting labor market practices—adopted ICT more slowly and also had slower TFP growth. Those findings are consistent with the notion that the uptake of ICT could affect measured TFP in the sectors using the ICT.[38]

37. In a different framework, Krueger and Kumar (2003) ask whether the different educational systems in the United States and Europe (especially Germany) may be responsible for their different growth experiences in the 1990s. See also Lynch and Nickell (2002).

38. In terms of standard growth-accounting, van Ark et al. (2002) compare the United States and the European Union by applying U.S. deflators for ICT and equipment. Earlier comparisons by Daveri (2002) and Schreyer (2000), using private sector sources for ICT investment and stocks, and Colecchia and Schreyer (2002), using national accounts data, find results broadly consistent with those of van Ark et al. who find that the European Union and the United States had similar ICT growth rates over 1980–2000. But the European Union had a lower *level* of ICT investment. Consequently, the income share of ICT is much lower in the European Union. As a result, van Ark et al. (2002) find a smaller direct ICT contribution via capital deepening in the European Union.

As discussed in Section 2, the Gust-Marquez regulatory variables look similar in the United States and the United Kingdom. But an open question is whether, for other reasons, U.S. society was better able to undertake the disruptions associated with reorganization than was the United Kingdom (or other countries).

5.2 THE CROSS-INDUSTRY PATTERN OF ICT USE IN THE UNITED STATES AND THE UNITED KINGDOM

A small number of U.S. and U.K. industries account for a large share of ICT use. For example, the finance/insurance and business services/real estate sectors have a disproportionate share of computers and software; communications uses a majority of communications equipment. Manufacturing, which accounts for about one-fifth of GDP in both countries, has only 14 to 16% of computers and software in the two countries.

Tables 6 and 7 show one measure of the importance of ICT capital—the ICT income share, i.e., the ratio of profits attributable to ICT capital to value added. Between 1990 and 2000, the income share of ICT in the United Kingdom increased by almost 50%, rising from 4.30% to 6.26%. The biggest rises occurred in communication (+10.1%), wholesaling (+3.5%), and nondurables (+2.66%). The overall share is now above the corresponding figure for the United States, 5.50%, which rose by much less in the 1990s. In short, on this measure, the United Kingdom has caught up.

These income shares are central for growth accounting because the contribution of ICT capital to output growth uses these shares as weights on growth in ICT capital services. These shares are now similar, which means that we expect a given growth in ICT capital to have the same impact on output growth. In addition, the GPT model above suggests that unobserved complementary capital should be closely related to observed share-weighted ICT capital growth (perhaps with an adjustment for the relative price of ICT).

5.3 CROSS-INDUSTRY EVIDENCE ON THE ROLE OF COMPLEMENTARY INVESTMENT

We now present some preliminary cross-sectional industry evidence for the United States and the United Kingdom that is, broadly speaking, consistent with the hypothesis that complementary investment associated with ICT has macroeconomic consequences. In particular, we explore the correlations between productivity growth (or the productivity acceleration) in the second half of the 1990s and various measures of ICT growth.

Such regressions are, of course, fraught with the potential for misspecification, given the uncertainty about how long it takes to build complementary capital and how long it takes for any spillovers to occur. In addition, given the difficulty of identifying valid instruments, all of our regression results are ordinary least squares (OLS); they capture any correlation between true non-ICT-related industry productivity growth and the accumulation of ICT capital, regardless of the direction of causation (if there is any causation at all). It follows that all our regressions need to be interpreted with a high degree of caution, and they should be interpreted in the spirit of data exploration. Nevertheless, the results suggest that the GPT model does help illuminate the effects of ICT on productivity.

We begin by estimating equation (10). One important difficulty in implementing this equation is that we don't know the length of time over which it should operate. The time lags depend on factors such as the time it takes to learn, innovate, and reorganize, which depends in large part on the adjustment costs associated with that complementary capital investment. Brynjolfsson and Hitt (2002) find evidence of long lags in firm-level data; Howitt (1998) calibrates a model to U.S. data and finds that the beneficial effects of a new GPT will not be detected in conventional national accounts data for more than 20 years.

To capture these notions in a loose way, we consider the following:

$$\Delta p_i^{1995-2000} = c_i + a\tilde{k}_i^{1995-2000} + b\tilde{k}_i^{1990-1995} + c\tilde{k}_i^{1980-1990} + \varepsilon_i$$

In this regression, $\tilde{k}^{1995-2000}$, for example, represents the average value of $\tilde{k}$ for computers and software over the period 1995 to 2000.[39] Thus, we regress average industry TFP growth over the 1995–2000 period on average share-weighted computer and software capital growth in the 1980s, early 1990s, and late 1990s. (We ignore the relative price terms in these regressions.)

We take this equation for each industry as a cross-sectional observation. This approach imposes an identical constant term on each industry, so that any industry-specific fixed effects show up in the error term.[40] Thus, this regression will tell us, simply as a matter of data description, whether we can relate productivity growth to relatively current as well as lagged ICT investment in the cross section. Because we are running an OLS regression, we cannot, of course, infer causation from the results. But this regression tells us whether productivity growth from 1995–2000 was larger in industries that had rapid share-weighted ICT growth in the late or early 1990s, the 1980s, or none of the above. (With minimal restrictions on the timing and stability; these are likely to differ across industries.) In the results that follow, we omit ICT-producing industries to focus on links between ICT *use* and TFP. (Including ICT producers generally has little

39. The regressions including communications equipment as part of ICT gave results that were less significant—arguably because of lack of sufficient adjustment for quality change in communications equipment.
40. We find similar results for a specification that removes these fixed effects by making the dependent variable the *change* in TFP growth from 1990–1995 to 1995–2000.

Table 6 UNITED STATES COMPUTER, SOFTWARE, AND COMMUNICATION SHARES OF VALUE-ADDED REVENUE (Percentage)

	1990				2000			
	Computer	Software	Communication	Total ICT	Computer	Software	Communication	Total ICT
Private nonfarm economy	1.35	1.24	1.70	4.29	1.60	2.31	1.59	5.50
Mining	0.18	0.15	0.32	0.65	0.27	0.36	0.13	0.77
Manufacturing	1.09	0.94	0.56	2.59	1.32	1.81	0.61	3.74
Nondurables	0.76	0.66	0.31	1.73	1.00	1.37	0.53	2.89
Durables	1.48	1.26	0.84	3.58	1.74	2.32	0.71	4.77
Construction	0.42	0.37	0.12	0.91	2.89	4.01	1.19	8.09
Transportation	0.16	0.14	1.52	1.82	0.64	0.87	2.44	3.95
Communication	1.23	1.09	30.51	32.83	1.70	2.51	24.81	29.01
Electric/gas/sanitary	1.33	1.14	3.18	5.65	1.25	1.66	3.10	6.01
Wholesale trade	2.78	2.48	0.87	6.12	4.37	5.34	1.19	10.91
Retail trade	1.03	0.85	0.20	2.08	1.04	1.35	0.31	2.69

Finance and insurance	3.35	3.56	1.16	8.06	2.60	5.22	0.87	8.69
Finance[1]	3.90	4.16	1.38	9.44	3.01	6.09	0.98	10.08
Insurance	1.97	2.06	0.59	4.62	1.55	2.99	0.61	5.15
Business services and real estate	1.98	1.86	0.64	4.48	1.87	2.08	0.47	4.43
Business services	4.75	4.48	0.95	10.17	3.44	3.82	0.70	7.96
Real estate	0.05	0.04	0.42	0.50	0.13	0.14	0.23	0.49
Other services	0.69	0.62	0.25	1.56	0.67	1.23	0.27	2.16
ICT-producing[2]	1.84	1.57	1.39	4.80	2.49	3.29	0.83	6.60
Non-ICT-producing	1.32	1.23	1.73	4.28	1.56	2.27	1.64	5.47
Well-measured ind.[3]	1.15	0.99	2.39	4.53	1.58	2.06	2.41	6.06
Well-measured (excluding ICT-producing)	1.08	0.94	2.53	4.55	1.51	1.96	2.59	6.06

1. "Holding and other investment offices" data were included in finance, and other services contains more services than had been previously defined for our calculations of productivity.
2. For the United States: ICT-producing includes industrial machinery and electronic and other electrical equipment sectors.
3. For the United States and the United Kingdom: Well-measured industries include mining, manufacturing, transportation, communication, electric/gas/sanitary and wholesale and retail trade.
Source: Authors' calculations using payments to ICT capital from the Bureau of Labor Statistics and nominal value added from the Bureau of Economic Analysis.

Table 7 UNITED KINGDOM: COMPUTER, SOFTWARE, AND COMMUNICATION SHARES OF VALUE-ADDED REVENUE (Percentage)

	1990				2000			
	Computer	Software	Communication	Total ICT	Computer	Software	Communication	Total ICT
Private nonfarm economy	1.97	1.58	0.75	4.30	2.82	2.59	0.85	6.26
Mining	0.04	0.11	0.22	0.37	0.02	0.22	0.11	0.35
Manufacturing	0.68	1.08	0.29	2.05	1.74	1.25	0.29	3.28
Nondurables	0.53	0.97	0.47	1.98	2.41	1.55	0.68	4.64
Durables	0.75	1.13	0.20	2.08	1.41	1.11	0.11	2.62
Construction	0.31	2.85	0.49	3.65	0.41	3.11	0.26	3.78
Transportation	0.35	0.35	0.02	0.73	1.10	1.32	0.02	2.44
Communication	1.12	0.22	6.85	8.19	5.51	2.03	10.72	18.26
Electric/gas/sanitary	0.78	0.65	0.83	2.25	1.34	1.10	0.86	3.30
Wholesale trade	2.99	1.55	0.89	5.43	4.74	4.12	0.55	9.40
Retail trade	1.03	0.95	1.28	3.26	1.21	1.46	0.55	3.22

Finance and insurance	5.51	5.90	0.05	11.46	4.75	8.53	0.09	13.37
Finance								
Insurance								
Business services and real estate	6.13	1.84	0.39	8.37	5.70	3.74	0.58	10.02
Business services								
Real estate								
Other services	1.55	1.20	1.37	4.12	1.58	1.88	1.16	4.61
ICT-producing[1]	0.81	1.87	1.21	3.88	2.79	2.61	0.83	6.23
Non-ICT-producing	1.49	1.25	0.60	3.34	2.74	2.57	0.82	6.13
Well-measured ind.[2]	0.91	0.90	0.90	2.71	2.00	1.59	1.05	4.64
Well-measured (excluding ICT-producing)	0.92	0.84	0.88	2.64	1.90	1.55	1.03	4.48

1. For the United Kingdom: ICT-producing comprises electrical engineering and electronics (SIC92 30-33)
2. For the United Kingdom: well-measured industries comprise mining, manufacturing, transportation, communication, electricity, water and gas supply, wholesale, retail trade, and waste treatment.

Figure 1 CAPITAL SHARE × CAPITAL GROWTH

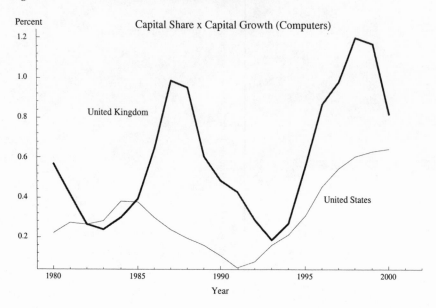

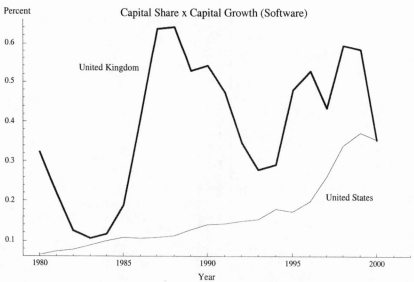

Table 8   ICT REGRESSIONS WITH CURRENT AND LAGGED ICT CAPITAL GROWTH[1]

	United States	United Kingdom
C	−0.001	−0.09
	(0.003)	(0.48)
$\tilde{k}_{1980-1990}$	4.1	1.39
	(7.2)	(3.56)
$\tilde{k}_{1990-1995}$	17.4	0.65
	(5.7)	(2.80)
$\tilde{k}_{1995-2000}$	−8.9	0.65
	(4.8)	(1.48)
Poorly*C	0.011	−0.18
	(0.0058)	(0.48)
Poorly* $\tilde{k}_{1980-1990}$	15.3	2.77
	(7.7)	(3.56)
Poorly* $\tilde{k}_{1990-1995}$	−8.1	−1.60
	(6.6)	(2.80)
Poorly* $\tilde{k}_{1995-2000}$	−10.1	−2.60
	(5.8)	(1.48)
R^2	0.38	0.10
Observations	49	28

1. Using $\tilde{k} = S_K \, \Delta \ln k$ as right-hand regressor, with computers and software as measure of capital. Robust standard errors in parentheses. We omit ICT-producing industries (this omission has relatively little effect on coefficients).

effect on coefficients.) We report results for only the measures of $\tilde{k}$ described above—i.e., for share weighted computer-and-software capital growth.

Figure 1 plots the individual components (computers and software capital) of this measure in the United Kingdom and the United States. The figure shows substantial fluctuations over time for $\tilde{k}$ in the United Kingdom and a more stable pattern for the United States, especially since 1990. This measure of $\tilde{k}$ drops the relative price terms from the alternatives discussed; regression results below appeared more stable with this measure than with the alternatives, although qualitative results were generally similar.

The first column of Table 8 shows that, for the United States, the data are reasonably consistent with the predictions of the theory section that, with long lags, ICT capital growth should be positively associated with TFP growth and that, controlling for past investments, contemporaneous ICT capital growth should be negatively associated with TFP growth. The data definitely want different coefficients across the well-measured and poorly measured groups, which we have addressed by interacting a poorly measured dummy with all right-hand-side variables.[41]

41. The point estimates give a reasonable summary of what happens when we estimate regressions for the two groups separately.

We find that, for both groups, ICT capital investments in the 1980s are positively correlated with the TFP acceleration in the late 1990s. For the poorly measured industries, ICT capital investments from the early 1990s were also positively associated with the TFP acceleration. In the late 1990s, by contrast, share-weighted capital growth is negatively correlated with the TFP acceleration, statistically significantly so for the poorly measured industries. The results for the poorly measured industries are consistent with the firm-level evidence in Bryjolfsson and Hitt (2002) and also suggest a lag length of about five years for U.S. firms.

These results are not driven by outliers. For example, two influential observations (based on the Belsley, Kuh, and Welsch hat matrix test)[42] are wholesale and retail trade. Because of the importance of those two industries in accounting for TFP growth, we experimented with omitting them. Doing so makes 1980s growth less important but 1990s growth more important—1990–1995 is more positive and 1995–2000 is more negative. These results could reflect that wholesale and retail trade have particularly long lags because of the importance of complementary capital. They may also be industries where endogeneity is particularly important. (For reasons unrelated to GPT arguments, ICT grew a lot in the late 1990s, just when the scale of complementary investment was waning.[43])

For the United Kingdom the same regression shows little.[44] Almost nothing is statistically significant, and the signs are reversed from what theory suggested. The lack of significance could reflect mismeasurement—the industry ICT capital stock data for the 1980s are not that reliable. But taken at face value, these results suggest that either the slowdown in U.K. TFP growth was not driven by complementary capital investment or that our ICT-based proxy for such investment works particularly poorly in the United Kingdom (perhaps because our specification is too simple). Another possibility is that the timing assumptions embedded in the estimating equation (on lags between observed ICT investment and unobserved complementary investments) do not match the U.K. experience.

42. One standard statistical test is to look at the diagonal of the hat matrix, $X'(X'X)^{-1}X'$. For a regression with k coefficients and n observations, Belsley, Kuh, and Welsch (1980) identify influential observations as those where the diagonal element of the hat matrix exceeds $2k/n$.

43. Using the Belsley, Kuh, and Welsch hat matrix test, influential observations include telephone and telegraph, wholesale and retail trade, depository and nondepository institutions, securities brokers, real estate, and business services. When those observations (which account for about one-third of GDP) are omitted, there is no evidence that poorly measured and well-measured industries look different—including the dummy variables would have only minor effects on coefficients or even standard errors. When these outliers are omitted, the data suggest that lagged growth of share-weighted computers and software are positively correlated with late 1990s TFP growth, whereas contemporaneous growth is negatively correlated with TFP.

44. Due to concerns about the data, we drop rail transport, leaving 29 industries.

Table 9 shows results from our second specification, equation (11), which we term the investment accelerator specification. As noted in the theory discussion, this equation may perform better if the complementary investment were closely correlated in time with the ICT investment. We can estimate this equation as a cross section for different time periods. When we do so, we find the right-hand side variables are insignificant. This finding is not surprising because the constant term in the specification differs across industries and may well be correlated with the explanatory variables. But a cross-section regression imposes a common constant. Hence we prefer to take first differences of both sides, thus eliminating the fixed effects. Our dependent variable is now the *acceleration* of TFP growth; i.e., average TFP growth in 1995–2000 minus average TFP growth in 1990–1995. The ICT and investment-deepening terms are defined analogously as changes in weighted growth rates. The estimating equation thus becomes:

$$\left(\Delta TFP_{i,\,1995-2000} - \Delta TFP_{i,\,1990-1995} \right) = c_i + a \left(\tilde{k}_{i,\,1995-2000} - \tilde{k}_{i,\,1990-1995} \right)$$
$$- b \left(\tilde{i}_{i,\,1995-2000} - \tilde{i}_{i,\,1990-1995} \right) + \varepsilon_i$$

Table 9 shows these results. For the United States, this equation shows little, basically reflecting the point made above, that the U.S. data want long lags.

By contrast, in the United Kingdom, the coefficients have the expected signs and are statistically significant. As expected, ICT capital deepening enters with a positive sign and is significant. Also as expected, investment deepening has a negative sign; we find that it too is significant. Three industries are influential according to the hat matrix, but dropping them has little effect on the results.

This result is highly suggestive, but there is an important qualification. Multiplying these means by their respective coefficients, we find that capital deepening would have raised TFP growth by 0.93% per annum on average, while investment deepening would have lowered it by 0.47% per

Table 9   INVESTMENT-ACCELERATION FORM OF ICT REGRESSION[1]

	United States	United Kingdom
$\left(\tilde{k}_{i,1995-2000} - \tilde{k}_{i,1990-1995} \right)$	0.21	4.41
	(2.27)	(1.02)
$\left(\tilde{i}_{i,1995-2000} - \tilde{i}_{i,1990-1995} \right)$	−0.04	−1.63
	(0.75)	(0.41)
R^2	0.01	0.41
Observations	49	28

1. Robust standard errors in parentheses. Constant term not shown. We omit ICT-producing industries (this omission has relatively little effect on coefficients).

annum, for a net positive effect of 0.46% per annum. So although investment deepening did serve to retard measured TFP growth, it cannot be said to account for the absolute fall in TFP growth.

On the other hand, one would expect endogeneity considerations to be particularly important in this equation, in a way that works against finding results consistent with the GPT hypothesis, even if true. In this specification, we regress the TFP acceleration on the contemporaneous investment acceleration. Because investment is endogenous, a positive industry-specific technology shock could lead to higher investment as well as higher TFP, thereby biasing the coefficient on investment upward. Hence, the true investment coefficient may be more negative than we find in our OLS regression.

In sum, the U.S. evidence is consistent with the notion that ICT investments affect measured productivity growth with a long (but variable) lag. Contemporaneously, they are correlated with a lot of diverted resources toward unmeasured complementary investment, and hence they are negatively correlated with output—once one controls for lagged growth rates. It appears that, in the United Kingdom, the rapid growth of ICT investment after 1995—which was higher than the growth of the ICT capital stock—appreciably retarded the measured growth of productivity. Comparing the second half with the first half of the 1990s, the change in TFP growth is positively and significantly related to the change in ICT capital deepening. But it appears significantly and negatively associated with ICT *investment* growth. In the long run, of course, ICT capital and investment must grow at the same rate. This finding suggests one reason that TFP growth in the United Kingdom will eventually recover, at least somewhat. The U.K. data suggest that the lags are much shorter—and that complementary investment was going on in the late 1990s. Although this effect is present, it is not large enough to explain the TFP slowdown in the United Kingdom in the late 1990s.

5.4 EXPLAINING THE U.K. EXPERIENCE

The basic story that we wish to tell based on our simple model of complementary capital investment is one where *measured* output growth is contemporaneously low when complementary investment is high, and it is high in periods after such investment has taken place and the stock of complementary capital is high. The theory also suggests that complementary capital investment will generally be high when observed investment in ICT capital times the share of such capital is high.

Apart from the evidence presented in Table 9, another reason we took this approach is that the aggregate data appear consistent with this story. Look at Figure 1 and the summary statistics by subsample for the United States and the United Kingdom given in Table 1. The regressions used the industry-level versions of the variable plotted in the top panel of Figure 1, the computer share times the growth rate of the computer stock, but we also plot the analogous series for software in the lower panel. We conclude that the United Kingdom had far larger swings in this key variable than did the United States, especially in the period before 1995. As we discussed before, the regressions with U.S. data support the hypothesis that the positive effects of IT investment and—we assume—complementary capital investment show up in measured output with a lag of about five years. (Two important industries in the United States, wholesale and retail trade, prefer longer lags, but these industries are not as important for explaining the U.K. experience as they are for explaining the U.S. experience.)

If investments become productive with roughly a five-year lag, Figure 1 shows that the broad outlines of the macro experience in the United Kingdom are consistent with the story that we are telling. Note that the United Kingdom had extremely high levels of $\tilde{k}$ for both computers and software in the 1985–1990 period, and both dropped sharply in the 1990–1995 period as the United Kingdom fell into a deep recession. Our story suggests that measured TFP growth in 1985–1990 should have been low, and measured growth in 1990–1995 should have been high. This is the pattern one finds in Table 1, where TFP growth in 1985–1990 was 1.2%, and growth in 1990–1995 was 1.6%. Note that this difference is almost certainly understated because the TFP numbers have not been corrected for cyclical mismeasurement coming from changes in utilization. The period of the late 1980s was a time of strong output and fixed investment growth (3.1 and 7%, respectively), while the corresponding figures for the early 1990s are 1.8 and –0.8%. It is amazing that a period with a deep recession should show an increase in measured TFP growth at all, and such a development indicates to us that the effects of IT and complementary capital investment may be quantitatively important.

If one accepts this story, then it should be unsurprising that the next five years were bad for measured TFP growth in the United Kingdom. The reason is twofold. First, the level of IT investment in the previous five years was low, so the contribution of complementary capital was presumably low. Second, the United Kingdom also had a steep increase in computer and software investment in the second half of the 1990s—in many ways a stronger surge than the one labeled historic in the United States. According to our story, this should also have been a time of high unmeasured investment in complementary capital. Both considerations have the effect of reducing measured TFP growth.

Some evidence is consistent with the idea that the United Kingdom was experiencing a surge of supply-driven growth in the period 1995–2000. Note that during this period the United Kingdom was going from a deep slump to a boom. The average growth rate of output was 1 percentage point, and that of investment was 7.2 percentage points, while unemployment fell a full 2.8 percentage points—to 6.7%, a level not seen for decades. And in the midst of this boom, the inflation rate also fell, by 1.4 percentage points—to 2.5%. Admittedly, it is not clear that embedding our story in a short-run macro model must lead to this result because we claim that TFP growth was higher than recorded, in turn because output growth was also higher than recorded, which should put extra upward pressure on prices. But it is suggestive in part because it is difficult to see how else one might reconcile the full set of facts.

Having said all this, it remains true that, although regression results for U.K. industries are somewhat consistent with this GPT story, the point estimates do not allow us to explain the recent growth and TFP experience based on investment in unmeasured complementary capital. That is, the regression suggests that the net effect of ICT is to raise, not lower, TFP growth when comparing the first and second halves of the 1990s.

But as we have already discussed, the form of the equation that appears to work better for the United Kingdom is also subject to larger endogeneity concerns, with a bias against finding support for the GPT view; this provides a potential, but so far only speculative, reconciliation. A second possibility is that the accumulation of complementary capital requires large inputs of skilled labor. This possibility suggests that our proxy for complementary investment may be too simple; we may also need to allow for cross-industry variations in skill intensity. Indeed, it could be that, even if complementary investment explains the divergent TFP performance, it is not, in fact, as closely linked to ICT capital accumulation in the United Kingdom as it is in the United States.

6. Conclusion

The "crime" or puzzle we investigated in this paper was the slowdown in U.K. productivity growth, both TFP and labor, in the second half of the 1990s, which coincided with rising U.S. productivity growth. We found that for the private nonfarm economy, the slowdown was nearly one percentage point. The slowdown was particularly marked in industries like wholesale and retail trade, that were among the major contributors to the U.S. improvement.

Many proposed explanations for the weak U.K. productivity performance seem insufficient. For example, the differences do not reflect differences in the importance of ICT production or a failure to account for falling labor quality. Nor do the genuine differences in national accounts methodology explain the differences: the U.K. slowdown persists even when the same methodology is applied to both countries.

Earlier work for the United States suggested that the disruption cost associated with investment might play a role because, in periods when investment is rising, such costs may reduce measured productivity growth. Investment accelerated even more sharply in the United Kingdom than in the United States in the second half of the 1990s, so this suspect has some explaining to do. We found that disruption costs could account for at most about one-third of the measured slowdown.

The most obvious suspects for the U.K. performance seem to have alibis, so we take an alternative path.[45] In particular, we believe that understanding why the United Kingdom has not yet seen a TFP acceleration requires that we understand why, in fact, the United States *did*. Our answer emphasizes ICT and the role of complementary investments and innovations induced by it. To many observers, ICT seems to be the major locus of innovation in recent decades, but at the same time, we find that most of the measured TFP acceleration took place outside the production of ICT goods. These two observations are consistent with the predictions of models of ICT as a general-purpose technology.

In particular, a pervasive theme of the microeconomic literature on ICT is the need for organizational change if full advantage is to be taken of the new technology. We modeled organizational change as the accumulation of intangible complementary capital, which means that the typical firm is also producing a stream of intangible output that constitutes gross investment in complementary capital. Some of this output, such as the production of own-account software, is now explicitly measured in the national accounts, but arguably much is not. To the extent that there is unmeasured output and unmeasured capital, conventional TFP growth will be a biased measure of true technical change. Growth in the complementary capital stock tends to raise measured TFP growth, but growth of complementary investment tends to reduce it by diverting resources from normal production. During the transition to a new steady state, the net bias can go either way, but the more that the growth rate of complementary investment (unmeasured output) exceeds that of complementary capital (unmeasured input), the more likely it is that measured TFP will be below the true rate of technical change. This GPT view also suggests that current productivity growth

---

45. In keeping with the mystery theme of this paper, now seems an appropriate time to quote Sherlock Holmes: "[W]hen you have excluded the impossible, whatever remains, however improbable, must be the truth." We are dumbfounded anew by Holmes's genius because we have never managed to exclude enough impossibles to reduce the improbable-but-true set to a singleton!

may be influenced by the accumulation of complementary capital in earlier periods.

A fundamental difficulty, of course, is that complementary investment and capital are unmeasured. Theory suggests, however, that observed ICT capital and investment should serve as reasonable proxies. In line with this GPT view, the U.S. industry data suggest that ICT capital growth is associated with industry TFP growth with long (and perhaps variable) lags of five to 15 years. Indeed, if we control for past growth in ICT capital, contemporaneous growth in ICT capital is negatively associated with TFP growth in the late 1990s. We find this result encouraging because, to our knowledge, no other empirical exercise has connected aggregate and industry-level U.S. TFP performance in the late 1990s either to the persuasive macro models of general-purpose technologies or to the stimulating micro empirical work that supports the GPT hypothesis.

The results for the United Kingdom are weaker. But we do find that, in the United Kingdom, the rapid growth of ICT investment after 1995, which was higher than the growth of ICT capital, appreciably retarded the measured growth of productivity. Comparing the second with the first half of the 1990s, the change in TFP growth is positively and significantly related to the change in ICT capital deepening. But it is significantly and negatively associated with ICT *investment* growth (the latter weighted by the investment-output ratio). These results are consistent with the notion that U.K. firms were accumulating complementary capital intensively in the late 1990s, in contrast with the U.S. accumulation much earlier. Hence, in this view, the U.K. economy most likely experienced strong underlying TFP growth despite the poor measured figures. But the point estimates suggest that, as a whole, ICT investment raised, not lowered, overall TFP growth in the United Kingdom in the late 1990s—i.e., they do not explain the pervasive TFP slowdown.

The results in this paper are suggestive, but it is too early to indict complementary capital as the sole perpetrator of the crime. Of course, it is always a challenge to provide incontrovertible proof of a hypothesis that implies that both inputs and output are unobserved! Nevertheless, several puzzles remain. In particular, if our hypothesis is correct, why did the United Kingdom invest later in complementary capital than did the United States? Even if they did invest later, why are the coefficients on contemporaneous ICT investment so low?

One hypothesis that we are considering in current research is that there may have been a shortage of skilled, college-educated managers to implement the necessary reorganizations earlier. This hypothesis would suggest that our model (and our empirical specification) is too simple: we need a third factor, skilled labor, to make complementary capital productive or else its accumulation cheaper. Certainly, the evidence that the skills premium has widened in the United Kingdom (as it did earlier in the United States) is potentially consistent with this view. This hypothesis also suggests that, on its own, ICT might be an inadequate proxy to capture fully the complementary investments we think are happening.

In addition, although labor and product market regulation generally appear similar, differences in competitive intensity could still play a role. A major contrast between the United States and the United Kingdom is in wholesale and retail trade. As we have seen, productivity rose sharply in these industries in the United States after 1995, but it fell in the United Kingdom. Some (e.g., Lovegrove et al., 1998) have blamed restrictive planning laws in the United Kingdom, which may have hampered the growth of so called big box retailing.[46] But it is not immediately clear why the major U.K. retailers (who also perform the wholesale function) should invest less in ICT for this reason alone: why would a comparatively low store size in a chain of supermarkets inhibit the retail firm from investing in computerized inventory control systems? However, if planning laws reduce competitive intensity by blocking entry, then they may inhibit investment too. In any event, the role of competitive intensity also seems a fruitful topic for future research.

Prepared for the NBER Macroeconomics Annual Conference, April 2003. We thank Olivier Blanchard, Ian Bond, Jeff Campbell, Mark Gertler, Elhanan Helpman, Dale Jorgenson, John Laitner, Jim Morsink, John Nichols, Ken Rogoff, Bob Triest, Gianluca Violante, and Christina Wang for helpful comments and discussions. We thank Shanthi Ramnath and Sunil Kapadia for superb research assistance. The views expressed in this paper are those of the authors and do not necessarily represent the views of others affiliated with the Federal Reserve System or the Bank of England.

REFERENCES

Aaronson, D., and D. Sullivan. (2001). Growth in worker quality. *Economic Perspectives*, Federal Reserve Bank of Chicago (25:4):53–74.

Abbade, J. (1999). *Inventing the Internet*. Cambridge, MA: The MIT Press.

Aghion, P., N. Bloom, R. Blundell, R. Griffith, and P. Howitt. (2002). Competition and innovation: An inverted U relationship. Cambridge, MA: National Bureau of Economic Research. NBER Working Paper 9269.

Baily, M. N., and R. Lawrence. (2001). Do we have a new e-conomy? *American Economic Review* 91:308–312.

Bakhshi, H., N. Oulton, and J. Thompson. (2003). Modelling investment when relative prices are trending: Theory and evidence for the United Kingdom. London: Bank of England. Working Paper 189. Available at www.bankofeng land. co.uk. (accessed January 8, 2004).

46. This is the term used to label very large retailers, typically selling from windowless, rectangular buildings surrounded by parking lots.

Basu, S., and J. G. Fernald. (2001). Why is productivity procyclical? Why do we care? In *New Developments in Productivity Analysis*, C. Hulten, E. Dean, and M. Harper (eds.). Cambridge, MA: National Bureau of Economic Research.

Basu, S., J. G. Fernald, and M. D. Shapiro. (2001). Productivity growth in the 1990s: Technology, utilization, or adjustment? *Carnegie-Rochester Conference Series on Public Policy* 55:117–165.

Basu, S., and M. Kimball. (1997). Cyclical productivity with unobserved input variation. Cambridge, MA: National Bureau of Economic Research. NBER Working Paper 5915 (December).

Bean, C., and N. Crafts. (1996). British economic growth since 1945: Relative economics decline . . . and renaissance? In *Economic Growth in Europe Since 1945*, N. Crafts and G. Toniolo (eds.). Cambridge, England: Cambridge University Press.

Belsley, D., E. Kuh, and R. Welsch. (1980). *Regression Diagnostics: Identifying Influential Data and Sources of Collinearity*. New York: Wiley.

Berners-Lee, T., with M. Fischetti. (1999). *Weaving the Web: The Past, Present and Future of the World Wide Web by Its Inventor*. London: Orion Business Books.

Bessen, J. (2002). Technology adoption costs and productivity growth: The transition to information technology. *Review of Economic Dynamics* 5(2):443–469.

Bosworth, B. P., and J. E. Triplett. (2002). "Baumol's Disease" has been cured: IT and multifactor productivity in U.S. services industries. Manuscript, Brookings Institution, Washington, D.C.

Bresnahan, T. F. (Undated). The mechanisms of information technology's contribution to economic growth. Paper prepared for presentation at the Saint-Gobain Centre for Economic Research.

Bresnahan, T. F., and M. Trajtenberg. (1995). General-purpose technologies: "Engines of growth"? *Journal of Econometrics* 65(Special Issue, January): 83–108.

Brookings Institution. (2002). Workshop on economic measurement service industry productivity: New estimates and new problems, May 17, 2002. Summary of the Workshop. http://www.brook.edu/es/research/projects/productivity/workshops/20020517_summary.pdf (accessed March 16, 2003).

Brynjolfsson, E., and L. M. Hitt. (2000). Beyond computation: Information technology, organizational transformation and business performance. *Journal of Economic Perspectives* 14(4):23–48.

Brynjolfsson, E., and L. M. Hitt. (2002). Computing productivity: Firm-level evidence. MIT Working Paper 4210-01 (Web site draft revised November 2002).

Brynjolfsson, E., and S. Yang. (2001). Intangible assets and growth accounting: Evidence from computer investments. Manuscript. Available at http://ebusiness.mit.edu/erik/itg01-05-30.pdf (accessed December 11, 2003).

Burriel-Llombart, P., and J. Jones. (2004). A quality-adjusted labour input series for the UK (1975–2002). Bank of England Working Paper, forthcoming.

Card, D., and R. B. Freeman. (2001). What have two decades of British economic reform delivered? Cambridge, MA: National Bureau of Economic Research. NBER Working Paper 8801.

Caselli, F. (1999). Technological revolutions. *American Economic Review* 89(March): 78–102.

Chandler, A. D., Jr. (1977). *The Visible Hand*. Cambridge, MA: Harvard University Press.

Colecchia, A., and P. Schreyer. (2002). ICT investment and economic growth in the 1990s: Is the United States a unique case? A comparative study of nine OECD countries. *Review of Economic Dynamics* 5(2):408–442.

Council of Economic Advisers. (2001). Annual report of the Council of Economic Advisers. In the *Economic Report of the President*, January.

Council of Economic Advisers. (2003). Annual report of the Council of Economic Advisers. In the *Economic Report of the President*, February.

Crafts, N., and M. O'Mahony. (2001). A perspective on UK productivity performance. *Fiscal Studies* 22(3):271–306.

Daveri, F. (2002). The new economy in Europe. *Oxford Review of Economic Policy* 18(Autumn):345–362.

David, P. A., and G. Wright. (1999). General-purpose technologies and surges in productivity: Historical reflections on the future of the ICT revolution. Manuscript. Available at www-econ.stanford.edu/faculty/workp/swp99026.pdf (accessed December 11, 2003).

Feldstein, M. (2001). Comments and analysis. In *The Financial Times*, June 28, p. 13.

Foster, L., J. Haltiwanger, and C. J. Krizan. (2002). The link between aggregate and micro productivity growth: Evidence from retail trade. Cambridge, MA: National Bureau of Economic Research. NBER Working Paper 9120.

Gordon, R. (2003). High tech innovation and productivity growth: Does supply create its own demand? Cambridge, MA: National Bureau of Economic Research. NBER Working Paper 9437.

Greenspan, A. (2000). Technology and the economy. Speech before the Economic Club of New York, January 13. Available at www.federalreserve.gov/board docs/speeches/2000 (accessed December 11, 2003).

Greenwood, J., and M. Yorokoglu. (1997). *Carnegie-Rochester Conference Series on Public Policy* 46:49–95.

Griliches, Z. (1994). Productivity, R&D, and the data constraint. *American Economic Review* 84(1):1–23.

Grimm, B. T., B. R. Moulton, and D. B. Wasshausen. (2002). Information processing equipment and software in the national accounts. Paper prepared for the NBER/CRIW Conference on Measuring Capital in the New Economy, April 26–27, 2002, Federal Reserve Board, Washington, D.C. Available at www.bea.gov/papers/IP-NIPA.pdf (accessed January 20, 2004).

Gust, C., and J. Marquez. (2000). Productivity developments abroad. *Federal Reserve Bulletin*, 86(10):665–681.

Gust, C., and J. Marquez. (2002). International comparisons of productivity growth: The role of information technology and regulatory practices. *Labour Economics* Special Issue on Productivity, Gilles Saint-Paul (ed.), forthcoming.

Hall, R. E. (2001). The stock market and capital accumulation. *American Economic Review* 91 (December):1185–1202.

Helpman, E., ed. (1998). *General Purpose Technologies and Economic Growth*. Cambridge, MA: MIT Press.

Helpman, E., and M. Trajtenberg. (1998). Diffusion of general purpose technologies. In *General Purpose Technologies and Economic Growth*, E. Helpman (ed.). Cambridge, MA: MIT Press.

Hobijn, B., and B. Jovanovic. (2001). The information-technology revolution and the stock market: Evidence. *American Economic Review* 91 (December): 1203–1220.

Hornstein, A., and P. Krusell. (1996). Can technology improvements cause productivity slowdowns? In *NBER Macroeconomics Annual*, Bernanke and Rotemberg (eds.). Cambridge, MA: National Bureau of Economic Research.

Howitt, P. (1998). Measurement, obsolescence, and general purpose technologies. In *General Purpose Technologies and Economic Growth*, E. Helpman (ed.). Cambridge, MA: MIT Press.

Jorgenson, D. W. (2001). Information technology and the U.S. economy. *American Economic Review* 91(March):1–32.

Jorgenson, D. W., M. S. Ho, and K. J. Stiroh. (2002). Growth of U.S. industries and investments in information technology and higher education. Manuscript. http://post.economics.harvard.edu/faculty/jorgenson/papers/jhscriw.pdf (accessed December 11, 2003).

Jorgenson, D. W., and K. J. Stiroh. (2000). Raising the speed limit: U.S. economic growth in the information age. *Brookings Papers on Economic Activity* 1:125–211.

Jovanovic, B., and P. L. Rousseau. (2003). Mergers as reallocation. Unpublished, NYU (February). Available at www.econ.nyu.edu/user/jovanovi/wave-35.pdf (accessed December 11, 2003).

Krueger, D., and K. Kumar. (2003). US–Europe differences in technology adoption and growth: The role of education and other policies. Manuscript prepared for the *Carnegie-Rochester Conference*, April.

Laitner, J., and D. Stolyarov. (2001). Technological change and the stock market. Manuscript, University of Michigan.

Lequiller, F. (2001). The new economy and the measurement of GDP growth. INSEE Working Paper G 2001/01, Paris. Available at www.insee.fr/en/nom_def_met/methodes/doc_travail/docs_doc_travail/g2001-16.pdf. (accessed January 8, 2004).

Lovegrove, N. C., S. Fidler, V. J. Harris, H. M. Mullings, W. W. Lewis, and S. D. Anthony (1998). Why is labor productivity in the United Kingdom so low? *The McKinsey Quarterly*, Number 4. Washington, D.C.: McKinsey Global Institute.

Lynch, L., and S. Nickell. (2002). Rising productivity and falling unemployment: Can the US experience be sustained and replicated?" In *The Roaring Nineties*, A. Krueger and R. Solow (eds.). New York: Russell Sage Foundation.

McKinsey Global Institute. (2001). US productivity growth 1995–2000: Understanding the contribution of information technology relative to other factors. San Francisco, CA: McKinsey Global Institute (October).

Nickell, S. (1996). Competition and corporate performance. *Journal of Political Economy* 104:724–746.

Nickell, S., and G. Quintini. (2001). The recent performance of the UK labour market. Talk given to the Economic Section of the British Association for the Advancement of Science, September 4, in Glasgow, Scotland. Available from www.bankofengland.co.uk (accessed December 29, 2003).

Nordhaus, W. D. (2002). Productivity growth and the new economy. *Brookings Papers on Economic Activity* 2:211–244.

Oliner, S. D., and D. E. Sichel. (2000). The resurgence of growth in the late 1990s: Is information technology the story? *Journal of Economic Perspectives* 14(Fall):3–22.

Oliner, S. D., and D. E. Sichel. (2002). Information technology and productivity: Where are we now and where are we going? *Economic Review*, Federal Reserve Bank of Atlanta 87(3):15–44.

O'Mahony, M., and W. de Boer. (2002). Britain's relative productivity performance: Updates to 1999. Final report to DTI/Treasury/ONS. Available at www.niesr.ac.uk (accessed January 5, 2004).

Oulton, N. (1995). Supply side reform and UK economic growth: What happened to the miracle? *National Institute Economic Review* 154(November):53–70.

Oulton, N. (2001a). Must the growth rate decline? Baumol's unbalanced growth revisited. *Oxford Economic Papers* 53:605–627.

Oulton, N. (2001b). ICT and productivity growth in the UK. London, England: Bank of England Working Paper 140. Available at www.bankofengland.co.uk (accessed December 29, 2003).

Oulton, N. (2002). ICT and productivity growth in the UK. *Oxford Review of Economic Policy* 18(3):363–379.

Oulton, N., and S. Srinivasan. (2003a). Capital stocks, capital services and depreciation: An integrated framework. London, England: Bank of England Working Paper 192. Available at www.bankofengland.co.uk (accessed December 29, 2003).

Oulton, N., and S. Srinivasan. (2003b). The Bank of England industry dataset. Manuscript. London, England: Bank of England. Available on request from authors.

Parker, R., and B. Grimm. (2000). Recognition of business and government expenditures for software as investment: Methodology and quantitative impacts, 1959–98. Washington, DC: Bureau of Economic Analysis. Available at www.bea.doc.gov (accessed December 29, 2003).

Schreyer, P. (2000). The contribution of information and communication technology to output growth: A study of the G7 countries. Paris: OECD. STI Working Papers 2000/2.

Schreyer, P. (2002). Computer price indices and international growth and productivity comparisons. *Review of Income and Wealth* 48(March):15–31.

Shapiro, M. (1986). The dynamic demand for capital and labor. *Quarterly Journal of Economics* 101(3):513–542.

Stiroh, K. J. (2002a). Are ICT spillovers driving the new economy? *Review of Income and Wealth* 48(1):33–58.

Stiroh, K. J. (2002b). Information technology and the U.S. productivity revival: What do the industry data say? *American Economic Review* 92(5): 1559–1576.

Tevlin, S., and K. Whelan. (2003). Explaining the investment boom of the 1990s. *Journal of Money, Credit and Banking* 35(1):1–22.

van Ark, B., J. Melka, N. Mulder, M. Timmer, and G. Ypma. (2002). ICT investment and growth accounts for the European Union, 1980–2000. Final report on *ICT and growth accounting* for the DG Economics and Finance of the European Commission, Brussels. Available at http://www.eco.rug.nl/GGDC/dseries/Data/ICT/euictgrowth.pdf (accessed December 29, 2003).

Wolff, E. N. (2002). Productivity, computerization, and skill change. Cambridge, MA: National Bureau of Economic Research. NBER Working Paper 8743.

Comment

OLIVIER BLANCHARD
MIT and NBER

This is a very ambitious, very careful, very honest paper. Unfortunately, ambition, care, and honesty are only necessary conditions for success. A bit of luck is also needed and, in this case, luck was not there. The case of U.K. missing productivity growth is not solved. But much is learned, and, building on the paper, more will be learned in the future. Let me first briefly summarize the three major points of the paper.

1. The Divergent Paths of TFP Growth in the United States and the United Kingdom

The basic facts laid out in Tables 4 and 5 of the paper, and reduced to their essence in Table 1 here, are striking. TFP growth in the IT-using sector increased substantially in the second half of the 1990s in the United States but decreased substantially in the United Kingdom. Given that the cyclical behavior of the two economies was largely similar over the decade, this suggests the need to look for structural rather than cyclical factors behind this divergence.

2. IT and Organization Capital

A preeminent role is given to IT for the performance of the U.S. economy in the second half of the 1990s, so this is a logical place to start looking. The authors point out the complex dynamic relation between IT investment, organization investment, and measured TFP.

Table 1 TFP GROWTH IN THE UNITED STATES AND THE UNITED KINGDOM IN THE 1990s (Percentage)

	1990–1995	1995–2000	Δ	Share in VA
United States				
Overall	0.9	2.1	1.2	
IT-producing	5.5	11.0	5.5	0.05
IT-using	0.6	1.5	**0.9**	0.95
United Kingdom				
Overall	2.6	1.3	−1.3	
IT-producing	3.9	10.8	6.9	0.03
IT-using	2.6	1.0	**−1.6**	0.97

Here again, it may be worth giving a bare-bones version of the more elaborate model in the paper. Suppose output depends only on organizational capital, C, and labor, N, and is used either for final goods, Y, or for investment in organizational capital, A. Organizational capital depreciates at rate δ:

$$Y = F(C, N) - A$$
$$C = A + (1 - \delta)C(-1)$$

True TFP growth is zero by construction. Measured TFP growth is given by:

$$g \equiv \left(\frac{CF_C}{Y}\right)\frac{\Delta C}{C} - \left(\frac{A}{Y}\right)\frac{\Delta A}{A}$$

Growth of unmeasured organization capital leads to an upward bias in measured TFP growth, and growth of unmeasured organization investment leads to a downward bias.

What is therefore the net effect of organization capital accumulation? Around the steady state, g can be rewritten as:

$$g \equiv \left(\frac{rC}{Y}\right)\frac{\Delta C}{C} - \left(\delta\frac{C}{Y}\right)\left(\frac{\Delta C}{C} - \frac{\Delta A}{A}\right)$$

In steady state $\Delta C/C = \Delta A/A$, so only the first term remains: measured TFP growth exceeds true TFP growth. Out of steady state, the net effect depends on the relation of the growth of capital to the growth of investment. A period of increasing investment is likely to lead to undermeasurement of true TFP growth. This can be seen more clearly by manipulating the previous equation to get:

$$g \equiv \left(r\frac{C}{Y}\right)\frac{\Delta C}{C} - \frac{C}{Y}(1 - \delta)\left[\sum_0^\infty (1 - \delta)^i \frac{\Delta^2 A}{A}(-i)\right]$$

Measured TFP growth depends positively on the growth rate of organization capital, negatively on the **change** in the growth rate of organization investment. I would have liked the authors to try a specification closer to the spirit of this specification, allowing for the rate of change of organization capital (or the proxy used for it), and a distributed lag in the rate of change of organization investment, constrained to have a sum of coefficients equal to zero. It would have made the results and the estimated dynamic structure perhaps easier to interpret.

3. Different IT Accumulation Paths in the United States and the United Kingdom?

The basic implication of the model is that a boom in organization invest-ment leads initially to a decrease in measured TFP, and only later to the promised increase. This suggests a potential explanation for the United Kingdom/United States difference: the boom in IT investment, and thus the boom in induced organization investment, happened earlier in the United States than in the United Kingdom. In the second half of the 1990s, the United States was already reaping the positive effects of high organi-zation capital, and so measured TFP growth was high. The United Kingdom, on the other hand, was still paying the cost of high organiza-tion investment, and measured TFP growth was accordingly low. Under this interpretation, the effects will turn positive, and the future may be brighter.

The authors take this hypothesis to the sectoral data, looking at the dynamic relation between TFP growth and proxies for organization capi-tal. This is where the data do not cooperate. The dynamic story appears to work decently for the United States. But it works extremely poorly for the United Kingdom. There is no evidence for a lag structure from IT to pro-ductivity growth along the lines suggested by the theory. The authors put a good face on the results, but one cannot conclude that the case has been solved. Let me take each of these points in turn, first focusing on the gen-eral line of arguments, then returning to the United States/United Kingdom comparison.

4. On the General Story

4.1 HOW WELL ESTABLISHED ARE THE BASIC TFP FACTS?

The first issue is a standard one. Even if one takes TFP growth numbers at face value, the question is, How much can be read in differences in sam-ple means over periods as short as five years? TFP growth varies a lot from year to year. Using the series constructed in the paper, the sample standard deviation of TFP growth over the last 20 years in the United Kingdom is 1.8%, implying a standard deviation for a five-year mean of about 0.8%. A difference of 1.4%, the number in the table for the difference between U.S. and U.K. productivity growth in the IT-using sector for 1995 to 2000, is not that significant. One could probably ask for more time to pass before feeling that there was a puzzle to be explained.

The second issue is that there are many decisions to be made in con-structing TFP growth (income or expenditure side, quality weighting of labor, and so on), and so different studies give different results. The authors of this paper conclude that TFP growth in the IT-using sector increased by 0.9% in the United States from 1990–1995 to 1995–2000 (and overall TFP growth, that is, TFP growth for the whole private nonfarm economy, increased over the same period by 1.2%). This appears to be at the high end of the range of available estimates.

At the low end is Robert Gordon (2000, Table 2), who concludes that there was roughly no increase in underlying TFP growth in the IT-using sector from 1992–1995 to 1995–1999, and a small (0.3%) increase for the whole private nonfarm economy. Next are Oliner and Sichel (2002, Table 4), with an increase of 0.3% in the IT-using sector, and an overall increase of 0.7%. Slightly higher is Jorgenson and Stiroh (2000), with an increase of 0.4% for the IT-using sector (1991–1995 to 1995–1998), and an overall increase of 0.6%. At the high end is the work reported in the *Economic Report of the President* (Council of Economic Advisers, 2001), with an increase of 1% for the IT-using sector, and an increase of 1.2% overall.

All the estimates are (weakly) positive; this is good news. But the magnitudes vary, and one wonders whether plausible variations on hedonic pricing of the IT-producing sector, and thus in the price of IT goods, could not change the allocation of TFP growth between IT-producing and IT-using sectors by a magnitude that would dominate the numbers reported in the previous paragraph and substantially affect the conclusions. This may not affect much the comparison of the United States and the United Kingdom. But it would affect the interpretation of the results: if there was no strong evidence of an increase in TFP growth in the IT-using sector, explanations based on unmeasured organization investment and capital lose a lot of their appeal.

4.2 WHAT ARE THE OUTPUT COSTS OF REORGANIZATION?

It is essential for the authors' thesis that high investment in organizational capital have substantial adverse effects on measured output, and therefore on measured TFP. A study by Lichtenberg and Siegel (1987) on the effects of mergers on TFP is relevant here. Not very surprisingly, they find that TFP in the merged firms goes from 3.9% below the conditional sectoral mean to 1.2% below after seven years. More relevant to the issue at hand, however, is their finding that the improvement is a steady one: there is no evidence of a temporary decrease in measured TFP before reorganization starts paying off.

This evidence is not totally conclusive. Reorganization after mergers may be very different from the types of changes triggered by new IT possibilities. But it makes one want to see more micro evidence that the accumulation of organization capital can have major adverse effects on measured output. This takes me to the next point.

4.3 RETAIL TRADE, THE McKINSEY STUDY, AND WAL-MART

As the authors point out, fully one-third of the increase in TFP growth from the first to the second half of the 1990s in the United States came from the retail trade sector. For this reason, the general merchandising segment, which represents 20% of sales in the sector, was one of the sectors examined in a McKinsey study (McKinsey Global Institute, 2001) aimed at understanding the factors behind U.S. TFP growth in the 1990s.

The study confirmed that there was indeed a large increase in productivity growth, with the growth rate of sales per hour increasing from 3.4% during 1987–1995 to 6.7% from 1995–1999, and it reached two main conclusions: first that more than two-thirds of the increase could indeed be traced to reorganization; second, that much of this reorganization came from the use of IT.

The study also provided a sense of what reorganization means in practice. Improvements in productivity were the result of "more extensive use of cross docking and better flows of goods/palleting; the use of better forecasting tools to better align staffing levels with demand; redefining store responsibilities and cross training of employees; improvements in productivity measurements and utilization rates at check-out." It also showed that, while innovations were first implemented by Wal-Mart, competitors were forced to follow suit, leading to a steady diffusion of these innovations across firms in the second half of the 1990s.

How does the story fit the authors' thesis? In some ways, very well: reorganization, linked with IT investment, clearly played a central role in the increase in TFP growth in the retail sector in the 1990s. But in other and more important ways, the evidence goes against the basic thesis of the paper: the major increase in IT capital took place in the second half of the 1990s. During that period, productivity growth and profits steadily increased. There is no discernible evidence of the adverse effects of organization investment on output, productivity, or profits.

5. Back to the United States and the United Kingdom

5.1 THE RELATIVE EVOLUTION OF IT SPENDING

Having stated their hypothesis, the authors proceed to test it using sectoral data. But a natural first step is just to look at the timing of IT investment in both the United States and the United Kingdom and see whether it fits the basic hypothesis.

The authors actually do it, but only in passing, in Figure 1. And what they show does not give strong support to the hypothesis. The figure plots the growth contribution of IT capital in the IT-using sector—constructed as the product of the share times the rate of growth of IT capital. If their hypothesis were right, one would expect to see high IT investment in the United States early on, and high IT investment in the United Kingdom only at the end of the sample. Actual evolutions are quite different. The United Kingdom appears to have two periods of high IT capital contributions: one in the late 1980s, the other in the late 1990s. It does not seem to be lagging the United States in any obvious way.

This impression is largely confirmed in work by others. Table 2 below is constructed from data in Colecchia and Schreyer (2002, Table 1). It also gives the contribution of IT spending to growth, measured as the product of the share times the rate of growth of IT capital for four subperiods, from 1980 to 2000. The numbers yield two conclusions.

First, the growth contribution of IT appears substantially lower in Europe than in the United States, a conclusion at odds with Figure 1 in the paper, which puts the IT contribution to growth in the United Kingdom, both in computers and software, above that in the United States. Much of the difference appears attributable to the multiplication by 3 by the authors of investment in software, and so the larger share of software in their data, relative to Colecchia and Schreyer. The adjustment may well be justified, but it is obviously rough and is a reminder of the many assumptions behind the data we are looking at.

Second, and more directly relevant here, the acceleration in IT appears to have been stronger at the end of the 1990s in the United States than in the three European countries. The contribution to growth roughly doubled in the last five years from an already high level. It also roughly doubled in the United Kingdom and France, but from a lower level. It increased, but far from doubled, in Germany. If these numbers are correct, and if investment in organization is indeed closely related to investment in IT, it is measured TFP growth in the United States that should have suffered the most from unmeasured investment in the late 1990s, not TFP growth in the United Kingdom.

5.2 WHOLESALE AND RETAIL TRADE AGAIN

The sectoral data in the paper give what looks like a promising lead for solving the case of missing productivity. Table 3, constructed from

Table 2   CONTRIBUTION OF IT TO GROWTH FOR FOUR COUNTRIES, 1980 TO 2000

	1980–1985	*1985–1990*	*1990–1995*	*1995–2000*
United States	0.44	0.43	0.43	0.87
United Kingdom	0.18	0.29	0.27	0.48
France	0.18	0.22	0.18	0.33
Germany	0.20	0.27	0.30	0.38

Tables 4 and 5 in the paper, summarizes the relevant information. The first and second columns report TFP growth in 1990–1995 and 1995–2000. The third shows the change in TFP growth. The fourth shows the share of the two sectors in value added. The last column shows the product of change and share, and shows therefore the contribution of the two trade sectors to the change in TFP growth in the two countries. In the United States, the contribution is 0.8%; in the United Kingdom, the contribution is –1.0%. From an accounting point of view, the evolution of TFP growth in just the trade sector accounts for close to half of the difference between the overall evolution of U.S. and U.K. TFP growth from the first to the second half of the 1990s.

This suggests looking at trade more closely. Indeed, the absolute numbers for U.K. TFP growth in both wholesale and retail for the second half of the 1990s are puzzling. Can it be that TFP growth was actually negative in the United Kingdom during that period? I checked the evolution of labor productivity, using OECD data from the STAN project. For wholesale and retail trade together, that source gives a growth rate of real value added of 3.2% a year, a growth rate for employment of 1.0%, so a rate of labor productivity growth of 2.2%. If the numbers are consistent with those used by the authors, this suggests an unusually high rate of capital accumulation during the period, capital that was not used very productively. This raises the question, Why was it used more productively in the United States?

Unfortunately, I do not know enough about the retail sector in the United Kingdom to give the answer or even help direct the search. In a related McKinsey project (McKinsey Global Institute, 2002) in which I participated, we looked at the evolution of labor productivity in the retail sector in the 1990s in Germany and France. Labor productivity was 1.1% for Germany, 1.5% for France, and 2% for the United States. For the first two countries, regulations affecting the rate at which various retail formats could grow seemed relevant. Such regulations appear much less relevant, however, for the United Kingdom in the 1990s.

Table 3   GROWTH CONTRIBUTIONS OF WHOLESALE AND RETAIL TRADE IN THE UNITED STATES AND THE UNITED KINGDOM

	TFP growth		Change	Share	Contribution
	1990–1995	1995–2000			
U.S. wholesale	1.7	5.4	3.7	9.2	0.3
U.S. retail	0.8	5.3	4.5	11.8	0.5
U.K. wholesale	3.3	3.2	–0.1	6.8	–0.0
U.K. retail	0.5	–1.2	–1.7	13.0	–0.2

5.3 CONVERGENCE?

An alternative way of looking at the United Kingdom/United States evolutions in the aggregate is that, for most of the postwar period, European TFP growth was high due to convergence. All Europe had to do was copy, not innovate. And this has largely come to an end.

The problem, as the authors mention, is that, in many countries, convergence has not been fully achieved. While several countries indeed have a level of output per worker close or even higher than the United States, this is not the case for the United Kingdom. According to Table 2 in the paper, U.K. output per worker stands at roughly 70% of the U.S. level.

Theory, however, predicts conditional convergence, not absolute convergence. A country with bad institutions (whatever this exactly means) will not achieve the same level of productivity as one with better institutions. I mention this not because it is a new insight, but because this seems to be happening in Europe. Several countries that were much poorer and had been converging for the past few decades seem now to be growing only at the European average, no longer catching up. Portugal and Greece come to mind, but the United Kingdom, in a less obvious way because the gap is much smaller and thus less visible, may be in the same predicament.

So, was it problems in the use of capital in the trade sector, or was it simply the end of convergence? We still do not know. But, thanks to the paper, we have a better sense of what to look for, and we have a number of lids to open. I wish the authors good luck in solving the case in the future.

REFERENCES

Colecchia, A., and Paul Schreyer. (2002). ICT investment and economic growth in the 1990s: Is the US a unique case? A comparative study of nine OECD countries. *Review of Economic Dynamics* 5(2):408–442.

Council of Economic Advisors. (2001). *Economic Report of the President.* Washington, D.C.: United States Government Printing Office (June).

Gordon, Robert. (2000). Does the "New Economy" measure up to the great inventions of the past? *Journal of Economic Perspectives* 14(4):49–74.

Jorgenson, Dale, and Kevin Stiroh. (2000). Raising the speed limit: US economic growth in the information age. *Brookings Papers on Economic Activity,* 1:125–235.

Lichtenberg, Frank, and Dan Siegel. (1987). Productivity and changes in ownership of manufacturing plants. *Brookings Papers on Economic Activity,* 3:643–673.

McKinsey Global Institute (2001). *US productivity growth 1995–2000. Understanding the contribution of information technology relative to other factors.* Washington, D.C.: McKinsey Global Institute.

McKinsey Global Institute. (2002). *Reaching high productivity growth in France and Germany.* Washington, D.C.: McKinsey Global Institute.

Oliner, Stephen, and Daniel Sichel. (2002). The resurgence of growth in the late 1990s: Is information technology the story? *Journal of Economic Perspectives,* 14(4):3–22.

Comment

GIOVANNI L. VIOLANTE
New York University and CEPR

1. Introduction

The exceptional productivity performance of the U.S. economy in the period 1995–2000 is well documented (see, for example, Jorgenson 2001): relative to the previous five years, total factor productivity (TFP) growth accelerated by 0.7% (and labor productivity growth by 1%) per year in 1995–2000. What are the sources of this sharp acceleration? Should we expect this higher TFP growth to be a long-term trend for the future, as some argue, or is it just a transitory phenomenon? Basu, Fernald, Oulton, and Srinivasan offer a comparative macroeconomics perspective to these important questions. They bring into the picture the experience of another country, the United Kingdom, which in many dimensions is similar to the United States.

From a long-run perspective, the U.S. and the U.K. economies stand at the same stage of development and share—unlike many other European countries—a similar institutional framework of labor and product markets. From a short-run perspective, the business cycle in the two economies in the 1990s was remarkably akin. I'd like to add that the United States and the United Kingdom were the only two among the developed economies that experienced a substantial rise in earnings inequality in the past 30 years, with analogous characteristics (e.g., both within and between skill groups).

Given these short-run and more structural affinities, one would expect a similar evolution of TFP growth in the 1990s for the U.K. economy. Instead, U.K. TFP growth decelerated by 0.5% (and labor productivity growth by 1%) per year from 1990–1995 to 1995–2000.

How do we explain the missing productivity growth in the United Kingdom (or the exceedingly high productivity growth in the United States)? Basu et al. build a convincing argument on two assumptions. First, because of unmeasured organizational capital that is complementary with information technology (IT) capital in production, TFP growth is mismeasured. Periods of strong investment in IT (and in the complementary organizational capital) are times where mostly output is unmeasured, so true TFP growth is underestimated, whereas periods where the economy has large stocks of IT and complementary capital are times where inputs are grossly undermeasured, and true TFP growth is overestimated. Second, IT investment boomed with a lag of 5 to 10 years in the

U.K. economy, relative to the U.S. economy. Thus, in 1995–2000, TFP growth was underestimated in the United Kingdom and overestimated in the United States, which explains, at least qualitatively, the gap.

This comment is organized into three parts: (1) an exploration of the role of convergence between the United Kingdom and the United States within a Solow-growth model; (2) a deeper look into the retail sector, where the TFP acceleration gap between the two countries is particularly striking; and (3) a quantitative exercise based on the model developed by Basu et al. in Section 4 of their paper.

2. Convergence

If one extends the comparison for the two countries back to the early 1980s (see Basu et al., Table 1), it emerges clearly that labor productivity growth was considerably faster in the United Kingdom until the mid-1990s. Basu et al. put it in plain words: "[T]he Europeans were catching up." The authors somewhat downplay the role of transition in their analysis, so here I try to assess if the fact that the United Kingdom was catching up is relevant in explaining the productivity acceleration gap. Intuitively, the transitional dynamics of the United Kingdom would naturally lead to a reduction in labor productivity growth as the economy approaches its steady state.

Think of the two countries (indexed by i) in terms of Solow-model economies with capital-embodied technical change: at time t the new investment goods $x_i(t)$ embody a productivity factor $A_i(t) = e^{\gamma_i t}$. The model can be summarized as:

$$x_i(t) = sy_i(t) = sk_i(t)^\alpha$$
$$k_i(t) = A_i(t)x_i(t) - (\delta + n)k_i(t)$$

where $k_i(t)$ is capital per worker, s is the savings rate, α is the income share of capital, δ is the depreciation rate, and n is the growth rate of the labor force. The thought experiment is as follows: start the two economies in 1980 with the same parameter vector (s, α, δ, v, γ) but assume that the United States is already on its balanced-growth path, while the United Kingdom is endowed with lower capital per worker, so it has a faster growth rate of labor productivity and slowly converges toward the U.S. level. In 1990 a technological breakthrough raises permanently capital-embodied productivity growth to γ' in the U.S. economy. From this simple exercise, one can learn the implied labor productivity growth in the United Kingdom in the period 1995–2000 under two scenarios: (1) the acceleration in technological change does not spill over to the United

Figure 1 CONVERGENCE BETWEEN THE UNITED KINGDOM AND THE
UNITED STATES IN A SOLOW MODEL ECONOMY

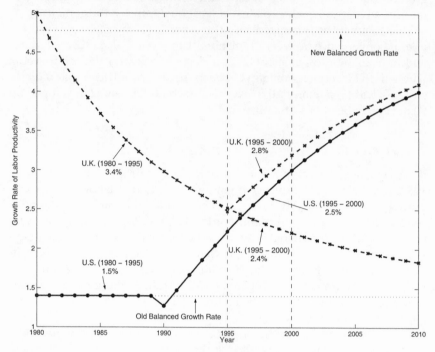

Kingdom and (2) the acceleration occurs with a lag of 5 years in the
United Kingdom.[1]

To calibrate the model, I set $\gamma = 1.7\%$ and $\gamma' = 5.7\%$ to match the data on
average labor productivity in the United States in the period 1980–1995 and
1995–2000, respectively. I chose the initial level of capital in the United
Kingdom so that along the transition in the period 1980–1995, average yearly
productivity growth is 3.4%, as documented in Table 1 by the authors.[2]

What can we conclude from this simple exercise on the role of catch-up
and transitional dynamics? Figure 1 shows that, under the first scenario,
the U.K. rate of labor productivity growth implied by the transitional
dynamics in 1995–2000 is 2.4%, which is well below 2.9%, the actual data
from Table 1. In the absence of a rapid technological spillover to the

---

1. The first scenario corresponds to a lag of 10 years or more, assuming that we are interested in the period until 2000.
2. The other parameters are set as follows: $s = 15\%$, $\alpha = 0.45$, $\delta = 5\%$, and $n = 1.5\%$. The somewhat high value of the capital share reflects the presence of human capital.

United Kingdom, pure convergence forces push the implied labor productivity too low compared to the data. Under the second scenario, labor productivity grows at an average yearly rate of 2.8%, thus the combination of the authors' view that the U.K. "implementation lag" is around 5 years together with catch-up forces explains the deceleration in full (in fact, it just overexplains it).[3]

An obvious question arises: Why did the United Kingdom adopt this more productive technology later? A satisfactory answer would require a full investigation. Here, I will limit myself to a brief speculation. In Table 3, Basu et al. document the educational characteristics of the labor force in the two countries. The difference with the United Kingdom does not lie so much in the average numbers of years of schooling, but rather in the fact that the United Kingdom has a much larger fraction of workers with specific skills associated with vocational training. At least since Nelson and Phelps (1966), numerous researchers argued that general education is a key force in technology adoption. In a recent mimeo, Krueger and Kumar (2003) embed the Nelson and Phelps mechanism into an equilibrium model and show that an acceleration in the growth rate of the frontier technology will increase the TFP growth gap between an economy with abundant general skills (like the United States) and an economy mostly endowed with specific skills (like the United Kingdom and most of the other European countries).

The careful reader will have noticed that the predictions of this exercise are relevant to explain the *labor productivity* acceleration gap between the two countries, but not the TFP growth differential. However, this is true only if all inputs are correctly measured. Suppose that the productivity improvements in investment goods captured by the factor $A(t)$ are completely missed by statisticians. In this case, measured total factor productivity $z(t)$ is obtained residually from the production relationship $y(t) = z(t)\hat{k}(t)^\alpha$, with $\hat{k}(t) = x(t) - (\delta + n)\hat{k}(t)$. In other words, $z(t)$ is an average of all past values of $A(t)$ weighted by the investment flow in each year.

What are the predictions of our simple calibrated model for TFP? Simulations under the same exact parametrization show that the model generates an acceleration in TFP growth for the United States of 1.5% and an acceleration in TFP growth for the United Kingdom of 0.3% under the first scenario and of 0.7% under the second scenario. Although the model produces larger accelerations in absolute value in the two economies (in particular, it does not generate a TFP deceleration for the United

---

3. Obviously, if all inputs are correctly measured, the predictions of this exercise are relevant only to explain the labor productivity acceleration gap between the two countries. TFP is constant over time.

Kingdom), it predicts a gap of roughly 1% between the two countries, in line with the data of Table 1.

3. Institutions in the Retail Sector

A comparison between Table 4 and Table 5 documenting the size of the TFP acceleration from 1990–1995 to 1995–2000 by industry in the two countries shows a relatively similar sectoral performance with one important exception: in the retail trade sector, TFP growth accelerated by 4.5% per year in the United States, whereas it decelerated by 1.9% per year in the United Kingdom. The authors note this puzzling divergence, but they do not search for its specific causes. It is clear, however, that an argument based on the dynamics of unmeasurable organizational capital is unlikely to account for the TFP acceleration gap in the retail industry. Tables 6 and 7 show that the share of IT investments in value added did not change much between 1990 and 2000 in either country in this sector.

A report of the McKinsey Global Institute (1998) sheds some light on the puzzle: between 1993 and 1996, fearing a massive "high-street flight" of retail stores toward the periphery of towns and cities, the U.K. government voted a series of planning restrictions establishing that local planning authorities should promote the development of small retail stores in town centers and restrict the concession of planning permissions for new stores or for the extension of existing stores outside town centers. By contrast, land regulations in the United States put no significant restrictions on retailers' location decisions.

As a result of these stringent planning guidelines, a large fraction of retail stores in the United Kingdom have suboptimal size and are not located optimally on the territory. McKinsey estimates the productivity loss associated with these strict regulations to be roughly 10% at the sectoral level, so the entire TFP deceleration in the U.K. retail sector (– 1.9% per year compounded over 5 years) could be explained through this channel. Retail trade is a large industry, accounting for about 12% of aggregate value added in both economies, thus these institutional restrictions alone can potentially explain over 60% of the differential TFP acceleration between the two countries.[4]

4. Complementary Capital

The equilibrium model of Section 4 allows Basu et al. to obtain the structural equation in equation (9) that relates the bias in TFP growth to the

---

4. Regulatory restrictions that have a significant impact on store size and productivity are not uncommon in other parts of the world. For example, in Japan, until 2000, the large-scale retail law limited greatly the entry of stores larger than 1,000 square meters.

change in the stock of complementary capital. Consider a special case of the model where $g = r$ (the growth rate of the economy equals the interest rate) and $\sigma = 1$ (a unitary elasticity between IT capital and the complementary organizational capital is necessary to have a balanced growth path in the model), then one can rewrite equation (9) as:

$$\Delta TFP_t^* - \Delta TFP_t = \frac{C}{Y^{NT}} \left(1 - r - \delta_c\right) \left[\Delta C_t - \Delta C_{t-1}\right] \tag{1}$$

where ΔTFP_t^* is true TFP growth in year t, C/Y^{NT} is the long-run (or steady-state) ratio of the stock of complementary capital to output produced in the non-IT industries, and δ_c is the depreciation rate of complementary capital. Given the assumptions made on the substitutability between IT capital and C capital in production, the growth rate of complementary capital at time t can be written also as:

$$\Delta C_t = \Delta K_t^{IT} + \Delta p_t \tag{2}$$

where ΔK_t^{IT} is the growth rate of IT capital, and Δp_t is the change in the price of new IT investment relative to non-IT output.

The authors use equations (1) and (2) as their statistical model in a series of cross-sectional regressions where different rates of IT investment across industries provide a source of variation to estimate the size of the bias in TFP growth due to the missing C capital. The results are encouraging, but not as sharp as one would hope. The main reason of the weak statistical significance, in my view, lies in the very same point the authors are trying to prove: if IT is truly a general-purpose technology, then we should expect similar investment rates across all industries, which makes the cross-sectional data not very informative. Indeed, Tables 6 and 7 show that, with the exclusion of a few outliers (like mining, real estate, and communications), the variability of investment rates in IT among industries is rather small.

I take a different approach for setting the complementary capital model in action. The spirit of the exercise will be as follows. From the data on IT capital and prices and from equation (2), one can construct growth rates of C capital for the whole decade 1990–2000 for both countries. Together with a common parametrization for the pair (δ_c, r), one can then compute the true TFP growth ΔTFP^* in the two countries for different values of the complementary capital output ratio, which is unobservable. Finally, assuming that the United Kingdom and the United States have the same long-run C/Y^{NT} ratio along their balanced growth (and this will be the case if the two economies differ only in the *timing* of the productivity shock, as in the convergence exercise), one can ask, What is the specific value of

Figure 2 GROWTH RATE OF COMPLEMENTARY CAPITAL

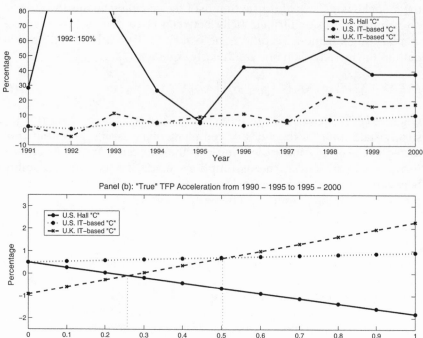

Panel (b): "True" TFP Acceleration from 1990 – 1995 to 1995 – 2000

C/Y^{NT} that rationalizes the TFP acceleration differential? In other words, given the scarcity of information contained in the industry-level data, and the fact that C capital is not directly measurable, the best we can do is engage in the art of "reverse engineering." I will express later a subjective judgment on the plausibility of the number obtained.

In the exercise, I will also use another indirect source of measurement of C capital growth constructed from Hall's (2001): the difference between the stock-market valuation of firms and the book value of their physical assets provides an implicit measure of the stock of intangibles in the U.S. economy.[5]

The top panel of Figure 2 plots ΔC_t in the United States measured through both IT-based and Hall's methods, and ΔC_t in the United Kingdom measured with the IT-based approach. The U.K. IT-based estimate of C capital growth is higher in the second half of the sample. The

---

5. Hall's data are available from http://www.stanford.edu/~rehall/. To my knowledge, there is no similar attempt to obtain an estimate of intangible capital for the U.K. economy.

IT-based measure of C capital growth for the United States is slightly increasing over time, albeit at a slower pace than the U.K. measure; instead Hall's U.S. C capital growth is much higher in the first half of the sample. Taken together, these numbers mean that the correction of the bias in TFP growth will go in the right direction.

The lower panel of Figure 2 plots—for a range of values of the C/Y^{NT} ratio—the true acceleration in TFP between 1990–1995 and 1995–2000 calculated using in equation (1) the three series for ΔC_t just constructed.[6] Note that when this ratio is zero, we obtain the measured ΔTFP of Table 1. The point where the U.S. and the U.K. lines cross corresponds to the value of the long-run C/Y^{NT} ratio that reconciles the measured U.S./U.K. differential in TFP acceleration with equal true TFP growth.

Using Hall's estimates for the growth in the stock of intangible capital in the United States in the 1990s, this value is 0.26, which corresponds to a true TFP deceleration of 0.1% per year in both countries. However, if the U.S. stock market were overvalued in the 1990s, this source of information on intangibles can be imprecise. The alternative IT-based measure of C capital for the United States proposed by the authors tells us that the long-run C/Y^{NT} ratio that solves the puzzle is around 0.5, which corresponds to a true acceleration of 0.7% per year in both economies.

How reasonable are these two numbers? I argue that they are quite plausible. To understand, it is useful to express them in terms of aggregate output Y (non-IT value-added Y^{NT} accounts for 95% of total output in the United States). Take the mean of these two estimates for C/Y, which is 0.35. Given the assumed depreciation rate, this number would imply that steady-state investment in C capital is less than 6% of output, very close to the current share of IT investment in U.S. data, which is around 7%. A C/Y ratio of 0.35 is a conservative estimate in light of the recent work by McGrattan and Prescott (2002, Table 2), who estimate the stock of intangible capital in the United States to be around 0.65 of aggregate gross domestic product (GDP) and, after reviewing the literature, conclude that a reasonable range for this ratio is between 0.5 and 1.

To conclude, this calculation provides support, from a different angle, to the authors' main argument: theory is *still* ahead of measurement. We have rich models suggesting that organizational capital plays an important role in macroeconomics, especially in phases of technological transformation, but we are lacking reliable direct measurements. However, I have also argued that one should not neglect more traditional explanations of productivity differentials, like convergence forces and institutions.

---

6. I have assumed that, in both countries, the depreciation rate for C capital δ_c is the same as the depreciation rate for IT used by the authors (16%), and that $r = 4\%$.

REFERENCES

Hall, Robert. (2001). The stock market and capital accumulation. *American Economic Review* 91(5, December)1185–1202.

Jorgenson, Dale W. (2001). Information technology and the U.S. economy. *American Economic Review* 91(1, March)1–32.

Krueger, Dirk, and Krishna B. Kumar. (2003). Skill-specific rather than general education: A reason for U.S.-Europe growth differences? Mimeo, Stanford University.

McGrattan, Ellen, and Ed Prescott. (2002). Taxes, regulations, and the value of U.S. corporations: A general equilibrium analysis. Research Department Staff Report 309, Federal Reserve Bank of Minneapolis.

McKinsey Global Institute. (1998). Driving productivity and growth in the UK economy. Available from http://www.mckinsey.com/knowledge/mgi/ (accessed April 3, 2003).

Nelson, Richard R., and Edmund S. Phelps. (1966). Investment in humans, technological diffusion and economic growth. *American Economic Review* 56(2):69–75.

Discussion

Several participants remarked on the role of the wholesale and retail trade in the authors' story. Mark Gertler suggested that the TFP slowdown in the United States appears to be partly associated with a slowdown in these sectors, which in turn implies that there is something important about these particular sectors that economists should try to understand. John Fernald remarked that the wholesale and retail trade contributed to three-fourths of the difference in TFP growth between the two countries. He also remarked that net entry alone—the entry of Wal-Mart and the exit of Kmart—explains the productivity performance of the retail sector. Robert Shimer counseled caution in the use of Wal-Mart as an example of the retail trade. He pointed out that by joining together successes such as Wal-Mart and failures such as Kmart, one would get a more realistic picture of the U.S. retail trade in the 1990s. In response to Olivier Blanchard's discussion, Nick Oulton noted that though planning regulations in the United Kingdom could lower the level of TFP, they should not affect the growth rate of TFP. He contended that the small size of individual stores should not affect the incentives for retail chains to invest in IT.

The theme of the choice of sample countries was raised by several participants. Mark Gertler questioned the authors' identification assumption that there are many macroeconomic similarities between the United Kingdom and the United States. He pointed out that according to the authors' Table 1, there was moderate growth in output and strong growth in investment in the United States between 1990 and 1995, but there was low output growth and no net investment in IT in the United Kingdom.

Athanasios Orphanides suggested that the authors expand their sample of two countries to include Australia. It was his view that this approach would help to deal with the identification issue pointed out by Mark Gertler because Australia experienced measured productivity growth even larger than that in the United States but was similar to the United Kingdom in terms of initial conditions and catching up in the 1990s. Kjetil Storesletten suggested that Germany and Sweden would be another interesting pair of countries to compare. He observed that there was a rapid acceleration of TFP growth in the 1990s in Germany, but little growth in IT investment. In the 1990s, Sweden, like the United States, saw sharply falling unemployment and an acceleration in TFP, along with widespread use of IT.

Several participants had concerns about data issues. Robert Shimer contended that the authors were wrong to dismiss the role of declining unemployment in explaining the differential behavior of TFP growth in the United States and the United Kingdom. He maintained that the bigger decline in unemployment in the United Kingdom, resulting in the long-term unemployed being drawn into employment, might contribute more than the authors estimated to the slow growth of TFP. Nick Oulton responded that the authors had controlled for the education characteristics as well as the gender and age of the labor force in the United Kingdom, so composition effects are unlikely to explain the differential TFP performance between the two countries. In response to Gianluca Violante's discussion of the aggregation of different qualities of labor, Susanto Basu agreed that big deviations from Cobb-Douglas do matter. He contended that the authors' aggregation procedure is not subject to this problem because they use a Törnqvist average of shares over time, rather than a pure Cobb-Douglas, to aggregate.

Mark Gertler was curious about whether there are any observable indicators of investment in complementary capital. In response to this question, Susanto Basu drew the attention of the audience to several firm-level studies associated with Brynjolfsson and co-authors from the pre-bubble period in the United States. These studies document that a $1.00 increase in IT investment is associated with a $5.00 increase in the stock-market value of a firm, suggesting the order of magnitude of complementary capital investments. The studies also indicate that returns to investments in IT are typically normal or low initially, but large with a five-year lag. He noted that this finding was consistent with the story of the paper.

Daron Acemoglu pointed out that the authors' lag story has additional first-order testable implications. He wondered whether investment in IT would have made sense with lags of the length necessary for the authors' story given that firms could have invested at the risk-free rate. Second, he asked whether a production function with decreasing returns to scale in factors other than the unobservable complementary capital would fit other features of the data.

Eva Nagypal commented that the authors do not discuss the distribution of TFP between newly created and existing firms. She suggested that differences in the composition of firms between the United States and the United Kingdom could explain the contrasting behavior of TFP in the two countries. While creation and destruction of establishments is similar in the two countries, growth in new establishments is much higher in the United States, and a large fraction of TFP growth is attributable to them.

Finally, the authors responded to some concerns of the discussants about data. Nick Oulton noted that differences between national accounts methodology in the United States and the United Kingdom make cross-country comparisons difficult. In particular, in the United Kingdom, software investment is misclassified as the purchase of an intermediate input, resulting in a substantial understatement of information and communications technology (ICT) investment as a whole. With an appropriate adjustment for this misclassification, the growth accounting contribution of ICT is similar in the United Kingdom and in the United States, even though stocks are smaller in the United Kingdom. In response to Olivier Blanchard's discussion, John Fernald pointed out that estimates of the acceleration in non-ICT production depend on whether the data used is product data or industry data. He commented that taking account of investment adjustment costs would strengthen the story that TFP growth took place mainly in non-ICT-producing sectors because sectors that were using IT, not producing it, experienced a surge in complementary investment that diverted resources.

Dirk Krueger and Fabrizio Perri
UNIVERSITY OF PENNSYLVANIA, NBER, AND CEPR; AND NEW YORK
UNIVERSITY, FEDERAL RESERVE BANK OF MINNEAPOLIS, NBER, AND CEPR

On the Welfare Consequences of the Increase in Inequality in the United States

1. Introduction

The sharp increase in wage and earnings inequality in the United States over the last 30 years is a well-documented fact. Katz and Autor (1999) summarize the findings of a large body of empirical research on this topic by concluding that "many researchers using a variety of data sets—including both household and establishment surveys—have found that wage inequality and skill differentials in earnings increased sharply in the United States from the late 1970s to the mid-1990s" (p. 1467). The objective of this paper is to analyze the welfare consequences of this sharp change in the wage distribution and the associated change in the earnings distribution.[1]

Our interest in welfare immediately forces us to look beyond the distribution of current wages. If a household's economic welfare depends on consumption and leisure enjoyed over that household's lifetime, as commonly assumed by economists, then an analysis of the welfare consequences of increasing wage inequality has to determine how current wages are related to disposable income, lifetime consumption, and hours worked. First, even if current wages perfectly determine lifetime earnings,

We thank Steven Davis, Mark Gertler, Ken Rogoff, and Kjetil Storesletten and seminar participants at UCLA and at the 2003 NBER Macroeconomics Annual conference for their useful comments. Krueger thanks the National Science Foundation for financial support under grant SES 0004376. The views expressed herein are those of the authors and not necessarily those of the Federal Reserve Bank of Minneapolis or the Federal Reserve System.
1. Our data stretches from 1972 to 2000. When we refer to the increase in inequality over the last 30 years, we mean the long-run trend within our sample period. Our data presented later show that inequality has not increased at a uniform pace throughout the last 30 years.

transfers among extended family members, friends, or the government may augment disposable income and thus increase consumption opportunities of families. Second, if a significant fraction of the variations in wages, and thus income, is due to variations in its transitory component and if some forms of credit markets are available to households, current wages or current income may not be the appropriate measure of lifetime resources of these households. This suggests that the distribution of consumption is a better indicator of the distribution of welfare. In addition, the distribution of consumption still does not constitute a sufficient statistic for the welfare distribution because high consumption in the light of low wages may be realized at the expense of long working hours and thus little leisure for household members. The objective of our analysis is to take all these elements into consideration in evaluating the welfare consequences of the increase in inequality in the United States.[2]

Our analysis is divided into two parts. In the first part we use data from the Consumer Expenditure (CE) survey for the years 1972–2000 to document the evolution of the U.S. cross-sectional variability of individual wages, household total earnings and disposable earnings, hours worked, and consumption. We find a substantial increase in wage inequality, total earnings inequality, and disposable earnings inequality. Total household earnings inequality increases slightly less than individual wage inequality, suggesting that longer hours might be used to compensate partly for declines in relative wages. We also find that inequality in disposable earnings (which include government taxes and transfers) increases by more than inequality in earnings, suggesting a reduction in the redistributive impact of these public policies. Despite all these developments, *consumption* inequality displays a very modest increase.

An important part of our analysis is the decomposition of the increase in cross-sectional inequality in the data into an increase in differences (estimated as persistent) between groups (e.g., college-educated and high school–educated households) and into an increase in idiosyncratic differences (estimated as less persistent) within each group (e.g., employed and unemployed).

In the second part of the paper, first we estimate stochastic processes for household earnings, consumption, and hours worked that are consistent with the evolution of the empirical cross-sectional distributions and with

2. Obviously a full evaluation of the welfare consequences of inequality is a complex task that depends on a large number of additional economic and social factors not considered here. Also, throughout the paper, we will treat long-run growth trends in consumption and leisure as orthogonal to changes in inequality. This approach implies that we will ignore all the effects that changes in inequality might have on these trends.

one-year relative mobility matrices from the CE. Then a standard lifetime utility framework, together with our estimates of the stochastic processes for the relevant variables, is employed to deduce the magnitude of welfare losses from increased inequality. In particular, our analysis focuses on the welfare consequences of two distinct aspects of the increase in inequality: (1) persistently higher differences between groups reduce relative mean resources of some groups and increase them for others, and (2) higher volatility within one group increases the risk faced by *all* groups of the population. Both aspects potentially have large welfare impacts; the upshot of our analysis is that the second aspect significantly affects the welfare of all groups, other things being equal, and that the first aspect determines the exact distribution of these welfare effects, reinforcing them for groups that do poorly and mitigating (or even offsetting) them for groups that do better. Our framework allows us to quantify the size of the welfare losses for many education and sex groups of the U.S. population. The estimates obtained using consumption and leisure processes are fairly robust to changes in the risk aversion parameter and are as large as 6% of lifetime consumption for some groups.

The paper is organized as follows. In the next section we briefly relate our study to the existing literature. The main descriptive statistics of the CE wage, earning, hours, and consumption distributions are summarized and interpreted in Section 3. The quantitative welfare analysis based on the empirical findings in that section is contained in Section 4, and Section 5 concludes. Additional details about the data used in the main body of the paper are discussed in the data appendix (Section 6).

2. Related Literature

What are the behavioral and welfare consequences of changes in the wage structure? Several strands of the existing literature provide partial answers to this question. First, a sizable literature, summarized in Blundell and MaCurdy (1999), investigates the behavioral response of labor supply to changes in wages and the employment status of the primary earner. We explicitly study hours worked by several members of the household, so the literature on the added worker effect, which studies the labor supply response of a spouse to the primary worker's job loss or job displacement, is relevant to our work. Whereas most studies find small effects (see, for example, Heckman and MaCurdy [1980] and Cullen and Gruber [2000]), Stephens (2002) argues that, once the labor supply response of spouses to an expected job loss of their partners and to permanently lower wages of partners following their displacement are taken into account, this response may be quite sizable.

Second, if changes in the wage structure translate into changes in a household's income process, how do these changes affect consumption? The complete consumption insurance hypothesis has a very strong prediction for the risk-sharing behavior among households. Under this hypothesis, the ratio of marginal utilities between two households is constant across time and states, even when individuals face idiosyncratic income uncertainty.[3] If preferences of all individuals are identical and can be represented by a constant relative risk aversion utility function that is separable across time and between consumption and leisure, then individual consumption growth rates move in tandem with aggregate consumption growth rates, unless tastes shift. Conditional on aggregate consumption growth rates, individual consumption growth rates would be uncorrelated with individual income growth rates, whether or not income fluctuations are temporary or permanent, expected or unexpected. As a consequence of full consumption insurance, the increase in variability of the idiosyncratic part of income (and if there is consumption insurance between observably distinct groups, even the increase in between-group variability) in itself does not have adverse welfare consequences. This hypothesis has been extensively tested empirically. Examples include Altug and Miller (1990); Mace (1991); Cochrane (1991); Nelson (1994); Townsend (1994); Attanasio and Davis (1996); and Hayashi, Altonji, and Kotlikoff (1996), with results that tend to reject the full consumption insurance hypothesis.

Full consumption insurance requires a sophisticated transfer or insurance system between individual households. (It can be achieved, for example, with a full set of Arrow securities that pay out contingent on individual income shocks.) In contrast, the second strand of the literature studying the map between income and consumption takes the permanent income hypothesis as a point of departure, which envisions a consumer in isolation attempting to self-insure against income fluctuations. The welfare consequences of increased income instability in this paradigm depend crucially on whether the income shocks are temporary or permanent because transitory shocks can be easily smoothed using (dis)saving. Hall and Mishkin (1982) decompose income into its transitory and permanent components and investigate whether, in fact, households smooth transitory income shocks to a higher degree than they smooth permanent income shocks. Blundell and Preston (1998) use this idea and income and consumption data to infer the extent to which income shocks are permanent. Finally, Heathcote et al. (2003) build a model based on the permanent income hypothesis to assess the wel-

---

3. See, e.g., Deaton (1992), Chapter 1.3.

fare consequences of the recent increase in wage inequality. They use model-predicted consumption paths implied by estimated wage processes in their welfare calculations.

Common to both strands of the literature is that researchers interpret consumption data through the lens of a particular economic model of financial markets (a complete set of contingent claims for the former strand, a single uncontingent bond in the latter). Finally, a descriptive literature does not take a stand on a particular economic model but rather documents changes in income and consumption distributions (and possibly interprets them). Examples include Cutler and Katz (1991a, 1991b), Johnson and Shipp (1991), Mayer and Jencks (1993), Johnson and Smeeding (1998), and Slesnick (1993, 2001).[4] In addition, the papers by Attanasio and Davis (1996), Dynarski and Gruber (1997), and us (Krueger and Perri, 2002) provide extensive descriptive analysis of cross-sectional household consumption data, but then go on to interpret and analyze these data from the viewpoint of an underlying theoretical model. Our approach will mostly follow this last descriptive tradition. The only theory we use is a period budget constraint to organize our data and an intertemporal utility function to evaluate the welfare consequences of changes in the wage distribution, in conjunction with observed consumption and leisure choices from the data directly.

Our thought experiment of assessing the welfare consequences of increased wage, income, and consumption inequality using microconsumption data is similar in spirit to the exercise conducted by Attanasio and Davis (1996). They quantify the welfare losses implied by incomplete consumption insurance between different education and cohort groups, relative to the complete consumption insurance benchmark. Behind the veil of ignorance (i.e., before knowing what cohort-education group one belongs to), agents have to be compensated by an increase of 1 to 3% of consumption (at all dates, in all states) for imperfect consumption insurance. In our analysis we study, in addition to imperfect between-group insurance, the welfare implications of within-group consumption variability and we document how the welfare consequences are distributed across the population (that is, we look once the veil of ignorance has been lifted). We find welfare losses of increased consumption inequality of similar magnitude for a large part of the population and conclude with Attanasio and Davis (1996) that these costs

---

4. Even policy circles and the popular press are occupied with the distribution of consumption. See Greenspan (1998) for an example of the former, and the book by Cox and Alm (1999) for an example of the latter.

are two orders of magnitude bigger than the costs of business cycles commonly derived in the macroeconomic literature (see, for example, Lucas, 1987).[5]

3. Descriptive Statistics

Before assessing the welfare consequences of increasing wage and income inequality, we want first to document the basic facts from the CE data that link wages to the economic variables that enter the utility function in our welfare analysis, namely, consumption and leisure (that is, all available nonsleep time minus hours worked per member of the household). A comment about our choice of the CE as our data source may be appropriate at this time. For detailed information on U.S. *individual* household consumption, the CE is the only available dataset. In addition, we want to investigate changes in the distribution of welfare associated with changes in the wage and earnings distribution, including the within-group variation. Thus, synthetic cohort techniques that make it feasible to combine several different datasets cannot be applied because these techniques average out all within-group (idiosyncratic) variation in the data.[6] The CE includes not only information about consumption, but also about hours worked and income, and indirectly about wages. It has a relatively small sample size (an average of 5000 households per quarter) and a short panel dimension (1 year), but it is the only available dataset that reports household-level observations for all economic variables needed for our study.

To organize the CE data we use a simple period-by-period budget constraint that reads, for an arbitrary household i, as:

$$c_{it} = y_{it} - s_{it}$$

where c_{it} are expenditures on consumption, y_{it} is income from all sources, and s_{it} is saving.

We divide net income y_{it} of the household into labor income net of taxes and capital income net of taxes. Let wages of household member j be denoted by w_{ijt}, and hours worked by that household member by h_{ijt}.

---

5. Krusell and Smith (1999), among others, use a model with many heterogenous agents to document the distribution of this cost across different income and wealth classes and find that the cost of business cycles is small for almost all population groups.
6. It needs to be acknowledged that with idiosyncratic variation, a potentially important amount of measurement error is contained in our dataset, which synthetic cohort techniques tend to average out. As long as the relative magnitude of these measurement errors do not change over time, however, our estimates of the changes in idiosyncratic variability of wages, earnings and consumption remain informative.

Finally let t_{it} denote direct labor income taxes paid by household i, and τ_{it} denote government transfers. Therefore:

$$y_{it} = \sum_j w_{ijt} h_{ijt} + \sum_k r_{ikt} a_{ikt} - t_{it} + \tau_{it} = ly_{it} - t_{it} + \tau_{it} + ky_{it}$$

Thus:

$$c_{it} = ly_{it} - t_{it} + \tau_{it} + ky_{it} - s_{it}$$

where ly_{it} is labor earnings before taxes and ky_{it} is capital income after taxes.

In our previous work (Krueger and Perri [2002]), we documented a significant increase in the cross-sectional variance of after-tax labor income (henceforth disposable earnings, or simply earnings) $ly_{it} - t_{it} + \tau_{it}$, without a correspondingly large increase in the variance of consumption. The cross-sectional variance of consumption is given by:

$$Var(c_{it}) = Var(y_{it}) + Var(s_{it}) - 2Cov(y_{it}, s_{it})$$
$$= Var(ly_{it} - t_{it} + \tau_{it}) + Var(ky_{it}) + Var(s_{it}) + \text{covariances}$$

Thus, to explore how wage inequality is related to inequality in hours worked and to consumption inequality, we have to explore (1) how wage inequality is related to hours inequality and disposable earnings inequality and (2) how disposable earnings inequality is related to consumption inequality (and thus inequality in savings).

3.1 FROM WAGE INEQUALITY TO DISPOSABLE EARNINGS INEQUALITY

Disposable earnings of household i at date t are given by:

$$ly_{it} = \sum_{j=1}^{J} w_{ijt} h_{ijt} - t_{it} + \tau_{it}$$

where j indexes members of the household receiving earnings. Throughout our empirical analysis, we will restrict ourselves to households for which $J \leq 2$. As Gottschalk and Moffitt (1994) and Katz and Autor (1999) document and we confirm below, wage inequality has increased significantly in the last 30 years. We also find that the inequality in wages translates in a quantitatively substantial way into inequality of disposable earnings.

3.1.1 *Wage Inequality*
In Figure 1, we plot the standard deviation of the natural logarithm of weekly wages from the CE, measured as the weekly earnings of the reference person of the household.[7] The figure shows a

---

7. The reference person in the CE is defined as the person who owns or rents the home in which the household members reside.

Figure 1 STANDARD DEVIATION OF LOG WEEKLY WAGES

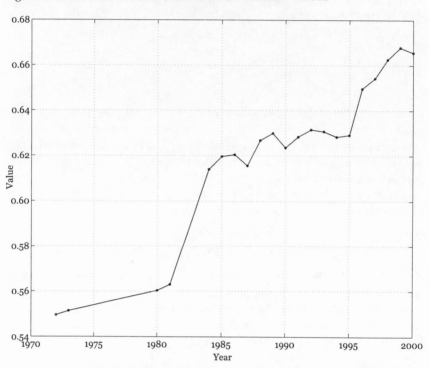

quantitatively significant increase in wage inequality: the percentage standard deviation of wages increases from around 55% in the early 1970s to around 67% at the end of the 1990s. We select only households that are classified as complete income respondents in the CE, that report positive consumption expenditures for each quarter in which they are in the sample, and whose reference person is between 20 and 64 years of age and has worked at least one week in the year. Also, to reduce measurement error, we exclude households whose reference person reports a weekly wage below $67, in constant 1982 dollars (equal to half of the 1982 minimum wage based on a 40-hour workweek). Finally, because we are interested in the welfare impact of the increase in wage dispersion, we divide the wage of the reference person by the number of adult equivalents in the household.[8]

Note that our sample includes households with low wages that are particularly vulnerable to the increase in inequality (for example, households

8. The number of adult equivalents is computed using the census equivalence scale.

whose reference person is not a full-time worker and households with female reference persons).[9] On the other hand, households with a reference person that never works during the year are not included in our wage distribution sample. Juhn, Murphy, and Topel (2002) argue that the number of such households is large and increased throughout the 1990s; they use the Current Population Survey (CPS) to impute wage data for individuals that are out of the labor force. The small sample of the CE does not allow us to follow the same procedure. We have consumption data for these households, however, and we will include them in the consumption distribution sample so that our consumption-based welfare analysis will take into account the effects of long jobless spells and labor force withdrawals described by Juhn et al. (2002).

We want to compare briefly our wage inequality findings with previous studies in the literature because some authors (for example, Cutler and Katz, 1991a) have questioned the reliability of CE wage and income data. To do so, we compute inequality measures in the CE for the wage distribution of male reference persons who work at least 40 weeks for at least 35 hours per week, the same selection criteria used by Katz and Autor (1999) to compute wage inequality measures for the Current Population Survey (CPS) and by Heathcote, Storesletten, and Violante (2003) for the Panel Study of Income Dynamics (PSID).

In Figure 2, we report the 90%–10% differential for male weekly log wages in the CE and the CPS (see Figure 4 in Katz and Autor, 1999). Notice that both the timing and the magnitude of the increase in inequality in the two samples are quite comparable. In Figure 3, we compare the increase in the standard deviation of log wages in our sample with the increase in the same measure in the CPS sample (Katz and Autor, 1999, Table 1) and the PSID sample (Heathcote et al., 2003, Table 2).[10] The figure confirms that both the timing and the magnitude of the increase in wage inequality are similar across the three datasets.[11]

3.1.2 Earnings Inequality   Wage inequality may be accentuated or mitigated by the endogenous labor supply decisions of the members of the

---

9. This sample selection strategy was suggested to us by our discussant Steve Davis.
10. All the series in Figures 2 and 3 are based on wages per person and not on per-adult equivalent wages (as the series in Figure 1).
11. Katz and Autor report only the standard deviation of log wages for 5 years. The level of the standard deviations is very similar in the CE and CPS, while it is slightly higher in the PSID (for example, in 1987 the standard deviation of log wages is 0.57 in the CE, 0.579 in the CPS, and 0.601 in the PSID). Small differences in levels are not surprising because levels are affected by the different top-coding thresholds in the datasets and by the potentially different extent of measurement error.

household. A decline in the primary earner's wage may induce other members of the household to start working or to work longer hours (the added worker effect). On the other hand, in the face of temporarily low wages, the primary wage earner may decide to substitute and work less today and work more in the future when wages have recovered. The map between wage and labor income inequality is therefore determined by the relative importance of these effects. Furthermore, changes in taxes and transfers can reduce or magnify the effect of changes in wages on disposable earnings. In Figure 4, we report inequality in total household earnings, $\Sigma_j w_{ijt} h_{ijt}$, and in disposable household earnings, $\Sigma_j w_{ijt} h_{ijt} - t_{it} + \tau_{it}$. The sample we select is exactly the same as the one chosen to compute wage inequality; as before, we divide every variable by the number of adult equivalent members of the household.

Figure 4 shows that total earnings inequality increases by a slightly smaller amount than wage inequality, consistent with moderate responses of labor supply to wage changes. Notice also that, not surprisingly, given the progressivity of the government tax and transfer system, disposable

Figure 2 WAGE INEQUALITY FROM CE AND CPS

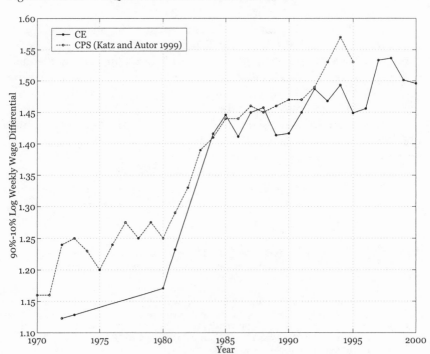

earnings inequality is significantly lower than inequality in total earnings. The gap between total earnings and disposable earnings inequality has declined over time. This decline suggests that the government tax and transfer system may have become less progressive over our sample period, which caused part of the increase in *disposable* earnings inequality.

Finally, for the purpose of this paper, it is important to understand whether the increase in earnings inequality stems from an increase in between- or within-group differences. The empirical decomposition we employ is simple and widely used (see Katz and Autor, 1999). To control for changes in the age and race composition of the population, first we regress each cross section of the raw data of disposable earnings on a constant, a quartic in the age of the household reference person and a race dummy. The cross section of the residuals is denoted by $y_t = \{\ln y_{it}\}_{i \in I}$. By construction y_t has zero cross-sectional mean for every t, and each observation is interpreted as percentage deviations of earnings of household i from the average earning of a household of the same age and the same race.

Figure 3 CHANGE IN WAGE INEQUALITY FROM CE, CPS, AND PSID

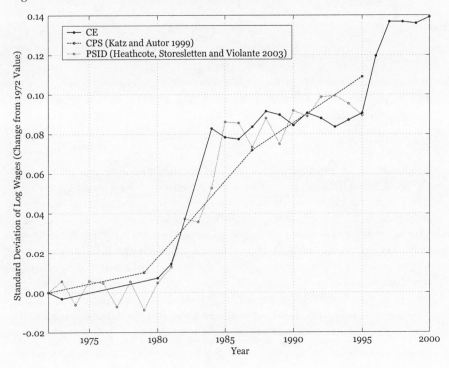

Figure 4 STANDARD DEVIATION OF LOG TOTAL AND DISPOSABLE
EARNINGS

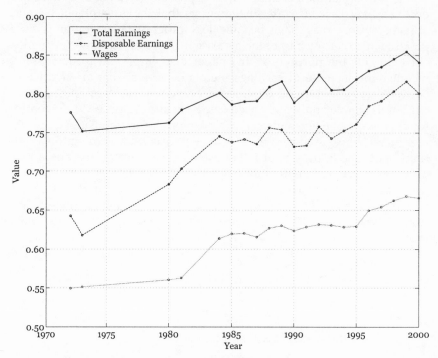

We then decompose each earning observation into a component y_{it}^g due
to observables (education and sex) and into a part due to unobservable,
purely idiosyncratic variation y_{it}^d:

$$\ln(y_{it}) = \ln(y_{it}^g) + \ln(y_{it}^d)$$

so that $y_{it} = y_{it}^g \, y_{it}^d$.[12] We chose education and sex to define groups because
the increase of the skill premium and the decline of the gender gap are the
two most important determinants of the changes of between-group earnings inequality in the last 30 years. We then assume that the unobservable
idiosyncratic component of earnings is orthogonal to the observable,
common-group component of earnings, so that we can find it by regressing $\ln(y_{it})$ on the years of education of the household reference person and
sex dummies. For each household observation $\ln(y_{it})$, we therefore obtain
two new observations, the predicted (by education and sex) value, $\ln(y_{it}^g)$
and the residual, $\ln(y_{it}^d)$. To understand their interpretation, consider, for

12. We decompose the logarithm of earnings because the standard deviation of the log of a
    variable has a cardinal interpretation, which makes our findings below easier to evaluate.

example, household i with $\ln y_{it} = -0.4$, $\ln (y_{it}^g) = -0.2$ and $\ln(y_{it}^g) = -0.2$; thus, this household has earnings 40% below the average earnings of a household with the same age and same race; half of this difference is explained by its education/sex characteristic and the other half is purely idiosyncratic variation.

From $\{\ln(y_{it}^g)\}$, we compute cross-sectional between-group variances σ_{gt}^2, and from $\{\ln(y_{it}^g)\}$, we compute cross-sectional idiosyncratic variances σ_{dt}^2. This procedure yields time series $\{\sigma_{gt}^2, \sigma_{dt}^2\}_{t \in T}$ of variances satisfying:

$$\sigma_{yt}^2 = \sigma_{gt}^2 + \sigma_{dt}^2 \tag{1}$$

for our sample period T.

Figure 5 shows the trends in between- and within-group earnings standard deviations. Note that within-group inequality accounts for a larger fraction of total inequality but that both the between- and the within-group component display a significant increase. Within-group inequality increases throughout the sample, while between-group inequality

Figure 5 DECOMPOSITION OF DISPOSABLE EARNINGS INEQUALITY

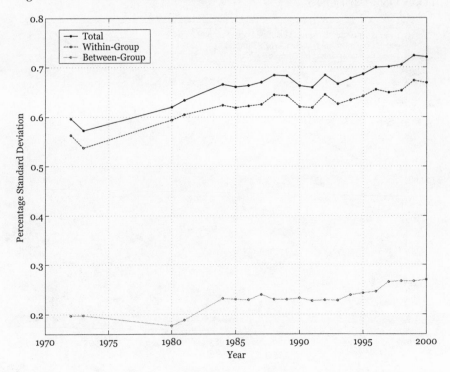

declines slightly in the 1970s (reflecting a reduction in the college premium) but increases significantly in the 1980s and 1990s. The patterns of both inequality measures from the CE are again similar to those from the CPS and the census data described by Katz and Autor (1999).

3.2 CONSUMPTION AND HOURS INEQUALITY

Our focus on welfare now leads us to investigate the evolution of the variables more directly connected to the lifetime utility of households, namely, consumption and leisure.

3.2.1 Consumption Inequality Figure 6 displays the trend in disposable earnings inequality (from Figure 5), together with two measures of consumption inequality. Both measures are standard deviations of household per adult equivalent nondurable consumption plus imputed services from durables. (This is the definition of consumption used

Figure 6 STANDARD DEVIATION OF LOG DISPOSABLE EARNINGS AND LOG CONSUMPTION

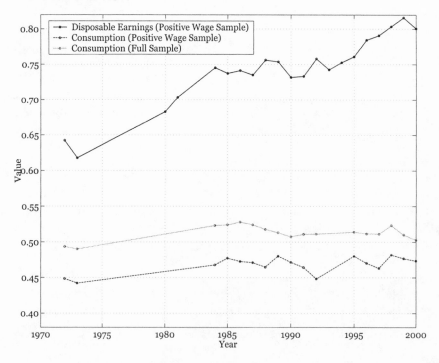

throughout the paper; see the data appendix and our earlier work [Krueger and Perri, 2002] for details about the construction of the consumption data.) The first measure, labeled consumption (Positive Wage Sample), is computed using the same sample selection criterion we use for wage and earnings inequality and does not include households with reference persons that do not work. The second measure, labeled consumption (Full Sample), includes all households that are complete income respondents, have a reference person between the ages of 20 and 64, and report positive consumption. Notice that the second sample is larger than the first (about 15% larger) and that it includes households whose reference person has left the labor force or is suffering a long unemployment spell. The picture shows that, although the *level* of inequality differs across the two samples, neither series of consumption inequality displays an increase comparable to the one registered for disposable earnings inequality. In Figure 7, we plot the average per-adult equivalent consumption of the household in the bottom, middle, and

Figure 7 CONSUMPTION BY SELECTED QUINTILES OF THE DISPOSABLE EARNINGS DISTRIBUTION

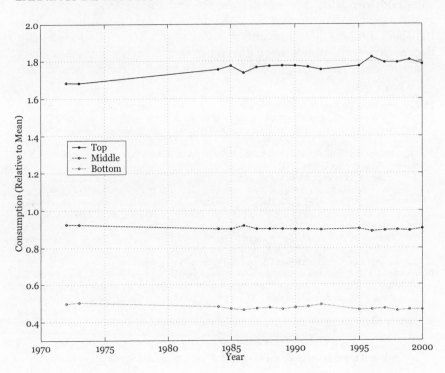

top quintile of the disposable earnings distribution (relative to average consumption in that year).[13]

Both figures confirm and extend our earlier findings (Krueger and Perri, 2002). During a period of strongly widening wage and earnings dispersion, there has been surprisingly little increase in consumption inequality.[14] In particular, households at the bottom of the earnings distribution have experienced only a mild reduction in their relative consumption, even though their relative earnings have declined substantially.

Note that, even though total consumption inequality has increased by only a small amount, this phenomenon is a result of two offsetting trends. We decompose—as we did for earnings—consumption inequality into within- and between-group inequality.[15] Figure 8 shows that the between-group component has increased substantially, by about the same magnitude as the increase in between-group earnings inequality. In stark contrast to earnings, *within-group* consumption inequality has, in fact, slightly declined. We draw two lessons from this decomposition, which will be crucial for interpreting our welfare calculations below. First, it is not true, as one may think from simply looking at overall consumption inequality, that the increase in earnings inequality had no impact on consumption inequality. Rather, it suggests that the increase in between-group earnings inequality (i.e., the increase in the skill premium) translates almost one to one into an increase of consumption inequality. Because between-group inequality tends to be highly persistent, it is likely to have important welfare consequences.[16] Second, the fact that

---

13. Consumption by earnings quintile is computed using the sample of all households that report positive consumption (full sample). If we restrict the sample to households with a reference person working at least one week, consumption by quintiles displays the same constant pattern.

14. We document that this fact is robust compared to various definition of consumption expenditures (Krueger and Perri, 2002). It is worth mentioning that our results are based on quarterly consumption expenditures reported in the CE interview survey. Attanasio (2002) presents some results from the CE diary survey (that is, the biweekly survey of expenditure data for items purchased on a daily or weekly basis) showing increasing consumption inequality. Additional work should be done to establish the exact source of the discrepancy between the two surveys. Another important concern with the CE consumption data is that their total does not match the National Income and Product Accounting total. Slesnick (2001) discusses some possible explanations for this phenomenon but concludes that a large part of the discrepancy between CE and NIPA is still unexplained.

15. We do the decomposition exactly as for income. We first control for changes in the age/race structure of the population by regressing the log of nondurable consumption plus services from durables on a quartic polynomial in the age of the reference person and on a dummy for his or her race. We then regress the residuals on the years of education and gender of the reference person of the household. The sample used consists of all households that report positive consumption.

16. This is a point that has been highlighted by Attanasio and Davis (1996). In the second part, we will provide an estimate of the persistence of between-group differences.

Figure 8 DECOMPOSITION OF CONSUMPTION INEQUALITY

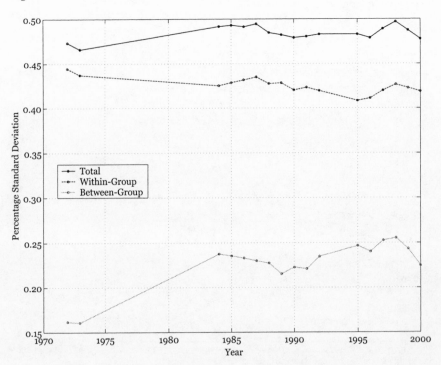

within-group disposable earnings inequality has increased while within-group consumption inequality has not indicates that the increase in within-group earnings variations has been effectively smoothed by households, possibly through some form of credit markets.[17]

3.2.2 Hours Inequality A household's lifetime utility depends on both the consumption and leisure it enjoys, so the number of hours worked by members of the household, by determining the hours available for leisure, is an important determinant of welfare. Therefore, in this section we present some evidence on how the distribution of hours worked across American households has changed. In Figure 9 we plot the percentage standard deviation of household yearly hours worked (per adult),

---

17. Blundell and Preston (1998), Heathcote et al. (2003), and we [Krueger and Perri, 2002] investigate the role of credit markets in generating this divergence between income and consumption inequality in detail.

Figure 9 STANDARD DEVIATION OF LOG WAGES AND OF LOG PER ADULT HOURS

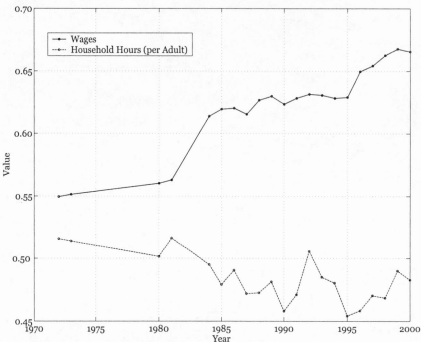

together with the standard deviation of wages of the reference person of the household.[18]

We observe that, despite the increase in wage dispersion, the variability in hours worked shows a moderate decline. If hours and consumption were uncorrelated, abstracting from any change in their trends, the reduction in hours dispersion would imply welfare gains. However, Figure 10 suggests that hours and consumption *are* correlated. It plots the number of per-person yearly hours worked for all households in our sample and for households in different quintiles of the consumption distribution.

Apart from the strong average increase in hours worked, whose causes and consequences we will not analyze here, the figure reveals two other facts.[19] First, households with high consumption work more hours;

---

18. We use the same sample we used for the wage and earnings distribution. We construct per-person hours worked by households in the following way: if a household consists of a single adult member, its hours worked are the hours worked in a year by that adult, and if the household consists of (at least) two adult members, average hours worked by the household are measured as total hours worked by both members divided by 2.

19. Inspection of the CE data immediately reveals that most of the average increase in hours worked is due to increased female labor force participation.

second, high-consumption households have increased their hours by less than low-consumption households. For example, in 1972–1973, households in the bottom quintile of the consumption distribution worked on average 28% less than households in the top quintile. In 1999–2000, the same ratio has fallen to 17%. In other words, Figure 10 suggests a positive, but falling, correlation between consumption and hours worked.

Figure 11 plots the correlation between hours and consumption (total, between-group component, and within-group component). The figure indeed shows a significant decline over time in the correlation between hours and consumption. This declining positive correlation explains the fall in hours variability and, together with constant consumption inequality, can generate negative welfare effects for low-consumption households, even if their relative consumption may not fall. More concretely, in the 1970s, the high correlation between consumption and hours implied that households with low consumption were compensated with high leisure. In the 1990s, the reduction in this correlation implies that households with relatively low consumption do not enjoy as much leisure as

Figure 10 YEARLY HOURS WORKED PER PERSON (AVERAGE AND BY SELECTED QUINTILES OF THE CONSUMPTION DISTRIBUTION)

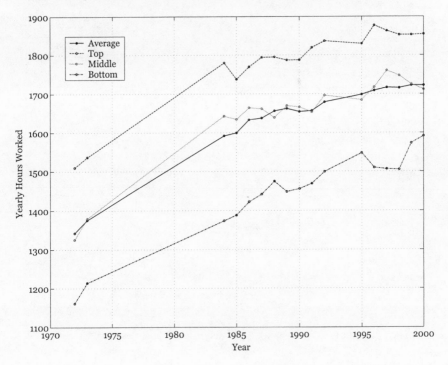

they used to and thus face potentially substantial welfare losses from this change over time. We will quantify the welfare consequences from a declining correlation in consumption and hours worked in the section containing our welfare calculation below.

3.3 SUMMARY

To summarize Section 3, the CE data suggest that the substantial increase in wage inequality has caused an increase in household earnings inequality of similar magnitude. The tax and transfer system has not mitigated this increase, so that it appears equally strong in disposable earnings. The *consumption* distribution data, on the other hand, suggest that low-consumption households did almost as well (relatively to the mean) in the late 1990s as they did in the 1970s.

This finding does not necessarily imply that the welfare effects of the increase in inequality are negligible. A closer investigation of consumption inequality reveals that households that suffer permanent relative

Figure 11 CORRELATION OF HOURS WORKED AND CONSUMPTION

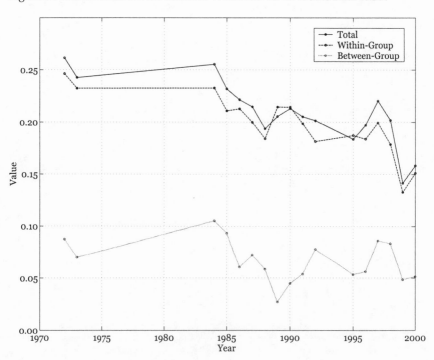

income falls (e.g., households with little education) experience substantial declines in relative consumption, with associated important welfare consequences.

In addition, the declining trend in the consumption–hours worked correlation suggests that one way through which low-consumption households maintain their relative consumption is by working longer hours, again with implied welfare losses. In the next section of the paper, we will try to quantify the size and exact distribution of these welfare effects.

4. Welfare Consequences of Increased Inequality

What are the welfare consequences of the trends in wage, income, and consumption inequality documented in the last section? To answer these questions explicitly, we now have to take a stand on how households value consumption and leisure, and we have to model, in a statistical or theoretical way, how a household's consumption and leisure processes changed as the variability of wages and earnings changed. The second step can be carried out in (at least) two different ways. Either one takes a stand on a particular theoretical model, feeds as input into the model two different earnings processes estimated from data (one reflecting increased earnings inequality), computes the corresponding consumption and labor supply allocations implied by the model, and then uses these allocations to compute the welfare gain and/or loss distribution from the change in the earnings (or wage) process.[20] Alternatively, one can specify or estimate a statistical model for consumption and labor supply (or leisure). The parameters governing these processes are allowed to be time dependent, so that the processes reflect the changes in the cross-sectional distribution of consumption and hours worked documented in the last section of the paper. We adopt the second approach in this paper.

We now discuss our exact estimation strategy, then we explain how we use our estimation results to answer the welfare question posed at the beginning of the paper, and finally we present our results.

4.1 MODELING HOUSEHOLD EARNINGS, CONSUMPTION, AND LEISURE PROCESSES

To carry our welfare analysis, we need stochastic processes for disposable earnings, consumption, and leisure. Take an arbitrary variable of interest from the last section, for concreteness, disposable earnings. In the empirical analysis, we discussed how each pre-filtered cross section $\ln(y_{it})$ can

---

20. Our earlier study (Krueger and Perri, 2002) and the study by Heathcote et al. (2003) take this approach.

be decomposed in a between-group $[\ln(y_{it}^g)]$ and a within-group part $[\ln(y_{it}^d)]$.

In this section, we specify time-series processes for both components of earnings. In particular, we assume that both $\ln(y_{it}^d)$ and $\ln(y_{it}^g)$ follow finite state Markov chains (of cardinality N) with possibly time-varying states Y_t^d and Y_t^g and with time-invariant transition matrices π^d, π^g.[21]

The states $\{Y_t^g\}_{t \in T}$ are determined by setting $Y_t^g(i)$ equal to the midpoint of the i-th quantile of the $\{\ln(y_{it}^g)\}$ sample for that period. By construction, our stochastic process matches, for every t, $N(N-1)/2$ quantile ratios of $\{\ln(y_{it}^g)\}$, its mean (by construction, equal to 0), but not necessarily its variance.[22] A similar construction yields the states $\{Y_t^d\}_{t \in T}$. Note that, because of the initial pre-filtering, there is no aggregate growth in the logs of any of our variables [i.e., $E_i(\ln x_{it}) = 0$, for every x and every t], which in particular removes aggregate consumption growth and growth in average hours worked. The welfare conclusions presented below have to be interpreted with this remark in mind, which we will address in the conclusion.

Finally, we use the panel dimension of the CE to estimate Markov transition matrices for the variables of interest, which will embody the persistence properties of our stochastic processes. For all observations $\{\ln(y_{it}^g)\}_{i,t}$ we group households into N relative classes delimited by $N-1$ uniformly spaced, time dependent quantiles: the first class is comprised of the bottom $1/N\%$ of the distribution in that quarter for that variable, the second class is comprised of the following $1/N\%$, etc. With this construction, the lowest class for $\{\ln y_{it}^g\}$ is interpreted as the group of households for which earnings explained by observables (gender and education) is lowest (i.e., households with female head and low education levels). We then search for all households for which we have observations in two consecutive periods and compute which relative class they belong to in the second period.[23] After repeating this proce-

---

21. In principle, our procedure could be used to estimate time-varying transition matrices. We have experimented with this for the time period 1984–2000 and found that the transition matrices display very little time variation. We therefore decided to use time-independent transition matrices in our analysis.
22. We find, however, that the ratio between the variance implied by the estimated process and the variance in the data is quite high (about 70%) and almost constant over time. It would have been easy to set the states of our stochastic process to match exactly the variance in the data, but we opted to match quantile ratios of the data because of our interest in the distribution of welfare losses. Our procedure is similar in spirit to the one used by Tauchen and Hussey (1991).
23. More precisely, a period is roughly three quarters because we use data from the second and fifth interview of a household in the CE to determine transitions. This timing comes closest to our notion of a period length of one year. Second, the only useful income observations for a household are contained in these interviews.

Table 1 THE PERSISTENCE OF THE ESTIMATED PROCESSES[1]

	Within-group	*Between-group*
Disposable earnings	0.76	0.97
Consumption	0.72	0.98

1. The reported measure of persistence is the value of the second largest eigenvalue of the transition matrices π^d and π^g.

dure for every period in the sample, the probability π_{ij}^g of transiting from class i to class j is computed as the total number of households transiting from i to j, divided by the total number of households starting in class i for the *entire* sample.[24] Using the same procedure for the sample $\{\ln(y_{it}^d)\}$ yields a transition matrix π^d. As a result of our estimation procedure, we obtain Markov processes for the group-specific as well as within-group components of earnings; we follow exactly the same procedures to construct time-series processes for household consumption. In Table 1 we report a summary measure of the persistence properties of the various processes we estimate. Note that the processes for between-group differences are significantly more persistent than the processes for within-group differences, so that changes in between-group inequality are more likely to have larger welfare effects.

For hours worked, we find that between-group inequality explains only a very small fraction of total variance (less than 0.5%), so the process for hours does not distinguish between the two components. In our welfare analysis, we will also study the case in which welfare is jointly determined by household consumption and hours worked. For this case, we specify a joint stochastic process for between-group consumption, within-group consumption, and hours worked. Because the correlation between hours and between-group consumption is fairly constant and close to 0 (see Figure 11), we assume that hours and between-group consumption are uncorrelated. However, we specify the parameters of the joint Markov chain for hours and within-group consumption so that the correlation between the two variables in the model matches exactly

24. Transitions of households between groups are rare and occur only if there are large swings in the returns to education, in the wage gender gap, or (the dominating reason) if households change the gender or the education of their reference person (through death, marriage, or divorce).

the falling cross-sectional correlation between the two variables in the data, as reported in Figure 11.[25]

In short, denote the estimated stochastic processes for earnings, consumption, and hours by $(Y, C, H,$ respectively) and the processes associated with no change in wage inequality (i.e., the process with states constant at their 1972 values) by $(\hat{Y}, \hat{L}, \hat{H},$ respectively). These are the necessary ingredients for the welfare calculations, which we describe next.

4.2 CALCULATING THE WELFARE CONSEQUENCES

We assume that households value streams of consumption c_t and leisure $l_t = 1 - h_t$ (where h_t are hours worked per household member, as a fraction of total nonsleep time) according to the lifetime utility function:

$$U(C, L) = E \sum_{t=0}^{\infty} \beta^t u(c_t, l_t)$$

We restrict the period utility function u to lie in the parametric class:

$$u(c, l) = \begin{cases} \dfrac{[c^\alpha l^{1-\alpha}]^{1-\sigma}}{1-\sigma} & \text{for } \sigma \neq 1 \\ \alpha \ln(c) + (1-\alpha)\ln(l) & \text{for } \sigma = 1 \end{cases}$$

where α, β and σ are preference parameters that govern the relative importance of consumption relative to leisure, time discounting, and the intertemporal elasticity of substitution, respectively.[26] Nested in this formulation are utility functions that depend on consumption alone ($\alpha = 1$).

Suppose that all economic variables follow Markov processes as estimated above, then we can write:

$$V(t, c, l) = u(c, l) + \beta E[V(t+1, c', l') | (c, l)] \tag{2}$$

Note that, conditional on knowing the function V, the conditional expectation can be evaluated because the stochastic processes for consumption and leisure have a Markov structure.[27] Also note that, for an arbitrary

---

25. The complete results of our estimation procedure are available on request from the authors.
26. Note that these utility functions have unit elasticity between consumption and leisure. With this class of utility functions, our welfare results are invariant to long-run deterministic average consumption growth.
27. This formulation implicitly assumes that households are infinitely lived. With finite lives, age becomes an additional state variable. The welfare consequences for a person living through the increase in inequality for only a finite number of periods is roughly proportional to the numbers reported below (such a household faces the same stochastic processes as our model households, simply for fewer periods). The proportionality factor is less than one and decreases with the remaining lifetime of a household.

individual with current consumption and leisure (c, l), expected lifetime utility is given by $V(t, c, l)$, which obviously depends on the time-varying stochastic process for consumption and leisure. Also note that this Bellman equation does not involve any maximization.

In particular, let $V(c, l)$ be the value function associated with the estimated stochastic processes, and let $\hat{V}(c, l)$ denote the value function associated with the stochastic processes if wage inequality had not increased (and thus the cross-sectional variances $[\sigma_{dt}^2, \sigma_{gt}^2]$ had remained the same).[28] More precisely, $\hat{V}$ is computed by employing the same transition matrices as for V, but under the assumption that the states of the Markov chains remain at their estimated 1972 values forever rather than change over time, in the way estimated above.

The welfare consequences of an agent with current state (c, l) in 1972 (the distribution of which we observe in our cross-sectional dataset) of the ensuing increase in wage inequality in the future is thus given by

$$W(c, l) = \| V(c, l) - \hat{V}(c, l) \|$$

where $\| \cdot \|$ is a particular metric. We let $W(c, l)$ equal the uniform percentage increase of consumption in each state of the world needed to make a household indifferent between the stochastic processes with more variability and the ones without, keeping leisure constant. What we want to document is the distribution of $W(c, l)$, that is, the distribution of the welfare consequences of the increase in wage inequality.

4.3 RESULTS

4.3.1 An Upper Bound   Suppose that households do not have access to any savings technology and do not value leisure.[29] Then consumption equals labor earnings y and, if we ignore irrelevant constants and suppress time indexation, equation (2) becomes:

$$V(y) = u(y) + \beta E[V(y') | y]$$

or more explicitly:

$$V(y^g, y^d) = \frac{[y^g y^d]^{1-\sigma}}{1-\sigma} + \beta E[V(y^{g'}, y^{d'}) | y^g, y^d]$$

---

28. We suppress the time index $t = 1972$.
29. The same results are obtained if households do not change their labor supply or if consumption and leisure are separable in the utility function.

and a similar definition for $\hat{V}(y^g, y^d)$ applies. The welfare criterion is given by:

$$W(y^g, y^d) = \|V(y^g, y^d) - \hat{V}(y^g, y^d)\|$$
$$= \left[\frac{\hat{V}(y^g, y^d)}{V(y^g, y^d)}\right]^{1/1-\sigma} - 1$$

The term $W(y^g, y^d)$ gives the percentage increase in consumption (or earnings) at the new, more unequal earnings process, at each contingency, necessary to make an agent with arbitrary current earnings $y = (y^g, y^d)$ indifferent between the old and the new wage (and thus earnings) process.[30] To compute this number, three steps have to be carried out:

1. Solve for the functions V and $\hat{V}$ using standard value function iteration, given time-series processes Y and $\hat{Y}$.
2. Draw arbitrary $y = (y^g, y^d)$ from the initial earnings distribution.
3. Evaluate $W(y^g, y^d)$.

Evidently steps 2 and 3 can be carried out easily for all y in the initial distribution of earnings, and thus the distribution of welfare consequences can be derived. These numbers provide an upper bound for the welfare consequences from increased earnings inequality because agents are assumed to be unable to smooth consumption via savings responses.

A simple example illustrates this basic procedure. Suppose that before 1972, earnings followed the simple continuous-state white-noise process:

$$\ln(y') = \hat{\mu} + \hat{\varepsilon}$$

where $\hat{\varepsilon} \sim N(0, \hat{\sigma}_\varepsilon^2)$. After 1972, the process changes to:

$$\ln(y') = \hat{\mu} + \varepsilon$$

with $\varepsilon \sim N(0, \sigma_\varepsilon^2)$, $\sigma_\varepsilon^2 = \gamma\hat{\sigma}_\varepsilon^2$, with $\gamma > 1$ and:

$$\mu = \hat{\mu} - \frac{1}{2}\hat{\sigma}_\varepsilon^2(\gamma - 1) < \hat{\mu}$$

Note that the adjustment of the mean of log earnings is required for the level of earnings to have the same mean before and after the change in its variance. For period utility being logarithmic, the value function V solves:

$$V(y) = \log(y) + \beta \int V(e^{\mu + \varepsilon}) d\Phi(\varepsilon)$$

30. For $\sigma = 1$, one can show that the welfare criterion, as defined above, is given by:
$$W(y^g, y^d) = \exp\left[(1 - \beta)\left(\hat{V}(y^g, y^d) - V(y^g, y^d)\right)\right] - 1$$

where Φ is the normal cumulative distribution function (cdf) with variance $\sigma_{\varepsilon}^2 = \gamma \hat{\sigma}_{\varepsilon}^2$. The function $\hat{V}$ solves the same equation, with Φ replaced by $\hat{Y}$, the normal cdf with variance $\hat{\sigma}_{\varepsilon}^2$. A simple guess-and-verify strategy shows that:

$$V(y) = \ln(y) + \frac{\beta}{1-\beta}\mu$$

$$\hat{V}(y) = \ln(y) + \frac{\beta}{1-\beta}\hat{\mu} > V(y)$$

In particular, if $\hat{v} = 0$ (which simply normalizes mean earnings), then:

$$W(y) = W = \exp\left(b(\hat{\mu}-\mu)\right) - 1$$

$$= \exp\left(\frac{\beta}{2}\right)\exp\left(\hat{\sigma}_{\varepsilon}^2(\gamma-1)\right) - 1 > 0$$

For this particular example, the welfare losses from increased earnings inequality are (1) independent of an agents' current earnings and (2) proportional to the increase of the variance of log earnings $\hat{\sigma}_{\varepsilon}^2(\gamma-1)$.

For a general stochastic earnings process and period utility function, of course, the value function cannot be solved by guess-and-verify methods and has to be computed numerically.[31] As a benchmark, an annual time discount rate of 4% and logarithmic utility are assumed. We then document how our welfare conclusions depend on the degree of risk aversion of households and discuss the role of the time discount rate for our results.

In Figure 12a, we plot the welfare losses implied by our estimated income processes from the CE. Each individual is characterized in 1972 by $(y^g, y^d) \in (Y^g, Y^d)$, where both Y^g and Y^d have cardinality 9. Thus, there are 81 distinct earnings classes, with equal population mass $\frac{1}{81}$. On the x axis we plot idiosyncratic earnings y^d as a fraction of average (idiosyncratic) earnings, and each of the separate 9 lines corresponds to one group-specific earnings level y^g. The y axis shows the welfare losses, in percentage consumption equivalent variation, implied by the increase in earnings inequality, as estimated by our processes.

We observe that the welfare losses implied by the increase in earnings inequality are potentially substantial, amounting to as much as 2% or more of consumption for more than half of the population, namely, the earnings-poor households in 1972. The welfare losses are declining (and substantially so) as one moves up the group-specific earnings distribution, to the extent that the highest two earnings groups (22% of the population)

---

31. Given the discrete nature of the income process, this computation can be done quickly and with precision using a standard value function iteration algorithm.

Figure 12 WELFARE LOSSES

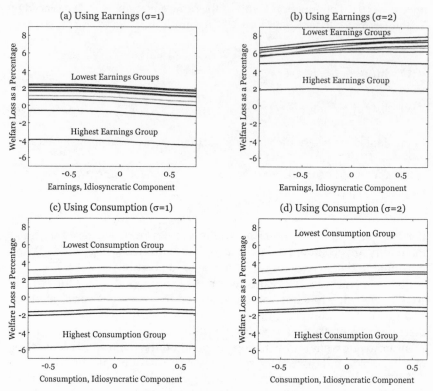

benefit from the increase in earnings inequality.[32] Welfare losses (or gains) are fairly uniform in the idiosyncratic income state, y^d, that a household starts with in 1972.

These findings can be interpreted as follows. The *aggregate* statistics show an increase in inequality in the last 30 years. An *individual* household in 1972 experiences two events: future changes in its expected mean earnings and more earnings risk in the future. Conditional on remaining in the same earnings class, high-earnings class households will enjoy increasing relative earnings, and low-earning classes will experience declining relative earnings. These outcomes are true for both the group component as well as the idiosyncratic component of earnings. From the figure, we observe, however, that the welfare losses differ substantially by

32. Note that, when we refer to welfare losses from inequality from now on, it is understood that individuals are affected directly only by changes in their relative earnings (and higher earnings uncertainty in the future), rather than by the change in the aggregate statistics per se.

groups but are fairly uniform with respect to the idiosyncratic earnings component. This difference is explained by the much higher persistence of the between-group earnings process compared to the idiosyncratic process documented in the last section. As a rough approximation, suppose that the group-earnings transition matrix is the identity matrix (so that all agents with probability of 1 stay in their earnings group) and the idiosyncratic earnings process is iid over time. Then welfare losses should vary greatly by group (because relative group earnings have diverged over time) but should be uniform across idiosyncratic states because everybody is equally negatively affected by the higher idiosyncratic earnings uncertainty. Figure 12 indicates that this first approximation provides fairly accurate intuition for the computed welfare numbers. The negative (uniform) impact of higher idiosyncratic *uncertainty* also explains why almost the entire population suffers welfare losses from increased earnings inequality, even though half the population experiences increases in relative earnings.

From the previous discussion, one would expect the welfare losses from increasing earnings inequality to rise with risk aversion of the household because higher idiosyncratic uncertainty is disliked more severely. That this is indeed the case is demonstrated by Figure 12b, which assumes a coefficient of relative risk aversion of $\sigma = 2$. Now the welfare losses become as high as 8% of consumption, and despite significant expected earnings increases, even the highest earnings group suffers welfare losses of about 2% due to the increase in future earnings (and thus, by construction, consumption) variability. To summarize, when judged from earnings data for a degree of risk aversion of $\sigma = 2$, commonly assumed in the macro and public finance literature, all groups of the population suffer welfare losses from increased earnings instability that more than outweigh the increase in relative incomes experienced by the highest earnings groups.

Before documenting how our results change if one uses consumption rather than earnings data for our welfare analysis, a brief discussion of the role of the time discount factor is in order. Our estimated transition matrices (in particular for the group component) are persistent, but not perfectly persistent, so that the unconditional probability of a household leaving its 1972 earnings state increases with time. With sizable time discounting of 4% per year, the welfare losses are affected by events along the transition period 1972–2000 (the increase in earnings inequality occurs gradually over this time period) and vary crucially with initial earnings states because earnings realizations in the early years of the transition largely determine welfare, as seen in Figure 12. If one were to choose very low time discounting (none in the limit), then households' welfare losses are determined largely (completely in the limit) by the change in the steady-state earnings distribution and would depend on neither a household's initial earnings position nor the transition path.[33] Since we want to document the distribution of welfare losses across different population groups, we chose a time discount rate of 4% that attributes substantial importance to initial conditions and transition paths. As a comparison, a time discount rate of 0.05% yields welfare losses, roughly uniform across the population, of about 1.4% for $\sigma = 1$ and 10.5% for $\sigma = 2$.

4.3.2 The Effects of Consumption Smoothing The previous section documented potentially large welfare costs of increased earnings inequality, under the assumption that households have no ability to smooth consumption intertemporally via self-insurance and/or formal and informal insurance arrangements. Calculations like these often form the explicit or implicit basis for concern expressed about the increase in inequality by researchers and policymakers.

As argued in the introduction, basing welfare evaluations of increased inequality on consumption data directly takes the mitigating effects of intertemporal smoothing opportunities, government transfer programs, and explicit or implicit insurance programs (such as transfers among members of the extended family) into account. Therefore, in this subsection, we repeat our previous analysis but now use estimated consumption processes from the CE instead of earnings processes. The Bellman equation becomes:

$$V(c) = u(c) + \beta E\left[V(c')|(c)\right] \tag{3}$$

which is solved as easily as in the previous subsection, under the maintained assumption that the estimated stochastic consumption processes have a Markov structure.

Again we start with the benchmark case of logarithmic utility and plot the welfare losses from increased consumption inequality in Figure 12c. Qualitatively, the welfare consequences are similar to the previous section: the consumption group to which a household belongs largely determines whether it ends up a loser or a winner of the increase in inequality. Again, the welfare consequences are fairly uniform across idiosyncratic consumption states. Quantitatively, however, some crucial differences in the results based on earnings observations emerge. The highest welfare losses now amount to slightly more than 5% of consumption, but only for

33. One may interpret this latter thought experiment and the welfare numbers as a household living behind the veil of ignorance: they don't know which income state they will be born into in the old, pre-1972 steady state and they don't know in which income state they end up in the in new, post-2000 steady state.

the consumption-poorest 10% of the population.[34] Note that, while maximal welfare losses from increased inequality when measured with consumption data are even higher than with earnings, a much larger fraction of the population (roughly 45%) now benefits sufficiently from the increase in relative group consumption to experience welfare gains from increased consumption inequality. This differential finding is due to the fact that the variability of the idiosyncratic component of *consumption* has remained relatively constant over time, very much in contrast to that of *earnings*. Therefore, the welfare consequences, when derived from consumption data, are almost exclusively determined by relative group consumption.[35]

For earnings, an increase in the risk aversion of households led to dramatically increased welfare losses from increased inequality, but when using consumption data, the welfare consequences of increased inequality are close to invariant to changes in a household's attitudes toward risk. Again, this finding is explained by the stable trend of the variance of the idiosyncratic consumption component. The welfare losses and gains in Figure 12d, computed for risk aversion of $\sigma = 2$, are almost indistinguishable from the corresponding figure 12c for $\sigma = 1$. Thus, in comparison to our findings for earnings, for a reasonable degree of risk aversion of $\sigma = 2$, consumption data do not suggest nearly as severe welfare losses as do earnings data. Repeating our calculations with a low time discount rate of 0.05% again results in welfare losses that are fairly uniform across the population, amounting to losses of 0.5% for $\sigma = 1$ and 1.6% for $\sigma = 2$, again significantly smaller than the corresponding numbers derived from earnings.

Our findings are consistent with Attanasio and Davis (1996), who document that a significant share of the increase in wage inequality between observably different groups is reflected in increases in consumption inequality between these groups. Our welfare numbers reproduce exactly this phenomenon. These results are also in line with findings in our earlier work (Krueger and Perri, 2002) because the idiosyncratic component of consumption inequality has not increased significantly over time and thus has not, to any noticeable extent, contributed to the welfare losses from increased inequality. Finally note that, to focus on the welfare effects of increased inequality, we have effectively detrended our data from

---

34. These high losses of the lowest consumption group compared to the more moderate losses of the lowest earnings group documented above are largely due to the timing of the transition, coupled with sizable time discounting: relative consumption for the lowest group drops early on and then stays constant, whereas relative earnings for the lowest group declines most dramatically only at the end of the 1972–2000 transition period.
35. Since the transition matrix for the group component of consumption displays very high persistence, increased *risk* in the between-group component is quantitatively of second-order importance.

aggregate consumption growth. Thus, our results are not to be interpreted as absolute standards of living having declined over the last 30 years for a large fraction of the population.

4.3.3 The Impact of Changes in Leisure In our empirical section we documented that, in light of increased wage variability, the relative labor supply of different groups in the population has changed, albeit only moderately so. In this section we extend our welfare analysis to incorporate these changes in relative labor supply and hence leisure. The Bellman equation for this augmented problem now becomes:

$$V(c,l) = u(c,l) + \beta E\,[V(c',l')/(c,l)] \tag{4}$$

Here, the expectations operator pertains to the joint Markov process for consumption c and leisure l. This Markov process may feature independence between c and l (our benchmark) or allow for dependence between consumption and leisure (a case that we will investigate as a sensitivity analysis).

Both the definition of welfare costs as well as their computation remain the same as in the previous subsection. We parametrize the period utility function as before, and choose a share parameter $\alpha = \frac{1}{3}$ and a nonsleep time endowment of 15 hours per person, per day.[36]

4.3.3.1 LABOR SUPPLY UNCORRELATED WITH CONSUMPTION How does the inclusion of leisure into the analysis change the magnitude of the welfare losses from increased inequality? To a first-order approximation, the magnitude as well as the distribution of these losses is unaffected by the incorporation of leisure into the analysis. Again, the consumption group a household belongs to in 1972 largely determines how it fares in terms of welfare, whereas the idiosyncratic consumption state, the leisure state, or the risk aversion of the household play only a minor quantitative role.[37]

---

36. In a static deterministic model with our preferences, an agent would choose to work exactly one-third of her nonsleep time if $\alpha = \frac{1}{3}$, independent of the wage. Note that the coefficient of relative risk aversion for consumption is now given by:

$$\frac{-cu_{cc}}{u_c} = \sigma\alpha + 1 - \alpha$$

When we report results for a particular risk aversion, we set σ, given $\alpha = \frac{1}{3}$, to the appropriate value to attain that risk aversion.

37. The reason that the leisure state is not an important determinant of the welfare losses is similar to the one for idiosyncratic consumption: we estimate labor supply, and hence leisure, to be not nearly as persistent as group consumption (roughly as persistent as idosyncratic consumption).

Because the hours and thus leisure distribution has become somewhat less dispersed between 1972 and 2000, the welfare losses from increased overall inequality are slightly mitigated by the presence of leisure in the utility function, but the reduction in welfare losses amounts to no more than 0.4% for any of the population groups, compared to the welfare losses reported in the last section based on consumption observations alone.

One has to bear in mind, though, that our estimation of stochastic processes for hours worked, as with consumption, effectively removed the positive trend in average hours worked by households. Therefore, our welfare numbers do not reflect the potentially adverse effect on well-being of longer hours worked by a large fraction of U.S. households.

4.3.3.2 LABOR SUPPLY CORRELATED WITH CONSUMPTION   In our empirical analysis, we found that the correlation between idiosyncratic consumption and leisure is negative and, more important, has declined in absolute value between 1972 and 2000. In other words, while low-consumption housseholds used to enjoy at least significantly higher leisure in 1972, this situation has become less pronounced in 2000. We now investigate whether allowing consumption and leisure to be correlated (and therefore allowing more extreme negative states over time—those with increasingly low relative consumption and decreasingly high leisure) modifies our result that the incorporation of leisure into the analysis leaves our welfare numbers roughly unaffected.

Figure 13 compares the welfare losses (or gains) implied by three utility and stochastic process specifications: consumption only (a subset of Figures 12c and 12d), consumption and leisure when uncorrelated (see the discussion in the previous subsection), and consumption and leisure processes that are correlated. The subpanels distinguish risk aversion and agents belonging to different consumption groups. All four panels contain the welfare losses of agents that start with the highest leisure state in 1972. Similar (but somewhat less pronounced) results are obtained for households starting in other leisure states in 1972.

For separable preferences (*CRRA* = 1), correlation between consumption and leisure does not change our findings from the previous section. As households become more averse to risk, however, welfare losses arising under the correlated consumption-leisure process actually exceed the corresponding number under the consumption-only process, by up to 0.5 percentage points (see Figure 13b). This finding is due to the higher likelihood of experiencing states with low consumption and fairly low leisure, compared to the situation in which consumption and leisure were modeled as independent processes. We conclude that, while the welfare numbers based on consumption alone tell most of the story, the incorporation of leisure may, when correlated with consumption, increase welfare losses from increased inequality to a quantitatively notrivial extent.

5. Conclusion

What are the welfare consequences of the increase in inequality in the United States between 1972 and 2000? In this paper we use a standard intertemporal utility function and wage, earnings, consumption, and hours-worked data from the Consumer Expenditure survey to answer this question.

Our main findings are twofold. First, welfare losses can be substantial, with significant variation of these losses across the population. Whereas households at the bottom of the consumption distribution suffer declines in welfare up to about 6% in consumption equivalent variation, households at the top end of the distribution enjoy sizable welfare gains of similar magnitude as the losses of the poorest agents. Overall, a majority of the population (based on consumption observations, roughly 60% of Americans) is on the losing side. The main part of these losses arises from the increase in between-group consumption inequality. The increase in the consumption/leisure correlation contributes to moderately higher

Figure 13 WELFARE LOSSES

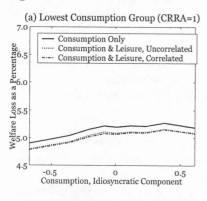

(a) Lowest Consumption Group (CRRA=1)

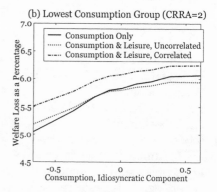

(b) Lowest Consumption Group (CRRA=2)

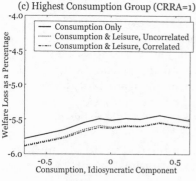

(c) Highest Consumption Group (CRRA=1)

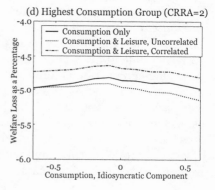

(d) Highest Consumption Group (CRRA=2)

welfare losses, an order of magnitude of 0.5% for most households. Second, while welfare losses from increased inequality are fairly sizable for a lot of U.S. households when based on consumption data, they are not nearly as big and affect not nearly as many households as an analysis based on earnings data alone would suggest (80% to 100% of the population losing up to 10%). In addition, the estimates of welfare losses based on consumption and leisure processes are fairly robust to different values of risk aversion, while those based on income processes are highly sensitive to that parameter.

To focus more precisely on the welfare effects of increasing inequality, we have ignored two important features of our data. First, there was substantial growth in average real household consumption; second, total hours worked by a typical household increased noticeably over the last 30 years. To the extent that these trends are causally linked to the trend in inequality, we have overstated (because of consumption growth) or understand (because of the decline in leisure) the welfare implications of the increase in inequality. Future empirical and theoretical work is needed to understand if, and to what extent, the trends in hours worked, in average consumption, and in the cross-sectional variance of consumption are causally related.

6. Data Appendix

Our statistics are based on repeated cross sections constructed from the interview surveys of the Consumer Expenditure (CE) survey for the years 1972–1973, 1980–1981, and 1984–2000, as provided by the Bureau of Labor Statistics. The 1972–1973 samples were conducted quarterly, but only annual totals were released; thus, for these years, we have only two cross sections, each reporting consumption and income for the year of the interview. The surveys from 1980 onward were conducted on a quarterly basis, so we have four cross sections for each year. Households report consumption expenditures for the quarter preceding the interview and income data for the year preceding the interview. A fraction of the households in the survey is interviewed for four consecutive quarters and reports consumption information in every quarter, as well as income and wage information in the first and last interview. For these households we can construct annual measures of wages, earnings, consumption, and number of hours from 1972–1973 until 2000.

6.1 WAGES, EARNINGS, AND HOURS

The definition of wages we use is the earnings of the reference person divided by the number of weeks worked by the person during the year.

We construct earnings of the reference person as her wages and salaries plus a fixed fraction of her self-employment farm and nonfarm income (the exact fraction is 0.864 and is taken from Diaz-Jimenez, Quadrini, and Rios-Rull [1997]). Household earnings simply sums the earnings of the reference person and her spouse. Disposable household earnings are computed as household earnings minus reported federal, state, and local taxes (net of refunds) and social security contributions paid by the household. We then add reported government transfers: in particular we add unemployment insurance, food stamps, and welfare receipts. Because the 1972–1973 CE does not report the number of hours worked per week by household members, only whether they are part- or full-time workers, hours worked by a person are computed as the number of weeks worked by that person times 20 if the person works part-time, or times 40 if the person works full-time. For the post-1980 sample, we compare the standard deviation of hours constructed in this way with the series constructed using actual weekly hours; the two series have very similar trends (although different levels).

6.2 CONSUMPTION

Our definition of consumption consists of nondurables plus imputed services from durables. It includes expenditures on nondurable goods and services, expenditures on household furnishings, and imputed services from houses and cars. Expenditures on nondurable goods and services include consumption expenditures for food, alcoholic beverages, tobacco, utilities, personal care, household operations, public transportation, gasoline and motor oil, apparel, education, reading, health services, and miscellaneous expenditures. Each component of consumption is deflated by its corresponding monthly consumer price index (CPI) from the Bureau of Labor Statistics.

Expenditures on household furnishings include items such as furniture, appliances, and floor coverings (e.g., rugs). The reason that we use expenditures and not imputed services is that no information is available in the CE for the value or the inventory of the stock of these furnishings, and the panel dimension of the CE is too short to carry out perpetual inventory techniques. With respect to vehicles, we impute services from cars in the following manner, following closely the procedure outlined by Cutler and Katz (1991b). From the CE data, we have expenditures for purchases of new and used vehicles. We also have data on the number of cars that a consumer unit possesses. For each year we first select all households that report positive expenditures for vehicle purchases and then run a regression of vehicle expenditures on a constant; age, sex, and education of the reference person of the consumer unit; total consumption expenditures, excluding vehicle expenditures of the consumer; the same variable squared; total income before taxes; family size; and quarter dummies. We use the estimated regression coefficients to predict expenditures for vehicles for all households in that quarter (i.e., for those who did and for those who did not report positive vehicle expenditures). Our measure of consumption services from vehicles is then the predicted expenditure on vehicles times the number of vehicles the consumer unit owns, times 1⁄32 (reflecting the assumption of average complete depreciation of a vehicle after 32 quarters), plus other expenditures for cars, such as insurance, maintenance, and finance charges. With respect to housing services, the CE provides information on rent paid for the residence of the consumer unit, including insurance and other out-of-pocket expenses paid by the renter. To impute housing services for those consumer households that own their residence, we use a variable from the CE that measures the market rent (as estimated by the reference person of the consumer unit) that the residence would command if rented out.[38] This variable is not available for the years 1980–1981 and 1993–1994; for these years we do not compute inequality measures for nondurables ND+ consumption expenditures.[39] As with nondurable consumption, all imputed services from consumer durables and housing are deflated with the corresponding CPI.

REFERENCES

Altug, S., and R. Miller. (1990). Household choices in equilibrium. *Econometrica* 58:543–570.
Attanasio, O. (2002). Consumption and income inequality: What do we know and what we can learn from it. UCL. Mimeo. University College London.
Attanasio, O., and S. Davis. (1996). Relative wage movements and the distribution of consumption. *Journal of Political Economy* 104:1227–1262.
Blundell, R., and T. MaCurdy. (1999). Labor supply: A review of alternative approaches. In *Handbook of Labor Economics*, O. Ashenfelter and D. Card (eds.). Amsterdam: Elsevier.
Blundell, R., and I. Preston. (1998). Consumption inequality and income uncertainty. *Quarterly Journal of Economics* 113:603–640.
Cochrane, J. (1991). A simple test of consumption insurance. *Journal of Political Economy* 99:957–976.
Cox, M., and R. Alm. (1999). *Myths of Rich & Poor: Why We're Better Off Than We Think*. New York: Basic Books.
Cullen, J., and J. Gruber. (2000). Does unemployment insurance crowd out spousal labor supply? *Journal of Labor Economics* 18:546–572.

---

38. Here is the exact question that the reference person of the CU is asked: "If you were to rent your home today, how much do you think it would rent for monthly, without furnishings and utilities?"
39. We experimented with using an imputation procedure similar to the one used for vehicles to obtain housing services for the four missing years. Results were very similar and are available from the authors on request.

Cutler, D., and L. Katz. (1991a). Macroeconomic performance and the disadvantaged. *Brookings Papers on Economic Activity* 1–74.

Cutler, D., and L. Katz. (1991b). Rising inequality? Changes in the distribution of income and consumption in the 1980s. *American Economic Review* 82:546–551.

Deaton, A. (1992). *Understanding Consumption*. Oxford, England: Clarendon Press.

Díaz-Giménez, J., V. Quadrini, and J. V. Ríos-Rull. (1997). Dimensions of inequality: Facts on the U.S. distributions of earnings, income, and wealth. *Federal Reserve Bank of Minneapolis Quarterly Review* 21:3–21.

Dynarski, S., and J. Gruber. (1997). Can families smooth variable earnings? *Brookings Papers on Economic Activity* 229–284.

Gottschalk, P., and R. Moffitt. (1994). The growth of earnings instability in the U.S. labor market. *Brookings Papers on Economic Activity* 217–272.

Greenspan, A. (1998). Opening remarks to the symposium on income inequality: Issues and policy options. Federal Reserve Bank of Kansas City.

Hall, R., and F. Mishkin. (1982). The sensitivity of consumption to transitory income: Estimates from panel data on households. *Econometrica* 50:461–481.

Hayashi, F., J. Altonji, and L. Kotlikoff. (1996). Risk sharing between and within families. *Econometrica* 64:261–294.

Heathcote, J., K. Storesletten, and G. Violante. (2003). The welfare implications of rising wage inequality in the US. Stockholm University. Mimeo. Institute for International Economic Studies IIES.

Heckman, J., and T. MaCurdy. (1980). A life cycle model of female labor supply. *Review of Economic Studies* 47:47–74.

Johnson, D., and S. Shipp. (1991). Trends in inequality using consumer expenditures: 1960 to 1993. Proceedings of the Section on Survey Research Methods, American Statistical Association 1–7.

Johnson, D., and T. Smeeding. (1998). Measuring the trends in inequality of individuals and families: Income and consumption. U.S. Bureau of Lasor Statistics. Working paper. Washington, D.C.:

Juhn, C., K. Murphy, and R. Topel. (2002). Current unemployment, historically contemplated. *Brooking Papers on Economic Activity* 1:79–136.

Katz, L., and D. Autor. (1999). Changes in wages structure and earnings inequality. In *Handbook of Labor Economics*. O. Ashenfelter and D. Card (eds.). Amsterdam: Elsevier.

Krueger, D., and F. Perri. (2002). Does income inequality lead to consumption inequality: Evidence and theory. Cambridge, MA: National Bureau of Economic Research. NBER Working Paper 9202.

Krusell, P., and A. Smith. (1999). On the welfare effects of eliminating business cycles. *Review of Economic Dynamics* 2:245–272.

Lucas, R. (1987). *Models of Business Cycles*. New York: Basil Blackwell.

Mace, B. (1991). Full insurance in the presence of aggregate uncertainty. *Journal of Political Economy* 99:928–956.

Mayer, S., and C. Jencks. (1993). Recent trends in economic inequality in the United States: income versus expenditures versus well-being. In *Poverty and Prosperity in the USA in the Late Twentieth Century*, D. Papadimitriou and E. Wolff (eds.). New York: St. Martin's Press.

Nelson, J. (1994). On testing for full insurance using Consumer Expenditure survey data. *Journal of Political Economy* 102:384–394.

Slesnick, D. (1993). Gaining ground: Poverty in the postwar United States. *Journal of Political Economy* 101:1–38.

Slesnick, D. (2001). *Consumption and Social Welfare.* Cambridge, England: Cambridge University Press.

Stephens, M. (2002). Worker displacement and the added worker effect. *Journal of Labor Economics* 20:504–537.

Tauchen, G., and R. Hussey. (1991). Quadrature-based methods for obtaining approximate solutions to nonlinear asset pricing models. *Econometrica* 59:371–396.

Townsend, R. (1994). Risk and insurance in village india. *Econometrica* 62:539–591.

Comment

STEVEN J. DAVIS
University of Chicago and NBER

Krueger and Perri set their sights on a major question: What are the welfare consequences of the pronounced rise in U.S. wage and income inequality in recent decades? Assumptions about the answer play an important role in many policy discussions and underlie much of the interest in wage and income inequality. I applaud the authors for tackling the question in a way that makes assumptions explicit and that facilitates constructive criticism. The authors also deserve much credit for grappling with the data on consumption inequality, a challenging task. As it turns out, however, I think that a compelling answer to the question awaits further research.

The authors describe trend changes in the distribution of household consumption expenditures using data from the Interview Survey component of the Consumer Expenditure (CE) survey. They find rising consumption inequality between groups defined by sex and educational attainment of the household head, but declining consumption inequality within groups. Overall consumption inequality changes little during the past three decades by their account—in striking contrast to a sharp rise in the inequality of wages, earnings, and disposable incomes.

They proceed to calculate welfare effects associated with certain changes in the consumption distribution. To do so, they specify and estimate stochastic processes for group-level and idiosyncratic components of consumption, and they postulate standard preferences over consumption paths.[1] They then compute, as of 1972, consumption-equivalent

Orazio Attanasio, David Autor, Erik Hurst, and Daniel Slesnick kindly supplied data for this comment and my remarks at the Macro-economics Annual Conference. Daniel Slesnick provided several useful observations about the Consumer Expenditure survey, and Erik Hurst provided valuable information about the Continuing Survey of Food Intakes by Individuals. Thanks also to Dirk Krueger and Fabrizio Perri for many helpful communications about their work.

1. Krueger and Perri also characterize the evolution of the hours-worked distribution, and some of their welfare calculations consider preferences defined over consumption *and* leisure. Their chief results involve consumption, however, and I limit my remarks to consumption-related issues.

welfare differences between estimated and counterfactual processes for consumption. They report these welfare differences as a function of education and initial position in the consumption distribution.

My remarks below develop two main themes. First, there are good reasons to doubt the basic characterization of consumption inequality trends offered by Krueger and Perri. Second, in their welfare analysis, they do not adequately model the uncertainty faced by households, which limits the usefulness of their welfare results.

1. Evaluating the Evidence on Trends in Consumption Inequality

Figure 6 in Krueger and Perri shows a striking divergence between the path of disposable earnings inequality and the path of consumption inequality. Figure 8 shows declining within-group consumption inequality in recent decades and, in particular, since 1987.[2] This decline is at odds with the strong rise in the within-group inequality of disposable earnings, as depicted in Figure 5.

To evaluate these empirical results, I proceed as follows. First, I consider whether they fit comfortably with other evidence on consumption responses to income shocks and conclude that they do not. Second, I note concerns about the quality of the Interview Survey component of the CE and the possibility that it yields an inaccurate picture of consumption inequality trends.[3] Third, I look to other sources of data on consumption inequality trends and find, in contrast to the CE Interview Survey, that they point to rising consumption inequality.

---

2. As a preliminary step, Krueger and Perri run cross-sectional regressions of consumption per adult-equivalent on a quartic polynomial in the household head's age and an indicator variable for his or her race. The consumption residuals from these regressions then serve as inputs to the remaining analysis. By allowing the coefficients on the age and race variables to vary freely by year in these regressions, Krueger and Perri sweep away potentially important changes in the consumption distribution. By constraining the age polynomial to have the same shape across education groups in each cross section, Krueger and Perri may obtain misleading characterizations of within-group inequality trends. For example, if the household distribution becomes more concentrated in education categories with similar age profiles, then the residual distribution tends to become less dispersed, even if there is no change in the distribution of consumption conditional on age and education. I ignore these issues in the main text.

3. Estimates of inequality in wages, earnings, and income are also subject to measurement problems, but the basic facts about U.S. trends in this regard are well established. Unlike the situation for consumption data, there are multiple, independent sources of data on wages, earnings, and income, and the most important sources have been heavily researched. Hence, I proceed under the assumption that the Krueger and Perri measures of trends in wage and earnings inequality are accurate descriptions of reality.

1.1 SELF-INSURANCE AND THE RELATIONSHIP OF CONSUMPTION INEQUALITY TO EARNINGS INEQUALITY

Consider the divergent paths of within-group earnings inequality (Figure 5) and within-group consumption inequality (Figure 8). The rise in within-group earnings inequality reflects some combination of greater dispersion in (the idiosyncratic components of) fixed earnings differences, persistent earnings shocks, and transitory shocks. Fixed effects and persistent shocks cannot be smoothed over the life cycle by borrowing and lending. Hence, a perspective on the data informed by permanent income theory leads one to anticipate a close relationship between persistent earnings shocks and consumption responses. Many other theories that entail incomplete sharing of consumption risks carry the same implication.[4]

This implication finds support in the observed relationship between group-level earnings shocks, which are highly persistent, and group-level consumption responses. For example, Figure 5 and 8 show similar trend increases in between-group earnings inequality and between-group consumption inequality. Attanasio and Davis (1996) find that persistent changes in relative wages among groups defined by birth cohort and education lead to roughly equal-size changes in consumption expenditures.

Many studies show that household consumption expenditures are sensitive to idiosyncratic earnings shocks. Two studies are especially pertinent here. First, Gruber (1997) investigates how consumption responses to unemployment vary with the generosity of unemployment insurance benefits. To estimate this relationship, he exploits the fact that the income replacement rates provided by unemployment benefits vary considerably across states and workers. Gruber's study is noteworthy for our purposes because the U.S. unemployment insurance system is not designed to insure against persistent earnings shocks—benefits typically expire after 26 weeks. So, insofar as the consumption response to unemployment varies with the replacement rate, households are not smoothing transitory income variation. Using Panel Study of Income Dynamics (PSID) data from 1968 to 1987, Gruber estimates that a 10-percentage-point rise in the replacement rate reduces the unemployment-induced fall in food expenditures by about 3 percentage points. This is a big effect, and it implies a big departure from effective self-insurance against transitory shocks. Gruber also notes that there has been a secular decline in the generosity of unemployment benefits

---

4. In principle, a properly structured portfolio of risky financial assets can insure against even the most persistent earnings shocks, but I am unaware of any evidence that households or their agents (e.g., pension fund managers) engage in this type of hedging behavior to a significant extent. Davis and Willen (2000) develop a theory of life-cycle portfolio choice with decision rules that exhibit this type of hedging behavior, and they present evidence that broadbased equity and bond funds have some limited potential as instruments for hedging occupation-level income shocks.

levels, which is a force for greater consumption inequality and increased sensitivity of consumption inequality to earnings inequality.

Second, Sullivan (2002) investigates whether households use unsecured debt to smooth consumption responses to unemployment spells. He relies on panel data from the PSID for 1984 to 1993 and the Survey of Program Participation for 1996 to 2000. Using a sample of unemployment spells that aims to isolate transitory earnings shocks, he finds that households with assets increase unsecured debt, on average, by about 10% of the earnings loss associated with unemployment. For households with low initial asset levels, however, unsecured debt does not respond to the income loss associated with unemployment. These households account for about 13 to 18% of the sample, depending on the definition of low assets. In addition, Sullivan finds that the consumption response to unemployment-induced income shocks is larger for households with lower asset levels. He estimates that expenditure on food and housing for households with little or no financial assets is five times more sensitive to unemployment-induced earnings losses compared to other households.

The Gruber and Sullivan studies indicate that many households do not effectively smooth transitory, idiosyncratic earnings shocks. Moreover, there are strong theoretical reasons, supported by empirical evidence, to think that households cannot smooth persistent earnings shocks. These considerations provide grounds for skepticism toward the Krueger and Perri evidence on consumption inequality trends, especially the decline in within-group consumption inequality coupled with strong increases in the within-group inequality of disposable earnings.

Conceivably, the effect of increased earnings inequality on within-group consumption inequality is overwhelmed by greater smoothing of transitory shocks. This interpretation is logically consistent, and it fits with the increasing availability of consumer credit, but the interpretation faces at least three problems. First, many households lack the financial means to smooth earnings shocks. Poorer households, in particular, often have little financial wealth, so they cannot draw on liquid assets to offset negative earnings shocks. Second, most forms of consumer credit carry high interest rates. Edelberg (2003, Table 1) reports mean consumer interest rates in 1998 of 8.0% per annum for first mortgages, 10.4% for second mortgages, 10.2% on auto loans, 14.5% for credit cards, and 12.9% for other consumer credit. Davis et al. (2003, Table 1) calculate that interest rates on unsecured forms of consumer credit exceed the three-year Treasury rate by 6 to 9 percentage points after netting out uncollected loan obligations. The high cost of consumer credit makes borrowing less useful for consumption smoothing, even when credit is available. The upshot of low financial wealth, incomplete access to credit markets, and high borrowing costs is that many households are poorly equipped to smooth even transitory earnings shocks.

Third, and perhaps most important, the effect of greater access to credit markets or other self-insurance devices must be large to rationalize Krueger and Perri's finding of a sharp divergence between within-group earnings inequality and within-group consumption inequality. Suppose that permanent shocks account for one-third of the rise in within-group earnings inequality. On that account alone then, Figure 5 suggests a secular rise of 3 or 4 log points in the standard deviation of consumption within groups. Instead, Figure 8 shows a decline of about 2 log points over the sample period. The implied gap between trend changes in earnings and consumption inequality is larger when we factor in a rising variance of transitory earnings shocks. This gap will be hard to explain in a model that matches the degree of consumption smoothing seen in the data.

1.2 CONCERNS ABOUT THE CE INTERVIEW SURVEY

The CE has two independent components, a quarterly Interview Survey and a weekly Diary Survey, each with its own questionnaire and sample. The two components differ, but overlap somewhat, in their coverage of expenditure categories. The Interview Survey covers a broad range of expenditure categories, but it is "designed to obtain data on the types of expenditures respondents can recall for a period of 3 months or longer" (www.bls.gov/cex/csxfaqs.htm). The Diary Survey focuses on frequently purchased smaller items such as food and beverages, housekeeping supplies, tobacco, nonprescription drugs, and personal-care products and services. Sample size in the Diary Survey is roughly one-third that of the Interview Survey. Following most previous research that uses CE micro data, Krueger and Perri rely on the Interview Survey.

The CE records out-of-pocket expenditures. Even when combined, the two CE components miss a big fraction of consumption (e.g., most health care). There are large and growing discrepancies between expenditures in the CE and Personal Consumption Expenditures (PCEs), as measured in the national income and product accounts. For example, Battistin (2003, Figure 1) reports a decline in the ratio of CE to PCE per-capita expenditures on nondurables and services from 0.79 in 1985 to 0.63 in 2000.[5] The CE-PCE gap and its growth over time are even larger when attention is restricted to the Interview Survey. This can be seen in Slesnick's (2001) Figure 3.2, which shows that the ratio of per-capita consumption in the CE Interview Survey to the PCE declines from 0.08 in 1973 to 0.56 in 1995.[6]

Slesnick (1992) investigates the discrepancy between CE and PCE consumption measures. He finds that only one-half of the CE-PCE gap

5. The CE-based measure of per-capita consumption in Battistin appears to reflect both the Interview and Diary surveys.
6. Slesnick confirms in a personal communication that his Figure 3.2 reflects CE data from the Interview Survey only.

reflects differences between the two sources in the definition of consumption, and the remaining half is unexplained. Underreporting in the CE (in covered expenditure categories) appears to be a major problem. The time period covered by Slesnick's study ends in 1989, after which the CE-PCE gap grew much larger. Battistin (2003) provides evidence that the quality of Interview Survey data on frequently purchased smaller items, housekeeping supplies, and personal-care products and services has declined over time, and that the decline has been "particularly accentuated" in the 1990s.

All of this leads me to question whether the CE provides a reliable basis for drawing inferences about trends in consumption inequality. Because the CE-PCE gap has expanded markedly over time, I am especially reluctant to accept Interview Survey evidence on consumption inequality trends during the 1990s. Of course, the large and growing discrepancy between CE and PCE consumption may partly reflect measurement problems in the national income accounts. It seems highly unlikely, however, that deterioration in the accuracy of the national income accounts can account for such a dramatic widening of the CE-PCE consumption gap.

1.3 CONSUMPTION INEQUALITY TRENDS IN OTHER DATA SOURCES

In light of my foregoing remarks, it seems appropriate to examine other data sources for evidence on consumption inequality trends. I do so, but my brief treatment merely scratches the surface of an important issue.

Attanasio (2002) compares the evolution of consumption inequality in the Interview and Diary Surveys. He plots the standard deviation of log consumption per household and per adult-equivalent for the overall population and for selected cohort-education groups. He finds that overall consumption inequality declines by about 2 log points from 1985 to 1998 in the Interview Survey, but it rises by 8 or 9 log points in the Diary Survey. His within-group plots also show rising inequality in the Diary Survey but flat or slightly declining inequality in the Interview Survey. Battistin (2003) reports similar results in his detailed analysis of the differences between the CE Diary and Interview Survey components. In short, the CE Diary Survey paints a picture of rising consumption inequality since 1985, in contrast to the flat or declining consumption inequality seen in Krueger and Perri's Figures 6 and 8.

Fisher and Johnson (2003) report Gini coefficients for consumption per adult-equivalent using data from the CE Interview Survey and the PSID. They impute total consumption for households in the PSID based on food expenditures, rent or mortgage, home ownership status and home value, utility expenses, demographic and family composition variables, the age and sex of the household head, and other variables. Table 1 reproduces their statistics for overall consumption inequality. From 1984 to 1999, the rise in overall consumption inequality is nearly twice as large in the PSID as in the CE Interview Survey. Consumption inequality declines over the 1990s according to the Interview Survey, but it rises from 1990 to 1994 and for the 1990s as a whole according to the PSID.

I also examined data on monthly food expenditures in the Continuing Survey of Food Intakes by Individuals (CSFII), which is conducted by the U.S. Department of Agriculture. The CSFII is a nationally representative sample with repeated cross sections for six years: 1989 to 1991 and 1994 to 1996. The survey response rate in the CSFII exceeds 85%, which compares favorably to CE response rates. See Aguiar and Hurst (2003) for a detailed description of the CSFII and an interesting analysis that exploits separate CSFII measures of food expenditures and food consumption (e.g., caloric intake). I make use of data on food expenditures only.

Following Krueger and Perri, I restrict my analysis sample to households with a head between 20 and 64 years of age. To measure "overall" consumption inequality, I compute the 90-10 differential and the standard deviation of the residuals from yearly cross-sectional regressions of log expenditures on controls for household size and a quartic polynomial in the household head's age. I follow the same procedure to measure within-group consumption inequality, except that the regressions also include dummy variables for the household head's education. For between-group inequality, I report estimated coefficients on the education variables.

As shown in Table 2, the CSFII shows a broad pattern of rising consumption inequality from 1989 to the mid-1990s. Overall inequality in food expenditures rises by about 8% from 1989 to 1996, within-group inequality rises by a bit less, and the education differentials expand in most cases.

Table 1   GINI COEFFICIENTS FOR CONSUMPTION PER ADULT EQUIVALENT, 1984–1999 (CEX INTERVIEW SURVEY COMPARED TO THE PSID)

Data source	*1984*	*1990*	*1994*	*1999*	*Change, 1984–1999*
PSID	.255	.243	.286	.278	9.1%
CEX	.267	.295	.289	.280	4.7%

Source: Reproduced from Table 3 in Fisher and Johnson (2003).

Table 2   INEQUALITY IN LOG MONTHLY FOOD EXPENDITURES,
1989 TO 1996 (U.S. HOUSEHOLDS WITH A HEAD BETWEEN 20 AND 64
YEARS OF AGE)

A. *Overall inequality (Controls for age of head and household size)*

	1989	1990	1991	1994	1995	1996
Log standard deviation	.505	.503	.528	.528	.523	.543
90-10 log differential	1.25	1.27	1.33	1.31	1.30	1.36

B. *Within-group inequality*

	1989	1990	1991	1994	1995	1996
Log standard deviation	.489	.491	.505	.507	.509	.526
90-10 log differential	1.23	1.24	1.26	1.28	1.22	1.29

C. *Between-group inequality*	*Log deviation from households with a college-educated head*		
	Head with some college	*Head with high school diploma*	*Head did not complete high school*
1989–1991 pooled sample	−.155	−.236	−.386
1994–1996 pooled sample	−.135	−.243	−.404

Source: Author's calculations using data from the *Continuing Survey of Food Intakes by Individuals*, U.S. Department of Agriculture.
1. Food expenditures are the head's report of household expenditures in the previous month on food purchased at the grocery store; food delivered into the home; and food purchased at restaurants, bars, cafeterias, and fast-food establishments.
2. All statistics are calculated from the "main sample" in the CSFII, a nationally representative sample of noninstitutionalized persons residing in U.S. households. The CSFII is a repeated cross section for the indicated years.
3. The analysis sample contains households with a head between 20 and 64 years of age and nonmissing observations for food expenditures and years of completed schooling. I deleted four observations that reported food expenditures in the previous month (in 1996 dollars) of less than $10.00, two of which reported no expenditures. The resulting sample ranges from 1076 observations in 1990 to 1352 observations in 1996.
4. "Overall inequality" is computed from residuals in yearly cross-sectional regressions of log food expenditures on controls for household size and a quartic polynomial in the head's age. "Within-group inequality" is computed from residuals in a regression specification that also includes dummy variables for the four indicated education categories. The log deviations reported under "Between-group inequality" reflect the coefficients on the education variables for the same regression specification, but also including year effects.

1. SUMMING UP

Krueger and Perri's characterization of consumption inequality trends is difficult to reconcile with other evidence on consumption responses to income shocks. Consumption measures based on the CE Interview Survey show signs of deteriorating quality, and they cover a steadily declining share of Personal Consumption Expenditures in the national income accounts. Three other sources of consumption data—the CE diary survey, the PSID, and the CSFII—show rising consumption inequality during the 1990s and are at odds with the message from the Interview Survey.[7] These observations cast doubt on Krueger and Perri's basic characterization of consumption inequality trends.

2. Calculating Welfare Consequences

2.1 SUMMARY OF THE KRUEGER AND PERRI PROCEDURE

It will be helpful to review the steps taken by Krueger and Perri in their welfare analysis. First, they obtain residuals from yearly cross-sectional regressions of log consumption on a constant and controls for the age and race of the household reference person. Second, they regress these residuals on the schooling and sex of the reference person, again by year. For each household-level observation, the second-stage regression expresses consumption as the sum of a predicted value and a residual value. Third, they sort predicted values into nine equal-size groups (each year). This sorting defines the sex-education "groups" to which households belong. Likewise, they sort residuals from the second-stage regressions into nine equal-size groups, which determines the household's relative position within its group.

Krueger and Perri then model the evolution of group-level and within-group components as independent nine-state Markov chains. They allow for time-varying states denoted by Y_t^g and Y_t^d and time-invariant transition matrices π^g and π^d, where g indexes the groups defined in the paragraph above and d indexes the within-group position. They set Y_t^g to the median of the predicted values in group g at t, and they set the values for Y_t^d in the same way. To estimate the elements of the nine-by-nine transition matrices, π^g and π^d, they use sample average transition rates from each state k to each state j.

The state vectors Y_t^g and Y_t^d, transition matrices π^g and π^d, and initial conditions for group membership and within-group position determine a stochastic path C for consumption. Given a utility function, the consumption path yields a welfare value $V(C)$. Altering one of the state vectors or transition matrices yields a different consumption path $\hat{C}$ and a different value $V(\hat{C})$. We can express the difference between $V(C)$ and $V(\hat{C})$ in consumption-equivalent terms by calculating the uniform percentage consumption variation Δ such that $V[(1 + \Delta)C] = V(\hat{C})$. The main welfare

---

7. The other sources of consumption data cover a much narrower range of expenditure categories than the Interview Survey, which could account for the discrepancy in consumption inequality trends. This possibility merits careful investigation, but my other observations in the main text suggest that there is more to the story.

experiment in Krueger and Perri's study involves a counterfactual path for the state vectors Y_t^g and Y_t^d. In particular, they generate $\hat{C}$ and $V(\hat{C})$ by fixing the state vectors at their 1972 values.

2.2 EVALUATING THE PROCEDURE

Calculations of this sort are potentially informative about the welfare consequences of changes in the process for consumption or earnings, and they can provide useful inputs into the analysis of inequality trends. The general approach is attractive because it requires one to be explicit about interpersonal and intertemporal utility comparisons, the economic environment that agents face, and the counterfactual scenario. These features facilitate communication and help to sharpen our thinking.

That said, the particular approach in this paper has important drawbacks. First, Krueger and Perri do not adequately model uncertainty about group-level consumption. They assume perfect foresight about the evolution of the state vector Y_t^g, so that uncertainty about group-level outcomes stems entirely from nonzero off-diagonal elements of π^g. In the data, the rank ordering of consumption (and earnings) for sex-education groups is extremely stable over time. In fact, π^g is essentially an identity matrix when estimated from data on households that have the same reference person in t and $t + 1$.[8] Of course, when π^g is the identity matrix, rising inequality translates directly into higher utility for groups with rising relative consumption and lower utility for those with declining relative consumption. That is basically what Krueger and Perri find.

In practice, they do not limit the sample to households with the same reference person in consecutive periods when estimating π^g. Instead, the identity and characteristics of the reference person can change in their sample, for example, because of a change in marital status or living arrangement.[9] This type of uncertainty is what Krueger and Perri capture in their specification of the group-level consumption and earnings processes. It is not what leaps to mind when policymakers and researchers ponder the welfare consequences of increased inequality among education groups.

Second, it is unwise to rely solely on the short-panel aspect of the CE to characterize uncertainty about group-level consumption and earnings. We know that relative consumption and earnings among education groups, for example, display large low-frequency movements, and that there is much uncertainty about these movements looking ahead. The

---

8. The authors confirm this fact in a personal communication. When estimated using households with no change in reference person, the diagonal elements of π^g range from .95 to .98.
9. Their estimate of π^g has important off-diagonal elements, although the diagonal elements remain large, ranging from .80 to .95.

panel aspect of the CE consists of two noisy observations, spaced nine months apart, on the same household. Expecting such data to identify an adequate statistical model for relative consumption movements among education groups is probably expecting too much.

Moreover, there is no need to rely (solely) on the short-panel aspect of the CE to estimate the group-level processes. Instead, one can exploit repeated cross sections in the CE (or other data source) to construct synthetic panel data on group-level outcomes. One can then follow groups defined by birth cohort and education over a period of 20 years or more. The long-panel aspect of such data makes them better suited for estimating the group-level processes, although nailing down the low-frequency properties remains a challenge.

It would also be useful to combine the CE with longer panel data from other sources to characterize the dynamics of the idiosyncratic components of consumption and earnings. For example, one could use the PSID to estimate the degree of persistence in idiosyncratic earnings or consumption changes and combine that information with the household-level changes observed in the CE. In this way, one could decompose within-group inequality trends into separate components associated with transitory and persistent household-level changes. See Blundell et al. (2002) for an analysis that combines cross-sectional data in the CE with panel data from the PSID.

To sum up, there are large gains from drawing on the information contained in CE-based synthetic panels and longer true panels in other data sources. This information can be used to provide richer, more compelling characterizations of the consumption and earnings processes, which are key inputs into the welfare calculations.

REFERENCES

Aguiar, Mark, and Erik Hurst. (2003). Consumption vs. expenditures. University of Chicago Graduate School of Business. Working Paper.
Attanasio, Orazio. (2002). Consumption and income inequality: What we know and what we can learn from it. Plenary Lecture, Society of Economic Dynamics Conference, New York (June).
Attanasio, Orazio, and Steven J. Davis. (1996). Relative wage movements and the distribution of consumption. *Journal of Political Economy* 104(6): 1227–1262.
Battistin, Erich. (2003). Errors in survey reports of consumption expenditures. Working Paper 03/07. London: The Institute for Fiscal Studies.
Blundell, Richard, Luigi Pistaferri, and Ian Preston. (2002). Partial insurance, information and consumption dynamics. London, England: Institute for Fiscal Studies. Working Paper 02/16.
Davis, Steven J., Felix Kubler, and Paul Willen. (2003). Borrowing costs and the demand for equity over the life cycle. Cambridge, MA: National Bureau of Economic Research. NBER Working Paper 9331. Revised version posted at gsbwww.uchicago.edu/fac/steven.davis/research/ (accessed July 20, 2003).

Davis, Steven J., and Paul Willen. (2000). Occupation-level income shocks and asset returns: Covariance and implications for portfolio choice. Cambridge, MA: National Bureau of Economic Research. NBER Working Paper 7905.

Edelberg, Wendy. (2003). Risk-based pricing of interest rates in consumer loan markets. University of Chicago, Department of Economics. Working Paper.

Fisher, Jonathan D., and David S. Johnson. (2003). Consumption mobility in the United States: Evidence from two panel data sets. U.S. Bureau of Labor Statistics. Working Paper.

Gruber, Jonathan. (1997). The consumption smoothing benefits of unemployment insurance. *American Economic Review* 87 (1, March): 192–205.

Slesnick, Daniel T. (1992). Aggregate consumption and saving in the postwar United States. *Review of Economics and Statistics.* 74 (4, November):585–597.

Slesnick, Daniel T. (2001). *Consumption and Social Welfare: Living Standards and Their Distribution in the United States.* Cambridge, England: Cambridge University Press.

Sullivan, James X. (2002). Borrowing during unemployment: Unsecured debt as a safety net. Northwestern University. Working Paper.

Comment

KJETIL STORESLETTEN
University of Oslo, Frisch Centre, and IIES

1. Introduction

This paper addresses the welfare consequences of the increase in inequality in the United States during the last three decades. By now, it is well established that since the 1970s there has been a substantial increase in inequality in wages and earnings. The focus of the empirical literature has been to decompose this rise in inequality into transient and permanent components. The motivation for this focus is that permanent shocks presumably have large welfare consequences, while transient shocks are regarded as (self-)insurable. However, this link between earnings and welfare implicitly requires assumptions about market structure and excludes risk-sharing devices that do not show up in wages or labor income (for example, in-kind transfers or means-tested price rebates).

Krueger and Perri pursue a different approach for quantifying the welfare costs of rising inequality by noting that welfare is not derived from income and wages, but rather from consumption and leisure. In particular, Krueger and Perri ask the following two questions: (1) How has inequality in consumption and leisure evolved? and (2) What are the welfare consequences of these changes?

I am very sympathetic to Krueger and Perri's idea of exploring the effects of rising inequality by putting more emphasis on allocations of consumption and leisure, and I believe it is a promising research approach.

Extending previous work (Krueger and Perri, 2002; Fernández-Villaverde and Krueger, 2002), Krueger and Perri document the first question using data from the Consumption and Expenditure Survey (CE). Next, they assess the welfare consequences using a novel approach. In this discussion I compare some of their findings with facts from alternative data. I then discuss two alternatives to Krueger and Perri's approach for evaluating the welfare consequences of the rising inequality.

2. Revisit Facts Using Alternative Data: PSID

The dataset that Krueger and Perri use, CE, focuses on consumption, and data on earnings and hours are arguably of lower quality than in the Panel Study of Income Dynamics (PSID) or in the Current Population Survey (CPS). However, Krueger and Perri document that the implications for wage inequality are comparable in the CE and other datasets (PSID and CPS).[1]

Using data from the PSID and CPS, Heathcote et al. (2003) document that hours inequality for men (excluding nonparticipants) has remained constant or experienced a small increase during this period. In contrast, Krueger and Perri find that inequality in hours per adult (i.e., average hours within the household) has declined over time.

One possible reason for this difference could be that even if all workers worked the same number of hours, changes in labor force participation (e.g., from one to two earners) would induce changes in hours inequality. Thus, the rise in female labor force participation may have caused the decline in hours inequality because of an increase in the average number of hours worked for women. Indeed, the number of hours worked for married women has increased during this period.[2]

---

1. Krueger and Perri argue that earnings inequality increases slightly less than wage inequality. If inequality is measured as the variance of log of earnings (instead of as the standard deviation of logs), however, earnings inequality increases slightly *more* (consistent with the finding of Heathcote et al. [2003] for the PSID).
2. Using data from the CPS, Jones et al. (2003) document that, while average hours worked for single men and women was relatively constant over this period, hours worked for married women rose sharply.

3. Welfare Effects of Rising Inequality

Given the facts on the evolution of consumption and hours inequality, Krueger and Perri examine the distribution of welfare effects of changes in inequality, conditional on initial state. They propose a novel, theory-free approach. They start by estimating an exogenous stochastic process for individual household consumption and leisure, exploiting the panel dimension in the CE data.[3] The data are detrended so that the welfare effects of changes in the process are due to changes in the higher-order moments only. They then assume a time-separable utility function over consumption, consumer durables, and leisure,

$$u\left(c, s, l\right) = \frac{1}{1 - \sigma} \left[(c^{\theta} s^{1 - \theta})^{\alpha} l^{1 - \alpha} \right]^{1 - \sigma},$$

and compute discounted utility given the time-varying processes for consumption and leisure.

The large dispersion in welfare effects are mainly driven by changes in between-group inequality and are hardly affected by changes in within-group inequality. One reason is that, conditional on group, the estimated processes for consumption and leisure are not very persistent. For example, holding group-specific characteristics constant, the autocorrelation of individual consumption is 0.72, lower than the autocorrelation for earnings.

This finding points, I believe, to a potential shortcoming of the Krueger and Perri approach. Assume that preferences are separable between consumption and leisure. The permanent income hypothesis then suggests that the marginal utility of consumption, and therefore consumption itself, should be very persistent. Why don't the data have this property? Of course, preferences may not be separable between consumption and leisure. However, there are good reasons to believe that the estimated persistence of consumption is biased downward due to measurement error. For example, Cogley (2002) suggests that measurement error in CE consumption biases upward the variance in individual consumption growth by one order of magnitude. Clearly, if the Krueger and Perri consumption process is mismeasured, it casts some doubt on their quantitative welfare findings.

---

3. Note that it is not the transition process between actual consumption levels that is estimated, but the transition probabilities between different consumption classes. This approach underestimates the consumption inequality and, in particular, the change in consumption inequality.

4. Alternative Route (i): A Theory-Free Approach

If one is to pursue a data-based, theory-free approach, why is it necessary to estimate a process for consumption and leisure instead of simply plugging in the actual data? In the spirit of Atkinson (1970), one could alternatively address the following welfare question: Under the veil of ignorance, what fraction of initial consumption would agents give up to get that allocation forever, relative to experiencing the subsequent evolution of inequality in consumption and leisure? Assuming that preferences are time-separable, it is only the dispersion in consumption and leisure that matters, and movements within the distribution are irrelevant. Thus, one could simply plug in the actual data observations and discount utility, given explicit assumptions about the utility function.

Pursuing this approach with the same data and utility function as Krueger and Perri used, the welfare losses, expressed as a fraction of lifetime consumption, are as follows:[4]

	c only	(c, l)	(c, s, l)
$\sigma = 1$	1.57%	1.48%	1.43%
$\sigma = 2$	2.54%	2.15%	1.94%

The first column refers to the welfare effects of the changes in inequality of nondurable consumption. The second and third columns add leisure and services from consumer durables. The key message of this list is that the average welfare loss is around 1 to 2%, which is in the same ballpark as the findings of Krueger and Perri.

5. Alternative Route (ii): A Structural Approach

The most serious critique of the Krueger and Perri approach is perhaps that the preferences are arbitrary because they are not necessarily consistent with the observed individual behavior. For example, the preferences considered by Krueger and Perri exhibit quite high individual labor elasticity (2 for $\sigma = 1$ and ⅔ for $\sigma = 2$). There are reasons to believe that the costs of changing inequality have been unevenly distributed across generations, with young in the 1980s shouldering the largest burden, an aspect absent in the infinite-horizon approach of Krueger and Perri.

4. The figures display the welfare loss of the changes in inequality after 1980 because the 1972–1973 CE data include fewer consumption items than the 1980–2000 data and are therefore not directly comparable.

An alternative route, pertinent for this criticism, would be to pursue a structural approach for quantifying the welfare costs. In particular, one could use an individual-specific wage or earnings process as a primitive, generate endogenous consumption and leisure allocations from a structural model, and subsequently use these findings to evaluate welfare consequences.

One paper pursuing this route is Heathcote et al. (2003). They estimate changes in the individual wage process in the United States using PSID data and document increases in the transitory, persistent, and permanent components of the wage process. They then formulate a standard life-cycle version of the permanent income hypothesis model with savings in one riskless bond and a consumption-leisure trade-off. The preferences are of the constant elasticity of substitution type and separable in time and between consumption and leisure. Their model is calibrated to capture key cross-sectional facts, resulting in quite plausible parameters (for example, a Frisch elasticity of 0.5 and a relative risk aversion for consumption of 1.5).[5] This model accounts for the salient features of the evolution in inequality, such as the evolution of the wage-hours correlation and the inequality in earnings, consumption, and hours. The fact that the preferences are consistent with the observed individual behavior makes the welfare calculation (including the particular utility function) less arbitrary, I believe.

Turning to welfare, Heathcote et al. (2003) find that, under the veil of ignorance but conditional on cohort, the welfare loss of changes in wage process is 2 to 5% of lifetime consumption for households entering the job market during 1970–2000, and around 1% for households entering the job market during the 1950s.[6]

REFERENCES

Atkinson, A. B. (1970). On the measurement of inequality. *Journal of Economic Theory* 2:244–63.
Cogley, T. (2002). Idiosyncratic risk and the equity premium: Evidence from the Consumer Expenditure survey. *Journal of Monetary Economics* 49:309–334.
Fernández-Villaverde, J., and D. Krueger. (2002). Consumption over the life cycle: Some facts from the CEX data. Stanford University. Mimeo.
Heathcote, J., K. Storesletten, and G. L. Violante. (2003). The cross-sectional implications of rising wage inequality in the United States. New York University. Mimeo.

5. In particular, Heathcote et al. (2003) match the standard deviation of changes in individuals' number of hours worked and the correlation between wages and hours worked.
6. The preference parameters used by Heathcote et al. (2003) differ from the Cobb-Douglas specification of Krueger and Perri that I used in Section 4. Repeating those calculations with the parameters of Heathcote et al., the CE data indicate a welfare loss of 1.9%.

Jones, L. E., R. E. Manuelli, and E. R. McGrattan. (2003). Why are married women working so much? Federal Reserve Bank of Minneapolis Staff Report.
Krueger, D., and F. Perri. (2002). Does income inequality lead to consumption inequality? Evidence and theory. Stanford University. Mimeo.

Discussion

Fabrizio Perri first responded to some of the discussion participants' concerns about data quality. He was aware of the fact that using different datasets produced different estimates of the increase in wage inequality in the sample period. He asserted that, although the estimates from the Consumer Expenditure (CE) survey are bigger than those obtained using the Current Population Survey (CPS), they are similar to those obtained using the Panel Study of Income Dynamics (PSID). Perri said that he was aware of the differences between the income and diary data from the CE, and said that the authors might consider using the diary data in the future. He also said that he was aware of the underreporting of both consumption and income in the CE. He also noted that as long as the income and consumption data come from the same sample, income inequality increases while consumption inequality remains flat. On the question of the identifiability of the stochastic process for between-group inequality, Perri agreed that using 1-year variation is not ideal. He pointed out that a large number of households are used to make the estimate, however, and that the results are not very different from what would be expected.

Annamaria Lusardi echoed the concerns of Steve Davis about the severity of measurement error in the CE. Responding to Steve Davis's comment that the CE and National Income and Product Accounts (NIPA) data do not match, she suggested that it is not obvious that the NIPA has the correct numbers. Fabrizio Perri responded that a big difference between the CE and the NIPA is that the CE does not include data on very rich people.

Annamaria Lusardi suggested that counting services from durables might yield a higher volatility of consumption. Eva Nagypal was concerned that the authors did not take account of the increase in assortative matching of spouses along observable characteristics over the sample period.

Several participants were concerned by the smoothness of the consumption data and suggested investigating this point further by examining the data on savings more closely. Annamaria Lusardi asked whether both savings and wealth data are consistent with the degree of consumption smoothing apparent in the data. She noted that wealth inequality increased a good deal in the 1990s. Deborah Lucas remarked that the authors hypothesize that the disconnect between consumption and income may be facilitated through financial markets. She was worried by the fact that the group that would have had to use financial markets to increase their consumption had almost no savings in the data and found this particularly troubling in light of the persistence of income shocks. Aart Kraay was struck by the fact that those in the bottom decile of savings rates in the data used in the paper had an average dissaving rate of 10% over 15 to 30 years. He wondered whether dissaving of this order of magnitude could be consistent with what is known about initial asset stocks. On the issue of savings rates, Fabrizio Perri responded that it was true that the gap in the savings rate widened over the sample period. However, he pointed out that the households in the bottom decile of savings rates in one year were not necessarily the same as the households in the bottom decile in other years because households with temporarily low realizations of income dissave, while those with temporarily high realizations save.

On the issue of the measurement of welfare, Fabrizio Perri reminded the participants that the welfare numbers in the paper are ex-post numbers. He noted that they answer the question, How bad has bad luck been for unlucky people? not How much would people have been prepared to pay in 1972 to avoid the future change in their income process? Jonathan Heathcote suggested using a welfare measure based on the assumptions of a utilitarian social-welfare function and separability over time and across consumption and leisure because this measure would require looking at the cross-section distribution of consumption and leisure alone. Fabrizio Perri responded that the welfare losses of increased inequality calculated in this way would be small because the increases in inequality in consumption and hours worked are small.

Mark Gertler speculated that there might be a link between the jump in between-group and within-group inequality around 1984 documented in the paper and the decline in macroeconomic volatility at that time documented by James Stock and Mark Watson in the *Macroeconomics Annual 2002*. Fabrizio Perri suggested that credit market changes could explain the smoothness of consumption relative to income and potentially also the decrease in macro volatility. Ken Rogoff pointed out that the improvement in credit markets was specific to the United States, whereas the decline in macroeconomic volatility was common to many developed countries. Fabrizio Perri pointed to the finding of Alberto Alesina and co-authors that inequality affects happiness in Europe but not in the United States as potential evidence that credit markets are less effective in facilitating consumption smoothing in Europe than in the United States.

Annette Vissing-Jorgensen
KELLOGG SCHOOL OF MANAGEMENT, NORTHWESTERN
UNIVERSITY, NBER, AND CEPR

Perspectives on Behavioral Finance: Does "Irrationality" Disappear with Wealth? Evidence from Expectations and Actions

1. Introduction

The contributions of behavioral finance are many. The field:

1. Documents price patterns that seem inconsistent with traditional finance models of efficient markets and rational investors.
2. Documents behaviors by investors that seem inconsistent with the advice of traditional finance theory.
3. Provides new theories for these patterns and behaviors, often based on behaviors documented in the psychology literature or observed in experiments.
4. Argues that if prices deviate from fundamentals due to the behavior of irrational investors, arbitrage by rational investors may not be able to force prices back to fundamentals. This part of the behavioral finance literature is referred to as the limits to arbitrage literature.

The most influential work on price patterns within the behavioral finance literature has concerned initial underreaction and (in some cases) subsequent overreaction of prices to new information. This work is described

I thank John Campbell, Owen Lamont, the editors, and the participants at the 2003 NBER Macroeconomics Annual Conference for their comments and suggestions. Special thanks to Karen Hess at Union Bank of Switzerland (UBS), David Moore at Gallup, and Ann Janda at Northwestern University for their help with the UBS/Gallup data, and to Justin Wolfers and David Lucca for help with the Survey of Consumer Attitudes and Behavior.

in Shleifer (2000) as well as in recent surveys of behavioral finance by (insiders) Barberis and Thaler (2003); Daniel, Hirshleifer, and Teoh (2002); and Hirshleifer (2001).

Defenders of the standard rational expectations, efficient markets asset pricing approach have argued that the evidence on underreaction and overreaction is unconvincing because (a) there are as many cases of initial overreaction as initial underreaction, and the evidence is not that solid statistically (Fama, 1998), and (b) if the documented price predictability was statistically solid and stable over time, mutual fund managers should be able to outperform the market substantially, on average, but are not (Rubinstein, 2001). On the modeling side, many have found references to the psychology literature or the experimental literature unconvincing. In some cases, it seems that too much is possible, in the sense that the literature provides evidence both in favor of a given behavioral bias as well as for the opposite bias. Furthermore, many have been skeptical of whether behavioral biases are present in real-world cases where individuals have had time to learn (by themselves or from prior generations), and in particular whether the wealthiest investors with large amounts at stake exhibit behavioral biases. The behavioral side has defended itself by arguing that prices may be far from the predictions of standard models even if (risk-adjusted) profit opportunities are not present. This is the case because arbitrage is limited. First, the mispricing may get worse in the short run (noise trader risk). This is especially a problem when investment is delegated to portfolio managers with short investment horizons (Shleifer and Vishny, 1997). Second, arbitrage is risky when it involves the whole stock market or when it involves individual stocks with no close substitutes. Third, arbitrage may involve substantial transactions costs or be hindered by costs of shorting stocks or restrictions on shorting stocks (e.g., by mutual funds). Barberis and Thaler (2003) provide a discussion of these limits to arbitrage. Abreu and Brunnermeier (2001, 2002) provide an additional argument for limited arbitrage. They show theoretically that it may be optimal for rational arbitrageurs to ride bubbles started by other investors.[1]

In this paper, I argue that direct evidence on investor beliefs and actions is valuable for determining whether assumptions made in behavioral asset pricing models are valid, and thus for determining which (if any) of the models are convincing explanations of the facts they set out to explain. Furthermore, to understand the causes of nonstandard beliefs and/or

---

1. In support of this theory, Brunnermeier and Nagel (2002) show that hedge fund portfolios were tilted heavily toward technology stocks during the stock-market boom of the late 1990s and that hedge funds started to reduce their exposure in the quarter prior to the price peaks of individual technology stocks.

actions, it is useful to distinguish between beliefs and actions that are present for wealthy investors and thus unlikely to be due to information or transactions costs, and beliefs and actions that are observed predominantly among less wealthy investors. This is also informative for determining whether a given bias is likely to have a substantial pricing impact. It is important to emphasize that biases affecting mostly low-wealth investors are nonetheless also important because these biases may have large effects on the utility of these investors.

I start in Section 2 by discussing the types of evidence about investors that would be valuable for understanding pricing anomalies. In Section 3 I provide new evidence on investor beliefs based on a dataset covering the period 1998–2002. Section 4 then turns to a set of investor behaviors that are inconsistent with the recommendations of standard finance theory and reviews evidence on whether these biases diminish substantially with investor wealth. Section 5 provides a rough calculation of how large information and transactions costs would be needed to explain one particular type of seemingly irrational investor behavior: limited participation in stock markets. Section 6 concludes.

2. The Value of Direct Evidence on Investor Beliefs and Actions

At the aggregate level, stock returns are predictable by the dividend-to-price ratio, the earnings-to-price ratio, the market-to-book ratio, the consumption-to-wealth ratio, and a host of other aggregate variables (see Campbell [2000] for a list of references). The direction of predictability indicates that future stock returns tend to be lower when the stock price is high relative to dividends and earnings. Within a rational agent framework, the interpretation of this is that investors' expected (and required) returns are low at such times. The alternative theory proposed by behavioral finance is overreaction of stock prices to news at the level of the aggregate stock market. According to overreaction theories, the returns expected by market participants are not unusually low when the price-to-dividend ratio is high.

The literature on the cross section of stock returns has identified many return patterns not predicted by standard models. Examples of overreaction include: (1) the market-to-book effect (low market-to-book or low price-to-dividend stocks have historically outperformed high market-to-book stocks [Fama and French, 1992, and earlier references cited therein]), (2) the small firm effect (small stocks have outperformed large stocks [Banz, 1981]), (3) long-run reversal (winners in the past three years perform worse than past three year losers over the following three years [DeBondt and Thaler, 1985]), and (4) the poor long-run performance of the stock of firms issuing new stock (Loughran and Ritter, 1995). Examples of underreaction include: (1) momentum (winners from the past 3 to 12 months continue to outperform losers from the past 3 to 12 months during the following six months (Jegadeesh and Titman, 1993), and (2) the post-earnings announcement drift (Bernard and Thomas, 1989).

Several risk-based models have been proposed for the cross-sectional return patterns. Berk, Green, and Naik (1999) provide a rational model based on growth options and time-varying risk that generates the market-to-book effect, the size effect, and the momentum effect. Gomes, Kogan, and Zhang (2003) provide a related investment-based explanation of the market-to-book effect and the size effect.

The behavioral finance literature also provides several possible explanations. In Barberis, Shleifer, and Vishny (1998), earnings are generated by a random walk process. However, investors think that shocks to earnings either are negatively correlated (regime 1) or positively correlated (regime 2). Investors update their beliefs based on observed earnings. Regime 1 is motivated by experimental evidence that people overweight their prior (conservatism), while regime 2 is based on experimental evidence that people believe in a law of small numbers (that is, they expect even short samples to reflect the population probabilities). The model generates momentum, long-term reversal, and cross-sectional forecasting power for scaled price ratios (i.e., initial underreaction followed by subsequent overreaction). A related model based on the law of small numbers is given in Rabin (2002). Daniel, Hirshleifer, and Subrahmanyam (1998) provide an alternative model based on overconfidence in private signals plus biased self-attribution. Overconfidence implies initial overreaction of prices to private information, while biased self-attribution implies that new public information supporting the investor's private information leads to even more overconfidence. This, on average, leads to further overreaction. The model thus explains medium-term momentum as well as long-run reversals. A third model is that of Hong and Stein (1999), in which two groups of agents interact to produce the same facts. Private information diffuses slowly among news watchers who therefore generate initial underreaction. Momentum traders in turn generate overreaction.

The above behavioral models base their main assumptions on experimental evidence or simply assume certain trading strategies of investors. They all rely on expectational errors of investors. To provide evidence on whether the pricing anomalies reflect mispricing due to expectational errors, a few papers have studied whether a large part of the profits from value and momentum strategies occur at subsequent earnings announcement dates (the following references are from Daniel, Hirshleifer, and

Teoh [2002]). La Porta, Lakonishok, Shleifer, and Vishny (1997) find that differences in postformation earnings announcement returns account for about one-quarter of the value effect. Jegadeesh and Titman (1993) find that during the first 7 months following the portfolio formation date a similar fraction of the profits from their momentum strategies is due to expectational errors. Jegadeesh (2000) shows that firms that issue seasoned equity do especially poorly around subsequent earnings announcement dates.

While these findings are suggestive of some mispricing, they do not conclusively rule out the possibility that rational stories based on time-varying expected returns could provide most of the explanation. They also do not help sort among different behavioral explanations. Directly analyzing investor expectations would be valuable. Several papers analyze measures of expected returns of equity analysts (see Brav, Lehavy and Michaely [2002] and references to earlier work therein). Careful modeling of analyst incentives is needed to interpret such evidence because analyst forecasts and the forecasts of professional macroeconomic forecasters have been shown to depend on the incentives provided by existing payment schemes (Hong, Kubik, and Solomon, 2000; Lamont, 2002). Consistent with this, Brav et al. (2002) find substantial differences between independent analysts and analysts with investment banking ties. For the independent analysts, they find that expected returns are higher for small stocks, consistent with the small-firm effect being a rational phenomenon driven by risk, whereas book-to-market has little effect on expected returns and momentum affects expected returns with the opposite sign of what a risk-based explanation of the momentum effect would suggest.

Evidence on the beliefs of investors gets around any incentive problems involved in interpreting analyst forecasts, and also does not need to assume that investor beliefs are driven by or correlated with analyst forecasts. This turns out to be important because my evidence based on investor beliefs suggests that investors' expected returns were high during the last part of the stock-market boom in the late 1990s, which is the opposite of what Brav et al. (2002) find for the independent analysts. The data on investor beliefs also allows me to provide evidence regarding some of the behavioral stories told to explain momentum and reversals. Specifically I provide evidence in favor of a version of the law of small numbers (an ingredient in the model of Barberis, Shleifer, and Vishny [1998]) by analyzing the cross section of investor beliefs. I also find support for biased self-attribution (an ingredient in the model of Daniel, Hirshleifer, and Subrahmanyam [1998]). I show that these biases are present and fairly strong even for high-wealth investors and thus that some pricing impact is likely.

As an alternative to evidence based on beliefs, analysis of investment patterns is informative for determining whether return puzzles are due to mispricing or to time-varying risk and expected returns. Grinblatt and Keloharju (2000) confirm that the momentum effect is present in Finland and then analyze whether more sophisticated investors tend to be more momentum oriented or less contrarian in their trades. They find strong support for this, suggesting either that momentum represents mispricing and that this mispricing is better understood by more sophisticated investors, or that high-momentum stocks are riskier in some yet to be identified way and that more sophisticated investors are better able to bear this risk. Cohen, Gompers and Vuolteenaho (2002) find that institutions buy shares from (sell shares to) individuals in response to positive (negative) cash-flow news. Again, this has two possible interpretations. Either institutions attempt to exploit under-reaction of prices to earnings announcements, the post-earnings announcement drift, or stocks with large positive (negative) earnings surprises are by some measure riskier (less risky) than stocks with small earnings surprises, and those who invest through institutions are better able to bear high risk. In the context of both studies, the ideal evidence would be a combination of these facts on trades, with evidence on whether or not the expected returns of institutions and households differed. If they did, that would provide further support for the mispricing interpretation.

Before turning to the evidence on investor beliefs, it is important to emphasize that the dataset I use covers only a short time period, 1998–2002, and mainly focuses on the aggregate stock market. While the large price movements makes this period particularly interesting, I view my results as simply suggestive. My evidence indicates that (1) expected returns were high at the peak of the market; (2) many investors thought the market was overvalued but would not correct quickly; (3) investors' beliefs depend on their own investment experience (a version of the law of small numbers); (4) the dependence of beliefs on own past portfolio performance is asymmetric, consistent with theories of biased self-attribution; and (5) investor beliefs do affect investors' stockholdings. Mainly, the purpose of providing this evidence is to illustrate the value that direct evidence on investor beliefs and actions can have in distinguishing rational theories of pricing anomalies from irrational ones, as well as for testing the assumptions of behavioral models using data for actual investors. While experimental evidence and references to the psychology literature are suggestive, such evidence certainly is more convincing if supplemented with facts about the beliefs and actions of investors.

3. Investor Beliefs from 1998 to 2002

3.1 DATA

My study of investor beliefs is based on the household level data underlying the Index of Investor Optimism. Since 1996, UBS and Gallup have conducted monthly telephone surveys of U.S. individual investors (an international dimension was added starting in 2002). Until February 2003, the UBS/Gallup data were proprietary. The data can now be purchased via the Roper Center at the University of Connecticut. UBS granted me access to the data in late 2002 so that I could undertake this study.

To be included in the survey, investors must have at least $10,000 in household financial assets defined as "stocks, bonds, or mutual funds in an investment account, or in a self-directed IRA or 401(k) retirement account." In 1996, about 1 in 3 households qualified as potential participants in the survey based on this criteria, increasing to about 4 in 10 households by the start of 2003. Using data from the 1998 Survey of Consumer Finances, households with $10,000 or more in financial assets owned more than 99% of stocks owned directly or indirectly by U.S. households, more than 99% of household financial wealth, and about 95% of household net worth.

The UBS Index of Investor Optimism is based on qualitative responses to a series of questions about optimism or pessimism regarding the investor's own investment and income outlook as well as about the stock market and other macroeconomic variables. In this study I focus on the more quantitative questions also included in the survey.

Each month about 1,000 investors are interviewed. The survey is not a panel, but given the relatively large number of investors interviewed each month, cohort analysis is possible. Information is collected about a host of expectational and demographic variables. Four questions about returns are of particular interest:

1. One-year own past return: "What was the overall percentage rate of return you got on your portfolio in the past twelve months?"
2. Expected one-year own return: "What overall rate of return do you expect to get on your portfolio in the next twelve months?"
3. Expected one-year market return: "Thinking about the stock market more generally, what overall rate of return do you think the stock market will provide investors during the coming twelve months?"
4. Expected ten-year market return: "And, what annual rate of return do you think the stock market will provide investors over the next ten years?"

Information on these variables is available for June, September, and December 1998, and then monthly from February 1999 to December 2002, with the exception that the expected ten-year market return is not asked about in June 1998 and various months of 2002. For 1998 and 1999, responses of less than 1% (including negative responses) are coded as one category. I set these values to zero.[2] I drop observations of expected market or own portfolio returns and of own past portfolio returns that are below –95% or above 95%.[3] I supplement the answers to these questions with background information on age, years of investing experience ("How long have you been investing in the financial markets?"), financial wealth (categorical), and household income (categorical).

To determine if expectations affect investment decisions, I consider special topical modules with information about portfolio shares (available for September 1998, February 2001, and May 2001), and about Internet stockholdings and expectations (available for March, June, and September 1999, and February, April, June, and July 2000).

Finally, to analyze investors' perceptions about misvaluation of the stock market and whether this is expected be corrected soon, I consider three additional questions:

1. Overvaluation perception: "Do you think the stock market is overvalued/valued about right/undervalued, or are you unsure?"[4]
2. Expected three-month market change: "Over the next three months, do you think the stock market will go up, go down, or remain about the same?"
3. Expected one-year market change: "A year from now, do you think the stock market will be higher than it is now, lower, or about the same?"

The overvaluation perception is available for most months of the survey since June 1998. The expected three-month market change is available from December 1998 to August 2000, and the expected one-year market change is available for September 1998 and from March 2000 onward.

3.2 WERE EXPECTED RETURNS HIGH IN THE LATE 1990s?

The UBS/Gallup data provide an opportunity to address several questions central to behavioral finance as well as traditional finance theory.

2. In the 1998 and 1999 data, fewer than 3% of responses for each of the four variables listed are in the less-than-1% category, suggesting that the lack of negative values for these years is not a substantial problem. To confirm this, I considered the data for January 2000, the first month where zero and negative values are available in noncategorical form. The average expected market return calculated by setting responses of less than 1% to zero differed by less than one-quarter percentage point from the value using the actual responses.

3. This approach was followed in some months in the data I received by Gallup. Also, it is not clear how responses of 100% or above were coded before year 2000.

4. This question is one of the few where respondents explicitly are allowed an "unsure" category.

I start by considering what the data from the recent stock-market experience can teach us about the reasons for predictability of aggregate stock returns. If investors have rational expectations and understand the historical relation between price-dividend ratios and future stock returns, then their expected stock returns should be low during the last years of the market boom when both price-dividend and price-earnings ratios reached historical highs (and appropriate measures of risk should be low at that time). On the contrary, if expected stock returns were high toward the end of the market boom, this would lend support to behavioral stories of overreaction. Prior work on this issue includes Shiller, Kon-Ya, and Tsutsui (1996), who used expectational data for institutional investors in Japan to help analyze expectations at and after the peak of the Nikkei index. Their results are hard to interpret. Japanese institutional investors expected one-year capital gains on the Nikkei index of about 10% at the peak of the market, which seems neither unusually high or not unusually low, but expectations then increased to levels of around 20% after the first year and a half of the Nikkei's decline.

Using the UBS/Gallup data, Figure 1a shows average expected one-year stock-market returns from June 1998 to December 2002. The graph uses survey weights to make results representative of the population. For reference, Figure 1b and c shows the time series for the NASDAQ and NYSE market indices.

The average expected one-year stock-market return increased from an average of 11.8% in 1998 to 15.8% in January 2000, and then declined dramatically to around 6% at the end of 2002. Thus, expected returns were high when the market was at its highest, counter to what the historical statistical relation would have predicted. The correlation at the monthly frequency between the average expected one-year stock-market return and the level of the NYSE is 64.6, and the corresponding correlation with the NASDAQ index is 78.0.[5] An ordinary least squares (OLS) regression (not shown) of the average expected one-year stock return on the NYSE index results in a coefficient of 0.035 with t statistic of 5.9. Using the NASDAQ index, the regression coefficient is 0.0024 with a t statistic of 8.6. Splitting the sample into investors with less than $100,000 in financial assets and investors with $100,000 or more (not shown), the average expected one-year stock returns are about 1% lower throughout the period for those with $100,000 or more in financial assets, but the time pattern is similar for the two groups.

This evidence suggests that, at least for this particular historical experience, prices and expected returns move together positively and thus that

5. These correlations are calculated using the NYSE and NASDAQ indices at the start of the month. Survey interviews are conducted during the first two weeks of the month.

Figure 1 AVERAGE EXPECTED ONE-YEAR AND TEN-YEAR STOCK MARKET
RETURNS, UBS/GALLUP DATA, AND THE LEVEL OF THE NYSE AND
NASDAQ INDICES 1998–2002

(a) Average Expected Stock Market Returns

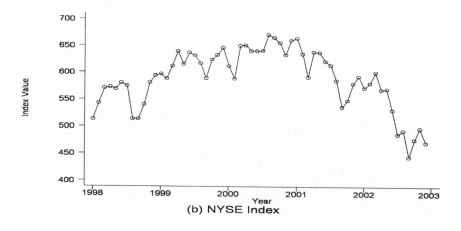

(b) NYSE Index

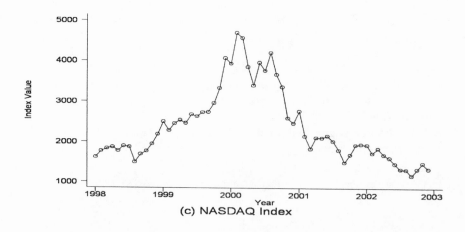

(c) NASDAQ Index

some amount of overreaction of prices may have been present.[6] The average expected ten-year stock-market returns, also shown in Figure 1, are much more stable over time. Given the small number of ten-year periods for which we have data, and the uncertainty about return predictability at this frequency, stable beliefs at the ten-year horizon seem rational.[7] Graham and Harvey (2001) study the stock-market return expectations of a smaller sample of chief financial officers (CFOs) for six quarters, starting in the second quarter of 2000. They also find that ten-year return expectations are more stable than one-year return expectations and that one-year return expectations move together positively with the realized market return.

3.3 DISAGREEMENT AND NOISE TRADER RISK

Standard finance theory suggests that expected stock-market returns should be similar across investors. While some investors may have private information about the returns on individual stocks, private information about the return on the whole market is less likely. Furthermore, to the extent that trading by better informed investors lead prices to reflect their information, others can learn from prices (Grossman and Stiglitz, 1980), reducing any belief heterogeneity further. In essence, because everyone, by assumption, believes in the same model of how expected stock returns are generated and are equally able to process information, any heterogeneity in beliefs requires both that some investors have private information about market returns and that noise traders or other impediments to learning prevent prices from revealing this information to all investors.

Behavioral finance theory, on the other hand, suggests that differences in expected returns across investors are likely. There is no presumption that all investors use the same model to form expected stock-market returns. Since Miller (1977), several models have considered the possible equilibrium effects of disagreement, emphasizing that in the presence of short-sales constraints, high disagreement leads to high prices and subsequent low returns. See Diether, Malloy, and Scherbina (2002) for references to this literature and for empirical evidence in favor of this theory based on analysts' earnings forecasts and the cross section of stock returns. Less is known about disagreement concerning aggregate stock-market returns and how investor beliefs begin to differ.

---

6. After completion of the final version of the paper I became aware that Fisher and Statman (2002) use the aggregate UBS/Gallup averages to emphasize this feature of investor beliefs.
    The following facts about investor beliefs exploit the household level UBS/Gallup data and are thus more novel. The household level data also allows one to confirm that the pattern shown in Figure 1(a) is present even for high wealth investors.
7. The average expected ten-year market returns are surprisingly high, however, relative to the average expected one-year market returns. Median ten-year return expectations also exceed median one-year return expectations, although not quite as dramatically.

Figure 2 CROSS-SECTIONAL STANDARD DEVIATION OF ONE-YEAR
EXPECTED STOCK RETURN (DISAGREEMENT), UBS/GALLUP DATA

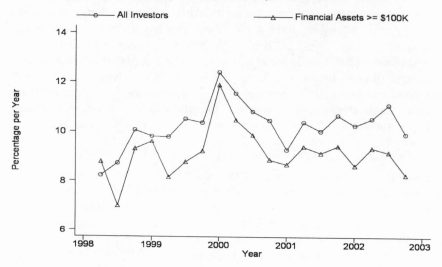

The time series of cross-sectional standard deviations is shown in
Figure 2.[8] In a cross section of investors, it is likely that some of the
observed differences in responses for expected stock-market returns simply reflect lack of knowledge about stock-market returns, rather than
firmly held beliefs on which the investor would place substantial trades.
This is confirmed by the fact that the cross-sectional standard deviation of
expected one-year stock-market returns is 10.3% for all investors in the
sample compared to 9.2% for those with $100,000 or more in financial
assets, who have a greater incentive to be informed about returns. These
numbers are averages over time of the quarterly cross-sectional standard
deviations. Figure 2 therefore shows both the disagreement across all
investors as well as the disagreement among those with $100,000 or more
in financial assets. Consistent with the findings of Diether, Malloy, and
Scherbina (2002) for the cross section of stocks, disagreement was highest
just prior to the market decline. It is important to emphasize, however,
that finding a positive relation between disagreement and subsequent
returns does not necessarily reflect the importance of short sales constraints.
Did a significant number of investors in fact want to short the market in
the late 1990s? De Long, Shleifer, Summers, and Waldmann (1990) and

8. The figure uses a quarterly data frequency. Results are similar when monthly average
returns are subtracted before calculating the quarterly cross-sectional standard deviations.
  Monthly cross-sectional standard deviations show the same patterns, but are a bit more
erratic, likely because a large number of observations is needed to estimate cross-sectional
standard deviations accurately.

Shleifer and Vishny (1997) emphasize how noise trader risk can limit arbitrageurs' willingness to take market-stabilizing positions. The risk that misvaluation may worsen will lead rational arbitrageurs to bet less heavily against the mispricing, more so the shorter the horizon of the arbitrageur. The argument of Abreu and Brunnermeier (2002) that it may even be optimal for arbitrageurs to attempt to ride bubbles rather than bet against them only serves to limit arbitrage further.

Shiller has collected expectations data that provide useful information on this issue. His data cover U.S. institutional investors and U.S. individual investors with net worth generally $250,000 or more.[9] While between 50 and 70% thought that U.S. stock prices were overvalued in 1998 and 1999 (calculated excluding those with "do not know" responses), about 70% expected the Dow Jones Industrial index to increase over the next year.

Figure 3 provides related information for the UBS/Gallup data, which covers a broader sample of individual investors and does not include institutions. As shown in Figure 3a, about 50% of investors thought the stock market was overvalued during the last two years of the boom, and typically less than 10% thought it was undervalued. Despite this, Figure 3b shows that only about 20% thought that the market would decline over the next three months/one year. (I use the three-month horizon from December 1998 up to February 2000, and the one-year horizon when it becomes available from March 2000 onward and for September 1998.) As shown in Figure 3c, even among those thinking the market was overvalued in 1999–2000, only about 25% thought it would decline. A similar pattern (not shown) is present for investors with $100,000 or more in financial assets. Along with the evidence on hedge fund holdings from Brunnermeier and Nagel (2002) mentioned above, the expectations data support the idea that noise trader risk matters.

Of course, there is an identification problem here. Short sales constraints could be the reason that few thought the market would go down in the near future. Mankiw, Reis, and Wolfers (2003, this volume) provide an interesting study of disagreement about inflation expectations based on data from the Survey of Consumer Attitudes and Behavior (SCAB). They find the same positive relation between the level of inflation and disagreement about next year's inflation rate that is present for stock-market returns. Since a high level of inflation is unrelated to short sales constraints for stocks, it is possible that a positive relation between the level of a series and the disagreement about the series in the future is a more general feature of expectations formation, for example, because households have less history on which to base their expectations when the series is at an unusually high value.

9. Shiller's analysis is available at http://icf.som.yale.edu/confidence.index (accessed June 3, 2003).

Figure 3 PERCEPTION OF MARKET VALUATION AND EXPECTED DIRECTION, UBS/GALLUP DATA

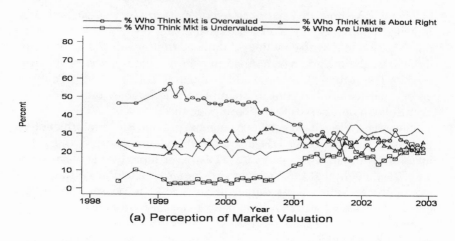

(a) Perception of Market Valuation

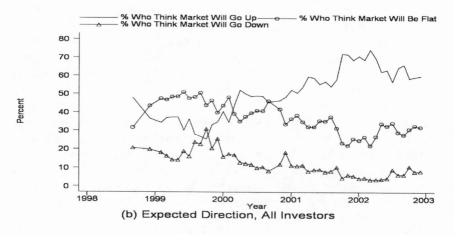

(b) Expected Direction, All Investors

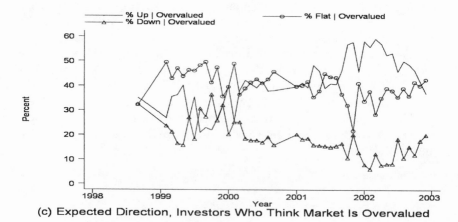

(c) Expected Direction, Investors Who Think Market Is Overvalued

3.4 THE DEPENDENCE OF INVESTOR BELIEFS ON THEIR OWN INVESTMENT EXPERIENCE

A unique feature of the UBS/Gallup data is that they provide a host of information about each individual investor in terms of demographics and past portfolio performance. These data allow further analysis of differences in beliefs. In this section I document that an investor's belief about future stock-market returns depends on the investor's own experience measured by age, years of investment experience, and own past (self-reported) portfolio returns. A behavioral interpretation of these facts is that they provide support for the law of small numbers emphasized by Barberis, Shleifer, and Vishny (1988) and Rabin (2002). (I discuss a possible rational story below.) Investors subject to this bias will expect even short samples to reflect the properties of the parent population and will thus have high expected returns after a period of high realized returns. However, the dependence of expected returns on investor age and experience makes this bias more precise by pointing to what defines the beginning of the (more) relevant small sample—the date the investor started investing in the market. The data also allow a more detailed analysis of how investors' expected market return and expected own portfolio return depend on the past return on their own portfolio to determine whether investors exhibit biased self-attribution, a key ingredient in the model of momentum and reversal of Daniel, Hirshleifer, and Subrahmanyam (1998).

Figure 4a plots the expected one-year stock-market returns of different investor age groups against time.[10] A strong relation between beliefs and age is apparent with young investors expecting substantially higher returns than middle-aged investors, who in turn are more optimistic than older investors. At the peak of the market, young investors, defined as those younger than 35 years, on average expected the market to do about 5 percentage points better over the next year than did older investors, those age 60 years or older. The difference narrows as the market declines. One would expect such narrowing because new data points should be weighted more by young investors who effectively have a shorter data sample. How much the gap narrows during the market downturn depends on whether one uses sample weights or not. Figure 4a uses sample weights, Figure 4b does not. Differences between age groups narrow more consistently when the data are not weighted within age groups.[11] Analyzing medians rather than means leads to similar patterns,

---

10. To have a reasonably large number of observations per age group per period, the figure shows quarterly average expectations rather than monthly average expectations.

11. It is not clear whether weighting is preferred. For calculating overall average expectations for each time period, weighting is appropriate. When considering the effect of a given investor characteristic on beliefs in a regression context, however, we know that OLS is efficient (other problems aside), and weighting observations by sampling probabilities leads to a less efficient estimator. Therefore, I do not use sample weights in the rest of the analysis.

Figure 4 AVERAGE EXPECTED ONE- AND TEN-YEAR STOCK-MARKET
RETURNS BY INVESTOR AGE, UBS/GALLUP DATA

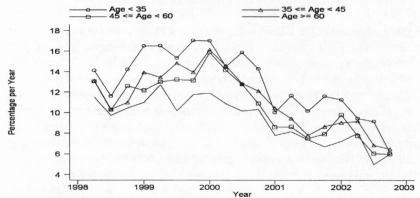

(a) Expected-One Year Stock Market Returns, Survey Weights Used

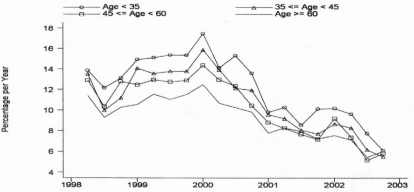

(b) Expected One-Year Stock Market Returns, Survey Weights Not Used

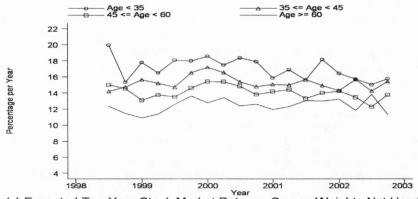

(c) Expected Ten-Year Stock Market Returns, Survey Weights Not Used

although the difference in median expectations of young and older house-holds at the peak of the market was around 2% compared to about 5% when focusing on means (except in the first quarter of 2000, where even the median difference increases to 5%). Figure 4c shows large age differ-ences in ten-year expected stock returns as well. Table 1, regression 1, shows that the age effect is statistically significant at the 5% level in almost all

Table 1   DETERMINANTS OF ONE-YEAR STOCK-MARKET RETURN EXPECTATIONS, UBS/GALLUP DATA, OLS REGRESSIONS[1]

Dependent variable: one-year expected stock-market return

Regressor	Regression 1		Regression 2		Regression 3	
	β	t-stat	β	t-stat	β	t-stat
Age*d983	−0.057	−2.03	−0.049	−1.25	−0.012	−0.40
Age*d984	−0.069	−2.27	−0.096	−2.24		
Age*d991	−0.115	−5.79	−0.158	−5.55	−0.020	−0.66
Age*d992	−0.082	−5.06	−0.088	−3.74	0.029	1.22
Age*d993	−0.104	−6.30	−0.098	−4.11	−0.037	−1.91
Age*d994	−0.088	−5.35	−0.084	−3.63	0.024	1.24
Age*d001	−0.125	−7.60	−0.113	−4.74	0.011	0.54
Age*d002	−0.091	−5.73	−0.081	−3.60	−0.001	−0.07
Age*d003	−0.102	−6.03	−0.114	−4.77	−0.006	−0.31
Age*d004	−0.100	−6.00	−0.055	−2.32	−0.029	−1.48
Age*d011	−0.055	−3.40	−0.056	−2.40	0.004	0.21
Age*d012	−0.053	−3.21	−0.053	−2.18	−0.031	−1.62
Age*d013	−0.026	−1.61	−0.020	−0.87	−0.034	−1.85
Age*d014	−0.061	−3.82	−0.066	−2.84	−0.019	−1.03
Age*d021	−0.049	−3.01	0.004	0.19	0.007	0.38
Age*d022	−0.056	−3.43	−0.050	−2.14	−0.033	−1.72
Age*d023	−0.052	−3.22	−0.019	−0.79	−0.038	−2.05
Age*d024	−0.001	−0.09	0.028	1.16	0.018	0.93
Experience*d983					−0.042	−1.06
Experience*d984						
Experience*d991					−0.072	−1.80
Experience*d992					−0.122	−4.05
Experience*d993					−0.042	−1.63
Experience*d994					−0.116	−4.52
Experience*d001					−0.114	−4.63
Experience*d002					−0.089	−3.84
Experience*d003					−0.093	−3.79
Experience*d004					−0.088	−3.57
Experience*d011					−0.103	−4.09
Experience*d012					−0.027	−1.13
Experience*d013					−0.019	−0.78
Experience*d014					−0.064	−2.62
Experience*d021					−0.060	−2.40

Table 1 CONTINUED

Regressor	Regression 1		Regression 2		Regression 3	
	β	t-stat	β	t-stat	β	t-stat
Experience*d022					−0.056	−2.32
Experience*d023					−0.016	−0.64
Experience*d024					−0.012	−0.49
Own past*d983					0.278	8.97
Own past*d984						
Own past*d991					0.301	10.86
Own past*d992					0.335	15.30
Own past*d993					0.374	22.42
Own past*d994					0.419	24.82
Own past*d001					0.369	28.77
Own past*d002					0.267	20.37
Own past*d003					0.311	20.16
Own past*d004					0.264	17.03
Own past*d011					0.117	9.74
Own past*d012					0.110	10.27
Own past*d013					0.114	9.75
Own past*d014					0.101	9.62
Own past*d021					0.173	14.92
Own past*d022					0.179	14.27
Own past*d023					0.167	15.73
Own past*d024					0.106	9.81
d983	13.038	9.42	12.367	5.95	6.618	4.55
d984	15.138	10.29	16.202	7.19		
d991	18.404	18.81	20.762	13.82	9.392	6.45
d992	17.118	21.20	16.834	13.34	7.609	7.15
d993	18.099	22.33	17.509	13.89	8.819	10.29
d994	17.461	21.42	17.213	14.05	6.457	7.42
d001	20.916	25.50	20.533	16.27	8.377	9.63
d002	17.311	21.83	16.398	13.75	9.106	11.05
d003	17.203	20.32	17.321	13.56	8.703	9.96
d004	16.052	19.31	13.357	10.58	10.392	12.42
d011	11.631	14.20	11.160	8.80	9.197	11.65
d012	11.404	13.64	11.081	8.60	10.200	12.61
d013	9.210	11.33	8.689	6.95	9.116	11.84
d014	10.745	13.08	10.601	8.38	9.388	12.10
d021	11.278	13.54	7.901	6.09	9.084	11.38
d022	10.605	12.87	9.496	7.48	9.875	12.17
d023	8.403	10.10	5.639	4.25	8.157	10.23
d024	5.890	7.00	3.764	2.89	5.379	6.53
	N = 39391		N = 17138		N = 31106	
	Adj. R2 = 0.503		Adj. R2 = 0.527		Adj. R2 = 0.590	

1. "Experience" refers to years of investment experience, "Own past" refers to the self-reported return on the investor's portfolio over the past year, 'dYYQ' is a dummy equal to 1 for year YY, quarter Q. Regression 1 and regression 3 is based on all investors, while regression 2 is for those investors with $100,000 or more in financial assets.

quarters. The coefficient on age is allowed to vary over time (by year and quarter), and time dummies are included separately. The negative effect of age on the expected stock-market return is strongest around the peak of the market. Table 1, regression 2, shows that the age effect is as strong for those with financial assets of $100,000 or more as for the full sample.

Additional evidence regarding the effect on beliefs of the stock-market returns observed by the investor him- or herself can be gained by considering the effect of years of investment experience within age groups. If the dependence of beliefs on age in fact is due to investors weighting stock-market returns they have observed more, then after a series of good stock returns, expected returns should be higher for those with low investment experience for a given age than for those with more years of experience. In Figure 5,

Figure 5 AVERAGE EXPECTED ONE-YEAR STOCK-MARKET RETURNS BY INVESTMENT EXPERIENCE WITHIN AGE GROUPS, UBS/GALLUP DATA

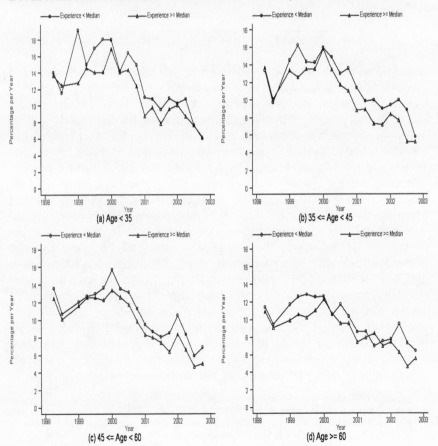

Figure 6 AVERAGE EXPECTED ONE-YEAR STOCK-MARKET RETURNS BY INVESTOR OWN PAST PORTFOLIO RETURN, UBS/GALLUP DATA

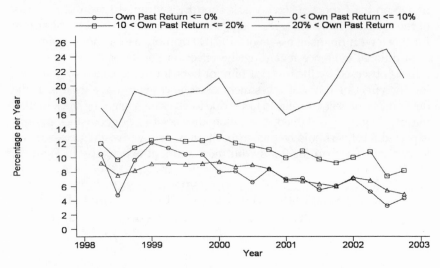

households are split into those with less than and more than median years of investment experience, within each age group. Over the time period covered by the UBS sample, the less experienced investors expect about 1 to 2% higher market returns, with no clear time pattern in this difference.

A final approach to analyzing how observed returns affect beliefs is to consider whether there is an effect of own past portfolio returns on expectations about the market return. This is strongly the case. I sort the respondents into four groups based on their reported own portfolio return over the past year. Figure 6 shows that, compared to those with reported own past returns between 0 and 10%, those with own past returns between 10 and 20% expected the market return over the next year to be about 3 to 4 percentage points higher, with the difference increasing to about 10 percentage points for those with own past returns above 20%.[12] To determine whether age, years of investment experience, and own past returns have independent effects on market expectations, Table 1, regression 3, provides regression results with all three variables included. Once experience and own past returns are included, the effect of age largely disappears. Thus, the higher expected returns of young investors seem to be driven mainly by their shorter average investment experience and the higher (actual or perceived) returns on their own portfolios during the stock-market boom. This leads to

---

12. Some of this effect could be due to measurement error in reported own past portfolio returns if those who exaggerate their past returns expect high market returns. The asymmetry of the effect of own past returns on expected market returns (and expected own returns) documented below is less subject to such problems.

two possible interpretations of the age effects on stock-market return expectations. The first is that investors are rational, but information about past market returns is costly. Then investors may rationally form expectations about future market returns based on their own actual past returns or, if such information is also costly, own perceived past portfolio returns. Because the young report higher own past returns, this would provide a rational explanation of the age effect. The second interpretation is that investors of different ages are equally informed about past market returns but, due to a behavioral bias, nonetheless use their own portfolio returns in forming beliefs about future market returns. The fact that the age effect is equally strong for the wealthiest half of the sample suggests that information costs are unlikely to be driving it and thus that a behavioral story is needed.

The data on inflation expectations from the SCAB can be used to determine whether the age dependence of expectations about stock-market returns generalizes to other aggregate variables.[13] The data also include each respondent's perception of what inflation was for things he or she buys during the past year. This is useful for distinguishing the above two interpretations of the age dependence of stock-market return expectations. If there is an age effect in inflation expectations but no difference in past perceived inflation (or the difference is the opposite of what is needed to explain the age effect in inflation expectations), that would be evidence against the rational costly information explanation of age effects in expectations about aggregate variables.

The SCAB asks respondents whether they think prices will go up, down, or stay the same over the next 12 months. From 1966–1979, respondents who expect price increases are asked for their expected inflation rate as a percentage. From 1980 onward, all respondents are asked for their expected inflation rate. Before the third quarter of 1977, all or some of the percentage responses are categorical. To construct a comparable time series of expected inflation rates, I assume that inflation is normally distributed in the cross section of respondents in each quarter or month (the survey is quarterly up to 1977 and monthly after that). I then estimate the cross-sectional mean and standard deviation based on the percentage of respondents who expect inflation to be below 5%, including those expecting no or negative inflation, and the percentage of respondents who expect inflation to be below 10%.[14] Figure 7 shows the expected inflation

---

13. See Souleles (2001) and Mankiw, Reis, and Wolfers (2003) for additional description of the data and analysis of heterogeneity in inflation expectations.
14. In principle, it would be more efficient to use all the inflation categories provided rather than only two pieces of information. In practice, a lot of the responses are at inflation rates of 0%, 3%, 5%, 10%, etc. A more sophisticated statistical approach would therefore need either to use a different distribution than the normal distribution or to model the rounding of the responses to popular values.

rate for the next 12 months, by age of respondent, for the period 1966–2001. The expectation plotted for a given year and age group is the cross-sectional average based on responses from all months of that year. Figure 7b shows similar series for 1975–2001 based on expected (annual) inflation over the next five to ten years. The actual inflation rate (based on the consumer price index for all urban consumers) is plotted in Figure 7c. Because survey interviews are spread out over the year, the actual inflation rate plotted is the annual inflation rate from July of the current year to July of the following year.

Figure 7 AVERAGE EXPECTED ONE-YEAR AND FIVE-TO-TEN-YEAR INFLATION RATES BY INVESTOR AGE, SURVEY OF CONSUMER ATTITUDES AND BEHAVIOR, AND THE ACTUAL INFLATION RATE FOR THE YEAR, 1966–2001

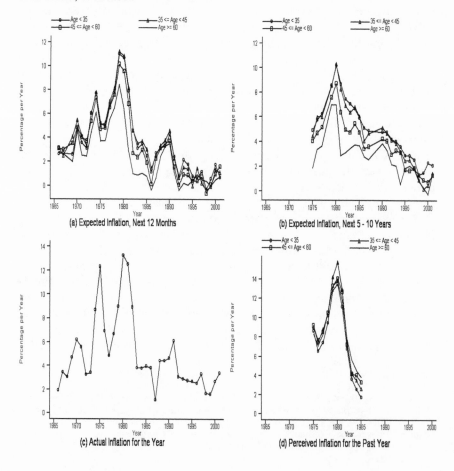

(a) Expected Inflation, Next 12 Months

(b) Expected Inflation, Next 5 - 10 Years

(c) Actual Inflation for the Year

(d) Perceived Inflation for the Past Year

Inflation expectations for the coming year peak in 1979 after a period of high actual inflation rates. In that year, the average expected inflation rate for the next 12 months of those under age 35 exceeded that of those age 60 or older by 2.5 percentage points. The difference widens to 4.9 percentage points in 1981, due to a more dramatic drop in expected inflation for older respondents in 1980 and 1981, and then gradually diminishes during the 1980s. For the years starting with 1980, where the expected percentage inflation rates are available for all households, a simple approach to test whether the age differences are significant is to run a pooled OLS regression of expected inflation rates on year dummies and on age interacted with year dummies, thus allowing the coefficient on age to differ by year (this approach is similar to that used for stock returns in Table 1). The regression, not included in a table for brevity, shows that age is significant at the 5% level in all years from 1980 to 1987. Overall, the age differences in expectations around the period of high inflation are quite similar to the evidence for stock-market return expectations. Figure 7b shows that a strong age pattern is also present in expectations about the level of inflation over the next five to ten years.

In some periods of the survey, households are asked for the inflation rate (for items they buy) over the past 12 months. Quantitative data, consistently defined across years, are available for 1975–1985. Time series for average perceived inflation rates are constructed using the same method as was used for the two forward-looking variables and are illustrated in Figure 7d. Notably, the youngest group generally have the *lowest* perceived inflation, while the ordering of the other three age groups depends on the year in question. A regression (not included in a table) of perceived inflation over the past 12 months on year dummies and on age interacted with year dummies can be run for 1980–1985 (again, percentage responses are available only in a noncategorical form for all respondents from 1980 onward). Perceived inflation is significantly *positively* related to age in each of these six years. Consistent with this, the negative effect of age on expected 12-month inflation is a bit stronger when controlling for perceived past inflation, which itself has a strong positive effect on expected inflation. Thus, the finding that the old expected much lower inflation than the young around 1980 is not driven by different perceptions about inflation over the past year. This again suggests that costs of acquiring information about the inflation level is not likely to explain the age difference in beliefs, consistent with the finding for stock return expectations that the age effect was equally strong for wealthier investors.

Further study of whether the young or the old have more accurate inflation and/or stock-market expectations would be interesting. Whether weighting recent data more is advantageous depends on the persistence of the series being predicted and thus could be expected to lead to improved accuracy for inflation but possibly decreased accuracy for stock returns. Given the quite short series of expectations on stock returns available in the UBS/Gallup data, I do not pursue the issue of forecast accuracy further.

3.5 BIASED SELF-ATTRIBUTION

Figure 8 illustrates that the dependence of expected one-year stock-market returns on the investor's own past portfolio return is asymmetric. Figure 8a is based on a regression (not included in a table) of market return expectations on age, experience, own past portfolio return, and time dummies.[15] The age and experience effects are allowed to vary by year and quarter, as in Table 1. The effect of own past portfolio return is now allowed to differ depending on whether the return was positive or negative and is allowed to vary by amount of financial wealth. The regression is estimated using data only from 2000–2002 where responses (for market and own return expectations and for own past portfolio returns) of less than 1% are not combined into one category. Figure 8a plots the predicted effect of own past portfolio returns on expected one-year market return. For those with financial wealth less than $100,000, an own past portfolio returns of 25% increases the expected market return by 10.4%, while an own past portfolio returns of –25% leads to an increase of 1.6%.[16] Thus, while positive own past portfolio returns leads to higher expected market returns, negative own past portfolio returns have a quite small and positive effect on expected market returns. The effect of positive own past returns is weaker for wealthier investors, but a 25% own past portfolio return still leads to an increase in the expected market return of as much as 6.7%, even for those with financial wealth of $500,000 or more. The difference to the lowest wealth group is significant at the 1% level. A diminished effect of positive own past returns was also found for higher income or higher education groups.

Several robustness checks are needed to determine if these findings reflect biased self-attribution. If they do, then the asymmetry results should be stronger for expected own portfolio returns than for expected market returns because the investor presumably is more likely to think that high own past portfolio returns are indicative of high future returns on his or her own portfolio than on the stock market as a whole. Figure 8b shows that this is indeed the case. The effect of positive own past returns

---

15. Note that by including time dummies, the effect of own past return on expected market returns is identified based on cross-sectional differences in own past returns, not based on time variation in own past returns.

16. Both these effects are significant at the 1% level. About 24% of own past portfolio returns for 2000–2002 are negative.

Figure 8 ESTIMATED EFFECT OF OWN PAST PORTFOLIO RETURN ON
EXPECTED ONE-YEAR STOCK-MARKET RETURN AND EXPECTED ONE-
YEAR OWN PORTFOLIO RETURN, UBS/GALLUP DATA

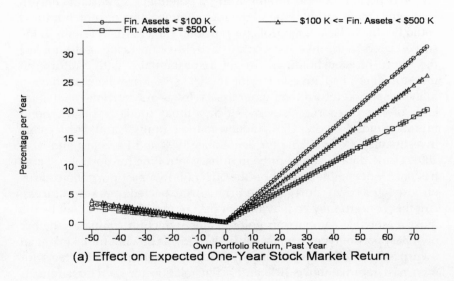

(a) Effect on Expected One-Year Stock Market Return

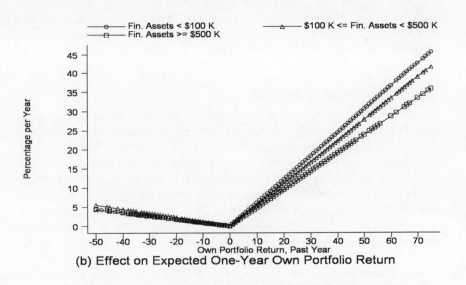

(b) Effect on Expected One-Year Own Portfolio Return

on expected own portfolio returns over the next year is about 50% larger than the effect on the expected one-year market return. When focusing on the expected own portfolio returns, a potentially important concern is whether the positive slope in the region of negative past own returns could be due to lack of controls for portfolio choice. The question in the survey refers to the investor's entire portfolio of financial assets, not just the return on stockholdings. To get a substantial negative return, an investor likely had invested a lot in stocks that are likely to have a higher expected return than other assets. Investors' portfolio shares for each of the categories "stocks, stock mutual funds," "bonds, bond mutual funds," "cash, CDs, money market funds," and "real estate investments" are available for September 1998 and February and May 2001. Using data for these three months, controlling for portfolio shares has only a negligible impact on the effect of own past portfolio returns on expected own portfolio returns (or expected market returns). Another concern may be that an own past return of zero may not be the most reasonable comparison point against which to evaluate whether own past portfolio performance is high or low. Allowing for a kink at an own past portfolio returns of 10% leads to strong positive effects for own past returns above 10% and a flat relation for own past returns below 10%.

Overall the results support the assumption of biased self-attribution made by Daniel, Hirshleifer and Subrahmanyam (1998). The finding that the effect diminishes in investor wealth or other measures of investor sophistication does suggest, however, that more work is needed to understand why some investors are more subject to this bias than others.

3.6 DO BELIEFS AFFECT ACTIONS?

The above results regarding investor beliefs would be of little interest if expectations reported to the survey are not correlated with investor choices. For the three months for which portfolio shares for broad investment categories are available, it is possible to determine whether investors with higher expected stock returns did in fact have higher equity portfolio shares.[17] Table 2 shows that this is strongly the case in the region of expected market returns up to 20%. This range covers over 95% of the investors used in the regression. As another piece of information about the link between expectations and portfolio holdings, Table 3 turns

---

17. Since the observed equity portfolio shares are in the range from 0 to 100%, I estimate the relationship using a two-sided Tobit model. The estimation also controls for age, investment experience, financial assets, education, and income because these factors may affect portfolio choice directly and, as discussed earlier, are correlated with expectations.

Table 2   EFFECT OF EXPECTATIONS ON STOCK HOLDINGS, 1998
(SEPTEMBER), 2001 (FEBRUARY, MAY), UBS/GALLUP DATA, TOBIT
REGRESSIONS

Dependent Variable: Percentage of Portfolio Held in Stocks

Regressor	β	t-statistic
Expected market return dummies (omitted = d $(E(r_M) \leq 0)$)		
d$(0 < E(r_M) \leq 5)$	2.729	0.84
d$(5 < E(r_M) \leq 10)$	4.648	1.51
d$(10 < E(r_M) \leq 15)$	10.164	2.88
d$(15 < E(r_M) \leq 20)$	10.191	2.30
d$(E(r_M) \geq 20)$	5.016	1.14
Time dummies (omitted = d9809)		
d0102	5.699	2.93
d0105	−7.883	−4.20
Age dummies (omitted = d(age < 30))		
d$(30 \leq$ age $< 40)$	0.517	0.15
d$(40 \leq$ age $< 50)$	−6.009	−1.68
d$(50 \leq$ age $< 60)$	−7.411	−1.98
d$(60 \leq$ age $< 70)$	−14.847	−3.48
d$($age $\geq 70)$	−22.754	−4.82
Experience dummies (omitted = d(experience ≤ 5 Years))		
d$(5 <$ experience $\leq 10)$	−2.195	−0.91
d$(10 <$ experience $\leq 15)$	1.354	0.49
d$(15 <$ experience $\leq 25)$	−5.686	−2.03
d$($experience $> 25)$	−0.374	−0.11
Financial asset dummy (omitted = d(financial assets < 100 K))		
d(financial assets $\geq$ 100 K)	3.793	2.06
Education dummies (omitted = d(≤ high school graduate))		
d(some college/technical college)	4.444	1.63
d(college graduate)	10.931	4.05
d(> college graduate)	10.146	3.64
Income dummies (omitted = d(income < 40 K))		
d$(40$ K $\leq$ income < 50 K)	−1.627	−0.45
d$(50$ K $\leq$ income < 60 K)	2.839	0.83
d$(60$ K $\leq$ income < 75 K)	−3.057	−0.94
d$(75$ K $\leq$ income < 100 K)	1.171	0.38
d(income $\geq$ 100 K)	−0.875	−0.28
Constant	51.601	9.64
N	2026	
N censored at 0	123	
N censored at 100	221	

to the relation between Internet stockholdings and expectations about
Internet stock returns. Information about Internet stockholdings are
included in six months of the survey spread out over 1999 and 2000.
Investors who expected Internet stocks to have much higher returns
than the stock market on average held as much as 25% more of their

Table 3   INTERNET STOCK HOLDINGS: TOBIT REGRESSION FOR
PERCENTAGE OF PORTFOLIO HELD IN INTERNET STOCKS, 1999 (MARCH,
JUNE, SEPTEMBER) AND 2000 (FEBRUARY, APRIL, JULY), UBS/GALLUP DATA

Dependent Variable: Percentage of Portfolio Held in Internet Stocks[1]

Regressor	β	t-stat	β	t-stat
Expected Internet stock return dummies (omitted = d(much higher))				
d(somewhat higher)	−7.787	−4.65	−8.049	−3.39
d(about same)	−18.039	−8.40	−18.462	−6.14
d(somewhat/much lower)	−25.151	−8.81	−22.560	−5.49
Perceived Internet stock risk dummies (omitted = d(much more risky))				
d(somewhat more risky)	4.674	2.89	4.290	1.83
d(about same risk)	4.955	2.31	4.723	1.58
d(somewhat less/much less risky)	7.276	2.27	9.325	2.19
Expected one-year stock market return (omitted = d(0 ≤ $E\ (r_M)$ < 5))				
d(0 < $E(r_M)$ ≤ 5)	−3.751	−0.80	4.961	0.69
d(5 < $E(r_M)$ ≤ 10)	−0.209	−0.05	5.135	0.79
d(10 < $E(r_M)$ ≤ 15)	3.835	0.91	8.672	1.32
d(15 < $E(r_M)$ ≤ 20)	7.147	1.60	11.896	1.71
d($E(r_M)$ ≥ 20)	8.337	1.84	12.427	1.73
Age dummies (omitted = d(age < 30))				
d(30 ≤ age < 40)	−8.730	−3.23	−9.565	−2.51
d(40 ≤ age < 50)	−17.359	−6.17	−15.247	−3.85
d(50 ≤ age < 60)	−15.801	−5.21	−9.877	−2.30
d(60 ≤ age < 70)	−21.640	−5.85	−17.218	−3.18
d(age ≥ 70)	−23.780	−5.33	−13.569	−2.10
Experience dummies (omitted = d(experience ≤ 5 years))				
d(5 < experience ≤ 10)	−6.816	−3.31	−7.961	−2.61
d(10 < experience ≤ 15)	−4.259	−1.80	−1.684	−0.49
d(15 < experience ≤ 25)	−2.669	−1.09	−2.770	−0.77
d(experience > 25)	−0.824	−0.27	3.995	0.91
Education dummies (omitted = d(≤ high school graduate))				
d(some college/technical college)	5.051	1.79	9.146	2.18
d(college graduate)	10.743	4.04	10.532	2.61
d(> college graduate)	11.755	4.33	8.810	2.13
Financial wealth dummy (omitted = d(financial assets < 100 K))				
d(financial assets ≥ 100 K)	9.617	5.94	6.039	2.61
Income dummies (omitted = d(income < 40 K))				
d(40 K ≤ income < 50 K)	6.829	1.83	5.155	0.93
d(50 K ≤ income < 60 K)	6.296	1.78	1.381	0.26
d(60 K ≤ income < 75 K)	10.491	3.14	6.825	1.35
d(75 K ≤ income < 100 K)	9.429	2.85	4.905	0.97
d(income ≥ 100 K)	19.768	6.08	13.134	2.63
Internet use dummies (omitted = d(never gets on Internet))				
d(gets on Internet, never purchased online)			8.209	2.57
d(gets on Internet, purchased online)			20.500	6.40
Constant	−32.806	−5.40	−44.982	−4.85
N/N cens. at 0/N cens. at 100	4164/1076/9		2084/445/2	

1. Regressions include time dummies. The table omits these for brevity.

portfolio in Internet stocks than those expecting Internet stock returns to be somewhat lower or much lower than the return on other stocks.[18] Lower perceived risk of Internet stocks relative to the risk of the market similarly has the expected positive effect on Internet stockholdings. Overall, the portfolio data thus show that investor actions are linked to their beliefs.

4. The Value of Correlating Irrational Actions with Wealth

In this section, I turn to the other main strand of the behavioral finance literature, which has focused on types of investor behavior that are inconsistent with the recommendations of standard finance models. Part of this literature is separte from the literature on pricing anomalies, while the pricing impact of other of these behaviors has been studied and linked to the pricing puzzles. Of course, even the behaviors listed below that may not have significant price impact are still important because such behaviors could have large effects on the utility of investors who act in supposedly irrational ways.

Investor behaviors that contradict the predictions of traditional finance models have been surveyed elsewhere (among others, see Barberis and Thaler [2003] and Daniel, Hirshleifer, and Teoh, [2002]). What I would like to focus on here is whether a given type of seemingly irrational behavior diminishes with investor wealth or with other measures of investor sophistication.

If the frequency or intensity of such behaviors diminishes substantially with wealth or sophistication, then two possibilities arise. The first possibility is that these behaviors are driven by information costs that likely have a large fixed component (once you understand diversification, you can apply your insights without cost to a larger portfolio). If they are driven in this way, then investors may be acting rationally given the costs they face. To confirm this, we would need to establish that the required information costs are not implausible, and to argue that the behavior exhibited is a reasonable response to lack of information. The latter is more likely to be satisfied in cases where the behavior involves too little action or too simple an action (e.g., lack of investment in some securities, lack of reallocation) than in cases where the behavior involves too much action (excessive trading). If information costs are to blame for seemingly irrational investor behavior, the policy recommendation would be increased investor education, especially for low-wealth and low-sophistication

---

18. It is not clear from the question asked whether the Internet portfolio share is the share of Internet stocks in the investor's equity portfolio or in his or her total financial asset portfolio.

investors who may not choose to become informed at their own cost. Of course, from an efficiency perspective, this would be the policy recommendation only if such education has positive externalities (i.e., that one educated investor can help another improve his or her choices) or can be provided more cheaply than the cost at which investors could have acquired the information on their own.

If behaviors that look irrational based on traditional finance theory diminish with wealth, a second interpretation is that psychological biases differ across individuals. Additional analysis of such cases would improve our understanding of the more fundamental determinants of the biases in beliefs and behavior and such correlations would need to be accounted for in models and calibrations of the likely pricing impact of such biases. To draw a parallel to the traditional finance literature, absolute risk aversion is typically thought and estimated to be decreasing in wealth. This does not mean that risk aversion is not a fundamental element of preferences or that risk-averse behavior is due to information costs, but it does mean that it is crucial for modeling and calibration whether or not this wealth dependency is accounted for. Correlating investor choices with other investor characteristics would also be helpful in this context.

Conversely, if a given irrational action remains equally frequent for high-wealth investors, then it is unlikely to be driven by information costs and is likely to have substantial impact on equilibrium prices. The behavioral finance literature is still not at the point where calibration of theoretical general equilibrium asset pricing models is done to determine the magnitude of the effects of nonstandard types of behavior on asset prices. I hope that work will progress to this stage as more information about investor expectations and actions becomes available and we get increasingly accurate estimates of the strength of the various biases.

Of course, it is important when considering the relation between biases and wealth to determine whether reverse causality could be driving the results. Some of the biases listed below are known to generate poor returns and thus low wealth. This means that one has to consider investors with vastly different wealth for comparisons to be robust to endogeneity issues; look at more exogenous measures of investor wealth and sophistication, such as labor income or education; or compare the behavior of different investor types, as in the earlier mentioned studies of trading behavior of households versus institutions, households versus foreign investors, and households versus hedge funds. An even better approach would be to consider the effects of exogenously provided information on investor behavior (examples of such studies are given in the next section).

A partial list of investor behavior not in accordance with standard finance theory includes those discussed in the following subsections. Some of these facts were documented by researchers in the rational camp. I include them to provide a more complete picture.

4.1 THE DISPOSITION EFFECT

This refers to a tendency of investors to delay selling investments on which they have incurred losses in the hope that they will recover their losses. This has been documented in the stock trades of individuals in the United States (Shefrin and Statman, 1985, and Odean, 1998), in the stock trades of Israeli individuals (Shapira and Venezia, 2001), in the stock trades of Finnish individuals and institutions (Grinblatt and Keloharju, 2001b), in the option exercise patterns of employees in the United States (Heath, Huddart, and Lang, 1999), and in sales patterns for homes (Genesove and Mayer, 2001).

The leading argument against the disposition effect being a rational phenomenon is that winners sold by individual investors subsequently outperform losers not sold (Odean, 1998). Behavioral researchers typically attribute the disposition effect to prospect theory (Kahneman and Tversky, 1979), with a reference price equal to the investor's purchase price. Based on experimental evidence, Kahneman and Tversky argued that utility should be defined not over wealth or consumption but over gains and losses, and that people are risk averse in the region of gains, but risk loving in the region of losses. Such preferences can induce the disposition effect because investors become risk loving in a security's payoff after a loss but not after a gain. An alternative behavioral story is a mistaken belief in mean-reversion. Odean (1999) argues against this by showing that the stocks purchased by individuals tend to be past winners. Grinblatt and Han (2002) consider the general equilibrium implications of the disposition effect. They construct a model where the momentum effect is driven by some investors exhibiting the disposition effect in their trading behavior. Goetzmann and Massa (2003) provide evidence that a disposition effect factor is priced in the cross section of daily stock returns.

Dhar and Zhu (2002) provide evidence about how the strength of the disposition effect depends on investor sophistication. Using U.S. data from a discount brokerage firm, they find that the disposition effect is only about half as strong for high-income, retired investors as for low-income investors working in nonprofessional jobs. Controlling for income and occupation, they also find a significant weakening of the disposition effect in investor age and in investor trading experience. Twenty percent of investors in their sample exhibit no disposition effect or exhibit a reverse disposition effect. Brown, Chapel, da Silva Rosa, and Walter

(2002) analyze the disposition effect using Australian data and find that the effect is weaker but still significant for investors taking large trading positions compared to others. Shapira and Venezia (2001) compare the disposition effect for accounts of independent investors and accounts of investors who have delegated portfolio management to a professional portfolio manager. The trades decided on by the investment professionals exhibit a weaker but still substantial disposition effect. In their study of the disposition effect in real estate transactions, Genesove and Mayer (2001) find that the disposition effect is twice as strong for owner-occupants as for (likely wealthier/more sophisticated) real estate investors. The evidence overall suggests that the disposition effect weakens substantially with investor wealth.

4.2 LIMITED DIVERSIFICATION OF STOCK PORTFOLIOS

French and Poterba (1991) emphasize that investors concentrate the vast majority of their equity portfolios in domestic stocks (the home bias puzzle). Coval and Moskowitz (1999) document a local equity preference in domestic portfolios of U.S. investment managers (home bias as home). Huberman (2001) reports a similar local stock preference by showing that the amount invested in local regional Bell phone companies far exceeds the amount invested in out-of-state regional Bell phone companies in most states. Grinblatt and Keloharju (2001a) report that home bias at home is also present among Finnish stockholders, while Massa and Simonov (2003) document it for Swedish investors. Benartzi (2001) analyzes stockholdings in employer stock and shows that employees invest 23% of their discretionary retirement plan contributions in company stock. Blume, Crockett and Friend (1974) and many subsequent papers have emphasized the low number of stocks held by many investors.

Coval and Moskowitz (2001) argue that informational advantages may motivate local holdings in their sample because fund managers earn an extra 2.67% per year from their local investments relative to their nonlocal investments. Benartzi (2001) shows that this is not the case for own company stockholdings. While employees tend to allocate more to company stock in firms that have done well in the past, retirement plans with higher discretionary contributions to own company stock do not outperform other plans. Benartzi also provides survey evidence that employees on average think high past returns will continue in the future and that only 16.4% of the respondents believe company stock is riskier than the overall stock market, measured by the likelihood of either investment losing half its value over the next five years.

The UBS/Gallup data provide a new opportunity to analyze the relationship between familiarity, expectations, and investments. For three months in 1999, the survey contains information about both Internet stockholdings, Internet stock return expectations, and Internet use. Table 4 shows that of those reporting that they use the Internet and have purchased something online, about 69% expected higher returns on Internet stocks than on other stocks, compared to 40% for those who did not use the Internet. Internet users also perceived Internet stocks to be riskier. This finding could be consistent with an information story where Internet use leads to cheaper or free information about Internet stocks because Internet stocks probably were riskier and therefore may have had higher expected returns than other stocks in 1999. The second regression in Table 3 shows, however, that even controlling for expected returns and risk (and a host of other variables), Internet use has a strong effect on Internet stockholdings, with those getting on the Internet and having purchased something online investing about 20% more in Internet stocks than those who do not use the Internet. This may be suggestive of an attention effect, where investors simply do not know about all stocks and invest in those stocks they—partly by accident—become aware of. Barber and Odean (2002) and Frieder and Subrahmanyam (2002) find evidence of an attention effect in the stock purchases of individual investors. If information is costly, the attention effect could be rational, although one could argue that any deviations of an investor's equity portfolio from the market portfolio is irrational.

I turn now to the relation between diversification and wealth/sophistication. Table 5 documents a relationship between home bias and investor income. The numbers are from the New York Stock Exchange (2000) and are based on a survey of 4842 investors in early 1999 (see Investment Company of America and the Securities Industry Association [1999]). The home bias is seen to diminish quite strongly with investor income, especially when it comes to directly held, non-U.S. stock or holdings of foreign stock through equity mutual funds in retirement accounts. Addressing home bias as home, Grinblatt and Keloharju (2001) show that the preference of Finnish investors for local stocks or for stocks with a chief executive officer (CEO) of their own cultural origin diminishes in investor sophistication as measured by the number of stocks held by the investors. Massa and Simonov (2003) find that the local stock preference of Swedish investors is driven purely by low-wealth investors.

Table 6 uses data from the 1998 and 2001 Survey of Consumer Finances to document that the number of stocks held in directly held equity portfolios is strongly increasing in the wealth of the household. While households with net worth below $100,000 hold on average just a couple of stocks in directly held stock portfolios (conditional on having any directly held stock), the average number of stocks increases to about 14 for

Table 4 PERCEPTIONS ABOUT RISK AND RETURN OF INTERNET STOCKS, BY INTERNET USE, 1999 (MARCH, JUNE, SEPTEMBER), UBS/GALLUP DATA

Overall, compared to investing in other common stocks, do you think that investing in selected Internet companies is . . .

	Much more risky	Somewhat more risky	About the same risk	Somewhat/ much less risky	Do not know	Number of observations
Never gets on Internet	21.22	37.08	24.65	9.65	7.40	933
Gets on Internet, never purchased online	26.52	37.55	25.81	8.10	2.02	988
Gets on Internet, purchased online	36.37	38.45	19.04	5.32	0.81	1108
Overall	28.49	37.74	22.98	7.56	3.24	3029

Again, compared to the return one can get from investing in other common stocks, do you think that the percentage return from investing in selected Internet companies is . . .

	Much higher	Somewhat higher	About the same	Somewhat/ much lower	Do not know	Number of observations
Never gets on Internet	12.33	28.08	33.90	11.58	15.11	933
Gets on Internet, never purchased online	17.61	36.34	29.05	10.73	6.28	988
Gets on Internet, purchased online	28.79	39.80	19.22	8.66	3.52	1108
Overall	20.07	35.06	26.64	10.23	7.99	3029

Table 5 EFFECT OF HOUSEHOLD INCOME ON HOME BIAS

Income	<$15 K	$15–25 K	$25–50 K	$50–75 K	$75–100 K	$100–250 K	> $250 K
Percentage of shareowners who have directly held, non-U.S. stock or an equity mutual fund holding non-U.S. stock inside a retirement account	11.9	11.5	27.7	35.9	38.1	42.3	38.5
Percentage of shareowners who have equity mutual funds holding non-U.S. equities, outside retirement accounts	26.2	23.3	21.8	29.3	30.0	34.8	39.2

Source: New York Stock Exchange (2000), based on Investment Company of America and the Securities Industry Association (1999).

Table 6 EFFECT OF HOUSEHOLD NET WORTH ON STOCK-MARKET PARTICIPATION AND DIVERSIFICATION OF DIRECTLY HELD EQUITY

Net worth	< $10 K	$10–50 K	$50–100 K	$100–250 K	$250–1 M	> $1 M	All
Percentage who hold stocks							
1998	16.2	42.3	46.9	59.7	81.0	91.9	48.9
2001	18.0	38.8	48.4	62.0	79.3	92.9	51.9
Mean (median) number of directly held stock conditional on owning stock directly							
1998	1.5 (1)	2.4 (1)	2.5 (2)	3.1 (2)	5.3 (3)	14.9 (8)	5.7 (2)
2001	1.7 (1)	1.9 (1)	2.6 (1)	3.0 (2)	6.0 (0)	13.3 (8)	6.3 (3)
Mean percentage of stocks held directly							
1998	12.9	12.1	15.9	20.3	25.7	35.9	20.6
2001	20.3	14.6	12.5	15.7	21.8	33.1	19.7

Source: Calculated using data from the 1998 and 2001 Survey of Consumer Finances (using survey weights).

households with a net worth of $1 million or more. In an earlier study (Vissing-Jorgensen, 1999), I argue that the percentage of equity owned by very poorly diversified investors in terms of the number of stocks is quite small. Goetzmann and Kumar (2001) analyze equity portfolio diversification using investor accounts at a particular brokerage firm and conclude that the majority of such investors are very poorly diversified. While analysis of brokerage accounts can be useful (for example, for analyzing the disposition effect) it is less compelling for analyzing diversification. Investors may use multiple brokers or hold most of their equity portfolios in mutual funds. Overall, investors with larger amounts of wealth or income, and thus greater incentives to become informed, hold better diversified portfolios than others.

4.3 LIMITED ASSET MARKET PARTICIPATION

A more extreme example of poor diversification is limited asset market participation. Many households have zero holdings of certain asset classes. The most well known is limited participation in stock markets. Other examples include holding no bonds or no investment real estate. The papers in the volume edited by Guiso, Haliassos, and Jappelli (2002) provide evidence that limited participation in markets for risky assets is prevalent in many countries. In Vissing-Jorgensen (2002) and in Section 5 below, I consider the role that costs of stock-market participation may play in providing a rational explanation for this. Heaton and Lucas (1999), Polkovnichenko (2001), I (Vissing-Jorgensen, 1998), and others have considered the equilibrium impact of limited participation on the equity premium. The consensus is that, in standard models where the equity premium is small with full participation, limited participation on its own will have some but not a dramatic effect on the equilibrium equity premium.

Table 6 illustrates that stock-market participation is strongly increasing in investor wealth and income. I return to this fact in Section 5.

4.4 NAÏVE DIVERSIFICATION OF RETIREMENT ACCOUNT CONTRIBUTIONS

Benartzi and Thaler (2001) document that the relative number of equity-type investment options offered in 401(k) plans affects the mean allocation to equities of plan participants. Investors in plans that are in the highest third in terms of percentage of equity-type investment options invest 64% on average in stocks, compared to 49% for investors in plans in the bottom third in terms of equity-type options. Experimental evidence roughly confirms these magnitudes and also suggests that this is driven by some investors choosing portfolio shares of $1/n$ for each plan option. A $1/n$ rule seems like a reasonable response to diversifying for an investor who understands the basic idea of diversification but not the exact differences between asset classes. Correlating this type of behavior with income or wealth would be informative for determining if a simple information explanation is likely.

4.5 STATUS QUO BIAS IN RETIREMENT ACCOUNT ALLOCATIONS

Ameriks and Zeldes (2001) analyze a ten-year panel of TIAA-CREF participants. Consistent with earlier findings of Samuelson and Zeckhauser (1988), they find that both changes in flow allocations and reallocation of accumulated assets are rare: 47% of individuals made no changes in flow allocations over a ten-year period; 73% made no changes in the allocation of accumulated assets. Ameriks and Zeldes suggest a rational explanation, namely, that individuals may face a nonmonetary fixed cost per transaction. If so, we would expect the status quo bias to diminish with the dollar amount invested, and thus with employee salary. The bias would also be expected to diminish with age or years of employment because a certain amount of free information about the value of reallocating arrives over time from interaction with colleagues and friends. Table 7 shows that these predictions are borne out in the data. The table is from Agnew, Balduzzi, and Sunden (2003), who analyze data from a large 401(k) plan. They find that employees with higher income and older employees place substantially more trades (changes in flow contributions and allocation of existing assets) and have a higher retirement asset turnover than younger employees and employees with lower income.

4.6 EXCESSIVE TRADING

In sharp contrast to the trading behavior in retirement plans, some investors trading though brokers or online trade frequently and on average

Table 7 EFFECT OF HOUSEHOLD SALARY AND AGE ON STATUS QUO BIAS IN RETIREMENT PLANS

Salary	Annual number of trades	Annual turnover, percentage	Age	Annual number of trades	Annual turnover, percentage
< $25 K	0.11	7.78	< 35	0.17	10.40
$25–50 K	0.16	10.80	35–44	0.27	17.14
$50 K–75 K	0.22	14.18	45–54	0.36	22.28
$75 K–100 K	0.39	23.11	55–64	0.60	36.93
≥ $100 K	0.66	39.43	65+	0.03	2.78

Source: Agnew, Balduzzi, and Sunden (2003), Tables 4 and 5.

lose money by trading as a result of the transaction costs involved. Odean (1999) finds an average monthly turnover rate of 6.5% in a sample of discount brokerage customers. He argues that trading by these investors is excessive because the stocks purchased perform worse on average than the stocks sold, implying that the trades are disadvantageous even before payment of commissions. Using a sample of accounts at a discount brokerage firm, Barber and Odean (2000) find that the average investor in their sample performs about the same as the S&P500 index before costs but underperforms the index by 1.5% per year after costs. Within the sample, those in the top quintile in terms of turnover underperform the index by 5.5% per year after costs. The authors argue that overconfidence motivates frequent trading.

Table 8 provides evidence on the dependence of trading in directly held stocks on wealth and income. Wealthier households trade much more than less wealthy households, with about one-quarter of the wealthiest group (those with 1 million or more in net worth) trading more than ten times per year. This could be interpreted as evidence that wealthier investors are more overconfident than others. This interpretation would

Table 8 EFFECT OF HOUSEHOLD NET WORTH ON TRADING FREQUENCY FOR DIRECTLY HELD STOCKS

Net worth	< $10 K	$10–50 K	$50–100 K	$100–250 K	$250–1 M	> $1 M	All
Percentage who hold stocks directly							
1998	3.2	8.3	13.8	21.5	43.1	68.6	19.2
2001	4.8	8.2	11.2	21.0	41.3	67.4	21.3
Percentage who bought or sold stocks in the last year, conditional on owning stock directly							
1998	6.4	17.8	12.9	16.7	35.7	61.3	22.8
2001	2.2	17.1	11.2	15.4	33.4	64.1	24.9
Percentage who traded 1–2 times							
1998	4.2	8.9	8.7	7.7	14.6	11.1	9.1
2001	0.7	7.5	4.7	9.2	11.6	12.7	8.5
Percentage who traded 3–10 times							
1998	0.9	5.7	3.6	6.3	12.1	22.6	7.8
2001	0.6	5.7	3.8	4.0	13.7	26.9	9.7
Percentage who traded >10 times							
1998	1.2	3.1	0.6	2.7	9.0	27.6	5.9
2001	0.9	3.8	2.6	2.2	7.8	24.5	6.7

Source: Calculated using data from the 1998 and 2001 Survey of Consumer Finances (using survey weights).

be consistent with the earlier evidence provided on biased self-attribution. Alternatively, high-wealth investors were seen to hold more shares on average, and that fact could be driving the results (portfolio turnover cannot be calculated in the survey of Consumer Finances). It would be interesting to correlate the dependence of underperformance due to frequent trading in Barber and Odean's (2000) study with wealth (or, better, labor income or education) to determine whether the wealthy are in fact trading more excessively than others with direct stockholdings or whether their frequent trading is rational. Coval, Hirshleifer, and Shumway (2002) document significant persistence in the performance of invididual investors buying and selling directly held stocks through a particular brokerage firm, suggesting that some do seem to have investment skill.

In sum, the evidence suggests that most of the seeming irrational investor behaviors are weaker for investors with higher wealth or income (frequent trading of directly held stocks being the main exception). This points to information or transactions costs as a potentially important contributing factor for these behaviors. I now turn to a simple calculation of the costs needed to explain one such behavior, namely, limited stock-market participation.

5. Costs of Stock-Market Participation

Information and/or transaction costs are a possible explanation for investor behavior that consists of inaction/too infrequent action/too simple action relative to the predictions of traditional finance theory. For each such behavior, however, it must be shown that the necessary costs are not implausibly large. In this section I give an example of how one might approach such a calculation in the case of stock-market participation. I start by considering which types of costs may be involved and then turn to an estimation of how large a per-period cost of stock-market participation would be needed to explain the choices of a substantial fraction of those who do not participate in the stock market.

5.1 COSTS FACED BY STOCK-MARKET INVESTORS

Consider the optimization problem of a household that maximizes expected lifetime utility given an exogenous stream of nonfinancial income and that faces the opportunity to invest in two assets: a risky asset and a riskless asset. The risky asset represents the stock market. The riskless asset is a catchall for less risky financial assets such as bonds, T-bills, bank accounts, etc. I assume it is free to invest in the riskless asset, whereas investing in stocks may involve several types of costs. First-time buyers likely incur an initial cost F^I representing the time/money spent understanding basic investment principles as well as acquiring enough information about risks and returns to determine the household's optimal mix between stocks and riskless assets. Add to that the cost of time spent setting up accounts. Subsequently, a per-period stock-market participation cost F^P may be incurred. This cost would include the value of time spent throughout the year determining if trading is optimal. With time-varying conditional asset return distributions, theory suggests that households should actively follow the stock market to form more precise expectations of future returns and change their portfolios accordingly. For households who attempt to gather information and thus benefit from buying individual stocks or subcomponents of the stock-market index, the cost of this would also be included in F^P. A more subtle part of F^P is that stocks complicate tax returns. According to Internal Revenue Service (IRS) numbers for 2002, households who have to fill out schedules D and D1 (the schedules for capital gains and losses) spend 8 hours and 34 minutes on average doing so. In addition to F^I and F^P, stock-market investors face a fixed cost of trading stocks, including the fixed part of brokerage commissions as well as the value of time spent implementing the trade. Investors also face variable (proportional) costs of trading stocks. For directly held stocks, this cost represents the bid-ask spread and the variable part of brokerage commissions.[19] Indirect holding of stocks also involve transaction costs. For load mutual funds, the front load paid on entry into the fund would enter the proportional trading costs. In addition, or as an alternative, some funds have contingent deferred sales loads requiring investors to pay a certain percentage of their initial investment if they sell their mutual fund shares before a given number of years. These again work as a variable cost. Annual expenses on mutual funds also reduce investor returns.[20]

The above discussion emphasizes the costs of acquiring and processing information as an important element of F^I and F^P. Several recent papers find evidence that households who report to be better informed about financial issues make portfolio decisions more in line with theoretical predictions by having a higher probability of owning risky financial assets and holding a larger number of financial asset classes (see Guiso and Jappelli [2002] for evidence based on Italian data; Alessie, Hochguertel, and van Soest [2002] for results based on Dutch data; and Eymann and

19. Jones (2001) documents a quite strong decline in NYSE average one-way transaction costs (commissions plus half of the bid-ask spread) since the mid 1970s, from around 1.10 percentage points in 1970 to around 0.20 percentage point in the late 1990s. Consistent with the importance of trading costs, turnover has increased dramatically over the same period (of course, reverse causality cannot be ruled out based on these aggregate data).
20. Investment Company Institute (2002) estimates average annual total shareholder costs (operating expenses plus distribution costs) for equity mutual funds of 2.26% in 1980, gradually declining to 1.28% in 2001.

Borsch-Supan [2002] for findings from German data). While these relations may not be causal, other papers suggest a causal effect of information on savings and portfolio choice. Chiteji and Stafford (2000) find that parental stockholding has a strong effect on the probability that children become stockholders, controlling for economic and demographic characteristics of the children as well as for bequests. This suggests an effect of education about financial matters on stock-market participation. Duflo and Saez (2002) study retirement plan choices among the employees in various departments of a particular university. They find that the decision to enroll in a tax-deferred account plan (and the choice of mutual fund vendor for people who enroll) is affected by the decisions of other employees in the same department. Information flow from colleagues is a plausible explanation for such effects. Hong, Kubik, and Stein (2003) provide related evidence of peer effects. Bernheim, Garrett, and Maki (2001) find that the savings rate of households who grew up in a state with a high school financial curriculum mandate is about 1.5 percentage points higher than for others, controlling for income and demographics. Bernheim and Garrett (2003) find similar effects for employer-based retirement education plans.

5.2 HOW LARGE ARE THE COSTS NEEDED TO EXPLAIN NONPARTICIPATION?

I now turn to a simple estimation of how large costs are needed to explain nonparticipation in the stock market by many households. I focus on the case with a fixed per-period participation cost F^P only, but discuss how an entry cost or transaction costs may affect the results. I first estimate how large a value of F^P is needed for participation costs to explain the majority of nonparticipants' choices not to participate in the stock market. This assumes that all nonparticipating households face the same value of F^P. Then I allow F^P to differ across households and estimate its cross-sectional distribution. The advantage of allowing heterogeneity in F^P is that it enables the framework to explain different participation choices of households with similar wealth and other observable characteristics.

Both estimations are based on estimating the benefits of stock-market participation for each household, taking as given its current level of financial wealth. The advantage of this simple approach over a more structural one is that it allows me to use the actual distribution of financial wealth in the data without providing a detailed model able to generate the observed distribution. The most closely related paper on costs of stock-market participation is Mulligan and Sala-i-Martin (2000). They focus on all interest-bearing assets and the per-period cost of investing in such assets. At an interest rate of 5%, they estimate the median cost of holding interest-bearing assets to be $111 per year. I focus on stockholdings only and present a theoretical argument to clarify the assumptions needed for the analysis of per-period participation costs. In addition, I consider a case where the cost is restricted to be the same for all nonparticipants so that one can identify the smallest cost needed to explain the choice of a given percentage of nonparticipants. Other related papers on investment costs and asset pricing are Luttmer (1999) and Paiella (1999), who focus on the costs needed to prevent households from adjusting their consumption from its current value (as opposed to reallocating existing financial wealth, as emphasized here).

5.2.1 *Theoretical Framework* My approach to estimating the benefits of stock-market participation relies on the definition of the certainty equivalent return to a portfolio. Start by considering a one-period setting with utility defined over end-of-period wealth and with no nonfinancial income. Consider a portfolio with stochastic net return r. If household i invests an amount W_i in the portfolio at the beginning of the period, end-of-period wealth is $W_i (1 + r)$. The certainty equivalent end-of-period wealth W_i^{ce} is given by[21]:

$$EU[W_i(1 + r)] = U(W_i^{ce}) \tag{1}$$

Correspondingly, the certainty equivalent return to the portfolio r_i^{ce} can be defined as:

$$EU[W_i(1 + r)] = U[W_i(1 + r_i^{ce})] \tag{2}$$

with the interpretation that the investor is indifferent between investing W_i in the risky portfolio with stochastic return r and investing it in a riskless portfolio with return r_i^{ce}. In a setting with participation costs of investing in the risky portfolio, replace initial wealth by $W_i^{Post} = W_i - F^P$. This wealth level then enters on the right side of the equation as well:

$$EU[W_i^{Post}(1 + r)] = U[W_i^{Post}(1 + r_i^{ce})] \tag{3}$$

If the risky portfolio consists of stocks and riskless assets in the fractions α_i and $1 - \alpha_i$, the above equation says that:

$$EU\left\{W_i^{Post}[1 + r_f + \alpha_i(r_s - r_f)]\right\} = U[W_i^{Post}(1 + r_i^{ce})] \tag{4}$$

where r_s is the stock return and r_f the riskless rate. Since the only risk in the portfolio of stocks and riskless assets stems from stocks, the certainty equivalent return to stocks $r_{s,i}^{ce}$ can be defined by the equation:

21. In the terminology of Pratt (1964), W_i^{ce} is given by $E[W_i (1 + r)] - \pi_i$, where π_i is the risk premium that makes the investor indifferent between receiving the stochastic amount $W_i (1 + r)$ and receiving the certain amount $E[W_i(1 + r)] - \pi_i$.

$$EU\{W_i^{\text{Post}}[1 + r_f + \alpha_i(r_s - r_f)]\} = U\{W_i^{\text{Post}}[1 + r_f + \alpha_i(r_{s,i}^{ce} - r_f)]\} \qquad (5)$$

which states that the investor is indifferent between investing fractions α_i and $1 - \alpha_i$ in a portfolio of stocks and riskless bonds and investing all of W_i^{Post} in a riskless asset with net return $r_f + \alpha_i (r_{s,i}^{ce} - r_f)$. If the household is risk averse, then r_i^{ce} is a number smaller than the expected net return on the risky portfolio $E[r_f + \alpha_i (r_s - r_f)]$. Therefore, if $\alpha_i > 0$ $r_{s,i}^{ce} < E(r_s)$. A household choosing $\alpha_i > 0$ furthermore reveals that $r_{s,i}^{ce} > r_f$.

Consider now the more realistic case where households live for multiple periods and have nonfinancial income. In this case, we can define the certainty equivalent stock return $r_{s,i,t+1}^{ce}$ by the following equation:

$$\max_{C_{it}} U(C_{it}) + \beta E_t V_{t+1}\{(W_{it}^{\text{Post}} - C_{it})[1 + r_{f,t+1} + \alpha_{it}(r_{s,t+1} - r_{f,t+1})] + Y_{i,t+1}\} =$$
$$\max_{C_{it}} U(C_{it}) + \beta E_t V_{t+1}\{(W_{it}^{\text{Post}} - C_{it})[1 + r_{f,t+1} + \alpha_{it}(r_{s,i,t+1}^{ce} - r_{f,t+1})] + Y_{i,t+1}\} \qquad (6)$$

where $V_{t+1}(W_{i,t+1})$ denotes the value function defined over date $t+1$ wealth and β is the discount factor. On the left side of this equation, the expectation is taken over $r_{s,t+1}$ and $Y_{i,t+1}$. On the right side, it is taken over $Y_{i,t+1}$ only because $r_{s,i,t+1}^{ce}$ is nonstochastic. In the above definition, consumption in period t is allowed to differ depending on whether the risky portfolio or the riskless portfolio is held. Below, however, I will need to assume that the chosen consumption for period t (but not for future periods) is approximately unaffected by the portfolio choice.

The certainty equivalent stock return can now be used to determine the value of participating in the stock market. Given the definition of $r_{s,i,t+1}^{ce}$, the household will choose to participate in the stock market in the current period if:

$$\max_{C_{it}} U(C_{it}) + \beta E_t V_{t+1}\left\{(W_{it}^{\text{Post}} - C_{it})\left[1 + r_{f,t+1} + \alpha_{it}(r_{s,i,t+1}^{ce} - r_{f,t+1})\right] + Y_{i,t+1}\right\}$$
$$> \max_{C_{it}} U(C_{it}) + \beta E_t V_{t+1}\left[(W_{it} - C_{it})(1 + r_{f,t+1}) + Y_{i,t+1}\right] \qquad (7)$$

where, as earlier, $W_{it}^{\text{Post}} = W_{it} - F^P$.

Below I consider two estimations. The first, estimation A, estimates the per-period cost sufficient to explain the choices of a given percentage of nonparticipants. The second more ambitious approach, estimation B, estimates the distribution of participation costs in the population.

5.2.2. *Estimation A: Homogeneous F^P* From equation (7), it follows that the gross benefit, as of time $t+1$, of participating in the stock market in period t is:

$$\text{Benefit}_{it} = \left(W_{it}^{\text{Post}} - C_{it}\right) \alpha_{it} \left(r_{s,i,t+1}^{ce} - r_{f,t+1}\right) \qquad (8)$$

under the simplifying assumption that period t consumption (but not future consumption) is unaffected by whether or not the household decides to enter the stock market.

On the cost side, the per-period cost of stock-market participation that could be avoided in period t by not entering, or entering in a subsequent period, reduces $W_{i,t+1}$ by:

$$\text{Avoidable cost}_{it} = F^P \left(1 + r_{f,t+1} \right) \tag{9}$$

A value of F^P $(1 + r_{f,t+1})$ greater or equal to Benefit$_{it}$ is sufficient to deter the household from participating in this period.[22] A lower value will also be sufficient if there are transactions costs (because the household would need to be able to recover these additional costs either in this period or in future periods of stock-market participation). In other words, if $x\%$ of nonparticipants have benefits less than y dollars in period t, then it is conservative to say that a per-period cost of $F^P = y$ is sufficient to explain the nonparticipation of $x\%$ of nonparticipants.

Under an additional assumption one can be more precise.

Assumption A: The per-period benefits of stock-market participation for observed nonparticipants are approximately the same across time periods for a given household i.

Most important, this assumes approximately constant holdings of financial wealth across periods for this group.[23] Then the entry condition states that the household should participate if:

Benefit$_{it}$ > F^P + annuity value of all stock-market
transaction costs for household i (10)

I will refer to the right side as the total participation cost, F_i^{Total}. The advantage of this is that it no longer ignores the potential importance of any initial entry cost F^I or transaction costs (but at the cost of the extra assumption needed). The annuity value is calculated over years of stock-market participation.[24] Under assumption A, one can then estimate the annualized value of total stock-market participation costs which is sufficient to explain the nonparticipation of $x\%$ of nonparticipants. One problem with assumption A is that there may be a life-cycle component to

---

22. Because $1 + r_{f,t+1}$ is close to 1, for simplicity I replace F^P $(1 + r_{f,t+1})$ by F^P in what follows.
23. This assumption clearly would make less sense for participants because they decided to enter the stock market at some point, which suggests that their financial wealth likely increased to make this optimal.
24. Note that, unlike F^I, F^P and the transaction costs, which are exogenous parameters in the household's problem, the total participation cost has an endogenous element because the number of periods of stock-market participation is chosen by the household.

financial wealth even for relatively low-wealth households. One could consider repeating the estimations below with middle-aged households to provide a more conservative estimate of the costs needed to explain nonparticipation.

The data for the estimation come from the Panel Study of Income Dynamics (PSID). I use the Survey Research Center sample of the PSID, which was representative of the civilian noninstitutional population of the United States when the study was started in 1968. The PSID tracks all original family units and their adult offspring over time. With low attrition rates, the sample therefore remains representative as long as offspring are included. To keep the sample representative of the U.S. population, I exclude the poverty sample and the Latino sample. Wealth information from the 1984, 1989, and 1994 supplements is used to calculate financial wealth, defined as the sum of cash (checking or savings accounts, money market bonds, or Treasury bills, including such assets held in individual retirement accounts [IRAs]), bonds (bond funds, cash value in life insurance policies, valuable collections, rights in trusts or estates), and stocks (shares of stock in publicly held corporations, mutual funds, or investment trusts, including stocks in IRAs). To identify entries for which imputations were used, I use the wealth information as given in the family files instead of the wealth supplement files. Imputed values for cash, bonds, or stocks can then be coded as missing. Topcoding of wealth or income variables is very rare in the PSID, and topcoded variables were left at their topcodes. Although in reality households can have a portfolio share for a given asset above one, the PSID wealth data does not allow one to observe this due to the way the wealth questions are formulated. For example, the questions asked concerning stockholdings are "Do you (or anyone in your family living there) have any shares of stock in publicly held corporations, mutual funds, or investment trusts, including stocks in IRAs?" and "If you sold all that and paid off anything you owed on it, how much would you have?" Thus, a household who had borrowed to invest more than its total financial wealth in stocks would be recorded as having a portfolio share for stocks of one. Similarly, it is not possible to identify short sales from these questions. To allow comparison of amounts for different years, wealth variables are deflated by the consumer price index (CPI) for all urban consumers, with 1982–1984 as the basis year. My earlier paper (Vissing-Jorgensen, 2002) contains summary statistics for the sample. Among households with positive financial wealth, the percentage who owns stocks is 28.4% in 1987, 37.0% in 1989, and 44.2% in 1994. Among all households in the sample, 23.7% own stocks in 1987, compared to 29.1% in 1989, and 36.4% in 1994.

To implement estimation A, I make three additional assumptions. First, I calculate the benefit of stock-market participation as $W_{it} \alpha_t \left(r^{ce}_{s,i,t+1} - r_{f,t+1} \right)$

Figure 9 STOCK-MARKET PARTICIPATION BENEFITS FOR
NONPARTICIPANTS, PSID

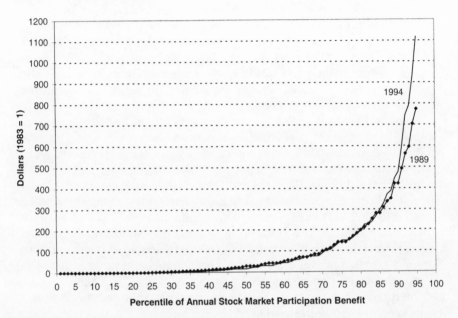

rather than $(W_{it}^{\text{Post}} - C_{it})\,\alpha_t\,(r_{s,i,t+1}^{ce} - r_{f,t+1})$. This overstates the benefits both
by assuming that no wealth must be set aside for current period
consumption and by replacing W_{it}^{Post} (financial wealth after participation
costs) with observed financial wealth. Second, I assume a value of
$r_{s,i,t+1}^{ce} - r_{f,t+1}$ of 0.04. With a historical equity premium around 7% and a
tax rate of, for example, 20 percentage points, the after-tax equity return
will be 5.6%.[25] Since the certainty equivalent excess return on stocks is risk
adjusted, 4% seems, if anything, to be a high value. Thus, both these
assumptions are conservative because they most likely overstate the benefits of stock-market participation and thus the costs needed to explain nonparticipation. Third, for the values of α_{it}, I assume that each nonparticipant
would have had a value of α_{it} equal to the average value for participants
in the PSID in that year (43.6 for 1989, 55.2 for 1994). Having calculated the
period t benefit of stock-market participation for each of the nonparticipants as $W_{it}\,\alpha_t\,0.04$, I calculate the percentiles of the cross-sectional distribution of this benefit in the set of nonparticipants. Figure 9 illustrates these

25. The exact tax rate is difficult to calculate because some stockholdings are in pensions
plans where returns accumulate tax-free and are taxed only on withdrawal.

percentiles and thus gives the minimum dollar amount necessary to explain the choices of various percentages of nonparticipants.

The curve labeled 1989 in Figure 9 shows the percentiles of the benefit distribution for those who were nonstockholders in 1989 (and in 1984 to be reasonably confident that the household did not participate in earlier periods). The benefits are calculated based on the households' 1989 financial wealth. Similarly the curve labeled 1994 is based on those who were nonparticipants in 1994 and 1989. For readability, the figure leaves out percentiles above the 95th percentile.

In both 1989 and 1994, half of nonparticipants had estimated real annual stock-market participation benefits of less than $30. The price index used to calculate the real values has a basis value of one on average over the years 1982–1984. Multiply dollar values in the figure by 1.817 to adjust them to January 2003 dollars. Thus, a per-period stock-market participation cost (or a total participation cost under assumption A) of around $55 in 2003 prices is enough to explain the nonparticipation of half the nonparticipants. This reflects the fact that these households had little or no financial wealth to invest. Of the nonparticipants in 1989 (and 1984), around 21% had no financial wealth. Of the nonparticipants in 1994 (and 1989), about 29% had no financial wealth.

Interpreting the per-period participation cost as the cost of additional time spent following the market and doing more complicated taxes, a cost of $55 translates into less than 4 hours at an hourly wage of $15 per hour. For both 1989 and 1994, a cost of $150 per year (about $275 in 2003 prices) is enough to explain the choices of 75% of nonparticipants.

5.2.3. *Estimation B: Heterogeneous F^P* Suppose now that F^P is allowed to differ across households and time. This improves the models' ability to explain different choices by households with similar observable characteristics. For now, assume again that F^I and transactions costs are zero. I return to the possible effects of these costs below.

Given the definition of the benefit of stock-market participation in equation (8), a simple approach to estimating the cross-sectional distribution of F^P at date t is as follows. Suppose that $\alpha_{it} = \alpha_t$ for all i, that $r^{ce}_{s,i,t+1} - r_{f,t+1}$ 0.04 $\forall i$, and that F^P_{it} is uncorrelated with financial wealth in the cross section of households. Given these assumptions, the stock-market participation condition states that household i should participate in period t if:

$$(W^{Post}_{it} - C_{it}) \, \alpha_t \, 0.04 > F^P_{it} \, (1 + r_{f,t+1}) \tag{11}$$

This condition is similar to the condition used by Mulligan and Sala-i-Martin (2000) in the context of the demand for interest-bearing assets more generally.

Since the incentive to participate is linear in financial wealth, one can estimate the cross-sectional distribution of F_{it}^P directly from the wealth distribution at date t. A simple nonparametric approach consists of calculating the percentage of households in different financial wealth groups who participate in the stock market. For example, if 27% of households with financial wealth of $10,000 participate, then 27% of these households must have participation costs below $10,000\alpha_t 0.04 = \$400\alpha_t$ [as in estimation A, replace $(W_{it}^{Post} - C_{it})$ with W_{it} and $F_{it}^P (1 + r_{f,t+1})$ with F_{it}^P]. Given the assumption that F_{it}^P is cross-sectionally uncorrelated with W_{it}, this implies that 27% of all households must have had participation costs below $400\alpha_t$. By splitting the sample into 10 wealth deciles and using this approach for each decile, one obtains 10 estimates of points on the cumulative distribution function (CDF) for the cross-sectional distribution of F_{it}^P.

How will the presence of an initial entry cost F^I or of transaction costs affect this estimation? Such costs imply that stock-market participation status becomes a state variable in the household's value function. This is the case because participating today affects the choices available tomorrow given the entry or transaction costs. In the example above where 27% of those with approximately $10,000 in financial wealth were stock-market participants, one can no longer be sure that this implies that 27% of the draws of F_{it}^P are below $400\alpha_t$. Let S_{it} be an indicator variable for whether household i participates in the stock market in period t. At date t, households can be split into four groups according to their participation choices at $t - 1$ and t: $(S_{i,t-1} = 0, S_{it} = 0)$, $(S_{i,t-1} = 0, S_{it} = 1)$, $(S_{i,t-1} = 1, S_{it} = 0)$, $(S_{i,t-1} = 1, S_{it} = 1)$. We would like to determine the percentage of the draws of F_{it}^P that are less than $400\alpha_t$. The group $(S_{i,t-1} = 0, S_{it} = 1)$ poses no difficulties. We can be sure that their F_{it}^P draw is less than $400\alpha_t$ (because their choice reveals that the period t benefit exceeds F^P plus any part of entry or transaction costs that must be covered by the period t benefits for entry to have been worthwhile). With the group $(S_{i,t-1} = 1, S_{it} = 0)$, we can be sure that their F_{it}^P draw is above $400\alpha_t$ because they have revealed that F_{it}^P exceeds their current period benefit of $400\alpha_t$ plus any future transaction costs they may save by staying in the market during this period.[26] The possible misclassifications arise for the groups choosing $(S_{i,t-1} = 0, S_{it} = 0)$ or $(S_{i,t-1} = 1, S_{it} = 1)$. Those choosing $(S_{i,t-1} = 0, S_{it} = 0)$ reveal only that $400\alpha_t$ is not sufficient to cover F_{it}^P plus any part of the entry and transaction costs that must be covered by a period t gain for entry to have been optimal. Thus, they reveal $F_{it}^P \geq \$400\alpha_t - z_{it}^{00}$ for some positive value z_{it}^{00}. Using the approach outlined above and classifying them all as having $F_{it}^P \geq \$400\alpha_t$

---

26. For example, a household with a temporary increase in consumption needs may decide to run down only nonstock wealth in this period and thus save the transaction costs involved in trading stocks.

leads one to overestimate the deciles of the cost distribution. However, those choosing $(S_{i,t-1} = 1, S_{it} = 1)$ lead to a counterbalancing bias: they reveal only that $\$400\alpha_t$ plus any future transaction costs they save by staying in the market during this period exceeds F_{it}^P; i.e., that $F_{it}^P \leq \$400\alpha_t + z_{it}^{11}$ for some positive value z_{it}^{11}. Thus, classifying them all as having $F_{it}^P \leq \$400\alpha_t$ leads one to understimate the deciles of the cost distribution. Overall, if an equal number of each of the $(S_{i,t-1} = 0, S_{it} = 0)$ households and the $(S_{i,t-1} = 1, S_{it} = 1)$ households are misclassified, then the approach outlined, assuming the absence of transaction costs, will lead to an unbiased estimate of the cross-sectional distribution of F_{it}^P. Because it is difficult to evaluate whether the two biases are likely to cancel each other, the cost distributions estimated below should be interpreted with some caution.

In both estimation A and B, one can allow for heterogeneity in α_{it} across households (rather than only across time). Nonparticipants may have chosen to stay out of the market due to a low optimal stock share conditional on participation. Accounting for heterogeneity based on a sample selection model has only small effects on the results, however, and for simplicity is therefore omitted from the results shown. Essentially, this is due to the fact that while the fit in models of the stock-market participation decision is quite high, models of the share invested in stocks conditional on participation typically has low explanatory power (possibly due to transaction costs of portfolio adjustment leading to substantial differences between optimal and observed portfolio shares for equity).

The results of estimation B are shown in Figure 10 for the sample of all households with positive financial wealth. Again assume that α_{it} (the actual or potential share of financial wealth invested in stocks) for each household equals the average value for participants in the PSID in that year (43.4 for 1984, 43.6 for 1989, and 55.2 for 1994). Households with no financial wealth provide no information about the participation cost in this approach because their benefit of stock-market entry is zero, assuming they cannot borrow or change their current consumption to invest in the stock market. The median per-period participation cost is around $350 (real 1982–1984 dollars) for 1994, around $500 for 1989, and around $800 for 1984. Even among very rich households, not all hold stocks, so the estimated CDF does not reach 1 at any wealth level (the point corresponding to the last wealth decile is not included in the graph but is also far below 1). This emphasizes the advantage of using a nonparametric approach because a parametric approach would impose the requirement that the CDF reaches 1. The economic implication is that participation costs are unlikely to be the explanation for nonparticipation among high-wealth households. More generally, if some of the nonparticipants at each wealth level have chosen not to hold stocks for reasons other than participation

Figure 10 ESTIMATED CDF OF PER-PERIOD STOCK-MARKET
PARTICIPATION COST, PSID

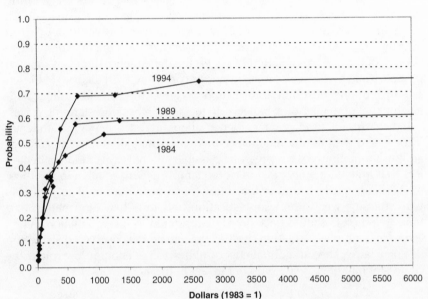

costs, my estimated CDF of the cost distribution will be shifted down
compared to the true CDF.

Overall the results of the estimations of stock-market participation costs
show that, while it is not reasonable to claim that participation costs can
reconcile the choices of all nonparticipants, modest costs are sufficient to
understand the choices of a large part of these households due to their
fairly low amounts of financial wealth.

6. Conclusion

Behavioral finance, and behavioral economics more generally, is a very
active area of research. The state of the literature is still one of exploration,
with little agreement among researchers on what the most important
investor biases are from an asset-pricing perspective.

In this paper I have argued that more direct evidence about the beliefs
and actions of investors would make behavioral theories more convincing
to outsiders, many of whom remain unconvinced that any of the multi-
tude of biases documented in the psychology literature and the experimental literature have much impact on asset prices (see Hirshleifer [2001]
for a thorough discussion of the evidence from psychology and experiments). To exemplify the potential value of such direct evidence, I have

analyzed new data from UBS/Gallup on investor expectations and stock-holdings for 1998–2002. The evidence suggests that, even for wealthy investors, (1) expected returns were high at the peak of the market; (2) many investors thought the market was overvalued but would not correct quickly; (3) investors' beliefs depend on their own investment experience (a version of the law of small numbers); (4) the dependence of beliefs on own past portfolio performance is asymmetric, consistent with theories of biased self-attribution; and (5) investor beliefs do affect their stockholdings, suggesting that understanding beliefs is in fact useful for understanding prices.

I then turned to existing evidence about investor behaviors that are inconsistent with traditional finance theory recommendations. Information and/or transaction costs represent a possible rational explanation of behaviors that involve too little action or too simple actions relative to the theoretical benchmark. I argued that many such behaviors tend to diminish with investor wealth and sophistication and thus that information and transaction costs should be seriously considered as an explanation. As an example, a simple calculation showed that, given the observed distribution of financial wealth, an annual cost of about $55 is enough to explain the choices of half of those who do not invest in the stock market.

REFERENCES

Abreu, D., and M. Brunnermeier. (2001). Bubbles and crashes. *Econometrica* 71(1):173–204.

Abreu, D., and M. Brunnermeier. (2002). Synchronization risk and delayed Arbitrage. *Journal of Financial Economics* 66:341–360.

Agnew, J., Balduzzi, P. L. and A. Sunden. (2003). Portfolio choice and trading in a large 401(k) plan. *American Economic Review* 93(1):193–215.

Alessie, R., S. Hochguertel, and A. van Soest. (2002). Household portfolios in the Netherlands. In *Household Portfolios*, L. Guiso, M. Haliassos, and T. Jappelli (eds.). Cambridge, MA:MIT Press, pp. 341–388.

Ameriks, J., and S. P. Zeldes. (2001). How do household portfolio shares vary with age? Working Paper, Columbia University.

Banz, R. W. (1981). The relationship between return and the market value of common stocks. *Journal of Financial and Quantitative Analysis* 14:421–441.

Barber, B. M., and T. Odean. (2000). Trading is hazardous to your wealth: The common stock investment performance of individual investors. *Journal of Finance* 55(2):773–806.

Barber, B. M., and T. Odean. (2002). All that glitters: The effect of attention and news on the buying behavior of individual and institutional investors. University of California, Davis. Working Paper.

Barberis, N., A. Shleifer, and R. Vishny. (1998). A Model of investor sentiment. *Journal of Financial Economics* 49:307–343.

Barberis, N., and R. Thaler. (2002). A survey of behavioral finance. In *Handbook of the Economics of Finance*, G. Constantinides, M. Harris, and R. Stulz (eds.). Forthcoming.

Benartzi, S. (2001). Excessive extrapolation and the allocation of 401(k) accounts to company stock. *Journal of Finance* 56(5):1747–1764.

Benartzi, S., and R. H. Thaler. (2001). Naive diversification strategies in defined contribution saving plans. *American Economic Review* March: 79–98.

Berk, J. B., R. C. Green, and V. Naik. (1999). Optimal investment, growth options and Security Returns. *Journal of Finance* 54:1553–1608.

Bernard, V. L., and J. K. Thomas. (1989). Post-earnings-announcement drift: Delayed price response or risk premium? *Journal of Accounting Research* 27:1–36.

Bernheim, B. D., and D. M. Garrett. (2003). The effects of financial education in the workplace: Evidence from a survey of households. *Journal of Public Economics* 87(7–8):1487–1519.

Bernheim, B. D., D. M. Garrett, and D. M. Maki. (2001). Education and saving: The long-term effects of high school financial curriculum mandates. *Journal of Public Economics* 80(3):435–465.

Blume, M. E., J. Crockett, and I. Friend. (1974). Stock ownership in the United States: Characteristics and trends. *Survey of Current Business* 54(11):16–40.

Brav, A., R. Lehavy, and R. Michaely. (2002). Expected return and asset pricing. Duke University. Working Paper.

Brown, P., N. Chappel, R. da Silva Rosa, and T. Walter. (2002). The reach of the disposition effect: Large sample evidence across investor classes. University of Sydney. Working Paper.

Brunnermeier, M. K., and S. Nagel. (2002). Arbitrage at its limits: Hedge funds and the technology bubble. Princeton University. Working Paper.

Campbell, J. Y. (2000). Asset pricing at the millennium. *Journal of Finance* 55(4):1515–1567.

Chiteji, N. S., and F. P. Stafford. (2000). Asset ownership across generations. Population Studies Center at the Institute for Social Research, University of Michigan. Research Report No. 00–454.

Cohen, R. B., P. A. Gompers, and T. Vuolteenaho. (2002). Who underreacts to cash-flow news? Evidence from trading between individuals and institutions. *Journal of Financial Economics* 66(2–3):409–462.

Coval, J. D., D. Hirshleifer, and T. Shumway. (2002). Can individual investors beat the market? Harvard Business School. Working Paper.

Coval, J., and T. J. Moskowitz. (1999). Home bias at home: Local equity preference in domestic portfolios. *Journal of Finance* 54:2045–2074.

Coval, J., and T. J. Moskowitz. (2001). The geography of investment: Informed trading and asset prices. *Journal of Political Economy* 4(109):811–841.

Daniel, K., D. Hirshleifer, and A. Subrahmanyam. (1998). Investor psychology and security market under- and overreactions. *Journal of Finance* 53(5):1839–1886.

Daniel, K., D. Hirshleifer, and S. H. Teoh. (2002). Investor psychology and capital markets: Evidence and policy implications. *Journal of Monetary Economics* 49:139–209.

DeBondt, W. F. M., and R. H. Thaler. (1985). Does the stock market overreach? *Journal of Finance* 40:793–808.

DeLong, J. B., A. Shleifer, L. Summers, and R. J. Waldmann. (1990). Noise trader risk in financial markets. *Journal of Political Economy* 98:703–738.

Dhar, R., and N. Zhu. (2002). Up close and personal: An individual level analysis of the disposition effect. Yale School of Management. Working Paper.

Diether, K., C. J. Malloy, and A. Scherbina. (2002). Differences of opinion and the cross section of stock returns. *Journal of Finance* 57:2113–2141.

Duflo, E., and E. Saez. (2002). Participation and investment decisions in a retirement plan: The influence of colleagues' choices. *Journal of Public Economics* 85:121–148.

Eymann, A., and A. Borsch-Supan. (2002). Household portfolios in Germany. In *Household Portfolios*, L. Guiso, M. Haliassos, and T. Jappelli (eds.) Cambridge, MA: MIT Press, pp. 291–340.

Fama, E. F. (1998). Market efficiency, long-term returns and behavioral finance. *Journal of Financial Economics* 49:283–306.

Fama, E. F., and K. R. French. (1992). The cross-section of expected stock returns. *Journal of Finance* 47(2):427–465.

Fisher, K. L., and M. Statman. (2002). Blowing bubbles. *Journal of Psychology and Financial Markets* 3(1):53–65.

French, K. R., and J. M. Poterba. (1991). Investor diversification and international equity Markets. *American Economic Review* 81(2):222–226.

Frieder, L., and A. Subrahmanyam. (2002). Brand perceptions and the market for common stock. UCLA. Working Paper.

Genesove, D., and C. Mayer. (2001). Loss aversion and seller behavior: Evidence from the housing market. 116(4):1233–1260.

Goetzmann, W. N., and A. Kumar. (2001). Equity portfolio diversification. Cambridge, MA: National Bureau of Economic Research. NBER Working Paper No. 8686.

Goetzmann, W. N., and M. Massa. (2003). Disposition matters: Volume, volatility and price impact of a behavioral bias. Cambridge, MA: National Bureau of Economic Research. NBER Working Paper No 9499.

Gomes, J. F., L. Kogan, and L. Zhang. (2003). Equilibrium cross-section of returns. *Journal of Political Economy* 111:693–732.

Graham, J. R., and C. R. Harvey. (2001). Expectations of equity risk premia, volatility and asymmetry from a corporate finance perspective. Fuqua School of Business. Working Paper.

Grinblatt, M., and B. Han. (2002). The disposition effect and momentum. UCLA. Working Paper.

Grinblatt, M., and M. Keloharju. (2000). The investment behavior and performance of various investor types: A study of Finland's unique data set. *Journal of Financial Economics* 55:43–67.

Grinblatt, M., and M. Keloharju. (2001a). How distance, language, and culture influence stockholdings and trades. *Journal of Finance* 56(3):1053–1073.

Grinblatt, M., and M. Keloharju. (2001b). What makes investors trade? *Journal of Finance* 56(2):589–616.

Grossman, S. J., and J. E. Stiglitz. (1980). On the impossibility of informationally efficient markets. *American Economic Review* 70(3):393–408.

Guiso, L., M. Haliassos, and T. Jappelli. (2002). Household portfolios. Cambridge, MA: MIT Press.

Guiso, L., and T. Jappelli. (2002). Households' portfolios in Italy. In *Household Portfolios*, L. Guiso, M. Haliassos and T. Jappelli (eds.). Cambridge, MA:MIT Press, pp. 251–290.

Heath, C., S. Huddart, and M. Lang. (1999). Psychological factors and stock option exercise. *Quarterly Journal of Economics* 114(2):601–627.

Heaton, J., and D. Lucas. (1999). Stock prices and fundamentals. In *NBER Macroeconomics Annual 1999*, B. Bernanke and J. J. Rotemberg (eds.). Cambridge, MA: MIT Press, pp. 213–242.

Hirshleifer, D. (2001). Investor psychology and asset pricing. *Journal of Finance* 64:1533–1597.

Hong, H. G., J. D. Kubik, and A. Solomon. (2000). Security analysts' career concerns and herding of earnings forecasts. *Rand Journal of Economics* 31:121–144.

Hong, H., J. D. Kubik, and J. Stein. (2003). Social interaction and stock market participation. *Journal of Finance* Forthcoming.

Hong, H., and J. C. Stein. (1999). A unified theory of underreaction, momentum trading, and overreaction in asset markets. *Journal of Finance* 54(6):2143–2184.

Huberman, G. (2001). Familiarity breeds investment. *Review of Financial Studies* 14(3):659–680.

Investment Company of America and the Securities Industry Association. (1999). Equity ownership in America. Washington, D. C.: Investment Company Institute.

Investment Company Institute. (2002). Total shareholder cost of mutual funds: An update. *Fundamentals*, 11(4):1–8.

Jegadeesh, N. (2000). Long-run performance of seasoned equity offerings: Benchmark errors and biases in expectations. *Financial Management* 29(3):5–30.

Jegadeesh, N., and S. Titman. (1993). Returns to buying winners and selling losers: Implications for stock market efficiency. *Journal of Finance* 48:65–91.

Jones, C. M. (2001). A century of stock market liquidity and trading costs. Columbia University. Working Paper.

Kahneman, D., and A. Tversky. (1979). Prospect theory: An analysis of decision under risk. *Econometrica* 46:171–185.

Lamont, O. A. (2002). Macroeconomic forecasts and microeconomic forecasters. *Journal of Economic Behavior and Organization* 48:265–280.

La Porta, R., J. Lakonishok, A. Shleifer, and R. W. Vishny. (1997). Good news for value stocks: Further evidence on market efficiency. *Journal of Finance* 52:859–874.

Loughran, T., and J. Ritter. (1995). The new issues puzzle. *Journal of Finance* 50:23–52.

Luttmer, E. G. J. (1999). What level of fixed costs can reconcile asset returns and consumption choices. *Journal of Political Economy* 107(5):969–997.

Mankiw, N. G., R. Reis, and J. Wolfers. (2003). Disagreement about inflation expectations. In *Macroeconomics Annual 2003*, M. Gertler and K. Rogoff (eds.). Cambridge, MA: MIT Press, pp. xxx–xxx.

Massa, M., and A. Simonov. (2003). Behavioral biases and portfolio choice. INSEAD. Working Paper.

Miller, E. (1977). Risk, uncertainty, and divergence of opinion. *Journal of Finance* 32:1151–1168.

Mulligan, C., and X. Sala-i-Martin. (2000). Extensive margins and the demand for money at low interest rates. *Journal of Political Economy* 108(5):961–991.

New York Stock Exchange. (2000). Shareownership 2000. Available at http://www.nyse.com/pdfs/shareho.pdf (accessed fund 3, 2003).

Odean, T. (1999). Do investors trade too much? *American Economic Review* 89(5):1279–1298.

Odean, T. (1998). Are investors reluctant to realize their losses? *Journal of Finance* 53(5):1775–1798.

Paiella, M. (1999). Transaction costs and limited stock market participation to reconcile asset prices and consumption choices. University College London. Working Paper.

Polkovnichenko, V. (2001). Limited stock market participation and the equity premium. University of Minnesota. Working Paper.

Pratt, J. W. (1964). Risk aversion in the small and the large. *Econometrica* 32:122–136.

Rabin, M. (2002). Inference by believers in the law of small numbers. *Quarterly Journal of Economics* 117(3):775–816.

Rubinstein, M. (2001). Rational markets: Yes or no? The affirmative case. *Financial Analysts Journal*, May/June, 57(3):15–29.

Samuelson, W., and R. J. Zeckhauser. (1988). Status quo bias in decision making. *Journal of Risk and Uncertainty*, 1 (March, 1):7–59.

Shapira, Z., and I. Venezia. (2001). Patterns of behavior of professionally managed and independent investors. *Journal of Banking and Finance* 25:1573–1587.

Shefrin, H., and M. Statman. (1985). The disposition to sell winners too early and ride losers too long: Theory and evidence. *Journal of Finance* 40(3): 777–790.

Shiller, R. J., F. Kon-Ya, and Y. Tsutsui. (1996). Why did the Nikkei crash? Expanding the scope of expectations data collection. *Review of Economics and Statistics* 78(1):156–164.

Shleifer, A. (2000). *Inefficient Markets: An Introduction to Behavioral Finance*, Oxford, England: Oxford University Press.

Shleifer, A., and R. Vishny. (1997). The limits to arbitrage. *Journal of Finance* 52:35–55.

Souleles, N. S. (2001). Consumer sentiment: Its rationality and usefulness in forecasting expenditure—Evidence from the Michigan micro data. *Journal of Money, Credit, and Banking*, forthcoming.

Vissing-Jorgensen, A. (1998). Limited stock market participation. Department of Economics, MIT. Ph.D. Thesis.

Vissing-Jorgensen, A. (1999). Comment on stock prices and fundamentals. *NBER Macroeconomics Annual 1999*. Cambridge, MA: The MIT Press, pp. 242–253.

Vissing-Jorgensen, A. (2002). Towards an explanation of household portfolio choice heterogeneity: Nonfinancial income and participation cost structures. Northwestern University. Working Paper.

Comment

JOHN Y. CAMPBELL
Harvard University and NBER

Almost 20 years ago, Robert Shiller, Lawrence Summers, and Richard Thaler challenged the finance profession to take seriously the possibility that investor behavior and asset prices deviate from the predictions of simple rational models. Since that time, behavioral finance has become one of the most active areas in financial economics, maturing to the point where it can be summarized in both popular and professional books (Shiller, 2000; Shleifer, 2000). Behavioral economics has had great success more generally, as illustrated by the award of the 2001 Clark Medal to Matthew Rabin and the 2002 Nobel Prize to Daniel Kahneman and

Vernon Smith, and behavioral finance is probably the most successful application of this approach.

In asset pricing, it is often hard to draw clear distinctions between behavioral and other research. Empirical researchers document systematic tendencies for some types of assets to outperform others, or for assets to perform better at some times than others. Very weak restrictions on asset markets ensure that these patterns can be explained by the properties of a stochastic discount factor that summarizes the rewards for taking on different kinds of risks. Behavioral finance models may derive the stochastic discount factor from nonstandard models of investor preferences, such as the prospect theory of Kahneman and Tversky (1979), but this can be hard to distinguish from more conventional models with features such as habit formation.

Behavioral finance is more distinctive in its insistence that we should try to measure the beliefs and actions of particular investors. We should not assume that investors' beliefs are homogeneous or rational, or that they deviate only idiosyncratically from a common set of rational beliefs. Rather, we should identify meaningful groups of investors and explore the possibility that these groups have different beliefs that induce them to trade with one another. Equilibrium asset prices emerge from the interactions of these heterogeneous investors.

Initially, the behavioral literature distinguished two groups of investors: rational investors and irrational noise traders. This raises the question of which investors play the role of noise traders. Much recent work has emphasized the distinction between individual investors, who may be particularly susceptible to cognitive limitations and psychological biases, and institutions, which seem likely to be more rational but may be limited in their risk-taking capacity. Vissing-Jorgensen's paper follows this tradition and examines a fascinating new dataset on the expectations of individual investors.

1. The UBS/Gallup Survey

The UBS/Gallup telephone survey has some inherent limitations. The most serious issue is whether respondents answer the survey questions accurately. Any survey that involves telephoning people at home in the evening is likely to elicit hasty or flippant responses. This is a particular problem here because the survey is relatively ambitious, going far beyond simple questions with binary answers such as yes/no or Republican/ Democrat. Accurate answers require both effort and comprehension. Questions about recent portfolio performance, for example, may require respondents to aggregate information from multiple brokerage and retirement accounts, while questions about expected future long-term returns require respondents to understand the difference between annual and cumulative returns. These problems do not mean that the data are worthless, but they do limit the weight that can be placed on the results.

A second limitation of the UBS/Gallup survey is that it is a series of cross sections and not a panel; thus, it cannot be used to track the expectations of particular individuals through time. Previous research has shown that the beliefs of different market participants may evolve in very different ways. Brav, Lehavy, and Michaely (2002), for example, look at the price targets issued by stock analysts and use these to construct analysts' return expectations. They argue that these numbers represent the expectations not only of the analysts themselves but also of the investors who follow them. They compare the price targets of analysts employed by sell-side brokerage firms (First Call data over the period 1997–2001, covering 7000 firms) with the price targets of independent analysts (Value Line data over a longer period—1987–2001—covering just under 3000 firms). They find that sell-side analysts' return forecasts increased with the level of the stock market in the late 1990s, while independent analysts' forecasts decreased throughout the 1990s. These discrepancies may be caused by honest differences of opinion, by differences in the horizon of the return forecast (one year for sell-side analysts, four years for independent analysts), or by the investment banking ties of sell-side analysts that induced them to tout the stocks of client companies. Regardless of the source, differences in analysts' opinions might well have led some individual investors to increase their return expectations in the late 1990s even while other investors were reducing their expectations.

2. The Distribution of Return Expectations

Although the UBS/Gallup survey is not a panel, there is much that can be learned from the cross-sectional distribution of return expectations within each month. Figure 2 in the paper shows that the cross-sectional standard deviation of return forecasts averages around 10%, comparable to the cross-sectional mean in Figure 1. Individual investors clearly do not have homogeneous expectations. In addition, the cross-sectional standard deviation appears to increase in the late 1990s, peaking in 2000, and then declines modestly. This pattern would be expected if some investors reacted to high returns in the late 1990s by increasing their return expectations, in the manner of sell-side analysts, while other investors decreased their expectations, in the manner of independent analysts.

Figure 2 also shows a great deal of variability in the cross-sectional standard deviation from month to month, and this tends to obscure the lower-frequency variation in disagreement. It would be good to know more about the possible sources of this high-frequency variation in the cross-sectional standard deviation of return expectations. For example, how much time-series variation would be expected just from sampling error if the true cross-sectional standard deviation is constant and 1000 households are interviewed each month?

The heterogeneity of investors' expectations raises difficult issues when one tries to summarize the survey results in a single average return expectation. The paper emphasizes an equal-weighted average, sometimes with an adjustment for the sampling methods used in the survey. This average, shown in Figure 1, increases in the late 1990s and declines after 2000. For the determination of asset prices, however, a wealth-weighted average is more relevant because wealthy investors have a much greater effect on asset demands than poor investors do. Vissing-Jorgensen reports that wealthy investors, with more than $100,000 in assets, have lower return expectations throughout the sample period but that their average expectations have the same time pattern shown in Figure 1.

If investors are constrained from selling shares short, or if they are reluctant to do so, then the most optimistic investors have a disproportionate influence on prices. The high level of disagreement about future stock returns throughout the sample, and particularly in 2000, indicates that this problem is relevant and that a wealth-weighted average return expectation understates the average demand for stocks by individual investors. Overall, the UBS/Gallup data suggest that optimism among individual investors was an important source of demand for stocks in the late 1990s. This raises the question of why individual investors were so optimistic in this period.

3. Irrational Extrapolation?

One plausible story is that individuals overreact to their recent past experience, irrationally extrapolating it into the future. According to this story, a series of favorable shocks during the 1990s set the stage for a speculative bubble at the end of the decade.

Although the UBS/Gallup survey does not follow investors through time, it does ask them to report their age, the number of years for which they have been investing, and their recent past portfolio returns. This feature of the data allows Vissing-Jorgensen to ask whether investors irrationally extrapolate their own past experience. She argues that if this is the case, then young and inexperienced investors should be more optimistic than older and experienced investors at the market peak because they place more weight on recent high returns in forming their expectations. The evidence, reported in Figures 4 and 5, turns out to be mixed. Young and inexperienced investors do have higher return expectations than do older and experienced investors at the market peak in 2000, but as the market falls in 2001 and 2002, the gap in expected returns narrows only for young investors and not for inexperienced investors.

Vissing-Jorgensen argues that reported past portfolio returns provide additional evidence of irrational extrapolation. Investors who report high past portfolio returns also expect higher future returns on the market (Figure 6), and the effect of past portfolio returns on expectations is stronger when those past returns are positive (Figure 8). Vissing-Jorgensen interprets the latter result as evidence for biased self-attribution; the human tendency to treat past success as meaningful evidence about one's skill and to treat past failure as random bad luck.

I believe that the results using past portfolio returns should be treated with caution. A first problem is that past returns are self-reported and may well reflect an investor's general optimism. A respondent who receives the UBS/Gallup telephone call when she is in a good mood may say that her portfolio has been doing well and that the market will do well in the future, whereas another respondent who is in a bad mood may give more pessimistic responses. This sort of correlated measurement error could account for the patterns shown in Figure 6.

A second problem is more subtle. The results shown in Figure 8 are based on a regression of the following form:

$$R_{it}^e = \alpha_t + \beta_t \text{age}_{it} + \gamma_t \text{ experience}_{it} + \theta_1 R_{i,t-1}^{P+} + \theta_2 R_{i,t-1}^{P-} + u_{it}$$

Here i denotes an individual respondent and t denotes a time period. The intercept and the coefficients on age and experience are all time-varying, but the coefficients on lagged positive portfolio return $R_{i,t-1}^{P+}$ and lagged negative portfolio return $R_{i,t-1}^{P-}$ are fixed. The regression is estimated over the period 2000–2002. Figure 8 reflects the fact that θ_1 is estimated to be large and positive, while θ_2 is estimated to be small and negative.

This regression is hard to interpret because past portfolio returns are not exogenous and are likely to be correlated with other determinants of return expectations that are omitted from the regression. Also, more investors had positive past portfolio returns in 2000 than in 2002. Thus, the separate coefficients on $R_{i,t-1}^{P+}$ and $R_{i,t-1}^{P-}$ may capture a change over time in the correlation between past portfolio performance and return expectations, rather than a true structural difference between the effects of positive and negative past returns. The signs of the coefficients could be explained, for example, if investors are exogenously optimistic or pessimistic and invest accordingly (optimists invest in stocks and pessimists invest in Treasury bills). In 2000, optimists had high past returns and reported high return expectations, while pessimists had mediocre past returns and reported low return expectations, generating a positive coefficient θ_1. In 2002, optimists had low past returns and reported high return expectations, while pessimists had mediocre past returns and reported low return expectations, generating a negative coefficient θ_2.

4. The Limitations of Behavioral Finance

Stepping back from the details of the empirical work in the paper, the difficulty in interpreting individual investors' optimism at the end of the 1990s illustrates the challenges that face behavioral finance. Compared with traditional models in financial economics, behavioral models often have a degree of flexibility that permits reinterpretation to fit new facts. Such flexibility makes it hard either to disprove or to validate behavioral models. For example, the theory of biased self-attribution does not make a clear prediction about individual investors' expectations of returns on the aggregate stock market. The theory says that investors interpret their past success as evidence of their skill, but it is not clear why people who have earned high returns in stocks and believe themselves to be skillful investors should necessarily expect the stock market to keep rising. They might just as well switch from one asset class to another in the belief that they have identified the next new trend.

The lack of theoretical discipline would not be a problem if empirical research on investor behavior indicated that individual investors are consistently biased in a particular direction. Unfortunately, this is not the case. While some behavior patterns are consistent with irrational extrapolation, others contradict it. Individual investors are keen to put their money in mutual funds that have performed well recently (Chevalier and Ellison, 1997; Sirri and Tufano, 1998), but they also tend to sell stocks that have performed well and hold on to those stocks that have performed badly (the disposition effect of Shefrin and Statman [1985] and Odean [1998]). While the mutual fund evidence is consistent with irrational extrapolation, it may also reflect the mechanism by which skillful fund managers are compensated (Berk and Green, 2002). The disposition effect is hard to reconcile with either the principles of rational investing or irrational extrapolation. It is sometimes attributed to prospect theory, combined with stock-level mental accounting, but this leaves an open question about the balance between these forces and the opposing force of irrational extrapolation.

The finance profession has learned a great deal from the detailed and careful empirical research on investor behavior that has been promoted by behavioral finance. Vissing-Jorgensen's paper is an excellent example of this type of research. I do not believe, however, that behavioral finance has yet been able to offer a coherent theoretical framework comparable to traditional finance theory. It is better thought of as a set of observed behaviors, particularly prevalent among individual investors with less experience and wealth, that can affect asset prices and, just as important, the financial well-being of these investors. Financial economists should take such behaviors seriously and should try to use financial education to reduce their incidence.

REFERENCES

Berk, J., and R. Green. (2002). Mutual fund flows and performance in rational markets. University of California Berkeley. Unpublished Paper.
Brav, A., R. Lehavy, and R. Michaely. (2002). Expected return and asset pricing. Duke University. Unpublished Paper.
Chevalier, J., and G. Ellison. (1997). Risk taking by mutual funds as a response to incentives. *Journal of Political Economy* 105:1167–1200.
Kahneman, D., and A. Tversky. (1979). Prospect theory: An analysis of decision under risk. *Econometrica* 46:171–185.
Odean, T. (1998). Are investors reluctant to realize their losses? *Journal of Finance* 53:1775–1798.
Shefrin, H., and M. Statman. (1985). The disposition to sell winners too early and ride losers too long: Theory and evidence. *Journal of Finance* 40:777–790.
Shiller, R. (2000). *Irrational Exuberance*. Princeton, NJ: Princeton University Press.
Shleifer, A. (2000). *Inefficient Markets: An Introduction to Behavioral Finance*, Oxford, England: Oxford University Press.
Sirri, E., and P. Tufano. (1998). Costly search and mutual fund flows. *Journal of Finance* 53:1589–1622.

Comment

OWEN A. LAMONT
School of Management, Yale University, and NBER

The U.S. stock market has experienced amazing upheaval in the past five years. Valuations seemed absurdly high in the period 1998–2000, especially for technology-related stocks. Many previously identified anomalies, particularly those relating to new issues, grew larger during the tech-stock mania episode. Other previously identified patterns relating to scaled prices (that is, price expressed as a ratio such as price/dividend or price/book value) seemed to go away entirely in the late 1990s, only to return with a vengeance in 2000–2002. This period will be studied by financial economists for years to come because it is an extraordinarily revealing episode full of important clues.

Vissing-Jorgensen discusses some fascinating evidence about this period, most of it derived from a continuing survey of investors from 1998–2002. Like all data, this data has limitations. First, all survey data should be regarded with skepticism and this type of survey more than most (I discuss this point further below). Second, it is a real shame this dataset starts in 1998 and does not include more of the pre-mania period. Despite these limitations, the data reveal many interesting facts that are useful for sorting out different hypotheses about the tech-stock mania.

Vissing-Jorgensen has done a great job in revealing the features of the data, taking what was undoubtedly a complicated and demanding task and making it look easy. There are many different ways this data could have been used, and I am convinced that the graphs, regressions, and statistical tests are accurately telling us what we need to know. Vissing-Jorgensen does many different things in the paper, but I am going to focus only on the main survey results and interpret them from my own perspective of what the tech-stock mania period was about.

1. Limitations of Survey Data

To me, survey data about expectations and beliefs is one of the weakest forms of data, just one rung above anecdotes in the quality ladder. I think we should always be suspicious of survey data on beliefs, especially involving abstract and intangible concepts (such as expected stock returns) that are unfamiliar to the respondents. This data is most useful when it is possible to cross-verify with data on actual (not self-reported) behavior observed by objective external measurement. I see survey evidence of this type as suggestive, but not definitive.

Fortunately, there is ample cross-verification for many of the patterns documented in the paper. For example, Figure 8 shows striking evidence for biased self-attribution (individuals believe good performance is due to their skill, but bad performance is due to luck). The fact that the performance is self-reported makes interpreting the results problematic. Fortunately, other evidence documents biased self-attribution. Barber and Odean (2002) document, using actual portfolio performance and actual trading, that investors who have done well in the past tend to increase their trading, consistent with the hypothesis that they believe themselves to be more skillful.

Having stated these reservations, let me say that I find nothing at all implausible in the results shown. They seem revealing about what was going through people's minds in real time. This survey is also potentially more reliable than surveys involving analyst expectations because these analysts have their own problems (most notably a pronounced optimistic bias).

2. Aggregate Expected Returns

There are three possible explanations for why the aggregate market was so extraordinarily high in the tech-stock mania period. The first explanation is the honest mistake hypothesis: investors believed that future profits would be extraordinarily high and set prices accordingly. As it turns out, this high-profit scenario did not occur, but perhaps at that time it was reasonable to forecast high profits. According to the honest mistake hypothesis, there is no special reason to think that investors believed that expected returns were either particularly high or particularly low in, say, March 2000. The honest mistake hypothesis appears to be the preferred explanation for true believers in the efficient market hypothesis.

The second explanation is the low expected return hypothesis. Under this hypothesis, everyone knew expected equity returns had fallen, but they were happy to hold stocks despite their lower returns. At the time, some asserted that the equity premium had fallen for various reasons: the increasingly broad ownership of stocks, lower economic risk, higher risk tolerance, more institutions to share risk, and demographic changes. The low expected return hypothesis is a bit shakier on explaining the dramatic fall in stock prices from 2000 to 2002, but perhaps for some reason the equity premium rose again. Like the honest mistake hypothesis, the low expected return hypothesis is consistent with frictionless efficient markets.

The third explanation is overpricing: investors set prices too high, either knowingly or unknowingly, and this overpricing was obvious to some set of rational and informed investors at the time. One particular version of the overpricing hypothesis is that some optimistic investors extrapolated returns into the future, not realizing that the market was overvalued. It could also be that many investors knew the market was overpriced but chose to buy stocks anyway. In either case, because mispricing is eventually corrected, the overpricing hypothesis predicts that when stocks are overpriced, subsequent long-term returns will be low as the correction takes place, which is exactly what happened.

Figure 1 refutes the low expected return hypothesis and also casts substantial doubt on the honest mistake hypothesis. Reported expected one-year returns were wildly optimistic in early 2000 and fell sharply in 2001 and 2002. This is exactly the opposite pattern required for the low expected return hypothesis. In reality, investors reported expectations were undoubtedly simply chasing past returns. This pattern is confirmed by a strong pattern in mutual fund flows: inflows also chase past returns. This return-chasing pattern occurs both in the cross section (top funds have big inflows) and in the time series (all stock funds have inflows when the stock market has done well). Indeed, one piece of confirming evidence for Figure 1 is that net flows to stock funds during this period roughly match the pattern of reported expected returns. In summary, naïve adaptive expectations appear to be an accurate model for many investors.

The honest mistake hypothesis takes another hit in Figure 3, which shows in early 2000 that about 50% of the respondents thought the market was overvalued, while less than 10% thought it was undervalued. If pessimists outnumber optimists by 5 to 1, that does not sound like an honest mistake. It sounds like many knew the market was too high, but for some reason they went along with the ride.

3. Heterogeneous Expectations and Short Sale Constraints

One of the most important contributions of the paper is its examination of differences of opinion among investors. Heterogeneity is an increasingly important topic in asset pricing as well as in macroeconomics (see the paper by Mankiw, Reis, and Wolfers in this volume, for example).

Combined with short sale constraints, differences of opinion can create overpricing. Short sale constraints are anything that inhibits investors from short selling securities; in the case of tech-stock mania, the main constraint was probably that pessimists thought that shorting tech stocks was too risky. In Figure 1, it is clear in hindsight that NASDAQ was too high at 3000 in 1999. But anyone shorting NASDAQ then would have suffered severe losses as NASDAQ went to 5000 in March 2000. As hedge fund manager Cliff Asness has commented about short sale constraints, "Our problem wasn't that we couldn't short NASDAQ in 1999, our problem was that we could and did."

As Miller (1977) pointed out, with short sale constraints, stock prices reflect only the views of the optimists. Thus, differences of opinion plus short sale constraints can lead to overpricing. Now, one reason opinions may differ is that some investors are irrationally optimistic—this is what I would call the behavioral finance explanation, and there is substantial evidence to support this view of tech-stock mania. However, Harrison and Kreps (1978) showed that even when all investors are rational but have different beliefs, overpricing can occur. Let me give an example of the Harrison and Kreps (1978) story. A remarkable property of this example, and one that fits well with the evidence given in the paper, is that everybody agrees that stocks are overpriced but they are still willing to hold stocks.

Suppose investor A and investor B have different beliefs about the prospects for the level of NASDAQ. Each investor knows what the other one believes, but they agree to disagree, so there is no asymmetric information. Now, it is a controversial issue in economic theory whether rational agents can agree to disagree, but let's leave that aside. Assume a simple setup with three dates, date 0, date 1, and date 2. For simplicity assume risk-neutral agents behaving competitively and a discount rate of zero. Assume also that there are sufficient numbers of type A and type B investors for each type to hold all of NASDAQ by themselves. Suppose it is currently date 0 and both investor A and investor B believe that NASDAQ is worth 2000 today. Specifically, they both believe that at date 2 it will be at 3000 with 50% probability and at 1000 with 50% probability. However, investor A thinks that at date 1, some news will arrive that will resolve all uncertainty, while investor B thinks there will be no relevant news released until date 2. This belief about the timing of news is the only disagreement between investor A and investor B (it is not necessary to state who, if either, is right in their beliefs). The Harrison and Kreps (1978) model has the remarkable property that, in the presence of short sale constraints, both investor A and investor B would be willing to hold NASDAQ at 2500 at date 0, despite the fact that they both think it is worth only 2000.

To get to this result, work backward from date 1, using the principle that with short sale constraints the optimist always sets the price. At date 1, if good news has arrived, then investor A will value NASDAQ at 3000, while investor B still thinks it is worth 2000; thus, the price will be 3000, investor A will hold all the asset, and investor B will hold none of it. If bad news arrives at date 1, the price will be 2000 and investor B will hold all of it. Because these two states happen with 50–50 probability, the date 0 expected price for date 1 is 2500. Thus at date 0, both investor A and investor B are willing to hold NASDAQ at a price of 2500. Although everyone thinks it is overvalued at date 0, they are willing to buy at date 0 because they believe they are following a dynamic trading strategy that will take advantage of the other guy. This example formalizes the notion of the greater fool theory of asset pricing. Note that, in this example, everyone agrees that long-term expected returns between date 0 and date 2 are low, and that a buy-and-hold strategy is a bad idea. If surveyed at date 0, both investor A and investor B would say that NASDAQ was overvalued relative to date 2 but fairly valued relative to date 1.

Key predictions of this story are that overpricing is highest when differences of opinion are highest, everyone agrees that prices are too high,
and trading volume is high because everyone is following dynamic trading strategies. Vissing-Jorgensen's evidence supports the first two predictions. Figure 2 shows disagreement peaked in early 2000, around the time
when stock prices peaked. Figure 1 shows that the majority of those who
had an opinion about the market thought it was overvalued. The third
prediction, about volume, is also supported by the events during this
period. Not only did tech stocks have high prices, they also had very high
volume. Volume on NASDAQ more than doubled between January 1999
and its peak in January 2001. Volume certainly seems like a key part of the
tech-stock mania story, and one that the honest mistake and low expected
return hypotheses cannot explain.

Another fact explained by the overpricing hypothesis is the high level
of stock issuance that occurred in 1998–2000. One interpretation is that
issuers and underwriters knew that stocks were overpriced and so rushed
to issue. Although Vissing-Jorgensen's survey does not include issuers,
evidence arising out of subsequent legal action against underwriters
(such as emails sent by investment-bank employees) is certainly consistent with the hypothesis that the underwriters thought the market was
putting too high a value on new issues. One way to think about issuance
is as a mechanism for overcoming short sale constraints. Both short selling and issuance have the effect of increasing the amount of stock that the
optimists can buy; both are examples of supply increasing in response to
high prices. Suppose you think lamont.com is overpriced in 1999. One
way to take advantage of this fact is to short the stock. In doing so, you
are selling overpriced shares to optimists. This action is risky, however,
because lamont.com might well double in price. A safer alternative action
is for you to start a new company that competes with lamont.com, call it
lamont2.com, and issue stock. This issue is another way to sell overpriced
shares to optimists.

4. Sources of Heterogeneity

Why might differences of opinion be more pronounced in 1998–2000 than
at other times? Miller (1977) presciently lists many of the characteristics
that lead to differences of opinion. The first is that the firm has a short
track record or has intangible prospects: "The divergence of opinion
about a new issue are greatest when the stock is issued. Frequently the
company has not started operations, or there is uncertainty about the success of new products or the profitability of a major business expansion"
(p. 1156).

The second is that the company has high visibility, so that there are many optimists: "Some companies are naturally well known because their products are widely advertised and widely consumed. . . . Of course, the awareness of a security may be increased if the issuing company receives much publicity. For instance, new products and technological breakthroughs are news so that companies producing such products receive more publicity" (p. 1165).

Tech stocks certainly fit both these criteria. Stocks like Amazon or AOL were familiar to the investing classes who used them, but unlike other familiar products (such as Coca-Cola), they had a short operating history, so that optimists could construct castles in the sky without fear of contradiction by fact. Vissing-Jorgensen reports survey data on Internet use that seems to fit this story. Those who used the Internet thought Internet stocks had higher expected returns than other stocks, and they were more likely to include Internet stocks in their portfolio.

Vissing-Jorgensen also documents another interesting fact: young investors expected higher returns than older (and wiser) investors. This fact illustrates another key principle of behavioral finance: there's a sucker born every minute. Folk wisdom on Wall Street often claims that overvaluation occurs when young and inexperienced investors (who did not live through the last bear market) come to dominate. Apparently there is some truth to this claim.

5. Conclusion

We need to understand the events of 1998–2002 if we are to have any hope of understanding how stock markets work. Economists have expended a lot of effort studying episodes such as the stock market crash of 1987, the crash of 1929, and various alleged bubbles such as tulip mania. We are fortunate that this particular episode is well documented. Any satisfactory explanation will need to explain the high level of prices, the high level of volume, the high level of stock issuance, and the forces that prevented pessimists from correcting prices. Vissing-Jorgensen's paper is a good first step in arriving at an explanation. Her results suggest to me that tech stocks were indeed identifiably overpriced in the tech-stock mania period.

REFERENCES

Barber, Brad M., and Terrance Odean. (2002). Online investors: Do the slow die first? *Review of Financial Studies* 15:455–487.

Harrison, J. Michael, and David M. Kreps. (1978). Speculative investor behavior in a stock market with heterogeneous expectations. *Quarterly Journal of Economics* 92:323–336.
Miller, Edward M. (1977). Risk, uncertainty, and divergence of opinion. *Journal of Finance* 32:1151–1168.

Discussion

Annette Vissing-Jorgensen agreed with the discussants that data reliability is an issue. However, she mentioned several pieces of evidence to support the fact that responses in the survey are not entirely noise. For example, respondents with higher market expectations put more in stocks than those with lower market expectations. Vissing-Jorgensen also suggested that the reliability of the survey data could be examined by looking at the length of time respondents took to complete the survey.

Rick Mishkin expanded on the comments of Owen Lamont about the structure of investment banking and the stock market bubble. He noted that bubbles occur when there is nonfundamental pricing of assets, but that this nonfundamental pricing can in fact be driven by institutions. He held that the U.S. stock market bubble of the 1990s was driven in part by a conflict of interest in investment banking between advice and sales. He mentioned that in Scandinavia and Japan, a combination of financial liberalization, government safety nets for the financial system, and poor prudential supervision had led to real estate bubbles. He recommended that policymakers should focus on institutions and regulation to understand and learn how to prevent bubbles. On this issue, Vissing-Jorgensen noted that the datasets described by John Campbell could be used to examine how price movements subsequent to earnings announcements depend on the independence of the analysts concerned.

Annamaria Lusardi was concerned by the implications of the paper's findings on the speed of learning for wealth accumulation. She speculated that the consequences for retirement savings could be substantial if investors do indeed learn very slowly. Vissing-Jorgensen responded that the fact that payoffs increase with wealth could be explained by costs of obtaining information. She noted that if this were indeed the case, it would suggest a role for investor education.

Mark Gertler was curious about whether survey respondents could be distinguished by frequency of trading. He pointed out that investors who adopt buy-and-hold strategies have less of an incentive to pay attention to the market and hence might have beliefs determined by outdated information. Vissing-Jorgensen said that it might be possible to perform this exercise eventually.

Kjetil Storesletten questioned the suggestion that short sale constraints could explain investor underperformance. He noted that if two-thirds of people expect the market to fall, there should be a substantial demand for short sales, and that this should lead to financial innovation. He suggested that it might not have been clear to investors at the time that there was a bubble. Vissing-Jorgensen responded that investors might not have been comfortable shorting the market because they thought that it would continue to go up before going down. She said that the bigger question was, Why are investor horizons so short? Owen Lamont commented that, for whatever reason, there are very few institutions allowing investors to go short. His view was that there was little demand for such institutions because psychological constraints made people reluctant to take negative positions, although they were quite happy to take zero positions.

Eva Nagypal was curious about how savings rates correlated with investor performance and behavior. Vissing-Jorgensen responded that those expecting high portfolio returns, i.e., of at least 20%, did save more but that otherwise there was no correlation between performance and savings.

N. Gregory Mankiw, Ricardo Reis,
and Justin Wolfers
HARVARD UNIVERSITY AND NBER; HARVARD UNIVERSITY; AND
STANFORD UNIVERSITY AND NBER

Disagreement About Inflation Expectations

1. Introduction

At least since Milton Friedman's renowned presidential address to the
American Economic Association in 1968, expected inflation has played a
central role in the analysis of monetary policy and the business cycle.
How much expectations matter, whether they are adaptive or rational,
how quickly they respond to changes in the policy regime, and many
related issues have generated heated debate and numerous studies. Yet
throughout this time, one obvious fact is routinely ignored: not everyone
has the same expectations.

This oversight is probably explained by the fact that, in much standard
theory, there is no room for disagreement. In many (though not all) textbook macroeconomic models, people share a common information set
and form expectations conditional on that information. That is, we often
assume that everyone has the same expectations because our models say
that they should.

The data easily reject this assumption. Anyone who has looked at survey data on expectations, either those of the general public or those of
professional forecasters, can attest to the fact that disagreement is substantial. For example, as of December 2002, the interquartile range of
inflation expectations for 2003 among economists goes from 1½% to 2½%.

We would like to thank Richard Curtin and Guhan Venkatu for help with data sources, and
Simon Gilchrist, Robert King, and John Williams for their comments. Doug Geyser and
Cameron Shelton provided research assistance. Ricardo Reis is grateful to the Fundacao
Ciencia e Tecnologia, Praxis XXI, for financial support.

Among the general public, the interquartile range of expected inflation goes from 0% to 5%.

This paper takes as its starting point the notion that this disagreement about expectations is itself an interesting variable for students of monetary policy and the business cycle. We document the extent of this disagreement and show that it varies over time. More important, disagreement about expected inflation moves together with the other aggregate variables that are more commonly of interest to economists. This fact raises the possibility that disagreement may be a key to macroeconomic dynamics.

A macroeconomic model that has disagreement at its heart is the sticky-information model proposed recently by Mankiw and Reis (2002). In this model, economic agents update their expectations only periodically because of the costs of collecting and processing information. We investigate whether this model is capable of predicting the extent of disagreement that we observe in the survey data, as well as its evolution over time.

The paper is organized as follows. Section 2 discusses the survey data on expected inflation that will form the heart of this paper. Section 3 offers a brief and selective summary of what is known from previous studies of survey measures of expected inflation, replicating the main findings. Section 4 presents an exploratory analysis of the data on disagreement, documenting its empirical relationship to other macroeconomic variables. Section 5 considers what economic theories of inflation and the business cycle might say about the extent of disagreement. It formally tests the predictions of one such theory—the sticky-information model of Mankiw and Reis (2002). Section 6 compares theory and evidence from the Volcker disinflation. Section 7 concludes.

2. Inflation Expectations

Most macroeconomic models argue that inflation expectations are a crucial factor in the inflation process. Yet the nature of these expectations—in the sense of precisely stating whose expectations, over which prices, and over what horizon—is not always discussed with precision. These are crucial issues for measurement.

The expectations of wage- and price-setters are probably the most relevant. Yet it is not clear just who these people are. As such, we analyze data from three sources. The Michigan Survey of Consumer Attitudes and Behavior surveys a cross section of the population about their expectations over the next year. The Livingston Survey and the Survey of Professional Forecasters (SPF) covers more sophisticated analysts—economists working

Table 1   SURVEYS OF INFLATION EXPECTATIONS

	Michigan survey	*Livingston survey*	*Survey of professional forecasters*
Survey population	Cross section of the general public	Academic, business, finance, market, and labor economists	Market economists
Survey organization	Survey Research Center, University of Michigan	Originally Joseph Livingston, an economic journalist; currently the Philadelphia Fed	Originally ASA/NBER; currently the Philadelphia Fed
Average number of respondents	Roughly 1000–3000 per quarter to 1977, then 500–700 per month to present	48 per survey (varies from 14–63)	34 per survey (varies from 9–83)
Starting date	Qualitative questions: 1946 Q1[1]; quantitative responses: January 1978	1946, first half (but the early data is unreliable)[1]	GDP deflator: 1968, Q4; CPI inflation: 1981, Q3
Periodicity	Most quarters from 1947 Q1 to 1977 Q4; every month from January 1978	Semi-annual	Quarterly
Inflation expectation	Expected change in prices over the next 12 months	Consumer Price Index (this quarter, in 2 quarters, in 4 quarters)	GDP deflator level, quarterly CPI level (6 quarters)

1. Our quantitative work focuses on the period from 1954 onward.

in industry and professional forecasters, respectively. Table 1 provides some basic details about the structure of these three surveys.[1]

Although we have three sources of inflation expectations data, throughout this paper we will focus on four, and occasionally five, series. Most papers analyzing the Michigan data cover only the period since 1978, during which these data have been collected monthly (on a relatively consistent basis), and respondents were asked to state their precise quantitative

1. For more details about the Michigan Survey, the Livingston Survey and the SPF, see Curtin (1996), Croushore (1997), and Croushore (1993), respectively.

Figure 1 MEDIAN INFLATION EXPECTATIONS AND ACTUAL INFLATION

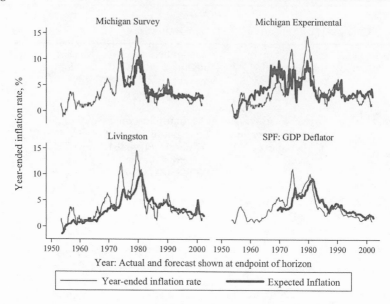

Year: Actual and forecast shown at endpoint of horizon

——— Year-ended inflation rate   ■■■■■ Expected Inflation

inflation expectations. However, the Michigan Survey of Consumer Attitudes and Behaviors has been conducted quarterly since 1946, although for the first 20 years respondents were asked only whether they expected prices to rise, fall, or stay the same. We have put substantial effort into constructing a consistent quarterly time series for the central tendency and dispersion of inflation expectations through time since 1948. We construct these data by assuming that discrete responses to whether prices are expected to rise, remain the same, or fall over the next year reflect underlying continuous expectations drawn from a normal distribution, with a possibly time-varying mean and standard deviation.[2] We will refer to these constructed data as the Michigan experimental series.

Our analysis of the Survey of Professional Forecasters will occasionally switch between our preferred series, which is the longer time series of forecasts focusing on the gross domestic product (GDP) deflator (starting in 1968, Q4), and the shorter consumer price index (CPI) series (which begins in 1981, Q3).

Figure 1 graphs our inflation expectations data. The horizontal axis refers to expectations at the endpoint of the relevant forecast horizon

2. Construction of this experimental series is detailed in the appendix, and we have published these data online at www.stanford.edu/people/jwolfers (updated January 13, 2004).

rather than at the time the forecast was made. Two striking features emerge from these plots. First, each series yields relatively accurate inflation forecasts. And second, despite the different populations being surveyed, they all tell a somewhat similar story.

By simple measures of forecast accuracy, all three surveys appear to be quite useful. Table 2 shows two common measures of forecast accuracy: the square root of the average squared error (RMSE) and the mean absolute error (MAE). In each case we report the accuracy of the median expectation in each survey, both over their maximal samples and for a common sample (September 1982–March 2002).

Panel A of the table suggests that inflation expectations are relatively accurate. As the group making the forecast becomes increasingly sophisticated, forecast accuracy appears to improve. However, Panel B suggests that these differences across groups largely reflect the different periods over which each survey has been conducted. For the common sample that all five measures have been available, they are all approximately equally accurate.

Of course, these results reflect the fact that these surveys have a similar central tendency, and this fact reveals as much as it hides. Figure 2 presents simple histograms of expected inflation for the coming year as of December 2002.

Here, the differences among these populations become starker. The left panel pools responses from the two surveys of economists and shows some agreement on expectations, with most respondents expecting inflation in the 1½ to 3% range. The survey of consumers reveals substantially greater disagreement. The interquartile range of consumer expectations stretches from 0 to 5%, and this distribution shows quite long tails, with 5% of the population expecting deflation, while 10% expect inflation of at

Table 2   INFLATION FORECAST ERRORS

	Michigan	Michigan experimental	Livingston	SPF–GDP deflator	SPF–CPI
Panel A: maximal sample					
Sample	Nov. 1974– May 2002	1954, Q4– 2002, Q1	1954, H1– 2001, H2	1969, Q4– 2002, Q1	1982, Q3– 2002, Q1
RMSE	1.65%	2.32%	1.99%	1.62%	1.29%
MAE	1.17%	1.77%	1.38%	1.22%	0.97%
Panel B: common time period (September 1982–March 2002)					
RMSE	1.07%	1.24%	1.28%	1.10%	1.29%
MAE	0.85%	0.95%	0.97%	0.91%	0.97%

least 10%. These long tails are a feature throughout our sample and are not a particular reflection of present circumstances. Our judgment (following Curtin, 1996) is that these extreme observations are not particularly informative, and so we focus on the median and interquartile range as the relevant indicators of central tendency and disagreement, respectively.

The extent of disagreement within each of these surveys varies dramatically over time. Figure 3 shows the interquartile range over time for each of our inflation expectations series. A particularly interesting feature of these data is that disagreement among professional forecasters rises and falls with disagreement among economists and the general public. Table 3 confirms that all of our series show substantial co-movement. This table focuses on quarterly data—by averaging the monthly Michigan numbers and linearly interpolating the semiannual Livingston numbers. Panel A shows correlation coefficients among these quarterly estimates. Panel B shows correlation coefficients across a smoothed version of the data (a five-quarter centered moving average of the interquartile range). (The experimental Michigan data show a somewhat weaker correlation, particularly in the high-frequency data, probably reflecting measurement error caused by the fact that these estimates rely heavily on the proportion of the sample expecting price declines—a small and imprecisely estimated fraction of the population.)

Figure 2 DISTRIBUTION OF INFLATION EXPECTATIONS

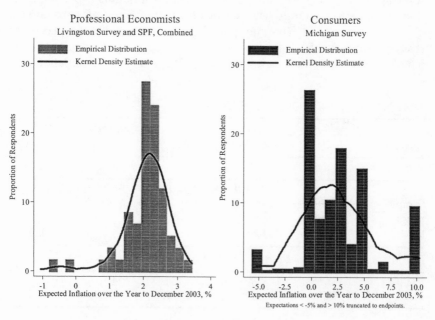

Figure 3 DISAGREEMENT OVER INFLATION EXPECTATIONS THROUGH
TIME

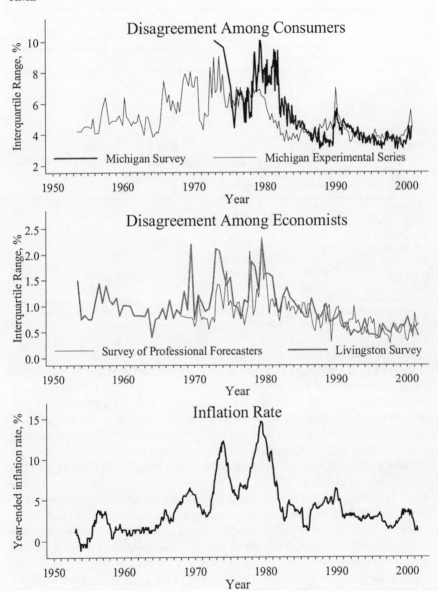

Date reflects when the forecast is made.

Table 3   DISAGREEMENT THROUGH TIME: CORRELATION ACROSS SURVEYS[1]

	Michigan	Michigan experimental	Livingston	SPF–GDP deflator	SPF–CPI
Panel A: actual quarterly data					
Michigan	1.000				
Michigan experimental	0.682	1.000			
Livingston	0.809	0.391	1.000		
SPF–GDP deflator	0.700	0.502	0.712	1.000	
SPF–CPI	0.667	0.231	0.702	0.688	1.000
Panel B: 5 quarter centered moving averages					
Michigan	1.000				
Michigan experimental	0.729	1.000			
Livingston	0.869	0.813	1.000		
SPF–GDP deflator	0.850	0.690	0.889	1.000	
SPF–CPI	0.868	0.308	0.886	0.865	1.000

1. Underlying data are quarterly. They are created by taking averages of monthly Michigan data and by linearly interpolating half-yearly Livingston data.

A final source of data on disagreement comes from the range of forecasts within the Federal Open Market Committee (FOMC), as published biannually since 1979 in the Humphrey-Hawkins testimony.[3] Individual-level data are not released, so we simply look to describe the broad pattern of disagreement among these experts. Figure 4 shows a rough (and statistically significant) correspondence between disagreement among policymakers and disagreement among professional economists. The correlation of the *range* of FOMC forecasts with the interquartile range of the Livingston population is 0.34, 0.54 or 0.63, depending on which of the three available FOMC forecasts we use. While disagreement among Fed-watchers rose during the Volcker disinflation, the range of inflation forecasts within the Fed remained largely constant—the correlation between disagreement among FOMC members and disagreement among professional forecasters is substantially higher after 1982.

We believe that we have now established three important patterns in the data. First, there is substantial disagreement within both naïve and expert

3. We are grateful to Simon Gilchrist for suggesting this analysis to us. Data were drawn from Gavin (2003) and updated using recent testimony published at http://www.federal-reserve.gov/boarddocs/ hh/ (accessed December 2003).

populations about the expected future path of inflation. Second, there are larger levels of disagreement among consumers than exists among experts. And third, even though professional forecasters, economists, and the general population show different degrees of disagreement, this disagreement tends to exhibit similar time-series patterns, albeit of a different amplitude. One would therefore expect to find that the underlying causes behind this disagreement are similar across all three datasets.

3. The Central Tendency of Inflation Expectations

Most studies analyzing inflation expectations data have explored whether empirical estimates are consistent with rational expectations. The rational expectations hypothesis has strong implications for the time series of

Figure 4 DISAGREEMENT AMONG THE FOMC

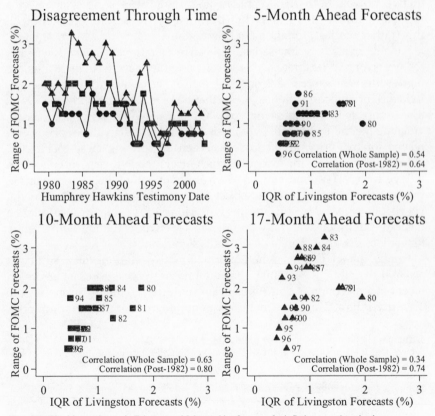

Humphrey-Hawkins testimony in February and July provides forecasts for inflation over the calendar year. Inflation concept varies.

expectations data, most of which can be stated in terms of forecast efficiency. More specifically, rational expectations imply (statistically) efficient forecasting, and efficient forecasts do not yield predictable errors. We now turn to reviewing the tests of rationality commonly found in the literature and to providing complementary evidence based on the estimates of median inflation expectations in our sample.[4]

The simplest test of efficiency is a test for bias: are inflation expectations centered on the right value? Panel A of Table 4 reports these results, regressing expectation errors on a constant. Median forecasts have tended to underpredict inflation in two of the four data series, and this divergence is statistically significant; that said, the magnitude of this bias is small.[5]

By regressing the forecast error on a constant and the median inflation expectation,[6] panel B of the table tests whether there is information in these inflation forecasts themselves that can be used to predict forecasting errors. Under the null of rationality, these regressions should have no predictive power. Both the Michigan and Livingston series can reject a rationality null on this score, while the other two series are consistent with this (rather modest) requirement of rationality.

Panel C exploits a time-series implication of rationality, asking whether today's errors can be forecasted based on yesterday's errors. In these tests, we regress this year's forecast error on the realized error over the previous year. Evidence of autocorrelation suggests that there is information in last year's forecast errors that is not being exploited in generating this year's forecast, violating the rationality null hypothesis. We find robust evidence of autocorrelated forecast errors in all surveys. When interpreting these coefficients, note that they reflect the extent to which errors made a year ago persist in today's forecast. We find that, on average, about half of the error remains in the median forecast. One might object that last year's forecast error may not yet be fully revealed by the time this year's forecast is made because inflation data are published with only one month lag. Experimenting with slightly longer lags does not change these results significantly.[7]

Finally, panel D asks whether inflation expectations take sufficient account of publicly available information. We regress forecast errors on recent macroeconomic data. Specifically, we analyze the inflation rate, the Treasury-bill rate, and the unemployment rate measured one month prior

---

4. Thomas (1999) provides a survey of this literature.
5. Note that the construction of the Michigan experimental data makes the finding of bias unlikely for that series.
6. Some readers may be more used to seeing regressions of the form $\pi = a + bE_{t-12}\pi_t$, where the test for rationality is a joint test of $a = 0$ and $b = 1$. To see that our tests are equivalent, simply rewrite $\pi_t - E_{t-12}\pi_t = a + (1 - b)E_{t-12}\pi_t$. A test of $a = 0$ and $b = 1$ translates into a test that the constant and slope coefficient in this equation are both zero.
7. Repeating this analysis with mean rather than median expectations yields weaker results.

Table 4   TESTS OF FORECAST RATIONALITY: MEDIAN INFLATION EXPECTATIONS[1]

	Michigan	Michigan-experimental	Livingston	SPF (GDP deflator)
Panel A: testing for bias: $\pi_t - E_{t-12}\,\pi_t = \alpha$				
α: mean error	0.42%	−0.09%	0.63%**	−0.02%
(Constant only)	(0.29)	(0.34)	(0.30)	(0.29)
Panel B: Is information in the forecast fully exploited? $\pi_t - E_{t-12}\,\pi_t = \alpha + \beta\, E_{t-12}\pi_t$				
β: $E_{t-12}\,[\pi_t]$	0.349**	−0.060	0.011	0.026
	(.161)	(.207)	(.142)	(.128)
α: constant	−1.016%*	−0.182%	0.595%	−0.132%
	(.534)	(.721)	(.371)	(.530)
Adj. R^2	0.197	−0.003	−0.011	−0.007
Reject eff.? $\alpha = \beta = 0$	Yes	No	Yes	No
(p-value)	(p = 0.088)	(p = 0.956)	(p = 0.028)	(p = 0.969)
Panel C: Are forecasting errors persistent? $\pi_t - E_{t-12}\,\pi_t = \alpha + \beta\,(\pi_{t-12} - E_{t-24}\pi_{t-12})$				
β: $\pi_{t-12} - E_{t-24}\,[\pi_{t-12}]$	0.371**	.580***	0.490***	0.640***
	(0.158)	(0.115)	(0.132)	(0.224)
α: constant	0.096%	0.005%	0.302%	−0.032%
	(0.183)	(0.239)	(0.210)	(0.223)
Adj. R^2	0.164	0.334	0.231	0.375
Panel D: Are macroeconomic data fully exploited? $\pi_t - E_{t-12}\pi_t = \alpha + \beta\, E_{t-12}\,[\pi_t]$ $+ \gamma\,\pi_{t-13} + \kappa\,i_{t-13} + \delta\,U_{t-13}$				
α: constant	−0.816%	0.242%	4.424%***	3.566%***
	(0.975)	(1.143)	(0.985)	(0.970)
β: $E_{t-12}\,[\pi_t]$	0.801***	−0.554***	0.295	0.287
	(0.257)	(0.165)	(0.283)	(0.308)
γ: inflation$_{t-13}$	−0.218*	0.610***	0.205	0.200
	(0.121)	(0.106)	(0.145)	(0.190)
κ: Treasury bill$_{t-13}$	−0.165**	−0.024	−0.319***	−0.321***
	(0.085)	(0.102)	(0.106)	(0.079)
δ: unemployment$_{t-13}$	0.017	−0.063	−0.675***	−0.593***
	(0.126)	(0.156)	(0.175)	(0.150)
Reject eff.? $\gamma = \kappa = \delta = 0$	Yes	Yes	Yes	Yes
(p-value)	(p = 0.049)	(p = 0.000)	(p = 0.000)	(p = 0.000)
Adjusted R^2	0.293	0.382	0.306	0.407
Sample	Nov. 1974– May 2002	1954, Q4– 2002, Q1	1954, H1– 2001, H2	1969, Q4– 2002, Q1
Periodicity	Monthly	Quarterly	Semiannual	Quarterly
N	290	169	96	125

1. ***, ** and * denote statistical significance at the 1%, 5%, and 10% levels, respectively (Newey-West standard errors in parentheses; correcting for autocorrelation up to one year).

to the forecast because these data are likely to be the most recent published data when forecasts were made. We also control for the forecast itself, thereby nesting the specification in panel B of Table 4. One might object that using real-time data would better reflect the information available when forecasts were made; we chose these three indicators precisely because they are subject to only minor revisions. Across the three different pieces of macroeconomic information and all four surveys, we often find statistical evidence that agents are not fully incorporating this information in their inflation expectations. Simple bivariate regressions (not shown) yield a qualitatively similar pattern of responses. The advantage of the multivariate regression is that we can perform an F-test of the joint significance of the lagged inflation, interest rates, and unemployment rates in predicting forecast errors. In each case the macroeconomic data are overwhelmingly jointly statistically significant, suggesting that median inflation expectations do not adequately account for recent available information. Note that these findings do not depend on whether we condition on the forecast of inflation.

Ball and Croushore (2003) interpret the estimated coefficients in a regression similar to that in panel D as capturing the extent to which agents under- or overreact to information. For instance, under the implicit assumption that, in the data, high inflation this period will tend to be followed by high inflation in the next period, the finding that the coefficient on inflation in panel D is positive implies that agents have underreacted to the recent inflation news. Our data support this conclusion in three of the four regressions (the Michigan series is the exception). Similarly, a high nominal interest rate today could signal lower inflation tomorrow because it indicates contractionary monetary policy by the Central Bank. We find that forecasts appear to underreact to short-term interest rates in all four regressions—high interest rates lead forecasters to make negative forecast errors or to predict future inflation that is too high. Finally, if in the economy a period of higher unemployment is usually followed by lower inflation (as found in estimates of the Phillips curve), then a negative coefficient on unemployment in panel D would indicate that agents are overestimating inflation following a rise in unemployment and thus are underreacting to the news in higher unemployment. We find that inflation expectations of economists are indeed too high during periods of high unemployment, again suggesting a pattern of underreaction; this is an error not shared by consumers. Our results are in line with Ball and Croushore's (2003) finding that agents seem to underreact to information when forming their expectations of inflation.

In sum, Table 4 suggests that each of these data series alternatively meets and fails some of the implications of rationality. Our sense is that these results probably capture the general flavor of the existing empirical literature, if not the somewhat stronger arguments made by individual authors. Bias exists but is typically small. Forecasts are typically inefficient, though not in all surveys: while the forecast errors of economists are not predictable based merely on their forecasts, those of consumers are. All four data series show substantial evidence that forecast errors made a year ago continue to repeat themselves, and that recent macroeconomic data is not adequately reflected in inflation expectations.

We now turn to analyzing whether the data are consistent with adaptive expectations, probably the most popular alternative to rational expectations in the literature. The simplest backward-looking rule invokes the prediction that expected inflation over the next year will be equal to inflation over the past year. Ball (2000) suggests a stronger version, whereby agents form statistically optimal univariate inflation forecasts. The test in Table 5 is a little less structured, simply regressing median inflation expectations against the last eight nonoverlapping, three-month-ended inflation observations. We add the unemployment rate and short-term interest rates to this regression, finding that these macroeconomic aggregates also help predict inflation expectations. In particular, it is clear that when the unemployment rate rises over the quarter, inflation expectations fall further than adaptive expectations might suggest. This suggests that consumers employ a more sophisticated model of the economy than assumed in the simple adaptive expectations model.

Consequently we are left with a somewhat negative result—observed inflation expectations are consistent with neither the sophistication of rational expectations nor the naïveté of adaptive expectations. This finding holds for our four datasets, and it offers a reasonable interpretation of the prior literature on inflation expectations. The common thread to these results is that inflation expectations reflect partial and incomplete updating in response to macroeconomic news. We shall argue in Section 5 that these results are consistent with models in which expectations are not updated at every instant, but rather in which updating occurs in a staggered fashion. A key implication is that disagreement will vary with macroeconomic conditions.

4. Dispersion in Survey Measures of Inflation Expectations

Few papers have explored the features of the cross-sectional variation in inflation expectations. Bryan and Venkatu (2001) examine a survey of inflation expectations in Ohio from 1998–2001, finding that women, singles, nonwhites, high school dropouts, and lower income groups tend to have higher inflation expectations than other demographic groups. They

Table 5   TESTS OF ADAPTIVE EXPECTATIONS: MEDIAN INFLATION EXPECTATIONS[1]

Adaptive expectations: $E_t\pi_{t+12} = \alpha + \beta(L)\,\pi_t + \gamma\,U_t + \kappa\,U_{t-3} + \delta\,i_t + \phi\,i_{t-3}$

	Michigan	Michigan-experimental	Livingston	SPF (GDP deflator)
Inflation				
β(1): sum of 8 coefficients	0.706*** (0.037)	0.635*** (0.085)	0.530*** (0.048)	0.581*** (0.054)
Unemployment				
γ: date of forecast	-0.633** (0.261)	-1.237** (0.488)	-0.755*** (0.192)	-0.405** (0.162)
κ: 3 months prior	0.585 (0.231)	0.555 (0.467)	1.055*** (0.185)	0.593*** (0.171)
Treasury bill rate				
δ: date of forecast	0.035 (0.038)	-0.053 (0.132)	0.143** (0.058)	0.069* (0.039)
φ: 3 months prior	-0.109** (0.045)	-0.052 (0.122)	0.100** (0.049)	0.144*** (0.047)
Reject adaptive expectations? (γ = κ = δ = φ = 0)	$F_{4,277} = 9.94$*** Yes	$F_{4,156} = 6.67$*** Yes	$F_{4,83} = 24.5$*** Yes	$F_{4,112} = 13.4$*** Yes
Adjusted R^2	0.922	0.539	0.916	0.929
N	290 (monthly)	169 (quarterly)	96 (semiannual)	125 (quarterly)

1. ***, **, and * denote statistical significance at the 1%, 5%, and 10% levels, respectively (Newey-West standard errors in parentheses; correcting for autocorrelation up to a year).

note that these differences are too large to be explained by differences in the consumption basket across groups but present suggestive evidence that differences in expected inflation reflect differences in the perceptions of current inflation rates. Vissing-Jorgenson (this volume) also explores differences in inflation expectations across age groups.

Souleles (2001) finds complementary evidence from the Michigan Survey that expectations vary by demographic group, a fact that he interprets as evidence of nonrational expectations. Divergent expectations across groups lead to different expectation errors, which he relates to differential changes in consumption across groups.

A somewhat greater share of the research literature has employed data on the dispersion in inflation expectations as a rough proxy for inflation uncertainty. These papers have suggested that highly dispersed inflation expectations are positively correlated with the inflation rate and, conditional on current inflation, are related positively to the recent variance of measured inflation (Cukierman and Wachtel, 1979), to weakness in the real economy (Mullineaux, 1980; Makin, 1982), and alternatively to lower interest rates (Levi and Makin, 1979; Bomberger and Frazer, 1981; and Makin, 1983), and to higher interest rates (Barnea, Dotan, and Lakonishok, 1979; Brenner and Landskroner, 1983). These relationships do not appear to be particularly robust, and in no case is more than one set of expectations data brought to bear on the question. Our approach is consistent with a more literal interpretation of the second moment of the expectations data: we interpret different inflation expectations as reflecting disagreement in the population; that is, different forecasts reflect different expectations.

Lambros and Zarnowitz (1987) argue that disagreement and uncertainty are conceptually distinct, and they make an attempt at unlocking the two empirically. Their data on uncertainty derives from the SPF, which asks respondents to supplement their point estimates with estimates of the probability that GDP and the implicit price deflator will fall into various ranges. These two authors find only weak evidence that uncertainty and disagreement share a common time-series pattern. Intrapersonal variation in expected inflation (uncertainty) is larger than interpersonal variation (disagreement), and while there are pronounced changes through time in disagreement, uncertainty varies little.

The most closely related approach to the macroeconomics of disagreement comes from Carroll (2003b), who analyzes the evolution of the standard deviation of inflation expectations in the Michigan Survey. Carroll provides an epidemiological model of inflation expectations in which expert opinion slowly spreads person to person, much as disease spreads through a population. His formal model yields something close to the Mankiw and Reis (2002) formulation of the sticky-information model. In an agent-based simulation, he proxies expert opinion by the average forecast in the Survey of Professional Forecasters and finds that his agent-based model tracks the time series of disagreement quite well, although it cannot match the level of disagreement in the population.

We now turn to analyzing the evolution of disagreement in greater detail. Figure 3 showed the inflation rate and our measures of disagreement. That figure suggested a relatively strong relationship between inflation and disagreement. A clearer sense of this relationship can be seen in Figure 5. Beyond this simple relationship in levels, an equally apparent fact from Figure 3 is that, when the inflation rate moves around a lot, dispersion appears to rise. This fact is illustrated in Figure 6.

In all four datasets, large changes in inflation (in either direction) are correlated with an increase in disagreement. This fanning out of inflation expectations following a change in inflation is consistent with a process of staggered adjustment of expectations. Of course, the change in inflation is (mechanically) related to its level, and we will provide a more careful attempt at sorting change and level effects below.

Figure 7 maps the evolution of disagreement and the real economy through time. The charts show our standard measures of disagreement,

Figure 5 INFLATION AND DISAGREEMENT

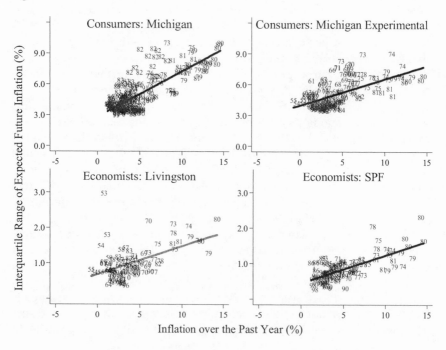

Figure 6 CHANGES IN INFLATION AND DISAGREEMENT

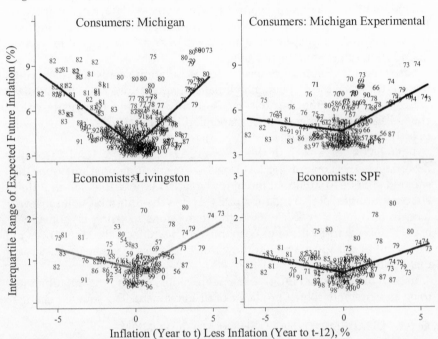

Inflation (Year to t) Less Inflation (Year to t-12), %

plus two measures of excess capacity: an output gap constructed as the difference between the natural logs of actual chain-weighted real output and trend output (constructed from a Hodrick-Prescott filter). The shaded regions represent periods of economic expansion and contraction as marked by the National Bureau of Economic Research (NBER) Business Cycle Dating Committee.[8]

The series on disagreement among consumers appears to rise during recessions, at least through the second half of the sample. A much weaker relationship is observed through the first half of the sample. Disagreement among economists shows a less obvious relationship with the state of the real economy.

The final set of data that we examine can be thought of as either a cause or consequence of disagreement in inflation expectations. We consider the dispersion in actual price changes across different CPI categories. That is, just as Bryan and Cecchetti (1994) produce a weighted median CPI by calculating rates of inflation across 36 commodity groups, we construct a weighted interquartile range of year-ended inflation rates across

8. We have also experimented using the unemployment rate as a measure of real activity and obtained similar results.

commodity groups. One could consider this a measure of the extent to which relative prices are changing. We analyze data for the period December 1967–December 1997 provided by the Cleveland Fed. Figure 8 shows the median inflation rate and the 25th and 75th percentiles of the distribution of nominal price changes.

Dispersion in commodity-level rates of inflation seems to rise during periods in which the dispersion in inflation expectations rises. In Figure 9, we confirm this, graphing this measure of dispersion in rates of price change against our measures of dispersion in expectations. The two look to be quite closely related.

Table 6 considers each of the factors discussed above simultaneously, reporting regressions of the level of disagreement against inflation, the squared change in inflation, the output gap, and the dispersion in different commodities' actual inflation rates. Across the four table columns, we tend to find larger coefficients in the regressions focusing on consumer expectations than in those of economists. This reflects the differences in the extent of disagreement, and how much it varies over the cycle, across these populations.

In both bivariate and multivariate regressions, we find the inflation rate to be an extremely robust predictor of disagreement. The squared change

Figure 7 DISAGREEMENT AND THE REAL ECONOMY

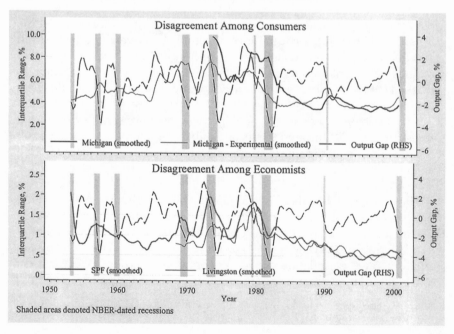

Shaded areas denoted NBER-dated recessions

Figure 8 DISTRIBUTION OF INFLATION RATES ACROSS CPI COMPONENTS

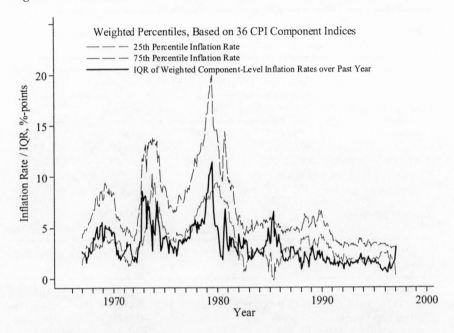

Figure 9 DISPERSION IN INFLATION EXPECTATIONS AND DISPERSION IN INFLATION RATES ACROSS DIFFERENT CPI COMPONENTS

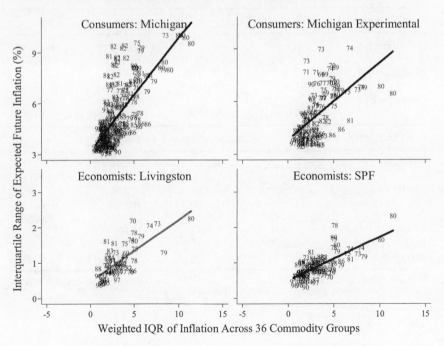

Table 6   DISAGREEMENT AND THE BUSINESS CYCLE: ESTABLISHING
STYLIZED FACTS[1]

	Michigan	Michigan-experimental	Livingston	SPF (GDP deflator)
Panel A: bivariate regressions (each cell represents a separate regression)				
Inflation rate	0.441***	0.228***	0.083***	0.092***
	(0.028)	(0.036)	(0.016)	(0.013)
ΔInflation-squared	18.227***	1.259**	2.682***	2.292**
	(2.920)	(0.616)	(0.429)	(0.084)
Output gap	0.176	−0.047	0.070**	−0.001
	(0.237)	(0.092)	(0.035)	(0.029)
Relative price	0.665***	0.473***	0.117**	0.132
variability	(0.056)	(0.091)	(0.046)	(0.016)
Panel B: regressions controlling for the inflation rate (each cell represents a separate regression)				
ΔInflation-squared	10.401***	0.814	2.051***	−0.406
	(1.622)	(0.607)	(0.483)	(0.641)
Output gap	0.415***	0.026	−0.062**	−0.009
	(0.088)	(0.086)	(0.027)	(0.013)
Relative price	0.268***	0.210	0.085**	0.099***
variability	(0.092)	(0.135)	(0.042)	(0.020)
Panel C: multivariate regressions (full sample)				
Inflation rate	0.408***	0.217***	0.066***	0.095***
	(0.028)	(0.034)	(0.013)	(0.015)
ΔInflation-squared	7.062***	0.789	1.663**	−0.305
	(1.364)	(0.598)	(0.737)	(0.676)
Output gap	0.293***	0.017	0.020	−0.007
	(0.066)	(0.079)	(0.032)	(0.014)
Panel D: multivariate regressions (including inflation dispersion)				
Inflation rate	0.328***	0.204***	0.044**	0.037***
	(0.034)	(0.074)	(0.018)	(0.011)
ΔInflation-squared	5.558***	−0.320	1.398	−0.411
	(1.309)	(2.431)	(0.949)	(0.624)
Output gap	0.336***	−0.061	0.013	0.006
	(0.067)	(0.117)	(0.039)	(0.018)
Relative price	0.237***	0.210	0.062	0.100***
variability	(0.079)	(0.159)	(0.038)	(0.022)

1. *** and ** denote statistical significance at the 1% and 5% levels, respectively (Newey-West standard
errors in parentheses; correcting for autocorrelation up to one year).

in inflation is highly correlated with disagreement in bivariate regressions, and controlling for the inflation rate and other macroeconomic variables only slightly weakens this effect. Adding the relative price variability term further weakens this effect. Relative price variability is a consistently strong predictor of disagreement across all specifications. These results are generally stronger for the actual Michigan data than for the experimental series, and they are generally stronger for the Livingston series than for the SPF. We suspect that both facts reflect the relative role of measurement error. Finally, while the output gap appears to be related to disagreement in certain series, this finding is not robust either across data series or to the inclusion of controls.

In sum, our analysis of the disagreement data has estimated that disagreement about the future path of inflation tends to:

- Rise with inflation.
- Rise when inflation changes sharply—in either direction.
- Rise in concert with dispersion in rates of inflation across commodity groups.
- Show no clear relationship with measures of real activity.

Finally, we end this section with a note of caution. None of these findings necessarily reflect causality and, in any case, we have deliberately been quite loose in even speaking about the direction of likely causation. However, we believe that these findings present a useful set of stylized facts that a theory of macroeconomic dynamics should aim to explain.

5. Theories of Disagreement

Most theories in macroeconomics have no disagreement among agents. It is assumed that everyone shares the same information and that all are endowed with the same information-processing technology. Consequently, everyone ends up with the same expectations.

A famous exception is the islands model of Robert Lucas (1973). Producers are assumed to live in separate islands and to specialize in producing a single good. The relative price for each good differs by island-specific shocks. At a given point in time, producers can observe the price only on their given islands and from it, they must infer how much of it is idiosyncratic to their product and how much reflects the general price level that is common to all islands. Because agents have different information, they have different forecasts of prices and hence inflation. Since all will inevitably make forecast errors, unanticipated monetary policy affects real output: following a change in the money supply, producers attribute some of the observed change in the price for their product to changes in relative rather than general prices and react by changing production.

This model relies on disagreement among agents and predicts dispersion in inflation expectations, as we observe in the data. Nonetheless, the extent of this disagreement is given exogenously by the parameters of the model. Although the Lucas model has heterogeneity in inflation expectations, the extent of disagreement is constant and unrelated to any macroeconomic variables. It cannot account for the systematic relationship between dispersion of expectations and macroeconomic conditions that we documented in Section 4.

The sticky-information model of Mankiw and Reis (2002) generates disagreement in expectations that is endogenous to the model and correlated with aggregate variables. In this model, the costs of acquiring and processing information and of reoptimizing lead agents to update their information sets and expectations sporadically. Each period, only a fraction of the population update themselves on the current state of the economy and determine their optimal actions, taking into account the likely delay until they revisit their plans. The rest of the population continues to act according to their pre-existing plans based on old information. This theory generates heterogeneity in expectations because different segments of the population will have updated their expectations at different points in time. The evolution of the state of the economy over time will endogenously determine the extent of this disagreement. This disagreement in turn affects agents' actions and the resulting equilibrium evolution of the economy.

We conducted the following experiment to assess whether the sticky-information model can capture the extent of disagreement in the survey data. To generate rational forecasts from the perspective of different points in time, we estimated a vector autoregression (VAR) on U.S. monthly data. The VAR included three variables: monthly inflation (measured by the CPI), the interest rate on three-month Treasury bills, and a measure of the output gap obtained by using the Hodrick-Prescott filter on interpolated quarterly real GDP.[9] The estimation period was from March 1947 to March 2002, and the regressions included 12 lags of each variable. We take this estimated VAR as an approximation to the model rational agents use to form their forecasts.

We follow Mankiw and Reis (2002) and assume that in each period, a fraction λ of the population obtains new information about the state of the economy and recomputes optimal expectations based on this new information. Each person has the same probability of updating their informa-

---

9. Using employment rather than detrended GDP as the measure of real activity leads to essentially the same results.

tion, regardless of how long it has been since the last update. The VAR is then used to produce estimates of future annual inflation in the United States given information at different points in the past. To each of these forecasts, we attribute a frequency as dictated by the process just described. This generates at each point in time a full cross-sectional distribution of annual inflation expectations. We use the predictions from 1954 onward, discarding the first few years in the sample when there are not enough past observations to produce nondegenerate distributions.

We compare the predicted distribution of inflation expectations by the sticky-information model to the distribution we observe in the survey data. To do so meaningfully, we need a relatively long sample period. This leads us to focus on the Livingston and the Michigan experimental series, which are available for the entire postwar period.

The parameter governing the rate of information updating in the economy, λ, is chosen to maximize the correlation between the interquartile range of inflation expectations in the survey data with that predicted by the model. For the Livingston Survey, the optimal λ is 0.10, implying that the professional economists surveyed are updating their expectations about every 10 months, on average. For the Michigan series, the value of λ that maximizes the correlation between predicted and actual dispersion is 0.08, implying that the general public updates their expectations on average every 12.5 months. These estimates are in line with those obtained by Mankiw and Reis (2003), Carroll (2003a), and Khan and Zhu (2002). These authors employ different identification schemes and estimate that agents update their information sets once a year, on average. Our estimates are also consistent with the reasonable expectation that people in the general public update their information less frequently than professional economists do. It is more surprising that the difference between the two is so small.

A first test of the model is to see to what extent it can predict the dispersion in expectations over time. Figure 10 plots the evolution of the interquartile range predicted by the sticky-information model, given the history of macroeconomic shocks and VAR-type updating, and setting $\lambda = 0.1$. The predicted interquartile range matches the key features of the Livingston data closely, and the two series appear to move closely together. The correlation between them is 0.66. The model is also successful at matching the absolute level of disagreement. While it overpredicts dispersion, it does so only by 0.18 percentage points on average.

The sticky-information model also predicts the time-series movement in disagreement among consumers. The correlation between the predicted and actual series is 0.80 for the actual Michigan data and 0.40 for the longer experimental series. As for the level of dispersion, it is 4 percentage points

Figure 10 ACTUAL AND PREDICTED DISPERSION OF INFLATION
EXPECTATIONS

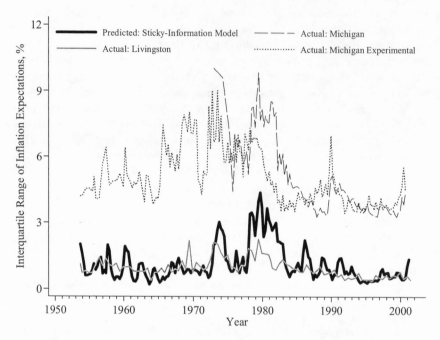

higher on average in the data than predicted by the model. This may be
partially accounted for by some measurement error in the construction of
the Michigan series. More likely, however, it reflects idiosyncratic heterogeneity in the population that is not captured by the model. Individuals in
the public probably differ in their sources of information, in their sophistication in making forecasts, or even in their commitment to truthful reporting in a survey. None of these sources of individual-level variation are
captured by the sticky-information model, but they might cause the high
levels of disagreement observed in the data.[10]

Section 4 outlined several stylized facts regarding the dispersion of
inflation expectations in the survey data. The interquartile range of
expected inflation was found to rise with inflation and with the squared
change in annual inflation over the last year. The output gap did not seem
to affect significantly the dispersion of inflation expectations. We reesti-
mate the regressions in panels A and C of Table 6, now using as the

10. An interesting illustration of this heterogeneity is provided by Bryan and Ventaku (2001),
who find that men and women in the Michigan Survey have statistically significant different expectations of inflation. Needless to say, the sticky-information model does not
incorporate gender heterogeneity.

Table 7   MODEL-GENERATED DISAGREEMENT AND MACROECONOMIC CONDITIONS[1]

	Multivariate regression	*Bivariate regressions*
Dependent Variable: Interquartile range of model-generated inflation expectations		
Constant	0.005***	
	(0.001)	
Inflation rate	0.127***	0.166***
	(0.028)	(0.027)
ΔInflation-squared	3.581***	6.702***
	(0.928)	(1.389)
Output gap	0.009	0.018
	(0.051)	(0.080)
Adjusted R²	0.469	
N	579	579

1. *** denotes statistical significance at the 1% level (Newey-West standard errors in parentheses; correcting for autocorrelation up to one year).

dependent variable the dispersion in inflation expectations predicted by the sticky-information model with a λ of 0.1, the value we estimated using the Livingston series.[11] Table 7 presents the results. Comparing Table 7 with Table 6, we see that the dispersion of inflation expectations predicted by the sticky-information model has essentially the same properties as the actual dispersion of expectations we find in the survey data. As is true in survey data, the dispersion in sticky-information expectations is also higher when inflation is high, and it is higher when prices have changed sharply. As with the survey data, the output gap does not have a statistically significant effect on the model-generated dispersion of inflation expectations.[12]

We can also see whether the model is successful at predicting the central tendency of expectations, not just dispersion. Figure 11 plots the median expected inflation, both in the Livingston and Michigan surveys and as predicted by the sticky-information model with λ = 0.1. The Livingston and predicted series move closely with each other: the correlation is 0.87. The model slightly overpredicts the data between 1955 and

11. Using instead the value of λ that gave the best fit with the Michigan series (0.08) gives similar results.
12. The sticky-information model can also replicate the stylized fact from Section 5 that more disagreement comes with larger relative price dispersion. Indeed, in the sticky-information model, different price-setters choose different prices only insofar as they disagree on their expectations. This is transparent in Ball, Mankiw, and Reis (2003), where it is shown that relative price variability in the sticky-information model is a weighted sum of the squared deviations of the price level from the levels expected at all past dates, with earlier expectations receiving smaller weights. In the context of the experiment in this section, including relative price dispersion as an explanatory variable for the disagreement of inflation expectations would risk confounding consequences of disagreement with its driving forces.

1965, and it underpredicts median expected inflation between 1975 and 1980. On average these two effects cancel out, so that over the whole sample, the model approximately matches the level of expected inflation (it overpredicts it by 0.3%). The correlation coefficient between the predicted and the Michigan experimental series is 0.49, and on average the model matches the level of median inflation expectations, underpredicting it by only 0.5%.

In Section 3, we studied the properties of the median inflation expectations across the different surveys, finding that these data were consistent with weaker but not stronger tests of rationality. Table 8 is the counterpart to Table 4, using as the dependent variable the median expected inflation series generated by the sticky-information model. Again, these results match the data closely. We cannot reject the hypothesis that expectations are unbiased and efficient in the weak sense of panels A and B. Recall that, in the data, we found mixed evidence regarding these tests. Panels C and D suggest that forecasting errors in the sticky-information expectations are persistent and do not fully incorporate macroeconomic data, just as we found to be consistently true in the survey data.

Table 9 offers the counterpart to Table 5, testing whether expectations can be described as purely adaptive. This hypothesis is strongly rejected—sticky-information expectations are much more rational than

Figure 11 ACTUAL AND PREDICTED MEDIAN INFLATION EXPECTATIONS

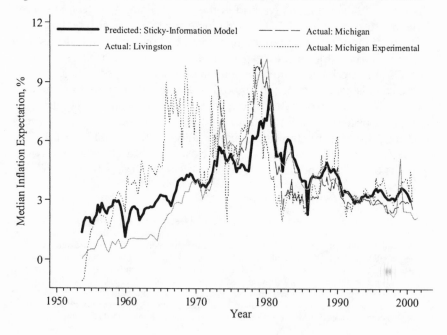

Table 8   TESTS OF FORECAST RATIONALITY: MEDIAN INFLATION EXPECTATIONS PREDICTED BY THE STICKY-INFORMATION MODEL[1]

Panel A: Testing for bias: $\pi_t - E_{t-12}\,\pi_t = \alpha$

Mean error	0.262%
(Constant only)	(0.310)

Panel B: Is information in the forecast fully exploited? $\pi_t - E_{t-12}\,\pi_t = \alpha + \beta\,E_{t-12}\,\pi_t$

β: $E_{t-12}\,[\pi_t]$	0.436*
	(0.261)
α: constant	−1.416%*
	(0.822)
Adj. R^2	0.088
Reject efficiency?	No
$\alpha = \beta = 0$	p = 0.227

Panel C: Are forecasting errors persistent? $\pi_t - E_{t-12}\,\pi_t = \alpha + \beta\,(\pi_{t-12} - E_{t-24}\,\pi_{t-12})$

$\pi_{t-12} - E_{t-24}\,[\pi_{t-12}]$	0.604***
	(0.124)
Constant	0.107%
	(0.211)
Adj. R^2	0.361

Panel D: Are macroeconomic data fully exploited? $\pi_t - E_{t-12}\,\pi_t = \alpha + \beta\,E_{t-12}\,[\pi_t] + \gamma\,\pi_{t-13} + \kappa\,i_{t-13} + \delta\,U_{t-13}$

α: constant	1.567%*
	(0.824)
β: $E_{t-12}\,[\pi_t]$	0.398
	(0.329)
γ: inflation$_{t-13}$	0.506***
	(0.117)
κ: Treasury bill$_{t-13}$	−0.413**
	(0.139)
δ: unemployment$_{t-13}$	−0.450***
	(0.135)
Reject efficiency?	Yes
$\gamma = \kappa = \delta = 0$	p = 0.000
Adjusted R^2	0.369

1. ***, **, and * denote statistical significance at the 1%, 5%, and 10% levels, respectively (Newey-West standard errors in parentheses; correcting for autocorrelation up to one year).

simple, backward-looking adaptive expectations. Again, this finding matches what we observed in the survey data.

Given how closely the predicted and actual dispersion of expectations and median expected inflation co-move, it is not surprising to find that the results in Tables 4, 5, and 6 are closely matched by the model-generated time series for disagreement in Tables 7, 8, and 9. A stronger test in the tradition of moment-matching is to see whether the sticky-information model can robustly generate the stylized facts we observe in the data. We verify this by implementing the following exercise. Using the residuals from our estimated VAR as an empirical distribution, we randomly draw 720 residual vectors and, using the VAR parameter estimates, use these draws to build hypothetical series for inflation, the output gap, and the Treasury-bill rate. We then employ the sticky-information model to generate a predicted distribution of inflation expectations at each date, using the procedure outlined earlier. To eliminate the influence of initial conditions, we discard the first 10 years of the simulated series so that we are left with 50 years of simulated data. We repeat this procedure 500 times, thereby generating 500 alternative 50-year histories for inflation, the output gap, the Treasury-bill rate, the median expected inflation, and the interquartile range of inflation expectations predicted by the sticky-information model with $\lambda = 0.1$. The regressions in Tables 4, 5, and 6, describing the relationship of disagreement and forecast errors

Table 9   TESTS OF ADAPTIVE EXPECTATIONS: MEDIAN INFLATION EXPECTATIONS PREDICTED BY THE STICKY-INFORMATION MODEL[1]

Adaptive expectations: $E_t \pi_{t+12} = \alpha + \beta(L)\, \pi_t + \gamma\, U_t + \kappa\, U_{t-3} + \delta\, i_t + \phi\, i_{t-3}$	
Inflation	1.182***
$\beta(1)$: sum of 8 coefficients	(0.100)
Unemployment	
γ : date of forecast	−0.561***
	(0.087)
κ : 3 months prior	0.594***
	(0.078)
Treasury bill rate	
δ : date of forecast	0.117***
	(0.026)
ϕ : 3 months prior	0.160***
	(0.027)
Reject adaptive expectations?	Yes
$(\gamma = \kappa = \delta = \phi = 0)$	p = 0.000
Adjusted R^2	0.954
N	579

1. *** denotes statistical significance at the 1% level. (Newey-West standard errors in parentheses; correcting for autocorrelation up to a year).

with macroeconomic conditions, are then reestimated on each of these 500 possible histories, generating 500 possible estimates for each parameter.

Table 10 reports the mean parameter estimates from each of these 500 histories. Also shown (in parentheses) are the estimates at the 5th and 95th percentile of this distribution of coefficient estimates. We interpret this range as analogous to a bootstrapped 95% confidence interval (under the null hypothesis that the sticky-information model accurately describes expectations). These results suggest that the sticky-information model robustly generates a positive relationship between the dispersion of inflation expectations and changes in inflation, as we observe in the data. Also, as in the data, the level of the output gap appears to be related only weakly to the dispersion of expectations.

At odds with the facts, the model does not suggest a robust relationship between the level of inflation and the extent of disagreement. To be sure, the relationship suggested in Table 6 does occur in some of these alternative histories, but only in a few. In the sticky-information model, agents disagree in their forecasts of future inflation only to the extent that they have updated their information sets at different points in the past. Given our VAR model of inflation, only changes over time in macroeconomic conditions can generate different inflation expectations by different people. The sticky-information model gives no reason to find a systematic

Table 10 MODEL-GENERATED DISAGREEMENT AND MACROECONOMIC CONDITIONS[1]

	Multivariate regression	Bivariate regressions
(Dependent Variable: Interquartile range of model-generated inflation expectations)		
Constant	1.027***	
	(0.612; 1.508)	
Inflation rate	−0.009	−0.010
	(−0.078; 0.061)	(−0.089; 0.071)
ΔInflation-squared	0.029***	0.030***
	(0.004; 0.058)	(0.005; 0.059)
Output gap	−0.019	−0.023
	(−0.137; 0.108)	(−0.163; 0.116)
Joint test on macro data	Reject at 5% level in 98.2% of histories	
Adjusted R^2	0.162	
N	588	588

1. *** denotes statistical significance at the 1% level. (The 5th and 95th percentile coefficient estimates across 500 alternative histories are shown in parentheses.) Adjusted R^2 refers to the average adjusted R^2 obtained in the 500 different regressions.

relationship between the level of inflation and the extent of disagreement. This does not imply, however, that for a given history of the world such an association could not exist, and for the constellation of shocks actually observed over the past 50 years, this was the case, as can be seen in Table 7. Whether the level of inflation will continue to be related with disagreement is an open question.

Table 11 compares the median of the model-generated inflation expectations series with the artificial series for inflation and the output gap. The results with this simulated data are remarkably similar to those obtained earlier. Panel A shows that expectations are unbiased, although there are many possible histories in which biases (in either direction) of up to one-quarter of a percentage point occur. Panel B shows that sticky-information expectations are typically inefficient, while panel C demonstrates that they induce persistent forecast errors. Panel D shows that sticky-information expectations also fail to exploit available macroeconomic information fully, precisely as we found to be true in the survey data on inflation expectations. The precise relationship between different pieces of macroeconomic data and expectation errors varies significantly across histories, but in nearly all of them there is a strong relationship. Therefore, while the coefficients in Table 11 are not individually significant across histories, within each history a Wald test finds that macroeconomic data are not being fully exploited 78.6% of the time. That is, the set of macro data that sticky-information agents are found to underutilize depends on the particular set of shocks in that history.

Table 12 tests whether sticky-information expectations can be confused for adaptive expectations in the data. The results strongly reject this possibility. Sticky-information expectations are significantly influenced by macroeconomic variables (in this case, the output gap and the Treasury-bill rate), even after controlling for information contained in past rates of inflation.

The sticky-information model does a fairly good job at accounting for the dynamics of inflation expectations that we find in survey data. There is room, however, for improvement. Extensions of the model allowing for more flexible distributions of information arrival hold the promise of an even better fit. An explicit microeconomic foundation for decisionmaking with information-processing costs would likely generate additional sharp predictions to be tested with these data.

6. A Case Study: The Volcker Disinflation

In August 1979, Paul Volcker was appointed chairman of the Board of Governors of the Federal Reserve Board, in the midst of an annual inflation

Table 11   TESTS OF FORECAST RATIONALITY: MEDIAN INFLATION
EXPECTATIONS PREDICTED BY THE STICKY-INFORMATION MODEL OVER
SIMULATED HISTORIES[1]

Panel A: Testing for bias: $\pi_t - E_{t-12}\,\pi_t = \alpha$

Mean error	0.057%
(Constant only)	(−0.264; 0.369)

Panel B: Is information in the forecast fully exploited? $\pi_t - E_{t-12}\,\pi_t = \alpha + \beta\,E_{t-12}\,\pi_t$

$\beta : E_{t-12}\,[\pi_t]$	0.308**
	(0.002; 0.6971)
α : constant	−1.018%
	(−2.879; 0.253)
Adjusted R^2	
Reject efficiency? $\alpha = \beta = 0$	Reject at 5% level in 95.4% of histories

Panel C: Are forecasting errors persistent? $\pi_t - E_{t-12}\,\pi_t = \alpha + \beta\,(\pi_{t-12} - E_{t-24}\,\pi_{t-12})$

$\beta : \pi_{t-12} - E_{t-24}\,[\pi_{t-12}]$	0.260***
	(0.094; 0.396)
α : constant	0.039%
	(−0.237; 0.279)
Adjusted R^2	0.072

Panel D: Are macroeconomic data fully exploited? $\pi_t - E_{t-12}\,\pi_t = \alpha + \beta\,E_{t-12}\,[\pi_t] + \gamma\,\pi_{t-13} + \kappa\,i_{t-13} + \delta\,U_{t-13}$

α : constant	−0.617%
	(−3.090; 1.085)
$\beta : E_{t-12}\,[\pi_t]$	0.032
	(−0.884; 0.811)
γ : inflation$_{t-13}$	0.064
	(−0.178; 0.372)
κ : Treasury bill$_{t-13}$	0.068
	(−0.185; 0.385)
δ : output gap$_{t-13}$	0.170
	(−0.105; 0.504)
Joint test on macro data ($\gamma = \kappa = \delta = 0$)	Reject at 5% level in 78.6% of histories
Adjusted R^2	0.070
N	569

1. *** and ** denote statistical significance at the 1% and 5% levels, respectively. (The 5th and 95th percentile coefficient estimates across 500 alternative histories are shown in parentheses.) Adjusted R^2 refers to the average adjusted R^2 obtained in the 500 different regressions.

Table 12   TESTS OF ADAPTIVE EXPECTATIONS: MEDIAN INFLATION
EXPECTATIONS PREDICTED BY THE STICKY-INFORMATION MODEL OVER
SIMULATED HISTORIES[1]

Adaptive expectations: $E_{t-12} \pi_t = \alpha + \beta (L) \pi_t + \gamma U_t + \kappa U_{t-3} + \delta i_t + \phi i_{t-3}$

Inflation	1.100**
$\beta(1)$: sum of 8 coefficients	(0.177; 2.082)
Output gap	
γ : Date of forecast	0.380**
	(0.064; 0.744)
κ : 3 months prior	−0.300
Treasury bill rate	(−0.775; 0.190)
δ : Date of forecast	0.063
	(−0.042; 0.165)
ϕ : 3 months prior	0.149
	(−0.111; 0.371)
Reject adaptive expectations?	Reject at 5% level
($\gamma = \kappa = \delta = \phi = 0$)	in 100% of histories
Adjusted R^2	0.896
N	569

1. ** denotes statistical significance at the 5% level. (The 5th and 95th percentile coefficient estimates across 500 alternative histories are shown in parentheses.) Adjusted R^2 refers to the average adjusted R^2 obtained in the 500 different regressions.

rate of 11%, one of the highest in the postwar United States. Over the next three years, using contractionary monetary policy, he sharply reduced the inflation rate to 4%. This sudden change in policy and the resulting shock to inflation provides an interesting natural experiment for the study of inflation expectations. The evolution of the distribution of inflation expectations between 1979 and 1982 in the Michigan Survey is plotted in Figure 12.[13] For each quarter there were on average 2,350 observations in the Michigan Survey, and the frequency distributions are estimated nonparametrically using a normal kernel-smoothing function.

Three features of the evolution of the distribution of inflation expectations stand out from Figure 12. First, expectations adjusted slowly to this change in regime. The distribution of expectations shifts leftward only gradually over time in the data. Second, in the process, dispersion increases and the distribution flattens. Third, during the transition, the distribution became approximately bimodal.

We now turn to asking whether the sticky-information model can account for the evolution of the full distribution of expectations observed in the survey data during this period. Figure 13 plots the distribution of

13. The Livingston and SPF surveys have too few observations at any given point in time to generate meaningful frequency distributions.

Figure 12 THE VOLCKER DISINFLATION: THE EVOLUTION OF INFLATION
EXPECTATIONS IN THE MICHIGAN SURVEY

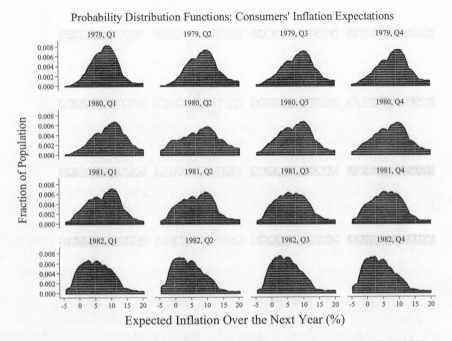

Probability Distribution Functions: Consumers' Inflation Expectations

Figure 13 THE VOLCKER DISINFLATION: THE EVOLUTION OF INFLATION
EXPECTATIONS PREDICTED BY THE STICKY-INFORMATION MODEL

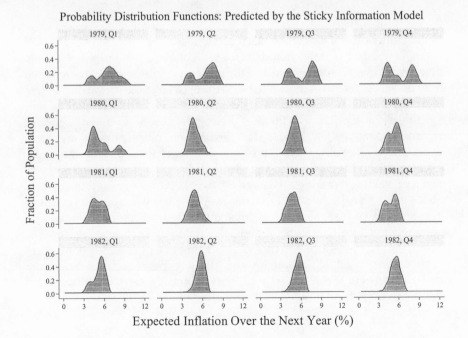

Probability Distribution Functions: Predicted by the Sticky Information Model

inflation expectations predicted by the VAR application of the sticky-information model described in Section 5.

In the sticky-information model, information disseminates slowly throughout the economy. As the disinflation begins, a subset of agents who have updated their information sets recently lower their expectation of inflation. As they do so, a mass of the cross-sectional distribution of inflation expectations shifts leftward. As the disinflation proceeds, a larger fraction of the population revises its expectation of the level of inflation downward, and thus a larger mass of the distribution shifts to the left. The distribution therefore flattens and dispersion increases, as we observed in the actual data.

The sudden change in inflation isolates two separate groups in the population. In one group are those who have recently updated their information sets and are now expecting much lower inflation rates. In the other are those holding to pre-Volcker expectations, giving rise to a bimodal distribution of inflation expectations. As more agents become informed, a larger mass of this distribution shifts from around the right peak to around the left peak. Ultimately, the distribution resumes its normal single peaked shape, now concentrated at the low observed inflation rate.

Clearly the sticky-information model generates predictions that are too sharp. Even so, it successfully accounts for the broad features of the evolution of the distribution of inflation expectations during the Volcker disinflation.

7. Conclusion

Regular attendees of the NBER Macroeconomics Annual conference are well aware of one fact: people often disagree with one another. Indeed, disagreement about the state of the field and the most promising avenues for research may be the conference's most reliable feature. Despite the prevalence of disagreement among conference participants, however, disagreement is conspicuously absent in the theories being discussed. In most standard macroeconomic models, people share a common information set and form expectations rationally. There is typically little room for people to disagree.

Our goal in this paper is to suggest that disagreement may be a key to macroeconomic dynamics. We believe we have established three facts about inflation expectations. First, not everyone has the same expectations. The amount of disagreement is substantial. Second, the amount of disagreement varies over time together with other economic aggregates. Third, the sticky-information model, according to which some people form expectations based on outdated information, seems capable of explaining many features of the observed evolution of both the central tendency and the dispersion of inflation expectations over the past 50 years.

We do not mean to suggest that the sticky-information model explored here is the last word in inflation expectations. The model offers a good starting point. It is surely better at explaining the survey data than are the traditional alternatives of adaptive or rational expectations, which give no room for people to disagree. Nonetheless, the model cannot explain all features of the data, such as the positive association between the level of inflation and the extent of disagreement. The broad lesson from this analysis is clear: if we are to understand fully the dynamics of inflation expectations, we need to develop better models of information acquisition and processing. About this, we should all be able to agree.

8. Appendix: An Experimental Series for the Mean and Standard Deviation of Inflation Expectations in the Michigan Survey from 1946 to 2001

The Michigan Survey of Consumer Expectations and Behavior has been run most quarters since 1946, Q1, and monthly since 1978. The current survey questions have been asked continuously since January 1978 (see Curtin, 1996, for details):

Qualitative: *"During the next 12 months, do you think that prices in general will go up, or go down, or stay where they are now?"*
Quantitative: *"By about what percent do you expect prices to go (up/down) on the average, during the next 12 months?"*

For most of the quarterly surveys from June 1966–December 1976, a closed-ended version of the quantitative question was instead asked as:

Closed: *"How large a price increase do you expect? Of course nobody can know for sure, but would you say that a year from now prices will be about 1 or 2% higher, or 5%, or closer to 10% higher than now, or what?"*

Prior to 1966, the survey did not probe quantitative expectations at all, asking only the qualitative question.

Thus, for the full sample period, we have a continuous series of only qualitative expectations. Even the exact coding of this question has varied through time (Juster and Comment, 1978):

• 1948 (Q1)–1952 (Q1): "What do you think will happen to the prices of the things you buy?"
• 1951 (Q4), 1952 (Q2)–1961 (Q1): "What do you expect prices of household items and clothing will do during the next year or so—stay where they are, go up or go down?"

- 1961 (Q2)–1977 (Q2): "Speaking of prices in general, I mean the prices of the things you buy—do you think they will go up in the next year or go down?"
- 1977 (Q3)–present: "During the next 12 months, do you think that prices in general will go up, or go down, or stay where they are now?"

Lacking a better alternative, we proceed by simply assuming that these different question wordings did not affect survey respondents.

We compile raw data for our experimental series from many different sources:

- 1948 (Q1)–1966 (Q1): unpublished tabulations put together by Juster and Comment (1978, Table 1).
- 1966 (Q2)–1977 (Q2): tabulations from Table 2 of Juster and Comment (1978).
- 1967 (Q2), 1977 (Q3)–1977 (Q4): data were extracted from Inter-university Consortium for Political and Social Research (ICPSR) studies #3619, #8726, and #8727, respectively.
- January 1978–August 2001: a large cumulative file containing microdata on all monthly surveys. These data were put together for us by the Survey Research Center at the University of Michigan, although most of these data are also accessible through the ICPSR.

These raw data are shown in Figure 14.

Figure 14 QUALITATIVE RESPONSES TO THE MICHIGAN SURVEY—LONG HISTORY

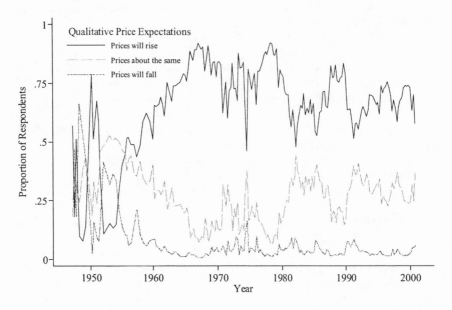

To build a quantitative experimental series from these qualitative data, we make two assumptions. First, note that a relatively large number of respondents expect no change in prices. We should probably not interpret this literally but rather as revealing that they expect price changes to be small. We assume that when respondents answer that they expect no change in prices, they are stating that they expect price changes to be less than some number, $c\%$. Second, we assume that an individual i's expectation of inflation at time t, π_{it}, is normally distributed with mean μ_t and standard deviation σ_t. Note especially that the mean and standard deviation of inflation expectations are allowed to shift through time, but that the width of the band around zero for which inflation expectations are described as unchanged shows no intertemporal variation (that is, there is no time subscript on c).

Consequently, we can express the observed proportions in each category as a function of the cumulative distribution of the standard normal distribution F_N; the parameter c; and the mean and standard deviation of that month's inflation expectations, μ_t, and σ_t,

$$\%Down_t = F_N\left(\frac{-c-\mu_t}{\sigma_t}\right)$$

$$\%Up_t = 1 - F_N\left(\frac{c-\mu_t}{\sigma_t}\right)$$

Thus, we have two independent data points for each month (*%Same* is perfectly collinear with *%Up+%Down*), and we would like to recover two time-varying parameters. The above two expressions can be solved simultaneously to yield:

$$\mu_t = c\left[\frac{F_N^{-1}(\%Down_t) + F_N^{-1}(1-\%Up_t)}{F_N^{-1}(\%Down_t) - F_N^{-1}(1-\%Up_t)}\right]$$

$$\sigma_t = c\left[\frac{2}{F_N^{-1}(1-\%Up_t) - F_N^{-1}(\%Down_t)}\right]$$

Not surprisingly, we can recover the time series of the mean and standard deviation of inflation expectations up to a multiplicative parameter, c; that is, we can describe the time series of the mean and dispersion of inflation expectations, but the scale is not directly interpretable. To recover a more interpretable scaling, we can either make an ad hoc assumption about the width of the zone from which same responses are drawn, or fit some other feature of the data. We follow the second approach and equate the sample mean of the experimental series and the corresponding quantitative estimates of median inflation expectations from the same survey over the shorter 1978–2001 period when both quantitative and qualitative data are available. (We denote the median inflation expectation by $\tilde{\pi}$.)[14] formally, this can be stated:

$$\sum_t^{1978-2001} \mu_t = \sum_t^{1978-2001} \tilde{\pi} \quad \text{which solves to yield:}$$

$$c = \frac{\displaystyle\sum_t^{1978-2001} \tilde{\pi}}{\displaystyle\sum_t^{1978-2001} \frac{F_N^{-1}(\%Down_t) + F_N^{-1}(\%1 - Up_t)}{F_N^{-1}(\%Down_t) - F_N^{-1}(\%1 - Up_t)}}$$

This assumption yields an estimate of $c = 1.7\%$. That is, the specific scaling adopted yields the intuitively plausible estimate that those expecting inflation between –1.7% and +1.7% respond that prices will stay where they are now. More to the point, this specific scaling assumption is not crucial to any of our regression estimates. It affects the interpretation of the magnitude of coefficients but not the statistical significance.

Thus, for our sample of T periods, with $2T + 1$ parameters and $2T + 1$ unknowns, we can estimate the time series of the mean and standard deviation of inflation expectations. As a final step, we rely on the assumption of normality to convert our estimate of the sample standard deviation into an estimate of the interquartile range.

Figures 1 and 3 show that the median and interquartile range of the constructed series move quite closely with the quantitative estimates over the period from 1978. Table 2 reports on the correlation of this series with other estimates.

REFERENCES

Ball, Laurence. (2000). Near-rationality and inflation in two monetary regimes. Cambridge, MA: National Bureau of Economic Research. NBER Working Paper 7988.
Ball, Laurence, and Dean Croushore. (2003). Expectations and the effects of monetary policy. *Journal of Money, Credit and Banking* 35(4): 473–484.
Ball, Laurence, N. Gregory Mankiw, and Ricardo Reis. (2003). Monetary policy for inattentive economies, *Journal of Monetary Economics*, forthcoming.
Barnea Amir, Amihud Dotan, and Josef Lakonishok. (1979). The effect of price level uncertainty on the determination of nominal interest rates: Some empirical evidence. *Southern Economic Journal* 46(2): 609–614.
Bomberger, William, and William Frazer. (1981). Interest rates, uncertainty and the Livingston data. *Journal of Finance* 36(3): 661–675.

---

14. It is just as valid to refer to the mean of this experimental series as the median expectation, given the assumption of normality.

Brenner, Menachem, and Yoram Landskroner. (1983). Inflation uncertainties and returns on bonds. *Economica* 50(200):463–468.

Bryan, Michael, and Stephen Cecchetti. (1994). Measuring core inflation. In *Monetary Policy*, N. Gregory Mankiw (ed.). Chicago: University of Chicago Press for NBER.

Bryan, Michael, and Guhan Venkatu. (2001). The curiously different inflation perspectives of men and women. Federal Reserve Bank of Cleveland Economic Commentary Series. Available at http://www.clev.frb.org/Research/Com2001/1015.pdf.

Carroll, Christopher. (2003a). Macroeconomic expectations of households and professional forecasters. *Quarterly Journal of Economics* 118(1):269–298.

Carroll, Christopher. (2003b). The epidemiology of macroeconomic expectations. In *The Economy as an Evolving Complex System, III*, Larry Blume and Steven Durlauf (eds.). Oxford, England: Oxford University Press.

Croushore, Dean. (1993). Introducing: The Survey of Professional Forecasters. Federal Reserve Bank of Philadelphia. *Business Review* November/December: 3–15.

Croushore, Dean. (1997). The Livingston Survey: Still useful after all these years. Federal Reserve Bank of Philadelphia. *Business Review* March/April: 15–27.

Cukierman, Alex, and Paul Wachtel. (1979). Differential inflationary expectations and the variability of the rate of inflation: Theory and evidence. *American Economic Review* 69(4):595–609.

Curtin, Richard. (1996). Procedure to estimate price expectations. University of Michigan Survey Research Center. Mimeo.

Friedman, Milton. (1968). The role of monetary policy. *American Economic Review* 58(1):1–17.

Gavin, William T. (2003). FOMC forecasts: Is all the information in the central tendency? Federal Reserve Bank of St Louis. Working Paper 2003–002A.

Juster, F. Thomas, and Robert Comment. (1978). A note on the measurement of price expectations. Institute for Social Research, University of Michigan. Unpublished manuscript.

Khan, Hashmat, and Zhenhua Zhu. (2002). Estimates of the sticky-information Phillips curve for the United States, Canada, and the United Kingdom. Bank of Canada Working Paper 2002–19.

Levi, Maurice, and John Makin. (1979). Fisher, Phillips, Friedman and the measured impact of inflation on interest. *Journal of Finance* 34(1):35–52.

Lambros, Louis, and Victor Zarnowitz. (1987). Consensus and uncertainty in economic prediction. *Journal of Political Economy* 95(3):591–621.

Lucas, Robert E., Jr. (1973). Some international evidence on inflation-output trade-offs. *American Economic Review* 63:326–334.

Makin, John. (1982). Anticipated money, inflation uncertainty and real economic activity. *Review of Economics and Statistics* 64(1):126–134.

Makin, John. (1983). Real interest, money surprises, anticipated inflation and fiscal deficits. *Review of Economics and Statistics* 65(3):374–384.

Mankiw, N. Gregory, and Ricardo Reis. (2002). Sticky information versus sticky prices: A proposal to replace the new Keynesian Phillips curve. *Quarterly Journal of Economics* 117(4):1295–1328.

Mankiw, N. Gregory, and Ricardo Reis. (2003). Sticky information: A model of monetary non-neutrality and structural slumps. In *Knowledge, Information and Expectations in Modern Macroeconomics: In Honor of Edmund S. Phelps*, P. Aghion, R. Frydman, J. Stiglitz, and M. Woodford (eds.). Princeton, NJ: Princeton University Press.

Mullineaux, Donald. (1980). Inflation expectations and money growth in the United States. *American Economic Review* 70(1):149–161.

Souleles, Nicholas. (2001). Consumer sentiment: Its rationality and usefulness in forecasting expenditure—Evidence from the Michigan micro data. *Journal of Money, Credit and Banking* forthcoming.

Thomas, Lloyd, Jr. (1999). Survey measures of expected U.S. inflation. *Journal of Economic Perspectives* 13(4):125–144.

Vissing-Jorgenson, Annette. (2003). Perspectives on behavioral finance: Does "irrationality" disappear with wealth? Evidence from expectations and actions. In *NBER Macroeconomics Annual 2003*, Mark Gertler and Kenneth Rogoff (eds.). Cambridge, MA: MIT Press.

Comment

ROBERT G. KING*
Boston University, NBER, and Federal Reserve Bank of Richmond

1. Expectations and Macroeconomics

Disagreement about inflation expectations, particularly controversies over the importance of these expectations for the relationship between real and nominal variables, has been a central topic in macroeconomics during the last three decades. Most analyses have taken inflation expectations—and other expectations about macroeconomic variables—as identical across agents, or they at least have taken the view that cross-sectional differences in beliefs are second-order for macroeconomic phenomena.

The view that average expectations are sufficient for most macroeconomic purposes is present in many diverse lines of research. In the early studies of Gordon (1970) and Solow (1969), inflation expectations were viewed as adaptive, but differences across agents in the speed of expectation adjustment were not stressed. Instead, this viewpoint was made operational by using simple distributed lag specifications as proxies for expectations, making beliefs about inflation depend only on a subset of available data despite the fact that it was generally more complicated in macroeconomic models. Famously criticized by Lucas (1972) and Sargent (1971), who employed rational expectations models with homogenous beliefs in their arguments, the adaptive expectations viewpoint has largely been replaced by rational expectations modeling. Following Lucas and Sargent, the specific form of rational expectations employed most frequently is that all information is common to agents.

* The views expressed in this comment are not necessarily these of The Federal Reserve Bank of Richmond or of The Federal Reserve System.

While the homogeneous expectations model has been dominant, it is important to remember that an earlier line of flexible price macroeconomic research during this period sought to use limited information constructs—the imperfect information models developed by Lucas (1973), Barro (1976), and others during the late 1970s and early 1980s—to rationalize monetary nonneutrality. In contrast to macroeconomic models incorporating rational expectations with common information, these setups featured incomplete adjustment of average beliefs precisely because individuals had limited and disparate information sets. The profession ultimately turned away from these models, however, for two reasons. First, their implications were fragile with respect to the specification of the nature and evolution of information sets. Second, it was difficult to believe that they explained the apparent nonneutrality of money stock measures in an economy like that of the United States, with readily available monetary statistics.

1.1 (MY) EXPECTATIONS

Recently, Mankiw and Reis (2002) have resurrected the idea that limited information—particularly infrequent adjustment of expectations—is important for the interplay of real and nominal variables. They do so within models in which firms are price-setters rather than participants in competitive markets like those envisioned by Lucas and Barro.

Because I cut my research teeth on the earlier generation of imperfect information models, I was delighted when Mark Gertler asked me to discuss a prospective paper in which these authors would explore the evidence for sticky expectations. I thought that it would be an excellent opportunity to think further about an important topic: what macroeconomic and microeconomic implications most sharply distinguish the sticky-expectations model of Mankiw and Reis (MR) from the popular sticky-price model that has been much employed in recent macroeconomic research. So I was excited to have the opportunity.

1.2 EXPECTATIONS ARE NOT ALWAYS FULFILLED

Conference organizers suggest topics to authors and sometimes get papers that are very different from those expected. Karl Brunner once asked Robert Lucas to write a survey of empirical evidence on the Phillips curve and got "Econometric Policy Evaluation: A Critique." My expectations were not fulfilled with this paper, but I am not disappointed. The Mankiw-Reis-Wolfers (MRW) paper is a fascinating description of various measures of survey inflation expectations. It documents how these measures vary through time; how they are related to the level of inflation; how they move over the course of business cycles; and how they evolved during an important episode, the Volcker deflation. It is sure to stimulate much interesting future research.

1.3 LINK TO THE STICKY-EXPECTATIONS MODEL

The sticky-expectations model of MR implies that macroeconomic shocks—particularly monetary policy shocks—have real effects because some agents adjust expectations and others don't. It also has the effect that monetary shocks cause dispersion in inflation expectations because some agents adjust their forecasts immediately when a shock occurs and others do so only gradually. This implication motivates the current paper: MRW want to find out whether there are important changes over time in the cross-sectional variability of expectations.

Now, there are other empirical implications of the sticky-expectations model that one might want to explore, both at the micro and macro levels. In the MR model, when a firm gets an opportunity to update its information, it chooses an entire *path* for future nominal prices that it will charge until its next information update.[1] To me, this *micro implication* flies in the face of one of the central facts that new Keynesian macroeconomics has long stressed, which is the tendency for many nominal prices to stay constant for substantial periods of time.[2]

And there are also *macro implications* of this adjustment pattern. Ball, Mankiw, and Romer (1988) use data on a large number of different countries to argue for sticky-price models rather than the alternative information-confusion model of Lucas. They argue that sticky-price models imply that the output-inflation trade-off should depend negatively on the average rate of inflation because high rates of inflation would induce firms to undertake more frequent adjustments. They argue that cross-country evidence strongly supports this implication, rather than Lucas's implication that the slope should depend on variability of inflation. Now, because a Mankiw-Reis firm sets a path of prices, it can neutralize the effects of the average inflation rate on its real revenues. Its incentives for frequency of information adjustment would therefore be unaffected by average inflation, just like Lucas's flexible price firm, because the MR firm's price is flexible with respect to forecasted inflation.

---

1. If a firm chose a nominal price that would be held fixed until the next receipt of information, then the MR model has the attractive characteristic that it simply collapses to the well-known Calvo (1983) model. Thus, the essential feature of the model is that the firm chooses a price plan rather than a price.
2. A notable and important exception is the practices of selective discounts, such as sales.

Each of these two implications of the MR model seems inconsistent with key facts long stressed by Keynesian macroeconomics, old and new. So if the MR model is the principal motivation for the MRW investigation, then the link is less than fully satisfactory.

1.4 INTELLECTUAL CURRENTS

There are other reasons for studying disagreement about inflation expectations. Stepping back, the MRW paper is part of recent work that is sometimes called behavioral macroeconomics and at other times called macroeconomics and individual decisionmaking. This work aims at (1) taking a careful look at how individuals actually make decisions at the individual level, and (2) developing hypotheses about behavior that are well-specified alternatives to those explored in earlier neoclassical studies of micro data. Work on behavioral macroeconomics in general and the MRW paper in particular is thus a timely and welcome contribution. But one must also bear in mind that survey reports of expectations are not quite the sort of behavior about which most economists—neoclassical or not—are prone to theorize about. They are not market actions, just statements.

1.5 REMEMBERING MUTH

Even if we take these measures as accurate indicators of individual expectations, it is important to remember Muth's (1961) original description of rational expectations. He noted that:

- "The hypothesis (is) . . . that expectations of firms . . . tend to be distributed, for the same information set, about the prediction of the theory . . . ."
- "The hypothesis asserts three things: (i) that information is scarce and the economic system generally does not waste it; (ii) the way that expectations are formed depends specifically on the structure . . . of the economy; (and) (iii) a 'public prediction' will have no effect . . . (unless it is based on inside information)."
- "It does *not assert* that the scratch work of entrepreneurs resembles the system of equations in any way; nor does it state that the predictions of entrepreneurs are perfect or that their expectations are all the same."

So Muth was comfortable with deviations of individual expectations from average, potentially of a systematic, type. He nevertheless chose to construct an economic model in which only average expectations mattered and to explore the implications of this model for the dynamics of agricultural prices.

1.6 CRITICAL QUESTION

As macroeconomists, we know that there are lots of types of heterogeneity in the world. We abstract from many in building our models, as Muth did. The key to successful macro model building is to put in heterogeneity that is important for the issue at hand and to leave out the rest. For example, in studying capital formation, one might think that it is important to take careful account of the age distribution of capital stocks because this distribution could aid in predicting the timing of firms' upgrades and replacements. One would like this age distribution of capital stocks to reflect underlying costs, presumably of a fixed sort, that keep firms from rapidly adjusting their capital stocks.

More specifically, one might think—as I did—that lumpy investment at the micro level would produce an important set of distributed lag effects on aggregate investment not present in standard neoclassical models. But the general equilibrium analysis of Thomas (2002) shows that this need not be the case: one carefully constructed model with a rich age distribution of capital stocks does not produce very different investment behavior than the simplest neoclassical model. So this form of heterogeneity did not turn out to be important in one particular setting.

By contrast, modern sticky-price models take heterogeneity in nominal prices, a comparable age distribution of prices, as a first-order phenomenon. Many such models produce *very* different real responses from those in flexible price models without a distribution of prices. While most of these studies impose a time-dependent pattern of price adjustment, the nonneutrality results of some sticky-price models survive the introduction of state dependent pricing.

So the critical question becomes, Is heterogeneity in beliefs important for macroeconomic models of the Phillips curve?

2. Expectations, Credibility, and Disinflation

To make the question asked above concrete within a particular model, I now consider a stylized model of the Volcker deflation, stimulated by the Mankiw-Reis-Wolfers discussion of this topic in Section 6 of their paper.

2.1 A STICKY–PRICE MODEL

For this purpose, I use a simple macroeconomic model consisting of an inflation equation for the private sector and a monetary policy rule that involves a specification of an inflation path. The examples are simplifications of the analyses of Ball (1994, 1995).

2.1.1 *Private Behavior*   The private sector inflation equation is:

$$\pi_t = E_t \pi_{t+1} + \phi y_t$$

where π_t is the inflation rate, $E_t\pi_{t+1}$ is the expectation of future inflation, y_t is a measure of the output gap, and ϕ is a slope coefficient that captures the structural effect that the output gap has on the inflation rate at a given expected future inflation rate.[3] As is well known, this specification—sometimes called the new Keynesian Phillips curve—can be derived from underlying microeconomic foundations with a stochastic price adjustment mechanism of the Calvo (1983) form.

2.1.2 *A Policy of Gradual Disinflation*   I also assume that the monetary authority takes whatever monetary actions are necessary to produce a gradual disinflation path:

$$\bar{\pi}_t = \begin{cases} \pi^h - gt \text{ for } t = 1, 2, \ldots T \\ \pi^l \text{ for } t > T \end{cases}$$

with $g = (\pi^h - \pi^l)/T > 0$. This rule specifies that inflation gradually declines from the high level π^h to the low level π^l over the course of T periods, with an identical change in the inflation rate taking place in each period.

2.1.3 *Imperfect Credibility and Expected Inflation*   I finally specify a sense in which the representative agent sees the policy as imperfectly credible. In each period, there is a probability α_t that the disinflation will be continued next period. If the disinflation is terminated, then inflation will return to the high level π^h and will stay there in all future periods. With this specification, expected future inflation takes the following form:

$$E_t \pi_{t+1} = \alpha_t \bar{\pi}_{t+1} + (1 - \alpha_t)\pi^h$$
$$= \alpha_t(\bar{\pi}_t - g) + (1 - \alpha_t)\pi^h$$

Within a successful deflation, the path of the output gap is therefore:

$$y_t = \frac{1}{\phi}[\pi_t - E_t \pi_{t+1}]$$
$$= \frac{1}{\phi}[\alpha_t g + (1 - \alpha_t)(\bar{\pi}_t - \pi^h)]$$

---

3. A coefficient β is sometimes inserted before expected future inflation. Because it is a quarterly discount factor, its value is just below 1 and it is omitted for simplicity in the discussion below.

This expression captures two effects familiar from Ball's work on sticky prices and deflation. First, a perfectly credible ($\alpha_t = 1$) deflation produces a boom in output. Second, if inflation is reduced in an imperfectly credible manner, then a recession will occur. For example, if the disinflation is completely incredible ($\alpha_t = 0$), then output declines in lock-step with inflation. It also highlights that the behavior of output depends importantly on the dynamics of beliefs that are here taken to be common across all agents, i.e., on the behavior of the α_t over time.

2.2 DYNAMICS OF A SUCCESSFUL DEFLATION

I now use this simple model to analyze an example of dynamics within a successful disinflation, which is assumed to take three years to complete and to reduce the inflation rate from 10% per year to 4% per year. In particular, I suppose that the beliefs about the disinflation are initially stubborn, with $\alpha_t = 0$ for three quarters, and then gradually rise until the disinflation is fully credible at its endpoint.

The particular assumptions and their implications for output are displayed in Figure 1. Inflation is assumed to decline gradually, as displayed in the top panel. The credibility of the disinflation rises through time.

Figure 1 DYNAMICS OF AN IMPERFECTLY CREDIBLE BUT ULTIMATELY SUCCESSFUL DEFLATION

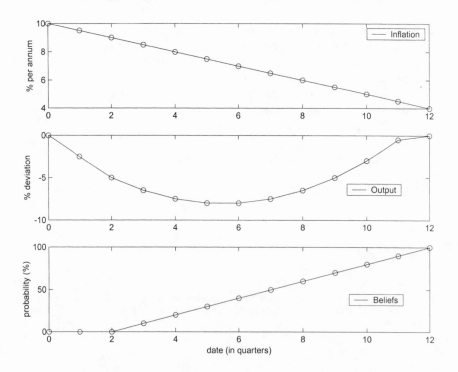

Output is initially not much affected but then declines because the disinflation is incredible.[4] As its credibility rises, the disinflation's real consequences evaporate.

2.3 REINTERPRETING THE MODEL

To this point, we have assumed that there is no disagreement about inflation expectations in the sense of Mankiw, Reis, and Wolfers. Suppose, however, that we now assume that there is such disagreement. A fraction α_t of the population is optimistic, believing that the disinflation will continue, while the remaining population members are pessimistic. Under this alternative interpretation, the dynamics of inflation and output are unaffected, but there would be variability in measures of disagreement similar to those considered in this paper: disagreement would be small at the beginning and end of the disinflation, while it would be higher in the middle. So, in this model, disagreement about inflation expectations can occur and evolve over time. But modeling these disagreements does not seem essential to understanding the episode.

2.4 CONNECTING WITH THE ACTUAL DISINFLATION EXPERIENCE

I think that the actual disinflation experience involved the following four features:

First, it was *widely discussed*: it is hard to imagine that agents didn't know that something was up.[5]

Second, it was *widely debated* on two dimensions. People disagreed about whether it would work and whether it was a good idea. The former suggests disagreement about expectations.

Third, there was some *uncertainty* about what was going on: people were not sure what the Federal Reserve was up to in terms of its long-range objectives for inflation.

Fourth, it was *imperfectly credible*. As Shapiro (1994) notes, the Volcker deflation is very different from the prior disinflation attempts by the

---

4. As the reader will note, the scale of the output effect depends entirely on the choice of the parameter ϕ. In drawing the graph, I chose a $\phi = .2$, which meant that a maximum output decline of about 2.5% occurred, although no vertical scale is included in the diagram. A choice of $\phi = .05$ would have alternatively brought about a maximum 10% decline in output. In models that derive ϕ from underlying micro structure, it is related to two deeper parameters: the effect of real marginal cost on inflation (which Gali and Gertler [1999] estimate to be about .05) and the elasticity of real marginal cost to the output gap. Dotsey and King (2001) discuss how some structural features of the underlying economy affect this latter feature. Values of this elasticity much less than 1 arise from models with elastic labor supply, variable capacity utilization, and intermediate inputs. Hence, small values of ϕ and large output effects are not hard to generate from modern sticky-price models.

5. This restates a common criticism of the Barro-Lucas–type incomplete information models, which my then-colleague Stan Engerman once summarized as "Don't the people in your economies have telephones?" and Ed Prescott later put as "People read newspapers."

Federal Reserve. Within a few years after each of the four prior episodes, inflation was reduced only temporarily and then returned to an even higher level within a few years.

During the Volcker deflation, long-term interest rates stayed high for a long time, much longer than any modern pricing model—including that of Mankiw and Reis—would predict, if there was not imperfect credibility about long-term inflation. Unraveling the nature of this episode is an important topic for research in monetary economics, but I am not convinced that understanding the dynamics of measures of disagreement about expectations is important for understanding the episode.

2.5 IMPERFECT CREDIBILITY VERSUS STICKY EXPECTATIONS

In terms of practical macroeconomics, one might ask whether I have drawn a distinction without a difference in my discussion. I don't think so. Sticky expectations are a structural feature of price dynamics for Mankiw and Reis and describe both normal situations and unusual events. Imperfect credibility is a feature of the macroeconomy and monetary policy, and is likely to be more important in some situations than others. So, the inflation-output trade-off during the Volcker deflation might give a poor guide to the nature of that trade-off in a current monetary policy context.

REFERENCES

Ball, Laurence. (1994). Credible disinflation with staggered price-setting. *American Economic Review* 84(1): 282–289.
Ball, Laurence. (1995). Disinflation with imperfect credibility. *Journal of Monetary Economics* 35(1): 5–23.
Ball, Laurence, N. Gregory Mankiw, and David Romer. (1988). The new Keynesian economics and the output-inflation trade-off. *Brookings Papers on Economic Activity* 1988(1): 1–82.
Barro, Robert J. (1976). Rational expectations and the role of monetary policy. *Journal of Monetary Economics* 2(1): 1–32.
Calvo, Guillermo. (1983). Staggered prices in a utility-maximizing framework. *Journal of Monetary Economics* 12(3): 383–398.
Dotsey, Michael, and Robert G. King. (2001). Production, pricing and persistence. Cambridge, MA: National Bureau of Economic Research. NBER Working Paper No. 8407.
Gali, Jordi, and Mark Gertler. (1999). Inflation dynamics: A structural econometric analysis. *Journal of Monetary Economics* 44(2): 195–222.
Gordon, Robert J. (1970). The recent acceleration of inflation and its lessons for the future. *Brookings Papers on Macroeconomics* 1:8–41.
Lucas, Robert E., Jr. (1972). Econometric testing of the natural rate hypothesis. In *The Econometrics of Price Determination*, Otto Eckstein (ed.). Washington, DC: Board of Governors of the Federal Reserve System.
Lucas, Robert E., Jr. (1973). Some international evidence on output inflation trade-offs. *The American Economic Review* 63(3): 326–334.

Mankiw, N. Gregory, and Ricardo Reis. (2002). Sticky information versus sticky prices: A proposal to replace the new Keynesian Phillips curve. *Quarterly Journal of Economics* 117(4): 1295–1328.

Muth, John F. (1961). Rational expectations and the theory of price movements. *Econometrica* 29(3):315–335.

Sargent, Thomas J. (1971). A note on the accelerationist controversy. *Journal of Money, Credit and Banking* 3(August):50–60.

Shapiro, Matthew D. (1994). Federal Reserve policy: Cause and effect. In *Monetary Policy*, N. G. Mankiw (ed.). Cambridge, MA: MIT Press.

Solow, Robert M. (1969). *Price Expectations and the Behavior of the Price Level*. Mancheser, UK: Manchester University Press.

Thomas, Julia K. (2002). Is lumpy investment relevant for the business cycle? *Journal of Political Economy* 110:508–534.

Comment

JOHN C. WILLIAMS
Federal Reserve Bank of San Francisco

This is an excellent paper that uncovers several novel and fascinating "stylized facts" about cross-sectional dispersion of inflation expectations based on surveys of households and economists in the United States. Of particular interest is the finding that the degree of dispersion is positively correlated with both the inflation rate and dispersion in relative prices. In addition, the authors propose a theory that can account for many of the empirical time-series regularities related to both the median and dispersion in surveys of inflation expectations. Given the central role of expectations in modern macroeconomic theory, this paper is certain to stimulate a wide range of theoretical and empirical research aimed at understanding heterogeneous expectations and their implications for the behavior of the economy. A question of immediate interest is whether the stylized facts regarding inflation expectations in the United States also describe expectations of other key macroeconomic variables, such as gross domestic product (GDP) and interest rates, and expectations data in other countries.

Throughout my discussion I will follow the authors' lead and treat surveys as representing reasonably accurate measures of agents' expectations. But it is worth keeping in mind that expectations derived from financial market data can differ in important ways from expectations taken from surveys. For example, as noted in the paper, Ball and Croushore (2001) document the insensitivity of the median value from surveys of inflation expectations to economic news. In contrast,

I would like to thank Kirk Moore for excellent research assistance

Gürkaynak et al. (2003) find that forward nominal interest rates are highly sensitive to economic news, and they provide evidence that this sensitivity is primarily related to the inflation component of interest rates. Because financial market participants "put their money where there mouths are," one is tempted to put greater faith in estimates taken from financial market data, even while recognizing the difficult measurement problems associated with extracting expectations from these data. Still, additional study and comparison of both sources of expectations data is needed to form a more complete picture of the properties of expectations.

The remainder of my discussion will focus on two topics: learning and model uncertainty. The first relates to is the real-time information that forecasters are assumed to possess. The second provides an alternative explanation of the evidence on dispersion in forecasters' inflation expectations based on the notion that there exists a range of competing forecast models. I find that model uncertainty provides an intuitively more appealing description of the form of disagreement among economists than that proposed in the paper.

The authors argue that the Mankiw and Reis (2002) sticky-information model can explain many of the properties of the median values and dispersion of surveys of inflation expectations. In this model, agents use a three-variable, 12-lag monthly vector auto regression (VAR), that includes inflation, the output gap, and the three-month T-bill rate, estimated over the entire postwar sample to generate forecasts.[1] Individual agents, however, update their expectations only at random intervals, with a 10% probability of an update in each month. Given this structure, the resulting median sticky-information forecast is closely related to the median of a geometrically weighted average of past inflation forecasts. The cross-sectional dispersion in forecasts reflects the dispersion of forecasts across vintages. In fact, there is absolutely no disagreement about forecasting methods; all the differences arise from the differences across vintages of forecasts that people are assumed to use.

I find the assumption that households and economists had access to the full-sample VAR estimates to be unrealistic: people in 1960 simply did not possess the knowledge of forecast model specification and

---

1. The use of the output gap in the forecasting VAR is problematic because of well-documented problems with real-time estimates of GDP and potential (or the natural rate of) output, issues emphasized by Orphanides (2001), Orphanides and van Norden (2002), and others. A preferable approach would be to use the unemployment rate or the real-time estimates of capacity utilization, which is the approach I follow in the model-based exercises reported in this discussion. As noted by the authors, their results are not sensitive to the use of the output gap in this application, so this criticism is intended more as a general warning.

Figure 1 IN SAMPLE VERSUS OUT-OF-SAMPLE FORECASTS

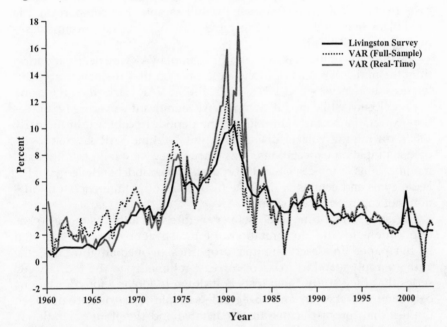

parameter estimates that we have accumulated over the subsequent 40 or more years. Instead, they needed to estimate and test models based on the limited data that they had on hand and that ran only back to the late 1940s.[2] By constructing the sticky-information model forecasts from a VAR estimated over the full sample, the authors are giving agents far more information, especially during the earlier part of the sample, than they had. A more palatable procedure would be to assume that agents estimate their models in real time, using the vintage of data available to them, and form forecasts accordingly.

VAR forecasts using the data available at the time track the Livingston Survey pretty closely through the 1960s and 1970s and do a much better job at this over that period than forecasts based on a VAR estimated over the full sample. The shaded gray line in Figure 1 shows the forecasts of consumer price index (CPI) inflation over the next four quarters from a real-time, three-variable VAR estimated over data from 1950 through

---

2. Data from the period of World War II was arguably of limited value for forecasting inflation because of the stringent price controls in place during the war.

the current quarter.[3] The dashed black line reports the corresponding fore-casts from a VAR estimated over the full sample. For comparison, the solid black line shows the Livingston Survey of expected price increases over the next 12 months.

The forecasts of the real-time and full-sample VARs are nearly identical from the mid-1980s on, but in the earlier period they display sizable dif-ferences. In the 1960s and 1970s, the real-time VAR tracks the Livingston Survey closely, while the full-sample VAR significantly overpredicts infla-tion expectations nearly throughout the period. In contrast, in the early 1980s, during the Volcker disinflation, the real-time VAR severely over-predicts inflation expectations. This discrepancy may reflect judgmental modifications to forecasts that incorporate extra-model knowledge of the Fed's goals and actions at the time (as well as other influences on infla-tion) not captured by the simple VAR.

The issue of real-time forecasts versus forecasts after the fact also has implications for the interpretation of forecast rationality tests reported in the paper. In describing the properties of median forecasts, the authors apply standard tests of forecast rationality to the four survey series that they study. Such tests boil down to looking for correlations between forecast errors and observable variables, the existence of which implies that forecast errors are predictable and therefore not rational. They consider four such tests. The simplest test is that for forecast bias, i.e., nonzero mean in forecast errors. A second test is for serial correla-tion in forecast errors in nonoverlapping periods. A third test, which I call the forecast information test in the following, is a test of correlation between forecast errors and a constant and the forecast itself. The final test, which I call the all information test, is a joint test of the correlation between forecast errors and a set of variables taken from the VAR described above, assumed to be in forecasters' information set.

They find mixed results on bias and forecast information tests, but rationality of the median value of surveys is rejected based on the serial correlation and all information tests. They then show that the median forecast predicted by the sticky-information model yields similar results—with forecast errors exhibiting positive serial correlation and a high rate of rejection of the forecast information and all information tests—providing support for that model.

An alternative interpretation of these results is that forecasters have been learning about quantitative macroeconomic relationships over time. The

---

3. I chose the CPI for this analysis because it sidesteps the issue of differences between real-time and final revised data in national income account price indexes, such as the GDP deflator. The CPI is not revised except for seasonal factors, and because I am focusing on four-quarter changes in prices, seasonal factors should be of little importance to the analysis.

tests are based on the correlations in the full sample and ignore the fact that forecasters, even those with the correct VAR model, had inaccurate estimates of these relationships at the time of their forecasts. Because of sampling errors in the forecaster's model, these tests are biased toward rejecting the null of rationality.[4]

Indeed, a wide variety of reasonable forecasting models, including a quarterly version of the VAR used in the paper (with the unemployment rate substituting for the output gap), yield a pattern of rejections similar to those seen in the survey data when one assumes that the forecasts were constructed in real-time using knowledge of the data correlations available at the time. Table 1 reports the results from rationality tests from several simple forecasting models. The first line of the table reports the results from the three-variable VAR with four quarterly lags, where the VAR is reestimated each period to incorporate the latest observed data point. This real-time VAR exhibits no bias over the past 40 years, but forecast rationality is rejected based on positive forecast error serial correlation and the two information tests. (For this test, I include the most recent observed value of the inflation rate, the unemployment rate, and the 3-month T-bill rate.) The results for other forecast models (the details of which I describe below) are also consistent with the evidence from the surveys. And as indicated in the bottom line of the table, the median forecast among these 10 forecasting models also exhibits the pattern of rejections seen in the survey data. This evidence suggests that forecasters use models in which the parameters change over time.

I now turn to the second half of the paper. The authors show that the sticky-information model provides a parsimonious theory of disagreement that is in accord, at least qualitatively, with the time-series pattern of disagreement seen in the survey data. In addition, the model can generate a positive correlation between disagreement and the inflation rate, also a prominent feature of the survey data.

The evidence for the sticky-information model from inflation expectations disagreement from household surveys, however, is not clear cut. The model cannot come close to matching the magnitude of the dispersion in household inflation expectations, for which the interquartile range (IQR)—that already excludes one half of the sample as outliers—can reach 10 percentage points! In Figure 10 of the paper, the difference between the measure of disagreement in the data and that predicted by

4. In addition to uncertainty about model parameters, the specification of forecasting models changes over time in response to incoming data, driving another wedge between the information set available to real-time forecasters and after-the-fact calculations of what forecasters "should have known." In models with time-varying latent variables such as the natural rates of unemployment and interest, this problem also extends to the real-time specification and estimation of the latent variable data-generating processes, as discussed in Orphanides and Williams (2002).

Table 1   REAL-TIME MODEL-BASED FORECASTS[1]

Description	RHS variables	Discounting of past data	RMSE	Bias	Error serial correlation	Forecast info.	All info.
					Tests of forecast rationality		
VAR	π, u, r	None	2.28	-0.11	0.42 ***	***	***
		0.015	2.06	-0.16	0.11	***	***
		0.030	2.09	-0.11	-0.01	***	***
Phillips curve	π, u	None	1.96	0.20	0.50 ***		***
		0.015	1.69	0.02	0.19	***	***
		0.030	1.72	-0.01	0.03	***	***
Autoregressive	π	None	1.92	0.46 *	0.46 ***		***
		0.015	1.73	0.09	0.16	**	***
		0.030	1.73	0.05	0.13	***	***
Random walk	π	—	1.79	0.01	0.17	***	***
Memo							
Median forecast			1.67	0.02	0.22 *	**	***

1. Forecast variable is the four-quarter percentage change in the CPI. Sample: 1960–2002; quarterly data. RMSE denotes root mean squared forecast error. Bias is the mean forecast error. One asterisk indicates an asymptotic p-value between 5 and 10 percent; two asterisks, between 1 and 5 percent; and three asterisks, below 1 percent. Error serial correlation reports the estimated coefficient on lagged forecast error in regression of forecast error on a constant and the lagged forecast error. Test I is a regression of forecast errors on a constant and the forecasted value. Test II is a regression of the forecast error on a constant, the forecasted value, the inflation rate, the Treasury-bill rate, and the unemployment rate. P-values based on Newey-West HAC standard errors.

the model is not constant over time and appears to be highly persistent. There's clearly something else going on here, with the sticky-information model capturing only part of the process of households' expectations formation.

The sticky-information model is closely linked to Chris Carroll's (2003) model, whereby households randomly come into contact with professional forecasts. I find his model to be a highly plausible description of expectations formation by households, who are unlikely to keep in constant touch with the latest macroeconomic data. But as a macroeconomic forecaster myself, I find it entirely implausible as a description of the behavior of business economists and professional forecasters surveyed in the Livingston Survey and the Survey of Professional Forecasters (SPF), respectively. Professional forecasters update their forecasts regularly and update their forecasting models at frequent intervals. The primary reason economists' forecasts disagree is not due to lags in formulating new forecasts, but instead is because economists themselves disagree about how to model the economy best![5] This is an aspect of dispersions in expectations entirely absent from the model in the paper.

In fact, there already exist theories of rational heterogeneity of beliefs that naturally yield expectations disagreement (see, for example, Brock and Hommes [1997], Branch [2003], and Branch and Evans [2003]). These theories assume that agents have at their disposal a range of forecasting models but are uncertain about which model or models to use. They update their model choice or priors over the various models based on forecasting performance. Idiosyncratic differences in agents' characteristics, say, different initial conditions in model priors and the costs for learning new models, implies that a range of models will be in use at any point in time.

This description matches closely the real-world practice of economic forecasting that recognizes the high degree of model uncertainty in forecasting. There exists many competing inflation forecast models, including time-series models, Bayesian VARs, reduced-form Phillips curves, and large-scale macroeconometric models in use at the same time. And for each model, several variants differ with respect to model specification and estimation, including the lag length of explanatory variables; treatment of latent variables; sample size; and the inclusion or exclusion of additional explanatory variables such as energy prices, import prices, price control dummies, sample, wages, productivity, etc. (compare Brayton et al. [1999] and Stock and Watson [1999]). These models have similarly good track

---

5. The disagreement seen in published forecasts is an imperfect measure of true disagreement. There are incentives both not stray too far from the consensus (Scharfstein and Stein, 1990; Lamont, 2002) as well as to stand out from the crowd (Laster et al., 1999).

records in terms of forecasting performance, but at times they can yield strikingly different forecasts. In practice, forecasters combine the forecasts from a subset of these models, along with extra-model information, to arrive at a point estimate forecast.

But why don't all forecasters arrive at the same forecast? For the same reason as in the theory sketched above: idiosyncratic differences between economists imply persistent deviations in modeling choices. One source of such differences might originate during graduate school training. For example, economists trained in the 1960s likely rely more heavily on structural macroeconometric models for forecasting, while those trained during the 1990s probably place more weight on Bayesian VARs. Because these models are about equally good in terms of forecasting accuracy, the pace of convergence to a single best mix of models is likely to be slow.

To illustrate how model uncertainty can lead to forecast disagreement conforming to the evidence presented in the paper, I construct an artificial universe of forecasters, each of whom is assumed to use one of the 10 forecasting models listed in Table 1. As seen in the table, these models have roughly similar out-of-sample forecast accuracy. In each case, the model is reestimated each period. The parameters are unrestricted. For each of the three main types of models, I consider three variants: one is estimated by standard ordinary least squares (OLS) and the second and third are estimated by weighted least squares (WLS), with the weights declining geometrically using the values 0.985 or 0.970, as indicated in the table. WLS estimation is designed as protection against structural change by downweighting old data (Evans and Honkapohja, 2001). The first main model is the VAR described above. The second model is a Phillips curve model that includes a constant, four lags of inflation, and two lags of the unemployment rate. The third model is a fourth-order autoregression. The set of models is completed with a simple random walk model where the forecast inflation over the next four quarters equals the inflation rate over the past four quarters.

The out-of-sample forecasting performance (measured by the root mean squared forecast error) of these various models is quite similar. The random walk model beats the other models without discounting, consistent with the findings of Atkeson and Ohanion (2001). The VAR model is the worst performer of the group, supporting Fair's (1979) finding that unrestricted VAR models tend to perform poorly out of sample. The Phillips curve model, with discounting, is the best performer of the group, and in all three cases the model with discounting outperforms the OLS version. Evidently, structural breaks are of great enough importance in this sample that protecting against such breaks outweighs the efficiency loss associated with discarding data (see Orphanides and Williams

[2004]). Finally, the median forecast from this set of 10 models performs better than any individual forecast, in line with the literature that averaging across forecast models improves performance (see Clement [1989] and Granger [1989] for surveys of this topic).

At times, these forecasting models yield different forecasts of inflation, as shown by the shaded region in Figure 2. The degree of disagreement across models widens appreciably around 1970, again in the mid-1970s, and most strikingly during the period of the disinflation commencing at the end of the 1970s and continuing into the early 1980s. The magnitude of disagreement across models is much smaller during the 1960s and from the mid-1980s through the end of the sample.

The time-series pattern seen in the interquartile range from these forecast models is similar to that seen in the Livingston Survey IQR, as depicted in Figure 3. During periods of stable and low inflation, forecast dispersion among these models is modest, but it spikes when inflation is high or changing rapidly, exhibiting the same pattern as in the IQR from the survey data. Of course, the purpose of this exercise is only to illustrate how model uncertainty can give rise to forecast disagreement similar to that seen in the survey data. As noted above, the extent of model disagreement extends beyond the set of models I have considered here,

Figure 2 MODEL UNCERTAINTY AND FORECAST DISAGREEMENT

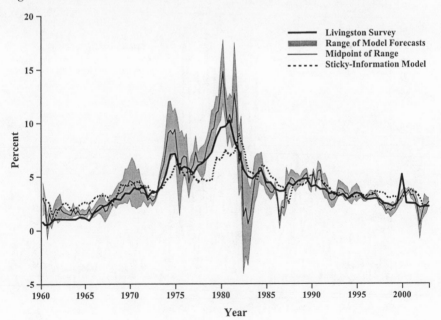

suggesting a wider range of disagreement than reported here. On the other hand, good forecasters will average various models, reducing the range of disagreement implied by individual models. Careful quantitative analysis of model-based forecast disagreement is left to future work.

Of course, there are many reasonable alternative explanations, in addition to the sticky-information model, for forecast disagreement among economists that conform to the main properties of inflation expectations highlighted in this paper. My goal was to provide an illustrative example of one such case. (Robert King's discussion of public disagreement regarding the Federal Reserve's ultimate inflation objective in this volume provides another.) To test these alternative theories against each other, it will be useful to examine evidence from expectations of a wider set of variables, including long-run inflation expectations, and from surveys in other countries. In addition, this paper has focused on a few moments in the survey data. The Livingston Survey and SPF are panel datasets that track the responses through time of individual forecasters. The panel aspect of this data is an untapped well of information that may help discern different theories of disagreement.

Finally, although expectations disagreement may be useful in discerning alternative models of expectations formation, it is unclear how quantitatively important disagreement on its own, even time-varying

Figure 3 FORECAST DISAGREEMENT

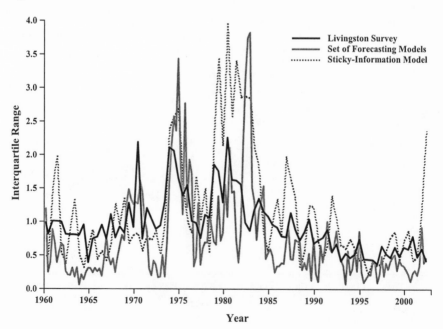

disagreement, is for the evolution of the aggregate economy, given a path for the mean expectation. The macroeconomic implications of time-varying disagreement provide another avenue of future research that is sure to be stimulated by this fine paper.

REFERENCES

Atkeson, Andrew, and Lee E. Ohanian. (2001). Are Phillips curves useful for forecasting inflation? *Federal Reserve Bank of Minneapolis Quarterly Review* 25(1): 2–11.
Ball, Laurence, and Dean Croushore (2001). Expectations and the effects of monetary policy. Federal Reserve Bank of Philadelphia. Research Working Paper: 01/12.
Branch, William A. (2003). The theory of rationally heterogeneous expectations: Evidence from survey data on inflation expectations. Department of Economics, College of William and Mary. Manuscript.
Branch, William A., and George W. Evans. (2003). Intrinsic heterogeneity in expectation formation. Department of Economics, College of William and Mary. Manuscript.
Brayton, Flint, John M. Roberts, and John C. Williams. (1999). What's happened to the Phillips curve? Board of Governors of the Federal Reserve System. Finance and Economics Discussion Paper Series: 99/49.
Brock, William A., and Cars H. Hommes. (1997). A rational route to randomness. *Econometrica* 65(5);1059–1160.
Carroll, Christopher D. (2003). Macroeconomic expectations of households and professional forecasters. *Quarterly Journal of Economics* 118(1):269–298.
Clement, Robert T. (1989). Combining forecasts: A review and annotated bibliography. *International Journal of Forecasting* 5(4):559–583.
Evans, George W., and Seppo Honkapohja. (2001). *Learning and Expectations in Macroeconomics.* Princeton, NJ: Princeton University Press.
Fair, Ray C. (1979). An analysis of the accuracy of four macroeconometric models. *Journal of Political Economy* 87(4):701–718.
Granger, Clive. (1989) Combining forecasts—Twenty years later. *Journal of Forecasting* 8:167–174.
Gürkaynak, Refet, Brian Sack, and Eric Swanson. (2003). The excess sensitivity of long-term interest rates: Evidence and implications for macroeconomic models. Board of Governors of the Federal Reserve System. Manuscript.
Lamont, Owen A. (2002). Macroeconomic forecasts and microeconomic forecasters. *Journal of Economic Behavior and Organization* 48(3):265–280.
Laster, David, Paul Bennett, and In Sun Geoum. (1999). Rational bias in macroeconomic forecasts. *Quarterly Journal of Economics* 114(1):293–318.
Mankiw, N. Gregory, and Ricardo Reis. (2002). Sticky information versus sticky prices: A proposal to replace the new Keynesian Phillips curve. *Quarterly Journal of Economics* 117(4):1295–1328.
Orphanides, Athanasios. (2001). Monetary policy rules based on real-time data. *American Economic Review* 91(4):964–985.
Orphanides, Athanasios, and Simon van Norden. (2002). The unreliability of output-gap estimates in real time. *Review of Economics and Statistics* 84(4):569–583.
Orphanides, Athanasios, and John C. Williams. (2002). Robust monetary policy rules with unknown natural rates. *Brookings Papers on Economic Activity* 2:63–145.

Orphanides, Athanasios, and John C. Williams. (2004). Imperfect knowledge, inflation expectations, and monetary policy. In *Inflation Targeting*, Michael Woodford, (ed.). Chicago, IL: University of Chicago Press.

Scharfstein, David S., and Jeremy C. Stein. (1990). Herd behavior and investment. *American Economic Review* 80(3):465–479.

Stock, James H., and Mark W. Watson. (1999). Forecasting inflation. *Journal of Monetary Economics* 44(2):293–335.

Discussion

A number of participants suggested alternative explanations for the disagreement across agents in inflation expectations documented by the authors, and they recommended that the authors test their theory against plausible alternatives. Olivier Blanchard suggested the possibility that people form inflation expectations based on small samples of goods. Inflation variability across goods could then drive dispersion in expectations. He noted that there is indeed a lot of inflation variability across goods. He pointed out that this story is consistent with the fact that there is more dispersion in inflation expectations when inflation is changing. He also speculated that women might buy different baskets of goods from men, hence explaining the difference in expected inflation between women and men in the Michigan Survey. Justin Wolfers explained that, in favor of Blanchard's story, people's assessment of past inflation is a good predictor of their inflation expectation. The caveat is that the extent of variation in the inflation that they think they have experienced is not rationalizable. Ken Rogoff pointed out that there is evidence of substantial inflation dispersion across cities within the United States. He suggested that this might favor the hypotheses of Blanchard and Williams: that individual forecasts might be made on the basis of different baskets.

Another explanation was suggested by Mike Woodford. He remarked that Chris Sims's theory of limited information-processing capacity could endogenously generate the co-movement of disagreement and other macro variables. Greg Mankiw responded that the sticky-information model is a close relation of Chris Sims's work, but that it is analytically more tractable and generates testable predictions more easily than the work of Sims.

Ken Rogoff asked whether a story about policy credibility could explain the fact that there is more disagreement when inflation is changing. He hypothesized that fat tails in the distribution could be due to expectations of more extreme histories than the United States has experienced. He noted that, in view of the historically higher inflation experienced by both developing countries and other OECD countries, such expectations were not necessarily unreasonable. He also remarked that few plays of the game have been experienced so far. Greg Mankiw objected that a credibility story would not be able to explain positive autocorrelated errors in forecasts. Robert Shimer responded that Markov switching in inflation regime and a small sample is sufficient to explain such autocorrelation. Ricardo Reis agreed with Rogoff that the inflation history of the United States was uneventful from the point of view of identification.

Athanasios Orphanides was concerned that the authors' sticky-information explanation for disagreement cannot reasonably explain disagreement among professional forecasters who have strong incentives to update their information regularly. He suggested that a more reasonable explanation would be disagreement about the model used to forecast inflation or about estimates of variables such as the natural rate of unemployment. As evidence that such disagreement is widespread, he cited the response of many forecasters in the SPF that they did not use an estimate of the NAIRU to forecast inflation. Robert Shimer agreed with Orphanides that professional forecasters were unlikely to have sticky information. Justin Wolfers responded to Orphanides that disagreement about models or the NAIRU is merely a richer version of the sticky-information explanation of why people stick to bad forecasts for long periods of time.

Mark Gertler said that examining the source of cyclical dispersion in expectations is important. He hypothesized that it may be due to something beyond sticky information or imperfect monetary policy credibility. He noted that, although the Fed is unlikely to suffer from sticky information or imperfect credibility, its Green Book forecasts in the late 1970s missed both the upsurge in inflation and the disinflation. He remarked that this forecast error is correlated with dispersion in inflation expectations and suggested that this avenue would be interesting to explore. Greg Mankiw asked Gertler whether the Green Book forecast errors were autocorrelated over the period covered by the paper. Gertler responded that, because inflation was relatively flat over the period, it is hard to distinguish autocorrelation.

The reliability of the data used by the authors concerned some participants. Rick Mishkin contended that household surveys should be regarded with skepticism. He noted that, in contrast to forecasters, who make their living from their expectations, households have no incentive to think hard about their survey responses. He suspected that respondents claiming to expect 10% inflation were unlikely to be behaving in a way consistent with this expectation, and that the level of dispersion in the survey responses was exaggerated. Mishkin also noted that there is a literature that documented incentives for forecasters to make extreme predictions to attract attention. Greg Mankiw responded that the fact that the cyclical response of expected inflation is as predicted by the model, and that disagreement co-moves strongly across different surveys suggests that they are picking up more than just noise. Mankiw agreed that the fact that private-sector forecasters are selling a product does affect the incentives they face compared with, for example, the Fed's Green Book forecast. Ken Rogoff noted that forecasters may try to avoid changing their predictions to maintain credibility.

Ricardo Reis stressed that the main point of the paper was to demonstrate the extent of disagreement across agents in inflation expectations. He remarked that nothing in macro theory so far can explain why there should be so much disagreement, and the paper explored a first possible explanation. Reis said that there is a large middle ground between adaptive and hyperrational expectations, and that the paper is an attempt to explore one possible alternative. Greg Mankiw concluded that the bottom line of the paper is that disagreement is widespread, and it varies over time with variables that interest macroeconomists. Hence, macro models should be consistent with disagreement of this type.

Pierpaolo Benigno and Michael Woodford
NEW YORK UNIVERSITY; AND PRINCETON UNIVERSITY

Optimal Monetary and Fiscal Policy: A Linear-Quadratic Approach

While substantial research literatures seek to characterize optimal monetary and fiscal policy, respectively, the two branches of the literature have largely developed in isolation, and on apparently contradictory foundations. The modern literature on dynamically optimal fiscal policy often abstracts from monetary aspects of the economy altogether and so implicitly allows no useful role for monetary policy. When monetary policy is considered within the theory of optimal fiscal policy, it is most often in the context of models with flexible prices. In these models, monetary policy matters only because (1) the level of nominal interest rates (and hence the opportunity cost of holding money) determines the size of certain distortions that result from the attempt to economize on money balances, and (2) the way the price level varies in response to real disturbances determines the state-contingent real payoffs on (riskless) nominally denominated government debt, which may facilitate tax-smoothing in the case that explicitly state-contingent debt is not available. The literature on optimal monetary policy has instead been mainly concerned with quite distinct objectives for monetary stabilization policy, namely, the minimization of the distortions that result from prices or wages that do not adjust quickly enough to clear markets. At the same time, this literature typically ignores the fiscal consequences of alternative monetary policies; the characterizations of optimal monetary policy obtained are thus strictly correct only for a world in which lump-sum taxes are available.

We would like to thank Stefania Albanesi, Marios Angeletos, Albert Marcet, and Ramon Marimon; seminar participants at New York University, Rutgers University, Universitat Pompeu Fabra, and the Macroeconomics Annual conference (2003), and the editors for helpful comments; Brad Strum and Vasco Curdia for research assistance; and the National Science Foundation for research support through a grant to the NBER.

Here we wish to consider the way in which the conclusions reached in each of these two familiar fields of study must be modified if one takes simultaneous account of the basic elements of the policy problems addressed in each. On the one hand, we wish to consider how conventional conclusions with regard to the nature of an optimal monetary policy rule must be modified if one recognizes that the government's only sources of revenue are distorting taxes, so that the fiscal consequences of monetary policy matter for welfare. And, on the other hand, we wish to consider how conventional conclusions with regard to optimal tax policy must be modified if one recognizes that prices do not instantaneously clear markets, so that output determination depends on aggregate demand, in addition to the supply-side factors stressed in the conventional theory of optimal taxation.

Several recent papers have also sought to consider optimal monetary and fiscal policy jointly, in the context of models with sticky prices; important examples include Correia et al. (2001), Schmitt-Grohé and Uribe (2001), and Siu (2001). Our approach differs from those taken in these papers, however, in several respects. First, we model price stickiness in a different way than in any of these papers, namely, by assuming staggered pricing of the kind introduced by Calvo (1983). This particular form of price stickiness has been widely used both in analyses of optimal monetary policy in models with explicit microfoundations (e.g., Goodfriend and King, 1997; Clarida et al., 1999; Woodford, 2003) and in the empirical literature on optimizing models of the monetary transmission mechanism (e.g., Rotemberg and Woodford, 1997; Gali and Gertler, 1999; Sbordone, 2002).

Perhaps more important, we obtain analytical results rather than purely numerical ones. To obtain these results, we propose a linear-quadratic approach to the characterization of optimal monetary and fiscal policy that allows us to nest both conventional analyses of optimal monetary policy, such as that of Clarida et al. (1999), and analyses of optimal tax-smoothing in the spirit of Barro (1979), Lucas and Stokey (1983), and Aiyagari et al. (2002) as special cases of our more general framework. We show how a linear-quadratic policy problem can be derived to yield a correct linear approximation to the optimal policy rules from the point of view of the maximization of expected discounted utility in a dynamic stochastic general-equilibrium model, building on our earlier work (Benigno and Woodford, 2003) for the case of optimal monetary policy when lump-sum taxes are available.

Finally, we do not content ourselves with merely characterizing the optimal dynamic responses of our policy instruments (and other state variables) to shocks under an optimal policy, given one assumption or another about the nature and statistical properties of the exogenous disturbances to our model economy. Instead, we also wish to derive policy rules that the monetary and fiscal authorities may reasonably commit themselves to follow as a way of implementing the optimal equilibrium. In particular, we seek to characterize optimal policy in terms of optimal targeting rules for monetary and fiscal policy, of the kind proposed in the case of monetary policy by Svensson (1999), Svensson and Woodford (2003), and Giannoni and Woodford (2002, 2003). The rules are specified in terms of a target criterion for each authority; each authority commits itself to use its policy instrument each period in whatever way is necessary to allow it to project an evolution of the economy consistent with its target criterion. As discussed in Giannoni and Woodford (2002), we can derive rules of this form that are not merely consistent with the desired equilibrium responses to disturbances, but that in addition (1) imply a determinate rational-expectations equilibrium, so that there are not other equally possible (but less desirable) equilibria consistent with the same policy; and (2) bring about optimal responses to shocks regardless of the character of and statistical properties of the exogenous disturbances in the model.

1. The Policy Problem

Here we describe our assumptions about the economic environment and pose the optimization problem that joint optimal monetary and fiscal policies are intended to solve. The approximation method that we use to characterize the solution to this problem is then presented in the following section. Additional details of the derivation of the structural equations of our model of nominal price rigidity can be found in Woodford (2003, Chapter 3).

The goal of policy is assumed to be the maximization of the level of expected utility of a representative household. In our model, each household seeks to maximize:

$$U_{t_0} \equiv E_{t_0} \sum_{t=t_0}^{\infty} \beta^{t-t_0} \left[\tilde{u}(C_t; \xi_t) - \int_0^1 \tilde{v}(H_t(j); \xi_t) dj \right] \tag{1}$$

where C_t is a Dixit-Stiglitz aggregate of consumption of each of a continuum of differentiated goods:

$$C_t \equiv \left[\int_0^1 c_t(i)^{(\theta-1)/\theta} di \right]^{\theta/(\theta-1)} \tag{2}$$

with an elasticity of substitution equal to $\theta > 1$, and $H_t(j)$ is the quantity supplied of labor of type j. Each differentiated good is supplied by a single monopolistically competitive producer. There are assumed to be many goods in each of an infinite number of industries; the goods in each industry j are produced using a type of labor that is specific to that industry, and they also change their prices at the same time. The representative household supplies all types of labor as well as consumes all types of goods.[1] To simplify the algebraic form of our results, we restrict attention in this paper to the case of isoelastic functional forms:

$$\tilde{u}(C_t;\xi_t) \equiv \frac{C_t^{1-\tilde{\sigma}^{-1}}\bar{C}_t^{\tilde{\sigma}^{-1}}}{1-\tilde{\sigma}^{-1}}$$

$$\tilde{v}(H_t;\xi_t) \equiv \frac{\lambda}{1+v}H_t^{1+v}\bar{H}_t^{-v}$$

where $\tilde{\sigma}, v > 0$, and $\{\bar{C}_t, \bar{H}_t\}$ are bounded exogenous disturbance processes. (We use the notation ξ_t to refer to the complete vector of exogenous disturbances, including $\bar{C}_t$, and $\bar{H}_t$.)

We assume a common technology for the production of all goods, in which (industry-specific) labor is the only variable input:

$$y_t(i) = A_t f(h_t(i)) = A_t h_t(i)^{1/\phi}$$

where A_t is an exogenously varying technology factor, and $\phi > 1$. Inverting the production function to write the demand for each type of labor as a function of the quantities produced of the various differentiated goods, and using the identity:

$$Y_t = C_t + G_t$$

to substitute for C_t, where G_t is exogenous government demand for the composite good, we can write the utility of the representative household as a function of the expected production plan $\{y_t(i)\}$.[2]

We can also express the relative quantities demanded of the differentiated goods each period as a function of their relative prices. This allows

1. We might alternatively assume specialization across households in the type of labor supplied; in the presence of perfect sharing of labor income risk across households, household decisions regarding consumption and labor supply would all be as assumed here.
2. The government is assumed to need to obtain an exogenously given quantity of the Dixit-Stiglitz aggregate each period and to obtain this in a cost-minimizing fashion. Hence, the government allocates its purchases across the suppliers of differentiated goods in the same proportion as do households, and the index of aggregate demand Y_t is the same function of the individual quantities $\{y_i(t)\}$ as C_t is of the individual quantities consumed $\{c_i(i)\}$, defined in equation (2).

us to write the utility flow to the representative household in the form $U(Y_t, \Delta_t; \xi_t)$, where:

$$\Delta_t \equiv \int_0^1 \left(\frac{p_t(i)}{P_t} \right)^{-\theta(1+\omega)} di \geq 1 \tag{3}$$

is a measure of price dispersion at date t, in which P_t is the Dixit-Stiglitz price index:

$$P_t \equiv \left[\int_0^1 p_t(i)^{1-\theta} di \right]^{1/(1-\theta)} \tag{4}$$

and the vector ξ_t now includes the exogenous disturbances G_t and A_t as well as the preference shocks. Hence, we can write equation (1) as:

$$U_{t_0} = E_{t_0} \sum_{t=t_0}^{\infty} \beta^{t-t_0} U(Y_t, \Delta_t; \xi_t) \tag{5}$$

The producers in each industry fix the prices of their goods in monetary units for a random interval of time, as in the model of staggered pricing introduced by Calvo (1983). We let $0 \leq \alpha < 1$ be the fraction of prices that remain unchanged in any period. A supplier that changes its price in period t chooses its new price $p_t(i)$ to maximize:

$$E_t \left\{ \sum_{T=t}^{\infty} \alpha^{T-t} Q_{t,T} \Pi(p_t(i), p_T^j, P_T; Y_T, \tau_T, \xi_T) \right\} \tag{6}$$

where $Q_{t,T}$ is the stochastic discount factor by which financial markets discount random nominal income in period T to determine the nominal value of a claim to such income in period t, and α^{T-t} is the probability that a price chosen in period t will not have been revised by period T. In equilibrium, this discount factor is given by the following equation:

$$Q_{t,T} = \beta^{T-t} \frac{\tilde{u}_c(C_T; \xi_T)}{\tilde{u}_c(C_t; \xi_t)} \frac{P_t}{P_T} \tag{7}$$

The function $\Pi(p, p^j, P; Y, \tau, \xi)$, defined in the appendix in Section 7, indicates the after-tax nominal profits of a supplier with price p, in an industry with common price p^j, when the aggregate price index is equal to P, aggregate demand is equal to Y, and sales revenues are taxed at rate τ. Profits are equal to after-tax sales revenues net of the wage bill, and the real wage demanded for labor of type j is assumed to be given by:

$$w_t(j) = \mu_t^w \frac{\tilde{v}_h(H_t(j); \xi_t)}{\tilde{u}_c(C_t; \xi_t)} \tag{8}$$

where $\mu_t^w \geq 1$ is an exogenous markup factor in the labor market (allowed to vary over time but assumed to be common to all labor markets),[3] and firms are assumed to be wage-takers. We allow for wage markup variations to include the possibility of a pure cost-push shock that affects equilibrium pricing behavior while implying no change in the efficient allocation of resources. Note that variation in the tax rate τ_t has a similar effect on this pricing problem (and hence on supply behavior); this is the sole distortion associated with tax policy in the present model.

Each of the suppliers that revise their prices in period t choose the same new price p_t^*. Under our assumed functional forms, the optimal choice has a closed-form solution:

$$\frac{p_t^*}{P_t} = \left(\frac{K_t}{F_t}\right)^{1/(1+\omega\theta)} \tag{9}$$

where $\omega \equiv \phi(1+v)-1 > 0$ is the elasticity of real marginal cost in an industry with respect to industry output, and F_t and K_t are functions of current aggregate output Y_t; the current tax rate τ_t; the current exogenous state ξ_t; and the expected future evolution of inflation, output, taxes, and disturbances, defined in the appendix.[4]

The price index then evolves according to a law of motion:

$$P_t = \left[(1-\alpha)p_t^{*1-\theta} + \alpha P_{t-1}^{1-\theta}\right]^{1/(1-\theta)} \tag{10}$$

as a consequence of equation (4). Substitution of equation (9) into equation (10) implies that equilibrium inflation in any period is given by:

$$\frac{1-\alpha\Pi_t^{\theta-1}}{1-\alpha} = \left(\frac{F_t}{K_t}\right)^{(\theta-1)/(1+\omega\theta)} \tag{11}$$

where $\Pi_t \equiv P_t/P_{t-1}$. This defines a short-run aggregate supply relation between inflation and output, given the current tax rate τ_t; current disturbances ξ_t; and expectations regarding future inflation, output, taxes, and disturbances. Because the relative prices of the industries that do not change their prices in period t remain the same, we can also use equation (10) to derive a law of motion of the form:

$$\Delta_t = h(\Delta_{t-1}, \Pi_t) \tag{12}$$

---

3. In the case where we assume that $\mu_t^w = 1$ at all times, our model is one in which both households and firms are wage-takers, or there is efficient contracting between them.
4. The disturbance vector ξ_t is now understood to include the current value of the wage markup μ_t^w.

for the dispersion measure defined in equation (3). This is the source in our model of welfare losses from inflation or deflation.

We abstract here from any monetary frictions that would account for a demand for central-bank liabilities that earn a substandard rate of return. We nonetheless assume that the central bank can control the riskless short-term nominal interest rate i_t, which is in turn related to other financial asset prices through the arbitrage relation:[5]

$$1 + i_t = [E_t Q_{t,t+1}]^{-1}$$

We shall assume that the zero lower bound on nominal interest rates never binds under the optimal policies considered below.[6] Thus, we need not introduce any additional constraint on the possible paths of output and prices associated with a need for the chosen evolution of prices to be consistent with a nonnegative nominal interest rate.

Our abstraction from monetary frictions, and hence from the existence of seignorage revenues, does not mean that monetary policy has no fiscal consequences because interest-rate policy and the equilibrium inflation that results from it have implications for the real burden of government debt. For simplicity, we shall assume that all public debt consists of riskless nominal one-period bonds. The nominal value B_t of end-of-period public debt then evolves according to a law of motion:

$$B_t = (1 + i_{t-1})B_{t-1} - P_t s_t \tag{13}$$

where the real primary budget surplus is given by:

$$s_t \equiv \tau_t Y_t - G_t - \zeta_t \tag{14}$$

Here τ_t, the share of the national product that is collected by the government as tax revenues in period t, is the key fiscal policy decision each period; the real value of (lump-sum) government transfers ζ_t is treated as exogenously given, as are government purchases G_t. (We introduce the additional type of exogenously given fiscal needs to be able to analyze the consequences of a purely fiscal disturbance, with no implications for the real allocation of resources beyond those that follow from its effect on the government budget.)

5. For discussion of how this is possible even in a cashless economy of the kind assumed here, see Woodford (2003, Chapter 2).
6. This can be shown to be true in the case of small enough disturbances, given that the nominal interest rate is equal to $\bar{r} = \beta^{-1} - 1 > 0$ under the optimal policy in the absence of disturbances.

Rational-expectations equilibrium requires that the expected path of government surpluses must satisfy an intertemporal solvency condition:

$$b_{t-1} \frac{P_{t-1}}{P_t} = E_t \sum_{T=t}^{\infty} R_{t,T} s_T \tag{15}$$

in each state of the world that may be realized at date t, where $R_{t,T} \equiv Q_{t,T} P_T/P_t$ is the stochastic discount factor for a real income stream.[7] This condition restricts the possible paths that may be chosen for the tax rate $\{\tau_t\}$. Monetary policy can affect this constraint, however, both by affecting the period t inflation rate (which affects the left side) and (in the case of sticky prices) by affecting the discount factors $\{R_{t,T}\}$.

Under the standard (Ramsey) approach to the characterization of an optimal policy commitment, one chooses among state-contingent paths $\{\Pi_t, Y_t, \tau_t, b_t, \Delta_t\}$ from some initial date t_0 onward that satisfy equations (11), (12), and (15) for each $t \geq t_0$, given initial government debt b_{t_0-1} and price dispersion Δ_{t_0-1}, to maximize equation (5). Such a t_0-optimal plan requires commitment, insofar as the corresponding t-optimal plan for some later date t, given the conditions b_{t-1}, Δ_{t-1} obtaining at that date, will not involve a continuation of the t_0-optimal plan. This failure of time consistency occurs because the constraints on what can be achieved at date t_0, consistent with the existence of a rational-expectations equilibrium, depend on the expected paths of inflation, output, and taxes at later dates; but in the absence of a prior commitment, a planner would have no motive at those later dates to choose a policy consistent with the anticipations that it was desirable to create at date t_0.

However, the degree of advance commitment that is necessary to bring about an optimal equilibrium is only of a limited sort. Let:

$$W_t \equiv E_t \sum_{T=t}^{\infty} \beta^{T-t} \tilde{u}_c(Y_T - G_T; \xi_T) s_T$$

and let $\mathcal{F}$ be the set of values for $(b_{t-1}, \Delta_{t-1}, F_t, K_t, W_t)$ such that there exist paths $\{\Pi_T, Y_T, \tau_T, b_T, \Delta_T\}$ for dates $T \geq t$ that satisfy equations (11), (12), and (15) for each T, that are consistent with the specified values for F_t, K_t, and W_t, and that imply a well-defined value for the objective U_t defined in equation (5). Furthermore, for any $(b_{t-1}, \Delta_{t-1}, F_t, K_t, W_t) \in \mathcal{F}$, let $V(b_{t-1}, \Delta_{t-1}, X_t; \xi_t)$ denote the maximum attainable value of U_t among the state-contingent

---

7. See Woodford (2003, Chapter 2) for the derivation of this condition from household optimization together with market clearing. The condition should not be interpreted as an a priori constraint on possible government policy rules, as discussed in Woodford (2001). When we consider the problem of choosing an optimal plan from among the possible rational-expectations equilibria, however, this condition must be imposed among the constraints on the set of equilibria that one may hope to bring about.

paths that satisfy the constraints just mentioned, where $X_t \equiv (F_t, K_t, W_t)$.[8] Then the t_0–optimal plan can be obtained as the solution to a two-stage optimization problem, as shown in the appendix (Section 7).

In the first stage, values of the endogenous variables x_{t_0}, where $x_t \equiv (\Pi_t, Y_t, \tau_t, b_t, \Delta_t)$, and state-contingent commitments X_{t_0+1} (ξ_{t_0+1}) for the following period, are chosen, subject to a set of constraints stated in the appendix, including the requirement that the choices $(b_{t_0}, \Delta_{t_0}, X_{t_0+1}) \in \mathcal{F}$ for each possible state of the world ξ_{t_0+1}. These variables are chosen to maximize the objective $\hat{J} [X_{t_0}, X_{t_0+1}(\cdot)](\xi_{t_0})$, where we define the functional:

$$\hat{J} [x_t, X_{t+1}(\cdot)](\xi_t) \equiv U(Y_t, \Delta_t; \xi_t) + \beta E_t V(b_t, \Delta_t, X_{t+1}; \xi_{t+1}) \tag{16}$$

In the second stage, the equilibrium evolution from period $t_0 + 1$ onward is chosen to solve the maximization problem that defines the value function $V(b_{t_0}, \Delta_{t_0}, X_{t_0+1}; \xi_{t_0+1})$, given the state of the world ξ_{t_0+1} and the precommitted values for X_{t_0+1} associated with that state. The key to this result is a demonstration that there are no restrictions on the evolution of the economy from period $t_0 + 1$ onward that are required for this expected evolution to be consistent with the values chosen for x_{t_0}, except consistency with the commitments X_{t_0+1} (ξ_{t_0+1}) chosen in the first stage.

The optimization problem in stage two of this reformulation of the Ramsey problem is of the same form as the Ramsey problem itself, except that there are additional constraints associated with the precommitted values for the elements of X_{t_0+1} (ξ_{t_0+1}). Let us consider a problem like the Ramsey problem just defined, looking forward from some period t_0, except under the constraints that the quantities X_{t_0} must take certain given values, where $(b_{t_0-1}, \Delta_{t_0-1}, X_{t_0}) \in \mathcal{F}$. This constrained problem can similarly be expressed as a two-stage problem of the same form as above, with an identical stage-two problem to the one described above. Stage two of this constrained problem is thus of exactly the same form as the problem itself. Hence, the constrained problem has a recursive form. It can be decomposed into an infinite sequence of problems, in which in each period t, $(x_t, X_{t+1}(\cdot))$ are chosen to maximize $\hat{J} [x_t, X_{t+1}(\cdot)] (\xi_t)$, subject to the constraints of the stage-one problem, given the predetermined state variables (b_{t-1}, Δ_{t-1}) and the precommitted values X_t.

Our aim here is to characterize policy that solves this constrained optimization problem (stage two of the original Ramsey problem), i.e., policy that is optimal from some date t onward given precommitted values for

8. In our notation for the value function V, ξ_t denotes not simply the vector of disturbances in period t, but all information in period t about current and future disturbances. This corresponds to the disturbance vector ξ_t referred to earlier in the case that the disturbance vector follows a Markov process.

X_t. Because of the recursive form of this problem, it is possible for a commitment to a time-invariant policy rule from date t onward to implement an equilibrium that solves the problem, for some specification of the initial commitments X_t. A time-invariant policy rule with this property is said by Woodford (2003, Chapter 7) to be "optimal from a timeless perspective."[9] Such a rule is one that a policymaker who solves a traditional Ramsey problem would be willing to commit to follow *eventually*, though the solution to the Ramsey problem involves different behavior initially because there is no need to internalize the effects of prior anticipation of the policy adopted for period t_0.[10] One might also argue that it is desirable to commit to follow such a rule immediately, even though such a policy would not solve the (unconstrained) Ramsey problem, as a way of demonstrating one's willingness to accept constraints that one wishes the public to believe that one will accept in the future.

2. A Linear-Quadratic Approximate Problem

In fact, we shall here characterize the solution to this problem (and similarly derive optimal time-invariant policy rules) only for initial conditions near certain steady-state values, allowing us to use local approximations in characterizing optimal policy.[11] We establish that these steady-state values have the property that if one starts from initial conditions close enough to the steady state, and exogenous disturbances thereafter are small enough, the optimal policy subject to the initial commitments remains forever near the steady state. Hence, our local characterization would describe the long-run character of Ramsey policy, in the event that disturbances are small enough, and that deterministic Ramsey policy would converge to the steady state.[12] Of greater interest here, it describes policy that is optimal from a timeless perspective in the event of small disturbances.

---

9. See also Woodford (1999) and Giannoni and Woodford (2002).

10. For example, in the case of positive initial nominal government debt, the t_0–optimal policy would involve a large inflation in period t_0 to reduce the pre-existing debt burden, but a commitment not to respond similarly to the existence of nominal government debt in later periods.

11. Local approximations of the same sort are often used in the literature in numerical characterizations of Ramsey policy. Strictly speaking, however, such approximations are valid only in the case of initial commitments X_{t_0} near enough to the steady-state values of these variables, and the t_0–optimal (Ramsey) policy need not involve values of X_{t_0} near the steady-state values, even in the absence of random disturbances.

12. Our work (Benigno and Woodford, 2003) gives an example of an application in which Ramsey policy does converge asymptotically to the steady state, so that the solution to the approximate problem approximates the response to small shocks under the Ramsey policy, at dates long enough after t_0. We cannot make a similar claim in the present application, however, because of the unit root in the dynamics associated with optimal policy.

First, we must show the existence of a steady state, i.e., of an optimal policy (under appropriate initial conditions) that involves constant values of all variables. To this end, we consider the purely deterministic case, in which the exogenous disturbances $\bar{C}_t$, G_t, $\bar{H}_t$, A_t, μ_t^w, ζ_t each take constant values $\bar{C}$, $\bar{G}$, $\bar{H}$, $\bar{A}$, $\bar{\mu}^w > 0$ and $\bar{\zeta} \geq 0$ for all $t \geq t_0$, and assume an initial real public debt $b_{t_0-1} = \bar{b} > 0$. We wish to find an initial degree of price dispersion Δ_{t_0-1} and initial commitments $X_{t_0} = \bar{X}$ so that the solution to the stage-two problem defined above involves a constant policy $x_t = \bar{x}$, $X_{t+1} = \bar{X}$ each period, in which $\bar{b}$ is equal to the initial real debt and $\bar{\Delta}$ is equal to the initial price dispersion. We show in the appendix (Section 7) that the first-order conditions for this problem admit a steady-state solution of this form, and we verify below that the second-order conditions for a local optimum are also satisfied.

Regardless of the initial public debt $\bar{b}$, we show that $\bar{\Pi} = 1$ (zero inflation), and correspondingly that $\bar{\Delta} = 1$ (zero price dispersion). Note that our conclusion that the optimal steady-state inflation rate is zero generalizes our result (Benigno and Woodford, 2003) for the case in which taxes are lump-sum at the margin. We may furthermore assume without loss of generality that the constant values of $\bar{C}$ and $\bar{H}$ are chosen (given the initial government debt $\bar{b}$) so that in the optimal steady state, $C_t = \bar{C}$ and $H_t = \bar{H}$ each period.[13] The associated steady-state tax rate is given by:

$$\bar{\tau} = s_G + \frac{\bar{\zeta} + (1 - \beta)\bar{b}}{\bar{Y}}$$

where $\bar{Y} = \bar{C} + \bar{G} > 0$ is the steady-state output level, and $s_G \equiv \bar{G}/\bar{Y} < 1$ is the steady-state share of output purchased by the government. As shown in Section 7, this solution necessarily satisfies $0 < \bar{\tau} < 1$.

We next wish to characterize the optimal responses to small perturbations of the initial conditions and small fluctuations in the disturbance processes around the above values. To do this, we compute a linear-quadratic approximate problem, the solution to which represents a linear approximation to the solution to the stage-two policy problem, using the method we introduced in Benigno and Woodford (2003). An important advantage of this approach is that it allows direct comparison of our results with those obtained in other analyses of optimal monetary stabilization policy. Other advantages are that it makes it straightforward to verify whether the second-order conditions hold (the second-order conditions that are required for a solution to our first-order conditions to be at

---

13. Note that we may assign arbitrary positive values to $\bar{C}$, $\bar{H}$ without changing the nature of the implied preferences as long as the value of λ is appropriately adjusted.

least a local optimum),[14] and that it provides us with a welfare measure with which to rank alternative suboptimal policies, in addition to allowing computation of the optimal policy.

We begin by computing a Taylor-series approximation to our welfare measure in equation (5), expanding around the steady-state allocation defined above, in which $y_t(i) = \bar{Y}$ for each good at all times and $\xi_t = 0$ at all times.[15] As a second-order (logarithmic) approximation to this measure, we obtain:

$$
U_{t_0} = \bar{Y}\bar{u}_c \cdot E_{t_0} \sum_{t=t_0}^{\infty} \beta^{t-t_0} \, \Phi\hat{Y}_t - \frac{1}{2} u_{yy} \, \hat{Y}_t^2 + \hat{Y}_t u_\xi \xi_t - u_\Delta \hat{\Delta}_t
$$
$$
+ \text{t.i.p.} + \mathcal{O}(\|\xi\|^3)
\tag{17}
$$

where $\hat{Y}_t \equiv \log(Y_t/\bar{Y})$ and $\hat{\Delta}_t \equiv \log \Delta_t$ measure deviations of aggregate output and the price dispersion measure from their steady-state levels.[16] The term *t.i.p.* collects terms that are independent of policy (constants and functions of exogenous disturbances) and hence is irrelevant for ranking alternative policies; $\|\xi\|$ is a bound on the amplitude of our perturbations of the steady state.[17] Here the coefficient:

$$
\Phi \equiv 1 - \frac{\theta - 1}{\theta} \frac{1 - \bar{\tau}}{\bar{\mu}^w} < 1
$$

measures the steady-state wedge between the marginal rate of substitution between consumption and leisure and the marginal product of labor, and hence the inefficiency of the steady-state output level $\bar{Y}$. Under the assumption that $\bar{b} > 0$, we necessarily have $\Phi > 0$, meaning that steady-state output is inefficiently low. The coefficients u_{yy}, u_ξ, and u_Δ are defined in the appendix (Section 7).

14. We (Benigno and Woodford, 2003) show that these conditions can fail to hold, so that a small amount of arbitrary randomization of policy is welfare-improving, but we argue that the conditions under which this occurs in our model are not empirically plausible.
15. Here the elements of ξ_t are assumed to be $\bar{c}_t \equiv \log (\bar{C}_t/\bar{C})$, $\bar{h}_t \equiv \log (\bar{H}_t/\bar{H})$, $a_t \equiv \log (A_t/\bar{A})$, $\hat{\mu}_t^w \equiv \log(\mu_t^w/\bar{\mu}^w)$, $\hat{G}_t \equiv (G_t - \bar{G})/\bar{Y}$, and $\hat{\zeta}_t \equiv (\zeta_t - \bar{\zeta})/\bar{Y}$, so that a value of zero for this vector corresponds to the steady-state values of all disturbances. The perturbations $\hat{G}_t$ and $\hat{\zeta}_t$ are not defined to be logarithmic so that we do not have to assume positive steady-state values for these variables.
16. See the appendix (Section 7) for details. Our calculations here follow closely those of our earlier work (Woodford, 2003, Chapter 6; Benigno and Woodford, 2003).
17. Specifically, we use the notation $\mathcal{O}(\|\xi\|^k)$ as shorthand for $\mathcal{O}(\|\xi, \bar{b}_{t_0-1}, \hat{\Delta}_{t_0-1}^{1/2}, \hat{X}_{t_0}\|^k)$, where in each case circumflexes refer to log deviations from the steady-state values of the various parameters of the policy problem. We treat $\hat{\Delta}_{t_0-1}^{1/2}$ as an expansion parameter, rather than $\hat{\Delta}_{t_0-1}$ because equation (12) implies that deviations of the inflation rate from zero of order ε only result in deviations in the dispersion measure Δ_t from one of order ε^2. We are thus entitled to treat the fluctuations in Δ_t as being only of second order in our bound on the amplitude of disturbances because, if this is true at some initial date, it will remain true thereafter.

Under the Calvo assumption about the distribution of intervals between price changes, we can relate the dispersion of prices to the overall rate of inflation, allowing us to rewrite equation (17) as:

$$U_{t_0} = \bar{Y}\bar{u}_c \cdot E_{t_0} \sum_{t=t_0}^{\infty} \beta^{t-t_0} \left[\Phi \hat{Y}_t - \frac{1}{2} u_{yy} \hat{Y}_t^2 + \hat{Y}_t u_\xi \, \xi_t - \frac{1}{2} u_\pi \pi_t^2 \right]$$
$$+ \text{t.i.p.} + \mathcal{O}(\|\xi\|^3) \tag{18}$$

for a certain coefficient $u_\pi > 0$ defined in the appendix, where $\pi_t \equiv \log \Pi_t$ is the inflation rate. Thus, we can write our stabilization objective purely in terms of the evolution of the aggregate variables $\{\hat{Y}_t, \pi_t\}$ and the exogenous disturbances.

We note that when $\Phi > 0$, there is a nonzero linear term in equation (18), which means that we cannot expect to evaluate this expression to second order using only an approximate solution for the path of aggregate output that is accurate only to first order. Thus, we cannot determine optimal policy, even up to first order, using this approximate objective together with approximations to the structural equations that are accurate only to first order. Rotemberg and Woodford (1997) avoid this problem by assuming an output subsidy (i.e., a value $\bar{\tau} < 0$) of the size needed to ensure that $\Phi = 0$. Here, we do not wish to make this assumption because we assume that lump-sum taxes are unavailable, in which case $\Phi = 0$ would be possible only in the case of a particular initial level of government assets $\bar{b} < 0$. Furthermore, we are more interested in the case in which government revenue needs are more acute than that would imply.

We (Benigno and Woodford, 2003) propose an alternative way of dealing with this problem; we use a second-order approximation to the aggregate-supply relation to eliminate the linear terms in the quadratic welfare measure. In the model that we consider, where taxes are lump-sum (and so do not affect the aggregate supply relation), a forward-integrated second-order approximation to this relation allows one to express the expected discounted value of output terms $\Phi \hat{Y}_t$ as a function of purely quadratic terms (except for certain transitory terms that do not affect the stage-two policy problem). In the present case, the level of distorting taxes has a first-order effect on the aggregate-supply relation (see equation [22] below), so that the forward-integrated relation involves the expected discounted value of the tax rate as well as the expected discounted value of output. As shown in the appendix, however, a second-order approximation to the intertemporal solvency condition in equation (15) provides another relation between the expected discounted values of output and the tax rate and a set of purely quadratic terms.[18] These two second-order approximations to the structural equations that appear as constraints in our policy problem can then be used to express the expected discounted value of output terms in equation (18) in terms of purely quadratic terms.

In this manner, we can rewrite equation (18) as:

$$U_{t_0} = -\Omega E_{t_0} \sum_{t=t_0}^{\infty} \beta^{t-t_0} \left\{ \frac{1}{2} q_y (\hat{Y}_t - \hat{Y}_t^*)^2 + \frac{1}{2} q_\pi \pi_t^2 \right\} + T_{t_0} + t.i.p. + \mathcal{O}(\|\xi\|^3) \quad (19)$$

where again the coefficients are defined in the appendix (Section 7). The expression $\hat{Y}_t^*$ indicates a function of the vector of exogenous disturbances ξ_t defined in the appendix, while T_{t_0} is a transitory component. When the alternative policies from date t_0 onward must be evaluated and must be consistent with a vector of prior commitments X_{t_0}, one can show that the value of the term T_{t_0} is implied (to a second-order approximation) by the value of X_{t_0}. Hence, for purposes of characterizing optimal policy from a timeless perspective, it suffices that we rank policies according to the value that they imply for the loss function:

$$E_{t_0} \sum_{t=t_0}^{\infty} \beta^{t-t_0} \left\{ \frac{1}{2} q_y (\hat{Y}_t - \hat{Y}_t^*)^2 + \frac{1}{2} q_\pi \pi_t^2 \right\} \quad (20)$$

where a lower value of expression (20) implies a higher value of expression (19). Because this loss function is purely quadratic (i.e., lacking linear terms), it is possible to evaluate it to second order using only a first-order approximation to the equilibrium evolution of inflation and output under a given policy. Hence, log-linear approximations to the structural relations of our model suffice, yielding a standard linear-quadratic policy problem.

For this linear-quadratic problem to have a bounded solution (which then approximates the solution to the exact problem), we must verify that the quadratic objective in equation (20) is convex. We show in the appendix (Section 7) that $q_y, q_\pi > 0$, so that the objective is convex, as long as the steady-state tax rate $\bar{\tau}$ and share of government purchases s_G in the national product are below certain positive bounds. We shall here assume that these conditions are satisfied, i.e., that the government's fiscal needs are not too severe. Note that, in this case, our quadratic objective turns out to be of a form commonly assumed in the literature on monetary policy evaluation; that is, policy should seek to minimize the discounted value of a weighted sum of squared deviations of inflation from an optimal

---

18. Since we are interested in providing an approximate characterization of the stage-two policy problem, in which a precommitted value of W_t appears as a constraint, it is actually a second-order approximation to that constraint that we need. This latter constraint has the same form as equation (15), however; the only difference is that the quantities in the relation are taken to have predetermined values.

level (here, zero) and squared fluctuations in an output gap $y_t \equiv \hat{Y}_t - \hat{Y}_t^*$, where the target output level $\hat{Y}_t^*$ depends on the various exogenous disturbances in a way discussed in the appendix. It is also perhaps of interest to note that a tax-smoothing objective of the kind postulated by Barro (1979) and Bohn (1990) does not appear in our welfare measure as a separate objective. Instead, tax distortions are relevant only insofar as they result in output gaps of the same sort that monetary stabilization policy aims to minimize.

We turn next to the form of the log-linear constraints in the approximate policy problem. A first-order Taylor series expansion of equation (11) around the zero-inflation steady state yields the log-linear aggregate-supply relation:

$$\pi_t = \kappa[\hat{Y}_t + \psi\hat{\tau}_t + c_\xi' \, \xi_t] + \beta E_t \pi_{t+1} \tag{21}$$

for certain coefficients $\kappa, \psi > 0$. This is the familiar new Keynesian Phillips curve relation.[19] It is extended here to account for the effects of variations in the level of distorting taxes on supply costs.

It is useful to write this approximate aggregate-supply relation in terms of the welfare-relevant output gap y_t. Equation (21) can be be written as:

$$\pi_t = \kappa[y_t + \psi\hat{\tau}_t + u_t] + \beta E_t \pi_{t+1} \tag{22}$$

where u_t is composite cost-push disturbance, indicating the degree to which the various exogenous disturbances included in ξ_t preclude simultaneous stabilization of inflation, the welfare-relevant output gap, and the tax rate. Alternatively we can write:

$$\pi_t = \kappa[y_t + \psi(\hat{\tau}_t - \hat{\tau}_t^*)] + \beta E_t \pi_{t+1} \tag{23}$$

where $\hat{\tau}_t^* \equiv -\psi^{-1}u_t$ indicates the tax change needed at any time to offset the cost-push shock, thus to allow simultaneous stabilization of inflation and the output gap (the two stabilization objectives reflected in equation [20]).

The effects of the various exogenous disturbances in ξ_t on the cost-push term u_t are explained in the appendix (Section 7). It is worth noting that under certain conditions u_t is unaffected by some disturbances. In the case that $\Phi = 0$, the cost-push term is given by:

$$u_t = u_{\xi 5}\hat{\mu}_t^w \tag{24}$$

where in this case, $u_{\xi 5} = q_y^{-1} > 0$. Thus, the cost-push term is affected only by variations in the wage markup $\hat{\mu}_t$; it does not vary in response to taste shocks, technology shocks, government purchases, or variations in

---

19. See, e.g., Clarida et al. (1999) or Woodford (2003, Chapter 3).

government transfers. The reason is that when $\Phi = 0$ and neither taxes nor the wage markup vary from their steady-state values, the flexible-price equilibrium is efficient; it follows that the level of output consistent with zero inflation is also the one that maximizes welfare, as discussed in Woodford (2003, Chapter 6).

Even when $\Phi > 0$, if there are no government purchases (so that $s_G = 0$) and no fiscal shocks (meaning that $\hat{G}_t = 0$ and $\hat{\zeta}_t = 0$), then the u_t term is again of the form in equation (24), but with $u_{\xi 5} = (1 - \Phi) \, q_y^{-1}t$, as we discussed in Benigno and Woodford (2003). Hence, in this case, neither taste nor technology shocks have cost-push effects. The reason is that in this isoelastic case, if taxes and the wage markup never vary, the flexible-price equilibrium value of output and the efficient level vary in exactly the same proportion in response to each of the other types of shocks; hence, inflation stabilization also stabilizes the gap between actual output and the efficient level. Another special case is the limiting case of linear utility of consumption ($\sigma^{-1} = 0$); in this case, u_t is again of the form in equation (24) for a different value of $u_{\xi 5}$. In general, however, when $\Phi > 0$ and $s_G > 0$, all of the disturbances shift the flexible-price equilibrium level of output (under a constant tax rate) and the efficient level of output to differing extents, resulting in cost-push contributions from all of these shocks.

The other constraint on possible equilibrium paths is the intertemporal government solvency condition. A log-linear approximation to equation (15) can be written in the form:

$$\hat{b}_{t-1} - \pi_t - \sigma^{-1} y_t = - f_t + (1 - \beta) E_t \sum_{T=t}^{\infty} \beta^{T-t} [b_y y_T + b_\tau (\hat{\tau}_T - \hat{\tau}_T^*)] \qquad (25)$$

where $\sigma > 0$ is the intertemporal elasticity of substitution of private expenditure, and the coefficients b_y, b_τ are defined in the appendix, as is f_t, a composite measure of exogenous fiscal stress. Here, we have written the solvency condition in terms of the same output gap and tax gap as equation (23) to make clear the extent to which complete stabilization of the variables appearing in the loss function of equation (20) is possible. The constraint can also be written in a flow form:

$$\hat{b}_{t-1} - \pi_t - \sigma^{-1} y_t + f_t = (1 - \beta)[b_y y_t + b_\tau (\hat{\tau}_t - \hat{\tau}_t^*)]$$
$$+ \beta E_t [\hat{b}_t - \pi_{t+1} - \sigma^{-1} y_{t+1} + f_{t+1}], \qquad (26)$$

together with a transversality condition.[20]

20. If we restrict attention to bounded paths for the endogenous variables, then a path satisfies equation (25) in each period $t \geq t_0$ if and only if it satisfies the flow budget constraint in equation (26) in each period.

We note that the only reason why it should *not* be possible to stabilize both inflation and the output gap completely from some date t onward is if the sum $\hat{b}_{t-1} + f_t$ is nonzero. The composite disturbance f_t therefore completely summarizes the information at date t about the exogenous disturbances that determines the degree to which stabilization of inflation and output is not possible; under an optimal policy, the state-contingent evolution of the inflation rate, the output gap, and the real public debt depend solely on the evolution of the single composite disturbance process $\{f_t\}$.

This result contrasts with the standard literature on optimal monetary stabilization policy, in which (in the absence of a motive for interest-rate stabilization, as here) it is instead the cost-push term u_t that summarizes the extent to which exogenous disturbances require that fluctuations in inflation and in the output gap should occur. Note that in the case when there are no government purchases and no fiscal shocks, u_t corresponds simply to equation (24). Thus, for example, it is concluded (in a model with lump-sum taxes) that there should be no variation in inflation in response to a technology shock (Khan et al., 2002; Benigno and Woodford, 2003). But even in this simple case, the fiscal stress is given by an expression of the form:

$$f_t \equiv h_\xi' \, \xi_t - (1 - \beta) E_t \sum_{T=t}^{\infty} \beta^{T-t} f_\xi' \, \xi_T \tag{27}$$

where the expressions $h_\xi' \, \xi_t$ and $f_\xi' \, \xi_t$ both generally include nonzero coefficients on preference and technology shocks, in addition to the markup shock, as shown in the appendix. Hence, many disturbances that do not have cost-push effects nonetheless result in optimal variations in both inflation and the output gap.

Finally, we wish to consider optimal policy subject to the constraints that F_{t_0}, K_{t_0} and W_{t_0} take given (pre-committed) values. Again, only log-linear approximations to these constraints matter for a log-linear approximate characterization of optimal policy. As discussed in the appendix, the corresponding constraints in our approximate model are pre-commitments regarding the state-contingent values of π_{t_0} and y_{t_0}.

To summarize, our approximate policy problem involves the choice of state-contingent paths for the endogenous variables $\{\pi_t, y_t, \hat{\tau}_t, \hat{b}_t\}$ from some date t_0 onward to minimize the quadratic loss function in equation (20), subject to the constraint that the conditions in equations (23) and (25) be satisfied each period, given an initial value $\hat{b}_{t_0-1}$, and subject also to the constraints that π_{t_0} and y_{t_0} equal certain pre-committed values (that may depend on the state of the world in period t_0). We shall first characterize the state-contingent evolution of the endogenous variables in response to exogenous shocks, in the rational-expectations equilibrium that solves this problem. We then turn to the derivation of optimal policy rules, commitment to which should implement an equilibrium of this kind.

3. Optimal Responses to Shocks: The Case of Flexible Prices

In considering the solution to the problem of stabilization policy just posed, it may be useful first to consider the simple case in which prices are fully flexible. This is the limiting case of our model in which $\alpha = 0$, with the consequence that $q_\pi = 0$ in equation (20), and that $\kappa^{-1} = 0$ in equation (23). Hence, our optimization problem reduces to the minimization of:

$$\frac{1}{2} q_y E_{t_0} \sum_{t = t_0}^{\infty} \beta^{t - t_0} y_t^2 \tag{28}$$

subject to the constraints:

$$y_t + \psi(\hat{\tau}_t - \hat{\tau}_t^*) = 0 \tag{29}$$

and equation (25). It is easy to see that in this case, the optimal policy is one that achieves $y_t = 0$ at all times. Because of equation (29), this requires that $\hat{\tau}_t = \hat{\tau}_t^*$ at all times. The inflation rate is then determined by the requirement of government intertemporal solvency:

$$\pi_t = \hat{b}_{t - 1} + f_t$$

This last equation implies that unexpected inflation must equal the innovation in the fiscal stress:

$$\pi_t - E_{t - 1} \pi_t = f_t - E_{t - 1} f_t$$

Expected inflation and hence the evolution of nominal government debt are indeterminate. If we add to our assumed policy objective a small preference for inflation stabilization, when this has no cost in terms of other objectives, then the optimal policy will be one that involves $E_t \pi_{t+1} = 0$ each period.[21] Thus, the nominal public debt must evolve according to:

$$\hat{b}_t = - E_t f_{t + 1}$$

---

21. Note that this preference can be justified in terms of our model, in the case that α is positive though extremely small. Then there will be a very small positive value for q_π, implying that reduction of the expected discounted value of inflation is preferred to the extent that this does not require any increase in the expected discounted value of squared output gaps.

If, instead, we were to assume the existence of small monetary frictions (and zero interest on money), the tie would be broken by the requirement that the nominal interest rate equal zero each period.[22] The required expected rate of inflation (and hence the required evolution of the nominal public debt) would then be determined by the variation in the equilibrium real rate of return implied by a real allocation in which $\hat{Y}_t = \hat{Y}_t^*$ each period. That is, one would have $E_t\pi_{t+1} = -r_t^*$, where r_t^* is the (exogenous) real rate of interest associated output at the target level each period, and so:

$$\hat{b}_t = -r_t^* - E_t f_{t+1}$$

We thus obtain simple conclusions about the determinants of fluctuations in inflation, output, and the tax rate under optimal policy. Unexpected inflation variations occur as needed to prevent taxes from ever having to be varied to respond to variations in fiscal stress, as in the analyses of Bohn (1990) and Chari and Kehoe (1999). This allows a model with only riskless nominal government debt to achieve the same state-contingent allocation of resources as the government would choose to bring about if it could issue state-contingent debt, as in the model of Lucas and Stokey (1983).

Because taxes do not have to adjust in response to variations in fiscal stress, as in the tax-smoothing model of Barro (1979), it is possible to smooth them across states as well as over time. However, the sense in which it is desirable to smooth tax rates is that of minimizing variation in the gap $\hat{\tau}_t - \hat{\tau}_t^*$, rather than variation in the tax rate itself.[23] In other words, it is really the tax gap $\hat{\tau}_t - \hat{\tau}_t^*$ that should be smoothed. Under certain special circumstances, it will not be optimal for tax rates to vary in response

22. The result relies on the fact that the distortions created by the monetary frictions are minimized in the case of a zero opportunity cost of holding money each period, as argued by Friedman (1969). Neither the existence of effects of nominal interest rates on supply costs (so that an interest-rate term should appear in the aggregate-supply relation in equation [29]) nor the contribution of seignorage revenues to the government budget constraint make any difference to the result because unexpected changes in revenue needs can always be costlessly obtained through unexpected inflation, while any desired shifts in the aggregate-supply relation to offset cost-push shocks can be achieved by varying the tax rate.

23. Several authors (e.g., Chari et al., 1991, 1994; Hall and Krieger, 2000; Aiyagari et al., 2002) have found that in calibrated flexible-price models with state-contingent government debt, the optimal variation in labor tax rates is quite small. Our results indicate this as well, in the case that real disturbances have only small cost-push effects, and we have listed earlier various conditions under which this will be the case. But under some circumstances, optimal policy may involve substantial volatility of the tax rate and indeed more volatility of the tax rate than of inflation. This would be the case if shocks have large cost-push effects while having relatively little effect on fiscal stress.

to shocks; these are the conditions, discussed above, under which shocks have no cost-push effects, so that there is no change in $\hat{\tau}_t^*$. For example, if there are no government purchases and there is no variation in the wage markup, this will be the case. But more generally, all disturbances will have some cost-push effect and will result in variations in $\hat{\tau}_t^*$. Then there will be variations in the tax rate in response to these shocks under an optimal policy. There will be no unit root in the tax rate, however, as in the Barro (1979) model of optimal tax policy. Instead, as in the analysis of Lucas and Stokey (1983), the optimal fluctuations in the tax rate will be stationary and will have the same persistence properties as the real disturbances (specifically, the persistence properties of the composite cost-push shock).

Variations in fiscal stress will instead require changes in the tax rate, as in the analysis of Barro (1979), if we suppose that the government issues only riskless indexed debt rather than the riskless nominal debt assumed in our baseline model. (Again, for simplicity we assume that only one-period riskless debt is issued.) In this case the objective function in equation (20) and the constraints in equations (25) and (29) remain the same, but $\underline{b}_{t-1} \equiv \hat{b}_{t-1} - \pi_t$, the real value of private claims on the government at the beginning of period t, is now a predetermined variable. This means that unexpected inflation variations can no longer relax the intertemporal government solvency condition. In fact, rewriting the constraint in equation (25) in terms of $\underline{b}_{t-1}$, we see that the path of inflation is now completely irrelevant to welfare.

The solution to this optimization problem is now less trivial because complete stabilization of the output gap is not generally possible. The optimal state-contingent evolution of output and taxes can be determined using a Lagrangian method, as in Woodford (2003, Chapter 7). The Lagrangian for the present problem can be written as:

$$L_{t_0} = E_{t_0} \sum_{t=t_0}^{\infty} \beta^{t-t_0} \left\{ \frac{1}{2} q_y y_t^2 + \varphi_{1t}[y_t + \psi\hat{\tau}_t] + \varphi_{2t}[\underline{b}_{t-1} - \sigma^{-1} y_t) \right.$$
$$\left. - (1 - \beta)(b_y y_t + b_\tau \hat{\tau}_t) - \beta(\underline{b}_t - \sigma^{-1} y_{t+1})] \right\} + \sigma\varphi_{2, t_0-1} y_{t_0} \qquad (30)$$

where φ_{1t}, φ_{2t} are Lagrange multipliers associated with the constraints in equations (29) and (26), respectively,[24] for each $t \geq t_0$, and $\sigma\varphi_{2,t_0-1}$ is the notation used for the multiplier associated with the additional constraint that $y_{t_0} = \bar{Y}_{t_0}$. The latter constraint is added to characterize optimal policy from a timeless perspective, as discussed at the end of Section 2; the

24. Alternatively, φ_{2t} is the multiplier associated with the constraint in equation (25).

particular notation used for the multiplier on this constraint results in a time-invariant form for the first-order conditions, as seen below.[25] We have dropped terms from the Lagrangian that are not functions of the endogenous variables y_t and $\hat{\tau}_t$, i.e., products of multipliers and exogenous disturbances, because these do not affect our calculation of the implied first-order conditions.

The resulting first-order condition with respect to y_t is:

$$q_y y_t = -\varphi_{1t} + [(1 - \beta)b_y + \sigma^{-1}]\varphi_{2t} - \sigma^{-1}\varphi_{2,t-1} \tag{31}$$

that with respect to $\hat{\tau}_t$ is:

$$\psi\varphi_{1t} = (1 - \beta)b_\tau \varphi_{2t} \tag{32}$$

and that with respect to b_t is:

$$\varphi_{2t} = E_t \varphi_{2,t+1} \tag{33}$$

Each of these conditions must be satisfied for each $t \geq t_0$, along with the structural equations (29) and (25) for each $t \geq t_0$, for given initial values $\underline{b}_{t0-1}$ and y_{t0}. We look for a bounded solution to these equations so that (in the event of small enough disturbances) none of the state variables leave a neighborhood of the steady-state values, in which our local approximation to the equilibrium conditions and our welfare objective remain accurate.[26] Given the existence of such a bounded solution, the transversality condition is necessarily satisfied so that the solution to these first-order conditions represents an optimal plan.

25. It should be recalled that, for policy to be optimal from a timeless perspective, the state-contingent initial commitment $\bar{y}_{t0}$ must be chosen so it conforms to the state-contingent commitment regarding y_t that will be chosen in all later periods, so that the optimal policy can be implemented by a time-invariant rule. Hence, it is convenient to present the first-order conditions in a time-invariant form.
26. In the only such solution, the variables $\hat{\tau}_t$, $\underline{b}_t$, and y_t are all permanently affected by shocks, even when the disturbances are all assumed to be stationary (and bounded) processes. Hence, a bounded solution exists only under the assumption that random disturbances occur only in a finite number of periods. However, our characterization of optimal policy does not depend on a particular bound on the number of periods in which there are disturbances, or which periods these are; to allow disturbances in a larger number of periods, we must assume a tighter bound on the amplitude of disturbances for the optimal paths of the endogenous variables to remain within a given neighborhood of the steady-state values. Aiyagari et al. (2002) discuss the asymptotic behavior of the optimal plan in the exact nonlinear version of a problem similar to this one, in the case that disturbances occur indefinitely.

An analytical solution to these equations is easily given. Using equation (29) to substitute for $\hat{\tau}_t$ in the forward-integrated version of equation (25), then equations (31) and (32) to substitute for y_t as a function of the path of φ_{2t}, and finally using equation (33) to replace all terms of the form $E_t\,\varphi_{2,t+j}$ (for $j \geq 0$) by φ_{2t}, we obtain an equation that can be solved for φ_{2t}. The solution is of the form:

$$\varphi_{2t} = \frac{m_b}{m_b + n_b}\,\varphi_{2,t-1} - \frac{1}{m_b + n_b}\,[f_t + \underline{b}_{t-1}]$$

Coefficients m_b, n_b are defined in the appendix (Section 7). The implied dynamics of the government debt are then given by:

$$\underline{b}_t = -\,E_t f_{t+1} - n_b\,\varphi_{2t}$$

This allows a complete solution for the evolution of government debt and the multiplier, given the composite exogenous disturbance process $\{f_t\}$, starting from initial conditions b_{t_0-1} and φ_{2,t_0-1}.[27] Given these solutions, the optimal evolution of the output gap and tax rate are given by:

$$y_t = m_\varphi\,\varphi_{2t} + n_\varphi\,\varphi_{2,t-1}$$

$$\hat{\tau}_t = \hat{\tau}_t^* - \varphi^{-1} y_t$$

where m_φ, n_φ are again defined in the appendix (Section 7). The evolution of inflation remains indeterminate. If we again assume a preference for inflation stabilization when it is costless, optimal policy involves $\pi_t = 0$ at all times.

In this case, unlike that of nominal debt, inflation is not affected by a pure fiscal shock (or indeed any other shock) under the optimal policy, but instead the output gap and the tax rate are. Note also that in the above solution, the multiplier φ_{2t}, the output gap, and the tax rate all follow unit root processes: a temporary disturbance to the fiscal stress permanently changes the level of each of these variables, as in the analysis of the optimal dynamics of the tax rate in Barro (1979) and Bohn (1990). However, the optimal evolution of the tax rate is not in general a pure random walk, as in the analysis of Barro and Bohn. Instead, the tax gap is an IMA(1,1) process, as in the local analysis of Aiyagari et al. (2002); the optimal tax

---

27. The initial condition for φ_{2,t_0-1} is chosen in turn so that the solution obtained is consistent with the initial constraint $y_{t_0} = \bar{y}_{t_0}$. Under policy that is optimal from a timeless perspective, this initial commitment is chosen in turn in a self-consistent fashion, as discussed further in Section 5. Note that the specification of φ_{2,t_0-1} does not affect our conclusions in this section about the optimal responses to shocks.

rate $\hat{\tau}t_t$ may have more complex dynamics, in the case that $\hat{\tau}_t^*$ exhibits stationary fluctuations. In the special case of linear utility ($\sigma^{-1} = 0$), $n_\varphi = 0$, and both the output gap and the tax gap follow random walks (both co-move with φ_{2t}). If the only disturbances are fiscal disturbances ($\hat{G}_t$ and $\hat{\zeta}_t$), then there are also no fluctuations in $\hat{\tau}_t^*$ in this case so that the optimal tax rate follows a random walk.

More generally, we observe that optimal policy smooths φ_{2t}, the value (in units of marginal utility) of additional government revenue in period t so that it follows a random walk. This is the proper generalization of the Barro tax-smoothing result, although it implies smoothing of tax rates in only fairly special cases. We find a similar result in the case that prices are sticky, even when government debt is not indexed, as we now show.

4. Optimal Responses to Shocks: The Case of Sticky Prices

We turn now to the characterization of the optimal responses to shocks in the case that prices are sticky ($\alpha > 0$). The optimization problem that provides a first-order characterization of optimal responses in this case is that of choosing processes $\{\pi_t, y_t, \hat{\tau}_t, \hat{b}_t\}$ from date t_0 onward to minimize equation (20), subject to the constraints in equations (23) and (25) for each $t \geq t_0$, together with initial constraints of the form:

$$\pi_{t_0} = \bar{\pi}_{t_0} \qquad y_{t_0} = \bar{y}_{t_0}$$

given the initial condition $\hat{b}_{t_0-1}$ and the exogenous evolution of the composite disturbances $\{\hat{\tau}_t^*, f_t\}$. The Lagrangian for this problem can be written as:

$$L_{t_0} = E_{t_0} \sum_{t=t_0}^{\infty} \beta^{t-t_0} \left\{ \frac{1}{2} q_y y_t^2 + \frac{1}{2} q_\pi \pi_t^2 + \varphi_{1t}[-\kappa^{-1}\pi_t + y_t + \psi\hat{\tau}_t + \kappa^{-1}\beta\pi_{t+1}] \right.$$
$$\left. + \varphi_{2t}[\hat{b}_{t-1} - \pi_t - \sigma^{-1}y_t - (1-\beta)(b_y y_t + b_\tau \hat{\tau}_t) - \beta(\hat{b}_t - \pi_{t+1} - \sigma^{-1}y_{t+1})] \right\}$$
$$+ [\kappa^{-1}\varphi_{1,t_0-1} + \varphi_{2,t_0-1}]\pi_{t_0} + \sigma^{-1}\varphi_{2,t_0-1}y_{t_0}$$

by analogy with equation (30).

The first-order condition with respect to π_t is given by:

$$q_\pi \pi_t = \kappa^{-1}(\varphi_{1t} - \varphi_{1,t-1}) + (\varphi_{2t} - \varphi_{2,t-1}) \tag{34}$$

that with respect to y_t is given by:

$$q_y y_t = -\varphi_{1t} + [(1-\beta)b_y + \sigma^{-1}]\varphi_{2t} - \sigma^{-1}\varphi_{2,t-1} \tag{35}$$

and that with respect to $\hat{\tau}_t$ is given by:

$$\psi \varphi_{1t} = (1 - \beta) b_\tau \varphi_{2t} \tag{36}$$

and finally that with respect to $\hat{b}_t$ is given by:

$$\varphi_{2t} = E_t \varphi_{2,t+1} \tag{37}$$

These together with the two structural equations and the initial conditions are to be solved for the state-contingent paths of $\{\pi_t, \hat{Y}_t, \tau_t, \hat{b}_t, \varphi_{1t}, \varphi_{2t}\}$. Note that the last three first-order conditions are the same as for the flexible-price model with indexed debt; the first condition in equation (34) replaces the previous requirement that $\pi_t = 0$. Hence, the solution obtained in the previous section corresponds to a limiting case of this problem, in which q_π is made unboundedly large; for this reason the discussion above of the more familiar case with flexible prices and riskless indexed government debt also provides insight into the character of optimal policy in the present case.

In the unique bounded solution to these equations, the dynamics of government debt and of the shadow value of government revenue φ_{2t} are again of the form:

$$\varphi_{2t} = \frac{\tilde{m}_b}{\tilde{m}_b + n_b} \varphi_{2,t-1} - \frac{1}{\tilde{m}_b + n_b} [f_t + \hat{b}_{t-1}]$$

$$\hat{b}_t = - E_t f_{t+1} - n_b \varphi_{2t}$$

although the coefficient $\tilde{m}_b$ now differs from m_b in a way also described in the appendix (Section 7). The implied dynamics of inflation and the output gap are then given by:

$$\pi_t = - \omega_\varphi (\varphi_{2t} - \varphi_{2t-1}) \tag{38}$$

$$y_t = m_\varphi \varphi_{2t} + n_\varphi \varphi_{2,t-1} \tag{39}$$

where m_φ, n_φ are defined as before, and ω_φ is defined in the appendix. The optimal dynamics of the tax rate are those required to make these inflation and output-gap dynamics consistent with the aggregate-supply relation in equation (23). Once again, the optimal dynamics of inflation, the output gap, and the public debt depend only on the evolution of the fiscal stress variable $\{f_t\}$; the dynamics of the tax rate also depend on the evolution of $\{\hat{\tau}_t^*\}$.

We now discuss the optimal response of the variables to a disturbance in the level of fiscal stress. The laws of motion just derived for govern-

ment debt and the Lagrange multiplier imply that temporary disturbances in the level of fiscal stress cause a permanent change in the level of
both the Lagrange multiplier and the public debt. This then implies a
permanent change in the level of output, which in turn requires (because
inflation is stationary) a permanent change in the level of the tax rate.
Since inflation is proportional to the change in the Lagrange multiplier,
the price level moves in proportion to the multiplier, which means a temporary disturbance to the fiscal stress results in a permanent change in the
price level, as in the flexible-price case analyzed in the previous section.
Thus, in this case, the price level, output gap, government debt, and tax
rate all have unit roots, combining features of the two special cases considered in the previous section.[28] Both price level and φ_{2t} are random
walks. They jump immediately to a new permanent level in response to a
change in fiscal stress. In the case of purely transitory (white noise) disturbances, government debt also jumps immediately to a new permanent
level. Given the dynamics of the price level and government debt, the
dynamics of output and tax rate then are jointly determined by the aggregate-supply relation and the government budget constraint.

We also find that the degree to which fiscal stress is relieved by a price-
level jump (as in the flexible-price, nominal-debt case) as opposed to an
increase in government debt and hence a permanently higher tax rate (as
in the flexible-price, indexed-debt case) depends on the degree of price
stickiness. We illustrate this with a numerical example. We calibrate
a quarterly model by assuming that $\beta = 0.99$, $\omega = 0.473$, $\sigma^{-1} = 0.157$, and
$\kappa = 0.0236$, in accordance with the estimates of Rotemberg and Woodford
(1997). We also assume an elasticity of substitution among alternative
goods of $\theta = 10$, an overall level of steady-state distortions $\Phi = \frac{1}{3}$, a
steady-state tax rate of $\hat{\tau} = 0.2$, and a steady-state debt level $\bar{b}/\bar{Y} = 2.4$ (debt
equal to 60% of a year's grass domestic product (GDP). Given the
assumed degree of market power of producers (a steady-state gross price
markup of 1.11) and the assumed size of the tax wedge, the value $\Phi = \frac{1}{3}$
corresponds to a steady-state wage markup of $\bar{\mu}^w = 1.08$. If we assume
that there are no government transfers in the steady state, then the
assumed level of tax revenues net of debt service would finance steady-
state government purchases equal to a share $s_G = 0.176$ of output.

Let us suppose that the economy is disturbed by an exogenous increase in
transfer programs $\hat{\zeta}$, equal to 1% of aggregate output, and expected to last
only for the current quarter. Figure 1 shows the optimal impulse response of
the government debt $\hat{b}$ to this shock (where quarter zero is the quarter of the

---

28. Schmitt-Grohé and Uribe (2001) similarly observe that in a model with sticky prices, the
optimal response of the tax rate is similar to what would be optimal in a flexible-price
model with riskless indexed government debt.

Figure 1 IMPULSE RESPONSE OF THE PUBLIC DEBT TO A PURE FISCAL
SHOCK, FOR ALTERNATIVE DEGREES OF PRICE STICKINESS

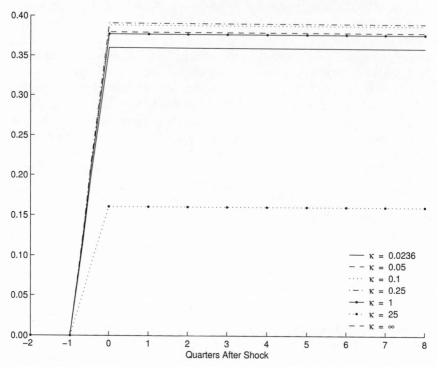

shock), for each of 7 different values for κ, the slope of the short-run aggregate-supply relation, maintaining the values just stated for the other parameters of the model. The solid line indicates the optimal response in the case
of our baseline value for κ, based on the estimates of Rotemberg and
Woodford; the other cases represent progressively greater degrees of price
flexibility, up to the limiting case of fully flexible prices (the case κ = ∞).
Figures 2 and 3 also show the optimal responses of the tax rate and the inflation rate to the same disturbance, for each of the same seven cases.[29]

We see that the volatility of both inflation and tax rates under optimal
policy depends greatly on the degree of stickiness of prices. Table 1
reports the initial quarter's response of the inflation rate, and the long-run
response of the tax rate, for each of the seven cases. The table also indi-

29. In Figure 1, a response of 1 means a 1% increase in the value of b_t, from 60% to 60.6% of
a year's GDP. In Figure 2, a response of 1 means a 1% decrease in τ_t, from 20% to 20.2%.
In Figure 3, a response of 1 means a 1% per annum increase in the inflation rate, or an
increase of the price level from 1 to 1.0025 over the course of a quarter (given that our
model is quarterly). The responses reported in Table 1 are measured in the same way.

Figure 2 IMPULSE RESPONSE OF THE TAX RATE TO A PURE FISCAL SHOCK

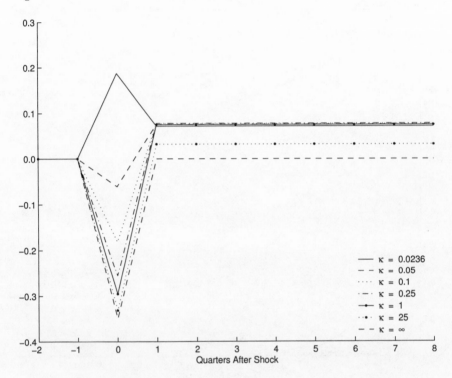

cates for each case the implied average time (in weeks) between price changes, $T \equiv (-\log \alpha)^{-1}$, where $0 < \alpha < 1$ is the fraction of prices unchanged for an entire quarter implied by the assumed value of κ.[30] We first note that our baseline calibration implies that price changes occur only slightly less frequently than twice per year, which is consistent with survey evidence.[31] Next, we observe that even were we to assume an aggregate-supply relation several times as steep as the one estimated using U.S. data, our conclusions with regard to the size of the optimal responses of the (long-run) tax rate and the inflation rate would be fairly similar. At the same time, the optimal responses with fully flexible prices are quite different:

30. We have used the relation between α and T for a continuous-time version of the Calvo model to express the degree of price stickiness in terms of an average time between price changes.
31. The indicated average time between price changes for the baseline case is shorter than that reported in Rotemberg and Woodford (1997), both because here we assume a slightly larger value of θ, implying a smaller value of α, and because of the continuous-time method used here to convert α into an implied average time interval.

Figure 3 IMPULSE RESPONSE OF THE INFLATION RATE TO A PURE
FISCAL SHOCK

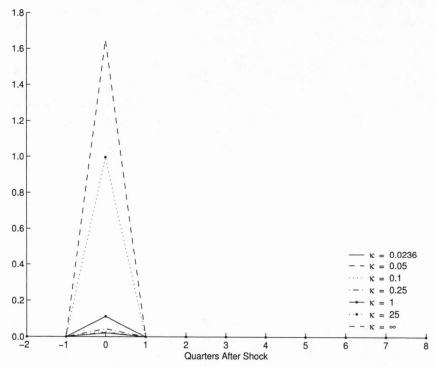

the response of inflation is 80 times as large as under the baseline sticky-price calibration (implying a variance of inflation 6400 times as large), while the long-run tax rate does not respond at all in the flexible-price case.[32] But even a small degree of stickiness of prices makes a dramatic difference in the optimal responses; for example, if prices are revised only every five weeks on average, the variance of inflation is reduced by a factor of more than 200, while the optimal response of the long-run tax rate to the increased revenue need is nearly the same size as under the baseline degree of price stickiness. Thus, we find, as do Schmitt-Grohé and Uribe (2001) in the context of a calibrated model with convex costs of price adjustment, that the conclusions of the flexible-price analysis are

---

32. The tax rate does respond in the quarter of the shock in the case of flexible prices, but with the opposite sign to that associated with optimal policy under our baseline calibration. Under flexible prices, as discussed above, the tax rate does not respond to variations in fiscal stress at all. Because the increase in government transfers raises the optimal level of output $\hat{Y}_0^*$, for reasons explained in the appendix (Section 7), the optimal tax rate $\hat{\tau}_0^*$ actually falls to induce equilibrium output to increase; under flexible prices, this is the optimal response of $\hat{\tau}_0$.

Table 1   IMMEDIATE RESPONSES FOR ALTERNATIVE
DEGREES OF PRICE STICKINESS

κ	T	$\hat{\tau}_\infty$	π_0
.024	29	.072	.021
.05	20	.076	.024
.10	14	.077	.030
.25	9	.078	.044
1.0	5.4	.075	.113
25	2.4	.032	.998
∞	0	0	1.651

quite misleading if prices are even slightly sticky. Under a realistic calibration of the degree of price stickiness, inflation should be quite stable,
even in response to disturbances with substantial consequences for the
government's budget constraint, while tax rates should instead respond
substantially (and with a unit root) to variations in fiscal stress.

We can also compare our results with those that arise when taxes are
lump-sum. In this case, $\psi = 0$, and the first-order condition in equation
(36) requires that $\varphi_{2t} = 0$. The remaining first-order conditions reduce to:

$$q_\pi \pi_t = \kappa^{-1}(\varphi_{1t} - \varphi_{1,t-1})$$

$$q_y y_t = -\varphi_{1t}$$

for each $t \geq t_0$, as in Clarida et al. (1999) and Woodford (2003, Chapter 7). In
this case the fiscal stress is no longer relevant for inflation or output-gap
determination. Instead, only the cost-push shock u_t is responsible for
incomplete stabilization. The determinants of the cost-push effects of
underlying disturbances and of the target output level $\hat{Y}_t^*$ are also somewhat different because in this case $\vartheta_1 = 0$. For example, a pure fiscal shock
has no cost-push effect nor any effect on $\hat{Y}_t^*$, and hence no effect on the
optimal evolution of either inflation or output.[33] Furthermore, as shown in
the references just mentioned, the price level no longer follows a random
walk; instead, it is a stationary variable. Increases in the price level due to
a cost-push shock are subsequently undone by a period of deflation.

Note that the familiar case from the literature on monetary stabilization
policy does not result simply from assuming that sources of revenue that do
not shift the aggregate-supply (AS) relation are available; it is also important
that the sort of tax that *does* shift the AS relation (like the sales tax here) is *not*
available. We could nest both the standard model and our present baseline
case within a single, more general framework by assuming that revenue can

---

33. See our work (Benigno and Woodford, 2003) for a detailed analysis of the determinants
of u_t and $\hat{Y}_t^*$ in this case.

be raised using either the sales tax or a lump-sum tax, but that there is an additional convex cost (perhaps representing collection costs, assumed to reduce the utility of the representative household but not using real resources) of increases in either tax rate. The standard case would then appear as the limiting case of this model in which the collection costs associated with the sales tax are infinite, while those associated with the lump-sum tax are zero; the baseline model here would correspond to an alternative limiting case in which the collection costs associated with the lump-sum tax are infinite, while those associated with the sales tax are zero. In intermediate cases, we would continue to find that fiscal stress affects the optimal evolution of both inflation and the output gap, as long as there is a positive collection cost for the lump-sum tax. At the same time, the result that the shadow value of additional government revenue follows a random walk under optimal policy (which would still be true) will not in general imply, as it does here, that the price level should also be a random walk; the perfect co-movement of φ_{1t} and φ_{2t} that characterizes optimal policy in our baseline case will not be implied by the first-order conditions except in the case that there are no collection costs associated with the sales tax. Nonetheless, the price level will generally contain a unit root under optimal policy, even if it will not generally follow a random walk.

We also obtain results more similar to those in the standard literature on monetary stabilization policy if we assume (realistically) that it is not possible to adjust tax rates on such short notice in response to shocks as can be done with monetary policy. As a simple way of introducing delays in the adjustment of tax policy, suppose that the tax rate τ_t has to be fixed in period $t - d$. In this case, the first-order conditions characterizing optimal responses to shocks are the same as above, except that equation (36) is replaced by:

$$\psi E_t \varphi_{1, t+d} = (1 - \beta) b_\tau E_t \varphi_{2, t+d} \tag{40}$$

for each $t \geq t_0$. In this case, the first-order conditions imply that $E_t \pi_{t+d+1} = 0$, but they no longer imply that changes in the price level cannot be forecasted from one period to the next. As a result, price-level increases in response to disturbances are typically partially, but not completely, undone in subsequent periods. Yet there continues to be a unit root in the price level (of at least a small innovation variance), even in the case of an arbitrarily long delay d in the adjustment of tax rates.

5. Optimal Targeting Rules for Monetary and Fiscal Policy

We now wish to characterize the policy rules that the monetary and fiscal authorities can follow to bring about the state-contingent responses to shocks described in the previous section. One might think that it suffices to solve for the optimal state-contingent paths for the policy instruments, but in general this is not a desirable approach to the specification of a policy rule, as discussed in Svensson (2003) and Woodford (2003, Chapter 7). A description of optimal policy in these terms would require enumeration of all of the types of shocks that might be encountered later, indefinitely far in the future, which is not feasible in practice. A commitment to a state-contingent instrument path, even when possible, also may not determine the optimal equilibrium as the locally unique rational-expectations equilibrium consistent with this policy; many other (much less desirable) equilibria may also be consistent with the same state-contingent instrument path.

Instead, we here specify targeting rules in the sense of Svensson (1999, 2003) and Giannoni and Woodford (2003). These targeting rules are commitments on the part of the policy authorities to adjust their respective instruments so as to ensure that the projected paths of the endogenous variables satisfy certain target criteria. We show that under an appropriate choice of these target criteria, a commitment to ensure that they hold at all times will determine a unique nonexplosive rational-expectations equilibrium in which the state-contingent evolution of inflation, output, and the tax rate solves the optimization problem discussed in the previous section. We also show that it is possible to obtain a specification of the policy rules that is robust to alternative specifications of the exogenous shock processes.

We apply the general approach of Giannoni and Woodford (2002), which allows the derivation of optimal target criteria with the properties just stated. In addition, Giannoni and Woodford show that such target criteria can be formulated that refer only to the projected paths of the target variables (the ones in terms of which the stabilization objectives of policy are defined—here, inflation and the output gap). Briefly, the method involves constructing the target criteria by eliminating the Lagrange multipliers from the system of first-order conditions that characterize the optimal state-contingent evolution, regardless of character of the (additive) disturbances. We are left with linear relations among the target variables that do not involve the disturbances and with coefficients independent of the specification of the disturbances that represent the desired target criteria.

Recall that the first-order conditions that characterize the optimal state-contingent paths in the problem considered in the previous section are given by subtracting equation (37) from equation (34). As explained in the previous section, the first three of these conditions imply that the evolution of inflation and of the output gap must satisfy the subtraction of equation (39) from equation (38) each period. We can solve this subtraction for the values of φ_{2t}, $\varphi_{2,t-1}$ *implied* by the values of π_t, y_t that are observed in an optimal equilibrium. We can then replace $\varphi_{2,t-1}$ in these two relations by the multiplier implied in this way by observed values of π_{t-1}, y_{t-1}. Finally, we can eliminate φ_{2t} from these two relations to obtain a necessary relation between π_t and y_t, given π_{t-1} and y_{t-1}, given by:

$$\pi_t + \frac{n_\varphi}{m_\varphi}\pi_{t-1} + \frac{\omega_\varphi}{m_\varphi}\left(y_t - y_{t-1}\right) = 0 \tag{41}$$

This target criterion has the form of a flexible inflation target, similar to the optimal target criterion for monetary policy in the model with lump-sum taxation (Woodford, 2003, Chapter 7). It is interesting to note that, as in all of the examples of optimal target criteria for monetary policy derived under varying assumptions in Giannoni and Woodford (2003), it is only the projected rate of change of the output gap that matters for determining the appropriate adjustment of the near-term inflation target; the absolute level of the output gap is irrelevant.

The remaining first-order condition from the previous section, not used in the derivation of equation (41), is equation (37). By similarly using the solutions for $\varphi_{2,t+1}$, φ_{2t} implied by observations of π_{t+1}, y_{t+1} to substitute for the multipliers in this condition, one obtains a further target criterion:

$$E_t\pi_{t+1} = 0 \tag{42}$$

(The fact that this always holds in the optimal equilibrium—i.e., that the price level must follow a random walk—has already been noted in the previous section.) We show in the appendix that policies ensuring that the subtraction of equation (42) from equation (41) hold for all $t \geq t_0$ determine a unique nonexplosive rational-expectations equilibrium.

This equilibrium solves the above first-order conditions for a particular specification of the initial lagged multipliers φ_{1,t_0-1}, φ_{2,t_0-1}, which are inferred from the initial values π_{t_0-1}, y_{t_0-1} in the way just explained. Hence, this equilibrium minimizes expected discounted losses from equation (20) given $\hat{b}_{t_0-1}$ and subject to constraints on initial outcomes of the form:

$$\pi_{t_0} = \bar{\pi}\left(\pi_{t_0-1}, y_{t_0-1}\right) \tag{43}$$

$$y_{t_0} = \bar{y}\left(\pi_{t_0-1}, y_{t_0-1}\right) \tag{44}$$

Furthermore, these constraints are self-consistent in the sense that the equilibrium that solves this problem is one in which π_t, y_t are chosen to satisfy equations of this form in all periods $t > t_0$. Hence, these time-invariant policy rules are optimal from a timeless perspective.[34] And they are optimal regardless of the specification of disturbance processes. Thus, we have obtained robustly optimal target criteria, as desired.

34. See Woodford (2003, Chapters 7 and 8) for additional discussion of the self-consistency condition that the initial constraints are required to satisfy.

We have established a pair of target criteria with the property that if they are expected to be jointly satisfied each period, the resulting equilibrium involves the optimal responses to shocks. This result in itself, however, does not establish which policy instrument should be used to ensure satisfaction of which criterion. Because the variables referred to in both criteria can be affected by both monetary and fiscal policy, there is no uniquely appropriate answer to that question. However, the following represents a relatively simple example of a way in which such a regime could be institutionalized through separate targeting procedures on the part of monetary and fiscal authorities.

Let the central bank be assigned the task of maximizing social welfare through its adjustment of the level of short-term interest rates, taking as given the state-contingent evolution of the public debt $\{\hat{b}_t\}$, which depends on the decisions of the fiscal authority. Thus, the central bank treats the evolution of the public debt as being outside its control, just like the exogenous disturbances $\{\xi_t\}$, and simply seeks to forecast its evolution to model correctly the constraints on its own policy. Here, we do not propose a regime under which it is actually true that the evolution of the public debt would be unaffected by a change in monetary policy. But there is no inconsistency in the central bank's assumption (because a given bounded process $\{\hat{b}_t\}$ will continue to represent a feasible fiscal policy regardless of the policy adopted by the central bank), and we shall show that the conduct of policy under this assumption does not lead to a suboptimal outcome as long as the state-contingent evolution of the public debt is correctly forecasted by the central bank.

The central bank then seeks to bring about paths for $\{\pi_t, y_t, \hat{\tau}_t\}$ from date t_0 onward that minimize equation (20), subject to the constraints in equations (23) and (25) for each $t \geq t_0$, together with initial constraints of the form equation (44) to equation (43), given the evolution of the processes $\{\hat{\tau}_t^*, f_t, \hat{b}_t\}$. The first-order conditions for this optimization problem are given by equations (34), (35), and (37) each period, which in turn imply that equation (41) must hold each period, as shown above. One can further show that a commitment by the central bank to ensure that equation (41) holds each period determines the equilibrium evolution that solves this problem, in the case of an appropriate (self-consistent) choice of the initial constraints (43) to (44). Thus equation (41) is an optimal target criterion for a policy authority seeking to solve the kind of problem just posed, and since the problem takes as given the evolution of the public debt, it is obviously a more suitable assignment for the central bank than for the fiscal authority. The kind of interest-rate reaction function that can be used to implement a flexible inflation target of this kind is discussed in Svensson and Woodford (2003) and Woodford (2003, Chapter 7).

Correspondingly, let the fiscal authority be assigned the task of choosing the level of government revenue each period that will maximize social welfare, taking as given the state-contingent evolution of output $\{y_t\}$, which it regards as being determined by monetary policy. (Again, it need not really be the case that the central bank ensures a particular state-contingent path of output, regardless of what the fiscal authority does. But again, this assumption is not inconsistent with our model of the economy because it is possible for the central bank to bring about any bounded process $\{y_t\}$ that it wishes, regardless of fiscal policy, in the case that prices are sticky.) If the fiscal authority regards the evolution of output as outside its control, its objective reduces to the minimization of:

$$E_{t_0} \sum_{t = t_0}^{\infty} \beta^{t - t_0} \pi_t^2 \tag{45}$$

But this is a possible objective for fiscal policy, given the effects of tax policy on inflation dynamics (when taxes are not lump-sum) indicated by equation (23).

Forward integration of equation (23) implies that:

$$\pi_t = \kappa E_t \sum_{T = t}^{\infty} \beta^{T - t} y_T + \kappa \psi E_t \sum_{T = t}^{\infty} \beta^{T - t} (\hat{\tau}_T - \hat{\tau}_T^*) \tag{46}$$

Thus, what matters about fiscal policy for current inflation determination is the present value of expected tax rates, but this in turn is constrained by the intertemporal solvency condition in equation (25). Using equation (25) to substitute for the present value of taxes in equation (46), we obtain a relation of the form:

$$\pi_t = \mu_t [\hat{b}_{t-1} - \sigma^{-1} y_t + f_t] + \mu_2 E_t \sum_{T = t}^{\infty} \beta^{T - t} y_T \tag{47}$$

for certain coefficients μ_1, $\mu_2 > 0$ defined in the appendix. If the fiscal authority takes the evolution of output as given, then this relation implies that its policy in period t can have no effect on π_t. However, it can affect inflation in the following period through the effects of the current budget on $\hat{b}_t$ (implied by (27)), which then affects π_{t+1} (according to (47)). Furthermore, because the choice of $\hat{b}_t$ has no effect on inflation in later periods (given that it places no constraint on the level of public debt that may be chosen in later periods), $\hat{b}_t$ should be chosen to minimize $E_t \pi_{t+1}^2$.

The first-order condition for the optimal choice of $\hat{b}_t$ is then simply equation (42), which we find is indeed a suitable target criterion for the fiscal authority. The decision rule implied by this target criterion is:

$$\hat{b}_t = - E_t f_{t+1} + \sigma^{-1} E_t y_{t+1} - (\mu_2 / \mu_1) E_t \sum_{T = t+1}^{\infty} \beta^{T - t - 1} y_T$$

which expresses the optimal level of government borrowing as a function of the fiscal authority's projections of the exogenous determinants of fiscal stress and of future real activity. It is clearly possible for the fiscal authority to implement this target criterion and doing so leads to a determinate equilibrium path for inflation, given the path of output. We thus obtain a pair of targeting rules, one for the central bank and one for the fiscal authority, that if both pursued will implement an equilibrium that is optimal from a timeless perspective. Furthermore, each individual rule can be rationalized as a solution to a constrained optimization problem that the particular policy authority is assigned to solve.

6. Conclusion

We have shown that it is possible to analyze optimal monetary and fiscal policy jointly within a single framework. The two problems, often considered in isolation, turn out to be more closely related than might have been expected. In particular, we find that variations in the level of distorting taxes should be chosen to serve the same objectives as those emphasized in the literature on monetary stabilization policy: stabilization of inflation and of a (properly defined) output gap. A single output gap can be defined that measures the total distortion of the level of economic activity, resulting both from the stickiness of prices (and the consequent variation in markups) and from the supply-side effects of tax distortions. This cumulative gap is what one wishes to stabilize, rather than the individual components resulting from the two sources; and both monetary policy and tax policy can be used to affect it. Both monetary policy and tax policy also matter for inflation determination in our model because of the effects of the tax rate on real marginal cost and hence on the aggregate-supply relation. Indeed, we have exhibited a pair of robustly optimal targeting rules for the monetary and fiscal authorities, respectively, under which both authorities consider the consequences of their actions for near-term inflation projections in determining how to adjust their instruments.

And not only should the fiscal authority use tax policy to serve the traditional goals of monetary stabilization policy; we also find that the monetary authority should take account of the consequences of its actions for the government budget. In the present model, which abstracts entirely from transactions frictions, these consequences have solely to do with the implications of alternative price-level and interest-rate paths for the real burden of interest payments on the public debt and not with any contribution of seignorage to government revenues. Nonetheless, under a calibration of our model that assumes a debt burden and a level of distorting taxes that would not be unusual for an advanced industrial economy, taking account of the existence of a positive shadow value of additional government revenue (owing to the nonexistence of lump-sum taxes) makes a material difference for the quantitative characterization of optimal monetary policy. In fact, we have found that the crucial summary statistic that indicates the degree to which various types of real disturbances should be allowed to affect short-run projections for either inflation or the output gap is not the degree to which these disturbances shift the aggregate-supply curve for a given tax rate (i.e., the extent to which they represent cost-push shocks), but rather the degree to which they create fiscal stress (shift the intertemporal government solvency condition).

Our conclusion that monetary policy should account for the requirements for government solvency does not imply anything as strong as the result of Chari and Kehoe (1999) for a flexible-price economy with nominal government debt, according to which surprise variations in the inflation rate should be used to offset variations in fiscal stress completely so that tax rates need not vary (other than as necessary to stabilize the output gap). We find that in the case of even a modest degree of price stickiness—much less than what seems to be consistent with empirical evidence for the United States—it is not optimal for inflation to respond to variations in fiscal stress by more than a tiny fraction of the amount that would be required to eliminate the fiscal stress (and that would be optimal with fully flexible prices); instead, a substantial part of the adjustment should come through a change in the tax rate. But the way in which the acceptable short-run inflation projection should be affected by variations in the projected output gap is substantially different in an economy with only distorting taxes than would be the case in the presence of lump-sum taxation. With distorting taxes, the available trade-off between variations in inflation and in the output gap depends not only on the way these variables are related to one another through the aggregate-supply relation but also on the way that each of them affects the government budget.

7. Appendix

7.1 DERIVATION OF THE AGGREGATE-SUPPLY RELATION (EQUATION (11))

In this section, we derive equation (11) and we define the variables F_t and K_t. In the Calvo model, a supplier that changes its price in period t chooses a new price $p_t(i)$ to maximize:

$$E_t \left\{ \sum_{T=t}^{\infty} \alpha^{T-t} Q_{t,T} \Pi(p_t(i), p_T^j, P_T; Y_T, \tau_T, \xi_T) \right\}$$

where α^{T-t} is the probability that the price set at time t remains fixed in period T, $Q_{t,T}$ is the stochastic discount factor given by equation (7) and the profit function $\Pi(\cdot)$ is defined as:

$$\Pi(p, p^j, P; T, \tau, \xi) \equiv (1-\tau)pY(p/P)^{-\theta}$$
$$- \mu^w \frac{\tilde{v}_h(f^{-1}(Y(p^j/P)^{-\theta}/A); \xi)}{\tilde{u}_c(Y-G;\xi)} \, P \cdot f^{-1}(Y(p/P)^{-\theta}/A) \qquad (48)$$

Here Dixit-Stiglitz monopolistic competition implies that the individual supplier faces a demand curve each period of the form:

$$y_t(i) = Y_t(p_t(i)/P_t)^{-\theta}$$

so that after-tax sales revenues are the function of p given in the first term on the right side of equation (48). The second term indicates the nominal wage bill, obtained by inverting the production function to obtain the required labor input, and multiplying this by the industry wage for sector j. The industry wage is obtained from the labor supply equation (8), under the assumption that each of the firms in industry j (other than i, assumed to have a negligible effect on industry labor demand) charges the common price p^j. (Because all firms in a given industry are assumed to adjust their prices at the same time, in equilibrium the prices of firms in a given industry are always identical. We must nonetheless define the profit function for the case in which firm i deviates from the industry price so we can determine whether the industry price is optimal for each individual firm.)

We note that supplier i's profits are a concave function of the quantity sold $y_t(i)$ because revenues are proportional to $y_t^{(\theta-1)/\theta}(i)$ and hence concave in $y_t(i)$, while costs are convex in $y_t(i)$. Because $y_t(i)$ is proportional to $p_t(i)^{-\theta}$, the profit function is also concave in $p_t(i)^{-\theta}$. The first-order condition for the optimal choice of the price $p_t(i)$ is the same as the one with respect to $p_t(i)^{-\theta}$; hence, the first-order condition with respect to $p_t(i)$ is both necessary and sufficient for an optimum.

For this first-order condition, we obtain:

$$E_t \left\{ \sum_{T=t}^{\infty} \alpha^{T-t} Q_{t,T} \left(\frac{p_t(i)}{P_T} \right)^{-\theta} Y_T \Psi_T(p_t(i), p_t^j) \right\} = 0$$

with

$$\Psi_T(p, p^j) \equiv \left[(1-\tau_T) - \frac{\theta}{\theta-1} \mu_T^w \frac{\tilde{v}_h(f^{-1}(Y_T(p^j/P_T)^{-q}/A_T); \xi_T)}{\tilde{u}_c(Y_T - G_T; \xi_T) \cdot A_T f'(f^{-1}(Y_T(p/P_T)^{-\theta}/A_T))} \frac{P_T}{p} \right]$$

Using the definitions:

$$u(Y_t;\xi_t) \equiv \tilde{u}(Y_t - G_t;\xi_t)$$

$$v(y_t(i);\xi_t) \equiv \tilde{v}(f^{-1}(y_t(i)/A_t);\xi_t) = \tilde{v}(H_t(i);\xi_t)$$

and noting that each firm in an industry will set the same price, so that $p_t(i) = p_t^j = p_t^*$, the common price of all goods with prices revised at date t, we can rewrite the above first-order condition as:

$$E_t\left\{\sum_{T=t}^{\infty}(\alpha\beta)^{T-t}Q_{t,T}\left(\frac{p_t^*}{P_T}\right)^{-\theta}Y_T\left[(1-\tau_T) - \frac{\theta}{\theta-1}\mu_T^w\frac{v_y(Y_T(p_t^*/P_T)^{-\theta};\xi_T)}{u_c(Y_T;\xi_T)}\right]P_T\right\} = 0$$

Substituting the equilibrium value for the discount factor, we finally obtain:

$$E_t\left\{\sum_{T=t}^{\infty}\alpha^{T-t}u_c(Y_T;\xi_T)\left(\frac{p_t^*}{P_T}\right)^{-\theta}Y_T\left[\frac{p_t^*}{P_T}(1-\tau_T) - \frac{\theta}{\theta-1}\mu_T^w\frac{v_y(Y_T(p_t^*/P_T)^{-\theta};\xi_T)}{u_c(Y_T;\xi_T)}\right]\right\} = 0 \quad (49)$$

Using the isoelastic functional forms given in previous sections, we obtain a closed-form solution to equation (49), given by:

$$\frac{p_t^*}{P_t} = \left(\frac{K_t}{F_t}\right)^{1/(1+\omega\theta)} \quad (50)$$

where F_t and K_t are aggregate variables of the form:

$$F_t \equiv E_t\sum_{T=t}^{\infty}(\alpha\beta)^{T-t}(1-\tau_T)f(Y_T;\xi_T)\left(\frac{P_T}{P_t}\right)^{\theta-1} \quad (51)$$

$$K_t \equiv E_t\sum_{T=t}^{\infty}(\alpha\beta)^{T-t}k(Y_T;\xi_T)\left(\frac{P_T}{P_t}\right)^{\theta(1+\omega)} \quad (52)$$

in which expressions:

$$f(Y;\xi) \equiv u_c(Y;\xi)Y \quad (53)$$

$$k(Y;\xi) \equiv \frac{\theta}{\theta-1}\mu^w v_y(Y;\xi)Y \quad (54)$$

and where in the function $k(\cdot)$, the vector of shocks has been extended to include the shock μ_t^w. Substitution of equation (50) into the law of motion for the Dixit-Stiglitz price index:

$$P_t = \left[(1-\alpha)p_t^{*1-\theta} + \alpha P_{t-1}^{1-\theta}\right]^{1/(1-\theta)} \quad (55)$$

yields a short-run aggregate-supply relation between inflation and output of the form in equation (11).

7.2 RECURSIVE FORMULATION OF THE POLICY PROBLEM

Under the standard (Ramsey) approach to the characterization of an optimal policy commitment, one chooses among state-contingent paths $\{\Pi_t, Y_t, \tau_t, b_t, \Delta_t\}$ from some initial date t_0 onward that satisfy:

$$\frac{1 - \alpha\Pi_t^{\theta-1}}{1 - \alpha} = \left(\frac{F_t}{K_t}\right)^{(\theta-1)/(1+\omega\theta)} \tag{56}$$

$$\Delta_t = h(\Delta_{t-1}, \Pi_t) \tag{57}$$

$$b_{t-1}\frac{P_{t-1}}{P_t} = E_t \sum_{T=t}^{\infty} R_{t,T}\, s_T \tag{58}$$

where:

$$s_t \equiv \tau_t Y_t - G_t - \zeta_t \tag{59}$$

for each $t \geq t_0$, given initial government debt b_{t_0-1} and price dispersion Δ_{t_0-1}, to maximize:

$$U_{t_0} = E_{t_0} \sum_{t=t_0}^{\infty} \beta^{t-t_0} U(Y_t, \Delta_t; \xi_t) \tag{60}$$

Here we note that the definition (3) of the index of price dispersion implies the law of motion:

$$\Delta_t = \alpha\Delta_{t-1}\Pi_t^{\theta(1+\omega)} + (1-\alpha)\left(\frac{1 - \alpha\Pi_t^{\theta-1}}{1 - \alpha}\right)^{-\theta(1+\omega)/(1-\theta)} \tag{61}$$

which can be written in the form in equation (57); this is the origin of that constraint.

We now show that the t_0–optimal plan (Ramsey problem) can be obtained as the solution to a two-stage optimization problem. To this purpose, let:

$$W_t \equiv E_t \sum_{T=t}^{\infty} \beta^{T-t} \tilde{u}_c(Y_T - G_T; \xi_T) s_T$$

and let $\mathcal{F}$ be the set of values for $(b_{t-1}, \Delta_{t-1}, F_t, K_t, W_t)$ such that there exist paths $\{\Pi_T, Y_T, \tau_T, b_T, \Delta_T\}$ for dates $T \geq t$ that satisfy equations (56), (57), and (58), for each T, that are consistent with the specified values for F_t, K_t, defined in equations (63) and (64), and W_t, and that imply a well-defined value for the objective U_t defined in equation (60). Furthermore, for any $(b_{t-1}, \Delta_{t-1}, F_t, K_t, W_t) \in \mathcal{F}$, let $V(b_{t-1}, \Delta_{t-1}, X_t; \xi_t)$ denote the maximum attainable value of U_t among the state-contingent paths that satisfy the constraints just mentioned, where $X_t \equiv (F_t, K_t, W_t)$.[35] Among these constraints is the requirement that:

$$W_t = \frac{b_{t-1}}{\Pi_t} \tilde{u}_c(Y_t - G_t; \xi_t) \tag{62}$$

for equation (58) to be satisfied. Thus, a specified value for W_t implies a restriction on the possible values of Π_t and Y_t, given the predetermined real debt b_{t-1} and the exogenous disturbances.

The two-stage optimization problem is the following. In the first stage, values of the endogenous variables x_{t_0}, where $x_t \equiv (\Pi_t, Y_t, \tau_t, b_t, \Delta_t)$, and state-contingent commitments X_{t_0+1} (ξ_{t_0+1}) for the following period, are chosen to maximize an objective defined below. In the second stage, the equilibrium evolution from period $t_0 + 1$ onward is chosen to solve the maximization problem that defines the value function $V(b_{t_0}, \Delta_{t_0}, X_{t_0+1}; \xi_{t_0+1})$, given the state of the world ξ_{t_0+1} and the precommitted values for X_{t_0+1} associated with that state.

In defining the objective for the first stage of this equivalent formulation of the Ramsey problem, it is useful to let $\Pi(F, K)$ denote the value of Π_t that solves equation (56) for given values of F_t and K_t, and to let $s(x; \xi)$ denote the real primary surplus s_t defined by equation (59) in the case of given values of x_t and ξ_t. We also define the functional relationships:

$$\hat{J}[x, X(\cdot)](\xi_t) \equiv U(Y_t, \Delta_t; \xi_t) + \beta E_t V(b_t, \Delta_t, X_{t+1}; \xi_{t+1})$$

$$\hat{F}[x, X(\cdot)](\xi_t) \equiv (1 - \tau_t) f(Y_t; \xi_t) + \alpha \beta E_t \{\Pi(F_{t+1}, K_{t+1})^{\theta-1} F_{t+1}\}$$

$$\hat{K}[x, X(\cdot)](\xi_t) \equiv k(Y_t; \xi_t) + \alpha \beta E_t \{\Pi(F_{t+1}, K_{t+1})^{\theta(1+\omega)} K_{t+1}\}$$

$$\hat{W}[x, X(\cdot)](\xi_t) \equiv \tilde{u}_c(Y_t - G_t; \xi_t) s(x_t; \xi_t) + \beta E_t W_{t+1}$$

where $f(Y; \xi)$ and $k(Y; \xi)$ are defined in equations (53) and (54).

Then in the first stage, x_{t_0} and $X_{t_0}+1(\cdot)$ are chosen to maximize:

$$\hat{J}[x_{t_0}, X_{t_0+1}(\cdot)](\xi_{t_0}) \tag{63}$$

over values of x_{t_0} and $X_{t_0}+1(\cdot)$ such that:

1. Π_{t_0} and Δ_{t_0} satisfy equation (57);
2. the values:

---

35. As stated previously, in our notation for the value function V, ξ_t denotes not simply the vector of disturbances in period t but all information in period t about current and future disturbances.

$$F_{t_0} = \hat{F}[x_{t_0}, X_{t_0+1}(\cdot)](\xi_{t_0}) \tag{64}$$

$$K_{t_0} = \hat{K}[x_{t_0}, X_{t_0+1}(\cdot)](\xi_{t_0}) \tag{65}$$

satisfy:

$$\Pi_{t_0} = \Pi(F_{t_0}, K_{t_0}) \tag{66}$$

3. the value:

$$W_{t_0} = \hat{W}[x_{t_0}, X_{t_0+1}(\cdot)](\xi_{t_0}) \tag{67}$$

satisfies equation (62) for $t = t_0$; and

4. the choices $(b_{t_0}, \Delta_{t_0}, X_{t_0+1}) \in \mathcal{F}$ for each possible state of the world ξ_{t_0+1}.

These constraints imply that the objective $\hat{J}[x_{t_0}, X_{t_0+1}(\cdot)]$ (ξ_{t_0}) is well-defined and that values $(x_{t_0}, X_{t_0+1}(\cdot))$ are chosen for which the stage-two problem will be well defined, whichever state of the world is realized in period $t_0 + 1$. Furthermore, in the case of any stage-one choices consistent with the above constraints, and any subsequent evolution consistent with the constraints of the stage-two problem, equation (66) implies that equation (56) is satisfied in period t_0, while equation (62) implies that equation (58) is satisfied in period t_0. Constraint 1 above implies that equation (57) is also satisfied in period t_0. Finally, the constraints of the stage-two problem imply that equations (56), (57) and (58) are satisfied in each period $t \geq t_0 + 1$; thus, the state-contingent evolution that solves the two-stage problem is a rational-expectations equilibrium. Conversely, one can show that any possible rational-expectations equilibrium satisfies all these constraints.

One can then reformulate the Ramsey problem, replacing the set of requirements for rational-expectations equilibrium by the stage-one constraints plus the stage-two constraints. Because no aspect of the evolution from period $t_0 + 1$ onward, other than the specification of $X_{t_0+1}(\cdot)$, affects the stage-one constraints, the optimization problem decomposes into the two stages defined above, where the objective in equation (63) corresponds to the maximization of U_{t_0} in the first stage.

The optimization problem in stage two of this reformulation of the Ramsey problem is of the same form as the Ramsey problem itself, except that there are additional constraints associated with the pre-committed values for the elements of X_{t_0+1} (ξ_{t_0+1}). Let us consider a problem like the Ramsey problem just defined, looking forward from some period t_0, except under the constraints that the quantities X_{t_0} must take certain given values, where $(b_{t_0-1}, \Delta_{t_0-1}, X_{t_0}) \in \mathcal{F}$. This constrained problem can also be expressed as a two-stage problem of the same form as above, with an identical stage-two problem to the one described above. The stage-one problem is also identical to stage one of the Ramsey problem, except that now the plan chosen in stage one must be consistent with the given values X_{t_0}, so that the conditions in equations (64), (65), and (67) are now added to the constraints on the possible choices of $(x_{t_0}, X_{t_0+1}(\cdot))$ in stage one. [The stipulation that $(b_{t_0-1}, \Delta_{t_0-1}, X_{t_0}) \in \mathcal{F}$ implies that the constraint set remains non-empty despite these additional restrictions.]

Stage two of this constrained problem is thus of exactly the same form as the problem itself. Hence, the constrained problem has a recursive form. It can be decomposed into an infinite sequence of problems, in which in each period t, $(x_t, X_{t+1}(\cdot))$ is chosen to maximize $\hat{J}[x_t, X_{t+1}(\cdot)](\xi_t)$, given the predetermined state variables (b_{t-1}, Δ_{t-1}) and the precommitted values X_t, subject to the constraints that:

1. Π_t is given by equation (66), Y_t is then given by equation (62), and Δ_t is given by equation 57;
2. the pre-committed values X_t are fulfilled, i.e.:

$$\hat{F}[x_t, X_{t+1}(\cdot)](\xi_t) = F_t \tag{68}$$

$$\hat{K}[x_t, X_{t+1}(\cdot)](\xi_t) = K_t \tag{69}$$

$$\hat{W}[x_t, X_{t+1}(\cdot)](\xi_t) = W_t \tag{70}$$

and

3. the choices $(b_t, \Delta_t, X_{t+1}) \in \mathcal{F}$ for each possible state of the world ξ_{t+1}.

Our aim in the paper is to provide a local characterization of policy that solves this recursive optimization, in the event of small enough disturbances, and initial conditions $(b_{t_0-1}, \Delta_{t_0-1}, X_t) \in \mathcal{F}$ that are close enough to consistency with the steady state characterized in the next part of this appendix.

7.3 THE DETERMINISTIC STEADY STATE

Here we show the existence of a steady state, i.e., of an optimal policy (under appropriate initial conditions) of the recursive policy problem just defined that involves constant values of all variables. We now consider a deterministic problem in which the exogenous disturbances $\bar{C}_t$, G_t, $\bar{H}_t$, A_t, μ_t^w, ζ_t each take constant values $\bar{C}$, $\bar{H}$, $\bar{A}$, $\bar{\mu}^w > 0$ and $\bar{G}$, $\bar{\zeta} \geq 0$ for all $t \geq t_0$, and we start from initial conditions $b_{t_0-1} = \bar{b} > 0$. (The value of $\bar{b}$ is arbitrary, subject to an upper bound discussed below.) We wish to find an initial degree of price dispersion Δ_{t_0-1} and initial commitments $X_{t_0} = \bar{X}$ so that the recursive (or stage-two) problem involves a constant policy $x_{t_0} = \bar{x}$, $X_{t+1} = \bar{X}$ each period, in which $\bar{b}$ is equal to the initial real debt and $\bar{\Delta}$ is equal to the initial price dispersion.

We thus consider the problem of maximizing:

$$U_{t_0} = \sum_{t=t_0}^{\infty} \beta^{t-t_0} U(Y_t, \Delta_t) \tag{71}$$

subject to the constraints:

$$K_t p(\Pi_t)^{(1+\omega\theta)/(\theta-1)} = F_t \tag{72}$$

$$F_t = (1-\tau_t) f(Y_t) + \alpha\beta\Pi_{t+1}^{\theta-1} F_{t+1} \tag{73}$$

$$K_t = k(Y_t) + \alpha\beta\,\Pi_{t+1}^{\theta(1+\omega)}\,K_{t+1} \tag{74}$$

$$W_t = u_c(Y_t)(\tau_t Y_t - \bar{G} - \bar{\zeta}) + \beta W_{t+1} \tag{75}$$

$$W_t = \frac{u_c(Y_t)b_{t-1}}{\Pi_t} \tag{76}$$

$$\Delta_t = \alpha\Delta_{t-1}\Pi_t^{\theta(1+\omega)} + (1-\alpha)p(\Pi_t)^{-\theta(1+\omega)/(1-\theta)} \tag{77}$$

and given the specified initial conditions $b_{t_0-1}, \Delta_{t_0-1}, X_{t_0}$, where we have defined:

$$p(\Pi_t) \equiv \left(\frac{1-\alpha\,\Pi_t^{\theta-1}}{1-\alpha}\right)$$

we introduce Lagrange multipliers ϕ_{1t} through ϕ_{7t} corresponding to the constraints in equations (72) through (77), respectively. We also introduce multipliers dated t_0 corresponding to the constraints implied by the initial conditions $X_{t_0} = \bar{X}$; the latter multipliers are normalized so that the first-order conditions take the same form at date t_0 as at all later dates. The first-order conditions of the maximization problem are then the following. The one with respect to Y_t is:

$$U_y(Y_t, \Delta_t) - (1-\tau_t)f_y(Y_t)\phi_{2t} - Ky(Y_t)\phi_{3t} - \tau_t f_y(Y_t)\phi_{4t} +$$
$$u_{cc}(Y_t)(\bar{G} + \bar{\zeta})\phi_{4t} - u_{cc}(Y_t)b_{t-1}\Pi_t^{-1}\phi_{5t} = 0 \tag{78}$$

The one with respect to Δ_t is:

$$U_\Delta(Y_t, \Delta_t) + \phi_{6t} - \alpha\beta\,\Pi_{t+1}^{\theta(1+\omega)}\,\phi_{6,t+1} = 0 \tag{79}$$

The one with respect to Π_t is:

$$\frac{1+\omega\theta}{\theta-1}p\left(\Pi_t\right)^{((1+\omega\theta)/(\theta-1))-1}p_\pi\left(\Pi_t\right)K_t\phi_{1,t}-\alpha(\theta-1)\Pi_t^{\theta-2}F_t\phi_{2,t-1}$$

$$-\theta(1+\omega)\alpha\Pi_t^{\theta(1+\omega)-1}K_t\phi_{3,t-1}+u_c(Y_t)b_{t-1}\Pi_t^{-2}\phi_{5t}$$

$$-\theta(1+\omega)\alpha\Delta_{t-1}\Pi_t^{\theta(1+\omega)-1}\phi_{6t}$$

$$-\frac{\theta(1+\omega)}{\theta-1}(1-\alpha)p\left(\Pi_t\right)^{(1+\omega\theta)/(\theta-1)}p_\pi\left(\Pi_t\right)\phi_{6t}=0 \qquad (80)$$

The one with respect to τ_t is:

$$\phi_{2t}-\phi_{4t}=0 \qquad (81)$$

The one with respect to F_t is:

$$-\phi_{1t}+\phi_{2t}-\alpha\Pi_t^{\theta-1}\phi_{2,t-1}=0 \qquad (82)$$

The one with respect to K_t is:

$$p\left(\Pi_t\right)^{(1+\omega\theta)/(\theta-1)}\phi_{1t}+\phi_{3t}-\alpha\Pi_t^{\theta(1+\omega)}\phi_{3,t-1}=0 \qquad (83)$$

The one with respect to W_t is:

$$\phi_{4t}-\phi_{4,t-1}+\phi_{5t}=0 \qquad (84)$$

And finally, the one with respect to b_t is:

$$\phi_{5t}=0 \qquad (85)$$

We search for a solution to these first-order conditions in which $\Pi_t=\bar{\Pi}$, $\Delta_t=\bar{\Delta}$, $Y_t=\bar{Y}$, $\tau_t=\bar{\tau}$, and $b_t=\bar{b}$ at all times. A steady-state solution of this kind also requires that the Lagrange multipliers take constant values. We also conjecture the existence of a solution in which $\bar{\Pi}=1$, as stated previously. Note that such a solution implies that $\bar{\Delta}=1$, $p(\bar{\Pi})=1$, $p_\pi(\bar{\Pi})=-(\theta-1)\alpha/(1-\alpha)$, and $\bar{K}=\bar{F}$. Using these substitutions, we find that (the steady-state version of) each of the first-order conditions in equations (78) to (85) is satisfied if the steady-state values satisfy:

$$\phi_1=(1-\alpha)\phi_2$$

$$\left[f_y(\bar{Y})-k_y(\bar{Y})-u_{cc}(\bar{Y}-\bar{G})(\bar{G}+\bar{\zeta})\right]\phi_2=U_y(\bar{Y},1)$$

$$\phi_3=-\phi_2$$

$$\phi_4=\phi_2$$

$$\phi_5=0$$

$$(1-\alpha\beta)\phi_6=-U_\Delta(\bar{Y},1)$$

These equations can obviously be solved (uniquely) for the steady-state multipliers given any value $\bar{Y} > 0$.

Similarly, (the steady-state versions of) the constraints in equations (72) to (77) are satisfied if:

$$(1 - \bar{\tau})u_c(\bar{Y} - \bar{G}) = \frac{\theta}{\theta - 1}\,\bar{\mu}^w v_y(\bar{Y}) \tag{86}$$

$$\bar{\tau}\bar{Y} = \bar{G} + \bar{\zeta} + (1 + \beta)\bar{b} \tag{87}$$

$$\bar{K} = \bar{F} = (1 - \alpha\beta)^{-1}k(\bar{Y})$$

$$\bar{W} = u_c(\bar{Y} - \bar{G})\bar{b}$$

Equations (86) and (87) provide two equations to solve for the steady-state values $\bar{Y}$ and $\bar{\tau}$. Under standard (Inada-type) boundary conditions on preferences, equation (86) has a unique solution $Y_1(\tau) > \bar{G}$ for each possible value of $0 \le \tau < 1$.[36] This value is a decreasing function of τ and approaches $\bar{G}$ as τ approaches 1. We note that, at least in the case of all small enough values of $\bar{G}$, there exists a range of tax rates $0 < \tau_1 < \tau < \tau_2 \le 1$ over which $Y_1(\tau) > \bar{G}\,/\tau$.[37] Given our assumption that $\bar{b} > 0$ and that $\bar{G}\,\bar{\zeta} \ge 0$, equation (87) is satisfied only by positive values of $\bar{\tau}$; for each $\bar{\tau} > 0$, this equation has a unique solution $Y_2(\tau)$. We also note that the locus $Y_1(\tau)$ is independent of the values of $\bar{\zeta}$ and $\bar{b}$, while $Y_2(\tau)$ approaches $\bar{G}/\tau$ as $\bar{\zeta}$ and $\bar{b}$ approach zero. Fixing the value of $\bar{G}$ (at a value small enough for the interval (τ_1, τ_2) to exist), we then observe that for any small enough values of $\bar{b} > 0$ and $\bar{\zeta} \ge 0$, there exist values $0 < \tau < 1$ at which $Y_2(\tau) < Y_1(\tau)$. On the other hand, for all small enough values of $\tau > 0$, $Y_2(\tau) > Y_1(\tau)$. Thus, by continuity, there must exist a value $0 < \bar{\tau} < 1$ at which $Y_1(\bar{\tau}) = Y_2(\bar{\tau})$.[38] This allows us to obtain a solution for $0 < \bar{\tau} < 1$ and $\bar{Y} > 0$, in the case of any small enough values of $\bar{G}$, $\bar{\zeta} \ge 0$ and $\bar{b} > 0$. The remaining equations can then be solved (uniquely) for $\bar{K} = \bar{F}$ and for $\bar{W}$.

---

36. There is plainly no possibility of positive supply of output by producers in the case that $\tau_t \ge 1$ in any period; hence, the steady state must involve $\bar{\tau} < 1$.
37. This is true for any tax rate at which $(1 - \tau)\,u_c(\bar{G}(\tau^{-1} - 1))$ exceeds $(\theta/(\theta - 1))\,\bar{\mu}^w v_y\,(\bar{G}/\tau)$. Fixing any value $0 < \tau < 1$, our Inada conditions imply that this inequality holds for all small enough values of $\bar{G}$. And if the inequality holds for some $0 < \tau < 1$, then by continuity it must hold for an open interval of values of τ.
38. In fact, there must exist at least two such solutions because the Inada conditions also imply that $Y_2(\tau) > Y_1(\tau)$ for all τ close enough to 1. These multiple solutions correspond to a Laffer curve result under which two distinct tax rates result in the same equilibrium level of government revenues. We select the lower-tax, higher-output solution as the one around which we compute our Taylor-series expansions; this is clearly the higher-utility solution.

We have thus verified that a constant solution to the first-order conditions exists. With a method to be explained below, we check that this solution is indeed at least a local optimum. Note that, as asserted previously, this deterministic steady state involves zero inflation and a steady-state tax rate $0 < \bar{\tau} < 1$.

7.4 A SECOND-ORDER APPROXIMATION TO UTILITY (EQUATIONS [17] AND [18])

We derive here equations (17) and (18), taking a second-order approximation to equation (60) following the treatment in Woodford (2003, Chapter 6). We start by approximating the expected discounted value of the utility of the representative household:

$$U_{t_0} = E_{t_0} \sum_{t = t_0}^{\infty} \beta^{t - t_0} \left[u(Y_t; \xi_t) - \int_0^1 v(y_t(i); \xi_t) di \right] \tag{88}$$

First, we note that:

$$\int_0^1 v(y_t(i); \xi_t) di = \frac{\lambda}{1 + \nu} \frac{Y_t^{1 + \omega}}{A_t^{1 + \omega} \bar{H}_t^\nu} \Delta_t = v(Y_t; \xi_t) \Delta_t$$

where Δ_t is the measure of price dispersion defined previously. We can then write equation (88) as:

$$U_{t_0} = E_{t_0} \sum_{t = t_0}^{\infty} \beta^{t - t_0} \left[u(Y_t; \xi_t) - v(Y_t; \xi_t) \Delta_t \right] \tag{89}$$

The first term in equation (89) can be approximated using a second-order Taylor expansion around the steady state defined in the previous section as:

$$
\begin{aligned}
u(Y_t; \xi_t) &= \bar{u} + \bar{u}_c \tilde{Y}_t + \bar{u}_\xi \xi_t + \frac{1}{2} \bar{u}_{cc} \tilde{Y}_t^2 + \bar{u}_{c\xi} \xi_t \tilde{Y}_t + \frac{1}{2} \xi_t' \bar{u}_{\xi\xi} \xi_t \\
&\quad + \mathcal{O}(\|\xi\|^3) \\
&= \bar{u} + \bar{Y} \bar{u}_c \cdot (\hat{Y}_t + \frac{1}{2} \hat{Y}_t^2) + \bar{u}_\xi \xi_t + \frac{1}{2} \bar{Y} \bar{u}_{cc} \hat{Y}_t^2 + \bar{Y} \bar{u}_{c\xi} \xi_t \hat{Y}_t \\
&\quad + \frac{1}{2} \xi_t' \bar{u}_{\xi\xi} \xi_t + \mathcal{O}(\|\xi\|^3) \\
&= \bar{Y} u_c \hat{Y}_t + \frac{1}{2} [\bar{Y} \bar{u}_c + \bar{Y}^2 \bar{u}_{cc}] \hat{Y}_t^2 - \bar{Y}^2 \bar{u}_{cc} g_t \hat{Y}_t + \text{t.i.p.} + \mathcal{O}(\|\xi\|^3) \\
&= \bar{Y} \bar{u}_c \left\{ \hat{Y}_t + \frac{1}{2} (1 - \sigma^{-1}) \hat{Y}_t^2 + \sigma^{-1} g_t \hat{Y}_t \right\} + \text{t.i.p.} + \mathcal{O}(\|\xi\|^3) \tag{90}
\end{aligned}
$$

where a bar denotes the steady-state value for each variable, a tilde denotes the deviation of the variable from its steady-state value (e.g., $\tilde{Y}_t \equiv Y_t - \bar{Y}$), and a circumflex refers to the log deviation of the variable from its steady-state value (e.g., $\hat{Y}_t \equiv \ln Y_t/\bar{Y}$). We use ξ_t to refer to the entire vector of exogenous shocks:

$$\xi'_t \equiv [\hat{\zeta}_t \; \hat{G}_t \; g_t \; q_t \; \hat{\mu}_t^w]$$

in which $\hat{\zeta}_t \equiv (\zeta_t - \bar{\zeta})/\bar{Y}$, $\hat{G}_t \equiv (G_t - \bar{G})/\bar{Y}$, $g_t \equiv \hat{G}_t + s_C \bar{c}_t$, $\omega q_t \equiv \nu \bar{h}_t + \phi(1 + \nu) a_t$, $\hat{\mu}_t^w \equiv \ln \mu_t^w/\bar{\mu}^w$, $\bar{c}_t \equiv \ln \bar{C}_t/C$, $a_t \equiv \ln A_t/\bar{A}$, $\bar{h}_t \equiv \ln H_t/H$. We use the definitions $\sigma^{-1} \equiv \tilde{\sigma}^{-1} s_C^{-1}$ with $s_C \equiv \bar{C}/\bar{Y}$ and $s_C + s_G = 1$. We have used the Taylor expansion:

$$\frac{Y_t}{\bar{Y}} = 1 + \hat{Y}_t + \frac{1}{2}\hat{Y}_t^2 + \mathcal{O}(\|\xi\|^3)$$

to get a relation for $\tilde{Y}_t$ in terms of $\hat{Y}_t$. Finally the term *t.i.p.* denotes terms that are independent of policy and may accordingly be suppressed as far as the welfare ranking of alternative policies is concerned.

We may similarly approximate $v(Y_t; \xi_t)\Delta_t$ by:

$$
\begin{aligned}
v(Y_t;\xi_t)\Delta_t &= \bar{v} + \bar{v}(\Delta_t - 1) + \bar{v}_y(Y_t - \bar{Y}) + \bar{v}_y(\Delta_t - 1)(Y_t - \bar{Y}) + (\Delta_t - 1)\bar{v}_\xi \xi_t \\
&\quad + \frac{1}{2}\bar{v}_{yy}(Y_t - \bar{Y})^2 + (Y_t - \bar{Y})\bar{v}_{y\xi}\xi_t + \mathcal{O}(\|\xi\|^3) \\
&= \bar{v}(\Delta_t - 1) + \bar{v}_y \bar{Y}\left(\hat{Y}_t + \frac{1}{2}\hat{Y}_t^2\right) + \bar{v}_y(\Delta_t - 1)\bar{Y}\hat{Y}_t + (\Delta_t - 1)\bar{v}_\xi \xi_t \\
&\quad + \frac{1}{2}\bar{v}_{yy}\bar{Y}^2\hat{Y}_t^2 + \bar{Y}\hat{Y}_t\bar{v}_{y\xi}\xi_t + \text{t.i.p.} + \mathcal{O}(\|\xi\|^3) \\
&= \bar{v}_y\bar{Y}\left[\frac{\Delta_t - 1}{1 + \omega} + \hat{Y}_t + \frac{1}{2}(1 + \omega)\hat{Y}_t^2 + (\Delta_t - 1)\hat{Y}_t - \omega\hat{Y}_t q_t \right. \\
&\quad \left. - \frac{\Delta_t - 1}{1 + \omega}\omega q_t\right] + \text{t.i.p.} + \mathcal{O}(\|\xi\|^3)
\end{aligned}
$$

We take a second-order expansion of equation (61) to obtain:

$$\hat{\Delta}_t = \alpha\hat{\Delta}_{t-1} + \frac{\alpha}{1 - \alpha}\theta(1 + \omega)(1 + \omega\theta)\frac{\pi_t^2}{2} + \text{t.i.p.} + \mathcal{O}(\|\xi\|^3) \tag{91}$$

This in turn allows us to approximate $v(Y_t; \xi_t)\Delta_t$ as:

$$v(Y_t;\xi_t)\Delta_t = (1 - \Phi)\bar{Y}u_c\left\{\frac{\hat{\Delta}_t}{1 + \omega} + \hat{Y}_t + \frac{1}{2}(1 + \omega)\hat{Y}_t^2 - \omega\hat{Y}_t q_t\right\}$$

$$+ \text{t.i.p.} + \mathcal{O}(\|\xi\|^3) \tag{92}$$

where we have used the steady state relation $\bar{v}_y = (1 - \Phi)\,\bar{u}_c$ to replace $\bar{v}_y$ by $(1 - \Phi)\,\bar{u}_c$, and where:

$$\Phi \equiv 1 - \left(\frac{\theta - 1}{\theta}\right)\left(\frac{1 - \bar{\tau}}{\bar{\mu}^\omega}\right) < 1$$

measures the inefficiency of steady-state output $\bar{Y}$.

Combining equations (90) and (92), we finally obtain equation (17):

$$U_{t_0} = \bar{Y}\bar{u}_c \cdot E_{t_0} \sum_{t = t_0}^{\infty} \beta^{t - t_0}[\Phi\hat{Y}_t - \frac{1}{2}u_{yy}\hat{Y}_t^2 + \hat{Y}_t u_\xi \xi_t - u_\Delta\hat{\Delta}_t]$$

$$+ \text{ t.i.p. } + \mathcal{O}(\|\xi\|^3) \tag{93}$$

where:

$$u_{yy} \equiv (\omega + \sigma^{-1}) - \Phi(1 + \omega)$$

$$u_\xi \xi_t \equiv [\sigma^{-1}g_t + (1 - \Phi)\omega q_t]$$

$$u_\Delta \equiv \frac{(1 - \Phi)}{1 + \omega}$$

We finally observe that equation (91) can be integrated to obtain:

$$\sum_{t = t_0}^{\infty} \beta^{t - t_0}\hat{\Delta}_t = \frac{\alpha}{(1 - \alpha)(1 - \alpha\beta)}\,\theta(1 + \omega)(1 - \omega\theta)\sum_{t = t_0}^{\infty}\beta^{t - t_0}\frac{\pi_t^2}{2}$$

$$+ \text{ t.i.p } + \mathcal{O}(\|\xi\|) \tag{94}$$

By substituting equation (94) into equation (93), we obtain:

$$U_{t_0} = \bar{Y}\bar{u}_c \cdot E_{t_0} \sum_{t = t_0}^{\infty} \beta^{t - t_0}[\Phi\hat{Y}_t - \frac{1}{2}u_{yy}\hat{Y}_t^2 + \hat{Y}_t u_\xi \xi_t - \frac{1}{2}u_\pi \pi_t^2]$$

$$+ \text{ t.i.p. } + \mathcal{O}(\|\xi\|^3)$$

This coincides with equation (18), where we have further defined:

$$\kappa \equiv \frac{(1 - \alpha\beta)(1 - \alpha)}{\alpha}\,\frac{(\omega + \sigma^{-1})}{1 + \theta\omega}$$

$$u_\pi \equiv \frac{\theta(\omega + \sigma^{-1})(1 - \Phi)}{\kappa}$$

7.5 A SECOND-ORDER APPROXIMATION TO THE AGGREGATE SUPPLY EQUATION (EQUATION [11])

We now compute a second-order approximation to the aggregate supply (AS) equation (56), or equation (11). We start from equation (50), which can be written as:

$$\tilde{p}_t = \left(\frac{K_t}{F_t}\right)^{1/(1 + \omega\theta)}$$

where $\tilde{p}_t \equiv p_t^*/P_t$. As we have shown (Benigno and Woodford, 2003), a second-order expansion of this can be expressed in the form:

$$
\frac{(1+\omega\theta)}{(1-\alpha\beta)}\,\hat{\tilde{p}}_t = z_t + \alpha\beta\frac{(1+\omega\theta)}{(1-\alpha\beta)}\,E_t(\hat{\tilde{p}}_{t+1}-\hat{P}_{t,t+1}) + \frac{1}{2}\,z_t X_t
$$
$$
- \frac{1}{2}(1+\omega\theta)\hat{\tilde{p}}_t Z_t + \frac{1}{2}\alpha\beta(1+\omega\theta)E_t\{(\hat{\tilde{p}}_{t+1}-\hat{P}_{t,t+1})Z_{t+1}\}
$$
$$
+ \frac{\alpha\beta}{2(1-\alpha\beta)}\,(1-2\theta-\omega\theta)\,(1+\omega\theta)E_t\{(\hat{\tilde{p}}_{t+1}-\hat{P}_{t,t+1})\hat{P}_{t,t+1}\}
$$
$$
+ \text{s.o.t.i.p.} + \mathcal{O}(\|\xi\|^3) \tag{95}
$$

where we define:

$$
\hat{P}_{t,T} \equiv \log(P_t/P_T)
$$
$$
z_t \equiv \omega(\hat{Y}_t - q_t) + \tilde{\sigma}^{-1}(\hat{C}_t - \bar{c}_t) - \hat{S}_t + \hat{\mu}_t^w
$$
$$
Z_t \equiv E_t\left\{\sum_{T=t}^{+\infty}(\alpha\beta)^{T-t}[X_T + (1-2\theta-\omega\theta)\hat{P}_{t,T}]\right\}
$$

and in this last expression:

$$
X_T \equiv (2+\omega)\hat{Y}_T - \omega q_T + \hat{\mu}_T^w + \hat{S}_T - \tilde{\sigma}^{-1}(\hat{C}_T - \bar{c}_T)
$$

where $\hat{S}_t = \ln(1-\tau_t)/(1-\bar{\tau})$. Here, s.o.t.i.p. refers to second-order (or higher) terms independent of policy; the first-order terms have been kept because these will matter for the log-linear aggregate-supply relation that appears as a constraint in our policy problem.

We next take a second-order expansion of the law of motion in equation (55) for the price index, obtaining:

$$
\hat{\tilde{p}}_t = \frac{\alpha}{1-\alpha}\pi_t - \frac{1-\theta}{2}\frac{\alpha}{(1-\alpha)^2}\pi_t^2 + \mathcal{O}(\|\xi\|^3) \tag{96}
$$

where we have used the fact that:

$$
\hat{\tilde{p}}_t = \frac{\alpha}{1-\alpha}\pi_t + \mathcal{O}(\|\xi\|^2)
$$

and $\hat{P}_{t-1,t} = -\pi_t$. We can then plug equation (96) into equation (95) to obtain:

$$
\pi_t = \frac{1-\theta}{2}\frac{1}{(1-\alpha)}\pi_t^2 + \frac{\kappa}{(\omega+\sigma^{-1})}\,z_t + \beta E_t\,\pi_{t+1} - \frac{1-\theta}{2}\frac{\alpha\beta}{(1-\alpha)}E_t\,\pi_{t+1}^2
$$
$$
+ \frac{1}{2}\frac{\kappa}{(\omega+\sigma^{-1})}z_t X_t - \frac{1}{2}(1-\alpha\beta)\pi_t Z_t + \frac{\beta}{2}(1-\alpha\beta)E_t\{\pi_{t+1}Z_{t+1}\}
$$
$$
- \frac{\beta}{2}(1-2\theta-\omega\theta)E_t\{\pi_{t+1}^2\} + \text{s.o.t.i.p.} + \mathcal{O}(\|\xi\|^3) \tag{97}
$$

We note that a second-order approximation to the identity $C_t = Y_t - G_t$ yields:

$$\hat{C}_t = s_C^{-1}\hat{Y}_t - s_C^{-1}\hat{G}_t + \frac{s_C^{-1}(1 - s_C^{-1})}{2}\,\hat{Y}_t^2 + s_C^{-2}\hat{Y}_t\hat{G}_t + \text{s.o.t.i.p.} + \mathcal{O}(\|\xi\|^3) \qquad (98)$$

and that:

$$\hat{S}_t = -\,\omega_\tau\hat{\tau}_t - \frac{\omega_\tau}{(1 - \bar{\tau})}\,\hat{\tau}_t^2 + \mathcal{O}(\|\xi\|^3) \qquad (99)$$

where $\omega_\tau \equiv \bar{\tau}\,/\,(1 - \bar{\tau})$. By substituting equations (98) and (99) into the definition of z_t in equation (97), we finally obtain a quadratic approximation to the AS relation.

This can be expressed compactly in the following form:

$$V_t = \kappa(c_x' \, x_t + c_\xi' \xi_t + \tfrac{1}{2}\, x_t' \, C_x x_t + x_t' C_\xi \xi_t + \tfrac{1}{2} c_\pi \pi_t^2) + \beta E_t V_{t+1}$$
$$+ \text{ s.o.t.i.p.} + \mathcal{O}\,(\|\xi\|^3) \qquad (100)$$

where we have defined:

$$x_t \equiv \begin{bmatrix} \hat{\tau}_t \\ \hat{Y}_t \end{bmatrix}$$

$$c_x' = [\Psi \quad 1]$$

$$c_x' = \begin{bmatrix} 0 & 0 & -\sigma^{-1}(\omega + \sigma^{-1})^{-1} & -\omega(\omega + \sigma^{-1})^{-1} & (\omega + \sigma^{-1})^{-1} \end{bmatrix}$$

$$C_x = \begin{bmatrix} \psi & (1 - \sigma^{-1})\psi \\ (1 - \sigma^{-1})\psi & (2 + \omega - \sigma^{-1}) + \sigma^{-1}(1 - s_C^{-1})(\omega + \sigma^{-1})^{-1} \end{bmatrix}$$

$$C_\xi = \begin{bmatrix} 0 & 0 & \psi\sigma^{-1} & 0 & 0 \\ 0 & \dfrac{\sigma^{-1}s_C^{-1}}{(\omega + \sigma^{-1})} & -\dfrac{\sigma^{-1}(1 - \sigma^{-1})}{(\omega + \sigma^{-1})} & -\dfrac{\omega(1 + \omega)}{(\omega + \sigma^{-1})} & \dfrac{(1 + \omega)}{(\omega + \sigma^{-1})} \end{bmatrix}$$

$$c_\pi = \frac{\theta(1 + \omega)}{\kappa}$$

$$V_t = \pi_t + \frac{1}{2}v_\pi \pi_t^2 + v_z \pi_t Z_t$$

$$Z_t = z_x' \, x_t + z_\pi \pi_t + z_\xi' \, \xi_t + \alpha\beta E_t \, Z_{t+1}\,.$$

in which the coefficients:

$$\psi \equiv \frac{\omega_\tau}{(\omega + \sigma^{-1})}$$

and:

$$v_\pi \equiv \theta(1+\omega) - \frac{1-\theta}{(1-\alpha)}$$

$$v_z \equiv \frac{(1-\alpha\beta)}{2}$$

$$v_k \equiv \frac{\kappa}{(\omega+\sigma^{-1})} \frac{\alpha\beta}{1-\alpha\beta} (1-2\theta-\omega\theta)$$

$$z'_x \equiv \left[(2+\omega-\sigma^{-1}) + v_\kappa(\omega+\sigma^{-1}) \quad -\omega_\tau(1-v_\kappa)\right]$$

$$z'_\xi \equiv \left[0 \quad 0 \quad \sigma^{-1}(1-v_k) \quad -\omega(1+v_k) \quad (1+v_k)\right]$$

$$z_\pi \equiv -\frac{\omega+\sigma^{-1}}{k} v_k$$

Note that in a first-order approximation, equation (100) can be written as simply:

$$\pi_t = \kappa[\hat{Y}_t + \psi\,\hat{\tau}_t + c'_\xi \xi_t] + \beta E_t \pi_{t+1} \tag{101}$$

where:

$$c'_\xi \xi_t \equiv (\omega + \sigma^{-1})^{-1}[-\sigma^{-1}g_t - \omega q_t + \hat{\mu}_t^w]$$

We can also integrate equation (100) forward from time t_0 to obtain:

$$V_{t_0} = E_{t_0} \sum_{t=t_0}^{\infty} \beta^{t-t_0} \kappa(c'_x x_t + \frac{1}{2} x'_t C_x x_t + x'_t C_\xi \xi_t + \frac{1}{2} c_\pi \pi_t^2)$$
$$+ \text{t.i.p.} + \mathcal{O}(\|\xi\|^3) \tag{102}$$

where the term $c'_\xi \xi_t$ is now included in terms independent of policy. Such terms matter when they are part of the log-linear constraints, as in the case of equation (61), but not when they are part of the quadratic objective.

7.6 A SECOND-ORDER APPROXIMATION TO THE INTERTEMPORAL GOVERNMENT SOLVENCY CONDITION (EQUATION [15])

We now derive a second-order approximation to the intertemporal government solvency condition. We use the definition:

$$W_t \equiv E_t \sum_{T=t}^{\infty} \beta^{T-t} \tilde{u}_c(Y_T; \xi_T) s_T \tag{103}$$

where:

$$s_t \equiv \tau_t Y_t - G_t - \zeta_t \tag{104}$$

and:

$$W_t = \frac{b_{t-1}}{\Pi_t} \tilde{u}_c(C_t; \xi_t) \tag{105}$$

First, we take a second-order approximation of the term $\tilde{u}_c(C_t; \xi_t)\, s_t$ to obtain:

$$
\begin{aligned}
\tilde{u}_c(C_t; \xi_t)s_t &= \bar{s}\bar{\tilde{u}}_c + \bar{\tilde{u}}_{cc}\bar{s}\tilde{C}_t + \bar{\tilde{u}}_c\tilde{s}_t + \bar{s}\bar{\tilde{u}}_{c\xi}\xi_t \\
&\quad + \frac{1}{2}\bar{s}\bar{\tilde{u}}_{ccc}\tilde{C}_t^2 + \bar{\tilde{u}}_{cc}\tilde{C}_t\tilde{s}_t + \bar{s}\tilde{C}_t\bar{\tilde{u}}_{cc\xi}\xi_t \\
&\quad + \tilde{s}_t\bar{\tilde{u}}_{c\xi}\xi_t + \text{s.o.t.i.p.} + \mathcal{O}(\|\xi\|^3) \\
&= \bar{s}\bar{\tilde{u}}_c + \bar{\tilde{u}}_{cc}\bar{s}\bar{C}\hat{C}_t + \bar{\tilde{u}}_c\tilde{s}_t + \bar{s}\bar{\tilde{u}}_{c\xi}\xi_t \\
&\quad + \frac{1}{2}\bar{s}(\bar{\tilde{u}}_{cc}\bar{C} + \bar{\tilde{u}}_{ccc}\bar{C}^2)\hat{C}_t^2 + \bar{C}\bar{\tilde{u}}_{cc}\hat{C}_t\tilde{s}_t \\
&\quad + \bar{s}\bar{C}\bar{\tilde{u}}_{cc\xi}\xi_t\hat{C}_t + \bar{\tilde{u}}_{c\xi}\xi_t\tilde{s}_t + \text{s.o.t.i.p.} + \mathcal{O}(\|\xi\|^3) \\
&= \bar{s}\bar{\tilde{u}}_c + \bar{\tilde{u}}_c[-\tilde{\sigma}^{-1}\bar{s}\hat{C}_t + \tilde{s}_t + \bar{s}\bar{\tilde{u}}_c^{-1}\bar{\tilde{u}}_{c\xi}\xi_t \\
&\quad + \frac{1}{2}\bar{s}\tilde{\sigma}^{-2}\tilde{C}_t^2 - \tilde{\sigma}^{-1}\tilde{s}_t\hat{C}_t \\
&\quad + \bar{s}\bar{C}\bar{\tilde{u}}_c^{-1}\bar{\tilde{u}}_{cc\xi}\xi_t\hat{C}_t + \bar{\tilde{u}}_c^{-1}\bar{\tilde{u}}_{c\xi}\xi_t\tilde{s}_t] \\
&\quad + \text{s.o.t.i.p.} + \mathcal{O}(\|\xi\|^3) \\
&= \bar{s}\bar{\tilde{u}}_c + \bar{\tilde{u}}_c[-\tilde{\sigma}^{-1}\bar{s}(\hat{C}_t - \bar{c}_t) + \tilde{s}_t \\
&\quad + \frac{1}{2}\bar{s}\tilde{\sigma}^{-2}\tilde{C}_t^2 - \tilde{\sigma}^{-1}\tilde{s}_t(\hat{C}_t - \bar{c}_t) - \tilde{\sigma}^{-2}\bar{s}\bar{c}_t\hat{C}_t] \\
&\quad + \text{s.o.t.i.p.} + \mathcal{O}(\|\xi\|^3)
\end{aligned}
\tag{106}
$$

where we have followed previous definitions and use the isoelastic functional forms assumed. Note that we can write $\bar{\tilde{u}}_c^{-1}\bar{\tilde{u}}_{c\xi}\xi_t = \tilde{\sigma}^{-1}\bar{c}_t$ and $\bar{C}\bar{\tilde{u}}_c^{-1}\bar{\tilde{u}}_{c\xi}\xi_t = -\tilde{\sigma}^{-2}\bar{c}_t$. Plugging equation (98) into equation (106), we obtain:

$$
\begin{aligned}
\tilde{u}_c(C_t; \xi_t)s_t &= \bar{s}\bar{\tilde{u}}_c[1 - \sigma^{-1}\hat{Y}_t + \sigma^{-1}g_t + \bar{s}^{-1}\tilde{s}_t + \frac{1}{2}[\sigma^{-1}(s_C^{-1} - 1) + \sigma^{-2}]\hat{Y}_t^2 \\
&\quad - \sigma^{-1}\bar{s}^{-1}(\hat{Y}_t - g_t)\tilde{s}_t - \sigma^{-1}(s_C^{-1}\hat{G}_t + \sigma^{-1}g_t)\hat{Y}_t] \\
&\quad + \text{s.o.t.i.p.} + \mathcal{O}(\|\xi\|^3)
\end{aligned}
\tag{107}
$$

by using previous definitions.

We recall now that the primary surplus is defined as:

$$s_t = \tau_t Y_t - G_t - \zeta_t$$

which can be expanded in a second-order expansion to get:

$$\bar{s}^{-1}\tilde{s}_t = (1 + \omega_g)(\hat{Y}_t + \hat{\tau}_t) - s_d^{-1}(\hat{G}_t + \hat{\zeta}_t) + \frac{(1 + \omega_g)}{2}(\hat{Y}_t + \hat{\tau}_t)^2$$

$$+ \text{ s.o.t.i.p.} + \mathcal{O}(\|\xi\|^3) \tag{108}$$

where we have defined $s_d \equiv \bar{s}/\bar{Y}$, $\omega_g = (\bar{G} + \bar{\zeta})/\bar{s}$ and $\hat{\zeta}_t = (\zeta_t - \bar{\zeta})/\bar{Y}$. Using equation (108) to substitute for $\tilde{s}_t$ in equation (107), we obtain:

$$\tilde{u}_c(C_t; \tilde{\xi}_t)s_t = \bar{s}\bar{\tilde{u}}_c \left[1 - \sigma^{-1}\hat{Y}_t + (1 + \omega_g)(\hat{Y}_t + \hat{\tau}_t) + \sigma^{-1}g_t - s_d^{-1}(\hat{G}_t + \hat{\zeta}_t)\right.$$

$$+ \frac{(1 + \omega_g)}{2}\hat{\tau}_t^2 + (1 + \omega_g)(1 - \sigma^{-1})\hat{\tau}_t\hat{Y}_t$$

$$+ \frac{1}{2}\left[1 + \omega_g + \sigma^{-1}(s_C^{-1} - 1) + \sigma^{-2} - 2\sigma^{-1}(1 + \omega_g)\right]\hat{Y}_t^2$$

$$- \sigma^{-1}[s_C^{-1}\hat{G}_t + (\sigma^{-1} - 1 - \omega_g)g_t - s_d^{-1}(\hat{G}_t + \hat{\zeta}_t)]\hat{Y}_t$$

$$\left. + \sigma^{-1}(1 + \omega_g)g_t\hat{\tau}_t\right] + \text{s.o.t.i.p.} + \mathcal{O}(\|\xi\|^3) \tag{109}$$

Substituting equation (109) in equation (103), we obtain:

$$\tilde{W}_t = (1 - \beta)\left[b_x'x_t + b_\xi'\xi_t + \frac{1}{2}x_t'B_x x_t + x_t'B_\xi \xi_t\right] + \beta E_t\tilde{W}_{t+1}$$

$$+ \text{s.o.t.i.p.} + \mathcal{O}(\|\xi\|^3) \tag{110}$$

where $\tilde{W}_t \equiv (W_t - \bar{W})/\bar{W}$ and:

$$b_x' = \left[(1 + \omega_g) \quad (1 + \omega_g) - \sigma^{-1}\right]$$

$$b_\xi' = \left[-s_d^{-1} \quad -s_d^{-1} \quad \sigma^{-1} \quad 0 \quad 0\right]$$

$$B_x = \begin{bmatrix} (1 + \omega_g) & (1 - \sigma^{-1})(1 + \omega_g) \\ (1 - \sigma^{-1})(1 + \omega_g) & (1 + \omega_g) + (s_C^{-1} - 1)\sigma^{-1} + \sigma^{-2} - 2\sigma^{-1}(1 + \omega_g) \end{bmatrix}$$

$$B_\xi = \begin{bmatrix} 0 & 0 & \sigma^{-1}(1 + \omega_g) & 0 & 0 \\ s_d^{-1}\sigma^{-1} & s_d^{-1}\sigma^{-1} - s_C^{-1}\sigma^{-1} & -\sigma^{-1}(\sigma^{-1} - 1 - \omega_g) & 0 & 0 \end{bmatrix}$$

We note from equation (110) that:

$$\tilde{W}_t \equiv (\hat{b}_{t-1} - \pi_t - \tilde{\sigma}^{-1}\hat{C}_t + \bar{c}_t) + \frac{1}{2}(\hat{b}_{t-1} - \pi_t - \tilde{\sigma}^{-1}\hat{C}_t + \bar{c}_t)^2$$
$$+ \mathcal{O}(\|\xi\|^3)$$

Substituting in equation (98), we obtain:

$$\tilde{W}_t \equiv \hat{b}_{t-1} - \pi_t - \sigma^{-1}(\hat{Y}_t - g_t) - \frac{\sigma^{-1}(1 - s_C^{-1})}{2}\hat{Y}_t^2 - \sigma^{-1}s_C^{-1}\hat{Y}_t\hat{G}_t$$
$$+ \frac{1}{2}(\hat{b}_{t-1} - \pi_t - \sigma^{-1}(\hat{Y}_t - g_t))^2 + \text{s.o.t.i.p.} + \mathcal{O}(\|\xi\|^3)$$

which can be written as:

$$\tilde{W}_t = \hat{b}_{t-1} - \pi_t + \omega_x' x_t + \omega_\xi' \xi_t + \frac{1}{2}x_t' W_x x_t + x_t' W_\xi \xi_t$$
$$+ \frac{1}{2}\left[\hat{b}_{t-1} - \pi_t + \omega_x' x_t + \omega_\xi' \xi_t\right]^2 + \text{s.o.t.i.p.} + \mathcal{O}(\|\xi\|^3)$$

where

$$w_x' = [0 \quad -\sigma^{-1}]$$

$$w_\xi' = [0 \quad 0 \quad \sigma^{-1} \quad 0 \quad 0]$$

$$W_x = \begin{bmatrix} 0 & 0 \\ 0 & (s_C^{-1} - 1)\sigma^{-1} \end{bmatrix}$$

$$W_\xi = \begin{bmatrix} 0 & 0 & 0 & 0 & 0 \\ 0 & -s_C^{-1}\sigma^{-1} & 0 & 0 & 0 \end{bmatrix}$$

Note that in the first-order approximation, we can simply write equation (110) as:

$$\hat{b}_{t-1} - \pi_t + w_x' x_t + w_\xi' \xi_t = (1 - \beta)\left[b_x' x_t + b_\xi' \xi_t\right]$$
$$+ \beta E_t\left[\hat{b}_t - \pi_{t+1} + w_x' x_{t+1} + w_\xi' \xi_{t+1}\right] \quad (111)$$

Integrating equation (110) forward, we obtain:

$$\tilde{W}_{t_0} = (1 - \beta)E_{t_0}\sum_{t=t_0}^{\infty}\beta^{t-t_0}\left[b_x' x_t + \frac{1}{2}x_t' B_x x_t + x_t' B_\xi \xi_t\right]$$
$$+ \text{t.i.p.} + \mathcal{O}(\|\xi\|^3) \quad (112)$$

where we have included $b_\xi' \xi_t$ in $t.i.p.$

7.7 A QUADRATIC POLICY OBJECTIVE (EQUATIONS [19] AND [20])

We now derive a quadratic approximation to the policy objective function. To this end, we combine equations (102) and (112) in a way that eliminates the linear term in equation (93). Indeed, we find ϑ_1, ϑ_2 so that:

$$\vartheta_1 b'_x + \vartheta_2 c'_x = a'_x \equiv [0 \quad \Phi]$$

The solution is given by:

$$\vartheta_1 = -\frac{\Phi \omega_\tau}{\Gamma}$$

$$\vartheta_2 = \frac{\Phi(1 + \omega_g)}{\Gamma}$$

where:

$$\Gamma = (\omega + \sigma^{-1})(1 + \omega_g) - \omega_\tau(1 + \omega_g) + \omega_\tau \sigma^{-1}$$

We can write:

$$E_{t_0} \sum_{t=t_0}^{\infty} \beta^{t-t_0} \Phi \hat{Y}_t = E_{t_0} \sum_{t=t_0}^{\infty} \beta^{t-t_0} [\vartheta_1 b'_x + \vartheta_2 c'_x] x_t$$

$$= -E_{t_0} \sum_{t=t_0}^{\infty} \beta^{t-t_0} \left[\frac{1}{2} x'_t D_x x_t + x' D_\xi \xi_t + \frac{1}{2} d_\pi \pi_t^2 \right]$$
$$+ \vartheta_1 \tilde{W}_{t_0} + \vartheta_2 \kappa^{-1} V_{t_0} + \text{t.i.p.} + \mathcal{O}(\|\xi\|^3)$$

where:

$$D_x \equiv \vartheta_1 B_x + \vartheta_2 C_x$$

and so on. Hence:

$$U_{t_0} = \Omega E_{t_0} \sum_{t=t_0}^{\infty} \beta^{t-t_0} \left\{ a'_t x_t - \frac{1}{2} x'_t A_x x_t - x'_t A_\xi \xi_t - \frac{1}{2} a_\pi \pi_t^2 \right\} + \text{t.i.p.} + \mathcal{O}(\|\xi\|^3)$$

$$= -\Omega E_{t_0} \sum_{t=t_0}^{\infty} \beta^{t-t_0} \left\{ \frac{1}{2} x'_t Q_x x_t + x'_t Q_\xi \xi_t + \frac{1}{2} q_\pi \pi_t^2 \right\} + T_{t_0} + \text{t.i.p.} + \mathcal{O}(\|\xi\|^3)$$

$$= -\Omega E_{t_0} \sum_{t=t_0}^{\infty} \beta^{t-t_0} \left\{ \frac{1}{2} q_y (\hat{Y}_t - \hat{Y}_t^*)^2 + \frac{1}{2} q_\pi \pi_t^2 \right\} + T_{t_0} + \text{t.i.p.} + \mathcal{O}(\|\xi\|^3) \qquad (113)$$

In these expressions, $\Omega = \bar{u}_c\,\hat{Y}$ and

$$Q_x = \begin{bmatrix} 0 & 0 \\ 0 & q_y \end{bmatrix}$$

with:

$$q_y \equiv (1 - \Phi)(\omega + \sigma^{-1}) + \Phi(\omega + \sigma^{-1})\frac{(1 + \omega_g)(1 + \omega)}{\Gamma}$$

$$+ \Phi\sigma^{-1}\frac{(1 + \omega_\tau)(1 + \omega_g)}{\Gamma} - \Phi\sigma^{-1}s_C^{-1}\frac{1 + \omega_g + \omega_\tau}{\Gamma}$$

We have defined:

$$Q_\xi = \begin{bmatrix} 0 & 0 & 0 & 0 & 0 \\ q_{\xi 1} & q_{\xi 2} & q_{\xi 3} & q_{\xi 4} & q_{\xi 5} \end{bmatrix}$$

with:

$$q_{\xi 1} = -\frac{\Phi\omega_\tau}{\Gamma}s_d^{-1}\sigma^{-1},$$

$$q_{\xi 2} = -\frac{\Phi\sigma^{-1}s_d^{-1}\omega_\tau}{\Gamma} + \frac{\sigma^{-1}s_C^{-1}\Phi(1 + \omega_g + \omega_\tau)}{\Gamma}$$

$$q_{\xi 3} = -(1 - \Phi)\sigma^{-1} - \frac{\sigma^{-1}\Phi(1 + \omega)(1 + \omega_g)}{\Gamma}$$

$$q_{\xi 4} = -(1 - \Phi)\omega - \frac{\omega\Phi(1 + \omega)(1 + \omega_g)}{\Gamma}$$

$$q_{\xi 5} = \Phi\frac{1 + \omega_g}{\Gamma}(1 + \omega)$$

and:

$$q_\pi = \frac{\Phi(1 + \omega_g)\theta(1 + \omega)(\omega + \sigma^{-1})}{\Phi\kappa} + \frac{(1 - \Phi)\theta(\omega + \sigma^{-1})}{\kappa}$$

We have defined $\hat{Y}_t^*$, the desired level of output, as:

$$\hat{Y}_t^* = -q_y^{-1}q_\xi'\xi_t$$

Finally:

$$T_{t_0} \equiv \bar{Y}\bar{u}_c[\vartheta_1\tilde{W}_{t_0} + \vartheta_2\kappa^{-1}V_{t_0}]$$

is a transitory component.

Equation (113) corresponds to equation (19). In particular, given the commitments on the initial values of the vector X_{t_0}, W_{t_0} implies that $\tilde{W}_{t_0}$ is given when characterizing the optimal policy from a timeless perspective. F_{t_0} and K_{t_0} imply that V_{t_0} and Z_{t_0} are also given. It follows that the value of the transitory component T_{t_0} is predetermined under stage two of the Ramsey problem. Hence, over the set of admissible policies, higher values of equation (113) correspond to lower values of:

$$E_{t_0} \sum_{t=t_0}^{\infty} \beta^{t-t_0} \left\{ \frac{1}{2} q_y (\hat{Y}_t - \hat{Y}_t^*)^2 + \frac{1}{2} q_\pi \pi_t^2 \right\} \tag{114}$$

It follows that we may rank policies in terms of the implied value of the discounted quadratic loss function in equation (114) which corresponds to equation (20). Because this loss function is purely quadratic (i.e., lacking linear terms), it is possible to evaluate it to second order using only a first-order approximation to the equilibrium evolution of inflation and output under a given policy. Hence, the log-linear approximate structural relations in equations (101) and (111) are sufficiently accurate for our purposes. Similarly, it suffices that we use log-linear approximations to the variables V_{t_0} and $\tilde{W}_{t_0}$ in describing the initial commitments, which are given by:

$$\hat{V}_{t_0} = \pi_{t_0},$$

$$\hat{W}_{t_0} = \hat{b}_{t_0-1} - \pi_{t_0} + w_x' x_{t_0} + w_\xi' \xi_{t_0}$$
$$= \hat{b}_{t_0-1} - \pi_{t_0} - \sigma^{-1}(\hat{Y}_{t_0} - g_{t_0})$$

Then an optimal policy from a timeless perspective is a policy from date t_0 onward that minimizes the quadratic loss function in equation (114) subject to the constraints implied by the linear structural relations in equations (101) and (111) holding in each period $t \geq t_0$, given the initial values $\hat{b}_{t_0-1}$, $\hat{\Delta}_{t_0-1}$, and subject also to the constraints that certain predetermined values for $\hat{V}_{t_0}$ and $\hat{W}$ (or alternatively, for π_{t_0} and for $\hat{Y}_{t_0}$) be achieved.[39] We note that under the assumption $\omega + \sigma^{-1} > \omega_\tau = \bar{\tau} / (1 - \bar{\tau})$, $\Gamma > 0$, which implies that $q_\pi > 0$. If:

$$s_C > \frac{\Phi \sigma^{-1}(1 + \omega_g + \omega_\tau)}{(1 - \Phi)(\omega + \sigma^{-1})\Gamma + \Phi(\omega + \sigma^{-1})(1 + \omega_g)(1 + \omega) + \Phi \sigma^{-1}(1 + \omega_g)(1 + \omega_\tau)}$$

then $q_y > 0$ and the objective function is convex. Because the expression on the right side of this inequality is necessarily less than one (given that $\Gamma > 0$), the inequality is satisfied for all values of s_G less than a positive upper bound.

7.8 THE LOG-LINEAR AGGREGATE-SUPPLY RELATION AND THE COST-PUSH DISTURBANCE TERM

The AS equation (101) can be written as:

$$\pi_t = \kappa[y_t + \psi \hat{\tau}_t + u_t] + \beta E_t \pi_{t+1} \tag{115}$$

---

39. The constraint associated with a predetermined value for Z_{t_0} can be neglected in a first-order characterization of optimal policy because the variable Z_t does not appear in the first-order approximation to the aggregate-supply relation.

where u_t is composite cost-push shock defined as $u_t \equiv c'_\xi \xi_t + \hat{Y}_t^*$. We can write equation (115) as:

$$\pi_t = \kappa[y_t + \psi(\hat{\tau}_t - \hat{\tau}_t^*)] + \beta E_t \pi_{t+1} \tag{116}$$

where we have further defined:

$$u_t = u'_\xi \xi_t \equiv \hat{Y}_t^* + c'_\xi \xi_t$$

where:

$$u_{\xi1} \equiv \frac{\Phi \omega_\tau}{q_y \Gamma} s_d^{-1} \sigma^{-1},$$

$$u_{\xi2} \equiv \frac{\Phi \sigma^{-1} s_d^{-1} \omega_\tau}{q_y \Gamma} - \frac{\sigma^{-1} s_C^{-1} \Phi (1 + \omega_g + \omega_\tau)}{q_y \Gamma}$$

$$u_{\xi3} \equiv - \Phi \sigma^{-2} \frac{(1 + \omega_\tau)(1 + \omega_g)}{q_y \Gamma(\omega + \sigma^{-1})} + \Phi \sigma^{-2} s_C^{-1} \frac{1 + \omega_g + \omega_\tau}{q_y \Gamma(\omega + \sigma^{-1})}$$

$$u_{\xi4} \equiv \omega \sigma u_{\xi3},$$

$$u_{\xi5} \equiv - \sigma u_{\xi3} + \frac{(1 - \Phi)}{q_y}$$

we finally define:

$$\hat{\tau}_t^* \equiv - \psi^{-1} u_t$$

so that we can write equation (101) as:

$$\pi_t^* = \kappa[(\hat{Y}_t - \hat{Y}_t^*) + \psi(\hat{\tau}_t - \hat{\tau}_t^*)] + \beta E_t \pi_{t+1} \tag{117}$$

which is equation (23).

7.9 THE LOG-LINEAR INTERTEMPORAL SOLVENCY CONDITION AND THE FISCAL STRESS DISTURBANCE TERM

The flow budget constraint in equation (111) can be solved forward to yield the intertemporal solvency condition:

$$\hat{b}_{t-1} - \pi_t - \sigma^{-1} y_t = - f_t + (1 - \beta) E_t \sum_{T=t}^{\infty} [b_y y_T + b_\tau(\hat{\tau}_T - \hat{\tau}_T^*)] \tag{118}$$

where f_t, the fiscal stress disturbance term, is defined as:

$$f_t \equiv \sigma^{-1}(g_t - \hat{Y}_t^*) - (1 - \beta)E_t \sum_{T=t}^{\infty} \beta^{T-t}[b_y \hat{Y}_T^* + b_\tau \hat{\tau}_T^* + b_\xi' \xi_T]$$

$$= \sigma^{-1}(g_t - \hat{Y}_t^*) - (1 - \beta)E_t \sum_{T=t}^{\infty} \beta^{T-t}[\omega_\tau^{-1} \Gamma \hat{Y}_T^* - (b_\xi' - b_\tau \psi^{-1} c_\xi') \xi_T]$$

This can be rewritten in a more compact way as:

$$f_t \equiv h_\xi' \xi_t + (1 - \beta)E_t \sum_{T=t}^{\infty} \beta^{T-t} f_\xi' \xi_T$$

where:

$$h_{\xi 1} \equiv -\frac{\Phi \omega_\tau}{q_y \Gamma} \frac{\sigma^{-2}}{s_d}$$

$$f_{\xi 1} \equiv \frac{\Phi}{q_y} \frac{\sigma^{-1}}{s_d} + \frac{1}{s_d}$$

$$h_{\xi 2} \equiv -\frac{\Phi \sigma^{-2} s_d^{-1} \omega_\tau}{\Gamma q_y} + \frac{\sigma^{-2} s_C^{-1} \Phi(1 + \omega_g + \omega_\tau)}{\Gamma q_y}$$

$$f_{\xi 2} \equiv \frac{\Phi \sigma^{-1} s_d^{-1}}{q_y} - \frac{\omega_\tau^{-1} \sigma^{-2} s_C^{-1} \Phi(1 + \omega_g + \omega_\tau)}{\omega_\tau q_y} + \frac{1}{s_d}$$

$$h_{\xi 3} \equiv \Phi \sigma^{-2} \frac{(1 + \omega_\tau)(1 + \omega_g)}{q_y \Gamma} - \Phi \sigma^{-2} s_C^{-1} \frac{1 + \omega_g + \omega_\tau}{q_y \Gamma}$$
$$+ \frac{(1 - \Phi)\omega \sigma^{-1}}{q_y} + \frac{\omega \sigma^{-1} \Phi(1 + \omega)(1 + \omega_g)}{\Gamma q_y}$$

$$f_{\xi 3} \equiv \frac{\omega_\tau^{-1} \Gamma(1 - \Phi)\sigma^{-1}}{q_y} + \frac{\omega_\tau^{-1} \sigma^{-1} \Phi(1 + \omega)(1 + \omega_g)}{q_y} - \sigma^{-1}(1 + \omega_\tau^{-1})(1 + \omega_g)$$

$$h_{\xi 4} \equiv -\frac{\sigma^{-1}(1 - \Phi)\omega}{q_y} - \frac{\sigma^{-1} \omega \Phi(1 + \omega)(1 + \omega_g)}{\Gamma q_y}$$

$$f_{\xi 4} \equiv \frac{\omega_\tau^{-1} \Gamma(1 - \Phi)\omega}{q_y} + \frac{\omega_\tau^{-1} \omega \Phi(1 + \omega)(1 + \omega_g)}{q_y} - \omega \omega_\tau^{-1}(1 + \omega_g)$$

$$h_{\xi 5} \equiv \sigma^{-1} \Phi \frac{(1 + \omega_g)(1 + \omega)}{q_y \Gamma}$$

$$f_{\xi 5} \equiv -\omega_\tau^{-1} \Phi \frac{(1 + \omega_g)(1 + \omega)}{q_y} + \omega_\tau^{-1}(1 + \omega_g)$$

7.10 DEFINITION OF THE COEFFICIENTS IN SECTIONS 3, 4, AND 5

The coefficients m_φ, n_φ, n_b, m_b, $\tilde{m}_b$, ω_φ are defined as:

$$m_\varphi \equiv -q_y^{-1} \psi^{-1}(1 - \beta)b_\tau + q_y^{-1}\left[(1 - \beta)b_y + \sigma^{-1}\right]$$

$$n_\varphi \equiv - q_y^{-1} \sigma^{-1}$$

$$n_b \equiv b_\tau (\psi^{-1} - 1)(m_\varphi + n_\varphi)$$

$$m_b \equiv - n_\varphi [(1 - \beta) b_\tau \psi^{-1} - (1 - \beta) b_y - \sigma^{-1}]$$

$$\tilde{m}_b \equiv \sigma^{-1} n_\varphi + \omega_\varphi - (1 - \beta)[b_\tau \psi^{-1} - b_y] n_\varphi + (1 - \beta) \psi^{-1} \kappa^{-1} b_\tau \omega_\varphi$$

$$\omega_\varphi \equiv - q_\pi^{-1} (\kappa^{-1}(1 - \beta) b_\tau \psi^{-1} + 1)$$

$$\phi \equiv \kappa^{-1} q_\pi^{-1} q_y$$

$$\gamma_1 \equiv \kappa^{-1} q_\pi^{-1} [(1 - \beta) b_y + \sigma^{-1}]$$

$$\gamma_2 \equiv \kappa^{-1} q_\pi^{-1} \sigma^{-1}$$

The coefficients μ_1 and μ_2 of Section 5 are defined as:

$$\mu_1 \equiv \frac{\kappa \psi}{(1 - \beta) b_\tau + \kappa \psi}$$

$$\mu_2 \equiv \frac{\kappa (1 - \beta)(b_\tau - \psi b_y)}{(1 - \beta) b_\tau + \kappa \psi}$$

7.11 PROOF OF DETERMINACY OF EQUILIBRIUM UNDER THE OPTIMAL TARGETING RULES

We now show that there is a determinate equilibrium if policy is conducted to ensure that the two target criteria:

$$E_t \pi_{t+1} = 0 \tag{119}$$

and:

$$\Delta y_t + \omega_\varphi^{-1}(m_\varphi + n_\varphi) \pi_t - \omega_\varphi^{-1} n_\varphi \Delta \pi_t = 0 \tag{120}$$

are satisfied in each period $t \geq t_0$. Note that equation (120) can be written as:

$$\Delta y_t = \gamma_3 \pi_t + \gamma_4 \pi_{t-1} \tag{121}$$

where:

$$\gamma_3 \equiv - \omega_\varphi^{-1} m_\varphi$$

$$\gamma_4 \equiv - \omega_\varphi^{-1} n_\varphi$$

Use equation (119), combined with:

$$\tau_t - \hat{\tau}_t^* = \kappa^{-1} \pi_t - \psi^{-1} y_t - \kappa^{-1} \beta E_t \pi_{t+1} \tag{122}$$

and:

$$E_t \Delta y_{t+1} = - \omega_\varphi^{-1} n_\varphi \pi_t$$

to eliminate $E_t \pi_{t+1}$, $E_t y_{t+1}$ and $\tau_t - \hat{\tau}_t^*$ from:

$$\hat{b}_{t-1} - \pi_t - \sigma^{-1} y_t + f_t = (1 - \beta)[b_y y_t + b_\tau (\hat{\tau}_t - \hat{\tau}_t^*)]$$
$$+ \beta E_t [\hat{b}_t - \pi_{t+1} - \sigma^{-1} \hat{y}_{t+1} + f_{t+1}]$$

Then equation (120) can be used to eliminate y_t from the resulting expression to obtain an equation of the form:

$$\hat{b}_t = \beta^{-1} \hat{b}_{t-1} + m_{41} \pi_t + m_{42} \pi_{t-1} + m_{43} y_{t-1} + \varepsilon_t$$

where ε_t is an exogenous disturbance. The system consisting of this equation plus equations (120) and (119) can then be written as:

$$E_t z_{t+1} = M z_t + N \varepsilon_t \tag{123}$$

where:

$$z_t \equiv \begin{bmatrix} \pi_t \\ \pi_{t-1} \\ y_{t-1} \\ \hat{b}_{t-1} \end{bmatrix} \quad M \equiv \begin{bmatrix} 0 & 0 & 0 & 0 \\ 1 & 0 & 0 & 0 \\ m_{31} & m_{32} & 1 & 0 \\ m_{41} & m_{42} & m_{43} & \beta^{-1} \end{bmatrix} \quad N \equiv \begin{bmatrix} 0 \\ 0 \\ 0 \\ n_{41} \end{bmatrix}$$

Because M is lower triangular, its eigenvalues are the four diagonal elements: 0, 0, 1, and β^{-1}. Hence, there is exactly one eigenvalue outside the unit circle, and equilibrium is determinate (but possesses a unit root). Because of the triangular form of the matrix, one can also easily solve explicitly for the elements of the left eigenvector:

$$v' = [v_1 \quad v_2 \quad v_3 \quad 1]$$

associated with the eigenvalue β^{-1}, where:

$$v_1 = (1 + \omega_g)[\psi^{-1} - 1] \beta \gamma_4 - (1 - \beta \sigma^{-1} \gamma_4) - (1 - \beta)(1 - \omega_g)(\kappa \psi)^{-1}$$
$$+ (1 + \omega_g)[\psi^{-1} - 1] \gamma_3,$$
$$v_2 = (1 + \omega_g)[\psi^{-1} - 1] \gamma_4$$
$$v_3 = (1 + \omega_g)[\psi^{-1} - 1]$$

By pre-multiplying the vector equation (123) by v', one obtains a scalar equation with a unique nonexplosive solution of the form:

$$v'z_t = -\sum_{j=0}^{\infty} \beta^{j+1} E_t \varepsilon_{t+j}$$

If $v_1 \neq 0$, this can be solved for π_t as a linear function of $\pi_{t-1}, y_{t-1}, \hat{b}_{t-1}$ and the exogenous state vector:

$$\pi_t = -\frac{1}{v_1} \hat{b}_{t-1} - \frac{v_2}{v_1} \pi_{t-1} - \frac{v_3}{v_1} y_{t-1} + \frac{1}{v_1} f_t \tag{124}$$

The solution for π_t can then be substituted into the above equations to obtain the equilibrium dynamics of y_t and $\hat{b}_t$, and hence of τ_t.

REFERENCES

Aiyagari, S. Rao, Albert Marcet, Thomas Sargent, and Juha Seppala. (2002). Optimal taxation without state-contingent debt. *Journal of Political Economy* 110(6):1220–1254.

Barro, Robert J. (1979). On the determination of public debt. *Journal of Political Economy* 87:940–971.

Benigno, Pierpaolo, and Michael Woodford. (2003). Inflation stabilization and welfare: The Case of a Distorted Steady State." New York, NY: New York University, Unpublished.

Bohn, Henning. (1990). Tax smoothing with financial instruments. *American Economic Review* 80:1217–1230.

Calvo, Guillermo. (1983). Staggered Prices in a Utility-Maximizing Framework. *Journal of Monetary Economics* 12:383–398.

Chari, V. V., Lawrence Christiano, and Patrick Kehoe. (1991). Optimal fiscal and monetary policy: Some recent results. *Journal of Money, Credit, and Banking* 23:519–539.

Chari, V. V., Lawrence Christiano, and Patrick Kehoe. (1994). Optimal fiscal policy in a business cycle model. *Journal of Political Economy* 102:617–652.

Chari, V. V., and Patrick J. Kehoe. (1999). Optimal fiscal and monetary policy. In *Handbook of Macroeconomics*, Vol. 1C, J. B. Taylor and M. Woodford (eds.). Amsterdam: North-Holland, pp. 1671–1745.

Clarida, Richard, Jordi Gali, and Mark Gertler. (1999). The science of monetary policy: A new Keynesian perspective. *Journal of Economic Literature* 37(4):1661–1707.

Correia, Isabel, Juan Pablo Nicolini, and Pedro Teles. (2001). Optimal fiscal and monetary policy: Equivalence results. Bank of Portugal. Unpublished Manuscript.

Friedman, Milton. (1969). The optimum quantity of money. In *The Optimum Quantity of Money and Other Essays*. Chicago: Aldine.

Gali, Jordi, and Mark Gertler. (1999). Inflation Dynamics: A Structural Econometric Analysis. *Journal of Monetary Economics* 44:195–222.

Giannoni, Marc, and Michael Woodford. (2002). Optimal interest-rate rules: I. General theory. Cambridge, MA: National Bureau of Economic Research. NBER Working Paper No. 9419.

Giannoni, Marc, and Michael Woodford. (2003). Optimal inflation targeting rules. In *The Inflation Targeting Debate*, B. S. Bernanke and M. Woodford (eds.). Chicago: University of Chicago Press.

Goodfriend, Marvin, and Robert G. King. (1997). The New Neoclassical Synthesis and the Role of Monetary Policy. In *NBER Macroeconomics Annual*, B. S. Bernanke and J. J. Rotemberg (eds.). Cambridge, MA: MIT Press, 231–283.

Hall, George, and Stefan Krieger. (2000). The tax smoothing implications of the federal debt paydown. *Brookings Papers on Economic Activity* 2:253–301.

Khan, Aubhik, Robert G. King, and Alexander L. Wolman. (2002). Optimal monetary policy. Cambridge, MA: National Bureau of Economic Research. NBER Working Paper No. 9402.

Lucas, Robert E., Jr., and Nancy L. Stokey. (1983). Optimal fiscal and monetary policy in an economy without capital. *Journal of Monetary Economics* 12:55–93.

Rotemberg, Julio J., and Michael Woodford. (1997). An optimization-based econometric framework for the evaluation of monetary policy. In *NBER Macroeconomic Annual 1997*, B. S. Bernanke and J. J., Rotemberg (eds.). Cambridge, MA: MIT Press, 297–346.

Sbordone, Argia M. (2002). Prices and unit labor costs: A new test of price stickiness. *Journal of Monetary Economics* 49:265–292.

Schmitt-Grohé, Stephanie, and Martin Uribe. (2001). Optimal fiscal and monetary policy under sticky prices. Rutgers University. Working Paper No. 2001–06.

Siu, Henry E. (2001). Optimal fiscal and monetary policy with sticky prices. Northwestern University. Unpublished Manuscript.

Svensson, Lars E. O. (1999). Inflation targeting as a monetary policy rule. *Journal of Monetary Economics* 43:607–654.

Svensson, Lars E. O. (2003). What is wrong with Taylor rules? Using judgment in monetary policy through targeting rules. *Journal of Economic Literature* 41(2):426–477.

Svensson, Lars E. O., and Michael Woodford. (2003). Implementing optimal policy through inflation-forecast targeting. In *The Inflation Targeting Debate*, B. S. Bernanke and M. Woodford (eds.). Chicago: Univ. of Chicago Press.

Woodford, Michael. (1999). Commentary: How should monetary policy be conducted in an era of price stability? Federal Reserve Bank of Kansas City, *New Challenges for Monetary Policy*, pp. 277–316.

Woodford, Michael. (2001). Fiscal requirements for price stability. *Journal of Money, Credit and Banking* 33:669–728.

Woodford, Michael. (2003). *Interest and Prices: Foundations of a Theory of Monetary Policy*. Princeton, NJ: Princeton University Press.

Comment

STEFANIA ALBANESI
Duke University

1. Introduction

Benigno and Woodford seek to offer an integrated analysis of optimal fiscal and monetary policy building on two branches of the literature. The

Prepared for the 2003 NBER Macroeconomics Annual Conference, April 4–5, 2003. I wish to thank Larry Christiano and Henry Siu for stimulating discussions.

first is the one on dynamic optimal taxation, stemming from the seminal contribution of Lucas and Stokey (1983).[1] The second part of the literature is on optimal monetary stabilization policy, for example, in Goodfriend and King (1997). Rotemberg and Woodford (1997) and Woodford (2000).[2] Both areas in the literature consider the problem of a benevolent government seeking to stabilize the response of economic outcomes to exogenous shocks with a combination of fiscal and monetary policies chosen once and for all at some previous date. The optimal taxation literature considers *fiscal* shocks, such as fluctuations in government expenditures, and rules out lump-sum taxes in the tradition of Ramsey (1927). Distortionary taxes generate wedges between marginal rates of transformation and marginal rates of substitution, and government policy becomes a source of frictions. The monetary stabilization literature, instead, considers environments where frictions are present even without government policy. These frictions are due to nominal rigidities and imperfect competition in product or labor markets. The corresponding wedges reduce the level of economic activity and may be subject to stochastic fluctuations, known as cost-push shocks. The government's only fiscal policy instrument is a lump-sum tax.

Both parts of the literature are characterized by an underlying tension. The fiscal shocks considered by the optimal taxation literature do not affect any wedges and should ideally be offset through lump-sum taxes. Yet the government has access only to distortionary fiscal instruments. The optimal stabilization literature considers fluctuations in wedges that could be offset with appropriate fiscal instruments acting on the same margins, but the government has access only to lump-sum taxes. Given this tension, monetary policy acquires an auxiliary role in responding to shocks. Lucas and Stokey show that it is optimal to respond to fiscal shocks by appropriately setting the state contingent returns on government debt. Taxes and real returns on government debt inherit the serial correlation structure of underlying shocks, and taxes are smooth, in the sense of having a small variance relative to fiscal shocks. Chari, Christiano, and Kehoe (1991, 1995) extend the analysis to monetary economies with risk-free debt and show that it is optimal to use state-contingent inflation as a fiscal shock absorber. They find that the standard deviation of optimal taxes is close to zero, while real returns on government debt are highly volatile for calibrated examples. In the monetary stabilization literature, rigidities in nominal prices and wages imply that

1. An excellent survey of this literature can be found in Chari and Kehoe (1999).
2. Additional important contributions in this literature are King and Wolman (1999); Kahn, King, and Wolman (2000); and Giannoni and Woodford (2002).

innovations in inflation reduce the average markups and increase equilibrium output. At the same time, nominal rigidities imply that inflation generates relative price distortions. The resulting trade-off between inflation and output stabilization implies that the volatility and persistence of optimal inflation will depend on the stochastic properties of the cost-push disturbances and on the degree of nominal rigidity. Hence, the interdependence between fiscal and monetary policy is generated in both branches of the literature by a lack of appropriate fiscal instruments. Given appropriate instruments, the government would be indifferent to the stochastic path of inflation.

Recent contributions to the optimal taxation literature, such as Correia, Nicolini, and Teles (2001); Schmitt-Grohé and Uribe (2001); and Siu (2001), have incorporated monopolistic competition and nominal price rigidity. Correia, Nicolini, and Teles (2001) assume that state-contingent bonds are available. Their theoretical analysis allows for fiscal shocks as well as cost-push shocks, and shows that the same equilibrium outcomes as those in a flexible price economy can be achieved. In addition, they describe the assumptions about fiscal instruments required for the path of inflation to be neutral to equilibrium outcomes, thus remarking the auxiliary role of inflation in this class of policy problems. Schmitt-Grohé and Uribe (2001) and Siu (2001) focus on government consumption shocks and do not allow for state-contingent debt, thus reinstating the role of inflation as a fiscal shock-absorber. With sticky prices, however, the benefits of volatile inflation must be balanced against the resource misallocation resulting from the associated relative price distortions. They find that, for government consumption processes with similar volatility to the postwar United States, the departures from optimal policy with flexible prices are striking. Optimal inflation volatility is close to zero, even for very small degrees of price rigidity. Tax rates and the real value of government debt exhibit random walk behavior, as in Barro (1979), regardless of the degree of auto-correlation of the underlying shocks. Siu (2001) also considers large fiscal shocks, such as fluctuations in government expenditure that would arise in an economy alternating between war and peace. He finds that optimal inflation volatility is high regardless of the degree of price stickiness for large fiscal shocks. The intuition for this is that the benefits of using inflation as a shock-absorber outweigh the costs of the resulting misallocation in this case. Hence, the stochastic properties of taxes and inflation in a Ramsey equilibrium with monopolistic competition and nominal rigidities can be understood as the outcome of a struggle between the costs of volatile inflation and the benefits of smoothing government outlays in the face of fiscal shocks.

Benigno and Woodford's main contribution is to allow for both fiscal and cost-push shocks. Their analytical results demonstrate that the different time-series behavior of optimal policies in flexible and sticky-price environments do not depend on the nature of the underlying shocks. With flexible prices, state-contingent inflation is used to offset fiscal shocks, implying volatile real debt returns. Because taxes are set to offset cost-push shocks and stabilize output, however, their variance is not necessarily small. With sticky prices, volatile inflation is costly and taxes are used to respond to both fiscal and cost-push shocks. Taxes and real debt returns have a unit root behavior, regardless of the stochastic properties of underlying shocks, and output cannot be stabilized. Benigno and Woodford's quantitative exercise is limited, however, to fiscal shocks. They find that the optimal response of inflation to a one-time increase in government expenditure is inversely related to the degree of price rigidity. This is not surprising, given the findings in the previous studies.

The rest of this comment expands on the previous discussion. In Section 2, I relate the analytical results in Benigno and Woodford to those in the literature on optimal taxation. The section discusses the benefits and costs of state-contingent inflation as a function of the volatility of exogenous shocks and raises several concerns about the solution method. Section 3 illustrates the notion of optimal policy from a timeless perspective with a simple example and relates it to limited commitment. I conclude with some questions for further research.

2. Optimal Policy with Nominal Rigidities

Benigno and Woodford (BW) adopt a standard new Keynesian framework with monopolistic competition in product markets and Calvo pricing. They allow for labor market frictions by assuming that a wage markup as well as a price markup are present, and they abstract from monetary frictions. There are four types of shocks: government consumption shocks, government transfer shocks, preference shocks, and wage markup shocks. The first three are common to the optimal taxation literature, while wage markup shocks are typically considered by the optimal monetary stabilization literature. The government's objective is to maximize the representative agent's lifetime utility. In the linear-quadratic problem, the government has two policy instruments; the tax rate on sales, $\hat{\tau}_t$, and the inflation rate, π_t.[3] These instruments are set to respond to a cost-push shock, u_t, and a fiscal shock, f_t. The variables u_t and f_t are not primitive shocks but a complex convolution of those primitive distur-

3. All variables denote percentage deviations from steady-state values.

bances. In particular, the primitive shocks contributing to the cost-push or fiscal shock depend on the available policy instruments and on the degree of price stickiness. However, the shock u_t can arise only if wage markup shocks are present.

The evolution of equilibrium outcomes in response to the shocks and government policy is summarized by the expectational Phillips curve:

$$\pi_t = \kappa\left[y_t + \psi\hat{\tau}_t + u_t\right]\beta E_t\pi_{t+1} \tag{1}$$

The expression in equation (1) makes clear that by setting the tax rate according to $\hat{\tau}_t^* = -u_t/\psi$, the government can completely stabilize output in the face of cost-push shocks because cost-push shocks and the tax rate on sales act on the same margin. Hence, fluctuations in equilibrium output away from the steady state behave according to:

$$y_t \sim (\hat{\tau}_t - \hat{\tau}_t^*)$$

The evolution of equilibrium outcomes and policy must also satisfy the government's intertemporal budget constraint:

$$\hat{b}_{t-1} + f_t - \pi_t - \sigma^{-1}y_t - (1-\beta)E_t\sum_{T=t}^{\infty}\beta^{T-t}(b_y y_t + b_\tau(\hat{\tau}_t - \hat{\tau}_t^*)) = 0$$

This equation clarifies that setting taxes equal to $\hat{\tau}_t^*$ requires inflation to respond fully to the fiscal stress shock.

The government strives to achieve three goals (see equation [20] in BW). The first two, output and inflation stabilization, appear directly in the objective function. The third goal is to minimize the intertemporal cost of raising government revenues measured by $\phi_{2,t}$, the multiplier on the government's intertemporal budget constraint. These goals are traded off based on the available policy instruments. In the monetary stabilization literature, taxes are lump-sum and $\phi_{2,t} = 0$. Hence, f_t does not influence y_t or π_t. However, u_t cannot be offset and $y_t \neq 0$.

In the optimal taxation literature, the stochastic properties of optimal policy depend on whether the returns on government debt are state contingent. In a monetary economy with nominal risk-free debt, bond returns can be made state contingent by setting the process for inflation appropriately. If no distortions are associated with inflation, as in the case with fully flexible prices, it is optimal to use inflation as a fiscal shock absorber:

$$\pi_t - E_{t-1}\pi_t = f_t - E_{t-1}f_t$$

$$\hat{b}_t = -E_t f_{t+1}$$

as in Chari, Christiano, and Kehoe (1991, 1995). Taxes can then be set to meet the output stabilization objective so that $\hat{\tau}_t = \hat{\tau}_t^*$ and $y_t = 0$. This implies that the cost of raising government revenues is equalized across states in each period:

$$\phi_{2,t} = \phi_{2,t-1}$$

Consequently, $\hat{\tau}_t$, π_t, and $\hat{b}_t$ inherit the stochastic properties of the underlying shocks. If the primitive shocks are stationary, tax rates, inflation, and the real value of government debt will also be stationary. The difference with a Ramsey model with only shocks to government spending is that smoothing the cost of raising fiscal revenues across states does not correspond to a smooth path of taxes. The volatility of the optimal taxes will depend on the volatility of the cost-push shocks.

With nominal risk-free debt and some degree of price rigidity, the properties of optimal fiscal and monetary policy resemble those in a real economy and risk-free debt, as in Barro (1979) and Aiyagari, Marcet, Sargent, and Seppala (2002). The optimal policy will smooth the cost of raising taxes over time, given the costs of fully smoothing it across states. This imparts a martingale behavior to the shadow cost of raising government revenues:

$$\phi_{2,t} = E_t \phi_{2,t+1} \tag{2}$$

Inflation does not fully respond to fiscal stress:

$$\pi_t = - \omega\phi(\phi_{2,t} - \phi_{2,t-1})$$
$$\hat{b}_t = - E_t f_{t+1} - \eta_b \phi_{2,t}$$

and taxes cannot be set to stabilize output fully:

$$y_t = m_\phi \phi_{2,t} + \eta_\phi \phi_{2,t-1} \neq 0$$

The unit-root behavior of the shadow cost of raising government revenues makes the equilibrium response of taxes, output, prices, and the real value of government debt to cost-push and fiscal shocks nonstationary, regardless of the autocorrelation properties of the primitive shocks.

2.1 DISCUSSION

While in a real economy with risk-free debt, the government has no alternative but to smooth the cost of raising distortionary revenues according to equation (2), in a monetary economy with nominal bonds, it is possible to make bond returns state-contingent in real terms by setting ex post inflation. If nominal rigidities are present, however, the government faces a trade-off between the costs of market incompleteness and the costs of volatile inflation. The properties of optimal policy will depend on the relative size of these costs. BW and previous studies focus on models in which the resource misallocation associated with volatile inflation increases with the degree of price stickiness. The costs of market incompleteness, on the other hand, should depend on the size and persistence of the primitive shocks. To understand this issue, it is useful to review the findings in Siu (2001) for a similar environment because BW's linear quadratic approach cannot be used to explore this aspect.[4]

Siu studies Ramsey policy in a cash-credit good economy with monopolistic competition in which a fraction of firms in each period sets their prices before current exogenous shocks are realized. The remaining firms set prices after the realization of the current exogenous shocks.[5] Government purchases, g, follow a two-state first-order Markov process with support: $[\underline{g}, \bar{g}]$ and $\underline{g} < \bar{g}$. Siu characterizes optimal policies as a function of the unconditional standard deviation of government purchases with a nonlinear numerical procedure. He finds that the optimal inflation volatility decreases with the degree of price stickiness for business-cycle fluctuations in g, while for g-processes designed to model an economy fluctuating between war and peace—large fiscal shocks—optimal inflation volatility is high regardless of the degree of price stickiness, as illustrated in Figures 1 and 2, reproduced from Siu.[6]

The percentage loss in output that occurs in the economy with sticky prices under the Ramsey policy corresponding to the flexible-price economy is a measure of the misallocation caused by volatile inflation. Figure 3 illustrates the behavior of this measure.[7] The horizontal axis measures L_s/L_f, the labor demand from sticky-price firms relative to flexible-price firms, and the vertical axis measures the corresponding misallocation. In each graph, the star on the left corresponds to a sequence $[g, \underline{g}]$; the one on the right corresponds to a sequence $[\bar{g}, \bar{g}]$.[8] When the current value of g is low, sticky-price firms have higher prices than flexible-price firms and $L_s/L_f < 1$. Concavity in production implies that the cost in terms of foregone output is very large for a large misallocation and decreases at a decreasing rate. The graphs suggest that the misallocation cost is large

4. The approximation is valid only for stochastic processes with an absorbing state and a small range. See Section 2.2 for further discussion.
5. The impact effect of a shock on the nominal price index in Siu's model is the same as the one in a model with Calvo pricing if the fraction of prices that remains unchanged in any period is set equal across the two models. In Siu's model, all remaining price adjustment takes place in the subsequent period, while the adjustment is smoothed across several periods with Calvo pricing.
6. The calibration is based on U.S. data for the twentieth century. The small-shock case matches fluctuations in government purchases that occur in the postwar United States. The transition probability between the $\bar{g}$ and $\underline{g}$ states is $\rho = 0.95$, and the standard deviation of g is 6.7%. For the large-shock case, the standard deviation is 21% and all other parameters are kept constant.
7. I thank Henry Siu for providing Figure 3 and Figure 4.
8. Given the assumed persistence of the government consumption process, these are the most likely sequences.

and increasing in the size of government spending shocks when the fluctuations in the spending shock are small, but it is small for large fiscal shocks. This pattern stems from the incentive for firms setting prices to frontload and set high prices to insure against the possibility of having negative profits. Because government consumption shocks are persistent, if the shock was high in the previous period, sticky-price firms will set high prices. If the shock in this period is high, inflation will be high under the Ramsey policy for the flexible-price economy, and the misallocation will be small. If the shock was low in the previous period, firms setting prices will still set them high. If the realized value of g is low, inflation will be low, which will give rise to a large misallocation. The tendency to frontload is a general feature of sticky-price models and is exacerbated when firms fix prices for longer periods of time.

Figure 4 plots the misallocation cost in consumption equivalents against the volatility of government consumption when 10% of firms have sticky prices. It raises steeply initially but then flattens out. The cost in terms of foregone consumption of not being able to smooth government

Figure 1 OPTIMAL INFLATION VOLATILITY FOR *SMALL* SHOCKS

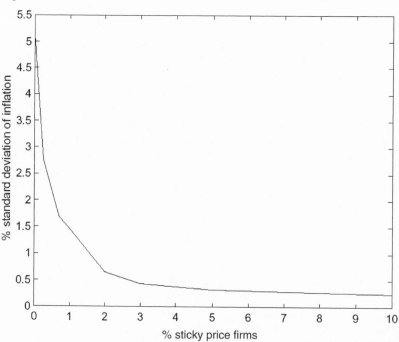

Reproduced from Siu (2001)

Figure 2 OPTIMAL INFLATION VOLATILITY FOR *LARGE* SHOCKS

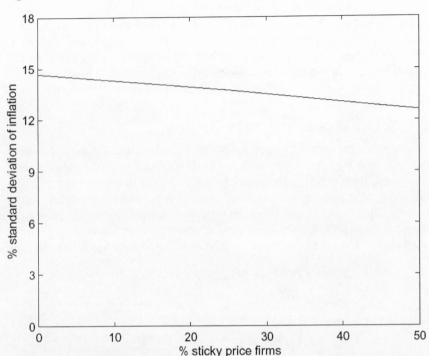

Reproduced from Siu (2001)

revenues across states as a function of the variability of government consumption shocks is also shown.[9] Not surprisingly it is increasing in the
variance of the shocks. This explains the finding that, for large government expenditure shocks, optimal inflation volatility is high even when a
large fraction of prices are fixed, while for business-cycle type fluctuations
in government consumption, optimal inflation volatility is close to 0. For
very small expenditure shocks, the costs of not using inflation to make
real bond returns respond to government consumption is low, as is inflation volatility in the Ramsey equilibrium for the flexible-price economy.
Because the distortion caused by taxation is first order, it will be optimal
to have a smooth path of taxes and volatile inflation.[10]

The role of the size of fiscal shocks for the stochastic behavior of taxes
and policy with nominal price rigidities raises several questions for future

9. This is the welfare loss in average consumption equivalents of using the Ramsey policy
   for the sticky-price economy in the flexible-price economy.
10. This is true in BW's model. Recall that the steady-state wedge between the marginal rate
    of substitution between consumption and leisure and the marginal product of labor, Φ,
    is positive if the initial level of public debt is positive.

research. Do these results depend on the nature of the shock? Would they differ if government transfers rather than government purchases were considered? Would the findings change for wage markup shocks? This issue is of interest because the consideration of wedge-type shocks is the novelty in BW's analysis. And last, what is the welfare cost of the lack of state-contingency relative to nonfiscal shocks? These questions cannot be addressed within BW's linear-quadratic approach, as I explain below.

2.2 THE LINEAR-QUADRATIC APPROACH

BW solve the optimal policy problem by analyzing the exact solution to a linear-quadratic problem, which should coincide with the solution to a linear approximation of the policy problem for the original economy. This amounts to a local approximation around a nonstochastic steady state. Chari, Christiano, and Kehoe (1995) provide several examples of inaccurate linear approximations in a similar context. They show that the inaccuracy is particularly severe for the computation of policies. In one

Figure 3 THE OUTPUT COST OF RELATIVE PRICE DISTORTIONS

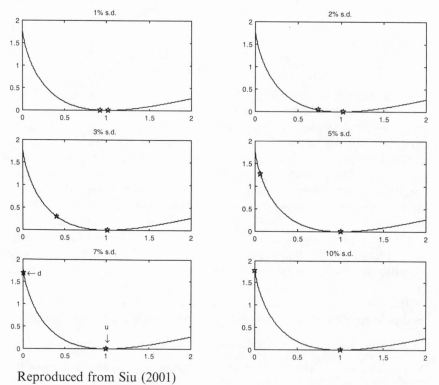

Reproduced from Siu (2001)

example, for which the analytical solution is available, they show that the linear approximation misses on basic statistics such as the mean and the standard deviation of tax rates. The degree of inaccuracy appears to increase with the curvature of preference and technology parameters and with the volatility of driving processes.

An additional and more severe concern arises in the model with sticky prices. Because equilibrium responses are nonstationary and the economy drifts away from the initial steady state permanently in response to shocks, the analysis must be limited to stochastic processes with a small range and with an absorbing state. This is a restrictive assumption for the purpose of studying stabilization policy from a quantitative standpoint. It rules out, for example, analyzing responses to business-cycle type fluctuations, which are naturally of interest in macroeconomics. More important, it raises the question of which steady state should be considered as a benchmark for the approximation. Aiyagari, Marcet, Sargent, and Seppala (2002) numerically characterize the Ramsey equilibrium for a real economy with risk-free debt, where the lack of state contingency of government

Figure 4 THE TRADE-OFF BETWEEN INFLATION AND TAX VOLATILITY

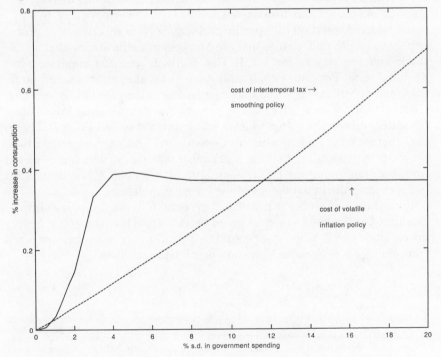

Reproduced from Siu (2001)

debt returns also imparts a unit root behavior to taxes and real variables.[11] They show that if the exogenous shock has an absorbing state, the analogue of $\phi_{2,t}$ converges to a value that depends on the realization of the path for the exogenous shocks when the economy enters the absorbing state. The incomplete markets allocation coincides with the complete markets allocation that would have occurred under the same shocks but for a different initial debt. They also consider the case in which the government expenditure process does not have an absorbing state. In this case, the analogue of $\phi_{2,t}$ converges to 0. Hence, the incomplete markets allocation converges to the first best allocation, and no distortionary taxes need to be raised without upper bounds on government asset accumulation.

3. Timeless Perspective and Limited Commitment

BW characterize the solution to the policy problem from a timeless perspective. This approach amounts to a particular recursive formulation of the optimal policy problem under commitment. As is well known, the Ramsey problem is not recursive in the natural state variables, which complicates the analysis substantially in the presence of stochastic shocks. It is possible, however, to formulate the Ramsey problem recursively by augmenting the set of natural state variables with a vector of costate variables, which depend on the specific problem. Solving this recursive problem gives rise to policy rules that are Markovian in the augmented set of states and the shocks for $t \geq 1$. This method was first suggested by Kydland and Prescott (1980) and was generalized by Marcet and Marimon (1999). Aiyagari, Marcet, Sargent, and Seppala (2002) and Siu (2001) also adopt a variant of this approach. The Ramsey equilibrium outcome depends on the values of exogenous state variables at time 0. There are different ways to deal with this dependence. The timeless perspective proceeds by suggesting that the Markovian policy rule, which is optimal from the standpoint of $t \geq 1$, is also optimal at time 0. This amounts to endogenizing the initial values of the exogenous states.

To see how this works in practice, it is useful to work through a simple example. Government policy is given by $\Pi_t = \{\tau_t, R_t\}$, where τ_t is a linear tax on labor and R_t is the state contingent bond return. Government consumption, g_t, is exogenous. Consumers solve the problem:

$$\max_{\{c_t, n_t, b_{t+1}\}_{t=0}^{\infty}} \sum_{t=0}^{\infty} \beta^t u(c_t, n_t) \text{ s.t.}$$
$$b_{t+1} \leq b_t R_t + (1 - \tau_t) n_t - c_t$$

11. Siu (2001) derives the constraint imposed on the set of attainable equilibria with sticky prices and shows that it is of the same nature as the one arising in the real economy with risk-free debt analyzed by Aiyagari, Marcet, Sargent, and Seppala (2002).

where b_t denotes holdings of government-issued bonds at time t. Their first-order conditions are:

$$u_{c,t} = \lambda_t$$
$$-u_{n,t} = \lambda_t(1 - \lambda\tau_t)$$
$$\lambda_t = \beta\lambda_{t+1}R_{t+1}$$

where λ_t is the multiplier on their budget constraint. A competitive equilibrium is a policy $\{\tau_t, R_t, g_t\}$ and an allocation $\{c_t, n_t, b_{t+1}\}_{t\geq0}$ in which allocation solves the consumer's problem given the policy, and the government budget constraint:

$$b_{t+1} + \tau_t n_t = b_t R_t + g_t$$

is satisfied. A Ramsey equilibrium is a competitive equilibrium that maximizes the representative consumer's lifetime utility.

The solution to the household problem clearly displays the potential for time inconsistency in the Ramsey problem: the fact that households have to choose b_{t+1} based on expectations of R_{t+1}; hence, the government might have an incentive to change R_{t+1} at $t + 1$. This time inconsistency makes the Ramsey problem nonrecursive in b_t. Despite this, it is possible to formulate the Ramsey problem recursively. For $t > 0$, the consumer's first-order conditions can be used to define a mapping from policy at time t to the competitive equilibrium allocation at time t and the shadow value of outstanding wealth, λ_t:

$$x_t \equiv (c_t, n_t, b_{t+1}) = d(b_t, \Pi_t, \lambda_t)$$
$$\lambda_t = h(\Pi_t, b_t, \lambda_{t-1})$$

The policy problem can then be rewritten as follows:

$$v(b, \lambda_{-1}) = \max_{\phi, x, \lambda}\{u(c, n) + \beta v(b', \lambda)\}$$
s.t. $\quad x = d(b, \Pi, \lambda)$
$$\lambda = h(\Pi, b, \lambda_{-1})$$
$$g \leq \tau n + b' - Rb$$

The solution to this problem is the function, $\hat{\Pi}$; (b, λ_{-1}), which represents a Markovian policy rule, in the state (b, λ_{-1}). The constraint $\lambda = h(\phi, b, \lambda_{-1})$ embeds the assumption of commitment because it ties today's choices to decisions made in the past by linking them through the costate variable λ. It is unusual because it goes back in time. The government solution to this problem selects the value of λ that the government wants to commit to because it induces future governments to choose the policy that is optimal from the standpoint of the current period.

Clearly, this procedure does not pin down the value of λ_0. This implies that the policy problem at time 0 is different from other periods. The policy problem at time 0 is:

$$\Pi_0(b_0) = \arg\max_{\phi_0, x_0, \lambda_0} u(c_0, n_0) + \beta v(b_1, \lambda_0)$$

s.t. $x_0 = d(b_0, \Pi_0, \lambda_0)$

$\quad\quad g \le \tau_0 n_0 + b_1 - R_0 b_0$

The policies chosen at at time 0 depend on initial conditions and influence the solution for all future periods. Adopting a timeless perspective involves removing this dependence on initial conditions by leave as is that the choice of λ_0 and of policy at time 0 is governed by the same Markovian rule that is optimal from time 1 onward. The system:

$$\Pi_0(b_0) = \hat\Pi(b_0, \lambda_{(-1)})$$

$$\lambda_0 = h(\Pi_0, b_0, \lambda_{(-1)})$$

defines an implicit equation for $\lambda_{(-1)}$ and λ_0. The second constraint pins down $\lambda_{(-1)}$ as a function of b_0 and λ_0, and the first constraint, which imposes consistency between the solution to the time 0 problem and the Markovian decision rule, pins down b_0. This procedure affects only the average level of taxes and does not alter the stochastic properties of the optimal policy. It is important to note that the recursive formulation of Ramsey problems discussed here does not imply that the resulting optimal choices are time consistent, even if it gives rise to Markovian policy rules. A government choosing policies sequentially under discretion would not make these choices. The discretionary solution would generate Markovian policy rules in the natural state, in this case, b_t.

This approach is appealing not only because it provides a tractable algorithm for solving Ramsey equilibria but also because it is related to a notion of limited commitment. Time inconsistency may arise in Ramsey models because private agents take certain actions before the government chooses policy and therefore must base their decisions on expectations of government policy. To ensure that the Ramsey equilibrium is implemented, it is not required that the government commits at time 0 to the entire path of future policy. A limited one-period-ahead commitment to those policies that influence expectations is, in general, enough. A recursive formulation of the Ramsey problem naturally identifies the minimum set of variables that the government must commit to. A drawback is that these variables are not primitive. They are rather complex functions related to the shadow value of government surpluses at the start of the following period. Hence, implementation of this solution with a simple strategy is incredibly valuable.

BW suggest that the optimal policy can be implemented with the flexible inflation target:

$$\pi_t + a\pi_{t-1} + b(y_t - y_{t-1}) = 0 \tag{3}$$

$$E_t \pi_{t+1} = 0 \tag{4}$$

They also propose a particular institutional arrangement associated with this rule. The monetary authority should have a mandate over both inflation and output stabilization. It should set interest rates so that equation (3) is met. The fiscal authority should have a mandate defined over inflation stabilization only and should set the path of debt so that equation (4) is met.

This institutional setup does relate to those proposed and implemented to tackle the potential time inconsistency problem in monetary policy.[12] It embeds a notion of independence because the monetary authority takes the path of government debt as given, and the fiscal authority takes the path of output as given. However, endowing the fiscal authority with a mandate over inflation stabilization seems rather unusual. One also wonders whether it would be viable because of the strong prevalence of political considerations in the dabate over fiscal policy.

4. Conclusion

The Ramsey literature and the optimal monetary stabilization literature have two important elements in common: the assumption of commitment and the auxiliary role of monetary policy. Woodford (2000) and Clarida, Gali, and Gertler (1999) have underlined how the optimal monetary stabilization policy under commitment differs in terms of stochastic responses from the policy under discretion. Woodford shows that inflation tends to overreact to cost-push shocks under discretion relative to commitment. This stabilization bias can arise even when no inflation bias is present. (By inflation bias, I mean a tendency for average inflation to be higher when the government cannot commit.) The stabilization bias arises due to the lack of alternative policy instruments (because lump-sum taxes cannot remove the distortions generated by cost-push shocks). Albanesi,

---

12. The central bank of New Zealand and most recently the central bank of Brazil follow a flexible inflation targeting scheme.

Chari, and Christiano (2002) show in a general equilibrium model with monetary frictions that the resource misallocation due to price dispersion may be large enough, with plausible parameters, to eliminate the inflation bias under discretion. They also show that multiple Markov equilibria are possible, giving rise to a potential for alternating high- and low-inflation regimes under discretion. It would be interesting to explore the joint role of monetary policies and distortionary taxation without commitment. Would the possibility of responding to cost-push shocks via fiscal policy remove the overreaction in inflation that occurs with lump-sum taxes? What is optimal inflation volatility in response to fiscal shocks under discretion? Is the misallocation resulting from the price dispersion associated with inflation sufficient to reduce the inflation bias in general?

The auxiliary role for monetary policy in these branches of the literature stems from the fact that, in these models, money is not essential. The optimal monetary stabilization literature often abstracts from money demand altogether. The Ramsey literature usually considers money in the utility function or cash-in-advance models. These assumptions are meant to stand in for some role for money that is not made explicit but ought to be. Instead, money is essential when spatial, temporal, and informational friction makes the use of money an efficient arrangement, as in the search-theoretic approach pioneered by Kiyotaki and Wright (1989, 1993).[13] The essential nature of money has implications for optimal monetary policy. For example, optimality of the Friedman rule generally occurs in Ramsey models. This result stems from the fact that money does not overcome any primitive friction, and agents use it for transactions because they are forced to. Hence, it is optimal to equate the return on money to that of other assets to minimize the distortions associated with this arrangement.[14] In environments where money is essential, the optimal monetary policy responds to changes in the distribution of liquidity needs. Levine (1991) and Kocherlakota (2003) show that, in this case, higher interest rates increase welfare.[15] Research on the properties of optimal monetary policy when money is essential is still in its infancy; however, this class of environments constitute the most natural laboratory for understanding the effect of monetary policy on the economy.

---

13. Additional contributions include Shi (1995), Trejos and Wright (1995), Kocherlakota (1998), and Wallace (2001).
14. I consider (in Albanesi, 2002) a costly nonmonetary transactions model with heterogeneous agents in which departures from the Friedman rule redistribute toward high-income households and the Friedman rule may not optimal.
15. See also Woodford (1990) for some related examples. Lagos and Wright (2002) show that optimality of the Friedman rule occurs in an environment where money is essential. In their model, however, the distribution of currency is degenerate.

REFERENCES

Aiyagari, S. Rao, Albert Marcet, Thomas J. Sargent, and Juha Seppälä. (2002). Optimal taxation without state-contingent debt. *Journal of Political Economy* 110(6): 1220–1254.

Albanesi, Stefania. (2002). Optimal and time consistent monetary and fiscal policy with heterogeneous agents. CEPR DP No. 3713.

Albanesi, Stefania, V. V. Chari, and Lawrence J. Christiano. (2002). Expectation traps and monetary policy. *The Review of Economic Studies* 70(4) 715–741.

Barro, Robert J. (1979). On the determination of public debt. *Journal of Political Economy* 87:940–971.

Chari, V. V., Lawrence J. Christiano, and Patrick Kehoe. (1991). Optimal fiscal and monetary policy: Some recent results. *Journal of Money, Credit and Banking* 23:519–539.

Chari, V. V., Lawrence Christiano, and Patrick Kehoe. (1995). Policy analysis in business cycle models. In *Frontiers of Business Cycle Research*, Thomas J. Cooley, (ed.). Princeton, NJ: Princeton University Press.

Chari, V. V., and Patrick J. Kehoe. (1999). Optimal fiscal and monetary policy. In *Handbook of Macroeconomics*, Volume 1, John B. Taylor and Michael Woodford (eds.). Amsterdam: Elsevier.

Clarida, Richard, Jordi Gali, and Mark Gertler. (1999). The science of monetary policy: A new Keynesian perspective. Cambridge, MA: National Bureau of Economic Research. NBER Working Paper No. 7147.

Correia, Isabel, Juan-Pablo Nicolini, and Pedro Teles. (2001). Optimal fiscal and monetary policy: Equivalence results. CEPR DP No. 3730.

Giannoni, Marc, and Michael Woodford. (2002). Optimal Interest-Rate Rules: I. General Theory. NBER Working Paper No. 9419, December.

Goodfriend, Marvin, and Robert G. King. (1997). The new neoclassical synthesis and the role for monetary policy. In *NBER Macroeconomics Annual 1997*, B. S. Bernanke and J. J. Rotemberg (eds.). Cambridge, MA: MIT Press, 402–417.

Kahn, Abhuk, Robert G. King, and Alexander Wolman. (2000). Optimal monetary policy. Boston University. Manuscript.

King, Robert G., and Alexander Wolman. (1999). What should monetary policy do if prices are sticky? In *Monetary Policy Rules*, John B. Taylor (ed.). Chicago: University of Chicago Press for NBER, 349–404.

Kiyotaki, Nobuhiro, and Randall Wright. (1989). A contribution to the pure theory of money. *Journal of Economic Theory* 53:215–235.

Kiyotaki, Nobuhiro, and Randall Wright. (1993). A search-theoretic approach to monetary economics. *American Economic Review* 83:63–77.

Kocherlakota, Narayana. (1998). Money is memory. *Journal of Economic Theory* 81:232–251.

Kocherlakota, Narayana. (2003). Societal benefits of illiquid bonds. *Journal of Economic Theory* 102:179–193.

Kydland, Finn, and Edward Prescott. (1980). Dynamic optimal taxation, rational expectations and optimal control. *Journal of Economic Dynamics and Control* 2:79–91.

Lagos, Ricardo, and Randall Wright. (2002). A unified framework for monetary theory and policy analysis. New York University. Manuscript.

Levine, David. (1991). Asset trading mechanisms and expansionary policy. *Journal of Economic Theory* 54:148–164.

Lucas, Robert E., and Nancy Stokey. (1983). Optimal fiscal and monetary policy in an economy without capital. *Journal of Monetary Economics* 12:55–93.

Marcet, Albert, and Ramon Marimon. (1999). Recursive Contracts. European Institute, EUI Working Papers in Economics 98/37.

Ramsey, F. P. (1927). A contribution to the theory of taxation. *Economic Journal* 37:47–61.

Rotemberg, Julio, and Michael Woodford. (1997). An optimization based framework for the evaluation of monetary policy. *NBER Macroeconomics Annual 1997*, B. S. Bernanke and J. J. Rotemberg (eds.). Cambridge, MA: NBER, 297–346.

Schmitt-Grohé, Stephanie, and Martin Uribe. (2001). Optimal fiscal and monetary policy under sticky prices. Rutgers University and University of Pennsylvania. Manuscript.

Shi, Shouyong. (1995). Money and prices: A model of search and bargaining. *Journal of Economic Theory* 67:467–496.

Siu, Henry. (2001). Optimal fiscal and monetary policy with sticky prices. University of British Columbia, Department of Economics. DP 02–13.

Trejos, Alberto, and Randall Wright. (1995). Search, bargaining, money and prices. *Journal of Political Economy* 103:118–141.

Wallace, Neil. (2001). Whither monetary economics? *International Economic Review* 42(4):847–870.

Woodford, Michael. (1990). The optimum quantity of money. In *Handbook of Monetary Economics* Volume II, Benjamin M. Friedman and Frank H. Hahn (eds.). Amsterdam: North Holland.

Woodford, Michael. (2000). Interest and prices. Princeton University. Manuscript.

Comment

GEORGE-MARIOS ANGELETOS
MIT and NBER

1. Introduction

The paper by Benigno and Woodford makes an important contribution to the theory of cyclical fiscal and monetary policies.

Following the tradition of Ramsey (1927), Barro (1979), and Lucas and Stokey (1983), the neoclassical literature on optimal fiscal policy has emphasized that, when taxation is distortionary, welfare is maximized if the government smoothes taxes across different periods of time and different realizations of uncertainty. To what extent, however, such smoothing is possible depends on the ability of the government to transfer budget resources from one date and state to another. If the government can trade a complete set of Arrow securities (or state-contingent debt), perfect smoothing across all dates and states is possible, implying that the

Prepared for the NBER Macroeconomics Annual Conference. I thank Oliver Blanchard and Ivan Werning for helpful comments and stimulating discussions.

optimal tax rate is essentially invariant (Lucas and Stokey, 1983; Chari, Christiano, and Kehoe, 1991). If instead insurance is unavailable, any innovation in fiscal conditions needs to be spread over time, implying that the optimal tax rate follows essentially a random walk (Barro, 1979; Aiyagari et al., 2002).

When the government cannot trade state-contingent debt, there might be other ways to obtain insurance. Bohn (1990) and Chari, Christiano, and Kehoe (1991) have argued that, when the government trades nominal bonds, unexpected variation in inflation may generate all the desirable variation in the real value of the outstanding public debt and may therefore replicate state-contingent debt. A serious caveat with this argument, however, is that it considers a world where prices are perfectly flexible and price volatility has no welfare consequences.

But when nominal prices are sticky, unexpected variation in the aggregate level of prices creates distortions in the allocation of resources and reduces welfare. The new Keynesian literature on optimal monetary policy has therefore stressed the importance of minimizing price volatility to minimize inefficiencies in the cross-sectoral allocation of resources.[1] Recent work by Schmitt-Grohé and Uribe (2001) and Siu (2001) shows that the conflict between insurance and price stability is likely to be resolved overwhelmingly in favor of the latter.[2] At the same time, the new Keynesian literature has noted that fiscal policy could, in principle, help stabilize output by offsetting cyclical variation in monopolistic distortions (price or wage markups), but has bypassed this possibility and instead focused on monetary policy.

The paper by Pierpaolo Benigno and Michael Woodford merges the new Keynesian paradigm of optimal monetary policy with the neoclassical paradigm of optimal fiscal policy. It examines the joint determination of optimal fiscal and monetary policy in the presence of incomplete insurance and sticky prices. Furthermore, it shows how one can start from a full-fledged micro-founded model and, through a long series of approximations, end with a simple linear-quadratic framework similar to the ad-hoc specifications used in the early contributions to both fiscal and monetary policy.

The welfare costs of business cycles in economies with sticky prices and incomplete markets and the consequent stabilization role of fiscal and monetary policy are important questions. The paper by Pierpaolo Benigno and Michael Woodford makes an important contribution in this

---

1. See, for example, Clarida et al. (1999), the excellent textbook by Woodford (2003), and the references therein.
2. This result is also verified by the findings of Benigno and Woodford.

direction. I have one concern, however, regarding the strategy of the paper. It is important to know that ad-hoc representations of the policy problem can be backed up by proper micro-foundations, but in their paper this comes at the cost of numerous linear-quadratic approximations, which I find hard to follow. The reduced-form analytic representation is hard to interpret. For example, all impulse responses are found to depend critically on a composite exogenous variable that the authors call "fiscal stress," but what exactly this variable is remains a mystery.

In the present discussion, I will attempt a simpler route. I will set up an ad-hoc framework from the very beginning. This will permit us to derive the essential results with less effort and more clarity. We will see that, when the government has access to either lump-sum taxation or complete insurance, the inflation rate is always zero, the output gap is always constant, and output stabilization is obtained only via fiscal policy. When instead there is incomplete insurance, the output gap has a unit root, like the tax rate and the level of government debt, and monetary policy complements fiscal policy in stabilizing the economy. Innovations in the inflation rate, the output gap, or the tax rate are driven by innovations in an exogenous fiscal stress variable, which simply measures the annuity value of government spending plus the subsidy that would have been necessary to implement the first best.

2. Optimal Fiscal and Monetary Policy: A Simple Model

2.1 SOCIAL WELFARE

We can approximate social welfare around the first-best outcome as:

$$u = -\sum_{t=0}^{\infty} \beta^t E_t \left[(y_t - y_t^*)^2 + \omega \cdot \pi_t^2 \right] \tag{1}$$

where y_t^* is an exogenous random variable representing the efficient (or first-best) level of output, whereas y_t and π_t are the endogenous actual levels of output and inflation. The last term in equation (1) reflects the welfare loss associated with the distortion in the cross-sectoral allocation of resources cause by a higher dispersion of prices.[3] The scalar $\omega \geq 0$ depends on how flexible prices are. If $1 - \alpha$ is the probability that a firm can adjust prices in any given period, so that α measures the degree of price stickiness, then $\omega = \omega(\alpha)$ is increasing in α; flexible prices correspond to $\alpha = 0$ and $\omega = 0$.

---

3. The implicit assumption is that the first-best level of inflation is zero.

2.2 MARKET EQUILIBRIUM

We can similarly summarize the market equilibrium with the following condition characterizing the equilibrium level of output:

$$y_t = -\psi\tau_t + \chi(\pi_t - \beta E_t\pi_{t+1}) + \varepsilon_t \tag{2}$$

where $\psi > 0$ and $\chi \geq 0$. The first term in equation (2) reflects the distortion of the tax on final output or the sale of intermediate goods. More generally, the first term can be interpreted as aggregate demand management via fiscal policy. The second term reflects the output effect of monetary policy when prices are sticky. The slope $\chi = \chi(\alpha)$ is increasing in α, the degree of price stickinees.[4] Provided $\chi > 0$, equation (2) gives the new Keynesian Phillips curve:

$$\pi_t = \beta E_t\pi_{t+1} + \frac{1}{\chi}(y_t - y_t^n)$$

where $y_t^n \equiv -\psi\tau_t + \varepsilon_t$ represents the natural level of output. Finally, the exogenous random variable ε_t captures what the literature has called a cost-push shock (e.g., Clarida et al. 1999). As will become clear, variation in ε_t is isomorphic to variation in y_t^*; either one reflects variation in markups and other shorts or distortions, namely, shocks that affect the natural level of output differently from the efficient level.

2.3 THE GOVERNMENT BUDGET

Suppose the government trades only one-period discount bonds, both real and nominal. For simplicity, I will ignore seigniorage and the fiscal effect of variations in either the growth rate of output or the real interest rate. I will also assume that the government freely adjusts the level of real bond issues but keeps the level of nominal bond issues constant at some level $\bar{d}$ (as a fraction of gross domestic product [GDP]), and treats $\bar{d}$ as a parameter. The government budget then reduces to the following equation:[5]

4. Provided $\chi > 0$, equation (2) gives the new Keynesian Phillips curve:

$$\pi_t = \beta E_t\pi_{t+1} + \frac{1}{\chi}(y_t - y_t^n),$$

where $y_t^n \equiv -\Psi\tau_t + \varepsilon_t$ represents the natural level of output.

5. To see this, let v_t and D_t denote the quantity of real and nominal bonds issued in the end of period t (as a fraction of GDP) and write the government budget as:

$$\left(v_t - 1 + \frac{D_{t-1}}{P_t}\right) + g_t = \tau_t + z_t + \left(\frac{1}{1+r_t}v_t + \frac{1}{1+R_t}\frac{D_t}{P_t}\right)$$

The first term represents the total real liabilities of the government in the beginning of period t, while the last term represents the revenue from the issue of new bonds. P_t is the price level, τ_t is the real interest rate, and R_t is the nominal interest rate. Next, let $1/P_t \approx (1 - \pi_t)/P_{t-1}$, $(1 + \tau_t)^{-1} \approx \beta$, $(1 + R_t)^{-1} \approx \beta(1 - E_t\pi_{t+1})$, and $D_{t-1}/P_{t-1} = D_t/P_t = \bar{d}$; and define $b_t \equiv v_t + D_t/P_t$. The budget constraint then reduces to equation (3).

$$b_{t-1} = [\tau_t + z_t + \bar{d}(\pi_t - \beta E_t \pi_{t+1}) - g_t] + \beta b_t \tag{3}$$

The term b_t denotes the total level of public debt (as a fraction of GDP), and τ_t denotes the tax rate on aggregate income. The initial value of debt is $b_{-1} = \bar{b}$. The term g_t denotes the level of government spending (also as a fraction of GDP) and follows a stationary Markov process with mean $Eg_t = \bar{g}$. The term $\bar{d}(\pi_t - \beta E_t \pi_{t+1})$ captures the gains from unexpected deflation of nominal debt. Finally, z_t captures any state-contingent lump-sum transfers the government potentially receives from the private sector. These may reflect either direct lump-sum taxation or various explicit and implicit kinds of insurance (other than the inflation of nominal debt). I will later distinguish three cases: (1) unrestricted lump-sum taxation, in which case z_t is a free control variable; (2) no lump-sum taxation but complete insurance, in which case z_t has to satisfy only the constraint $E_{t-1} z_t = 0$; (3) no lump-sum taxation and no insurance, in which case $z_t = 0$ in all periods and events.

2.4 THE RAMSEY PROBLEM

The government seeks to maximize social welfare subject to its budget constraint and the equilibrium condition for aggregate economic activity. Hence, the Ramsey problem is given by:

$$\min E_0 \sum_{t=0}^{\infty} \beta^t \left[(y_t - y_t^*)^2 + \omega \pi_t^2 \right] \tag{4}$$

$$\text{s.t. } y_t = -\psi \tau_t + \chi(\pi_t - \beta E_t \pi_{t+1}) + \varepsilon_t$$

$$b_{t-1} - \beta b_t = \tau_t + z_t - g_t + \bar{d}(\pi_t - \beta E_t \pi_{t+1})$$

The Lagrangian of this problem can be written as $\mathcal{L} = \sum_{t=0}^{\infty} \beta^t E_t [L_t]$, where:

$$L_t \equiv \frac{1}{2} \left[(y_t - y_t^*)^2 + \omega \pi_t^2 \right] - \mu_t \left[\chi(\pi_t - \beta \pi_{t+1}) - (y_t + \psi \tau_t + \varepsilon_t) \right]$$
$$+ \lambda_t \left[(b_{t-1} - \beta b_t) - (\tau_t - g_t + z_t) - \bar{d}(\pi_t - \beta \pi_{t+1}) \right] \tag{5}$$

$\mu_t \geq 0$ represents the shadow value of real resources and $\lambda_t \geq 0$ represents the shadow cost of the government budget.[6] Taking the First order conditions (FOCs) with respect to y_t, π_t, b_t, and τ_t, and using the last one to substitute for μ_t, we conclude to the following optimality conditions.[7]

---

6. Note that the exogenous disturbances of the economy are given by $s_t = (y_t^*, \varepsilon_t, g_t)$ and the endogenous variables $(\pi_t, \tau_t, y_t, b_t)$ are contingent on $s^t = (s_0, \ldots, s_t)$. Along the optimal plan, however, the history in the beginning of period t can be summarized by $(\mu_{t-1}, \lambda_{t-1})$. See Marcet and Marimon (2001).

7. To be precise, equation (7) holds for $t \geq 1$. Period $t = 0$ is special for the usual reason, namely, that expectations formed in the past are now sunk.

$$y_t - y_t^* = - \frac{1}{\psi} \lambda_t \tag{6}$$

$$\pi_t = \frac{1}{\omega} \left(\frac{\chi}{\psi} + \bar{d} \right) (\lambda_t - \lambda_{t-1}) \tag{7}$$

$$\lambda_t = E_t \lambda_{t+1} \tag{8}$$

These conditions, together with the equilibrium output condition in equation (2), the budget constraint in equation (3), and the initial condition $b_{-1} = \bar{b}$, pin down the optimal policy plan.

Note that equations (7) and (8) imply $E_t \pi_{t+1} = 0$. Note also that both the optimal output gap and the optimal inflation rate are determined merely by the shadow cost of government budget resources (the multiplier λ_t). Finally, equation (8) states that the shadow cost of government budget resources follows a random walk. This property reflects intertemporal smoothing, which is possible as long as the government can freely borrow and lend in riskless bonds. How large is the variance of the innovation in λ_t depends critically on how much insurance the government may obtain against the fiscal consequences of business cycles.

2.5 THE FIRST BEST

Suppose for a moment that the government had unlimited access to lump-sum taxation. This means that the government can freely choose z_t. The FOC, with respect to z_t, implies $\lambda_t = 0$, for all periods and events. That is, the shadow cost of the government budget is always zero, reflecting simply the fact that there is unrestricted lump-sum taxation. It follows that:

$$y_t - y_t^* = 0 \qquad \text{and} \qquad \pi_t = 0 \tag{9}$$

meaning that there is complete output and price stabilization exactly at the first-best levels.

The first-best outcome is implemented by setting the tax rate so that the aggregate supply condition is satisfied at the efficient level of output with zero inflation. This gives:

$$\tau_t = \tau_t^* \equiv - \frac{1}{\psi} (y_t^* + \varepsilon_t) \tag{10}$$

The sum $y_t^* + \varepsilon_t$ measures the overall distortion in the economy due to monopolistic competition or other market imperfections, and τ_t^* represents the Pigou tax (or subsidy) that corrects any such distortion and implements the first-best outcome. (In the case of monopolistic distortions, output is inefficiently low, and therefore $\tau_t^* < 0$, meaning that the government uses a subsidy to offset the monopolistic distortions.) Finally, to balance the government budget, we can pick the level of lump-sum taxes so that they are enough to finance the level of government spending, plus the interest payments on the initial public debt, plus the subsidy that implements the first-best level of output. That is, we let $z_t = (g_t - \tau_t^*) + (1 - \beta)\bar{b}$.

2.6 OPTIMAL POLICY WITH COMPLETE MARKETS

Suppose now that lump-sum taxation is not available, but the government can issue state-contingent debt (or otherwise replicate full insurance). The government chooses z_t subject to the constraint $E_{t-1} z_t = 0$. The FOCs with respect to z_t, together with equation (8), now imply $\lambda_t = \bar{\lambda} > 0$ for all periods and events. That is, the shadow value of tax revenues is positive (because taxation is distortionary) but constant across all periods and events (because markets are complete). It follows that:

$$y_t - y_t^* = -\frac{1}{\psi}\bar{\lambda} < 0 \qquad \text{and} \qquad \pi_t = 0 \tag{11}$$

This outcome is now obtained by setting:

$$\tau_t = \frac{1}{\psi^2}\bar{\lambda} + \tau_t^* \tag{12}$$

where $\tau_t^* \equiv -\frac{1}{\psi}(y_t^* + \varepsilon_t)$ is again the Pigou tax that would implement the first best, and letting

$$z_t = (g_t - \tau_t) - (\bar{g} - \bar{\tau}) \tag{13}$$

where $\bar{g} \equiv E g_t$ and $\bar{\tau} \equiv E \tau_t$. That is, variation in z_t absorbs any business-cycle variation in either the level of government spending or the subsidy that implements the first-best level of output. Finally, to compute $\bar{\lambda}$, note that the government budget clears if and only if $\bar{\tau} = \bar{g} + (1 - \beta)\bar{b}$, which together with equation (12) implies:

$$\bar{\lambda} = \psi^2[(1 - \beta)\bar{b} + (\bar{g} - \bar{\tau}^*)] \tag{14}$$

That is, the (constant) shadow cost of budget resources is proportional to the interest cost of public debt, plus the annuity value of government spending, plus the annuity value of the subsidy that would be necessary to implement the first best. It follows that the (constant) output gap is higher the higher the initial level of public debt, the higher the average level of government spending, or the higher the monopolistic distortion in the economy. Finally, substituting equation (14) in equation (12), we infer:

$$\tau_t = \bar{\tau} + (\tau_t^* - \bar{\tau}^*) \tag{15}$$

where $\bar{\tau} = \bar{g} + (1 - \beta)\,\bar{b}$. Note that $\bar{\tau}$ corresponds to the optimal tax rate in a neoclassical economy, such as in Barro (1979) or Lucas and Stokey (1983). In the presence of a Keynesian business cycle, the optimal tax rate inherits in addition a cyclical component, the latter being the cyclical variation in the Pigou subsidy that would have implemented the first-best level of output. Fiscal policy can thus eliminate the inefficient business cycle by simply offsetting the cyclical variation in the monopolistic (or other) distortion.

To see how fiscal policy works under complete markets, consider a negative shock in the output gap (a shock that reduces the natural rate of output more than the first-best level). The government can offset this shock and fully stabilize the output gap by simply lowering the rate of taxation while keeping the price level constant. This policy leads to a primary deficit, but the latter is totally covered by an increase in state-contingent transfers. Hence, the government does not need to issue any new public debt, and the stabilization policy has no fiscal consequences for the future.

2.7 OPTIMAL POLICY WITH INCOMPLETE MARKETS

Finally, consider the case that the government cannot obtain any insurace. It is useful to define the variable:

$$f_t \equiv (1 - \beta) \sum_{j=0}^{\infty} \beta^j E_t (g_{t+j} - \tau_{t+j}^*) \tag{16}$$

which measures the annuity value of government spending plus the annuity value of the subsidy that is necessary to implement the first best, and let $\xi_t \equiv f_t - E_{t-1} f_t$ denote the innovation in this variable. (The term f_t corresponds to the mysterious object that Benigno and Woodford call the fiscal stress variable.) After some tedious algebra, we can show that the shadow value of budget resources satisfies:

$$\lambda_{t-1} = \psi^2 [(1 - \beta) b_{t-1} + E_{t-1} f_t] \qquad \text{and} \qquad \lambda_t - \lambda_{t-1} = \eta \xi_t \tag{17}$$

for some constant $\eta > 0$. That is, the shadow cost of budget resources is proportional to the interest cost of public debt, plus the annuity value of government spending, plus the annuity value of the subsidy that would be necessary to implement the first best; the innovation in the shadow cost of budget resources is proportional to the innovation in the fiscal stress variable f_t. It follows that any transitory change in f_t results in a permanent change in λ_t, which manifests the effect of intertemporal tax smoothing. Finally, using equation (17) together with the equations (6) to (8), we conclude with the following impulse-response functions:

$$\pi_t = \varphi_\pi \xi_t, \tag{18}$$

$$y_t - y_{t-1} = (y_t^* - y_{t-1}^*) - \varphi_y \xi_t \tag{19}$$

$$\tau_t - \tau_{t-1} = (\tau_t^* - \tau_{t-1}^*) + \varphi_\tau \xi_t \tag{20}$$

for some constant $\varphi_\pi, \varphi_y, \varphi_\tau > 0$. It follows that inflation is white noise.[8] The output gap and the tax rate, however, follow a martingale plus a stationary component, which is proportional to the change in the output gap (that is, the distance from the first best). This cyclical component of optimal fiscal and monetary policy is absent in the neoclassical paradigm (Barro, 1979; Lucas and Stokey, 1983) and arises here because cyclical variation exists in the extent of distortions in the economy. Finally, the coefficients $\varphi_\pi, \varphi_y,$ and φ_τ are decreasing in $\bar{d}$, reflecting the fact that a higher level of nominal debt permits the government to obtain more insurance with less inflation volatility.

To see how fiscal policy works under incomplete markets, consider a negative shock in the output gap (a shock that reduces the natural rate of output more than the first-best rate). Contrary to what was the case with complete markets, the government cannot fully stabilize the output gap and keep the price level constant at the same time. Because complete insurance is no longer available, lowering the contemporaneous rate of taxation necessarily results in a primary deficit that has to be financed by an increase in public debt and thus an increase in future taxes. The government thus finds it optimal to lower the tax rate by less than what it would have done under complete markets, that is, by less than what is necessary to offset the negative cyclical shock. And because fiscal policy can no longer do it all, it becomes optimal to use monetary policy also for the purpose of output stabilization. Actually, an unexpected increase in inflation not only stimulates aggregate demand but also lowers the real value of nominal public debt and thus eases fiscal conditions. Nonetheless, monetary policy cannot do it all either. Because inflation surprises distort the cross-sectoral allocation of resources, the government finds it optimal to raise inflation by an amount less than what would be necessary to stabilize output fully and cover the primary deficit. Overall,

8. Note that the white-noise result for inflation is not robust to the introduction of lags in fiscal policy. The martingale property for fiscal policy and the output gap, however, is likely to be robust to more general frameworks.

both fiscal and monetary policy are now used to stabilize output, but the negative cyclical shock is only partly offset and results in a permanent increase in the level of public debt and thereby in a permanent increase in taxes and a permanent reduction in output.

3. Conclusion

I conclude with some important (at least in my view) open questions about fiscal policy over the business cycle.

First, the theory suggests that there are important welfare gains to be made if the government traded state-contingent debt (or at least gains of the same order of magnitude as the gains from eliminating business cycles). And if state-contingent debt is not available, our models predict that the government could obtain insurance by appropriately designing the maturity structure of public debt (Angeletos, 2002) or the cyclical properties of consumption taxes (Correia et al., 2002). Similarly, the government could replicate more insurance with less cyclical variation in inflation by issuing a lot of nominal debt and at the same time investing in real assets to keep the overall level of public debt at the desired level. Yet none of these forms of insurance appear to play an important role in practice. Why not?[9]

Second, the implications of incomplete insurance become even more interesting once we abandon the simple linear-quadratic framework. If the lack of insurance is due to exogenous reasons, then a precautionary motive dictates that the government should accumulate a large amount of assets to use it as a buffer stock against cyclical shocks (Aiyagari et al., 2002). If instead the lack of insurance is due to the government's own moral hazard, then a desire to minimize the costs of providing future governments with optimal incentives dictates that the government should accumulate a large amount of debt (Sleet, 2002). But which of the two opposite predictions should we follow?

Third, consider the comparison of fiscal and monetary policy as instruments for managing the business cycle. The simple model presented here, the more elaborate models of Correia et al. (2002) or Benigno and Woodford, and probably any model we teach our graduate students share the prediction that fiscal policy cannot do all (if markets are complete) or most (if markets are incomplete) of the job of stabilizing the economy. One could even argue that fiscal policy is superior to monetary policy in

---

9. Moral hazard in government behavior is only part of the answer: If it were severe enough to explain complete lack of insurance, one would also expect the government customarily to default on (domestic) public debt, which is not the case in reality.

stabilizing the economy because its effectiveness does not depend on the extent of nominal rigidities. In practice, however, fiscal policy is quickly dismissed on the basis that it takes time to implement changes in fiscal policy and even more time for these changes to have an effect on economic activity. But where is the hard proof for this? And even if there are important lags involved in discretionary cyclical fiscal policy, why don't we undertake the necessary reforms to reduce them, or why don't we redesign the existing automatic stabilizers to implement the optimal cyclical variation in fiscal policy? Or why should a systematic fiscal policy rule have a weaker and slower impact on market incentives than a systematic monetary policy rule? Similarly, cyclical fiscal policy may have a differential impact on different sectors of the economy, but this is equally true for monetary policy. I am not totally convinced that monetary policy is intrinsically more effective as an instrument for managing the business cycle, I believe that we should carefully investigate the alleged asymmetries between fiscal and monetary policies, and I wonder if it is mostly a historical coincidence that economists and policymakers alike have been obsessed with monetary policy.[10]

Finally, consider the nature of the shocks that justify policy intervention. The conventional wisdom is that we should try to stabilize the actual level of output, or the gap between the actual level and some smoother level (the empirically measured natural rate). The theory instead dictates that we should stabilize the gap between the actual and the first-best level of output because it minimizes welfare losses. What is more, the canonical model predicts that productivity and taste shocks move the actual and the first-best level of output proportionally, in which case there is no inefficient business cycle and thus no reason for countercyclical policy.[11] The resolution to this unappealing theoretical prediction has been to introduce ad hoc shocks that perturb directly the gap between the actual and the first-best level of output.[12] It remains an open question what exactly these shocks are, and why they may be highly correlated with the actual level of output, in which case only the conventional wisdom and the common policy practice would be justifiable.

---

10. For the possibility that sunspots (or self-fulfilling expectations) determine which policy instruments are effective and actively used in equilibrium, see Angeletos, Hellwig, and Pavan (2003).

11. See Woodford (2003) for an extensive analysis of this issue.

12. These shocks are commonly called cost-push shocks, although they may have little to do with real-life cost-push shocks, such as an increase in oil prices, which are bound to affect both the actual and the first-best level of output and may have an ambiguous effect on the level of the distortion in the economy. See Blanchard (2003) for a critical assessment.

REFERENCES

Aiyagari, S. Rao, Albert Marcet, Thomas Sargent, and Juha Seppala. (2002). Optimal taxation without state-contingent debt. *Journal of Political Economy*, 110(6):1220–1254.

Angeletos, George-Marios. (2002). Fiscal policy without state-contingent debt and the optimal maturity structure. *Quarterly Journal of Economics* 117:1105–1131.

Angeletos, George-Marios, Christian Hellwig, and Alessandro Pavan. (2003). Coordination and policy traps. Cambridge, MA: National Bureau of Economic Research. NBER Working Paper No. 9767.

Barro, Robert J. (1979). On the determination of public debt. *Journal of Political Economy* 87:940–971.

Blanchard, Olivier. (2003). Comments on "Inflation targeting in transition economies: Experience and prospects." by Jiri Jonas and Frederic Mishkin. MIT. Mimeo.

Bohn, Henning. (1990). Tax smoothing with financial instruments. *American Economic Review* 80:1217–1230.

Chari, V. V., Lawrence Christiano, and Patrick Kehoe. (1991). Optimal fiscal and monetary policy: Some recent results. *Journal of Money, Credit, and Banking* 23:519–539.

Clarida, Richard, Jordi Gali, and Mark Gertler. (1999). The science of monetary policy: A new Keynesian perspective. *Journal of Economic Literature* 37:1661–1707.

Correia, Isabel, Juan Pablo Nicolini, and Pedro Teles. (2002). Optimal fiscal and monetary policy: Equivalence results. CEPR Discussion Paper No. 3730.

Lucas, Robert E., Jr., and Nancy L. Stokey. (1983). Optimal fiscal and monetary policy in an economy without capital. *Journal of Monetary Economics* 12:55–93.

Marcet, Albert, and Ramon Marimon. (2001). Recursive Contracts. University of Pompeu Fabra Mimeo.

Ramsey, Frank. (1927). A Contribution to the Theory of Taxation. *Economic Journal* 48:47–61.

Schmitt-Grohé, Stephanie, and Martin Uribe. (2001). Optimal fiscal and monetary policy under sticky prices. Rutgers University. Working Paper No. 2001–06.

Siu, Henry E. (2001). Optimal fiscal and monetary policy with sticky prices. Northwestern University. Mimeo.

Sleet, Christopher. (2002). Optimal taxation with private government information. University of Iowa. Mimeo.

Woodford, Michael. (2003). *Interest and Prices: Foundations of a Theory of Monetary Policy*, Princeton, NJ: Princeton University Press.

Discussion

Participants as well as discussants were concerned by the generality of the authors' local linear-quadratic approximation approach. Mike Woodford responded to the discussion of Stefania Albanesi that the advantage of this approach over the approaches of Siu, Schmitt-Grohé, and other authors is that analytic solutions for optimal policies can be obtained, and optimal responses to shocks with general stochastic properties can be calculated. He noted that the disadvantage of the linear-quadratic approach is that very large shocks cannot be analyzed. Stefania Albanesi noted that the linear-quadratic approximation is thus less likely to be appropriate for analyzing the problems facing developing countries where shocks are larger. Ken Rogoff said that, while on the one hand, analytic results can be useful for building intuition, on the other hand, it may not be possible to answer every important question analytically.

Robert Hall was worried that the results of the paper place a huge weight on the Calvo price adjustment mechanism and the Dixit-Stiglitz-Spence model of imperfect competition. He questioned whether this is how economies really work and whether the results are robust to more general assumptions. Mike Woodford agreed that the results are subject to assumptions about the form of distortions, including the form of sluggish price adjustment. He noted that the aim of the paper is to analyze the effect of sluggish price adjustment on optimal fiscal policy, something that the literature has not investigated before. He also remarked that the framework is quite flexible in allowing various distortions to be added or taken away.

Andrés Velasco was curious about the generality of the model result that debt indexation is undesirable. Mike Woodford responded that when prices are sticky, nominal debt is desirable, but the degree to which unexpected inflation is optimally used to achieve state contingency is limited. Stefania Albanesi elaborated that the cost of not having state-contingent debt depends on the size of shocks. When shocks are of the business-cycle variety, as in the authors' framework, the costs of not having state-contingent debt are small. Marios Angeletos remarked that it would be optimal to have nominal debt but real assets. To add to Stefania Albanesi's point, Angeletos noted that in the authors' exercise, the difference between nominal and indexed debt is small because the optimal volatility of inflation is, in any case, almost zero.

Several participants were curious about the ability of the authors' framework to nest important policy concerns. John Williams asked whether the linear-quadratic framework can allow for realistic distortions such as the nonneutrality of the U.S. tax system with respect to inflation. Mike Woodford responded that this can indeed be integrated into the framework. Mark Gertler remarked that the old-fashioned argument that lags in the implementation of fiscal policy make monetary policy a more appropriate stabilization instrument was not taken account of by the authors' framework. He was curious about the effect on optimal policy of allowing for such. Mike Woodford responded that delays in fiscal policy implementation are indeed realistic and can be included. He said that even with lags in the implementation of fiscal policy, optimal monetary policy in the case of distortionary taxation is not the same as when all taxes are lump sum because, with distortionary taxation, there is a nonzero shadow value of additional resources to the government that the monetary authority should take into account. On this question, Marios Angeletos noted that in the linear-quadratic framework, thinking of fiscal and monetary policy as independent is actually not a bad approximation. Where shocks are big, however, this is much less likely to be an appropriate assumption.

Ken Rogoff pointed out that political economy concerns were absent from the authors' model, while in the real world, fiscal policy has effectively been dismissed as a tool of stabilization because the degree of commitment available to fiscal authorities is so limited. He was curious about what type of institutional framework the authors envisaged for implementing the optimal fiscal policy. Kjetil Storesletten suggested that the authors do more to confront the time-consistency issue and work out the time-consistent policy for their framework. Mike Woodford responded that this could be done but that, in reality, governments appear to have some ability to accept constraints on fiscal policy, as shown by their reluctance to tax existing capital.

Arminio Fraga, Ilan Goldfajn, and André Minella

PARTNER, GAVEA INVESTIMENTOS; PONTIFICAL
CATHOLIC UNIVERSITY OF RIO DE JANEIRO; AND CENTRAL
BANK OF BRAZIL

Inflation Targeting in Emerging Market Economies

1. Introduction

The performance of inflation-targeting regimes around the world has been positive. Average inflation in both emerging markets and developed economies is substantially lower after the adoption of the inflation-targeting regime than immediately before its adoption (Figure 1).[1] However, emerging market economies (EMEs) have had a relatively worse performance. In these countries, deviations from both central targets and upper bounds are larger and more common.[2] This outcome suggests that either inflation targeters in EMEs are less committed to their targets or inflation targeting in these countries is a more challenging task than in developed ones. The latter explanation is related to the more volatile macroeconomic environment and to weaker institutions and credibility in these countries, which in turn lead to more acute trade-offs than the existing ones in developed economies.

We thank the participants in the NBER Eighteenth Annual Conference on Macroeconomics, especially Mark Gertler, Robert Hall, Frederic Mishkin, and Kenneth Rogoff, and seminar participants at Princeton University for their comments. We are also grateful to Fabia A. de Carvalho, Eduardo Loyo, and Marcio I. Nakane for their suggestions; to Thaís P. Ferreira and Myrian B. S. Petrassi for research assistance; and to Marcileide A. da Silva, Pedro H. S. de Sousa, and Raquel K. de S. Tsukada for assistance with data. The views expressed are those of the authors and not necessarily those of the Banco Central do Brasil.

1. Bernanke, Laubach, Mishkin, and Posen (1999); Mishkin and Schmidt-Hebbel (2002); and Corbo, Landerretche, and Schmidt-Hebbel (2002) have found evidence of additional gains stemming from inflation targeting. Ball and Sheridan (2003) have found no evidence that inflation-targeting countries have enjoyed better performance in the OECD.
2. The deviations of inflation from central targets and from the upper bounds of targets were 81% and 167% higher than in developed economies, respectively (table available on request to the authors).

Under inflation targeting, EMEs have the challenge of breaking the vicious circle between, on one side, low credibility and more fragile institutions and, on the other side, higher macroeconomic instability and vulnerability to external shocks. It is a long process that involves acquiring credibility as a monetary policy institution committed to price stability in the context of higher instability.

This paper assesses inflation targeting in EMEs compared to that in developed economies and develops applied prescriptions for the conduct of monetary policy and inflation-targeting design. We verify that EMEs have faced more acute trade-offs than developed countries have: both output and inflation are more volatile, and the inflation level is higher. The explanation for the different performance of EMEs relies on the presence of more fragile institutions and imperfect credibility, and on the nature and magnitude of the shocks that hit these economies.

There are several instances where these more acute trade-offs emerge. Take the case of a sudden stop in the inflow of capital to an EME leading to a substantial depreciation of the currency (e.g., in 2002, Brazil was faced with a negative swing of US$30 billion—or 6% of gross domestic product (GDP)—in capital flows relative to an already difficult 2001, which led to a nominal depreciation of 50%). Even in a context of good initial conditions—low pass-through and 12-month forward inflation expectations on track—this event led to a breach of the inflation target and, given some inertia, to a worsening of both inflation expectations and actual future inflation (Brazil's target of 4% was breached with an inflation of 12.5%, and 12-month forward inflation expectations were 11.0% at the end of

Figure 1 INFLATION BEFORE AND AFTER ADOPTION OF INFLATION TARGETING (IT)

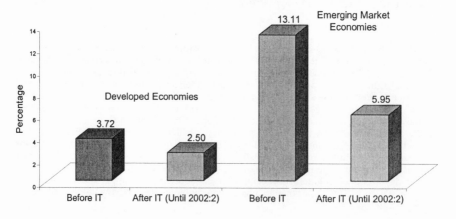

December 2002). In this context, what is the optimal response to these types of shocks? Should one take 24 months or longer to converge to the target, even when building credibility and reputation is still important?

In general, in the more volatile environment in EMEs, some applied and theoretical issues deserve attention. (1) How can the country build credibility when faced with larger shocks? And how can it balance flexibility and credibility in such an instance? (2) How does an inflation-targeting regime work in a disinflation process? And in a credibility-building process? (3) How can a country deal with shocks that represent important changes in relative prices? (4) Should bands be wider and the central points of inflation targets be higher in EMEs? (5) How should International Monetary Fund (IMF) conditionality be designed with an inflation-targeting country?

This paper discusses these monetary policy issues. Its focus, therefore, is more applied. For that purpose, our analysis is based on empirical findings for EMEs and, in particular, on our own experience at the Banco Central do Brasil (BCB), besides the use of simulations of a model to guide our discussions. In a way, because the case of Brazil represents the first stress test of an inflation-targeting regime, the lessons learned may someday be useful for other countries.

We stress the role of communication and transparency as crucial for the process of building credibility. This paper lays out the main issues and, as a by-product, also includes two applied proposals. The first is a transparent procedure that a central bank under inflation targeting can apply and communicate when facing strong supply shocks. The second is a design of a monitoring structure for an inflation-targeting regime under an IMF program.

The paper is organized as follows. Section 2 presents some stylized facts about EMEs and developed countries. It contains a statistical comparison of the conduct and results of monetary policy in EMEs and developed countries. Section 3 presents a theoretical model of a small open economy, which is employed to simulate the effects of some shocks and changes in inflation targets. Section 4 discusses some reasons why EMEs face higher volatility. It analyzes the challenge of constructing credibility and reducing inflation levels, analyzes the effect of large external shocks, and addresses issues on fiscal and financial dominance. Section 5 addresses how to deal with shocks.

2. Stylized Facts About Inflation Targeting in Emerging Market Economies

In this section we present basic stylized facts comparing the volatilities of inflation, output, exchange rates, and interest rates, and the average of inflation and output growth in emerging markets and developed

Table 1   INITIAL TARGETS AND INFLATION AROUND ADOPTION OF
INFLATION TARGETING (12-MONTH ACCUMULATED INFLATION)

	Date of adoption inflation targeting	First target	Inflation right before IT adoption	Inflation 12 months after IT adoption
Developed economies				
Australia	Apr 1993	2% – 3%	1.22	1.74
Canada	Feb 1991	3% – 5%	6.83	1.68
Iceland	Mar 2001	2.5% (–1.5% + 3.5%)	4.05	8.72
New Zealand	Mar 1990	3% – 5%	7.03	4.52
Norway	Mar 2001	2.5	3.64	1.10
Sweden	Jan 1993	2% (± 1%)	1.76	1.70
Switzerland	Jan 2000	≤ 2%	1.63	0.90
United Kingdom	Oct 1992	1% – 4%	3.57	1.35
Average		**2.8**	**3.72**	**2.71**
Median		**2.5**	**3.61**	**1.69**
Emerging market economies				
Brazil[1]	Jun 1999	8% (± 2%)	3.15	6.51
Chile	Jan 1991	15% – 20%	27.31	19.47
Colombia	Sep 1999	15%	9.22	9.35
Czech Republic	Jan 1998	5.5% – 6.5%	9.98	3.5
Hungary	Jun 2001	7% (±1%)	10.78	4.87
Israel	Jan 1992	14% – 15%	18.03	10.74
Mexico	Jan 1991	≤13%	18.61	11.03
Peru	Jan 1994	15% – 20%	39.49	13.71
Poland	Oct 1998	≤9.5%	10.44	8.82
South Africa[2]	Feb 2000	3% – 6%	2.65	7.77
South Korea	Jan 1998	9%(±1%)	6.57	1.46
Thailand	Apr 2000	0% – 3.5%	1.04	2.47
Average		**10.3**	**13.11**	**8.31**
Median		**9.3**	**10.21**	**8.30**

1. In Brazil, the inflation of the period previous to the adoption of inflation targeting was in part a result of the overappreciation of the domestic currency.
2. First target established for 2002.

economies.[3] We have faced two difficulties in defining the differences between the two country groups. First, some differences exist across EMEs; therefore, not all characteristics that we list are common to all these economies. Because they are present in a significant part of the group, however, we call them stylized facts. Second, in most EMEs, the adoption of inflation targeting is recent, making it difficult to draw conclusions and to apply econometric methods. Table 1 shows the dates of adoption for

3. The assessment of the experiences of some countries and of some issues involved in the design of inflation targeting can be found in Bernanke, Laubach, Mishkin, and Posen (1999); Truman (2003); Mishkin and Schmidt-Hebbel (2002); Schmidt-Hebbel and Werner (2002); Corbo and Schmidt-Hebbel (2001); and Minella, Freitas, Goldfajn, and Muinhos (2002).

Table 2   VOLATILITY AND AVERAGE OF SELECTED VARIABLES FOR 1997:1–2002:2

Countries	Inflation	*Volatility of basic variables*			*Average*	
		Exchange rate*	GDP growth†	Interest rate	GDP growth	Inflation
Developed economies						
Australia	2.05	0.13	1.96	0.58	4.78	5.89
Canada	0.83	0.04	1.30	1.14	3.57	1.96
Iceland	2.45	0.15	3.13	3.02	4.17	4.05
New Zealand	1.21	0.16	3.61	1.47	3.09	1.65
Norway	0.77	0.10	2.25	1.46	2.66	2.44
Sweden	1.11	0.12	2.41	0.44	2.58	1.24
Switzerland	0.54	0.08	1.14	0.92	1.79	0.85
United Kingdom	0.92	0.06	0.79	1.13	2.61	2.46
Average	**1.24**	**0.11**	**2.07**	**1.27**	**3.16**	**2.57**
Median	**1.02**	**0.11**	**2.11**	**1.13**	**2.88**	**2.20**
Emerging market economies						
Brazil	2.09	0.15‡	2.06	7.06	1.81	5.89
Chile	1.30	0.17	3.25	—	3.11	3.88
Colombia	5.43	0.25	3.38	10.02	0.81	12.51
Czech Republic	3.46	0.09	2.73	5.81	1.81	5.31
Hungary	4.09	0.16	—	1.13	—	11.21
Israel	3.18	0.10	3.36	3.34	2.98	4.35
Mexico	5.98	0.07	3.17	7.26	4.05	11.72
Peru	3.04	0.11	3.45	5.50	2.11	3.89
Poland	4.13	0.11	2.40	4.14	3.85	8.40
South Africa	2.13	0.26	1.11	3.65	2.26	6.51
South Korea	2.36	0.14	6.38	5.52	4.31	3.73
Thailand	3.25	0.14	6.13	6.72	0.08	2.88
Average	**3.37**	**0.15**	**3.40**	**5.47**	**2.41**	**6.69**
Median	**3.22**	**0.14**	**3.25**	**5.52**	**2.26**	**5.60**

Data source: International Financial Statistics, IMF (quarterly data).
* The coefficient of variation (standard deviation/average).
† Growth rate measured comparing the current quarter to the quarter of the previous year.
‡The period 1999:1–2002:2. For 1997:1–2002:2, the value is 0.31.

emerging and developed economies. The number of inflation targeters among developing and developed economies amounts to 12 and 8, respectively. Most of the developed countries adopted inflation targeting between 1990 and 1993, whereas the majority of the developing countries adopted it from 1998 onward.

We consider two samples. The first refers to the period after the adoption of inflation targeting in each country. The objective is to compare countries with the same regime. Because the periods across countries are different, however, the world macroeconomic environment is

Figure 2 VOLATILITIES OF SELECTED VARIABLES OF THE PERIOD
1997–2002 (AVERAGE OF STANDARD DEVIATION)

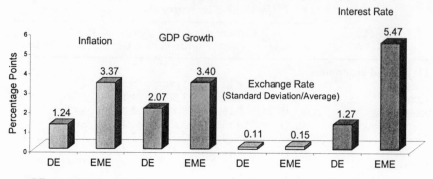

DE = developed economies.
EME = emerging market economies.

different as well. Then we consider a second sample that refers to a recent period, which includes Asian, Brazilian, and Russian crises: 1997 to mid-2002, which we refer to as a fixed sample. In this case, some countries are inflation targeters in the whole sample, whereas others are just in part of it. Table 2 and Figure 2 record the data for the second sample.[4]

In both samples, the data indicate that, in comparison to developed economies, the volatilities of all variables (inflation, the exchange rate,[5] output, and the interest rate) and the inflation level are higher in EMEs. The more challenging trade-off faced by EMEs is illustrated in Figure 3, which shows the combination of the variability of output growth and inflation for each country for 1997:1 to 2002:2.

3. Model

We develop a small open economy model to illustrate the main points raised in the paper. The objective is to simulate the effects of some shocks and changes in inflation targets. The model combines features of Batini, Harrison, and Millard's (2003) and McCallum and Nelson's (2000) formulations.

Imports enter as intermediate goods, in contrast to most of the open economy literature, which typically uses a model with imports as consumption goods. As stressed by McCallum and Nelson (2000), a

4. The data referring to the first sample is available on request to the authors.
5. For the inflation-targeting sample, the measured exchange-rate volatility is similar.

Figure 3 TRADE-OFF VOLATILITIES OF OUTPUT AND INFLATION (1997:1–2002:2)

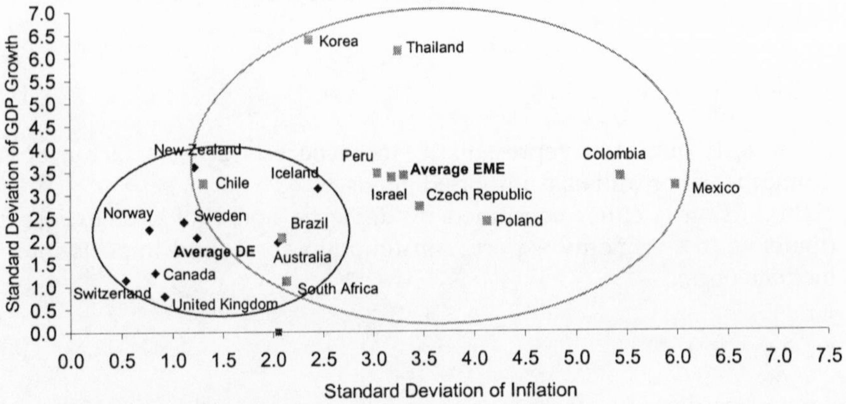

DE = developed economies.
EME = emerging market economies.

specification where imports are entered as intermediate goods captures better the features of the data. In comparison to models where imports enter as consumption goods, such as in Galí and Monacelli (2002), McCallum and Nelson's (2000) model generates a lower and more delayed correlation between exchange-rate changes and the inflation rate, closer to that observed in the data. Furthermore, intermediate goods are the major items in imports. Table 3 records the share in imports of goods classified by use for five countries. On average, consumption goods represent only 21.3% of the total imports, whereas capital and intermediate goods shares are 29.5% and 46.2%, respectively. Because no imported consumption goods are included in the model, there is no distinction between domestic and consumer price index (CPI) inflation, which is different from Svensson (2000) and Galí and Monacelli (2002).

The model is derived from the optimization of infinitely lived households and firms. We present directly the log approximation of the variables around the nonstochastic flexible-price steady state. Lowercase variables represent log-deviations from their steady-state values.[6] We present here only the most important equations of the model.[7] The economy is

6. $x_t = \log(X_t) - \log(X_t^{SS})$, where X_t^{SS} is the steady-state value for X_t, and log is the natural logarithm. Because $\log(1 + r_t) \approx r_t$, the lowercase variables represent percentage deviations from the steady state.
7. The derivation of the model from the optimization of households and firms, and all the equations resulting from the log-linearization are available on request to the authors.

comprised of households, firms (owned by the households), and government. Firms produce differentiated consumption goods using a Cobb-Douglas production function:

$$y_t = a_t + \alpha n_t + (1 - \alpha) m_t \tag{1}$$

where y_t is output, a_t represents a stochastic productivity factor, n_t is (domestic) labor, and m_t is imported goods.

Production is either consumed by domestic households or exported (therefore, the economy exports consumption goods and imports intermediate ones):

$$y_t = s_c c_t + s_x x_t \tag{2}$$

where c_t is domestic consumption, x_t is exports, $s_c = (1 - X^{SS}/Y^{SS})$, and $s_x = X^{SS}/Y^{SS}$.

The aggregate demand equations are:

$$c_t = E_t c_{t+1} - \frac{1}{\gamma_c} (i_t - E_t \pi_{t+1}) + \varepsilon_{ct} \tag{3}$$

$$x_t = n q_t + y_t^* \tag{4}$$

where i_t is the nominal interest rate; E_t is the expectations operator; inflation is $\pi_t = p_t - p_{t-1}$; p_t is the price level; γ_c is the inverse of the intertemporal elasticity of substitution for consumption; ε_{ct} is a shock to preferences; η is the elasticity of substitution between domestic and foreign goods; q_t is the real exchange rate, defined as $q_t = s_t + p_t^* - p_t$; s_t is the nominal exchange rate, defined as the price in domestic currency of a unit of foreign currency; p_t^* is the foreign price level; and y_t^* is the output of the rest

Table 3   IMPORTS CLASSIFIED BY USE (2001)

Countries	Consumption	Capital	Intermediate (including fuel)	Total
Australia	30.2 %	21.3 %	48.5 %	100.0 %
Brazil	12.8 %	26.6 %	60.6 %	100.0 %
Chile	19.8 %	21.0 %	59.3 %	100.0 %
Mexico	19.8 %	57.7 %	22.5 %	100.0 %
New Zealand*	24 %	21 %	40 %	85 %
Simple Average	21.3 %	29.5 %	46.2 %	

*1999. Part of imports not classified by use.
Data source: Central banks and national institutes of statistics.

of the world. The asterisk (*) indicates a variable of the rest of the world. All variables of the rest of the world are treated as exogenous in the model.

The model has domestic and foreign bonds, both private. Domestic bonds are denominated in domestic currency and are held only by domestic residents. Foreign bonds are denominated in foreign currency, and their prices include a stochastic country risk premium. The derived uncovered interest rate parity condition (UIP) is presented below:

$$i_t - i_t^* = E_t s_{t+1} - s_t + \zeta_t \tag{5}$$

where i_t^* is the interest rate in the rest of the world, and ζ_t is the country risk premium.

Firms maximize the difference between expected marginal revenue and unit cost. There is price rigidity: only a fraction of the firms are allowed to adjust prices each period. The choice of the optimum price for the firm yields $\pi_t = \beta E_t \pi_{t+1} + \lambda v_t$, where β is a discount factor, and v_t is the real unit cost given by:[8]

$$v_t = \alpha w_t + (1 - \alpha) p_{Mt} - a_t - p_t \tag{6}$$

where w_t is wage, and p_{Mt} is the price of imports in domestic currency, defined as $p_{Mt} = s_t + p_{Mt}^*$ (p_{Mt}^* is the price of imports in foreign currency). Note that inflation is affected by the exchange rate via the price of intermediate goods.

Nevertheless, this formulation of the Phillips curve delivers some counterfactual results, as stressed in Galí and Gertler (1999) and Fuhrer (1997). It implies that current changes in inflation are negatively related to the lagged output gap; that is, a positive output gap would lead to a reduction in the inflation rate in the following period. In contrast, the empirical evidence is that a positive output gap is followed by an increase in the inflation rate over the cycle. Moreover this formulation implies that, with perfectly credible announcements, a disinflation is costless.

These empirical results have motivated some authors to work with a hybrid Phillips curve: besides the expected inflation term, the equation also contains a lagged term for inflation. In this paper, we do not have a special concern about the specific derivation for the persistence in

8. $\lambda = \dfrac{(1 - \theta)(1 - \beta\theta)}{\theta}$ where θ is the probability of the firm not adjusting its price in period t.

inflation.[9] As in Galí and Gertler (1999), one possibility is to consider that there is a fraction of backward-looking firms.[10]

In addition, we can also postulate a cost-push shock. This term could reflect changes in the markup resulting from movements in the price elasticity of demand over the cycle or in tax rates. It could also be used as a proxy for the case of change in relative prices across sectors.[11] The resulting aggregate supply equation is:

$$\pi_t = \gamma_f E_t \pi_{t+1} + \lambda v_t + \gamma_b \pi_{t-1} + \mu_t \tag{7}$$

where $\gamma_b + \gamma_f = 1$.

We assume that the shocks follow stationary univariate autoregressive processes of an order of 1.

The interest rate is the policy instrument. Monetary policy is given by a Taylor-type simple rule or by optimal simple rules. In the latter, the optimal coefficients are obtained by the minimization of the standard central bank's intertemporal loss function that penalizes deviations of the output gap ($\tilde{y}_t$) and inflation from their targets:

$$\frac{1}{2} E_t \left\{ \sum_{i=0}^{\infty} \beta^i \left[w_y \left(\tilde{y}_{t+i} \right)^2 + \left(\pi_{t+i} - \pi_{t+i}^T \right) \right] \right\} \tag{8}$$

where w_y is related negatively to the aversion to inflation variability,[12] π_t^T is the inflation target, and $\tilde{y}_t = y_t - \bar{y}_t$ ($\bar{y}_t$ is the potential output, defined as the output that would prevail in the case of full price flexibility). The

---

9. Fuhrer and Moore (1995) have generated inflation persistence assuming that agents care about relative wages over the life of the wage contract. Roberts (1997, 1998) has found some empirical evidence that expectations are less than perfectly rational: a fraction of the agents would have adaptive expectations or there would be a partial adjustment of expectations (these would adjust only gradually to the fully rational value). Galí and Gertler (1999) have found that the fraction of backward-looking firms is statistically significant, although not quantitatively important.

10. For simplification, we are assuming that λ is not affected by the presence of the backward-looking term.

11. For example, in the case of Brazil, there has been an important change in relative prices in the last years that is only partially related to the exchange rate and the movement of international prices.

12. In the simulations, we have considered different values for w_y. We are not concerned about the derivation of this parameter based on microfoundations. This objective function can be derived from a household utility function in the presence of price rigidity (Rotemberg, and Woodford, 1999; Woodford, 2003). Woodford (2003) has also derived the objective function in the case where prices are indexed to a lagged price index between the occasions on which they are reoptimized. The objective function includes a quasi-differenced inflation rate term rather than the inflation rate itself. We have used the usual objective function based on the following grounds: (1) the objective function is used only to get an idea of the optimal coefficients in the central bank's reaction function; (2) in practice, this objective function seems to be used more often by central banks.

interest rate is restricted to react to selected variables. We use the algorithm in Dennis (2002) to estimate the optimal simple rule.[13]

4. Explaining the Higher Volatility

The conduct of monetary policy in EMEs faces at least three major challenges: (1) building credibility; (2) reducing the level of inflation; and (3) dealing with fiscal, financial, and external dominance. The presence of low credibility, inflation levels greater than the long-term goal, and large shocks results in higher volatility of output, inflation, and the interest rate. Fiscal and financial dominance issues also have implications for these variables. In this section, we show how all these elements can help explain the stylized facts presented previously. The explanation for the different performance of EMEs relies on the presence of more fragile institutions and imperfect credibility, on the necessity of reducing inflation levels, and on the nature and magnitude of the shocks that hit these economies.

4.1 BUILDING CREDIBILITY AND REDUCING INFLATION RATE LEVELS

Institutions in emerging economies tend to be weaker than those in developed economies. Central banks are no exception. In this context, the adoption of inflation targeting represents an effort to enhance the credibility of the monetary authority as committed to price stability.

Nevertheless, building credibility takes time. During this transition period, the central bank's actions not only have to be consistent with the inflation-targeting framework, but they also have to take into account that private agents do not fully trust that the central bank will act accordingly. Private agents have concerns about the commitment of the central bank to the target itself and to its reaction to shocks. In the first case, given the history of low credibility, private agents assign some positive probability that the central bank will renege on its commitment to the targets. As a result, the expected inflation and consequently the actual inflation tend to be higher than with a perfectly credible monetary authority. Similarly, when the economy is hit by an inflationary shock, private agents do not trust completely that the central bank will react strongly. As a consequence, the central bank incurs a cost of trust building because it has to react to curb the inflationary pressures stemming from low credibility and has to prove that it is committed to the new regime. During some period, the volatility of the interest rate and output will be higher and, because the central bank also takes into account output costs, the inflation volatility also tends to be higher when compared to a situation of full credibility.

13. The explanation of the calibration of the model is available on request to the authors.

Figure 4 12-MONTH INFLATION RIGHT BEFORE IT ADOPTION

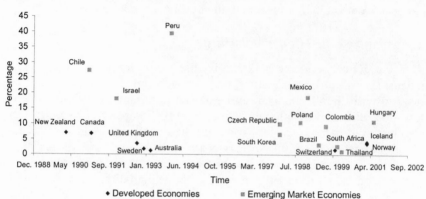

Imperfect credibility concerning the fulfillment of the targets becomes more important when we consider that the role of inflation targeting in emerging economies goes beyond assuring that inflation is kept at approximately its long-term level. It must first assure that inflation converges to low levels. In fact, emerging market countries have had to face much higher initial inflation rates than have developed countries. Table 1 showed the inflation around the moment of adoption of inflation targeting (right before and after), and the initial targets. When inflation targeting was adopted, the average inflation in the developed countries was 3.7%, whereas in the EMEs, it was 13.1%.[14] The values are also shown in Figure 4. Half of the developing economies had a two-digit inflation rate when implementing inflation targeting. In the case of Peru, Chile, Israel, and Mexico, the inflation rate was 39.5%, 27.3%, 18.0%, and 18.6%, respectively.

The differences are even clearer when we consider the first targets that were established (Figure 5). In developed economies, the maximum upper bound for the target was 6%, with an average of 2.8% for the central target. For developing economies, however, the highest upper bound reached 20%, and the average was 10.3%.

Because inflation was higher than the long-term goal, the targets were decreasing in time. Figure 6 shows the evolution of the central target average for both country groups. They are relatively stable for developed economies, and they are decreasing for EMEs.

If inflation targeting is adopted in an economy with an inflation rate significantly higher than the long-term goal, the central bank has to con-

---

14. The low inflation rate in Brazil that prevailed prior to the adoption of inflation targeting was partly a result of an overvalued exchange rate.

duct an active policy to bring inflation down that leads to output costs. The reduction in inflation faces two obstacles, which result in costly disinflation and higher volatility of inflation and output: (1) the already mentioned imperfect credibility, and (2) the presence of some degree of inflation persistence, resulting from some backward-looking behavior in price setting. The presence of backward-looking behavior may be due to factors such as indexed wage contracts, and adaptive expectations. In particular, in Brazil, the adjustment of regulated prices such as electricity and telephone service follows a contractual rule that implies a high degree of persistence.

Figure 5 FIRST CENTRAL TARGET ADOPTED

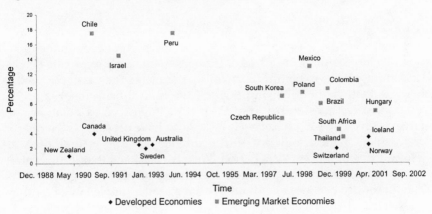

Figure 6 INFLATION TARGET AVERAGES—CENTRAL POINTS

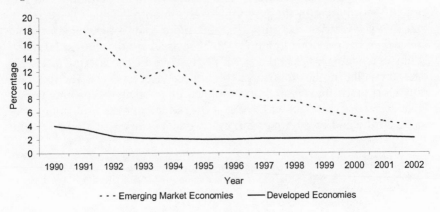

Decreasing targets are a source of possible nonfulfillment of targets because it is difficult to assess the current backward-looking behavior and the speed of future convergence of inflation expectations. The higher deviations from the targets in EMEs may then be related to the variability of shocks as well as to the fact that inflation targeting was typically adopted when inflation was significantly higher than the long-term goal.

To have some indication of the speed of inflation convergence and of the output costs involved, we have simulated the case of a reduction in the inflation targets with imperfect credibility. To focus on this issue, we have used the closed economy version of the model previously presented ($\alpha = 1$, $s_c = 1$). The result is a standard model. The aggregate supply curve without the backward-looking term can be written as:

$$\pi_t = \beta E_t \pi_{t+1} + \lambda^* \tilde{y}_t$$

where $\lambda^* \equiv \lambda(\gamma_c + \gamma_n)$. The central bank announces a reduction in the inflation rate target from π^{To} to π^{Tn} as of the current quarter, but private agents do not fully believe that this change is permanent. They assign a probability b_t that, at the following quarter, the central bank reneges on its announcement and returns to π^{To}. Therefore, the expected inflation rate target is given by $E_t \pi_{t+1}^T = b_t \pi^{To} + (1 - b_t)\pi^{Tn}$. We have considered the case of an optimal monetary policy under discretion.[15] The central bank is allowed to reoptimize every period. We have assumed that if the central bank maintains the new target, the probability of reneging on its announcement declines over time. We have used a simple law of motion: $b_{t+1} = \rho_b b_t$, where $0 \leq \rho_b < 1$.[16]

Figure 7 shows the impulse responses of the output gap and inflation to a reduction of 3 percentage points in the inflation target for the cases of imperfect and perfect credibility. If we compare the first announced targets to the inflation in the previous twelve months (Table 1), we verify that many countries had initial targets more than 3 percentage points lower than the previous inflation. We have assumed that the initial probability of reneging is 0.8, and $\rho_b = 0.8$. Because we are considering quarterly data, the latter implies that, at the end of the year, $b_t = 0.41$. The inflation rate refers to the four-quarter accumulated inflation above the new target. We assume that inflation was stable at the old target before the announcement. At the end of the first year, in the case of imperfect credibility, the

---

15. We have not shown the results under commitment because it is less reasonable to assume that private agents believe the central bank is committed and, at the same time, does not keep its commitment.

16. The derivation is available on request to the authors.

Figure 7 IMPERFECT CREDIBILITY: IMPULSE RESPONSES TO A 3
PERCENTAGE POINT INFLATION TARGET REDUCTION

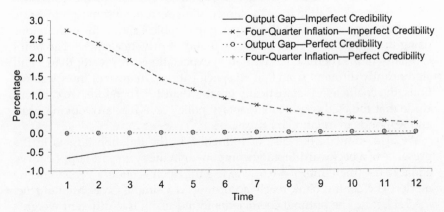

inflation rate is still 1.42 percentage points above the new target, and the
output gap presented a reduction of 0.49%, on average.[17] Therefore, even
assuming a relatively rapid reduction in the degree of imperfect credibility,
the inflation rate converges only gradually to the new target. In the case of
perfect credibility, inflation expectations converge automatically to the
new target. As a result, inflation also converges immediately to the new
target, and this movement does not require any output gap reduction.

Similar reasoning is applied when the economy is hit by an inflationary
shock. The possibility that the central bank will not be tough for enough
time increases inflation expectations, thus requiring a higher output
reduction. The result is a higher volatility of inflation, output, and the interest rate.

As stressed by Svensson (2002), the economy incurs higher output
variability at the beginning of the regime to gain credibility, but it benefits later from an improved trade-off with lower output and inflation
variability, and the central bank can then be a more flexible inflation
targeter. In the case of Brazil, the construction of credibility has been a
process that combines reactions to inflationary pressures and increased
transparency to the public. The Banco Central do Brasil has reacted to
inflation expectations in a way that is consistent with the inflation-targeting
framework. Minella, Freitas, Goldfajn, and Muinhos (2003)[18] have estimated

17. In this simulation, we are assuming that the relative output weight in the objective function is equal to 0.3. If we increase it to 1.0, the effect is significant on the output response
but low on the inflation path: the inflation rate is 1.45, and the output gap has a reduction of 0.15% on average.
18. That paper is an updated and shorter version of Minella, Freitas, Goldfajn, and Muinhos
(2002).

a reaction function for the BCB for the first three-and-a-half years of inflation targeting. It relates the interest rate to deviations of the 12-month
ahead expected inflation from the target, allowing also for some interest-rate
smoothing and reaction to the output gap.[19] Table 4 shows the estimations
using the inflation forecast of the BCB and of private agents.[20] The point
estimates of the coefficient on inflation expectations are greater than 1 and
significantly different from 0 in all specifications. In most of the specifications, the coefficient is statistically greater than 1.[21] Therefore, we can conclude that the BCB conducts monetary policy on a forward-looking basis
and responds to inflationary pressures.

We also simulate the case of reduction in the inflation targets in the
presence of a backward-looking component in the aggregate supply curve
equal to 0.4 (therefore, $\gamma_f = 0.6$). We use the open economy version of the
model. The central bank reacts according to a simple expectational rule:
$i_t = 1.5 \, E_t \pi_{t+1}$. The optimal coefficients found using two different weights
on the output gap in the objective function, $w_y = 0.3$ and $w_y = 1.0$, are 1.79
and 1.34, respectively.[22] As in the case of imperfect credibility, inflation
decreases slowly to the new target, and the optimal output gap is negative. With a 3 percentage point reduction in the inflation target, inflation
is 0.78 percentage point above the target at the fourth quarter, and the output gap reduction is 0.55% on average in the first year. In the case of a
purely forward-looking aggregate supply curve, inflation converges automatically to the new target.

Because the inflation-targeting regime is supposed to affect inflation
expectations, we can consider the possibility that the backward-looking
component in the price adjustment becomes less important as credibility
increases. The share of backward-looking firms could become smaller
and/or firms could give less consideration to past inflation when adjusting prices. Either situation would reduce the degree of persistence in

---

19. They have estimated the equation $i_t = \alpha_1 i_{t-1} + (1 - \alpha_1)(\alpha_0 + \alpha_2 (E_t \pi_{t+j} - \pi_{t+j}^*) + \alpha_3 y_{t-1})$, where
    i_t is the Selic rate decided by the monetary policy committee (Copom), $E_t \pi_{t+j}$ equals
    inflation expectations, and π_{t+j}^* is the inflation target, where j = 12, and y_t is the output
    gap.
20. Private agents' expectations are obtained from a survey that the Investors Relation
    Group (Gerin) of the BCB conducts among banks and non-financial companies.
    (Available at www.bcb.gov.br. Market Readout and Market Expectations Time Series of
    Investor Relations Section).
21. The point estimates vary, however, across specifications. Using private agents' expecta-
    tions (sample 2000:1–2002:12), the point estimates are around 2.1 to 2.3, whereas with
    BCB expectations (sample 1999:6–2002:12), they are 3.5 and 5.7. The p-values for the test
    that the coefficient is equal to 1 are 0.150, 0.101, 0.012, and 0.040 in specifications I, II, III,
    and IV, respectively.
22. Cecchetti and Ehrmann (1999) have found a value between 0.32 and 0.41 for inflation-
    targeting countries. Batini, Harrison, and Millard (2003) have used 1.0 (including also a
    term for the interest rate in the objective function).

Table 4   ESTIMATION OF REACTION FUNCTION OF THE BANCO
CENTRAL DO BRASIL: DEPENDENT VARIABLE: TARGET FOR THE
NOMINAL SELIC INTEREST RATE (MONTHLY DATA)[1]

Regressors	Using central bank inflation expectations (1999:7–2002:12)		Using market inflation expectations (2000:1–2002:12)	
	I	II	III	IV
Constant	1.65	3.06*	4.58***	5.38**
	(1.08)	(1.59)	(1.52)	(2.07)
Interest rate (t–1)	0.90***	0.82***	0.71***	0.67***
	(0.06)	(0.09)	(0.09)	(0.12)
Inflation expectations	5.70*	3.54**	2.32***	2.09***
(deviations from	(3.20)	(1.51)	(0.53)	(0.53)
the target)				
Output gap(t–1)		–0.36*		–0.10
		(0.21)		(0.15)
R^2	0.9129	0.9160	0.9205	0.9214
Adjusted R^2	0.9084	0.9094	0.9157	0.9140
LM test for autocorrelation of residuals (p-values)				
1 lag	0.7853	0.7210	0.6586	0.6411
4 lags	0.6831	0.5298	0.5362	0.3991

1. Standard error in parentheses. *, ** and *** indicate the coefficient is significant at the 10%, 5%, and 1% levels, respectively.
Source: Minella, Freitas, Goldfajn, and Muinhos (2003).

inflation. Minella, Freitas, Goldfajn, and Muinhos (2003) have estimated a simple aggregate supply curve for the low inflation period in Brazil to assess if the inflation-targeting regime was accompanied by some structural change.[23] They regress inflation rate on its own lags, the unemployment rate (lagged one period), and the exchange-rate change in 12 months (lagged one period).

Table 5 records the results when including only one lag for inflation and when including two. The regression also includes dummy variables that multiply the constant and lagged inflation for the inflation-targeting period,[24] and a dummy that assumes the value of 1 for the last three months of 2002. Without adding this last dummy, the residuals in both specifications present serial correlation. Actually, the end of 2002 is a peculiar period, one that does not fit a simple Phillips curve. The authors find that the backward-looking term has decreased. The point estimate of the autoregressive coefficient decreases from 0.56 to 0.10 in

23. The procedure is similar to the one in Kuttner and Posen (1999).
24. Dummies for the inflation-targeting period that multiply unemployment and the exchange rate do not enter significantly; therefore, they were excluded from the estimation.

Table 5   ESTIMATION OF AGGREGATE SUPPLY CURVE: DEPENDENT
VARIABLE: MONTHLY INFLATION RATE (1995:08–2002:12)[1]

Regressors	I	II
Constant	0.65*	0.70*
	(0.36)	(0.36)
Dummy constant[†]	0.34***	0.51***
	(0.12)	(0.14)
Inflation rate (t–1)	0.56***	0.62***
	(0.11)	(0.15)
Inflation rate (t–2)		–0.09
		(0.14)
Dummy inflation rate (t–1)[†]	–0.46***	–0.43*
	(0.17)	(0.19)
Dummy inflation rate (t–2)[†]		–0.35*
		(0.20)
Unemployment (t–1)	–0.08	–0.09*
	(0.05)	(0.05)
Exchange rate change (t–1) (12-month average)	0.08*	0.09**
	(0.04)	(0.04)
Dummy 2002Q4[‡]	1.42***	1.47***
	(0.26)	(0.25)
R^2	0.5593	0.6022
Adjusted R^2	0.5271	0.5624
LM test for autocorrelation of residuals (p-values)		
1 lag	0.6646	0.7022
4 lags	0.2218	0.3599

1. Standard error in parentheses. *, ** and *** indicate the coefficient is significant at the 10%, 5%, and 1% level, respectively. Since exchange rate change refers to the 12-month change, the sample starts in 1995:08 to avoid the inclusion of data of the period before the stabilization.
†Dummy has value 1 in the inflation-targeting period (1999:06–2002:12), and 0 otherwise. It multiplies the associated variable.
‡Dummy has value 1 in 2002:10–2002:12, and 0 otherwise.
Source: Minella, Freitas, Goldfajn, and Muinhos (2003).

the inflation-targeting period when compared to the previous period of low inflation (specification I).[25]

4.2 DOMINANCE ISSUES: FISCAL, FINANCIAL, AND EXTERNAL

We deal here with three elements that seem to be potential features of EMEs: weak fiscal regimes, the risks associated with poorly regulated financial systems, and large external shocks. Each of these problems can lead to a form of dominance: fiscal, financial, or external. In the case of fiscal and financial dominance, the problems that arise on the monetary policy front are quite

25. This result is in line with the findings in Kuttner and Posen (2001). Using a broad dataset of 191 monetary frameworks from 41 countries, they found that inflation targeting reduces inflation persistence.

similar: the fear that one or both regimes will break down increases the probability that the government will inflate in the future, and therefore increases expected inflation. This in turn increases the challenge of establishing a solid monetary anchor. The external dominance refers to the vulnerability to external shocks, which results in higher macroeconomic volatility.

4.2.1 *Fiscal Dominance* The success of inflation targeting or any other monetary regime requires the absence of fiscal dominance. Therefore, implementation of inflation targeting must be accompanied by a strong fiscal regime. But even with that, in the case of past weaknesses, it takes time for government to gain the full confidence of private agents. This fear of fiscal dominance affects inflation expectations, requiring a tighter monetary policy, which in turn negatively affects the fiscal balance.

The challenge, therefore, is to build fiscal and monetary regimes that reinforce one another. The evidence we have thus far on this issue is promising, but it may be too early to celebrate. Schaechter, Stone, and Zelmer (2000) show that the fiscal imbalance at the time inflation targeting was adopted was lower in developing countries.

4.2.2 *Financial Dominance* A problem for the conduct of monetary policy can arise when there is fear that a tightening may lead to a financial crisis. This may come as a consequence of a weak and/or overleveraged financial system and may bring about the expectation that monetary policy will not be conducted with the goal of defending the nominal anchor of the economy. This problem can be characterized as a form of dominance, which we can name financial dominance. For example, Goldfajn and Gupta (2003) have found that, in the aftermath of currency crises, an economy that faces a banking crisis (1) has a lower probability of choosing a tight policy, and (2) when tight monetary policy is adopted, the probability of a successful recovery is lower.[26]

Banking sector weaknesses, and financial vulnerabilities in general, played a key role in the Asian crisis of 1997. This type of fragility may also be an issue when the financial system exhibits a significant presence of government-owned banks, either because these banks may themselves be weak or because the government may use its banks unwisely. Just as in the case of fiscal dominance, it is necessary to work toward a strong fiscal regime; in the case of financial dominance, care must be taken to make sure the regulation and supervision of the financial system is sound and permanent.

26. They have used a dataset of currency crises in 80 countries for the period 1980–1998.

Another issue is the predominance of short-term financial contracts and lower financial depth in EMEs, which tend to weaken the monetary policy transmission mechanisms.[27] According to Schaechter, Stone, and Zelmer (2000), the ratio of liquid liabilities to GDP was on average 51.0% in EMEs and 72.0% in developed countries in 1997. The ratio of private credit to GDP was 63.9% and 81.0%, respectively. As Taylor (2000) stresses, without longer-term markets, short-term interest rates will have to move more quickly. Therefore, we tend to observe higher interest-rate volatility.

4.2.3 *External Dominance: Sudden Stops*   Another possible explanation for the volatility shown in Section 2 is the existence of larger shocks in EMEs. External shocks tend to play a more important role in EMEs than they do in developed countries. EMEs are subject to sudden stops in capital inflows. These shocks significantly affect the exchange rate, and consequently the inflation rate, leading to higher interest rates to curb the inflationary pressures. As a result, these economies tend to present a higher volatility of interest rates and exchange rates.

Of course, sudden stops themselves may reflect weaker fundamentals, which translate into lower credit ratings, among other problems. On the other hand, the presence of large and frequent external shocks generates greater instability in the economy and may jeopardize the fulfillment of the targets, which in turn may negatively affect the credibility of the regime. This may be seen as a form of external dominance. It must be addressed through the strengthening of the fundamentals of the economy, such as, in the case of inflation targeting, a fairly clean exchange-rate float (by that, we mean the absence of an exchange-rate target) and in general a sufficient degree of openness and flexibility.

The data presented in Table 2 confirmed the higher volatility of the interest rate in EMEs. For the exchange rate, the data is less clear but points to a higher volatility. The coefficient of variation (the ratio of the standard deviation to the average) is 0.15 in EMEs and 0.11 in developed economies. There are some differences, however, within the group of developing economies. Brazil, Chile, Hungary, Peru, and South Africa presented significantly greater exchange-rate volatility. The average of the coefficient of variation of the five countries is 0.22.

To try to measure the importance of external shocks, we have run vector autoregression (VAR) estimations for selected countries. We have used monthly and quarterly data of four variables: industrial production (or GDP), the consumer price index, the interest rate, and the exchange rate.

---

27. Actually, there are two opposite effects in the case of short-term contracts: the wealth effect of change in the interest rates is lower, but changes in the interest rates affect the cost of outstanding debt more quickly.

We have used a Cholesky decomposition with the order mentioned. We have considered two specifications: (1) all variables in log level, and (2) the price and exchange rate in first log-difference. We have estimated for three periods: a large period (which varies across countries but in general starts in the 1980s), the period before the adoption of inflation targeting, and the inflation-targeting period. (All of them end in mid-2002.) Table 6 records the values for the variance error decomposition of the interest rate and price level (or inflation rate), considering a 12-month or 4-quarter horizon, for the inflation-targeting period. In particular, we show the percentage of the forecast error of the interest rate and prices (or inflation) that is explained by shocks to the exchange rate. In Brazil and South Africa, shocks to the exchange rate explain a significant part of the forecast error of interest rate and prices. In Brazil, they explain 49% of the interest rate forecast errors and 18% of the price forecast error (this figure is not statistically significant though). South Korea has similar results using monthly data, mainly for the interest rate. On the other hand, for the developed economies and for Mexico, the estimations indicate that the exchange rate does not play an important role.

Exchange-rate fluctuations do not always reflect the pressure of the external shocks because of policy responses, which include interest-rate changes and direct intervention in the exchange-rate market. Some emerging markets opt not to allow the exchange rate to reflect the extent of the external shocks. Some of the arguments are related to fear of floating (Calvo and Reinhart, 2002).[28] In addition to inflationary pressures, significant exchange-rate fluctuations have other implications for the economy, such as uncertainty concerning prices and the value of dollar-denominated liabilities and assets. Huge depreciations of the domestic currency may affect the financial solvency of firms and financial institutions. In this case, the central bank may have additional goals in its objective function. According to Amato and Gerlach (2002), several reasons may make it appropriate for EMEs to give importance to the exchange rate beyond that related to its inflationary effects: (1) with less developed foreign exchange markets, large shocks or capital flows cause significant volatility in the exchange rate if they are neglected by policies; (2) in economies with a poor history of monetary stability, the exchange rate tends to be a focal point for inflationary expectations; (3) exchange-rate fluctuations may have a large impact on the relative profitability of firms across sectors; and (4) foreign currency borrowing may be significant.

---

28. Reinhart and Rogoff (2002) have developed a system of reclassifying historical exchange-rate regimes. They have found that regimes that were officially classified as floating in reality use a form of de facto peg.

Therefore, it is worth examining the spread over treasuries of the foreign currency denominated debt of the country as another indicator of external shocks. Table 7 shows the average and volatility of the spread of the emerging market bond index plus (EMBI+) over the U.S. Treasury for Brazil, Colombia, Mexico, Peru, Poland, and South Korea. Except for Poland, the standard deviation is always higher than 118 basis points. In the case of Brazil, it reaches 377 basis points in the inflation-targeting period.

Table 6   VARIANCE ERROR DECOMPOSITION AFTER ADOPTION OF INFLATION TARGETING (12-MONTH OR 4-QUARTER HORIZON) (PERCENTAGE); VAR WITH FOUR VARIABLES: INDUSTRIAL PRODUCTION (GDP), CPI, INTEREST RATE, AND EXCHANGE RATE

	Estimation in levels for price and exchange rate		Estimation in first difference for price and exchange rate	
	Shocks to the exchange rate explaining the forecast error for the interest rate	Shocks to the exchange rate explaining the forecast error for inflation	Shocks to the exchange rate explaining the forecast error for the interest rate	Shocks to the exchange rate explaining the forecast error for inflation
Monthly Data[†]				
Developed Economies				
Canada	1	0	1	1
Sweden	2	8	4	6
United Kingdom	0	17	10	5
Emerging Market Economies				
Brazil	49*	18	8	29*
Mexico	2	1	0	0
South Africa	36*	25*	36*	25
South Korea	26*	7	32	9
Quarterly Data[‡]				
Developed Economies				
Australia	12	3	1	11
Canada	0	1	2	2
New Zealand	11	3	4	3
Sweden	4	1	4	10
United Kingdom	0	0	1	1
Emerging Market Economies				
Brazil	57*	35	10	20
Mexico	1	0	1	12
South Korea	3	3	5	8

*Indicates that the value is significant at the 5% level.
[†]New Zealand and Australia do not have cpi and industrial production on a monthly basis.
[‡]The sample for South Africa is too short.

As a result of these external pressures, we tend to observe a higher volatility of output, interest rates, and the exchange rate, and the possibility of nonfulfillment of targets tends to be higher. In the case of Brazil, the significant depreciation of the domestic currency was the main factor behind the nonfulfillment of the inflation targets in 2001 and 2002. The nominal exchange rate in Brazil accumulated an increase of 84.7% during 2001 and 2002 (a depreciation of the domestic currency of 45.9%), representing a real depreciation of 44.6%.

We use the model to simulate the effects of a shock to the real exchange rate of 45%, but instead of using the UIP condition, we use an autoregressive process for the real exchange rate (with an autoregressive coefficient equal to 0.5). As before, the central bank reacts according to a simple expectational rule: $i_t = 1.5E_t \pi_{t+1}$, and the coefficient on lagged inflation is 0.4.

Figure 8 shows the impulse responses. At the end of the fourth quarter, the four-quarter accumulated inflation reaches 5.16%, and the output gap reduction is on average 6.80% in the first year. Therefore, even with a significant output gap reduction, any existing inflation target would be breached. If we consider the inflation target for Brazil in 2002 of 4%, then with this simulation, the inflation rate would reach 9.7%, distant even from the upper bound of 6.5%.

The existence of this possibility of breaching the targets due to large shocks leads us to analyze important issues in the design of inflation targeting in emerging markets. The next section explores how to deal with higher volatility in an inflation-targeting regime.

Table 7   EMBI+ (BASED ON MONTHLY AVERAGE)

Country	1997:01–2002:12*			After IT adoption until 2002:12[†]		
	Average	Standard deviation	Coefficient of variation (s.d./ average)	Average	Standard Deviation	Coefficient of variation (s.d./ average)
Brazil	879.35	389.07	0.44	987.14	377.82	0.38
Colombia	651.18	118.48	0.18	648.04	123.83	0.19
Mexico	443.40	150.03	0.34	408.37	130.19	0.32
Peru	601.75	120.64	0.20	601.75	120.64	0.20
Poland	233.03	38.17	0.16	232.65	35.88	0.15
South Korea	236.37	145.39	0.62	236.37	145.39	0.62

*Colombia: 1999:05–2002:12. Peru: 1998:01–2002:12. Poland: 1998:01–2002:12. South Korea: 1998: 05–2002:12. For Brazil and Mexico, the data for 1997 refers to EMBI.
[†]South Korea: 1998:05–2002:12.

5. How to Deal with Higher Volatility?

The central element of the inflation-targeting regime is the public announcement of a numerical target for inflation. As Mishkin (2002) stresses, however, inflation targeting comprises much more than that. It also involves (1) an institutional commitment to price stability as the primary goal of monetary policy, to which other goals are subordinated; (2) the use of many variables for the instrument policy decision; (3) increased transparency of monetary policy strategy; and (4) an increased accountability of the central bank.

The issues presented in the previous section imply important challenges for monetary policy. The key aspect is how to build credibility in the conduct of monetary policy and in the inflation-targeting regime itself, and at the same time remain flexible enough to avoid unnecessary output costs that could lead to a perception that the regime is too costly. Communication and transparency become crucial.

One of the most appealing features of inflation targeting is the flexibility it allows monetary policy when the economy is confronted with shocks. For instance, in dealing with a supply shock, the professional consensus among academic economists and central bankers is that a central bank should accommodate the direct price-level impact of the shock while calibrating monetary policy to avoid further rounds of price increases. In practice, however, this approach may come at a cost. The central bank's commitment to low inflation may be questioned if the nature of the shock and the appropriateness of the policy response are not clear

Figure 8 IMPULSE RESPONSES TO A 45 PERCENTAGE POINT REAL EXCHANGE RATE SHOCK

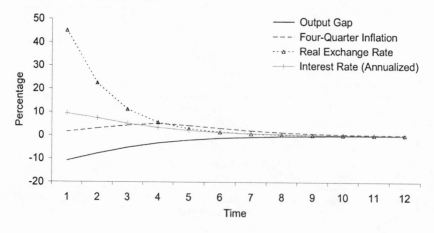

to most observers. The solution to this conundrum is to provide enough information to the public to clarify that the policy response is the right answer to a well-understood problem.

In general, the optimal response depends on the nature of the shock, on several economic parameters and elasticities, and on the preferences of society relative to the inflation versus output gap volatility trade-off. At a basic level, it is crucial therefore that the central bank make an effort to identify the size and nature of the shocks, focusing in particular on whether one is dealing with supply or demand shocks, temporary or permanent shocks, and the size and inflationary impact of the shocks. Once the shocks are identified, the central bank can choose a monetary policy response that will deliver the chosen feasible pair of inflation and output gap paths.

Inflation-targeting central banks have developed several tools to deal with these issues. They involve the inflation-targeting design, transparency, adjusted targets, and a change in the IMF conditionality.

5.1 TARGET BANDS, HORIZONS, AND PERSISTENCE OF SHOCKS

The possibility that large shocks may cause target breaches leads to an important feature in the design of the inflation-targeting regime: the size of the band around the central point of the target. Tighter bands tend to signal a preference for lower inflation volatility relative to lower output volatility. The band is typically seen as a barrier not to be broken.

In a world of perfect information, however, where all shocks are precisely identified, there is no role for bands around the inflation target. Deviations from the point target would occur as an optimal response to shocks, given the parameters of the economy and the inflation aversion of society. An optimal response to a very large shock may demand large deviations from the central point of the target, sometimes beyond the upper bound of the target. The same holds for the horizon over which inflation is allowed to deviate from the target when the economy is hit by shocks. This horizon should also be determined according to the type, size, and persistence of the shock as well as the parameters mentioned above.

So why do countries opt to include target bands? While some countries may treat the band limit as a strict barrier not to be broken, in our view the bands should be treated mainly as a communications device. The bands should be considered mainly as checkpoints, with the central bank explaining clearly the reasons for the nonfulfillment of the targets. This discussion is not easily translated, however, into operational guidelines that can be implemented by the central bank. As a result, it is necessary that the assumptions underlying the decisionmaking process of the central bank be communicated clearly. This approach means being explicit about a fairly precise path of inflation on the way back to the targeted level to avoid losing the confidence of economic agents. Transparency therefore plays the key role of imposing enough discipline on the central bank to avoid the temptations depicted in the time-consistency literature.[29]

In practice, the size of the bands varies across countries: 1 percentage point in Australia and Israel; 3 percentage points in South Africa; 3.5 in Iceland; and 4 in Brazil for 2002, and 5 for 2003 and 2004. What should be the size of the bands? One possibility would be to keep them large enough to allow the inflation rate within the bands in most of the circumstances if monetary policy is conducted efficiently. Given some variability of shocks in the economy, inflation should be inside the bands in most, say, 90%, of the cases. Using the model, and assuming some variance for the shocks, we obtain the standard deviation of inflation (given some optimal rule). If we assume that the random shocks are normally distributed, we would find a band size corresponding to 1.65 standard deviations of inflation.

The recurrent presence of larger shocks may also recommend higher central targets. As shown in Figure 6, the difference between the targets of EMEs and developed countries has decreased, but it is still positive. In 2002, the central point target for EMEs was 3.7%, whereas for developed countries it was 2.2%. The higher target reflects not only higher past inflation but also the greater vulnerability to external shocks. One possible reason is the asymmetric effects of supply shocks. Given greater downward price rigidity, deflationary shocks tend to have a lower effect in inflation than do inflationary shocks. As a consequence, with higher shocks, this bias tends to be higher.

The issue of the magnitude of the response to shocks leads us also to the discussion of the horizon to be used in the inflation-targeting framework. As emphasized by Svensson (2002), in practice, flexible inflation targeting (where some weight is given to output stabilization) means aiming to achieve the inflation target at a somewhat longer horizon. Because EMEs are more subject to larger shocks, their target horizon should naturally be longer. A danger here, of course, is that if the central bank is still building credibility, longer horizons could be interpreted as lenience, thus affecting the central bank's reputation.

In practice, there is no magic number for the horizon that a central bank should use to guide its reaction to supply shocks. It should be long

---

29. It seems these days that the important lesson of the time-consistency literature has reached most central banks. In fact, one finds a substantial number of central bankers around the world who seem to act like the inflation-averse central bankers in Rogoff (1985).

enough to allow the workings of the monetary policy transmission mechanisms and some degree of smoothing of the effects of the shock. On the other hand, it should be short enough to neutralize part of its inflationary effect and allow convergence of inflation expectations to the target. At any rate, it is crucial that the central bank's response be clearly explained to avoid reputational risk. Section 5.3 presents the procedure adopted by the BCB in dealing with a series of large shocks during the years 2001 and 2002.

5.2 MONETARY POLICY COMMITTEES, MEETING MINUTES, AND AN INFLATION REPORT

To stress the importance of the existence of a monetary policy committee (MPC) may sound unnecessary to most observers in more advanced economies, but it is not a trivial matter in the EMEs. Until one such committee was created in Brazil, for example, monetary policy decisions were made on an ad-hoc basis, typically at the end of a board meeting, at the end of the day, when everyone was already quite exhausted, and often without the benefit of proper preparation and analysis. An MPC that meets regularly, on a monthly basis, has created a proper environment for what, after all, is the key role of a central bank: to run monetary policy. The MPC meetings have become a ritual that provides those responsible for setting policy with a well-informed decisionmaking environment. It moves board members away from their otherwise hectic day-to-day schedules of meetings and phone calls and allows them to focus on the task at hand.

A crucial aspect of inflation targeting is the ability to enhance the credibility of the policymaking process and, as a result, to achieve the desired goals with minimum costs. The timely publication of the detailed minutes of MPC meetings is a key ingredient for an effective communications strategy. In emerging economies, where credibility is typically lower than one would like, the benefits of publishing this information can be substantial.

In addition to monthly meeting minutes, most inflation-targeting central banks also publish a quarterly inflation report where their views on economic prospects and, in particular, on inflation trends are presented in detail.[30] Again, for EMEs, these reports play a key role, serving the purpose of minimizing uncertainty about the central bank's analysis and goals. Inflation reports are appropriate vehicles for the central bank to present its views on complex issues such as the degree of exchange-rate

---

30. For an assessment of inflation reports by inflation-targeting central banks, see Fracasso, Genberg, and Wyplosz (2003).

pass-through, the degree of inflationary persistence, the workings of the transmission mechanism, and so on.

5.3 SHOCKS AND ADJUSTED TARGETS

The recent experience of Brazil with inflation targeting during turbulent times serves to illustrate the practical application of the general guidelines and principles discussed above. This section summarizes the methodology currently used in Brazil. It calculates the inflationary impact of current supply shocks as well as the secondary impact of past shocks (due to inertia in the inflation process). The idea is simply to accommodate the direct impact of current shocks and to choose a horizon to weed out the secondary impact of past shocks.

When facing shocks, the BCB initially considers the nature and persistence of the shock. Then it builds different inflation and output trajectories associated with different interest-rate paths. Based on its aversion to inflation variability, it chooses the optimal path for output and inflation. Banco Central do Brasil (2003) has published this path and also the outcome of different paths. This is in line with Svensson's (2002) recommendations.[31]

If shocks are large and/or persistent, however, their inflationary effects may last one year or more. The optimal inflation path may imply a 12-month ahead inflation superior to the previous annual target. Therefore, in this situation, because the BCB would not be targeting the previous inflation target, it uses an adjusted target. More specifically, the target is adjusted to take into account primary effects of change in relative prices and of past inertia that will be accommodated. The new target is publicly announced. Although there is a credibility loss stemming from the target change itself, the gains in terms of transparency and communication are more significant. Private agents know the target pursued by the BCB. Keeping the old target would affect the credibility of the BCB because it could be considered unattainable. In the concept of the adjusted target, the primary effect of the shock to regulated-price inflation, and the inflation inertia inherited from the previous year to be accommodated in the current year, are added to the target previously set by the government. Facing cost shocks, such as the increase of regulated prices above the inflation of the other prices of the economy, monetary policy should be calibrated to accommodate the direct impact of shocks on the price level but to fight their secondary effects. Furthermore, because the BCB also takes into account output costs, the inertial impacts of the previous year's inflation should not necessarily be fought completely.

31. Svensson's (2002) recommendations also involve publishing the corresponding instrument-rate plan.

Indeed, significant shocks, such as increases in the price of regulated utilities and the exchange rate, have been one of the main challenges faced by the BCB. Since the implementation of the Real Plan in July 1994, regulated-price inflation has been well above the market-price inflation for various reasons. Since the start of the inflation-targeting period, the ratio of regulated prices to market prices rose 31.4% (1999:7–2003:2). As long as there is some downward rigidity in prices, changes in relative prices are usually translated into higher inflation. If these increases are treated as a supply shock, monetary policy should be oriented toward eliminating only their secondary impact on inflation while preserving the initial realignment of relative prices. Therefore, the efforts of the BCB to quantify the first-order inflationary impact of the regulated-price inflation have become particularly important because they help to implement monetary policy in a flexible manner, without losing sight of the larger objective of achieving the inflation targets.

The first-order inflationary impact of the shock to regulated items is defined as the variation in regulated prices exceeding the target for the inflation rate, weighted by the share of regulated prices in the IPCA (consumer price index) and excluding the effects of the inflation inertia from the previous year and of variations in the exchange rate:

$$ShA = (\pi_{adm} - \pi^*) * \omega_{adm} - (IA + CaA) \tag{9}$$

where ShA = first-order inflationary impact of regulated prices

π_{adm} = inflation of regulated prices

π^* = target for the inflation

ω_{adm} = weight of regulated prices in the IPCA

IA = effect of inertia in the previous year on the evolution of regulated prices

CaA = effect of the exchange-rate variation on the evolution of regulated prices

The effect of inflation inertia is excluded because inflation propagation mechanisms should be neutralized by the monetary policy over a period deemed to be appropriate (again, based on inflation aversion and other parameters). The exchange-rate variation is excluded because it is affected by monetary policy and could reflect demand shocks. If the effect of exchange-rate changes were automatically included, monetary policy would be validating any inflationary pressure coming from the exchange rate (including demand pressures). Therefore, in defining the shock to regulated prices, only the component of relative price change that is predetermined or backward-looking, and therefore cannot be affected by monetary policy in the short run, is preserved as a first-order supply shock.

Table 8   ADJUSTED TARGETS FOR 2003 AND 2004

Itemization	2003	2004
(a) Target for inflation set by the government	4.0	3.75
(b) Regulated-price shocks[1]	1.7	1.1
(c) Inertia not to be fought in the current year[2]	2.8	0.6
Inherited inertia from the previous year (total)	4.2	1.0
of regulated prices	1.4	0.4
of market prices	2.8	0.6
(d) Adjusted targets = (a) + (b) + (c)	8.5	5.5

1. For the calculation of the shock, the effect of inertia and the exchange rate on regulated-price inflation is deducted.
2. The inertia not to be fought in the current year corresponds to ⅔ of the inertia inherited from the previous year. Source: Banco Central do Brasil (2003).

Table 8 shows how this methodology was applied to Brazil for inflation in 2003 and 2004.[32] The target established by the government for 2003 is 4%. However, the regulated-price shocks are estimated at 1.7%. This value represents the expected contribution for the overall inflation of a change in relative prices that is not related to the inflation inertia from the previous year and to the exchange-rate change. Since these first-round effects should not be neutralized, they are added to the target of the BCB, leading to an adjusted target of 5.7%.

Furthermore, the BCB also takes into account the nature and persistence of the shocks and the output costs involved in the disinflationary process (the output weight in the objective function is greater than zero). In this case, the BCB decided to fight against one-third of the inertia inherited from the previous year. This inertia is estimated at 4.2%. Therefore, we have to add 2.8% to the target, leading to an adjusted target of 8.5%, which was publicly announced.

The decision to pursue an inflation trajectory based on these adjusted targets considers that monetary policy will be able to lead inflation to converge to the target tolerance interval in two years. We should stress, however, that two years is not a magic number. It depends on the size and type of the shock. Figure 9 draws the actual and expected path for inflation (Banco Central do Brasil, 2003). The trajectory is compatible with the (end-of-year) adjusted targets.

Other trajectories with steeper decreases of inflation imply an excessive loss of output. Simulations indicate that a trajectory of inflation that reaches 6.5% in 2003, the ceiling of the target tolerance interval, would

32. See Banco Central do Brasil (2003). For a more detailed explanation of the methodology, see Freitas, Minella, and Riella (2002).

imply a 1.6% drop in GDP. A trajectory that reaches the center of the target, 4%, in 2003, would imply an even larger decline in GDP (−7.3%).

One could argue that the decision to neutralize the shock in a longer time horizon, based on an evaluation of the size and persistence of the shock, may lead to time-consistency issues: too much accommodation in the short run could lead to a loss of credibility in the long run. In fact, it is essential that the whole procedure be explained publicly in detail so that the agents can judge effectively whether the size and persistence of the shock justify the decision taken by the central bank. It is the transparency, therefore, that imposes enough discipline to avoid time-consistency issues.

In the inflation-targeting design, a core inflation measure or the establishment of escape clauses has also been used or suggested as a way of dealing with shocks and volatilities. The main argument contrary to the use of core inflation is that it is less representative of the loss of the purchasing power of money at a given point in time. Agents are concerned about the whole basket of consumption. In the case of Brazil, exclusion of the regulated price items would leave out more than 30% of the representative consumption basket. In this sense, private agents may question a monetary policy that is not concerned about the overall consumer price index.

In general, there are two advantages to the use of the adjusted target procedure. First, the core inflation measure is not necessarily isolated from the effect of shocks. For example, the large depreciation shock of the Brazilian economy in 2002 led to a core inflation—calculated by the symmetric trimmed mean method—of 8.8%, way above the inflation target. Second, the construction of the adjusted target is directly based on the idea that monetary policy should neutralize second-order effects of supply shocks and accommodate the first-round effects, and on the fact that some

Figure 9 TWELVE-MONTH INFLATION

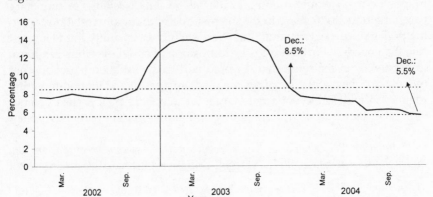

weight to output volatility should be assigned in the objective function. Therefore, the principles under which the monetary policy is conducted become more transparent.

In the case of escape clauses, the circumstances under which the central bank can justify the nonfulfillment of the targets are set in advance. It has more similarities with the adjusted target procedure than with the use of a core inflation measure because it does not exclude items from the inflation target but defines circumstances in which the breach of targets can be justified. The main advantages of the adjusted target procedure are the following: (1) it is a forward-looking procedure, (2) it defines clearly the new target to be pursued by the central bank, and (3) it explains how the new target is measured.

5.4 IMF PROGRAMS AND CONDITIONALITY

This section focuses on the IMF conditionality in the case of a country under an inflation-targeting regime.[33] We stress two issues: (1) the diminished role of net domestic assets (NDA) conditionality, and (2) how to insert inflation performance as a criterion for the assessment of a monetary policy stance.

5.4.1 NDA Conditionality Versus Inflation Targeting
Brazil was the first country under an inflation-targeting system to have an agreement with the IMF. From a theoretical point of view, the NDA conditionality, which is usually the one found in the agreements to evaluate the stance of monetary policy, is not adequate for an inflation-targeting regime because it harms transparency and can force the central bank to take unnecessary monetary policy actions.

Money demand is unstable, and the monetary aggregates seem to be poor predictors of inflation. Therefore, autonomous increases in the level of money demand would require, in the case of NDA ceilings or monetary base targeting, an increase in the interest rate without any inflation-targeting policy purpose. We would then observe higher volatility in the interest rate than needed. Furthermore, the imposition of an NDA ceiling can harm transparency in the sense that it would add to the inflation target another monetary policy goal. One of the main advantages of an inflation-targeting regime is the definition of a clear target for monetary policy. The existence of another target affects the credibility of the main goal of monetary policy.

5.4.2 Inflation Performance As a Criterion for the Assessment of a Monetary Policy Stance
In place of NDA targets, inflation performance emerges as a

33. See also Blejer, Leone, Rabanal, and Schwartz (2002), and Bogdanski, Freitas, Goldfajn, and Tombini (2001).

natural criterion for the assessment of a monetary policy stance. Of course, because inflation targets focus on inflation forecasts, assessing inflation outcomes has to account for the shocks that hit the economy. At least two issues have to be addressed in the case of an IMF program: the frequency of the assessments (reviews), and the criteria on which to base the targets.

IMF programs have quarterly reviews, whereas in an inflation-targeting framework, inflation performance is assessed at longer horizons. The use of annualized quarterly inflation figures as targets is not recommended because they are more volatile and subject to the strong influence of temporary shocks. Brazil has used a 12-month inflation as the monetary quarterly target in the technical memorandum of understanding with the IMF. It also includes inner and outer bands of 1.0 percentage point and 2.5 percentage points, respectively, both above and below the central targets. Figure 10 shows the targets agreed to by the IMF and the BCB in the second review of Brazil's performance in March 2003. The target for the 12-month inflation of the quarter following the agreement considers the inflation verified in the three previous quarters plus an estimate for the next quarter inflation. If an important shock hits the economy in the next quarter, however, inflation may breach the target.

The path of the targets with the IMF should be consistent with the annual targets of the inflation-targeting regime. This approach is in line with the forward-looking or pre-emptive nature of the inflation-targeting system. At the same time, it eliminates the problem of the effect of quarterly figures because the time horizon for the inflation target could be defined as four quarters. Eventual (predicted) pickups of inflation during the year should not alter the monetary policy committee decisions, provided inflation is expected to converge to the target and provided shocks in one year keep affecting inflation in the following year, but only through the direct channel, that is, via the autoregressive component of inflation.

Figure 10 INFLATION TARGETS (CENTRAL POINT AND UPPER AND LOWER BOUNDS) AGREED WITH THE IMF

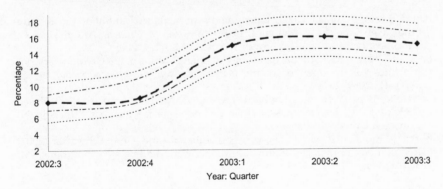

The main difficulty arises with the necessity of agreement between the IMF and the central bank concerning the model used and the associated risks, and reaching this agreement may also be time consuming. Therefore, it also involves the construction of credibility by the forecast-making process of the central bank.

In the agreements between Brazil and the IMF, the inflation forecasts made by the BCB have been used as an important criterion for the definition of the targets. However, the revisions are still made on a quarterly basis based on the actual inflation. The reasons for the nonfulfillment of targets have been explained thoroughly to the public and to the IMF.

6. Conclusion

Inflation targeting in EMEs has been relatively successful but has proven to be challenging. The volatility of output, inflation, the interest rate, and the exchange rate has been higher than in developed countries. Several issues have led these economies to face this less favorable trade-off. The process of building credibility, the necessity of reducing inflation levels, the dominance issues, and the larger shocks have all played an important role. To deal with this more volatile environment, we recommend (1) high levels of communication and transparency, (2) target bands treated mainly as communications devices, (3) a methodology for calculating the convergence path following a shock (adjusted targets), and (4) better IMF conditionality under inflation targeting.

REFERENCES

Amato, Jeffery D., and Stefan Gerlach. (2002). Inflation targeting in emerging market and transition economies: Lessons after a decade. *European Economic Review* 46:781–790.
Ball, Laurence, and Niamh Sheridan. (2003). Does inflation targeting matter? Cambridge, MA: National Bureau of Economic Research. NBER Working Paper No. 9577.
Banco Central do Brasil. (2003). Open-letter sent by Banco Central do Brasil's governor, Henrique de C. Meirelles, to the minister of Finance, Antonio Palocci Filho. Available at www.bcb.gov.br (accessed March 6, 2003).
Batini, Nicoletta, Richard Harrison, and Stephen P. Millard. (2003). Monetary policy rules for an open economy. *Journal of Economic Dynamics and Control* 27(11–12):2059–2094.
Bernanke, Ben S., Thomas Laubach, Frederic S. Mishkin, and Adam S. Posen. (1999). *Inflation Targeting: Lessons from the International Experience.* Princeton, NJ: Princeton University Press.
Blejer, Mario I., Alfredo M. Leone, Pau Rabanal, and Gerd Schwartz. (2002). Inflation targeting in the context of IMF-supported adjustment programs. IMF Staff Papers 49(3):313–338.

Bogdanski, Joel, Paulo S. de Freitas, Ilan Goldfajn, and Alexandre A. Tombini. (2001). Inflation targeting in Brazil: Shocks, backward-looking prices, and IMF conditionality. Central Bank of Brazil. Working Paper Series No. 24.

Calvo, Guillermo, and Carmen Reinhart. (2002). Fear of floating. *Quarterly Journal of Economics* 117(2):379–408.

Cecchetti, Stephen G., and Michael Ehrmann. (1999). Does inflation targeting increase output volatility? An international comparison of policymakers' preferences and outcomes. Cambridge, MA: National Bureau of Economic Research. NBER Working Paper No. 7426.

Corbo, Vittorio, Óscar Landerretche, and Klaus Schmidt-Hebbel. (2002). Does inflation targeting make a difference? *Inflation Targeting: Design, Performance, Challenges*, In Norman Loayza and Raimundo Soto (eds.). Santiago, Chile: Central Bank of Chile, 221–269.

Corbo, Vittorio, and Klaus Schmidt-Hebbel. (2001). Inflation targeting in Latin America. Central Bank of Chile. Working Paper No. 105.

Dennis, Richard. (2002). Solving for optimal simple rules in rational expectations models. Federal Reserve Bank of San Francisco. Mimeo, Sept. *Journal of Economic Dynamics & Control* (forthcoming).

Fracasso, Andrea, Hans Genberg, and Charles Wyplosz. (2003). How do central banks write? An evaluation of inflation reports by inflation-targeting central banks. Geneva Reports on the World Economy Special Report 2. Geneva, Switzerland: International Center for Monetary and Banking Studies (ICMB); London: Center for Economic Policy Research (CEPR).

Freitas, Paulo S. de, André Minella, and Gil Riella. (2002). Metodologia de Cálculo da Inércia Inflacionária e dos Efeitos dos Choques dos Preços Administrados. Notas Técnicas do Banco Central do Brasil No. 22. English translation in Banco Central do Brasil. (2002). *Inflation Report* 4(2):123–128.

Fuhrer, Jeffrey. (1997). The (un)importance of forward-looking behavior in price specifications. *Journal of Money, Credit, and Banking* 29(3):338–350.

Fuhrer, Jeffrey, and Georger Moore. (1995). Inflation persistence. *Quarterly Journal of Economics* 110(1):127–159.

Galí, Jordi, and Mark Gertler. (1999). Inflation dynamics: A structural econometric analysis. *Journal of Monetary Economics* 44:195–222.

Galí, Jordi, and Tommaso Monacelli. (2002). Monetary policy and exchange rate volatility in a small open economy. Cambridge, MA: National Bureau of Economic Research. NBER, Working Paper No. 8905.

Goldfajn, Ilan, and Poonam Gupta. (2003). Does monetary policy stabilize the exchange rate following a currency crisis? IMF Staff Papers 50(1):90–114.

Kuttner, Kenneth N., and Adam S. Posen. (1999). Does talk matter after all? Inflation targeting and central bank behavior. Federal Reserve Bank of New York. Staff Report No. 88.

Kuttner, Kenneth N., and Adam S. Posen. (2001). Beyond bipolar: A three-dimensional assessment of monetary frameworks. *International Journal of Finance and Economics* 6:369–387.

McCallum, Bennett T., and Edward Nelson. (2000). Monetary policy for an open economy: An alternative framework with optimizing agents and sticky prices. *Oxford Review of Economic Policy* 16(4):74–91.

Minella, André, Paulo S. de Freitas, Ilan Goldfajn, and Marcelo K. Muinhos. (2002). Inflation targeting in Brazil: Lessons and challenges. Central Bank of Brazil. Working Paper Series No. 53.

Minella, André, Paulo S. de Freitas, Ilan Goldfajn, and Marcelo K. Muinhos. (2003). Inflation targeting in Brazil: Constructing credibility under exchange rate volatility. *Journal of International Money and Finance* 22(7):1015–1040.

Mishkin, Frederic. (2000). Inflation targeting in emerging market countries. *American Economic Review* 90(2):105–109.

Mishkin, Frederic, and Klaus Schmidt-Hebbel. (2002). A decade of inflation targeting in the world: What do we know and what do we need to know? In Norman Loayza and Raimundo Soto (eds.). *Inflation Targeting: Design, Performance, Challenges*. Santiago, Chile: Central Bank of Chile, 171–219.

Reinhart, Carmen M., and Kenneth S. Rogoff. (2002). The modern history of exchange rate arrangements: A reinterpretation. Cambridge, MA: National Bureau of Economic Research. NBER Working Paper No. 8963. Quarterly Journal of Economics (forthcoming).

Roberts, John M. (1997). Is inflation sticky? *Journal of Monetary Economics* 39:173–196.

Roberts, John M. (1998). Inflation expectations and the transmission of monetary policy. Board of Governors of the Federal Reserve System. Finance and Economics Discussion Paper Series, no 98/43, October.

Rogoff, Kenneth. (1985). The optimal degree of commitment to an intermediate monetary target. *Quarterly Journal of Economics* 100(4):1169–1189.

Rotemberg, Julio J., and Michael Woodford. (1999). Interest-rate rules in an estimated sticky price model. In John B. Taylor (ed). *Monetary Policy Rules*. NBER Business Cycles Series, Vol. 31. Chicago and London: University of Chicago Press, pp. 57–119.

Schaechter, Andrea, Mark P. Stone, and Mark Zelmer. (2000). Adopting inflation targeting: Practical issues for emerging market countries. International Monetary Fund. Occasional Paper No. 202.

Schmidt-Hebbel, Klaus, and Alejandro Werner. (2002). Inflation targeting in Brazil, Chile, and Mexico: Performance, credibility and the exchange rate. Central Bank of Chile. Working Paper No. 171.

Svensson, Lars E. O. (2000). Open-economy inflation targeting. *Journal of International Economics* 50:155–183.

Svensson, Lars E. O. (2002). Monetary policy and real stabilization. Princeton University Mimeo. Paper presented at "Rethinking Stabilization Policy", a symposium sponsored by the Federal Reserve Bank of Kansas City and held at Jackson Hole, Wyoming, August 29–31, 2002.

Taylor, John B. (2000). Using monetary policy rules in emerging market economies. Stanford University. Mimeo.

Truman, Edwin M. (2003). *Inflation targeting in The World Economy*. Washington, D.C.: Institute for International Economics.

Woodford, Michael. (2003). *Interest and Prices: Foundations of a Theory of Monetary Policy*. Princeton NJ: Princeton University Press.

Comment

ROBERT E. HALL
Stanford University and NBER

A nation dealing with its central bank is a leading example of principal-agent mechanism design in an imperfectly understood environment. As this interesting paper shows, the problems are tougher in an emerging market economy such as Brazil, especially during the transition toward freer markets.

The central bank seeks to deliver low average inflation, but it will inevitably miss its inflation target at times—often for good reasons. The challenge is to design rules and incentives that achieve the general goal but do not impose unrealistic harsh penalties when an event stands in the way of the immediate achievement of the goal. Whiffs of inflation should be excused if they arise for good reasons rather than dereliction.

Flexible inflation targeting has a good reputation these days as the correct way for citizens to manage their central bank. Commitment to strict rules such as pegging the currency to another country's or a discretion-free Taylor rule has not fared well in practice, and modern analysis suggests that strict rules could never perform satisfactorily. These problems do not occur if instead, the central bank should be given an overall inflation target and be expected to achieve the target unless some extraordinary event occurs outside the bank's control; in which case, the bank should explain why it missed its target and on what path it will return to the target.

Brazil has operated under a wonderfully flexible inflation-targeting regime for several years, as we learn in this paper. The current overall target is 4% per year. Current inflation in Brazil is about 14%. Is this 1970s-style central-bank irresponsibility, or is the 10-percentage-point gap the result of an intelligent response to special circumstances?

Table 8 of the paper lays out a formula by which the citizens of Brazil can decide if 14% inflation is acceptable under the 4% target regime, shown in line (a). Line (b) gives the bank 1.7 percentage points of slack because of rising prices associated with liberalization—the removal of subsidies that kept some prices unrealistically low. Line (c) grants the bank 2.8 more percentage points of slack because of excess inflation in the previous year. Whatever excess is brought over by way of inertia from the previous year, only one-third is to be squeezed out this year. The rest will wait until future years. The logic is that erasing all inherited inflation immediately would depress real activity excessively.

Table 8 would permit 8.5% inflation, not the actual rate of 14%. The remaining 5.5 percentage points are explained in Figure 9. The target applies at the end of the year. Forecasted inflation from December 2002 to December 2003 is on target, at 8.5%, because the forecast calls for a rapid decline in inflation in the fall of 2003. By the time this volume is in print, the Brazilian public will know if the target was actually met.

The paper makes a compelling argument in favor of the flexibility of the formula underlying the Brazilian process for adjusting the target. Liberalization is creating highly desirable turbulence in the economy, which needs to be recognized in setting inflation targets. And the instability of exchange rates in emerging market economies also differentiates them from the advanced economies, such as Britain, which have much tighter inflation targets.

The paper is equally compelling about the desirability of adjusting the target to account for special forces rather than adjusting the price index. Public acceptance of the targeting procedure is surely weakened if the products whose prices rise most rapidly are removed from the official price index. I think this argument also extends to advanced economies—the use of core or stripped inflation measures had a lot to do with the loss of control of the price level in the United States in the 1970s, for example.

The complexity and sophistication underlying Table 8 are remarkable. In the 1980s, when I dabbled in monetary policy and inflation-targeting rules, I would not have dreamt of proposing something as academic as the procedure embodied in line (c) of the table.

It's fascinating that Brazil has so far outstripped the International Monetary Fund (IMF), which is living in the deep past by trying to enforce inflation targets through limits on the growth of liquid assets. Because successful disinflations are almost always accompanied by large increases in the holdings of liquid assets, the IMF policy is perverse. I'm delighted to learn that the Brazilian team was able to talk the IMF out of this type of discredited policy.

The Brazilian public faces a difficult task in deciding if the gap between target and actual current performance is the result of diligence in following the rules or is misconduct. The public may find the logic behind Table 8 and Figure 9 a contrivance to hide bad performance. On the one hand, the process will be less subject to manipulation if the rules for granting exceptions are well established in advance—the basic logic of committed monetary policy rules. On the other hand, painful experience has demonstrated the need to keep the process flexible so that the economy can deal with the blow that comes from an utterly unexpected direction.

The authors share the enthusiasm for transparency that pervades the modern literature on monetary policy. The public needs to know what the central bank is doing now, what it plans to do in the future, and what it expects the resulting inflation rate to be. I'm impressed by this logic. But I'm also impressed by the success of the U.S. Federal Reserve in achieving desirably low inflation under a regime with almost total opacity. It appears that a small amount of actual performance substitutes for a great deal of transparency.

Many commentators on monetary policy have pointed to the benefit of testing monetary policy against outside forecasts of inflation. Figure 9 illustrates the potential value of these forecasts. The bank's claim that it is entitled to the extra 5.5 percentage points of slack rests on the realism of the forecast. Certainly, in the United States, comparison to the consensus or to individual reputable inflation forecasts would prevent the Fed from taking an unrealistic position about future inflation should our economy find itself in the situation of the recent Brazilian economy, which suffered from simultaneous large shocks from currency depreciation and liberalization.

Comment

FREDERIC S. MISHKIN
Columbia University and NBER

The paper by Arminio Fraga, Ilan Goldfajn, and André Minella is a thoughtful and important paper on inflation targeting in emerging market economies. Not only does it add substantially to the literature on how to conduct monetary policy in these economies, but as I will argue below, it has important lessons for monetary policy in advanced economies.

Because I have so little to be critical about, my comments will focus on expanding some themes discussed in the paper. Specifically, first, I will examine why emerging market economies are so different from advanced economies and why this affects thinking about monetary policy. Then I will address several issues for inflation targeting in emerging market economies discussed in the paper: target bands, transparency and formality, response to shocks, and International Monetary Fund (IMF) conditionality.

1. Why Emerging Market Economies Are So Different from Advanced Economies

This paper, along with a recent paper I have written with Guillermo Calvo (Calvo and Mishkin, 2003), rightfully emphasizes that emerging market economies (EMEs) are fundamentally different from advanced economies, and this distinction is important in designing appropriate monetary policy regimes. EMEs have five fundamental institutional differences from advanced economies that are crucial to sound theory and policy advice:

1. Weak fiscal institutions (what the paper refers to as "fiscal dominance").
2. Weak financial institutions, including government prudential regulation and supervision (what the paper refers to as "financial dominance").

3. Low credibility of monetary institutions.
4. Liability dollarization.
5. Vulnerability to sudden stops of capital inflows (what the paper refers to as "external dominance").

Advanced countries are not immune to problems with their fiscal, financial, and monetary institutions (the first three items in the list above), but there is a major difference in the degree of the problem in EMEs. Weak fiscal, financial, and monetary institutions make emerging market countries vulnerable to high inflation and currency crises, which are not only a source of high volatility but also mean that the real value of domestic money cannot be taken for granted. As a result, EMEs have much of their debt denominated in foreign currency, usually dollars, hence leading to what is called liability dollarization. As (Mishkin, 1996) and Calvo (2001) have pointed out, liability dollarization is what leads to an entirely different impact of currency crises on the economy in emerging market versus advanced countries. In emerging market countries, a sharp real currency depreciation raises the value of liabilities in local currency, thus causing the net worth of corporations and individuals, especially those whose earnings come from the nontradables sector, to fall. This serious negative shock to corporations' and individuals' balance sheets then increases asymmetric information problems in credit markets, leading to a sharp decline in lending and an economic contraction. It should be noted, however, that not all emerging market countries (e.g., Chile, and South Africa) suffer from liability dollarization in a serious way (see Eichengreen, Hausmann, and Panizza, 2002).

A dominant phenomenon in emerging market countries is a sudden stop, a large negative change in capital inflows, which appear, as a general rule, to contain a large unanticipated component (see Calvo and Reinhart, 2000). It is more likely to hit EMEs because of their weak fiscal and financial institutions, and a sudden stop leads to a sharp contraction of investment and the aggregate economy. The effect of sudden stops on individual countries is by no means uniform and appears to have much to do with initial conditions. For example, Chile had low debt relative to Argentina and did not suffer from liability dollarization, and thus was much less affected by the sudden stop in 1997–1998 than was Argentina, which suffered a serious dislocation.

This paper illustrates that these institutional differences result in a much more complicated environment for executing monetary policy by conducting illustrative simulations using a dynamic new Keynesian model. These simulations show that low credibility of monetary institutions leads to slower convergence of inflation to targeted levels and a higher cost of disinflation. In addition, low credibility leads to higher volatility of inflation, output, and interest rates. The simulations also show that sudden stops, as represented by an exchange-rate shock, also lead to higher volatility of inflation output and interest rates.

One conclusion from the above discussion is that institutional reforms are especially critical to successful macroeconomic performance in EMEs. Rounding up the usual suspects provides the following list: (1) improvements in prudential supervision, (2) limits on the government safety net for the financial system, (3) discouragement of currency mismatch for the economy as a whole, (4) increased trade openness, (5) improvements in fiscal relationships between the central government and the provinces and increases in fiscal transparency, and (6) public/institutional commitments to price stability and central bank independence. I will not discuss these institutional reforms here because that would take my discussion to far afield. I do want to emphasize, however, that fundamental institutional reform is far more critical to macroeconomic success than is the choice of monetary policy regime (a point emphasized in Calvo and Mishkin [2003]). Inflation targeting or other monetary policy regimes, including hard exchange rate pegs such as a currency board or dollarization, are not a panacea.

Central banks in EMEs can encourage institutional reform, and the Banco Central do Brasil has been active in this regard. A central bank in an EME can only do so much, however, and it has to take weak institutions as given in deciding how to conduct monetary policy. The bottom line is that being a central banker is much tougher in EMEs than it is in advanced economies.

2. Issues in Inflation Targeting in EMEs

The tougher institutional environment that central bankers in EMEs face is important in policy design with regard to four issues discussed in the paper: target bands, transparency and formality, response to shocks, and IMF conditionality.

2.1 TARGET BANDS

The paper advocates target bands for inflation targets that are wide to accommodate the higher volatility in EMEs and suggests that the bands should be seen as checkpoints. Although the paper's position on these issues is reasonable, there is a subtlety here that needs to be emphasized.

The use of target bands has a dangerous aspect. Floors and ceilings of bands can take on a life of their own in which there is too great a focus on the breach of the floor or ceiling rather than on how far away actual inflation is from the midpoint of the target range. As discussed in Bernanke et al. (1999) and Mishkin and Schmidt-Hebbel (2002), too great a focus on breaches of the floors or ceilings can lead to the so-called instrument instability problem, in which the attempts of policymakers to keep inflation within the target range cause policy instruments, such as short-term interest rates or exchange rates, to undergo undesirably large fluctuations. A focus on avoiding short-term breaches of the bands can also lead to suboptimal setting of monetary policy and controllability problems in which the inflation target is more likely to be missed in the medium term. Both of these problems have arisen in the New Zealand inflation-targeting regime.

One solution to these problems is to use a point target rather than a target range. There is still a need, however, for a trigger mechanism to support accountability for the central bank. Indeed, this is exactly what the Bank of England has done: it has a point target for inflation of 2% and the requirement that if the inflation rate is more than 1 percentage point above or below this target, then it has to issue a public letter to the government explaining why inflation has moved so far from the target, what policy actions will be taken to deal with the situation, and what will be the expected path of inflation back to the 2% target. This procedure puts the focus on the midpoint of a target range and not too much on the edges of the target range.

Having a wide target range with the edges of the range seen as checkpoints, as advocated in the paper, can be consistent with the Bank of England procedure and can avoid the problem of too much focus on the edges of the range. However, this requires that the focus always stay on the midpoint of the range and that the edges of the bands are interpreted only as checkpoints and not hard targets that cannot be breached. I think Fraga, Goldfajn, and Minella are advocating this approach, but it is important that EMEs be aware that the use of a target range requires some sublety in the communication process to avoid instrument instability and controllability problems.

2.2 TRANSPARENCY AND FORMALITY

This paper rightfully emphasizes that the weaker credibility of monetary policy institutions in EMEs requires even more transparency and formality in the inflation-targeting regime than in advanced economies. Because the public is more skeptical of monetary authorities in EMEs, the central bank can strengthen its credibility by providing even more information to the public with measures like the following: releasing minutes of central bank deliberations quickly; publishing the central bank's forecasts; and publishing a clear and frank inflation report that outlines the goals and limitations of monetary policy, how the numerical values of the inflation targets are determined, how the targets are to be achieved, and the reasons for deviations from the targets.

Fraga, Goldfajn, and Minella also emphasize that a formal process for monetary policy decisions with regularly scheduled meetings of a monetary policy committee (which in turn has a high level of proper preparation and economic analysis) is not only crucial to effective decisionmaking but is also crucial to establishing credibility for the central bank. This point almost seems obvious, but as the authors emphasize, many central banks in EMEs have not followed this procedure in the past.

It is important to note that the Banco Central do Brasil has been a leader in advancing transparency and formality in EMEs. Before the Brazilian central bank adopted inflation targeting, many central banks in EMEs were skeptical that they could put in place a full-fledged inflation-targeting regime with high levels of transparency and formality. This is one reason that some of these central banks engaged in a gradual approach to implementing inflation-targeting regimes, with the Bank of Mexico being a prominent example. However, in 1999, the Banco Central do Brasil, under Arminio Fraga, has paved the way for other central banks in EMEs by implementing a full-fledged inflation-targeting regime with all the bells and whistles of transparency and formality within four months of the initial announcement of inflation targeting. This achievement was extraordinary and has helped hasten the adoption of inflation targeting in many EMEs.

2.3 RESPONDING TO SHOCKS

A key theme of the paper is that EMEs face much bigger shocks than advanced economies do, which complicates the conduct of monetary policy. How should inflation-targeting central banks in EMEs respond to shocks? When shocks drive inflation away from the target, what horizon should be used for returning to the target? For Brazil, these questions have not been academic: Brazil experienced a major exchange-rate shock in 2002, prior to the election of the new president, that caused a major overshoot of its inflation target.

The discussion in the paper on how to respond to shocks gets it exactly right. The first point the paper makes is that the response to a shock and the horizon over which the central bank plans to get the inflation rate back on target depends on the nature and persistence of the shock. In other words, an optimizing framework in which output and inflation fluctuations are minimized requires that the horizon for hitting an inflation goal is shock dependent. Thus, the procedure for responding to a shock derived from an optimizing framework requires the following four steps: (1) identify the nature and persistence of the shock; (2) estimate the first- and second-order effects of the shock, depending on the type of shock; (3) calculate the optimal response, depending on weights on inflation versus output fluctuations in the central bank's objective function; and (4) explain to the public why the particular path of inflation has been chosen.

The paper provides an excellent discussion of how the Banco Central do Brasil has responded to a large shock when it adjusted its inflation targets in early 2003. First, the central bank estimated the regulated-price shock to be 1.7%. Then taking into account the nature and the persistence of past shocks, it estimated the inertia from past shocks to be 4.2%, of which two-thirds was to be accepted, resulting in an additional adjustment of 2.8%. Then the central bank added these two numbers to the previously announced target of 4% to get an adjusted inflation target for 2003 of 8.5% (4% + 1.7% + 2.8%). The adjusted target was then announced in an open letter sent to the minister of finance in January 2003. The letter explained that getting to the nonadjusted target of 4% too quickly would entail far too high a loss of output. Specifically, the letter indicated that an attempt to achieve an inflation rate of 6.5% in 2003 was expected to entail a decline of 1.6% of gross domestic product (GDP), while trying to achieve the nonadjusted target of 4% was expected to lead to an even larger decline in GDP of 7.3%.

The procedure followed by the Banco Central do Brasil has several important advantages and is a textbook case for central bank response to shocks. First, the procedure has tremendous transparency, both in articulating why the initial inflation target was missed and also in showing how the central bank is responding to the shock and its plans to return to its longrun inflation goal. This degree of transparency helps minimize the loss of credibility from the missed target and the need to adjust the shortterm inflation target. Second, the central bank recognized that not adjusting the inflation target was just not credible because the market and the public clearly recognized that inflation would overshoot the initial target. Thus, adjusting the target publicly was absolutely necessary to retain credibility for the central bank because to do otherwise would have signaled to the markets that the central bank was unwilling to be transparent. Third, by discussing alternative paths for the inflation rate and the reasons that the particular path using the adjusted target was chosen, the central bank could demonstrate that it is not what King (1996) has referred to as an inflation nutter who cares only about controlling inflation and not about output fluctuations. By its procedure of outlining that lower inflation paths would lead to large output losses, the Banco Central do Brasil demonstrated that it is not out of touch with the concerns of the public because it indeed does care about output losses, just as the public and the politicians do.

2.4 LESSONS FOR ADVANCED COUNTRIES

Although the discussion in the paper and the experience of Banco Central do Brasil in responding to shocks has important lessons for the conduct of monetary policy in other EMEs, it also has important lessons for the conduct of monetary policy in advanced economies. Inflation-targeting central banks in advanced economies have often adopted a horizon for their inflation targets of two years or so, with the Bank of England being a prominent example. This approach can give the impression that the horizon for inflation targets is fixed, which could mean that inflation targeting will not be flexible enough. After all, our models tell us that optimal monetary policy will surely adjust the target horizon for inflation depending on the nature and persistence of shocks, a key point made by the paper. Indeed, critics of inflation targeting in advanced economies have pointed to the rigidity of the inflation-targeting regimes with a fixed horizon as an important reason for not adopting inflation targeting.

Until now, the use of a specific horizon like two years has not been a problem for inflation targeting in advanced economies like the United Kingdom because inflation has not been subject to big shocks and it has remained close to the target level. In this case, having the horizon for the target equal to the policy horizon (i.e., the time it takes for monetary policy to affect inflation), which is about two years, is consistent with optimal monetary policy. As Svensson (1997) demonstrates, however, if the inflation rate is shocked away from its long-run target, then the target horizon should be longer than the policy horizon. Although this situation has not occurred yet for inflation targeters in advanced economies, one day a big shock to inflation will come (as it already has in Brazil). Then for monetary policy to minimize output and inflation fluctuations optimally, the target horizon will need to be longer than two years and to vary depending on the nature of the shock.

Central banks in advanced economies are aware of this issue. For example, in the United Kingdom, the inflation-targeting regime stipulates that if inflation is knocked more that 1 percentage point away from its target of 2%, then the Bank of England will specify the path of inflation and the length of time that it will take to get back to the 2% target. Thus, there is a provision for flexibility in which the target horizon can be varied when big shocks hit the inflation process. There are two problems that may arise, however, when a big shock hits the economy. The first is that the two-year horizon may have become so fixed in the mind of the public and/or the central bank that the central bank may not respond flexibly enough to a large shock. The second is that a big shock may occur that the central bank expects will drive inflation outside the band around the inflation target, but inflation is still within the band for the time being. Even though inflation is not yet outside the target range, the two-year horizon for hitting the inflation targets is unlikely to remain appropriate. Instead, the central bank will need to adopt a procedure like the Banco Central do Brasil has followed to set appropriate policy instruments in which the horizon and path for inflation are adjusted depending on the nature and persistence of the shock. This kind of flexible response would be harder to accomplish if the fixed time horizon is in place when inflation at first remains within the target range.

Because EMEs like Brazil have already been subjected to large shocks that require changes in the horizon for inflation targets, they illustrate that central banks in advanced economies have to take this contingency into account when designing their inflation-targeting systems. A lesson in this paper is that to minimize output and inflation fluctuations optimally, central banks in both advanced and emerging market economies need to make it clear, even before it is necessary, that the horizon for inflation targets needs to be flexible and will vary depending on the nature and persistence of shocks, and that they will be ready to use procedures like the one the Banco Central do Brasil has followed recently.

Stating that they are ready to use a procedure like the one the Banco Central do Brasil has used has another important advantage for central banks in advanced as well as emerging market economies. A well-known conundrum for central bankers in both advanced and emerging market economies is that many of them don't like to talk about output fluctuations when discussing monetary policy. They fear that doing so encourages the public and the politicians to demand that the central bank focus on fighting declines in output, with the result that the pursuit of the price stability goal will be compromised. The problem with central banks unwillingness to discuss output fluctuations is that the public may begin to see the central bank as having different preferences than they do, which can erode support for the central bank. By acknowledging that a procedure like the one followed by the Banco Central do Brasil will be used when large shocks hit the economy, a central bank can make it clear that it does care about output fluctuations and is not an inflation nutter. This approach has the advantage that it will promote support for central bank independence and the inflation-targeting regime. It also shows that the central bank cares about output fluctuations in a forward-looking context because it highlights decisions that the central bank will make about the future path of inflation and the horizon over which inflation will return to target. It therefore clarifies that the central bank is focusing on output fluctuations in a long-term context, which is necessary for avoiding the time-inconsistency problem.

2.5 IMF CONDITIONALITY

The paper contains a brief section on IMF conditionality and I have a few comments about this topic. When a country obtains loans under an IMF program, it is subject to conditions that require evaluation of the monetary policy stance. In the past, a key element of this conditionality was ceilings on the growth rate of net domestic assets. As pointed out by Fraga, Goldfajn, and Minella, conditionality based on net domestic assets makes little sense in an inflation-targeting regime. Net domestic assets conditionality, which is derived under the IMF's financial programming framework, is based on an outdated theory: the monetary approach to the balance of payments (see Mussa and Savastano, 1999), which requires that the growth rate of monetary aggregates be closely linked to inflation. However, the linkage between monetary aggregates and inflation is almost always found to be weak when inflation rates are reasonably low, as is the case for EMEs that have adopted inflation targeting. As a result, targets for net domestic assets are likely to lead to the inappropriate setting of monetary policy instruments and are likely to decrease monetary policy transparency.

In an inflation-targeting regime, it seems natural to replace net domestic asset conditionality with assessment of the country's inflation performance. Indeed, this is what the IMF moved to in evaluating monetary policy under its program for Brazil when inflation targeting was adopted in 1999. The IMF program has conducted quarterly reviews on Brazil's performance in meeting its inflation targets, but there is still a problem that the IMF evaluation is essentially backward-looking (Blejer, Leone, Rabanal, and Schwartz, 2001). Inflation targeting is inherently forward-looking, so how can IMF conditionality be modified to be more forward-looking? One approach would be for the IMF to monitor monetary policy institutions. Specifically, the IMF conditions could focus on the degree of central bank independence, whether the central bank mandate focuses on price stability as the long-run overriding goal of monetary policy, and whether transparency and accountability of the central bank is high. As part of this monitoring, the IMF could conduct a careful assessment of central bank procedures, the legitimacy of its forecasting process and whether the central bank provides adequate explanations for misses of its inflation targets.

In a sense, this shift in approach is similar to the shift in approach that has occurred in bank supervision in recent years. In the past, bank supervision was also quite backward-looking because it focused on the current state of banks' balance sheets. However, this backward-looking approach is no longer adequate in today's world, in which financial innovation has produced new markets and instruments that make it easy for banks and their employees to make huge bets easily and quickly. In this new financial environment, a bank that is quite healthy at a particular point in time can be driven into insolvency extremely rapidly from trading losses, as was forcefully demonstrated by the failure of Barings in 1995. Thus, bank examinations have now become far more forward-looking and now place much greater emphasis on evaluating the soundness of a bank's management processes with regard to controlling risk. Similarly, the IMF could shift its conditionality to focus on the management processes in central banks to keep inflation under control.

3. Conclusion

The paper by Fraga, Goldfajn, and Minella is important not only because it has useful lessons for how inflation targeting should be conducted in emerging market countries but also because it has valuable lessons for advanced countries. The Banco Central do Brasil has been a leader in developing best-practice inflation targeting for emerging market countries, sometimes under extremely difficult conditions.

This topic reminds me of an incident at the Federal Reserve Bank of Kansas City's Jackson Hole conference, where top central bankers from all over the world congregate every August. The recently departed Rudi Dornbusch, who we all miss, made the provocative statement that "there are no competent central bankers in Latin America." Of course, what Dornbusch was getting at was that the environment for conducting effective monetary policy in Latin America is difficult, to say the least. What this paper demonstrates is that, in fact, some of the most competent central bankers are in Latin America, and we have a lot to learn from them.

REFERENCES

Bernanke, Ben S., Thomas Laubach, Frederic S. Mishkin, and Adam S. Posen. (1999). *Inflation Targeting: Lessons from the International Experience*. Princeton, NJ: Princeton University Press.
Blejer, Mario I., Alfredo M. Leone, Paul Rabanal, and Gerd Schwartz. (2001). Inflation targeting in the context of IMF-supported adjustment programs. IMF Working Paper No. 01/31.
Calvo, Guillermo A. (2001). Capital markets and the exchange rate: With special reference to the dollarization debate in Latin America. *Journal of Money, Credit, and Banking* 33(2):312–334.
Calvo, Guillermo A., and Frederic S. Mishkin. (2003). The mirage of exchange rate regimes for emerging market countries. *Journal of Economic Perspectives*, 17(4):99–118.
Calvo, Guillermo A., and Carmen M. Reinhart. (2000). When capital flows come to a sudden stop: Consequences and policy. In *Reforming the International Monetary*

and Financial System, Peter B. Kenen and Alexander K. Swoboda (eds.). Washington, DC: IMF.

Eichengreen, Barry, Ricardo Hausmann, and Ugo Panizza. (2002). Original sin: The pain, the mystery, and the road to redemption. Presented at the conference Currency and Maturity Matchmaking: Redeeming Debt from Original Sin. Inter-American Development Bank. Washington, DC, November 21–22.

King, Mervyn. (1996). How should central banks reduce inflation? Conceptual issues. *Achieving Price Stability.* Federal Reserve Bank of Kansas City, 53–91.

Mishkin, Frederic S. (1996). Understanding financial crises: A developing country perspective. Annual World Bank Conference on Development Economics, World Bank 29–62.

Mishkin, Frederic S., and Klaus Schmidt-Hebbel. (2002). One decade of inflation targeting in the world: What do we know and what do we need to know? In *Inflation Targeting: Design, Performance, Challenges,* Norman Loayza and Raimundo Soto (eds.), Central Bank of Chile, Santiago 2002, 117–219.

Mussa, Michael, and Miguel Savastano. (1999). The IMF approach to economic stabilization. *NBER Macroeconomics Annual 1999,* Cambridge, MA: MIT Press, 79–121.

Svensson, Lars E. O. (1997). Inflation forecast targeting: Implementing and monitoring inflation targets. *European Economic Review* 41:1111–1146.

Discussion

A number of participants asked for clarification on the conduct of monetary policy by the Brazilian central bank. Mark Gertler noted that Alan Greenspan spent his first years in charge of monetary policy, successfully building his reputation. This situation could potentially be a problem, however, if expectations about monetary policy and the reputation of the Fed become tied to his personality. He asked whether the head of the central bank in Brazil faced similar problems. He was skeptical that the publication of details of state-contingent targets could successfully substitute for the reputation of Arminio Fraga, speculating that there might be considerable leeway for discretion within the published targets. Gertler asked whether the target paths published by the Brazilian central bank are based on specific models or on individual judgement. Arminio Fraga responded that the fact that there is room for discretion makes transparency extremely important, and thus it is important that the specific models used to generate the target paths are published. Ken Rogoff speculated that if target inflation rates in emerging markets were to reflect the size of the shocks those countries are likely to face, the target rates should be substantially higher. Arminio Fraga responded that the Brazilian central bank gave a good deal of thought to this issue. He noted that the central bank had not wanted the target to be high enough to include expectations of a violent change in regime because this consideration might have triggered indexation clauses. Andrés Velasco suggested an alternative approach to accommodating big supply shocks in emerging markets without loss of credibility. He suggested that the central bank focus only on the element of the price level that does not depend on the exchange rate. He was curious about why the Brazilian central bank had not followed this approach. Arminio Fraga responded that the exchange rate affects all sectors of the economy and also that the exchange rate may be driven by the usual type of fundamentals as well as by supply shocks.

Arminio Fraga disagreed with the proposal in Robert Hall's discussion that the central bank explicitly announce its preferences. Among other problems, he felt that this approach still leaves open issues of time consistency and is difficult to explain to the public. However, he said that the central bank of Brazil is still trying to refine its approach and is currently thinking of explaining decisions in terms of a unit shock and how the shock will be handled over time. Rick Mishkin was also of the view that publishing the objective function of the central bank is not a sensible idea. In response to Robert Hall's discussion of external forecasts, Arminio Fraga said that outside forecasts tended to lag and that there was a lot of herding behavior. Mike Woodford was not convinced that targeting external forecasts would be better than targeting internal forecasts because outsiders' beliefs about central bank credibility affect their forecasts, while the central bank has full information about its own credibility. However, he noted that external forecasts are useful to the central bank forecasts as indicators of expected inflation. Robert Hall responded that this comment was reasonable, but that his point was that central banks shouldn't offer excuses; they should offer performance.

The difference in the challenges faced by monetary policy in developing and developed countries was discussed by several participants. Arminio Fraga noted that a history of weak institutions makes managing regime change more difficult in developing countries than it is in developed countries. In contrast to the events prior to Lula's election in Brazil, the transition from Clinton to Bush in the United States did not pose any problems for the Federal Reserve. Rick Mishkin agreed, noting that the job of the central bank is made much more difficult if the fiscal authority misbehaves. He pointed out that in the United States, the Fed benefits greatly from a stable and favorable policy environment. By contrast, central banks in developing countries have to work much harder on institutionalization and transparency because the policy environment tends to be much less favorable. Ken Rogoff remarked that Brazil's achievement in bringing inflation under control was very significant, especially in light of the fact that Brazil had experienced the second highest cumulative inflation rate of any country since 1970: over 1 quadrillion percent. He speculated that, just as the Bundesbank seemed to have gained credibility from Germany's hyperinflation history, Brazil's central bank might also be able to benefit to some extent from the country's past.

A number of participants expressed the view that developed countries could learn from Brazil's experience. Ken Rogoff was of the view that the problem of credibility in monetary policy has not been solved, contrary to what a lot of people think. He noted that high productivity growth in recent years has made low inflation possible relatively painlessly. He speculated that the combination of high debt–GDP ratios and the old-age problem in Europe and Japan may incite these countries to inflate in the future. Rogoff also remarked that the ratio of science to art in central banking needs to be increased, and that the only difference between the Fed's conduct of monetary policy in the 1970s and today is in its communications strategy. Rick Mishkin noted that, although it is hard for central banks to explain technical details to the public, transparency about the effect of the output gap on the inflation target is a good idea. He observed that this topic is currently missing from the discussion of inflation targeting in advanced countries but could be crucial if a large shock does occur. Mike Woodford supported Mishkin's comment that the paper offers lessons for developed countries with low inflation. In particular, he said that a fixed horizon for achieving an inflation target is undesirable because the horizon should clearly depend on the persistence and nature of the shocks.

Carl Walsh noted that in the area of monetary economics, the interchange between policymakers and theory has been productive in the past few years. He observed that the table of state-contingent paths used by the Brazilian central bank to explain its actions can be interpreted as the optimal targeting rule from Benigno and Woodford. He noted that difficulty in explaining either the table or the rule is that the coefficients of the reaction function depend on many structural parameters, about which there is uncertainty. This situation makes it hard to be explicit or transparent about how output affects the inflation target. In response to Carl Walsh, Mike Woodford was optimistic that the Benigno and Woodford paper provides a useful framework for framing justifications for deviations from the target, particularly from the point of view of external monitoring by the International Monetary Fund (IMF).